THE
SELECTED LETTERS
OF

Dolley Payne Madison

Edited by

David B. Mattern

and

Holly C. Shulman

University of Virginia Press

CHARLOTTESVILLE AND LONDON

The publication of this volume has been supported by a grant from the
National Historical Publications and Records Commission.

UNIVERSITY OF VIRGINIA PRESS

First published 2003

1 3 5 7 9 8 6 4 2

LIBRARY OF CONGRESS CATALOGING-IN-PUBLICATION DATA

Madison, Dolley, 1768–1849.
   [Correspondence. Selections]
   The selected letters of Dolley Payne Madison / edited by
David B. Mattern and Holly C. Shulman.
     p.   cm.
   Includes index.
   ISBN 0-8139-2152-X (cloth : alk. paper)
   1. Madison, Dolley, 1768–1849 — Correspondence.   2. Madison,
James, 1751–1836 — Correspondence.   3. Presidents' spouses — United
States — Correspondence.   I. Mattern, David B., 1951–   II. Shulman,
Holly Cowan.   III. Title.
E342.1.M18 A4 2003
973.5′1′092 — dc21

                                      2002028940

To Ralph Ketcham

Contents

Illustrations

Acknowledgments

The editors would like to thank all those who contributed to the preparation of this volume, including our research assistants, Scott Taylor, Victoria Scott, Amy Rider Minton, and Kristin Celello; Susan Lyman of Charleston, S.C., and Mary Black of Fincastle, Va., for sharing their family letters; J. C. A. Stagg for his close reading and criticism of the manuscript; Ellen J. Barber for her painstaking preparation of the manuscript; and the following individuals: Cindy Aron, Catherine Allgor, Sara Lee Barnes, Brian P. Conway, Charlotte Crystal, Mary Gilliam, Lewis Gould, Richard Holway, Ralph Ketcham, Cynthia Kierner, Ann Lane, Susan Holbrook Perdue, Herbert Sloan, and the staff of the Papers of James Madison.

We would also like to thank Ryan Hyman, Macculloch Hall Historical Museum; Brian J. Lang, Dumbarton House of the National Society of the Colonial Dames of America; J. Stephen Catlett, the Greensboro Historical Museum; Karin Wittenborg, Michael Plunkett, and the staff of the Alderman Library at the University of Virginia; Wendy Wiener, Octagon House; Mary Ellen Chijioke, Friends Historical Library of Swarthmore College; Mary Giunta and Timothy D. W. Connelly, the National Historical Publications and Records Commission; and the staffs of the following institutions: the Arthur and Elizabeth Schlesinger Library on the History of Women in America, Harvard University, the Manuscript Room of the Library of Congress, and the Museum of the American Architectural Foundation.

Editorial Method

This edition of the selected letters of Dolley Payne Madison follows the editorial protocols of the Papers of James Madison project at the University of Virginia. Considerable effort has been made to render the printed texts as literal, faithful copies of the original manuscripts, but some exceptions must be noted. The dateline has been placed at the head of the document, regardless of its position in the original manuscript. Superior letters have been brought down, and confusing punctuation has been eliminated. The first letter of a sentence is invariably capitalized. Obvious slips of the pen, such as repeated words, have been silently corrected. A long dash or gap has been interpreted to indicate a new paragraph. Beyond these exceptions, alterations are noted in textual footnotes.

Missing or illegible characters and words in a damaged or torn manuscript are restored by conjecture within angle brackets. Ellipsis dots within angle brackets indicate indecipherable portions of the manuscript; other ellipses are in the originals. Words consistently spelled incorrectly, as well as variant or antiquated spellings, are left as written; however, misspellings that may appear to be printer's errors are corrected through additions in square brackets or followed by the device [sic]. Brackets used by Dolley Payne Madison and other correspondents have been rendered as parentheses.

A note following each document gives its provenance as well as additional information to be gleaned from the letter and its cover, such as dockets or other markings. This is also where the physical condition of the letter, if pertinent, is described. Annotations follow the provenance note.

Some letters in this edition are transcriptions made by Dolley Madison's niece Mary E. E. Cutts, who corrected spelling and grammar, cut sections, and occasionally merged two or more separate letters into one. Despite these problems, the editors have included them as the closest approximation of the originals where the latter do not exist.

Persons referred to in these pages are identified whenever possible in the biographical directory.

The letters in this edition have been chosen to tell the story of Dolley Madison's life and include letters that represent all aspects of her correspondence. They offer a representative sample of the letters she wrote and received from the 1790s through her death in 1849. While roughly three hundred letters have been chosen for this volume, the entire corpus of known Dolley Madison letters is being compiled for a forthcoming digital edition. This electronic version is being produced by the Dolley Madison Project through the auspices of the Virginia Center for Digital History, the Electronic Text Center, and the University of Virginia Press, all at the University of Virginia, and with the support of the National Endowment for the Humanities and the Virginia Foundation for the Humanities and the endorsement of the National Historical Publications and Records Commission.

Depository Symbols

In the provenance note following each document the first entry indicates the source of the text. If the document was in private hands when copied for this edition, the owner and date are normally indicated. If the document was in a private or public depository in the United States, the symbol listed in the Library of Congress's *MARC Code List for Organizations* (Washington, D.C., 2000) is used. Where the symbol DLC stands alone, it indicates the Madison Papers in the Library of Congress. The location symbols for depositories used in this volume are as follows:

CLU-C	University of California, Los Angeles, William Andrews Clark Memorial Library
CSmH	Henry E. Huntington Library, San Marino, California
CtHi	Connecticut Historical Society, Hartford
DCHi	Historical Society of Washington, D.C.
DLC	Library of Congress, Washington, D.C.
DNCD	National Society of the Colonial Dames of America, Dumbarton House, Washington, D.C.
ICHi	Chicago Historical Society
ICN	Newberry Library, Chicago
InHi	Indiana Historical Society, Indianapolis
InU	Indiana University, Bloomington

IU	University of Illinois, Urbana
KyHi	Kentucky Historical Society, Frankfort
MB	Boston Public Library
MCR-S	Radcliffe College, Schlesinger Library on the History of Women in America, Cambridge, Massachusetts
MdHi	Maryland Historical Society, Baltimore
MHi	Massachusetts Historical Society, Boston
MiD	Detroit Public Library
MiU-C	University of Michigan, William L. Clements Library, Ann Arbor
MnHi	Minnesota Historical Society, St. Paul
MoSHi	Missouri Historical Society, St. Louis
NBuU	State University of New York, Buffalo
NcGG	Guilford College, Dolley Madison Memorial Association, Greensboro, North Carolina
NHi	New-York Historical Society, New York City
NIC	Cornell University, Ithaca, New York
NjMoHP	Morristown National Historical Park, Morristown, New Jersey
NjP	Princeton University, Princeton, New Jersey
NN	New York Public Library, New York City
PCarlD	Dickinson College, Carlisle, Pennsylvania
PHi	Historical Society of Pennsylvania, Philadelphia
PPPrHi	Presbyterian Historical Society, Philadelphia
PPRF	Rosenbach Foundation, Philadelphia
THi	Tennessee Historical Society, Nashville
TxU-Hu	Harry Ransom Humanities Research Center, University of Texas, Austin
Vi	Library of Virginia, Richmond
ViHi	Virginia Historical Society, Richmond
ViU	University of Virginia, Charlottesville
WHi	State Historical Society of Wisconsin, Madison

Abbreviations

DPM	Dolley Payne Madison.
FC	File copy. Any version of a letter or other document retained by the sender for his own files and differing little if at all

from the completed version. A draft, on the other hand, is a preliminary sketch, often incomplete and varying frequently in expression from the finished version. Unless otherwise noted, both are in the sender's hand.

JM   James Madison.

Ms   Manuscript. A catchall term describing numerous reports and other papers that are not letters.

RC   Recipient's copy. The copy of a letter intended to be read by the addressee. If the handwriting is not that of the sender, this fact is noted in the provenance.

RG   Record Group.

Tr   Transcript. A copy of a manuscript, or a copy of a copy, customarily handwritten and ordinarily not by its author or by the person to whom the original was addressed.

Short Titles for Books and Other Frequently Cited Materials

Annals of Congress   *Debates and Proceedings in the Congress of the United States . . . (42 vols.; Washington, D.C., 1834–56).*

ASP   *American State Papers: Documents, Legislative and Executive, of the Congress of the United States . . . (38 vols.; Washington, D.C., 1832–61).*

PJM   William T. Hutchinson et al., eds., *The Papers of James Madison* (1st ser., vols. 1–10, Chicago, 1962–77, vols. 11–17, Charlottesville, Va., 1977–91).

PJM-PS   Robert A. Rutland et al., eds., *The Papers of James Madison: Presidential Series* (4 vols. to date; Charlottesville, Va., 1984–).

PJM-SS   Robert J. Brugger et al., eds., *The Papers of James Madison: Secretary of State Series* (6 vols. to date; Charlottesville, Va., 1986–).

PMHB   *Pennsylvania Magazine of History and Biography.*

Riverside   G. Blakemore Evans, ed., *The Riverside Shakespeare* (Boston, 1974).

Senate Exec. Proceedings   *Journal of the Executive Proceedings of the Senate of the United States of America* (3 vols.; Washington, D.C., 1828).

Shaw and Shoemaker	R. R. Shaw and R. H. Shoemaker, comps., *American Bibliography: A Preliminary Checklist for 1801–1819* (22 vols.; New York, 1958–66).
VMHB	*Virginia Magazine of History and Biography.*
WMQ	*William and Mary Quarterly.*

The Selected Letters
of
Dolley Payne Madison

Introduction

IN 1924 A POPULAR AND PROLIFIC BIOGRAPHER NAMED GAMALIEL
Bradford wrote an essay about Dolley Madison for a collection he was assembling entitled *Wives*. Bradford was a much admired writer at the beginning of the twentieth century who crafted psychological portraits he called "psychographs." He wanted to picture the soul, the character, and the personality of the human being, to discover the temperament, demeanor, and mood. He chose biography, he explained, because it "is the story of life." "When we read biography," he said, "we are holding up the mirror to our own hearts."[1]

Wives was a volume devoted to women who "would probably have lived quiet, utterly unknown lives except for their masculine connections," he wrote a friend. Bradford liked writing about women. "When you come to study them," he observed, "you often find them more interesting than the men." In making up his list of subjects, Bradford decided on several president's wives and included Dolley Madison. But he found writing about her hard slogging. He simply could not get to know her. "Spent a whole morning," he wrote in his journal in 1924, "in the hope of finding some touch that might make Dolly Madison stand out a little more vividly." He was exasperated, as he "found nothing for that purpose."[2] In reading his essay, we feel his

1

frustration. "It is hardly fair to infer that the woman had no inner life because we hear nothing of it," he argued, almost as if in dialogue with himself, "but it is safe to assume that the rush of external impressions left her little time to brood upon her own soul, its nature or its workings." He had read what he could find and discovered "little of inward experience."[3]

Yet by 1924 there had appeared two volumes of her letters. Lucia B. Cutts, the granddaughter of Dolley's beloved sister Anna Payne Cutts, compiled the first edition, which was entitled *Memoirs and Letters of Dolly Madison* and published in 1886. She declared that her object was to "lay before the public a series of private letters, written, without the most remote idea of publication, by a woman to her nearest and dearest relations." She promised that these letters would "furnish an exact transcript of the feeling of the writer, in times of no ordinary trial."[4] In fact, however, Lucia B. Cutts was careful to lay before the reading public an edited version of her great-aunt, bowdlerizing the letters she included in order to present the most attractive image of her ancestor.

Nearly thirty years later a Washington, D.C., historian named Allen C. Clark collected and published an expanded version of Dolley's letters entitled *Life and Letters of Dolly Madison.* Like Cutts, Clark swore he was presenting a wholly truthful portrait. His goal, he explained, was to let the reader decide whether "the unfading fame of Mrs. Madison has its foundation more on fact or more on fancy." And yet his adoration shines forth in the first sentence of his book: "The incomparable Dolly!" He continues: "The queens of our chosen kings are a long line . . . but Queen Dolly sparkles the most."[5] He too cut, edited, and reshaped her letters.

Not only had these two books been published by the time Bradford set to work, but a host of essays and book-length biographies of Mrs. Madison already existed. Some of the writers, such as Harriet Upton, Mary Logan, and Sarah K. Bolton, were reform activists looking for models for young American women. Ella Kent Barnard was interested in Dolley's Quaker background.[6] Some of these biographers took themselves seriously as historians; others were popular novelists. Most, however, wrote hagiography. None could have informed Bradford about her inner life. Their evaluations of her career reveal their goals and their sources.

All these writers seem happy to have assessed Dolley Madison's contributions within rather narrow definitions of what best suited a woman's public activity. Her first biographer and her contemporary, Margaret Bayard Smith, admired her, in the end, because of her "warm heart, that lent its glow to her cheek and its sparkle to her eye," and "the kindness and benevolence of her disposition." Lucia B. Cutts pictured her as "ambitious in that she endeavored to make her husband's administration a brilliant and successful one." Ella Kent Barnard respected her for her "ready tact" and "kind and loving thoughtfulness." Maud Wilder Goodwin, writing for a late nineteenth-century series on women for the Daughters of the American Revolution, agreed with Bradford that Mrs. Madison "lived very much upon the surface of things" but added that the president's wife was "charming and magnetic." Elizabeth Fries Ellet, the scholar who first introduced women's history to American readers in her *Women of the American Revolution,* envisioned Dolley as a perfect hostess, an American queen who dressed simply and furnished her house plainly while making her hospitality and charity "bounteously liberal."[7]

More recently, historians have taken this portrait and turned it on its head. The early scholars defined Dolley Madison's role as smoothing James Madison's path, lending him social sophistication, establishing a gathering place for the city's elite through her parties, and blending European fashion with American simplicity: she became a jewel in her husband's crown. Current historians argue instead that through her parties she invented a public space, invited everyone of importance—both men and women—to participate, provided the environment for networking and the building of interest groups, and then, using her feminine charms, manipulated and guided a fractious Congress. In so doing, she achieved a political goal that her husband could not attain. As one recent historian has written, "Like Thomas Jefferson, Dolley attracted the members, cajoling, charming, and bullying them, in a gracious way of course."[8] Both of these interpretations are based on the same sources.

There has yet to be a good biography of Dolley Madison. Although some of the existing attempts make enjoyable reading, they all portray her as the nation's hostess, the wife who charmed the nation and its capital, the strong and courageous patriot who guarded the White House against the British until she fled with George Washington's portrait under her arm and her husband's papers stuffed in her carriage. This is the woman who has lent her name to snacking cakes and ice cream. None of the biographies captures her inner life or discusses the range of her emotions and thoughts. The reason for this lies in large measure with Dolley Payne Todd Madison herself.

It was a hot August day in 1834 when Dolley Madison received a letter from her old Washington friend Margaret Bayard Smith.[9] Smith had agreed to write a biographical sketch of Mrs. Madison for a new four-volume work, *The National Portrait Gallery of Distinguished Americans.* Few women were to be found in any of the volumes, and few women were asked to write for the project. The third volume, scheduled for publication in 1836, was to include essays on both James and Dolley Madison. No other woman was to be included in that volume. It was an important assignment, even for so distinguished a writer as Smith. As Smith began researching her subject, she asked Dolley to jot down her memories, outline her family history, and lend Smith some copies of her letters. Who were her parents, where had she grown up, what kind of education had she received, when had she moved to Philadelphia, and who were her siblings? The former First Lady responded with a brief account of her early history: birth, parents, education, first and second marriages. But it was very slight information indeed, and despite repeated requests and promises, Dolley sent her biographer little more.[10]

There were, of course, practical reasons for her reserve. She was busy caring for her increasingly ill husband and shouldering the burdens of housekeeping as well as receiving streams of visitors. Indeed she explained to Smith that she would have to "plead also my constant engagements of different sorts at home." But her reasons may have been both more complicated and more typical of her generation than her preoccupations as a housewife might indicate. Biographers during the Early Republic strove to proclaim America's virtue and glory to their fellow Americans and to the world; they wanted to instill the values they saw in the founding fathers in the nation as a whole.[11] In this environment the public side of great personages was important, but not their private lives. Public figures, including James Madison, destroyed their personal correspondence, and many of Dolley's surviving letters instruct their recipients to burn them. As one contemporary biographer wrote, "Private character is much more an object of individual curiosity, than of general interest, or public importance. A representative of it may amuse and entertain; but it is rarely calculated to improve." Thus Dolley told her niece Mary Cutts that she could not give Smith "anything of importance *in my own Eyes*," adding that she found "egotism . . . so repugnant to my nature that I shrink from recording my own feelings, acts or doings."[12]

And yet while Dolley Madison stonewalled her biographer, she was careful to provide her with one particular letter. She wanted Smith to have the letter she had mailed her sister in August 1814 describing her own heroic actions during the British attack on Washington. She was insistent that Smith receive it, telling her nieces, "If you have lost it or omitted to give it to her, it will be much to my injury."[13] As a result, what stands out most in Smith's short biography of Dolley is that single letter. The rest of the sketch Smith wrote largely from her own memory. She had, after all, resided in Washington since

4

the beginning of the Jefferson administration and had been good friends with the Madisons for over three decades. She knew what social life was like in the early days of the city and how Dolley had conducted herself as First Lady. She remembered what the president's mansion had looked like before it was burned, and she had visited Montpelier, the Madison plantation in Orange County, Virginia. Smith included no direct quotes in her work. But she did reprint this one letter.

We may never know the contents of the original letter. Dolley Madison sent Smith only a copy of it, not the original. She wrote Smith that her letters were with her sister Lucy Washington Todd in Kentucky, and that she was "unwilling to have them exposed to the Mail," but she told Mary Cutts that "the original is nearly torn to bits by the mice" (although she gave no indication how she knew this if the letter was in Kentucky).[14] We might expect that in a moment of such stress she would have written in a more dashed and hurried fashion than usual, and yet there is a more formal quality to this letter as it was printed than is evident in most of her writing. Moreover, there are details included that she would not have needed to tell her sister. And we know that Dolley was not committed to telling Smith the truth, for she had already written in a letter that she had been born in North Carolina "whilst my Parents were there on a visit of one year to an Uncle," when in truth the Paynes had migrated to a Quaker community in central North Carolina and had remained there for three years before moving back to Virginia. Four years later she would write to an unknown correspondent that her husband had wanted her to read over his letters "and if any letter — or line — or word struck me as being calculated to injure the feelings of any one or wrong themselves that I would withdraw them or it." As a consequence, she admitted, she had made "slight corrections," as she felt these were "consonant to his wishes."[15]

But the letter of August 1814 is about courage and bravery. It is about one woman's determination to prevail against the enemy and champion American independence. Americans still carry the image of Dolley Madison saving the icons of the nation. When asked what they know about Dolley Madison, most Americans today recall her stand in Washington against the enemy, her courage, and her rescue of the portrait of the nation's greatest leader and founding hero, George Washington.[16]

She stamped her own legend. Her reticence, while appropriate for a woman of her time and station, served more than one purpose. Again and again she instructed her correspondents to burn her letters. She knowingly and carefully protected her personal and inner life. And she was careful about her public face.

From the very beginning, the editors of *The Papers of James Madison* considered acquiring the correspondence of Dolley Madison a critical part of their mission, and the project has continued to collect her letters over the past forty years. We are indebted to them in every way. Many of these letters were kept by their recipients and handed down over the generations. Some of the most personal letters, however, exist only because one of Dolley Madison's favorite nieces, Mary E. E. Cutts, transcribed them. They are not the same as the originals—Mary Cutts corrected spelling and grammar, deleted sections, and merged letters—but we are fortunate to have them. We now have copies of about two thousand of her letters in our collection. Some of these letters are invitations and thank-you notes, brief replies and responses. But others, especially her letters to her sisters Anna and Lucy, reveal her inner thoughts and anxieties. These are letters that, in the words of Gamaliel Bradford, picture her soul, character, and personality. They describe her close attachment to her family, her fears and her physical pain, her moments of pleasure, and her experiences of grief.

But the letters of Dolley Madison do more than that. Over the past generation both the general public and historians have become increasingly interested in the role of the First Lady and the ways in which women have exerted political power and helped define the nature of American society. The role of the First Lady emerged out of the constitutional design of the U.S. presidency. From the outset the president was not only the chief executive of the federal government; he was the head of state. As such, he presided over the nation's ceremonial functions, and he lived where he worked. The social life of the president, therefore, became intertwined with his political power. Once the national capital moved to Washington, D.C., and the White House became the center of the executive branch of the government, the president's social and ceremonial role became increasingly important. Within this context James and Dolley Madison fabricated the symbols of power and authority consistent with their republican ideology in a way that suited the First Lady as well as the president. In part this partnership of effort was deliberately fostered by James Madison, who was shy and retiring in public. But it was largely a consequence of Dolley Madison's strength, graciousness, and political perspicacity. Through her conduct she defined republican manners and created republican rituals that affirmed the political legitimacy of her husband. Historians have finally begun to write about this subject. But the new historiography is based on the old sources and presents the story of Dolley Madison as the flip side of the same coin. This volume presents the new sources needed to make a fresh examination of old narratives.[17]

A collection of letters is a kind of autobiography, diary, or journal. Thus *The Selected Letters of Dolley Payne Madison* tells her story in her own voice. The letters reveal her private life: her loving sisters and her profligate son, her pleasures in Washington and her heartache at selling Montpelier. Many of the letters are so immediate that her emotions stand up from the page.

We have divided her life into five periods that trace the arc of her life and its inherent drama. The first period, covering her childhood and youth, extends from her birth in 1768 through 1801, when, as the wife of James Madison, she moved to the new capital of Washington, D.C. The second period covers those years when James was secretary of state and Dolley became the most important woman in the new city and new society. The third period contains her years of triumph, the White House years, from 1809 to 1817. The fourth, from 1817 to 1836, encompasses her years of country retirement, from the Madisons' return to Montpelier to the death of her husband. The final period coincides with her widowhood, those years of loss and deprivation when, desperately poor, she returned to Washington to live off her fame and her friends. She died in July 1849.

These letters present Dolley Madison's trials and triumphs and make it possible to do what Gamaliel Bradford could never accomplish: to gain admittance to her mind and her private emotions and to understand the importance of her role as the national capital's first First Lady.

1. Richard Hutch, "Explorations in Character: Gamaliel Bradford and Henry Murray as Psychobiographers," *Biography: An Interdisciplinary Quarterly* 4 (fall 1981): 313; see also Edward Wagenknecht, *Gamaliel Bradford* (Boston, 1982), esp. chap. 5; Bradford to C. B. Porter, 12 Aug. 1930, *The Letters of Gamaliel Bradford, 1918–1931*, ed. Van Wyck Brooks (Boston, 1934), 339 n. 1.

2. Gamaliel Bradford, *Wives* (New York, 1925), xi; Bradford to Marvin Sprague, 17 June 1924, *Letters of Gamaliel Bradford*, 193–94; Van Wyck Brooks, ed., *The Journal of Gamaliel Bradford, 1883–1932* (Boston, 1933), 371.

3. Bradford, *Wives*, 129. Bradford's essay on DPM was first printed in the first issue of the *Virginia Quarterly Review*, in April 1925.

4. Lucia B. Cutts, *Memoirs and Letters of Dolly Madison* (Boston, 1886), 2.

5. Allen C. Clark, *Life and Letters of Dolly Madison* (Washington, D.C., 1914), [i], 7.

6. Harriet Upton, *Our Early Presidents: Their Wives and Children* (Boston, 1890); Mary Logan, *The Part Taken by Women in American History* (Wilmington, Del., 1912); Sarah K. Bolton, *Famous Leaders among Women* (New York, 1895); Ella Kent Barnard, *Dorothy Payne, Quakeress* (Philadelphia, 1909).

7. Margaret Bayard Smith, "Mrs. Madison," in *The National Portrait Gallery of Distinguished Americans*, ed. James Herring and James B. Longacre (4 vols.; Philadelphia, 1836), 3:1; Cutts, *Memoirs*, 72; Barnard, *Dorothy Payne*, 114; Maud Wilder Goodwin, *Dolly Madison* (New York, 1896), 70, 73; Elizabeth Fries Ellet, *The Women of the American Revolution* (2 vols.; New York, 1848–50); Ellet, *The Court Circles of the Republic* (1869; rept. New York, 1975), 83. For Ellet herself, see Scott E. Casper, "An Uneasy Marriage of Sentiment and Scholarship: Elizabeth F. Ellet and the Domestic Origins of American Women's History," *Journal of Women's History* 4 (1993): 10–35.

8. Catherine Allgor, *Parlor Politics: In Which the Ladies of Washington Help Build a City and a Government* (Charlottesville, Va., 2000), 73, 81.

9. The 25 Aug. 1834 heat wave was reported in the Baltimore *Chronicle and Daily Marylander* on 8 Sept. 1835.

10. DPM to Smith, 31 Aug. 1834. For the *National Portrait Gallery of Distinguished Americans,* Herring and Longacre commissioned essays from among a wide range of their contemporaries. On 11 Sept. 1834 Smith's husband, Samuel Harrison Smith, in a short note to JM (DLC) mentioned "transmitting the enclosed letter for Mrs. Madison." Although DPM did not preserve this correspondence, we can presume that Margaret Bayard Smith was asking for more materials, as she may also have done indirectly through Mary and Dolley Cutts.

11. DPM to Margaret Bayard Smith, 17 Jan. 1835, DLC: J. Henley Smith Papers. For biography in the Early Republic, see Scott E. Casper, *"Constructing" American Lives: Biography and Culture in Nineteenth-Century America* (Chapel Hill, N.C., 1999).

12. Charles Caldwell, quoted in Casper, *"Constructing" American Lives,* 61; DPM to Mary E. E. Cutts, 2 Dec. 1834.

13. DPM to Mary E. E. Cutts and Dolley P. Madison Cutts, 2 Jan. 1836, MCR-S.

14. DPM to Smith, 17 Jan. 1835, to Mary E. E. Cutts, October 1835.

15. DPM to Smith, 31 Aug. 1834; *PJM* 1:xvii.

16. For a fuller discussion, see David B. Mattern, "Dolley Madison Has the Last Word: The Famous Letter," *White House History* 4 (fall 1998): 38–43. The legend that DPM saved the Declaration of Independence, while not true, was depicted repeatedly in illustrations throughout the late nineteenth and twentieth centuries, a fact that reflects her mythic status as America's great heroine of the War of 1812.

17. See Allgor, *Parlor Politics;* Jan Lewis, "Politics and the Ambivalence of the Private Sphere: Women in Early Washington, D.C.," in *A Republic for the Ages,* ed. Donald R. Kennon (Charlottesville, Va., 1999), 122–51; Fredrika J. Teute, "Roman Matron on the Banks of Tiber Creek: Margaret Bayard Smith and the Politicization of Spheres in the Nation's Capital," ibid., 89–121; Barbara Carson, *Ambitious Appetites: Dining, Behavior, and Patterns of Consumption in Federal Washington* (Washington, D.C., 1990); Susan Branson, *These Fiery Frenchified Dames: Women and Political Culture in Early National Philadelphia* (Philadelphia, 2001).

First page of Dolley Payne Madison's letter to her son, John Payne Todd, 9 April 1823. (Courtesy of Albert and Shirley Small Special Collections Library, University of Virginia Library)

A miniature of Dolley Payne Madison by James
Peale (1748–1831) done in 1794. (Prints and
Photographs Division, Library of Congress)

Eliza Collins Lee, painter unknown. (From
Allen C. Clark, *The Life and Letters of Dolly
Madison* [Washington, D.C., 1914])

Dolley Payne Madison by Gilbert Stuart, painted in 1804. (White House Historical Association)

James Madison by Gilbert Stuart, painted in 1804. (Courtesy of Colonial Williamsburg Foundation)

View of the White House from Blodgett's Hotel, an 1803 watercolor by
Nicholas King (1771–1812), first surveyor of Washington, D.C.
(Huntington Library, San Marino, California)

In 1812 William Chappell engraved this picture of Dolley Payne Madison. (Prints and Photographs Division, Library of Congress)

James Madison as fourth president of the United States. Engraved by
David Edwin (1776–1841) from a portrait painted by Thomas Sully
(1783–1872). (Prints and Photographs Division, Library of Congress)

Benjamin Henry Latrobe made this wash print of the White House after it had been burned. In the foreground is Saint John's Episcopal Church, which he designed. (Prints and Photographs Division, Library of Congress)

Montpelier as it looked during the Madisons' retirement, engraved by
J. F. E. (John Francis Eugene) Prud'homme for the title page of James B.
Longacre and James Herring's *The National Portrait Gallery of Distinguished
Americans* (Philadelphia, 1836). Prud'homme took this image from a
drawing by John G. Chapman (1808–1889). (Prints and Photographs
Division, Library of Congress)

J. F. E. Prud'homme made this engraving from a drawing by James Herring after a portrait of Dolley Madison by Joseph Wood painted in 1817, during the Madisons' retirement years at Montpelier. (Prints and Photographs Division, Library of Congress)

James B. Longacre drew this portrait of James Madison in July 1833, and a student of his, Thomas B. Welch (1814–1874), engraved it for *The National Portrait Gallery of Distinguished Americans.* Andrew Jackson and Nicholas Trist urged the reluctant Madison to sit for it, the last life portrait of him known to have survived. (Prints and Photographs Division, Library of Congress)

Dolley Payne Madison, painted in oil by William S. Elwell, 1848. (Courtesy of the National Portrait Gallery, Smithsonian Institution/Art Resource, N.Y.)

John Payne Todd by Kurtz. (From Allen C.
Clark, *The Life and Letters of Dolly Madison*
[Washington, D.C., 1914])

Dolley Madison and Annie Payne, photographed by Mathew Brady
in 1848. (Courtesy of the Greensboro Historical Museum)

Quaker
Beginnings

1768-1801

DOLLEY PAYNE WAS BORN ON 20 MAY 1768 IN WHAT IS TODAY GUILFORD County, North Carolina, on an otherwise uneventful day in a tumultuous decade. In 1763 the Seven Years' War had ended. Since then the country had passed the milestones marking the path to the American Revolution: Sugar Act and Stamp Act, Declaratory Act and Townshend Acts. In the spring of 1768, protest began to escalate; by that fall resistance was spreading, and the British were shipping troops to North America. For the Paynes, however, 1768 was the year their first girl was born, in the midst of their struggles to make a living in a small Quaker community in North Carolina.

The many blanks in her early years have been filled with myths, oral histories, and family legends—some of which were of her own making. In August 1834 she wrote to her friend Margaret Bayard Smith, "My family are all Virginians except myself, who was born . . . on a visit of one year to an Uncle." Mrs. Madison carefully explained that "their families on both sides, were among the most respectable citizens of the state." [1] No family letters survive from the first twenty-five years of her life, and only the circumstances and context of her early life can be recounted.

Mary and John Payne were both Virginians. Their families were rooted in Hanover County, north of Richmond. Dolley Madison's mother's family had prospered: Mary Coles was descended on one side from Isaac Winston, an early Virginia Quaker and the grandfather of Patrick Henry, and on the other side from William Coles, a Quaker immigrant from Wexford County in southeastern Ireland. By the 1760s the Winstons and the Coleses were members of Virginia's planter elite. Dolley Madison's father's family, neither wealthy nor Quaker, were Anglicans of middling success. Unlike the Winstons and Coleses, the Paynes left behind no record of letters, plantation mansions, or public accomplishments, but according to family legend John Payne's father was a planter of sufficient substance to give the newlyweds both land and slaves. The Anglican John Payne and the Quaker Mary Coles were married in 1761. Three years later John Payne applied for membership in and was admitted to the Cedar Creek Meeting in Hanover County.

It was as Quakers that the Paynes moved south and west. North American colonists were streaming to the southern frontier. A phenomenal growth in population had doubled the number of colonists between 1750 and 1770 — from one million to two. Old settlements seemed overcrowded; long-cultivated farmland became expensive. So the colonists beat a path down into the North Carolina piedmont. The population of North Carolina soared until, by 1770, it was the fourth-largest colony in North America.[2]

The Quakers participated in this generational restlessness, moving in communities to preserve their religious customs and escape the corrupting influences of more settled areas, as well as to take advantage of economic opportunity. Migration to North Carolina meant a shift into a more intensely Quaker, less cosmopolitan atmosphere; it demonstrated a voluntary commitment to Quaker ideals. Members of the eastern Virginia meetings were the most likely in the entire colony to migrate, probably because these were the meetings most influenced by their non-Quaker neighbors, and of these, Cedar Creek was the largest community. Eleven Quaker families, including the Paynes, moved from the Cedar Creek Meeting in Hanover County to what was then Rowan County, North Carolina, and the New Garden Meeting in 1766–67.[3] Thus John Payne sold his Virginia land and bought property in the North Carolina wilderness. Three years later Dolley Payne was born.

Whatever their dreams, the family did not prosper. If North Carolina was the scene of extraordinary growth, it was also the site of exceptional disorder. The colonial government was weak, and the conflict between backcountry and tidewater, known as the Regulator movement, created havoc, especially in

Rowan County and surrounding areas. Land claims became hard to enter, disputes difficult to win, and by 1768 Regulators were breaking up courts and dragging attorneys through the streets. A year later the Paynes made the atypical decision to return to Virginia.[4] The move proved costly; in selling their North Carolina farm, they lost nearly a third of their capital. Perhaps their decision to return was simply a rational response to the chaos of the era; perhaps Mary Payne could not bear to live so far from her beloved Winstons and Coleses; perhaps John Payne failed in business, as he was later to do in Philadelphia; perhaps the Paynes found that they disliked living in a conformist and isolated Quaker community. Whatever the reason—or reasons—they reversed their route and traveled back to Virginia.

At this point accounts of the Payne family diverge. There are stories that they bought or rented Scotchtown, a plantation in Hanover County, from Patrick Henry, who was a relative of Mary Payne's, or that they sold it to him after residing there for only a year. In some versions of the story, they moved to the Coles Hill plantation, owned by Isaac Coles Sr., also in Hanover County. Two people named Mary and John Payne became clerks in the Cedar Creek Meeting, were put in charge of recording the manumission of slaves, and signed documents dated between 1775 and 1782. If these were Dolley Payne's parents, then it was sometime before 1775 when the family returned to Hanover County and to their life in the Quaker community near the Coles, Winston, and Payne families.[5] They remained there throughout the Revolutionary War.

Biographers either have not discussed Dolley Payne's early schooling or have asserted that she received a good education as a young girl in Virginia. There is, however, little mention of schools in the records of the Virginia Friends. By 1784 the Virginia Yearly Meeting had voted to establish schools in the state, and the Cedar Creek Meeting did so in 1791, after Dolley was grown. Her letters suggest that she received only a rudimentary education.[6]

The Paynes owned slaves, as did their Quaker relatives the Winstons and the Coleses, but by the middle of the eighteenth century, the institution had become increasingly troublesome to many Virginia Quakers. The Quaker minister John Griffith wrote in 1765 that "the life of religion is almost lost where slaves are numerous . . . the practice being as contrary to the spirit of Christianity as light is to darkness," and Quaker communities began to look for solutions to this moral dilemma. The issue was not simply whether a meeting or its members opposed the institution; in the 1760s emancipation was illegal in Virginia except by special government act. If Quakers freed their slaves, non-Quakers could and did seize them, declare them runaway slaves, and sell them again into bondage.[7] It was not simply a dilemma for individuals and communities but a moral crisis without a clear legal solution.

The answer came in 1782, when the Virginia legislature declared manumission legal under a broader set of circumstances. Quakers in the state were presented with a choice: they could keep their slaves and leave the Society of Friends, or they could emancipate their slaves and remain in the fold. On 21 February 1783 the Paynes freed their slaves and applied for admission to the Philadelphia Meeting. The certificate of membership was granted on 12 April 1783.

By the late 1770s the Paynes had already begun considering ways to escape the dilemma of slavery by uprooting the family again. This time they would move not from one southern rural community to another but to the largest and most sophisticated city in the colonies: Philadelphia. They tested the waters, visiting first in 1779 and again two years later. Their eldest son, Walter, established himself there as an advanced scout for the family early in 1783. That year the Paynes emancipated their slaves, shifted their belongings, and became Philadelphians.[8] John Payne launched a new career as a laundry-starch merchant.

By the time they moved to Philadelphia, they had eight children: four boys and four girls. The first son, Walter, was born in the early 1760s. After Walter, the Paynes had William Temple and Isaac, but little is known about either of them. After Dolley was born in 1768, there were three more girls. Lucy, born in 1777, was eventually married twice, first to George Steptoe Washington, nephew of George Washington, and second to Thomas Todd, a U.S. Supreme Court justice from Kentucky. Anne, called Anna, was born in 1779; she married Richard Cutts, a congressman from Saco, Maine. The youngest girl, Mary Coles Payne, was born in 1781. She also married a politician, John George Jackson, a congressman from western Virginia. The baby of the family was John Coles Payne, born in 1782. The only boy to survive into his thirties, John became an endless source of anxiety for Dolley, who tried to take care of him.[9] He finally settled down and married, living for years on the Madison family plantation until he and his family moved to Illinois.

Philadelphia was a leading commercial center, with a large carrying trade; it was a magnet for immigrants from overseas. Noisier and richer than any other American urban area at that time, it had innumerable small shops and the largest outdoor market in the country. The city stretched from the Delaware River on the east to the Schuylkill River on the west; the population numbered around thirty-nine thousand and was growing.[10]

The 1780s, however, was not an easy time to adapt to new circumstances. War had taken its toll, and Philadelphia shared in the national economic turmoil of the decade. The local economy had been forced to convert from maritime commerce to war-related manufacturing and back again. Paper money had become worthless. Spiraling costs and contracting trade imposed crushing expenses on small businessmen. Overseas demand for produce shipped through Philadelphia fell dramatically after 1785, as the ports of the West Indies, whose trade had provided so much revenue for Philadelphia merchants before the war, remained shut to American ships. To make matters worse, the Confederation Congress had moved in 1783, first to New Jersey and then to New York. Houses stood empty—ghostly witnesses to hard times. While Philadelphia's wealthy continued to enjoy the glamour of their own society, the decade proved ruinous for many of the city's residents—including John Payne.[11]

Even during these years of hardship and turmoil, Philadelphia was a well-planned city whose central streets were paved and edged with raised brick sidewalks. Like all cities of the era, it was dirty and unsanitary, but sections of the town presented an attractive appearance, with brick buildings and sidewalks shaded by rows of buttonwood, willow, and poplar trees. The houses of the upper crust, modeled on London mansions, had elegant staircases, furniture imported from Great Britain, chairs upholstered in silk, and walls adorned with the best French wallpaper. These were homes well suited for the dances, dinners, and receptions that mushroomed when the city became the new nation's capital in 1790.[12]

Dolley Payne was fifteen when her family moved to Philadelphia. She seems to have been a dazzling young woman. Years later Anthony Morris, one of her oldest friends, wrote to her niece Anna Payne about the young Dolley. It was the "bright dawn of her splendid day," he remembered. "She came upon our comparatively cold hearts in Philada, suddenly & unexpectedly with all the delightful influences of a Summer Sun . . . with all the warm feelings, & glowing fancies of her Native State." She was lovely: "her complexion seemed from Scotland, and her soft blue Eyes from Saxony." And most of all he extolled her for her "stately step, and the sweet engaging Smile."[13]

Elizabeth Drinker, a member of a prominent Quaker family, occasionally noted in her diary the activities of the Paynes, especially Dolley and her brother Walter. By 1784 Walter was courting the eldest Drinker child, Sarah, while Dolley was paired off with a young man named Jacob Downing, a flour merchant who would later marry Sarah Drinker. Late that year Walter set sail for Great Britain, and Elizabeth Drinker never again mentioned him; he probably died at sea.[14] Walter had been the family's emissary to Philadelphia; Walter had moved into elite Quaker society. His loss was the first of a series of tragedies to befall the family over the next decade.

As the family business began to slide downhill, it was difficult for Dolley Payne to make her peace with Quaker criticism. The matronly guardians of behavior chided her for the cut of her gown and the shape of her cap and imposed upon her a formality she found stifling. Twenty-five years later, back in the city for a knee operation, she wrote her sister Anna that seeing these old acquaintances "brought to my mind the time when our society used to control me entirely, and debar me from so many advantages and pleasures." [15]

By 1789 Dolley's father's business had collapsed, and the Pine Street Meeting had expelled him for insolvency.[16] It was in this environment that Dolley became engaged to her first husband, John Todd, a Quaker lawyer and a member of the Pine Street Meeting. On 7 January 1790 they wed. His father was a teacher, and he was a young man with good prospects rather than actual affluence. His brother, James Todd, was a bank clerk. The Pine Street Meeting granted its approval, and on the appointed day the two stood up and declared their vows. Then the contracting parties and the gathered witnesses signed the marriage certificate. The signers were respectable Philadelphia Quakers all: Drinkers and Walns, Pembertons and Collins, Biddles and Logans.[17]

Times continued hard for the Paynes. After losing his business, John Payne became seriously depressed and eventually retreated to his bedroom, where he remained until he died on 24 October 1792. To keep the family afloat financially, Mary Payne converted their home into a boardinghouse for members of the federal government temporarily residing in Philadelphia. Family legend has it that John Payne had urged his eldest daughter to marry John Todd, perhaps hoping she could thereby salvage the family's fortunes.[18] Dolley's sister Lucy helped shortly after her father's death when, at the age of fifteen, she eloped with George Steptoe Washington, nephew of the president, George Washington. The marriage allowed Mary Payne to give up her boardinghouse and leave Philadelphia for George Steptoe Washington's home in Virginia, Harewood, taking with her the two youngest Payne children, Mary Coles and John Coles, while Anna remained in Philadelphia with Dolley.

Whatever the burdens, John and Dolley Todd set up house. In November 1791 they moved to the northeast corner of Fourth and Walnut, into a three-story brick house with two rooms to a floor. John Todd established his law practice in the first-floor front room and gave another room to his apprentice. It was a modest middle-class house that feels cramped to visitors today.[19] The following February, Dolley gave birth to her first child, John Payne Todd, and in the summer of 1793 to her second, William Temple Todd. It is soon after this that the letters in this volume begin, on 30 July 1793. John Todd was away from home on a law case, but he sent a short note to his wife to tell her how and where he was and to chat about his two boys. The next month a yellow-fever epidemic engulfed the city. It was not the only epidemic of the decade, nor was it the worst, but it entered into public memory as a plague.[20]

Contemporary accounts of the epidemic are horrendous. Fear ran rampant. No one understood the disease—why it occurred, how to prevent it or cure it or respond to it. Faced with this nightmare, husbands abandoned their wives, and wives forsook their husbands. Children were orphaned; whole families were wiped out. At first people lit bonfires, but when the city's doctors said that did no good, they began to use gunpowder—until the sound of explosions became so depressing that that too was stopped. Between 6 and 8 percent of the resident population died, or about five thousand people.[21] Panic spread to other East Coast cities. New York and New Jersey passed laws forbidding citizens of Philadelphia to cross their borders. Federalists feared that Republicans would drive the government out of Philadelphia, and Thomas Jefferson confidently concluded that "yellow fever will discourage the growth of great cities in the nation."[22]

One of the young men reading law with John Todd that summer was Isaac Heston, a member of a respectable Philadelphia Quaker family. Todd sent Dolley, Anna, and the two sons off to the country but stayed in town himself. He tried to persuade his parents to leave, but they would not go. The yearly Quaker meeting was held. The need for lawyers was great, so Todd kept Heston with him, and when Heston fell ill, Todd would not leave him. On 19 September Heston wrote his brother Abraham. "You can not immagin the situation of this city," he despaired. "They are dieing on our right hand & on our Left. We have it oposit us, in fact, all around us, great are the number that are Calld to the grave, and numbered with the silent Dead." Though healthy enough to write on the nineteenth, Isaac Heston was soon gone.[23] John Todd Sr. died on 2 October and James Todd fled, renting space for his mother outside the city, but she too expired, on 12 October, before she could leave. John Todd left in mid-October but died on 14 October, the same day his younger son perished.

For Dolley Payne Todd these years brought enormous personal loss: her brother Walter, her father, her husband, her baby, her in-laws, and in 1795 her two remaining elder brothers.[24] The sense of deprivation and anxiety never left her.

And so Dolley Payne Todd became a widow. At first she struggled, nearly alone and with slim financial resources until her husband's estate was settled. Deeply concerned, her mother wrote to the Todd family nurse that Dolley was "in debt for the burial of her babe & nearly moneyless."[25] Dolley fought with her brother-in-law, James Todd, over her rights and inheritance from both her husband and her father-in-law. William W. Wilkins, a suitor and a lawyer, assisted her, and James Todd settled. There is no indication of any further communication between Dolley and Todd, although after he died she helped his children, especially her nephew, Samuel Todd.

Dolley moved back to her own house in Philadelphia and remained a member of the Quaker community. By then, however, her ties to the community were already frayed: her father had been expelled, her sister Lucy had married out, and her mother and younger siblings had gone to live at Harewood. Her brother-in-law had proved combative in a time of crisis. Moreover, if Quaker society before the yellow-fever epidemic had partially policed its members by moral censure communicated through gossip, the number and kind of rumors that sped through the city during the plague made even the appearance of unsanctioned behavior increasingly fraught with difficulty. When it became clear that she was about to marry again, Wilkins wrote her that she ought to be careful in making her marriage settlement on her son Payne, for whatever she did could open her up to criticism. She followed his advice.

She was twenty-five years old, a young woman with suitors and the financial stability that the settlement of John Todd's estate had given her. A Mr. Groves was in the "pouts" about her, and Wilkins himself had been smitten. Years later Anthony Morris remembered her as "the first & fairest representative of Virginia, in the female society of Philada, and she soon raised the mercury there in the thermometers of the Heart to fever heat." She had become one of the most eligible young women in Philadelphia. In 1794 James Madison, a forty-three-year-old congressman from Virginia, asked his friend Aaron Burr—who had once boarded with Mary Payne—to introduce him to the widow Todd. By June the courtship had advanced to the point that Catharine Coles wrote to Dolley that Madison was dreaming of her at night and desired "that your Heart will be calous to every other swain but himself."[26]

A member of a Virginia planter family, Madison was seventeen years her senior and a long-standing bachelor, although he had been engaged to the teenaged daughter of a New York congressman in 1783.[27] With a towering intellect and penetrating mind, he was a wonderful conversationalist who loved intimate gatherings and hated large ones. He had played a major role in framing the U.S. Constitution and drafting the Bill of Rights and was representing his central Virginia district in the U.S. House of Representatives. In the First

Federal Congress, he had been a key member of the Washington administration. George Washington greatly relied on his advice on a vast array of issues related to the conduct of the infant government. Madison drafted Washington's inaugural address and then wrote the response from the House of Representatives. When the Senate responded, he composed Washington's reply as well. By 1794 Thomas Jefferson had retired to Monticello, and James Madison had become the leader of the emerging Republican Party, a political force often referred to in the mid-1790s as "Madison's Party." [28]

On 15 September the two were quietly wed at Harewood, the home of Lucy and George Steptoe Washington near Berkeley Springs, Virginia (now W.Va.). If she had any regrets or fears, she left no record of them. We can only ponder the significance of her letter to Eliza Collins Lee on her wedding night. She originally signed this letter Dolley Payne Todd, then crossed that out, and wrote: "Dolley Madison! Alass!" But the letter is torn at this point and her meaning rendered undecipherable.

Dolley Todd, now Dolley Madison, had married a non-Quaker before the end of the requisite year of mourning. On 12 December 1794 she was expelled from the Society of Friends. She had left behind her the closed environment of the Quakers and the stolid world of her late husband. She had become the wife of a slave-owning Virginia planter, moving from the provincial world of observant Quakers to the cosmopolitan world of politics, affluence, and gaiety.

The material conditions of her life demonstrated her shift in circumstances. She moved to more fashionable quarters in Philadelphia, a large and comfortable three-story house on Spruce Street, with its brick sidewalks, branching elm trees, and hitching posts every ten feet to keep horses off the sidewalks. Through James Monroe, then serving as minister to France, the Madisons imported carpets, china, and furniture from Europe; they had more furniture sent from Montpelier, along with slaves to act as household staff. A French clock for their mantle and silk for curtains, barrels of hams and of corn—all arrived in good time.[29] The household included not only the Madisons and Payne Todd but also Anna Payne and at times James's youngest sister, Fanny.

With a few important exceptions—most notably Eliza Collins Lee, Betsy Pemberton, and Anthony Morris—those who had once peopled Dolley's world in Philadelphia disappeared from her life, and a new set of actors entered onto her stage. Her new environment contained balls and parades and festivals attending the opening of Congress or the birthday of George Washington; there were dances, plays, and visits.[30] But if it was gay, this world was also politically charged; every social action was freighted with the overtones of class, region, and politics. Philadelphia was the national capital during a decade in which party conflict increasingly escalated over both domestic issues, such as Alexander Hamilton's proposals for the assumption and funding of the national debt, and international issues, such as the Jay treaty with Great Britain. The knitting together of people and politics, the personal and the political, was to dominate Dolley's social world for much of the rest of her life, especially the years from 1801 to 1817. It began in Philadelphia soon after her marriage to James Madison and is easily glimpsed through her friendship with Sally McKean, the daughter of Pennsylvania politician Thomas McKean, who in 1798 scandalized the city by converting to Roman Catholicism and marrying the Spanish minister to the United States, Carlos Fernando Martínez de Yrujo.[31]

Thomas McKean was a leading Pennsylvania jurist and statesman. A signer of the Declaration of Independence, by the 1790s he was chief justice of the state supreme court and a leader of the emerging Republican Party. He was also a self-made man who, no matter how many dinners and balls he gave or attended, found it impossible to gain entry into the inner circles of Philadelphia's elite. McKean first broke with the Washington administration over Alexander Hamilton's financial plans for the assumption and funding of the national debt. The Senate ratification of the Jay treaty in the summer of 1795 completed his disenchantment. By the election of 1796, he found himself particularly distressed at what he considered the apostasy of his old friend John Adams, whom he now considered a dangerous monarchist.

At the same time the friendship between Dolley Madison and Sally McKean was growing. The age difference of nine years makes it likely that the two women first got to know each other through Anna Payne.[32] By August 1797, the date of the first surviving letter between them, Sally was part of Dolley's social world, swept up in the politics of the city and the times. The fact that Yrujo was courting Sally became woven into the city's political feuds. It was Spanish policy to oppose any rapprochement between Great Britain and the United States; Yrujo accordingly expressed his government's displeasure over the terms of the Jay treaty. For Federalists who supported the Washington administration and the Jay treaty, the alliance between McKean and Yrujo provided an opportunity to turn social gossip into political ammunition. Although most Philadelphia newspapers ignored Sally McKean's marriage to Yrujo, the arch-Federalist William Cobbett, writing for his paper, *Porcupine's Gazette,* ran editorial after editorial trumpeting the couple's alleged rudeness, profanity, and drunken domestic quarrels.[33]

The tone of Sally McKean's letter of 3 August 1797 demonstrates the role these political disputes played within the world of women. Dolley had written to Sally from Montpelier, asking for the Philadelphia gossip about the new Adams administration. McKean, who had a sharp wit, responded with a highly political and gossiping letter, a mixture of humor, fun, and fury against Yrujo's and her father's enemy. She began with a vicious description of Abigail Adams—"with her hawks eyes"—and a nasty portrait of John Adams himself, who was too awkward to know or observe the protocols of society. McKean went on to insult Secretary of State Timothy Pickering, adding that her beloved Yrujo had given "Tim a very good dose" in his diplomatic notes. Continuing with insider Philadelphia chatter, she closed her letter with a scandalous tale about the Spanish consul general, José Ignacio de Viar. It was all good gossip in a world where politics was part of daily life and where opponents were to be lashed and lampooned while one's own party and husband were admired and protected. But gossip provides a forum where women have few other direct channels through which to articulate their political opinions. The gossip we read in these letters hints at the larger social and political issues addressed through behind-the-hand chatter at the social gatherings.

When John Adams was elected president in late 1796, James Madison announced his retirement. Tired and frustrated with incessant party battles, he and Dolley left for Montpelier, the family estate of five thousand acres in Orange County, Virginia, once Adams was inaugurated in March 1797. The family's stated expectation was to remain in Virginia, living quietly in the country, but as John Adams had observed to his wife Abigail in January, "It seems the Mode of becoming great is to retire." He continued, "Madison I suppose after a Retirement of a few Years is to become President or V.P. It is marvelous how political Plants grow in the shade." [34]

In 1797 both of James Madison's parents were still alive. Increasingly, however, James took over the running of the farm from his father, who was elderly and failing and frequently traveled to local spas for his health. James Madison Sr. had married Nelly Conway in 1749; they had twelve children, including five who died in infancy or childhood.

James Madison Jr. was the first, born in 1751, and was a child of about nine when his parents began building the house that became Montpelier, which James's great-nephew once described as "a plain rectangular structure, with a hall running through the center having two rooms on each side." [35] He had three brothers and three sisters who survived. Of Francis, two years younger than James, there is little record. He lived close by, married Susanna Bell in 1772, had at least nine children, and died in 1800. His children were remembered in James's will. The next brother, Ambrose, died in 1793. He had married Mary Willis Lee and had been the heir apparent of the Montpelier plantation, so his death was a particular blow to the family. Last among the boys was William, who was much younger than James and outlived him by nearly a decade. William settled on a plantation in Orange County, married Frances Throckmorton, and had ten children. He would later create trouble in the family, but these earlier decades of family life gave no foreshadowing of this role. Of Madison's sisters, Nelly died in 1802, Sarah lived until 1843, and Frances died in 1823. Nelly married Isaac Hite, moved to Winchester, Virginia, and seems to have been quite close to James, as was her husband. Sarah married Thomas Macon, whose plantation adjoined Montpelier. Fanny was the baby of the family, twenty-three years younger than James and six years younger than Dolley. In 1800 she married a local doctor, Robert H. Rose, and they too had a large family.

James Madison Jr. brought his new family to the house occupied by his parents. Almost immediately he began planning to enlarge the dwelling to accommodate both families and to make the house more elegant. He rearranged rooms and added another wing about thirty feet long to the south of the house, as well as new halls and staircases, creating a duplex for the two Madison families. The size of the renovation is reflected in James's order for 190 windowpanes for French windows and enough brass hinges for eight doors. The younger Madisons' portion of the house now included a new dining room, a large central room, and two additional rooms. He also installed a front portico adorned with Tuscan columns, in the process transforming the house from a Georgian building into a larger mansion in the neoclassical Federal style. This was a mansion more worthy of a planter-politician with a new wife and family, a man who was the "squire of Montpelier." [36]

The house sits on a knoll and then commanded a beautiful view of fields and orchards and the Blue Ridge Mountains to the west. As a Washington friend, Anna Maria Thornton, observed in 1802, the mountain view was constantly changing depending on the clouds and the angle of the sun, giving the visitor "a very agreeable and varied object, sometimes appearing very distant, sometimes much separated & distinct and often like rolling waves." One of Dolley's nieces remembered years later that there were "successions of landscapes [which] varied at every turn, from the wildest to the most cultivated." Looking down from the portico, she went on, one could see "immense waving fields of grain, tobacco &c. in sight, the mountains cultivated, tho' so many miles distant." [37]

Although James Madison had retired with the intention of leaving politics behind him, he remained intensely engaged with national issues. With Madison's retirement and Jefferson's election to the vice presidency, Jefferson became leader of the Republican Party. The two men remained close political colleagues as well as friends, as party animosities became increasingly hostile. When John Adams pushed through the Alien and Sedition Acts, Madison reacted with alarm, labeling the alien bill "a monster that must forever disgrace its parents."[38] In 1798 Madison wrote the Virginia Resolutions, and in April 1799 he returned to active politics with his election to the Virginia General Assembly.[39] The Madisons went to Richmond in December for the 1799–1800 session of the state legislature.

Dolley Madison's life during these years was devoted to her family, and the couple spent most of their time at Montpelier. They socialized with the local gentry: the Taylors, Barbours, and Pendletons. She was busy raising her young son and caring for her teenaged sister. The family paid annual visits to Thomas Jefferson at Monticello. They were there in September 1797 but did not stay long enough to visit Enniscorthy, a plantation not far from Monticello where several of Dolley's Coles cousins lived. Instead they rushed back to Montpelier to be with some of James's sisters, who were paying an annual visit to the family, and to wait for Dolley's mother and sisters to arrive. Did the Madison family—either James's parents or his many siblings—embrace her as a member of their family, and she them? Were these years of contentment or struggle? Certainly she remained in her later years far closer to her own family than to her husband's.

One other aspect of their marriage deserves mention here. Though all evidence points to a warm, affectionate, and even passionate physical relationship between husband and wife, the marriage remained childless. Historians have speculated, based on Dolley's successful pregnancies in her first marriage, that the cause of their childlessness lay with James. Given modern insights into infertility, the story is perhaps more complicated than that; there is one ambiguous reference to Dolley's being pregnant in 1809 when she was forty-one. The two delighted in their many nieces and nephews, and the lack of children of their own was undoubtedly a great disappointment to them.[40]

In 1800 the nation held its fourth presidential election, and Thomas Jefferson was a candidate. By late November the voting had concluded, but the results were not yet counted; nevertheless, Jefferson had begun talking to Madison about the shape of the new administration should he be the victor. On his way back to Washington, Jefferson stopped off at Montpelier for a private talk, and they seem to have agreed at this time that, were Jefferson elected, Madison would become secretary of state.[41]

In mid-February 1801, however, Madison's father died. Madison wrote Jefferson on 28 February, "Altho' the exact degree of agency devolving on me now remains to be known, a crowd of indispensable attentions must necessarily be due from me."[42] The Madisons did not arrive in Washington, D.C., until 1 May, two months after Jefferson's inauguration.

Jefferson's election was not unexpected, nor was his choice of James Madison as his secretary of state. But this decision would profoundly alter Dolley Madison's life. Before then her world had revolved around Philadelphia and then Virginia. With a small child to rear, she must have anticipated the quiet life of a member of the rural elite. James Madison's decision to join the Jefferson administration in 1801 changed all that: it thrust her onto the national stage.

1. DPM to Margaret Bayard Smith, 31 Aug. 1834.

2. Bernard Bailyn, *Voyagers to the West* (New York, 1986), 16; A. Roger Ekirch, *"Poor Carolina": Politics and Society in Colonial North Carolina, 1729–1776* (Chapel Hill, N.C., 1981), 6–7; Larry D. Gragg, *Migration in Early America: The Virginia Quaker Experience* (Ann Arbor, Mich., 1980), 39.

3. Susan Mary Forbes, "'As Many Candles Lighted': The New Garden Monthly Meeting, 1718–1774" (Ph.D. diss., Univ. of Pennsylvania, 1972), 147; James Pinckney Pleasant Bell, *Our Quaker Friends of Ye Olden Time* (Lynchburg, Va., 1905), 183; Hiram H. Hilty, *New Garden Friends Meeting: The Christian People Called Quakers* (Greensboro, N.C., 1983), 8–9. The Cedar Creek Meeting lost 250 more members than it gained in the eighteenth century because of this population transfer (Gragg, *Migration in Early America,* 40).

4. Ekirch, *"Poor Carolina,"* 164–65; Maldwyn A. Jones, "The Scotch-Irish in British America," in *Strangers within the Realm: Cultural Margins of the First British Empire,* ed. Bernard Bailyn and Philip D. Morgan (Chapel Hill, N.C., 1991), 309.

5. Bell, *Our Quaker Friends,* 130–35.

6. Spotswood Hunnicutt, "Quakerism in Colonial Virginia" (M.A. thesis, College of William and Mary, 1957), 67–68.

7. Gragg, *Migration in Early America,* 64; John H. Russell, *The Free Negro in Virginia, 1619–1865* (Baltimore, 1913), 43.

8. Elaine Forman Crane et al., eds., *The Diary of Elizabeth Drinker* (3 vols.; Boston, 1991), 1:343, 384, 410, 411. Quakers who left Virginia over the issue of slavery generally settled in the Northwest Territory, especially after 1787. The Paynes were unusual in their choice of Philadelphia. While their earlier move to North Carolina had been a retreat into a more self-contained and Quaker-dominated world, their move to Philadelphia placed them in a complex and worldly environment. See Gragg, *Migration in Early America,* 65, 76–78.

9. William B. Coles, *The Coles Family of Virginia* (Baltimore, 1989), 64–65.

10. Richard G. Miller, *Philadelphia—The Federalist City: A Study of Urban Politics, 1789–1801* (Port Washington, N.Y., 1976), 4.

11. Ellis Paxson Oberholtzer, *Philadelphia: A History of the City and Its People* (Philadelphia, 1912), 308; Ronald Schultz, *The Republic of Labor: Philadelphia Artisans and the Politics of Class, 1720–1830* (New York, 1993), 116–17.

12. Richard G. Miller, "The Federal City, 1783–1800," in *Philadelphia: A 300-Year History*, ed. Russell F. Weigley (New York, 1982), 172–73, 177; Miller, *Philadelphia*, 4.

13. Anthony Morris to Anna Payne, 26 June 1837, *Records of the Columbia Historical Society* 44–45 (1942–43): 217–20.

14. Crane et al., *Diary of Elizabeth Drinker* 1:xi, xxvii, 431 and n. 22.

15. DPM to Anna Cutts, 19 Aug. 1805.

16. Quaker meetings usually expelled members for their actions, rather than for their thoughts or beliefs. The actions considered so obnoxious as to warrant discipline or expulsion reveal something about Quaker values. Stirring up public controversy and marrying outside the faith, for example, were grounds for expulsion. Other causes indicate the importance of moderation: excessive drinking, even a single instance of drunkenness, the use of profane language, gambling, or card playing. Another sufficient cause was the failure to repay lenders, which would have been a result of John Payne's insolvency. See Forbes, "Many Candles Lighted," 124–29.

17. *Philadelphia Directory* for 1797 and 1799; Hunnicutt, "Quakerism in Colonial Virginia," 64–65; Barnard, *Dorothy Payne*, 70–71.

18. Cutts, *Memoirs*, 9, 10.

19. Agnes Downey Mullins, Ruth Matzkin Knapp, and Charles G. Dorman, "Descriptive List of Proposed Furnishings," in "Structural Report of the Todd House," sec. 1, 1, sec. 4, 1–31 (copy at Papers of James Madison).

20. See J. Worth Estes, "Introduction: The Yellow Fever Syndrome and Its Treatment in Philadelphia, 1793," in *A Melancholy Scene of Devastation: The Public Response to the 1793 Philadelphia Yellow Fever Epidemic*, ed. J. Worth Estes and Billy G. Smith (Canton, Mass., 1997), 1–18.

21. John Bach McMaster, *The Life and Times of Stephen Girard, Mariner and Merchant* (2 vols.; Philadelphia and London, 1918), 1:212; Susan E. Klepp, "'How Many Precious Souls Are Fled?': The Magnitude of the 1793 Yellow Fever Epidemic," in *Melancholy Scene*, 166; see also J. H. Powell, *Bring Out Your Dead: The Great Plague of Yellow Fever in Philadelphia in 1793* (Philadelphia, 1949); Mathew Carey, *A Short Account of the Malignant Fever Lately Prevalent in Philadelphia* (1794; rept. New York, 1970); Paul G. Sifton, "'What a Dread Prospect . . .': Dolley Madison's Plague Year," *PMHB* 87 (1963): 182–88.

22. Billy G. Smith, "Comment: Disease and Community," in *Melancholy Scene*, 159.

23. Edwin B. Bronner, "Letter from a Yellow Fever Victim, Philadelphia, 1793," *PMHB* 86 (1962): 205.

24. Elizabeth Drinker wrote on 5 Jan. 1796: "I heard this evening of the deaths of two of Molly Paynes sons, Temple and Isaac, the latter offended a man in Virginia, who some time afterward shot him with a pistol, of which wound he dyed" (Crane et al., *Diary of Elizabeth Drinker* 1:638).

25. Mary Payne to Margaret Hervey, 24 Oct. 1793, in Sifton, "What a Dread Prospect," 185.

26. Anthony Morris to Anna Payne, 26 June 1837, *Records of the Columbia Historical Society* 44–45 (1942–43): 217–20; Catharine Coles to DPM, 1 June 1794.

27. James Morton Smith, *The Republic of Letters* (3 vols.; New York, 1995), 2:847.

28. Ibid., 881.

29. *PJM* 16:39, 174, 197, 435; Ralph Ketcham, *James Madison* (New York, 1971), 378–86.

30. Ketcham, *James Madison*, 384.

31. G. S. Rowe, *Thomas McKean: The Shaping of an American Republicanism* (Boulder, Colo., 1978), 295, 300, 460 n. 15.

32. See the letters from Sally McKean to Anna Payne written in 1796 in Cutts, *Memoirs*, 18–23.

33. Rowe, *Thomas McKean*, 265, 284–87, 289–305.

34. *PJM* 17:xix.

35. W. W. Scott, *A History of Orange County, Virginia* (Richmond, 1907), 208.

36. Smith, *Republic of Letters* 2:968; Conover Hunt-Jones, *Dolley and the "Great Little Madison"* (Washington, D.C., 1977), 61–66; Ketcham, *James Madison,* 389.

37. "Diary of Anna Thornton," 5 Sept. 1802, DLC: Thornton Papers; Mary Cutts, "Memoir," DLC: Cutts Collection.

38. *PJM* 17:133–34.

39. Smith, *Republic of Letters* 2:1108.

40. Ketcham, *James Madison,* 386–87; Joseph Dougherty to Thomas Jefferson, 15 May 1809, DLC: Jefferson Papers: "Mr. Barry is painting in the Presidents house, but Mrs Madison cannot abide the smell of the paint: that may be on account of her pregnancy, but I think she will bring forth nothing more than dignity."

41. Irving Brant, *James Madison* (6 vols.; Indianapolis and New York, 1941–61), 4:27.

42. *PJM* 17:475.

From John Todd Jr.

My dear Dolley,   CHESTER July 30th. 1793.

I found it extremely warm riding yesterday Afternoon and got safely housed near the eleven Mile Stone on the Road before the heavy Gust came on. I proceeded on to Chester after it had abated and got there about five o'Clock—I have a Prospect of seeing home before fifth Day Afternoon from the present Prospect of Business if ⟨I⟩ do not try W. West's Cause. I hope my dear ⟨D⟩olley is well & my sweet little Payne can lisp *Mama* in a stronger Voice than when his Papa left him—I wish he was here to run after Mrs. Withy's Ducks he would have fine sport—Let the Boys be attentive to the office and Business. I have no Doubt of my Dear Dolleys Assistance when necessary. Thine forever

John Todd Junr.

RC (Macculloch Hall Historical Museum, Morristown, N.J.). Torn by removal of seal.

To James Todd

4th day Evening 9 oclock [October 1793]

Oh my dear Brother what a dread prospect has thy last Letter presented to me! A reveared Father in the Jaws of Death, & a Love'd Husband in perpetual danger—I have long wished for an oppertunity of writeing to thee & enquireing what we could do? I am almost destracted with distress & apprihension—is it two late for their removal? or can no interfearance of their Earthly friends rescue them from the two general fate? I have repeatedly Entreated

24

John to leave home from which we are now unavoidably Banished—but alass he cannot leave his Father.

I did not receive thy first Letter & am in ignorence of the particulars thee Mentions—pray write me soon again—I wish much to see you, but my Child is sick, & I have no way of geting to you.

My best Love to Ailez & the little ones—believe me sincearly & affectinately thyne.

D P Todd

RC (Macculloch Hall Historical Museum, Morristown, N.J.). Addressed to James Todd at Darby.

To James Todd

Second day Morn 8 oClock

My dear Brother [28 October 1793]

An opportunity offering this Morning to thee, I have sent on thy Letter & request a copy of our Fathers Will, as our seperation may be soon & a conveyance from Wilmington will not be so conveniant—the papers, also of my Husband contained in the Trunk.

I was hurt My dear Jamy that the Idea of his Lib[r]ary should occur as a proper source for raising money. Book's from which he wished his Child improved, shall remain sacred, & I would feel the pinching hand of Poverty before I disposed of them.

I have not time to say much but trust in Heaven "all will be rite" & that our homes may yet afford us a plentiful assilum—with Love to you all

D P Todd

RC (Macculloch Hall Historical Museum, Morristown, N.J.). Docketed as received 28 Oct. 1793.

To James Todd

7th Febry. 94.

As I have already suffered the most serious Inconvenience from the unnecessary Detention of my part of my Mother in Law's property and of the Receipt Book and papers of my late Husband—I am constrained once more to request—and if a request is not sufficient—to *demand* that they may be delivered this day—as I cannot wait thy return from the proposed Excursion without material Injury to my Affairs. The bearer waits for thy answer.

Dolley P. Todd

RC (Macculloch Hall Historical Museum, Morristown, N.J.). Addressed to James Todd at Chestnut Street. Note at bottom in an unidentified hand: "Received the above about one oClock whilst Alex Todd and Jeremiah Cresson were employed in finishing the Division of Furniture."

Will of Dolley Payne Todd

[PHILADELPHIA, 13 May 1794]

I Dolley P: Todd being at present in the City of Philadelphia do publish and declare this to be my last will and testament.

I give to my brother John two hundred and fifty Dollars to be paid or by my executors put to interest for his use one Year after My decease—To my Aunt Lucy Winston I give my gold Watch and all my books—my wearing apparel and personal ornaments to be divided equally among my sisters including Isaac's wife—I direct sixty Dollars to be laid out in a gold Watch to be presented to my brother Isaac—To my brother Walter I give two hundred and fifty dollars to be paid one year after my death—The foregoing pecuniary legacies to be paid only out of my personal estate after the payment of my debts. And to this end, I direct that all the residue of my personal estate be converted into money as soon as possible after my death.

I give to my Mother Two hundred and fifty dollars per annum, during her life; the first payment to be made at the expiration of one Year after my death: but if by any Means my estate should be so reduced that this annuity should exceed the one fourth part of the net income thereof, then instead of the said annuity, she shall after such deficiency shall appear, and be declared by either of my executors, be paid quarterly the one fourth part of the clear income of my estate.

All the residue of my Estate real and personal I give to my son John Payne Todd his heirs and assigns forever, but if my son should die before he shall have attained the age of twenty one years, then and immediately after his death, I give my house, lot and stables at the Corner of fourth and Walnut Streets to my Mother during her life, and after her death, I give the same to my three Sisters Lucy, Anna and Mary: The annuity above given to my Mother is to cease upon the death of my son under the age of twenty one.

And in Case of such death of my son under Age, I farther direct that my executors the survivor or survivors of them shall sell all the residue of my real estate and that the proceeds thereof together with what may remain of my personal estate be equally divided among my brothers then living and the issue of such as may have died leaving issue, such issue to take the Parent's Share only.

I appoint my Mother, my brother in Law George S: Washington, and William W. Wilkins of the City of Philadelphia to be my executors, and Aaron Burr to be the sole Guardian of my son. And as the education of my son is to him and to me the most interesting of all earthly concerns, and far more important to his happiness and eminence in Life than the increase of his estate, I direct that no expense be spared to give him every advantage and improvement of which his Talents may be susceptible. In testimony whereof I have hereunto subscribed my name and set my seal this thirteenth Day of May in the Year one thousand seven hundred and Ninety four.

Dolley P. Todd

Sealed, signed published and declared by the said D. P: Todd as and for her last will and testament in the presence of us who have hereunto at her request subscribed our Names as witnesses there being an erasure from the word *"Upon"* 28th line to the word *"the"* 29th. line, first page, made before the execution & signature

Catherine Coles
Sarah Pemberton
Wm Preston

RC (NjMoHP). In a clerk's hand, signed by DPM.

From Catharine Coles

PHILADELPHIA 1 June 1794

I told you my Dear Cosen that I should not stay very Long here after you was gone we propose Leaveing this next Wednesday for New york.

Now for some News all the good Folks in this House are well only Cosen Sally[1] is sikish, Capn Preston[2] is gone, Sukey & Mrs Grenup are all so. Mr Grove is in the Pouts about you, tell Anny[3] I have not seen Mr Porter so I cant tell how he Looks, the General is pretty so so, J—— B—— Round the Corner is melancholy, Lawrance[4] has made me his Confidant Poor Fellow I fear he will not meet with Suckcess, now for Mad——[5] he told me I might say what I pleas'd to you about him to begin, he thinks so much of you in the day that he has Lost his Tongue, at Night he Dreames of you & Starts in his Sleep a Calling on you to relieve his Flame for he Burns to such an excess that he will be shortly consumed & he hopes that your Heart will be calous to every other swain but himself he has Consented to every thing that I have wrote about him with Sparkling Eyes, Monroe goes to France as Minister Plenipo. M—— has taken his House do you like it. Poor Coln Bur[6] has Lost his Wife he is gone to New York. Dont you think that I have wrote anough for this time adieu. Mr Coles Joins m⟨e⟩ in affectionate Love to you your Mother & Sisters & remember us to all frien⟨ds.⟩ Your Sincere friend

Catharine Coles

RC (ViU: Dolley Madison Papers). Addressed by Catharine Coles to Mrs. Todd in Virginia. Docketed by Dolley Payne Todd. On the cover is written, in unknown hands, "Wm. W. Wilkins Esqr." and "Mrs. Coles Letters must be directed to the care of Mr. James Thompson of New York." Printed in *PJM* 15:342.

1. Sarah Coles.
2. William Preston.
3. Anna Payne.
4. Probably John Lawrence, a gentleman who lived at 197 Chestnut Street (*PJM* 15:343 n. 7).
5. James Madison.
6. Aaron Burr.

From James Madison

ORANGE Aug: 18. 94.

I recd. some days ago your ⟨p⟩recious favor from Fredg. I can not express, but hope you will conceive the joy it gave me: The delay in hearing of your leaving Ha⟨n⟩over which I regarded as the only ⟨s⟩atisfactory proof of your recove⟨r⟩y, had filled me with extreme ⟨. . . dis⟩quietude, and the co⟨mmun⟩ication of the welcome event was ⟨e⟩ndeared to me by the *stile* in which it was conveyed. I hope you will never have another *de⟨li⟩beration,* on that subject. If the sentiments of my heart can gua⟨r⟩antee those of yours, they assure me there can never be a caus⟨e⟩ for it. Is it not cruel that I should be obliged to mingle w⟨ith⟩ the deliciou⟨s . . .⟩ your letter the pain ⟨. . .⟩ I cannot ⟨di⟩smiss my fears that his illness may at least be prolonged. ⟨O⟩n the most favorable supposition, I can not venture to expect that he will be able to travel in less than 10 or 12 days. I should not hesitate to set out without him, tho' in several respects inconvenient, were it not forbidden by his utter ignorance of our language, and my being the only ⟨pe⟩rson here who knows a word of his; ⟨so⟩ that in case his ⟨il⟩lness should continue his distress as well as that of those around him would be inexpressible; to say noth⟨in⟩g of the difficulty of followi⟨n⟩g me in the event of his getting wel⟨l.⟩ This adverse incident is t⟨he⟩ more mortifying, as I had spared ⟨n⟩o efforts and made some sacrifices, to meet you at ⟨. . .⟩ than I hoped when we ⟨par⟩ted. I limited ⟨. . .⟩

⟨. . .⟩ set out. If he so far recovers that I can leave him, without being a⟨ble⟩ in a few days, according to appearances, to travel, I shall then endeavo⟨r⟩ to proceed without him, and let him make his way after me as well as he can: In the mean time, allow me to hope that this unavoidable delay, will not extend its influence to the epoch most ⟨. . . an⟩d to repeat the claim ⟨wh⟩ich I apprised ⟨. . .⟩

RC (DLC). Damaged by folds, the RC consists of three portions of pages. Printed in *PJM* 15:351.

From William W. Wilkins

PHILADELPHIA August 22nd. 1794.

I will not delay a Moment my ever dear and valued friend to reply to your last interresting Epistle.[1] Flattered as I am by your Condecension in consulting me on this important Occasion and truly and disinterestedly solicitous for your Welfare—the Task I undertake is far from being a painful one. As your friend I feel not the least Hesitation in forming my Opinion—ought I then to feel any Reluctance in communicating it?

Mr M——n is a Man whom I admire. I knew his Attachment to you and did not ther⟨efor⟩e content myself with taking his Character from the Breath of popular Applause—but ⟨consul⟩ted those who knew him intimately in private Life. His p⟨ersonal⟩ Character therefore I have every reason to believe is good and amiable. He unites to the great Talents which have secured him public Approbation those engaging Qualities that contribute so highly to domestic Felicity. To such a Man therefore I do most freely consent that my beloved Sister be united and happy.[2]

Yes my dear and amiable Julia you have my fullest and freest Approbation of the Step you are about to take. No Wish is dearer to my Heart than your Happiness & Heaven is my Witness that nothing is less selfish than my Attachment to you. That I have not been insensible to your Charms ought not I think to be regarded as a Fault—few persons in similar Situations would not have felt their irresistible Influence; but none I will venture to say could have mingled in their Emotions more true Respect and more fraternal Affection than I have.

With respect to the Settlement on your Son—I will give ⟨yo⟩u my Sentiments frankly. You are placed in a critical Situation in this Affair—the Eyes of the World are upon you and your Enemies have already opened their Mouths to censure and Condemn you. I hope you will disappoint them—I believe you will now be just—for you have hitherto always been generous. I must confess I conceive it to be your duty to make some Settlement upon him and I know you too well to doubt your Inclination to do it. The only Question can be to what Amount and in what Manner shall this Settlement be made.

Mr. M——n is as I am informed a Man of genteel tho not of large property. He has a right to expect some part but does not want the whole of your Estate. I would suggest therefore that your House and Stables situate in Fourth Street be previously to your Marriage conveyed to Trustees in Trust to receive the Rents Issues and profits during the Minority of your Son and apply the same first to discharge the Sum of £350 with the Interest (being the Remaining Sum due of the purchase Money & which ought to be regarded as an Incumbrance on the premises) & in the second place to the support & Education of your Son (stipulating if you please that for this purpose the payments of the proceeds be made to your future Husband and yourself as it is to be presumed your Son will always remain under your joint Care and Protection) and in trust farther to convey the premises to your Son in fee Simple upon his arriving to the Age of twenty one Years—but if he should die before he attains that Age to convey to yourself and your Heirs.

Your Son as a residuary Legatee of his Grand Father will be intitled to something—but the Amount of this Legacy is wholly uncertain. The provision which I had mentioned will in your Circumstances be a generous one— I only fear it will be thought unreasonably great. But those who know Julia as well as ⟨I do⟩ will look for Conduct at once maternally affectionate and exaltedly bountiful.

If I have given my Opinion with too much freedom—I earnestly solicit your pardon. I am sensible that neither Age or Wisdom or Relationship authorize me to advise—but your own Command has opened my Lips and Friendship bids me be sincere. With the truest—warmest Wishes for your Happiness I am my dear Julia ever & affectionately yours

Wm. W. Wilkins

My Respects to Mrs. Payne. Hallowell[3] informs me that he considered himself *obliged* to pay the money to Isaac[4] & has paid it to his Order. Compliments to Miss Anna. I must beg her pardon for detaining these Letters so long in my possession as I expected daily to hear from you & wished to dispatch in one packet. I shall attend as usual to your Affairs till my power is revoked.

RC (DLC: DPM Papers). Addressed by Wilkins to Dolley Payne Todd, "Martinsburg / Virginia / Particular Care of / Geo. [Steptoe] Washington Jun Esqr." Printed in *PJM* 15:351–53.
    1. Letter not found.

2. The remainder of this sentence, crossed through but faintly legible, reads: "⟨and am Satisfied?⟩ that an honorable asylum is offered to my gentle friend who has been so undeservedly and so vindictively persecuted and over whose Safety I have long anxiously watched!"

3. John Hallowell (1768–1839) was a Philadelphia Quaker lawyer (Crane et al., *Diary of Elizabeth Drinker* 3:2158).

4. This was DPM's brother Isaac Payne, who died in Norfolk, Va., later in 1794 (*PJM* 15: 353 n. 6).

To Eliza Collins Lee

HAIR-WOOD[1]—September the 16th.[2] [1794]

I receav'd your precious favour from Bath & should have indulged myself in writing an answer but for the excessive weakness In my Eyes—And as a proof my dearest Eliza of that confidence & friendship which has never been interrupted betwe[e]n us I have stolen from the family to commune with you—to tell you in short, that in the cource of this day I give my Hand to the Man who of all other's I most admire—You will not be at a loss to know who this is as I have been long ago gratify'd In haveing your approbation—In this Union I have every thing that is soothing and greatful in prospect—& my little Payne will have a generous & tender protector.

A Settlement of all my real property with a considerable Adition of Money is made upon him with Mr. M——s full approbation—This I know you feel an Interrest in or I should not have troubled you with it—you also are acquainted with the unmerited sensure of my Enimys on the subject.

Mr. & Mrs. L. Lee[3] have left the neighbourhood to our great regret as we wished much their presence to day, they being the only Family Invited except *his* sister & Brother Washington—but how shall I express the anxiety I feel to see you? That friend whose goodness, at many interresting periods I have greatfully experienced would now rejoice us by a sight of her—tell your dear Lee that he must not suplant D P T in your Affections but suffer her whilst she deserves it to share with him your ever valuable Esteem—Adeiu! Adeiu.

It is yet uncertain whether we shall see you before the meeting in Phila. Mama, Madison, Lucy, G[e]orge Anna and Hariot[4] joine in best love to ⟨yo⟩u & yours.

Dolley Payne Todd

Evening.

Dolley Madison! Alass!

RC (DLC: DPM Papers). Addressed by Dolley Payne Todd to Eliza Lee in Loudoun County, "favour'd by Mr. J. Armistead." Last page damaged, probably removing part of postscript. Printed in *PJM* 15:357.

1. Harewood was George Washington Steptoe's estate near Charles Town, in what is now Jefferson County, W.Va.

2. DPM first wrote "15th," then altered the date to read "16th."

3. Ludwell Lee was the son of Richard Henry Lee. His wife Flora was a member of the Steptoe family (ibid., 358 n. 5).

4. Harriot Washington (1776–1822) was George Steptoe Washington's sister (ibid., 358 n. 9).

From "Signora Catoni" (Sally McKean)

PHILADELPHIA, August 3d. –97.

I hasten to thank you my Dearest Sister (for so hereafter I intend to stile you, as I cannot bear the dry, affected stile of—Dear Madam,) as you really are my sister in affection—for your charming letter dated the 23d of June— which was handed me by our friend *Brent*,[1] in the first place you ask me for a description of the Drawing room, I now hasten to give it you—that we have none at all—for that old what shall I call her[2]—with her hawks eyes, gave out that the weather was too warm, and it would affect her nerves, they must be very delicate of course, but I suppose we shall have it in full splendor in the fall: her, and her Caro sposa, accompanied by Miss Smith—a neice of hers, and who I suppose will sett up for the Miss Custis of the place—but there I defy her—for she is not young, and confounded ugly, have sett of a few days ago, for Boston, where I suppose they want to have a little fuss made with them for dear knows they have had none made here. But I must give you an anecdote about the elegance of his manners, and very great attention on the fourth of July, the *foreign Ministers,* the members of the Cincinata, and some few Members of Congress, waited on him in the morning, and he was so polite as to put his hat on—before them, but after a little while he recollected himself and took it off—and appeared quite fright[e]ned at his absence, some of the Gentlemen were going to put theirs on also; in order to keep him company—only they thought it too warm—Pray tell me now—was ever our former *President* known to behave in that manner—no you will say—because he was a Gentleman: the conclusion I have drawn from it is—that he meant to introduce a new custom and for its elegance and politeness—it exceeds any thing I ever saw, or have even heard of happening in any of the Courts of Europe, the only Ladies who visited *his Right Honorable* Lady—was Madame Freire,[3] and forlorn Mrs Wolcott. There has been a confounded peice of work here lately with Blount and our Dear friend Robert List—n,[4] but before this time you must be acqua[int]ed with the particulars, if not by the news paper—you must have been by old Amey who came and worried me to Death till I told her all about it she said please *God* as soon as she got home she would write you all about it the very first thing she did. The Man Tim——Pick—[5] has been behaving in a very devlish manner—but our amiable friend the Chevalier—has written a very excellent letter,[6] address'd to him and which gives Tim a very good dose. It is allow'd by every body to be exceedingly well written, and to contain the naked truth—Oh! you cannot have any idea what a noise it has made some of the Timothy gang says he is worse than Genett, Fauchett, or Adett[7]—but on the other hand all the clever fellows say that nothing can be better than it is, and that the Minister deserves well of his Country for it. You ask me if he and Viar still talk of visiting Virginia, the Chevalier does—but I beleive not very shortly—as he is to sett of next week for Boston, and some other places he means I beleive to travel thro' before he returns here—as for Viar I know it is impossible, as he has some business which requires his presence here, and I beleive our friend Fatio will also remain here—we are going to lose Nancy Emlen—she is to be married very shortly to a Mr Russel from Boston. I beleive you saw him last winter, he is very rich, but ugly as the Devil. Our friend Molly Wh—ton[8] is still very much enamour'd of Fatio, but I beleive his heart is made of something harder than ice ore it would melt—Mr and Mrs Buckley—Sally Wall that used to be—has sett of for Lisbon a few days ago—and I should not be much astonish'd if the Vessel was to sink, containing such a load of sin—and impudence as Smith of S.C. on board—who has gone as our Minister to Portugal[9]—I received a letter a day or two ago from Mrs Jaudenes, she tells me she is delighted with Spain—she writes from Mayorca—she says also, that they [*sic*] Ladies there occasionally dress as they do here—but they wear very rich dresses and a great many jewels—she desires her remembrance to you—Mr J——s health is compleatly restored, and the Children are all well. I received letters a few days ago—from Anne and Polly—they were handed me by the all killing all elegant and accomplish'd Beau Dawson[10]—who strikes me dumb with Admiration whenever he appears—The Chevalier sends his love to you—and also our friend Fatio—as for Viar—I have not seen him these two or three days— The Ch——r is in excellant health and spirits—and looks very well, but [I] beleive as you say that he misses Nelly—I am very sorry for her accident but she must bear it like a Christian—Bless me what a letter I have written you— but remember you must write me in return very soon all the news of Virginia—Swanick has call'd his creditors together and given up every thing— the old Lady is in a great deal of trouble—and looks very thin—they are to move in a ⟨few?⟩ days in a small house opposite the new Chappel poor Meclare is in rather dull spirits—he [*crossed out*] I sincerely pity him—I shall write to morrow to the girls—my paper warns me that It is time to conclude—I therefore take its advice by signing myself your sincere and affectionate friend—

Signora Catoni[11]

I dont venture to put any other name as there is something of the nature of treason contain'd in my letter. Mrs. Liston resides in the country I have not seen her pretty face for some time.

4th. August. I cannot seal this without giving you a little anecdote of Viar, which I have just heard and which accounts for my not seeing him these two, or three days, he has been making love to the wife of a servant who formerly lived with Mr Jaudenes, and he afterward lived with the Chevalier—The wife is a remarkable pretty woman, but no great things in point of character, the husband lives at service. He came home a few days ago to see her—it was at twelve oclock at noon—and behold—verily, he caught the old goat, with his wife, and in not the most decent situation—so the fellow very politely took him by the nose and saluted him with kiks till the corner of the next Street. He is going to make him pay a devlish large sum of money, or else he says he will prosecute him, it has made a confounded noise, the Emlens, and Moll Wharton—all the shoemakers and in fact all the town knows it.

RC (MdHi). Addressed to "Mrs. D. P. Maddison near Orange Court House Via, Fredericksburg, Virginia."
1. Richard Brent.
2. Abigail Adams.
3. This was the wife of Cypriano Riberio Freire, Portuguese minister to the United States.
4. Robert Liston.
5. Timothy Pickering.
6. The chevalier de Yrujo's letter to Pickering is printed in *ASP, Foreign Relations* 2:87–89.
7. Edmond Charles Genet, Jean Antoine Joseph Fauchet, and Pierre Auguste Adet were successively French ministers to the United States.
8. This may have been Martha Wharton (c. 1769–1821), daughter of Samuel and Sarah Lewis Wharton, who married Samuel B. Shaw in 1801 (Crane et al., *Diary of Elizabeth Drinker* 3:2229).
9. William Loughton Smith.
10. John Dawson.
11. Catoni: pertaining to, or resembling, Cato the censor; thus, severe (*OED*).

From James Madison

My dearest,   RICHMOND Monday night December 2d. 1799
Neither the chart of your uncle, or the memory of your brother could save me from two errors on our way down, we made out, notwithstanding to reach

Town before sunset. I found at Mr. Watson's a room prepared for me,[1] and an empty one immediately over it, but they are both in a style much inferior to what I had hoped. You must consequently lower your expectations on this subject as much as possible before you join me, which I shall look for about the time you suggested. I have found it more convenient to let Sam remain until tomorrow morning, than to start him today. He will be able to execute the journey in one day with ease, with an empty carriage. I have procured for your Uncle, a paper, which is for tomorrow morning, in which there is an account of the success of the Republicans in Holland—against the British and Russians, particularly the latter.[2] He will see also, the first fruits of the session in the change of the Speaker and clerk. Colonel Smith had eighty and odd votes, against fifty odd, and Mr. Wirt ninety odd against forty odd.[3] The former Chaplain and Sergent at Arms were reelected. Present me affectionately to all around you—always and truly yours

J. Madison Jr.

Tr (MCR-S: Mary Estelle Elizabeth Cutts Papers).

    1. JM had been elected a delegate to the Virginia General Assembly for the 1799–1800 session. The Madisons were in Richmond from early December 1799 until late January 1800. For JM's account for lodging at George Watson's, see *PJM* 17:358–59.

    2. The defeat of the Anglo-Russian expedition in Holland on 19 Sept. 1799 was reported in the Philadelphia *Aurora General Advertiser* on 30 Nov. 1799 (ibid., 286 n. 3).

    3. The election of Republicans Larkin Smith and William Wirt as speaker and clerk, respectively, of the House of Delegates was part of a purge of Federalists from public office in Virginia (ibid., 285 n. 2).

To Eliza Collins Lee

Janny 12th: [1800]

How shall I approach thee, my dearest Eliza after this tedious seperation, & long silence? Not I trust as a mear correspondent, but as an early friend who does not now recollect thee, without tears of affection.

A prospect of meeting thee which is now clouded with disappointment, was my first inducement to visit Richmond—having heard that Mr. Lee's family would certainly be with him. I have found the place, however, to my surprise, a most agreable one—the society is delightful—many ladys joine in my regret that you are not with us—among others our accomplished friend Mrs. J Mayo.

Mr. L. tells me you have 2 little ones—I would give the world to see them— why will you not come to Orange? Make an Effort my dear Girl to visit us—

& if your Heart is unaltered towards me you will Immagin the happiness such a favour would occation—My time to write is so short that I can only add *our* affectionate salutations.

D. P. Madison

Pray write me & kiss the children

RC (DLC: DPM Papers).

From John G. Jackson

CLARKSBURG Septr 25th 1800

I now commence, my good Friend, a correspondence, which I hope will continue to our last moments, or until I intentionally forfeit your well wishes, ⟨. . .⟩ in my next Letter I may be permitted to address you by the tender appellation of Sister, which next to calling Polly mine,[1] will afford me the highest gratifi⟨cation⟩ especially when I am convinced of your unma⟨. . .⟩ friendship, and look up to you as the tutelary Angel of my dear Polly—you have no doubt heard by my Letter from Morgantown of my victory in the Law suits, thank heaven, I am clear of litigation again, and if the most undeviating rectitude will keep me so, I flatter myself it will be the last; as well as it is the first time I was ever engaged as a principal. The lands worth $5 or 6 which were conveyed in trust to secure the payment of a sum of money to me I bought for 152 cents per acre—so much for my promised information.

Could you believe it—my favorite Kate even, while I was absent deserted her dearest Friends and has taken refuge in the arms of Doctr Williams,[2] ⟨he⟩ is however very per⟨. . .⟩ promises ⟨. . .⟩ forgive her not to do so again, as the Doctr. is a good Republican, and their primary principle *is to do good* I am disposed to be lenitive and accept her concessions as sufficient à produire laction d'excuser.[3]

Before you receive this Letter I shall be on my way to see you, & if asked why this versatility? answer I see no necessity to procrastinate my happiness any longer. I have therefore to entreat you my dear Dora, let nothing *on your part* be wanting to accelerate the wished for day—I refer you to Polly for further information—My Sisters join their Love with mine

John G Jackson

Present me to your good Husband

RC (DLC: Thomas J. Jackson Papers). Torn by removal of seal.

1. Mary (Polly) Payne, youngest of DPM's sisters, married John G. Jackson sometime between October 1800 and January 1801 (Stephen W. Brown, *Voice of the New West* [Macon, Ga., 1985], 10).

2. Dr. William Williams married Catherine, one of Jackson's sisters, in August 1800.

3. The sense of this French phrase is that Jackson is willing to pardon his sister.

A Washington
Education

1801-1809

THE MADISONS ARRIVED IN WASHINGTON ON 1 MAY 1801. DOLLEY
Madison was then thirty-three years old, her husband fifty-one. She was not
classically beautiful, but she had a compelling presence. Gilbert Stuart's portrait of her, painted during this period, shows a woman who is full-bodied and
voluptuous, with dark hair curling in ringlets to frame her oval face. The New
York politician Samuel Latham Mitchill described her as having "a most engaging countenance, which pleases not so much from mere symmetry or
complexion as from expression." And the writer and novelist Margaret Bayard Smith portrayed her as a "stately person" with a "lofty carriage."[1]

It was not just her physical attractiveness or her elegance that drew others
to her, however, but a generosity of spirit, warmth, and genuineness. She
made people feel comfortable without effacing herself, and she commanded
attention without dominating it. Perhaps the key to her social success was her
ability to communicate an interest in others. She was young, gay, enthusiastic,
and immensely sociable. Even so critical an observer as the British diplomat
Augustus John Foster, whose standards were set by the British nobility, described her as "so perfectly good-tempered and good-humoured that she rendered her husband's house as far as depended on her agreeable to all parties."[2]

She loved society, and it seems to have taken her very little time to grow into her new position as wife of the American secretary of state. It became part of her longer education for the role of First Lady. First she spent two years as the wife of a congressman in Philadelphia, where she both observed and partook in some of the society events surrounding official government life. Next she served for four years as mistress of a Virginia plantation, where attendance at dinners and entertainments would have equaled, if not surpassed, the numbers that turned out for social dinners and balls in early Washington. Finally during these eight years, absorbing impressions both positive and negative, she began deciding what she would imitate and what she would reject were she to become the wife of the president of the United States.

Unlike Jefferson, the Monroes, and the Adamses, the Madisons traveled very little and had never been abroad. Rather, the couple shuttled between their plantation in Orange County, Virginia, and their home in Washington, with an occasional visit to a nearby friend or relative. This insularity intensified Dolley Madison's concentration on her immediate roles: wife of the secretary of state and mistress of Montpelier. It also helped her to create a special blend of high fashion and popular American culture. She interpreted European dress, manners, and food through a purely American filter.

And there was herself: gracious, attractive, gregarious, warm, and charming. As early as 28 May 1801—a month after the Madisons had arrived in Washington and two days after they had moved into their own home there— Margaret Bayard Smith reported meeting the Madisons at a dinner at the President's House. Before and after the meal, Smith sat "in the drawing-room with Mrs. M and her sister, whose social disposition soon made us well acquainted with each other." But then, Smith wrote, "it is impossible for an acquaintance with them to be different."[3]

During these eight years Dolley Madison would learn to navigate between different worlds. She would be a key member of Washington "society." She would often serve as Thomas Jefferson's hostess on the relatively few occasions when he found it necessary to include women at his dinner table. She would mix with congressmen and townspeople, cabinet officials and diplomats, those who were her friends and those who were the administration's political enemies.

When the Madisons first arrived in Washington, they stayed in the White House. Jefferson would have been pleased to have them remain there, for as a widower with neither of his daughters in residence, he lived with his private secretary, Meriwether Lewis, the two men rattling around the executive mansion "like two mice in a church."[4] But the Madisons wanted their own quarters, so on 26 May they moved out, as Jefferson wrote his daughter Martha, "to commence housekeeping" in a dwelling on Pennsylvania Avenue, a four-block stroll in the direction of Georgetown.[5] By the time the Madisons went back to Montpelier for their summer retreat—from late July until early October—they had already decided to relocate. Decent housing was hard to find; unable to get the house they really wanted, they settled on a three-story brick residence at 1333 F Street, next door to William and Anna Maria Thornton and only two blocks east of the White House. William Thornton, who had made all the arrangements for them, described the house as larger than the Thorntons' with a light and dry kitchen. It had enough space, Thornton advised, for the whole Madison household. There was a cellar for wine and one for coal, and a year later the owner agreed to build a brick stable for the Madisons' horses and carriage. F Street between Thirteenth and Fifteenth was a good place to live, moreover, as it was one of the few areas of the city where there were a number of large brick houses clustered together. They remained there for the next seven years.[6]

The city itself, between the Potomac and Anacostia Rivers, had been built on a tract of land that in the 1780s and early 1790s had been a lovely spot with small streams gliding between old oaks. By 1800, however, it had already become blighted, as scrubby underbrush, barren lots, and hovels replaced the trees. Contemporary descriptions are filled with dust and poverty. A Connecticut congressman, John Cotton Smith, remembered nearly half a century later that, with two or three exceptions, the city was composed of brand-new houses that had been thrown up too quickly to be comfortable, let alone elegant. In a city of 6,000 acres, only 109 buildings were constructed of brick; the other 263 were of wood and mostly squalid.[7]

In 1800 there were about 3,000 people living in Washington itself, excluding the older towns of Georgetown and Alexandria and the surrounding areas encompassed within the official boundaries of the District of Columbia. By 1810 the population had jumped to 8,121 and a decade later to 13,117.[8] The statistics vibrate with the sound of hammers and saws and the arrival of people in the new nation's capital. After 1801 Congress refused to spend money on city improvements, and city services quickly became inadequate. Many streets remained little more than paths, and traveling from one location in town to another meant riding for miles over rutted roads covered with deep mud or thick dust. At night the same journey was worse, as potholes and tree stumps became dangerous obstacles in the dark. Foster, secretary to the British legation in Washington, wrote to his mother in disgust that he had gone one night to a party only to have his carriage "overturned in a gully." Without congressional support the city could not even construct adequate waterworks and had to content itself with digging wells in the public squares and hiring a pump mender.[9]

These conditions allowed Dolley Madison to play a role in Washington that she could never have played in an older city. In Philadelphia, the previous seat of the federal government, there was a long-established elite to which she did not belong. Washington, however, was brand-new. When the Madisons moved there in 1801, the city's upper crust was drawn from those few who had enough money to live well and had chosen to reside there. According to Margaret Bayard Smith—who was a great partisan of Jefferson and not an objective observer—Washington society during the Jefferson administration quickly knit into a "close and intimate circle," as the residents were drawn together by "the necessity of mutual aid and accommodation." Foster, who disdained America, agreed with her. Despite its desolation and inconveniences, he wrote, Washington was "the most agreeable town to reside in for any length of time" in the United States. The president and his cabinet ministers, he explained, "are generally very hospitable." [10]

Dolley's correspondence in this chapter contains many references to members of Washington society. Some, like Thomas Law and William Thornton, had relocated to Washington as pioneers and speculators. Others, like Joseph Nourse and Thomas Tingey, had moved to the city to join the small corps of civil servants. A handful of congressmen had brought their families, like Richard Cutts, who in 1804 married Dolley's sister Anna Payne. Jefferson's administration included Secretary of War Henry Dearborn and his wife, whom Jefferson described as "plain and excellent people," both "without ceremony." [11] And finally a few diplomats joined society's ranks. This very mixed establishment was well suited to a raw nation that was devoted to republican principles. Members of the diplomatic corps might come from well-established families with aristocratic connections, as Foster did, but Henry Dearborn was born without money or social status.

The Madisons dined with all of them, took tea with them, met them at the races, and went on day excursions with them. They invited some of them to visit Montpelier during the summer months. The same social pattern is evident in the correspondence of Margaret Bayard Smith. On 26 April 1803, for example, Smith's husband, editor of the *National Intelligencer*, the city's Republican newspaper and the voice of the administration, wrote that he had just returned "from a dinner party at General Dearborn's, where I met with Mrs. Madison and Mrs. Duval." And on 26 December 1802 Mrs. Smith told her sister, "Since my last letter to you, I have unexpectedly been in a good deal of company." She had dined "twice at the President's, three times at Mr. Pichons and they have dined twice here, four times at Mrs. Tingeys and once at Genl. Mason's." It was a social whirl. "I have drank tea out three or four times and declined several invitations to balls."[12]

Washington society was complicated by the bitter partisanship displayed by the Republicans and Federalists, not only in the halls of Congress but also on Washington's muddy streets and in its elegant parlors. From the mid-1790s on, the two parties engaged in character assassination and vicious personal attacks. Jefferson complained that he had become "the property of the newspapers, a fair target for every man's dirt." In 1798 a Connecticut Federalist congressman, Roger Griswold, insulted a Vermont Republican, Matthew Lyon, while both men were sitting in the House chamber. Infuriated, Lyon spat in Griswold's face, who then beat Lyon with a cane on the floor of the House. Discord remained the rule, rather than the exception, throughout the Jefferson and Madison administrations.[13]

Jefferson's solution was to banish political partisanship from White House society. He abolished the Federalist administrations' teas and levees that had been open to members of both parties. He received his guests at dinners instead. He sat them at round tables, thus avoiding all symbol of rank, and he kept most of these affairs small and all-male. As a widower Jefferson seldom considered the distaff side of society, and by containing the size of his dinners, he could exert more personal control. He carefully invited only Federalists one day and only Republicans the next. His parties were known for their elegant food, fine French wines, good talk—and lack of rancor.[14]

If she became the wife of a president, Dolley Madison would have to solve the problem of political warfare in other ways. Only 7 congressmen out of about 130 representatives and 34 senators brought their wives to Washington for the winter of 1807–8.[15] It was not only that congressmen might come and go at the will of the electorate, or that few brought their wives to the capital, but that those who did so resided in the city for only four or five months a year. Those wives who did come to Washington generally filled a social niche secondary to that of other members of the city's upper crust. Their stays were too short to enable these wives to become intimate members of Washington "society." Despite the small size of the city, there were thus layers of intensity of relationships and concentric rings of inclusiveness. Jefferson had to deal with the men; Dolley did not have to deal with their wives. How she would include the legislators as the wife of the president would be part of her education.

Social relations were further complicated by contemporary international relations. The first year and a half of the Jefferson administration witnessed a brief period of peace in Europe while France and Great Britain, like prize-fighters sent to their corners, rested before reengaging in a struggle that would not end until 1815. In May 1803, however, Great Britain—using the pretext of France's violation of its treaty obligations—declared war. The immediate issues were Great Britain's command of the seas, France's increasing domination of Europe, and the question of who would profit from the coming breakup of Spanish America. Three camps emerged: Great Britain, France and its satellites, and the neutral nations, whose numbers diminished over the years, leaving the United States as the most important neutral in the Atlantic world. Long before the War of 1812, the United States was caught up in the maelstrom of the European war.

The complexities of foreign affairs meant different things to James and Dolley Madison. For James the situation entailed engagement in a series of elaborate negotiations with France, Great Britain, and Spain over neutral rights, revolution in Saint-Domingue (Haiti), the depredations of the Barbary States, and American claims to Spanish West Florida. For Dolley, however, it posed a different problem: how to navigate between the official representatives of mutually hostile foreign powers within the framework of her role as hostess and leading member of Washington society.

Dolley Madison was already acquainted with members of the diplomatic corps. She had socialized with some of them in Philadelphia during the early years of her marriage to James Madison, especially with members of the Spanish mission after her friend Sally McKean married the Spanish minister, Carlos Fernando Martínez de Yrujo. When the Danish minister, Peder Blicherolsen, wrote a letter bidding the secretary of state farewell on 21 June 1803, he thanked Madison for "all the unaffected proofs of goodness and partiality which You and the highly amiable Mrs. Madison have favoured me with during my several visits to the Federal City." And he added, "Particularly at the last, I should most probably without Mrs. Madisons Generosity have been poisoned: If it was not too old fashiond, I should here have a fine opportunity to drop a few words about Nectar, Divinities, Goddesses etc." [16] In 1803, however, the war intervened. In addition, Jefferson attempted to change the rules of diplomatic etiquette.

Washington was home only to the diplomatic missions of France and, after 1803, Great Britain and Denmark. Initially both France and Great Britain were represented by their chargés d'affaires, Louis-André Pichon (residing in Washington) and Edward Thornton (residing in Philadelphia), respectively. Both nations replaced these men with ministers: Great Britain dispatched Anthony Merry in 1803; David Erskine took his place in 1806. In 1805 France deputed Louis-Marie Turreau de Garambouville, who remained in Washington until 1810. These distinctions of status carried with them burdens of diplomatic protocol. The social life of the diplomatic corps was governed by rules that reflected both diplomatic rank and the current condition of international relations. The small size of Washington society, moreover, amplified the importance of every event. Who was introduced to whom, by whom, and in what order could cause a scandal. Who was seated where at a dinner party could provoke a crisis. Parties, receptions, and dinners could serve as instruments of foreign policy. As James Madison observed in 1804, "Questions of this sort were known to have . . . been sources of the most serious and scandalous consequences."[17] Dolley Madison would be swept into conflict through the social protocols of foreign affairs.

Thomas Jefferson further complicated these issues when he established a new republican code of behavior. The Federalist administrations of Washington and Adams had adopted the broad outlines of European protocol. Jefferson felt deeply that these customs were inappropriate for a republic. In part he was responding to a domestic constituency that saw Federalist rules of social intercourse as monarchical pretense. As Foster wrote, "The President's popularity was unfortunately connected with his manners as well as his acts."[18] In part Jefferson was acting out of his own imperatives. The new nation, he believed, should express its republican theory of government in its pattern of official behavior, and this demanded a more egalitarian etiquette.

Jefferson's solution was the rule of "pell-mell." In 1804 he spelled out his ceremonial guidelines. "In social circles," he wrote, "all are equal, whether in, or out, of office, foreign or domestic; & the same equality exists among ladies as among gentlemen." As part of his campaign of republican etiquette, Jefferson flouted contemporary rules of attire. He eliminated drawing-room evenings and invited guests to small, informal, and usually all-male dinners. As James Madison wrote Monroe in early 1804, "The present administration as you know has not been disposed to cherish ceremony of any kind, and a relaxation of it has been favored by the removal of the Govt. from large Cities."[19] When Peder Pedersen, the Danish chargé d'affaires, moved his nation's mission from Philadelphia to Washington and paid his respects to the president, Jefferson received him in slippers. But Pedersen was a chargé d'affaires, a bachelor, the representative of a small nation, and perhaps an easygoing man; he never objected to this treatment.[20]

For Dolley Madison the combination of international hostilities, Jeffersonian protocol, and Washington society became personal through a series of events in late 1803 and early 1804 known as the Merry affair. Anthony Merry, the new British minister, arrived in Washington in late 1803 with his new bride, Elizabeth Death Merry. He was rather drab, dour, and very meticulous; she was striking and handsome, literate and intellectual, but haughty and discontented with America, and perhaps especially so with the provinciality of Washington, D.C. When Merry arrived he shifted the British official presence from Philadelphia, a city of some refinement, to the new national capital. It was an important diplomatic move, and it lent added significance to Merry's first meeting with Jefferson.

Merry's first interview with the president, however, was not auspicious. Dressed, as Foster wrote his mother, "all bespeckled with the spangles of our gaudiest Court Dress," Merry called on Jefferson, who received the British minister in casual dress and slippers.[21] It was as if the president had conflated his personal domestic household with his public space. Perhaps this confusion arose out of the dual role of the White House itself as private home and public domain. Whatever the reason, Anthony Merry was deeply insulted. A few days later Jefferson asked Merry and his wife to dine at the White House. According to the rules of protocol, Jefferson should have escorted Mrs. Merry to the dinner table. Instead he turned to Dolley Madison, took her arm, and ushered her in. When no man offered his arm to Mrs. Merry, her husband did the honors, and to their mutual mortification they walked into the dining room together. To make matters even worse, Jefferson had also invited Louis-André Pichon, the representative of Great Britain's enemy and a diplomat of lower rank. A few days later the Madisons had the Merrys to dine. Acting in accordance with Jefferson's rules of pell-mell, James offered his arm to Hannah Gallatin, the wife of the secretary of the treasury. Again the Merrys were offended. Twice insulted, they turned the matter into an international incident. The Merrys refused all further official invitations from Jefferson and the Madisons. Merry allied himself with the Spanish and accused the administration of exhibiting partiality toward France. As Rosalie Stier Calvert, wife of the wealthy Maryland planter George Calvert, wrote to her mother, "It made a huge uproar—as much as if a treaty had been broken!"[22]

At the social events that constituted the Merry affair—first at the president's mansion and then at the Madisons' house—Dolley found herself a pawn in Jefferson's chess game of domestic politics and foreign relations. The president's mode of operation, his manipulation of manners regardless of its personal effect on others, suited neither of the Madisons. And yet she must also have understood Jefferson's reasoning. In May 1804, months after the Merry incident, Sally McKean Yrujo wrote her old friend Anna Cutts, "We dined a few days since at the President's who to do away with all ideas of Etiquette handed the Lady who happened to be next to him when dinner was announced." As she explained, it was "the only mode he could adopt to avoid distinctions which would be viewed with a jealous eye in this land of Equality."[23] If the American-born wife of the Spanish minister, a woman who was close to both Dolley and her sister Anna, understood Jefferson's motives so clearly, then certainly Dolley must have too.

James Madison quickly wrote letters to both the past and present American ministers to Great Britain exploring the issue, although, as he wrote Monroe, "I blush at having put so much trash on paper." According to Margaret Bayard Smith's biographical sketch of Dolley published in *The National Portrait Gallery*, Mrs. Merry poured her humiliation and wrath on Dolley when she described dinner at the Madisons as "more like a harvest-home supper, than the entertainment of a Secretary of State." Dolley, Smith wrote, replied that "she thought abundance was preferable to elegance; that circumstances formed customs, and customs formed taste; and as the profusion, so repugnant to foreign customs, arose from the happy circumstance of the super-abundance and prosperity of our country, she did not hesitate to sacrifice the delicacy of European taste, for the less elegant, but more liberal fashion of Virginia."[24] But Smith wrote her sketch thirty years after the event. She was eager to put Mrs. Madison in the very best light, to depict Dolley as a courageous symbol of patriotic America.

In a half-dozen letters to her sister Anna, Dolley made her own comments on Elizabeth Merry. By the late spring of 1804, the two women were on visiting terms, and they had even become friends of a sort by the early summer of 1805. But Mrs. Madison also considered Mrs. Merry strange. She kept to herself. She was a loner who tended to be moody and had a temper—a personality type that the very sociable Dolley may have found difficult.

Read in a larger context, these letters show the kind of relationship Dolley Madison maintained with all the wives of the European diplomats. She made no distinction between those married to ministers and those wed to chargés d'affaires, nor did she differentiate according to their backgrounds. She was very friendly with Emilie Pichon, and she was also close to Mme Turreau, wife of the subsequent French minister, who came from a humble background and whose husband was rumored to beat her. The Spanish minister's wife was her old and great friend Sally McKean, who continued to write to her after the Yrujos left the United States. Dolley frequently mentioned David Erskine and his wife.[25] Pedersen, Foster, and Thornton were bachelors. She displayed an equanimity, generosity, and warmth to all. Dolley might have become friendly with, even an intimate friend of, Mrs. Merry—despite the difficulties created by hostile international relations—had Elizabeth Merry wanted the friendship as well. After all, James Madison worked well with Anthony Merry, despite the social problems.

It is not her public role, however, but her personal concerns that dominate these letters. The circumstances of her family remained difficult. Although Dolley had found financial security and a position in Virginia society—and perhaps even emotional support—with her marriage to James Madison, it is easy to speculate that all the losses she had sustained before she met him had shaped her. She had become a warm, sociable, and comforting woman in part because she needed to love and be loved; but she reserved her most intense emotions for her immediate family. It is this inner self that is expressed in these letters.[26]

During her first few years in Washington, life proceeded without any major problems or shifts in her daily routine. Her sisters Mary and Lucy were safely married. Her mother remained mostly with Lucy but spent time with all of her daughters. Her son Payne was still quite young, and whatever lack of restraint or dissipation he may have exhibited could simply be chalked up to youthful ways. And Anna—her favorite sister, who had lived with her since her marriage to John Todd and to whom she referred as her "daughter-sister"—still lived with the Madisons in their home on F Street.

Then on 30 March 1804 Anna married Richard Cutts. A congressman from a wealthy family in Saco, Maine (still part of the state of Massachusetts), Cutts had first been elected to the House of Representatives in 1801. The marriage proved a pivotal event for Dolley. She had raised Anna almost as her child, and she had no daughter of her own. Anna's departure left Dolley feeling vulnerable and torn. Outwardly she seemed calm and behaved normally. She wrote notes of introduction for Anna and her husband to people they might want to meet as they traveled north. But inwardly she grieved, and in her letters to her sister she was absolutely clear about the pain she felt at their separation. It was not mitigated by the fact that the Cuttses would live in Washington when Congress was in session.

In 1805 Dolley began a long bout with an ulcerated knee, which soon needed serious medical attention. That summer she went to Philadelphia to be treated by the eminent doctor Philip Syng Physick, who bound her knee into splints and kept her confined to bed. There she remained, under her doctor's supervision, until November. For much of that time, James remained by her side—writing but also relaxing—until September, when the press of official business called him back to Washington.

It was the only time in their marriage that the Madisons spent more than a day or two apart, and their often-quoted letters have a tenderness that speaks of mutual affection, even of passion. Their letters convey a physical longing hidden behind a humorous and good-natured banter about Mrs. Madison's old Philadelphia friend Betsy Pemberton and her flirtation with Dolley's cousin Isaac A. Coles. Again and again James wrote of kisses and her sweet lips, mixing playful humor with sexual innuendos. For her part Dolley clearly missed the attentions of her husband. Her concern for his health when they entered the city together at the end of July 1805, stopping near where she had fled the yellow-fever epidemic in 1793, reveals her anxiety that James—like John Todd—might die. "I thought all was over with me," she wrote Anna on 29 July; "I could not fly to him & aid him as I used to do—but Heaven in its mercy restored him next Morng."

Dolley was in physical pain during this period and worried that she might have to sustain surgery or, worse, that she would never be able to walk again. It is significant that she wrote of her agony to her sister Anna, but not to her husband. Perhaps this fact simply reflects the extent to which she had recovered. But that seems unlikely. The tone of her letters to each is quite different. The ordeal lasted half a year, but by late November she had finally recovered and returned home to Washington.

By 1805 her only surviving brother, John C. Payne, had become an alcoholic and a reckless gambler. The Madisons, worried about his habits and his friends, cast about for a solution. In 1806 they sent him to Tripoli as secretary to the American consul there, George Davis. She received few letters from her brother while he was abroad, but her second letter from him left her clearly concerned.[27]

In 1806 two of her nieces died, and she wrote her mother of her profound sorrow. In 1807 her mother passed away. A year later her sister Mary succumbed to tuberculosis after years of illness.[28] By 1808 her once-large family had been reduced to her two surviving sisters, Anna and Lucy, her brother John, her son, and her husband. The letters in this section reflect the extent of her pain and loss.

1. Samuel Latham Mitchill to Catherine Mitchill, 3 Jan. 1802, quoted in Clark, *Life and Letters of Dolly Madison*, 49; Margaret Bayard Smith's novel, *A Winter in Washington* (New York, 1824), quoted in Clark, *Life and Letters of Dolly Madison*, 53.

2. Augustus John Foster, *Jeffersonian America: Notes on the United States of America Collected in the Years 1805-6-7 and 11–12*, ed. Richard Beale Davis (San Marino, Calif., 1954), 155.

3. Margaret Bayard Smith, *The First Forty Years of Washington Society*, ed. Gaillard Hunt (New York, 1906), 29. The sister referred to was Anna Payne.

4. Dumas Malone, *Jefferson and His Time* (6 vols.; Boston, 1948–81), 4:40.

5. The Madisons may have moved into one of the "Six Buildings" in square 74 of the city plan,

which also temporarily housed the offices of the Department of State. See Allan Clark, *Greenleaf and Law in the Federal City* (Washington, D.C., 1901), 141; Brant, *Madison* 4:490 n. 12; Ketcham, *James Madison,* 409. For their move out of the White House, see Jefferson to Martha Jefferson Randolph, 28 May 1801, *The Family Letters of Thomas Jefferson,* ed. Edwin Morris Betts and James Adam Bear Jr. (Columbia, Mo., 1966), 202.

6. *PJM-SS* 1:113 n. 1, 3:341.

7. George Watterston, "Recollections of Early DC," *National Intelligencer,* 26 Aug. 1847; John Cotton Smith, "Recollections of Early Washington," ibid., 20 Aug. 1847; Wilhelmus Bogart Bryan, *A History of the National Capital* (2 vols.; New York, 1914–16), 1:355.

8. Constance McLaughlin Green, *Washington: Village and Capital, 1800–1878* (Princeton, N.J., 1962), 21. In 1800 the capital had 123 free blacks and 623 slaves; in 1810, 867 free blacks and 1,437 slaves; and in 1820, 1,796 free blacks and 1,945 slaves.

9. Augustus John Foster to Elizabeth Foster, 4 Dec. 1807, in Marilyn Kay Parr, "Augustus John Foster and the 'Washington Wilderness'" (Ph.D. diss., George Washington Univ., 1987), 310; Green, *Washington,* 38–42.

10. Smith, "Mrs. Madison," 3; Foster, *Jeffersonian America,* 84.

11. Richard Alton Erney, *The Public Life of Henry Dearborn* (New York, 1979), 45. Jefferson noted the congressmen who had brought their wives to Washington for the winter of 1807–8 in a letter to his daughter Martha (Betts and Bear, *Family Letters,* 315, 316 n. 1).

12. Smith, *First Forty Years,* 33, 35.

13. Merrill D. Peterson, *Thomas Jefferson and the New Nation: A Biography* (New York, 1970), 569, 592.

14. Malone, *Jefferson and His Time* 4:375.

15. Betts and Bear, *Family Letters,* 316 n. 1. This number presumably did not include those wives of Federalists residing in Georgetown. For congressional living patterns, see James Sterling Young, *The Washington Community, 1800–1828* (New York, 1966).

16. Peder Blicherolsen to JM, 21 June 1803, *PJM-SS* 5:109–10. Blicherolsen referred to his "visits to the Federal City" because the Danish mission to the United States did not move from Philadelphia to Washington until Peder Pedersen took over later in 1803.

17. JM to James Monroe, 19 Jan. 1804, DLC: Rives Collection, Madison Papers.

18. Foster, *Jeffersonian America,* 51.

19. Jefferson, "Etiquette of the Court of the U.S.," in Malone, *Jefferson and His Time* 4:499–500; JM to James Monroe, 19 Jan. 1804, DLC: Rives Collection, Madison Papers.

20. Foster, *Jeffersonian America,* 54.

21. Parr, "Augustus John Foster," 97.

22. Rosalie Stier Calvert to Mme H. J. Stief, 29 Dec. 1803, *Mistress of Riversdale: The Plantation Letters of Rosalie Stier Calvert, 1795–1821,* ed. Margaret Law Callcott (Baltimore, 1991), 70.

23. Sally McKean Yrujo to Anna Cutts, May 1804, MCR-S: Mary Estelle Elizabeth Cutts Papers.

24. JM to James Monroe, 19 Jan. 1804, DLC: Rives Collection, Madison Papers; Smith, "Mrs. Madison," 4.

25. DPM to Anna Maria Thornton, 18 May 1808. The Erskines, however, were unusual representatives of the British government. She was American; he was extremely informal of manner. Augustus John Foster wrote of David Erskine that "he would have gone in Boots to visit the President but for me. & cares nothing about driving o⟨ut⟩ . . . in a dirty Hack without a Servant" (Foster to Elizabeth Foster, 1–3 Sept. 1807, in Parr, "Augustus John Foster," 307–8).

26. For women's emotions during the Early Republic, see, in particular, Jan Lewis, *In Pursuit of Happiness: Family and Values in Jefferson's Virginia* (New York, 1983).

27. DPM to John C. Payne, 21 Sept. 1809.

28. DPM to an unidentified correspondent, 7 Nov. 1807; John G. Jackson to DPM, 8 May 1808.

From Anna Maria Thornton

My dear Friend   Tuesday August 24th. 1802

Your welcome letter came at last, but not 'till I had been much disappointed at not receiving one the post before, the recital of your fatigues acquitted you, and I rejoiced that you were well enough to write even then, you must indeed have had a painful Journey, but you say you spent three happy days, that was sufficient to make amends for it had it been even more disagreeable. I am in the midst of Walsingham's lamentable tale,[1] I believe he has inspired me with some of his melancholy, & if you had not said you admired it I wou'd say I hate it, what a gloomy what a *"sombre"* mind must hers have been that wrote it— but she was unhappy. I always think we have sorrows & troubles enough of our own, without having the spirits depressed by the relation of fictitious Woes— and seek for books that will enliven & make me more chearful.

To your kind enquiries of when we are coming, I can only say as soon as we can, that is my husband's answer to me—We cannot set out 'till after the 30th. I know—depend upon it our inclination is not wanting, to make us set out immediately, business which must always give way to pleasure, will only cause our delay—I hope by the end of next week, we shall turn our backs on this dull tho' Great City, and greet with Joy, our beloved Friends beyond the mountains. Pray don't let Mr M. have the trouble of sending for pompey at present, it is impossible for him to travel, it will be well if he lives, we have every thing done for him that we can think of—he has certainly been very much abused, he has broken out in large sores, which have the appearance of a surfeit, we have been from the farm a week, but heard on Sunday that he was a little better. Amy bears your absence better than I expected, she was at Church twice last Sunday, and says she really believes she may be induced to stay here—I gave her some wool, and she immediately carded & spun it & is now knitting it, I believe this has contributed to make her more easy, by giving her employment. She comes in two or three times a day but does not teaze us at all. Dr. May has been to pay her two or three visits—He hovers about like a troubled spirit in search of "lost repose." Tell my dear Annie, that I thank her for her kind remembrance, that the Guitarre speaks in sweet tones when she touches it I doubt not, but she has not made it speak to me & I am jealous of it & every body she has written to.

You will be visited by Mr Thornton, & Mr Olsen, and perhaps by Pichon but certainly not by his family, who have no idea of quitting George Town. We have been gratified by seeing the celebrated Stewart,[2] he came down with

Mr Thornton and was here every day while he staid, he was in search of a house and talks of coming this winter with his family—I hope he may, I shall then hope to get some good pictures to copy after—He denies most pointedly having painted the picture in the President's house, and says he told Genl: Lee that he did not paint it—but he had bargained for it.

It is twelve days since I have heard from you, if I don't receive a letter to-morrow, I shall be in a very *bad humour.* Part of the Tingey family, and Mr & Mrs Wingate and Miss Dalton & G. Dearborn drank tea with us yesterday— all the Dearborn's except George set off this morning for Frederick, to return on Thursday or Friday—they go for the sake of the ride & change of air— Mrs D. has been poorly. If you want any thing that we can take you, you will have time enough to let me know after the receipt of this. Dr. T. went to Marl-bro' on Sunday I expect him home this Evening—he suffered for more than ten days but is again recovered—I take the liberty of sending you all his kind remembrance, if he was here he wou'd desire it. Mama & I join in best regards to you, your worthy husband—Sister—& little Payne. I was surrounded by work & *deep* in Walsingham, but could neither work nor read till I had written to you—I now return to them—Julie de Beaumont relieved from Prison— nothing but misery & distress pervades this work.

I write with freedom & carelessness, expecting that none but the partial eye of my dear Mrs M. will see what I write—Yrs. most affectionately

Anna Maria Thornton

We keep Jemmy with us, he behaves very well.

RC (ViU). Docketed by JM.

    1. Mary Robinson, *Walsingham; or, The Pupil of Nature* (4 vols.; London, 1797).

    2. The celebrated painter Gilbert Stuart (1755–1828) moved to Washington, D.C., from Germantown, Pa., in the summer of 1803. The next year he painted portraits of both JM and DPM (Charles Merrill Mount, *Gilbert Stuart, A Biography* [New York, 1964], 242, 251).

To Eliza Collins Lee

Thursday Morng. [6 January 1803]

It seems my dearest friend, that the language of regret, must allways be mine! Here has been a little groupe, who joined sincerely, in my anxious wishes for your arrival—the Presidents daughters, Lucy Anna & myself & al-tho two of them ware personally strangers they were prepared to give you their hearts—yes, this is the very company who have sigh'd for you, but they are gone—& you cannot come!

Mr. Lee tells me that your sweet children are not verry ill, & I will yet hope, if the weather clears off mildly, & the roads mend that you will visit us. Lucy with her little ones have been with us 2 months, but fear are on the point of going home, as Mr. Washington came down last sunday with his mouth full of persuasion, to entice her back saying that his dreary days & miserable nights ware not to be supported, & she like her flexible sex gave up the rest of the winter for *his accomodation.* In doing this she takes from the City half its charms (in my Eye) unless indeed her place is supply'd by you my other sister—I hear that friend Collins has been to visit you—oh that she had come thro Washington, that my eyes could have seen her once more.

We have had Mrs. Stewart with us—she is much attatched to you & expected fully to see you—she left this, on Monday last for Phila. We have many agreable strangers here, & every body seems disposed to keep up that hospitable intercourse which forms the best trait in the character of any place— I am writeing with the worst of pens & very carlessly, under the impression that will throw it into the fire—when Mr. Lee arrived yesterday we were seting off to Pichons where we had been engaged a week—but he did not come to stay a moment I found—on this day Mr. M & Mr. Jefferson are setling a most important peice of Political business.[1] We entreated to have the honour of entertaining your Husband & I now wait to receive him—if he does not gratify me by dining with us I shall pronounce him cerimonious—& what is worse (to me) indifferent to your poor friend—I was so foolish as to fall the other day & strain my ankle but by the care of an attentive Phisian I am able to walk slowly about.

Accept my dearest Eliza the united affection of us all—but remember, that to no one individual, are you more dear than to your

D P M

RC (DLC: Dolley P. Madison Papers). Addressed to "Mrs. R. B. Lee Alexandria." Date assigned on the basis of internal evidence.

1. The "important peice of Political business" was probably JM and Thomas Jefferson's decision to send James Monroe as special envoy to France to purchase New Orleans for the United States. Monroe and U.S. minister Robert R. Livingston instead acquired the entire Louisiana Territory in April 1803 (Jefferson to Monroe, 10 Jan. 1803, in Paul Leicester Ford, ed., *The Writings of Thomas Jefferson* [10 vols.; New York, 1892–99], 8:188).

To Anna Cutts

26 Apr. 1804.

Tho few, are the days, passed since you left me my dearest Anna they have been spent in anxious impatience to hear from you—your letter from

Baltimore releaved my mind & the one from Phila. (this hour receav'd) gives me the greatest pleasure—To trace you & your dear Husband in that regretted City, where we have spent our early years to find that even there, you can recollect with affection the solatary being you have left behind, reflects a ray of brightness on my *sombre prospect*—I will now give you a little sketch of times here—I shut myself up from the Morg you entered the stage, & wrote Mama P. & Lucy until Saturday 3 oClock when we went in the rain to dine with Marshall Brent on Sunday Morng. Nelly[1] went to Alexandria to return in a week— all our acquaintance call'd in to see me on the different mornings—those few I saw seemed all to sympathise with me in your loss—but unamiously thought you verry happy in haveing so amiable a conducter thro life, in which I most heartily joined them—I drank Tea with Tingys & Mrs Forrest which is the amot. of my visits made—a letter from the President anounced the death of poor Maria[2] & the consequent Misery it has occasion'd them all—this is among the many proofs my dr. Sister of the uncertainty of life! A girl so young, so lovely—all the efforts of her Father docters & friends availed nothing—I have a long letter from Mama, but it being in part to John I forbear to inclose it—she recieav'd our last, but not the one before it which was so full—she wishes a few lines from Mr Cutts—you ⟨. . . wri⟩te her—she cant move a mus⟨cle?⟩ no way to come to me this summer ⟨. . .⟩ make every effort to send for her, being determin'd she shall meet you here in the Fall—John has given out all thought of going abroad I belieave, as he seems *already reinstated* with his old *friends*—I presented your love to our neighbours who beg me to give you both a great deal from them—I will see the others soon to whom I will say what you wish—I have locked up your little Trunk in the Store room.

I am delighted with the kind attention you meet from our old accquaintance & have no doubt but that you will meet a gratful welcome in all the other places you ar[e] destind to visit—remember me to McKeans & to Sally say a great deal for I feel a tenderness for her & her Husband independent of curcumstances[3]—I am glad you would not accept the Chamber tho' I could not suppose you would. Poor Sophie! my love to her. I am charmed with the ⟨. . .⟩ for which you must ⟨. . .⟩ & I thank you sincearly for the things you mention— my dr. Anna if you will get me a light shaul a douzn yds. of fashionable handsome broad ribbon a pr or 2 of gloves to inclose to M & any thing else which you know I want I will immediately inclose you a bill on Moiland or Lewis who both owe M mony for the amot. of what you may think proper to buy me—I trust you will find Riggs or some other oppertunity for The bonit &c. Write me all about your visits to Dallass and the company—what they say or do—Bonopartee & so forth—Mrs. Pichon is sick & will certainly leave this country—or rather there is a new Minister comeing[4]—Madison says he will

53

write to Mr. Cutts—he read your letter & said the offer you both make to oblidge him justifies his good oppinion of your kindness & affection—he bids me say he loves you dearly—Adeiu—No one shall lay Eyes on your letters.

RC (ViU). Ms torn.
    1. This was Nelly Conway Madison (1781–1865), daughter of Ambrose Madison and JM's favorite niece, who married Dr. John Willis (Ketcham, *James Madison*, 460).
    2. Thomas Jefferson's daughter Maria Jefferson Eppes died on 17 April 1804 at the age of twenty-five soon after the birth of her third child (Malone, *Jefferson and His Time* 4:411–17).
    3. The "circumstances" to which DPM here refers is the quarrel between Yrujo and the Jefferson administration. Following Spanish protests over the U.S. purchase of the Louisiana Territory that had roiled Spanish-American relations in 1803, the passage of the Mobile Act on 24 Feb. 1804 provoked several more intemperate letters of protest from Yrujo. In April, Yrujo left Washington for Philadelphia without calling on JM—a breach of diplomatic decorum—leaving his wife to go alone to say goodbye to DPM (Brant, *Madison* 4:188–212).
    4. Mme Pichon had recently lost a child. The new French minister was Gen. Louis-Marie Turreau, who arrived at Annapolis on 16 Nov. 1804, bringing official notice of Pichon's recall (ibid., 4:266, 269).

To Anna Cutts

[ca. 8 May 1804]

⟨ . . . ⟩ [t]hanks—you dont speak of the long letter I wrote you—but still I hope you have it, nothing has occured since I wrote worth your knowing—I continue to miss you both, & to lament a seperation from you, who could have made my happiness—but when I read your letters & see you in those charming places enjoying yourself, & every advantage, I reflect on my own selfishness & strive to be reconciled—the P. has not yet return'd but is expected in a day or 2 ⟨. . .⟩ finished—& hers ⟨. . .⟩ nearly done—quite pritty he has made us. Nelly still at Allexandria—I had a few lines from Mama yesterday—all ware well—the fashionable talk here is of Mrs. Law & her affairs [1]—she expects soon to be fixed on a Farm by herself & the observations are terribly against her—give my love to Mrs. Morton & tell her I don't know what—write me all about every thing that concerns you in Boston.

May 8th. I should have sent you a letter for N. York but you say you will tell me from thence how to direct & lest you should leave that city before mine could reach it I will write to Boston where I trust it will find you both my dear Sister well & happy—I inclosed your's to Mama, & had the pleasure to get a long letter from her last night she says Dolley has been ill but is mending all the rest well—she has sent John a Deed for the Kentucky Land & he'l sell it if he can & go into some business—we all continue well & alone. I have a letter from Mrs Deblois who laments not seeing you & begs me to come to see her—one from Nelly including an invitation from the Fitzhue family to visit them—I think of rideing over tomorrow with John—M not haveing leasure to go—Nelly will come back with me she says—& as I cant avoide her visit I shall make the best of it—she speaks most affectinately of you both & intends to write to you—Polly got home well & is prepareing to come back she has not written to me yet—I have given her a full acct of your Marriage & leaveing me—G. Dearborn it is said is comeing back in a day or 2 to marry Peggy— Wm Burrel has arrived to succeed Hervey with the P. who is still expected[2]— Mrs. Forrest sends you much love & intends to write you when I hear from you again—pray write me a great deal my dear you know of what importance a particular detail of all that you ⟨me⟩et with is to me—Mr. M John & Payne join me in the most affectinate love & wishes for you both—your ever

D P M

RC (MCR-S: Mary Estelle Elizabeth Cutts Papers). Top third of first two pages torn off.

1. Married to Thomas Law in 1796, Eliza Parke Custis Law separated from him in 1804. The gossip about the couple became intense (Clark, *Greenleaf and Law in the Federal City*, 285–86).

2. Lewis Harvie and William Burwell served as Jefferson's private secretaries (Malone, *Jefferson and His Time* 4:368, 414, 419).

To Anna Cutts

May 20th [1804]

All your letters my dearest Anna arrived safe—every one of which gave me aditional satisfaction—your last from New Haven leads me to hope you now, safe arrival [*sic*] in Boston where you will have reciev'd 2 long one's from me directed to that place.

We are still as when I wrote, except that I have passed 2 days in Alexanda. & brought Nelly back with me—& a great uncertainty of our going to Orange until July which I am heartily sorry for—as this place seems not natural or scarsly agreable without you—Debloises said a great deal about you & intend to write you they did not think amiss of your not visiting them, but rather regretted they had not all of them come over to see you before your departure— I passed one day at Fitzhughs by their pressing invitation & was much pleased with their polite attentions. A great many of the inhabitants call'd on me whilst there & the Dalton & Deblois'es put me in mind of Aunt & Unkle's, quite engrossed with new friends and acquaintan[c]es—there verry senses turned with novelty &c—John went with me & we ware both delighted to get out of the bustle & return to our peaceful home—I have had but little company—about 3 afternoons we had all the *remainder* of our friends—the Dearbourns have got well & are lively & affectinate. Mrs. Tingy has been at the point of Death but is now a little better—I have had a long & affectinate letter from the Marchioness where she speaks of you like a good friend—Oh Anna you little know the triumph I feel when I hear of you & you[r] beloved Husband in the stile that many speak of you—if Payne was a Man Married & gone from me I could not feel more sensibly every thing that regarded him than I do, what concerns you both—I have had no letter from Mama since I wrote last, which was last week—I hope she is well & will be with me soon—I suspect Nelly will not go until we do, as she has no one to conduct her—Wm. Burrel is at the Presidents *he* came back some days ago & I have been with M to drink Tea with him. He was delighted to see me enquired after you & behaved with great cleaverness. His Philosiphy ennables him to bear his loss better than I expected.

Steward has taken an admirable picture of Mr. Madison—his & mine are finished—Mrs R Smiths is nearly done but she does not like it tho tis verry like her—pray write me directly from Boston as I am anxious to have your jurnal from thence—I have enclosed your letters except the last to Mama—I told you how delighted I was with my bonit & other things you sent me—I mean to send you on Money before the fall to get me many pretty things for the winter—I will tell you all the news as it occurs—I sent you a letter from Mrs Thornton.

Nelly says she will write you by tomorrows post she sends you both much love—send her some in return—Madison Payne & John join me in great affection to you both adeiu my dear Sister ever yours

I have not a line from Polly yet!

RC (MCR-S: Mary Estelle Elizabeth Cutts Papers).

To Anna Cutts

WASHING. May 25th. 1804.

Long before this my dear Sister & Brother are safe & happy in Boston. I sigh for a letter to tell me so. Yours from N. Haven I answered a few days ago—since then I received ⟨. . .⟩ inclose'd letter. I am quite uneasy for our beloved Mother who is now quite sick by her attendance on poor little Dolley[1] whose Eyes are in great danger—lovely blossom! Heaven send she may recover—

Mama is now at the Sulpher Springs with her & I have sent her a remittance to keep them both there until they both recover—They are (Mama & Lucy) verry anxious to meet me in Orange, & I expect will do so in answer to my offer to send a Carriage for them now—they say they cant come directly— G. W. is verry unwell—talks of a voyage to the West Indias for his symtom of consuption.

We have no prospect of going Home until july—the Publick business will not allow Ms absence—we go on just as usial—we have had 2 partys this week Duval's & Dearborns—tonight at Thorntons—tomorrow night here—Mrs. Loid Mrs. Masons sister will be here with a sister of Mrs. Prentis Smith & the little Circle left in the City. Kitty Murry still in G. T. She & Mrs. ⟨Murry?⟩ send you a great deal of love—Mrs. Pichon has been in Baltimore 2 weeks—she moves to the Seven Buildings as soon as she returns. Mrs. Merry is still the same strange ⟨lasse?⟩. She hardly associates with any one—allways rideing on Horse back.

I told you about my visit to Alexandria—Nelly is writeing I hope she will amuse you with something new, as I can see nor hear of anything worth re-citeing—John is well & reads your letters—I tell him to write you but you know his indolence in that emploimt.

I met judge Linton at Dearborn's last night he was particular in his enquirys & expressions of regard for you—Mrs. Forrest intends to write to you—M is verry busy & allways tells me to give you his best love &c. Payne is at school he has written to you but it is so bad that I tell him to write again.

Adeiu my dear Anna allways your Affectinate Sister

Hervey has gone to live in Richmond—Mr. Burral his sucessor is a good deal like him in all but temper—the P. does not entertain company yet.

RC (MCR-S: Mary Estelle Elizabeth Cutts Papers). Some words obscured by water damage.
    1. The daughter of Mary Payne and John G. Jackson, Dolley Jackson, then aged four, was with her grandmother Mary Coles Payne.

To Anna Cutts

[May–June] 1804

⟨. . .⟩ how delighted I should be to accompany you to all the charming places you mention—to see all the kind people & to play loo with Mrs Knox—I have scarsly played since you left us—I find it disagreable unless the partys are pleasant & therefore decline.

G. Dearborn & Peggy go on as usial, he allways there but nothing said of when it is to be. Mrs. Tingy has got almost well again & is just the same dame she used to be—I had a letter from Old Amey who has been at the point of Death. She desired to know all about you & the others of our family—I wrote her a few lines yesterday—I have not had a line from the Marchioness lately. Have you an answer to yours? Mrs. Pichon Forrest Murray Mrs. Mason send their love to you—If I should see Mrs. Merry again I will tell her but she calld & took leave a few days ago. The weather prevents her setting off.

Mr. M is overwhelm'd with business—the British, French & Spanish infringements are all under his pen—he expects Genl. Armstrong every day (who is to suceed Livingston) to receave his instructions[1]—M wishes to write Mr. C. but has not a moment—he sends you his affectinate love—as we all do to you both—continue to write me dr. Sister. I hope you will be highly pleased with the ⟨place?⟩ & connections you are now going amongst. Farewell for the present I shall write again in a day or 2. Tell me you recceiv'd my last, indeed all as I am anxious lest they be lost.

Mount Vernon has been sett on fire five different times & tis suspected some malicious persons are determined to reduce it to ashes—Oh the wickedness of Men & women. I'm affraid to accept their invitations.

No mortal but Mama see's your letters.

I'm much pleased with Mrs. Morton's & Mr Ps Poetry. I've known the time when . . . I could write two—I'm glad you take no more snuf—but I must.

RC (MCR-S: Mary Estelle Elizabeth Cutts Papers).
    1. In May 1804 Jefferson appointed John Armstrong to replace Robert R. Livingston as minister to France. The Armstrongs left for France on 5 Sept. 1804 (C. Edward Skeen, *John Armstrong, Jr., 1748–1853* [Syracuse, N.Y., 1981], 51).

To Anna Cutts

My dearest Anna   16th. july [1804]
    Yours from Main reached me yesterday, I need not say how happy I am at your de[s]cription of persons & places & at the knowledge of your felicity— we go to O. this week I am now in the midst of packing—Payne continues weak & sick—my prospects rise & fall to sadness as this precious Child recovers or declines! I shall do as you wish precisely, with your papers, trunks Books &&: so be easy on that head, no eye but your sisters shall go over our family letters. I have already sent yours to Mrs. Deblois.

I have just now a letter from our Mother but I cant send it to you—she says they are all tolerably well now—but *that incorrigable* Man has broke her Pheaton to peices borrowd. her money & now will not take the least trouble in procureing a conveyance for her to O. John will sett out for her the day after we go—in a Hack, in order to bring her to me with little Dolley. Hariot[1] & her family are at Hairwood for the summer poor dear Lucy to be confined there makes my heart ake she cant leave them to visit me, but she is determind to meet you here in the fall—Mr. M says his business will not allow him to go before tuesday next which is not so soon as I thought when I begun this—I'm affraid Nelly[2] will come back to sett of with us—I wish she had never come on, as it is terribly inconvenient to take her now Payne is so weak & sick & the roads are so bad we are about to hire a Hack & horses—I feel as dull as if the world rested on my shoulders, & have you no longer to complain to or help me out. John is all but frantick to sett of for Mama since her last letter—tis something like the one she wrote us when in Jefferson once before. G. W. is better but still talks of going to the springs.[3] You have herd no doubt of the terrible duel & end of poor Hamilton.[4] I sent the P. word by M of your offer of servises & about the glass—I believe N is engaged to the Doct. but when or where they'l Marry I know not, as I dont mean to interest myself or take any trouble in *their* affairs—The President has just sent us an invitation for the day after tomorrow when I ⟨. . .⟩

Farewell my dear sister write me often as I shall often write you—I have another long letter from the Marchioness she says she has written to you—she is the same thing as ever—I have not herd from Old Amey a long time—she had been verry ill when she wrote last. I'm affraid she is dead! Merry's have been 10 days in Baltimore & their coachman dyed there & 3 other servants ill—I'm told the Smiths are devoted to her—Mrs. Pichon after the loss of her child sett of to Phila. They intend to return & come to Orange this summer—The Neighbours all send their love to you—I hear Bonoparte & Lady are delighted at N. York & mean to ⟨. . .⟩ time—adeiu again.

RC (MCR-S: Mary Estelle Elizabeth Cutts Papers). Last two pages torn.

1. Harriot Washington.

2. Nelly Conway Madison Willis.

3. The burgeoning development of the "Virginia Springs" in the early nineteenth century was due to their popularity among the southern gentry, who commonly "took" the waters to restore their health as well as to enjoy fashionable society (Charlene M. Boyer Lewis, *Ladies and Gentlemen on Display: Planter Society at the Virginia Springs, 1790–1860* [Charlottesville, Va., 2001], 59–62).

4. On 11 July 1804 Aaron Burr fatally wounded Alexander Hamilton in a duel.

To Elizabeth Parke Custis Law

My dear Mrs Law   WASHINGTON Octor. 17th. 1804.

Mr. Madison is willing to take David for 400 dolrs. to be paid at the end of one year from the time of his comeing into service with lawful interest from that date, it being understood that at the expiration of five years he is to become free, & that in the mean time Mr. M. is to be his owner. If these terms are satisfactory, you will be so good as to have the contract prepared & on his appearing with it, Mr. Madison will send you his obligation for the price.

RC (NN: James Madison Papers).

To Anna Cutts

22d May [1805]

Yours of the 12th. my dear Anna was handed me last night, I am rejoiced allways to hear from you, & am glad you have recovered all my letters, the last with Lucy's inclosed, you have by this time—I could tell you a great deal about these french people, but must forbear some things which could not fail to divert you—they are very agreable on the whole & make to me a vast addition to the comfort of this place—we see each other every day almost (that is Madame) she speaks no english but we understand each other well [1]—She is good natured & inteligent generous plain & curious—we ride walk together & visit sans cerimoni—I never visit her in her chamber but I crack my sides a laughing—I wish I could tell you on paper at what—she shews me every thing she has, & would fain give me of *every thing*—she decorates herself according to the french Ideas & wishes me do so two—in short I love the woman for her singularitys which are [s]carcely known to others—you would be surprized to hear my improvement in the language—she says she allways understands me—she is very anxious to see my "belle Seur" as she stiles you—I have before told you about the men—we have ⟨. . .⟩ usial at this season, we ⟨. . .⟩ ⟨Turners?⟩ the other day & met all the Lee's Eliza speaks affectinately of you & so does all your acquaintances—I must send you a little of olsen's lace either for my darling Julia or your self—it is not uncommon but pritty—I see & hear little of your caps tho I dun the Damsels when e're I see them—every body visits Madame & are makeing partys for her—I am allways the better on such occasions, as I must go of course.

Oh Anna I am dying to come to your Country—if I could be with you now how glad it would make me—tell ⟨. . .⟩ Mama & Dolley are well also John two, but he dont write—Mama says she will—I am sorry you have not all the seed—I will get you all for next summer—nothing new from Orange or from our sisters or Aunt.

I shall wait a few days for some muslin expected in order to try my skill on a little cap for you & put on the Olsen lace for a christening orniment, if I should be disappointed Il send the lace in my next letter—Mrs. & Doct. Bartlett are just discovered ⟨. . .⟩ stills & I instantly call'd ⟨. . .⟩ adeiu—

RC (MCR-S: Mary Estelle Elizabeth Cutts Papers). Ms torn.
    1. DPM referred here to the wife of the French minister to the United States, Louis-Marie Turreau de Garambouville.

To Anna Cutts

My dearest Anna   June 4th. [1805]

I now write you from my bed to which I have been confined for Ten days with a sad knee—it became a painful tumour, & 2 Doctrs ware call'd in, & their applications of caustick & so forth gives me hopes of geting well but heaven knows when as it promises to be tedious.

I reccd. your last this morng. which was very acceptable, but it made me extreamly sorry, to find you ware still sick, tho such things are common they are not the less terrible—I hope a month or 6 weeks will bring you a comfort & a cure. I shall be all anxiety for you my dear, you must have a good Doctor & do as he bids you. Mama Mr. M Payne & Dolley are all here & quite well. John has been sick but recovering. Mama & Dolley will of course go with us to Orange & return with us to this place—we hear from Lucy & Polly they are all well—& now my dear I must tell you of Mrs. Merrys airs, I told you we had been unusially intimate—she had met the french here & had been verry sociable with Madame but the other Eveg. she came in high good humour to pass three hours with her patient, as she stiled me, when Merran call'd in & mention'd that the Genel. & his family ware walking near the house. Mrs. M instantly took the alarm said they ware waiting for her to depart in order to come in, seazed her shaul & in spite of all I could say marched of with great dignity, & more passion, you know when she chuses she can get angry with persons as well as [circumstances.

61

Yesterday we had brother George, Thornton and Lawrence Washington to spend the day. Mamma and Madison dined at Young's. I was confined to bed, John presided below and the sound of Virginia hilarity echoed][1] thro the House—George says Lucy is not in the way & that he'l bring her & his children to pass 2 months with me in Orange—he caughs continually & is hoarse look's thin in his person but has no Idea of dying—since I wrote you 2 days ago I have heared sad things of Turreau—that he whiped his wife & abused her before all his servants—dont breath it in your country, as it will make them all so odious as *he* deserves to be. I pity her sincearly as I believe her an amiable & sensible woman—I have just had a letter from Mount Vernon inviteing me there, but alass it seems as if I should walk no more! I have tryed in vain to draw the paturn of my sleves—I'l try to get Mr Thornton to do it for you, it [is] a large one & not fit for little things—Our best affection for you both.

RC and Tr (MCR-S: Mary Estelle Elizabeth Cutts Papers).
1. Text within square brackets taken from the transcript made by Mary Cutts.

To Anna Cutts

29th july [1805]

My beloved sister if she has reccd. my last from W. will be unhappy to find that I was obliged to take this jurney in such a dangerious season, but it proved a verry pleasant one, as I was easier rideing than in any other position & my health & spirits revived every day that I rode we breakfasted at Greys this Morng. & I now write from my bed at Francis' Hotell[1]—but Oh how dismal are all things to my veiw in this place without you, & I in this sad condition—but Doct. Physick has seen it, & says he will cure me in a month—this aught to comfort me—but Anna, if I was not affraid of death I could give way to most immoderate greaf. I feel as if my heart was bursting. No Mother no Sister—but fool that I am—here is my beloved Husband siting anxiously by me & who is my unremiting Nurse—but you know how delicate he is I tremble for him—on our way one night he taken very ill with his old bilious complaint. I thought all was over with me, I could not fly to him & aid him as I used to do—but Heaven in its mercy restored him next Morng. & he would not pause until he heared my fate from Doctr. P. I left our dear Mother overwhelm'd with distress on my acct. but I have written all the way we came & from hence today, so that I hope she is in good spirits now—I will not send this to night hopeing that tomorrow I may be able to console you & myself.

RC (ViU).

1. The Madisons approached Philadelphia from the west, stopping to eat at Gray's Ferry, where DPM had fled in 1793 during the yellow-fever epidemic, and where her first husband and second child had died. They then went on to Francis's Union Hotel, located at 13 South Fourth Street in Philadelphia.

To Anna Cutts

My dear sister.   wednesday 31st. july [1805]

We are at exellent lodgings in Sanson street,[1] & I feel quite like another being—My knee is better. Doct. P. has splintered it, that is fixed a bark nearly a yd. long & with a bandage has bound it so tight that I cannot even lift it from the bed—not a step can I take—but this process is to cure it without any thing, we hope, & the Doct. thinks—I'm in no pain but from the fixed position—I have had the world to see me—Mr. Mrs. Lenox Miss Keen Mr. & Mrs. Hair McKeans Sally Marquis & Mrs. Maultby—Mrs Rush Steward &c. & every body of every description to see M. We have invitations to the Houses of one Douzn gentry but withstand all to be ⟨at ease here.⟩ I have your letter since I got here, it revived me but you had 2 to receive from me, one with a cambrick cap, & the one written the day before I left W—M. is quite well & sends his love to you both as I do—I can not write half I wish as I'm laying in bed & dare not cannot sit up—Write me as soon as possible. I have heard from Mama—she is well & now easy about me—she will go on to Unkles soon, where we shall follow when Im well—I will write you in a day or 2. all about every thing.

RC (MCR-S: Mary Estelle Elizabeth Cutts Papers). Words in angle brackets supplied from the transcript made by Mary Cutts.

1. The Madisons took lodgings on Walnut Street between Seventh and Eighth Streets, where Quaker philanthropist William Sansom had built a row of houses on the north side (*PJM* 17:293 n. 1).

To Anna Cutts

My dearest Anna.   19 August [1805]

The letter from your own pen was a joyfull one to me, as it convinced me that you must be well—how is our little tinker, & what is his name[1]—I am still in bed, & can write but badly—you ask me who is kindest to me here, & I can tell you that among a numerious sett the Pembertons bear of[f] the palm—I can never forget Betsy she has been as you would have been to me. Not a day but I rec[e]ive additional marks of hers & Nancy affection—I wish Waddel would come if he is worthy of Betsy, as she is two lovely in all respects to be lost, by celibicy—well my dear to our own affairs—my poor knee is yet but indifferent—so tedious it is to heal that I am at times lowspiritted—yet Docr. P says it will & must soon be well—he has apply'd caustick 3 times to the wou⟨nd⟩ since I wrote you which is a sad thing to feel, but it does every thing that the knife could do, it removes all impediments to a cure—but it increases the work of healing & causes this delay—I have not seen where I am yet & the longer I stay the less I care for the vanities of the place—but I shall enjoy them much two well at last, I suspect—I have not heard from Polly, but am quite anxious nor can I immagin the reason, I sent you Lucys last—I expect Mama has left W, as the Post of to day has brought me no letter from her—indeed I hope she has gone to Unkles, as the Town could not so well agree with them—I had a visit last night from Nancy Miflin & Sally Lane, who remonstrated with me—on seeing so much company—they said that it was reported that half the City of Phila had made me visits—this lecture made me recollect the times when *our Society* used to controle me entirely & debar me from so many advantages & pleasures—& tho so entirely from their clutches, I really felt my ancient terror of them revive to disiagreable degree. This crowde, more like the attendence of a New Play, has really become tiresome, yet, I can not help it—nor can all my vanity, make it any longer more than tolerable—I had a thousand times rather be in your Chamber with ⟨. . .⟩ babe & self than to see the string of this Morg. Marchioness Mother & sister Mrs. G. Harison, Steward, Donaldson & Leiper the butlers & Mrs. Dallass—Generally in the morng. I see more than these, in the afternoon & eveg. a greater number—I have this moment a Packet from Mama—she is well & intends to sett of this day one from Aunt she says Unkle & Isaack ware seting off to see if they could do any thing for me.

Amey is by me send love to both of you & the baby—adeiu dear

RC (ViU). Incomplete. Damaged by tear.

1. James Madison Cutts was born on 29 July 1805 (Coles, *Coles Family of Virginia*, 179).

To James Madison

23d: October 1805

A few hours only have passed since you left me my beloved, and I find nothing can releave the oppression of my mind but speaking to you in this *only* way.

The Docter called before you had gone far and with an air of sympathy wished you could see how much better the knee appeared—I could only speak to assure him it felt better—Betsey Pemberton and Amy are sitting beside me and seem to respect the grief they know I feel, at even a short seperation from one who is all to me—I shall be better when Peter returns, not that any length of time could lessen my just regret, but an assurance that you are well and easy will contribute to make me so. I have sent the books and note to Mrs: Dallas—B. Pemberton puts on your hat to divert me, but I cannot look at her.

24th: of October. What a sad day! The watchman announced a cloudy morning at one o'clock, and from that moment I found myself unable to sleep from anxiety for thee my dearest husband—detention cold and accident seemed to menace thee! B. Pemberton who lay beside me administered three or four drops of Laudinum, it had some effect before the Dr: came, who pronounced a favorable opinion on the knee.

Yesterday the Miss Gibbons called upon me, in the evening Mrs: Dallas and daughter with Mrs: Stuart and Nancy Pemberton. Every one is kind and attentive.

25th: This clear cold morning will favor your journey and enliven the feelings of my darling! I have nothing new to tell you—Betsey and myself sleep quietly together and the knee is mending. I eat very little and sit precisely as you left me. The doctor during his very short visits, talks of you, he says he regards you more than any man he ever knew and nothing could please him so much as passing his life near you—sentiments so congenial with one's own, and in *such cases*, like dew drops on flowers, exhilarate as they fall! The Governor, I hear, has arrived and is elated with his good fortune.[1] General Moreau is expected in town in a few days, to partake of a grand dinner the citizens are about to give him.[2]

Adieu, my beloved, our hearts understand each other—In fond affection thine

Dolley P. Madison

Tr (MCR-S: Mary Estelle Elizabeth Cutts Papers). Tr taken by Mary Cutts.

1. Thomas McKean had been reelected governor of Pennsylvania.

2. Jean-Victor Moreau, one of France's most able general officers, was implicated in a royalist plot and banished by Napoleon in May 1804. Moreau left France for Spain in June of that year, and after nearly a year's residence in Cádiz, he sailed for Philadelphia on 4 July 1805, arriving there on 25 Aug. Soon thereafter he settled his family at Morrisville, Pa., and kept winter quarters in New York City. He visited Washington, D.C., in April 1812 and left New York for Europe on 20 June 1813 (Pierre Savinel, *Moreau, rival republicain de Bonaparte* [Rennes, France, 1986], 156–57, 164–66, 194, 196–97).

To James Madison

My dearest husband,   26th: of October 1805

Peter returned safe, with your letter, and cheared me with a favorable account of your prospect of getting home in the stage. I was sorry you could not ride further in our carriage, as you would have felt less fatigue—In my dreams of last night, I saw you in your chamber, unable to move, from riding so far and so fast—I pray that an early letter from you may chase away the painful impression of this vision—I am still improving and shall observe strictly, what you say on the subject of the Doctor's precepts, he has given me no new instructions—Betsey sends you love and kisses in *return,* with "a word to Cousin Isaac."

28th: I have the letters this moment which you enclosed at Washington, I rejoice to find you there and I see that you can write—shall now expect the next post with impatience, by that you will speak of yourself. The Marquis and Marchoness came to see me yesterday, with several other ladies—I am getting well as fast as I can, for I have the reward in view of seeing my beloved when I do. Please enclose Mamma's letter with those of the other friends you will send me tomorrow—Anna's was dated on the 14th: before she received my last, I have every reason to expect her the end of this week. Tell me if Mrs. Randolph is expected and all the other news, you shall have time and patience to give me. I have written you every day since we parted, but am so shut up that I can say nothing to amuse, when I begin to ride, shall become a more interesting correspondant. Doctor Physic has had a letter from Mrs: Merry at Baltimore, written in great gaity. Did you see the Bishop or engage a place for Payne? Farewell, until tomorrow my best friend! Think of thy wife! who thinks and dreams of thee!

                                                                    D.

Tr (MCR-S: Mary Estelle Elizabeth Cutts Papers). Tr made by Mary Cutts.

From James Madison

My dearest,   WASHINGTON, October 28th: 1805

I reached the end of my journey on Saturday evening; without accident and in good health. I found your friends here all well. Payne arrived about an hour after I did. I enclose a letter from him with several others. During my halt at Baltimore, I made two efforts to see Bishop Carroll, but without success. General Smith had not returned to town from his country seat. I could do nothing therefore towards getting a birth for Payne in the seminary of Mr. Dubourg.[1] I have lost no time however in making an attempt for the purpose, by a request which is gone in a letter to Bishop Carroll, and if his answer authorizes me, I shall take immediate steps for preventing any further loss of time. Dr: Willis has signified to Gooch, that he wishes if we should not load the waggon ourselves on its return from Washington, to provide a conveyance for some of his furniture and will with that view contribute a pair of horses to the team. May I not assent to this arrangement, without inconvenience to our own plans? Let me know as soon as possible. Dr: and Miss Park had before my arrival gone to Alexandria, they are to return hither tomorrow. I hope you did not fail to execute my commission as to Miss Pemberton. I had the pleasure of dining yesterday with Cousin Isaac at the President's and can venture to say that ⟨. . .⟩

Present my best respects to Dr: Physic, and let me know that I shall soon have you with me, which is most anxiously desired by your ever affectionate

James Madison

This is the first mail that has been closed since my arrival

Tr (MCR-S: Mary Estelle Elizabeth Cutts Papers). Tr made by Mary Cutts.

1. John Payne Todd had been attending the school established by Walter Dulaney Addison (1769–1848), the founder of St. John's Episcopal Church in Georgetown. In 1805 JM arranged with John Carroll, the first Roman Catholic bishop in the United States, to send him to St. Mary's College in Baltimore, a new school for both Protestant and Roman Catholic boys directed by Father Louis Dubourg (Bryan, *History of the National Capital* 1:88; Brant, *Madison* 4:289).

To James Madison

PHILA: 30th: October 1805

I have this moment perused with delight thy letter, my darling, with its enclosures—to find you love me, have my child safe and that my mother is well, seems to comprise all my happiness—You consult me on the subject of Dr: Willis's request, which I should assuredly comply with—I do not know as yet what we have to send home, but I shall be ever desirous to oblige Nelly and every other of our connexions. The knee is acquiring strength every day but my nerves are often weak—the Doctor ordered me some drops yesterday which I took—he also directed me to eat meat and drink porter, I take but a morsel of either, having no appetite. I walk about the room and expect a few days more will enable me to ride, no inflamation and the little incission nearly fast, so that you may expect me to fly to you as soon—ah! I wish I could say how soon! I had a visit from Mr: Lewis yesterday, who repeated most pressingly his wife's invitation. I gave him the reason I had in store for resisting the many temptations held out for my removal to their house.

Madam Pichon writes me an affectionate letter and begs me to accept a pair of earrings for her sake. I suppose you may have them if they are not with the letter. I am punctual in delivering to Betsey your commands she insists in adding a postcript to this which I am not to see, but she must go home to dinner and I must not miss the post. You will continue to write me and say whether you get all mine—adieu, my beloved

your Dolley.

Tr (MCR-S: Mary Estelle Elizabeth Cutts Papers). Tr made by Mary Cutts.

To James Madison

MONDAY NIGHT PHILADELPHIA [30 October 1805]
I received, my dear Husband's, two last letters this morning, one enclosing Anna's and the other a commission from the President to procure several articles for Mrs: Randolph, which I shall now be able to do by riding to the shop doors, he did not send money but I can get them notwithstanding, as General Morland[1] has paid me $100—and I have the sum you sent.

How I grieved at the loss of your estimable friend Judge Jones. I hope it was not his son who fought the duel—Anna will not be here until the 18th: or 20th: of the month, owing to the illness of her nourse. I have had many ladies to see me today, Mrs: Lenox and Miss Keen came to invite me to a party and were very pressing, but I could not think of it—and this evening General Tourrea[u] and two or three frenchmen with him, I declined seeing them as you were absent and I upstairs, the General sent word up that he was anxious to see and speak to me, but I resolved not to admit a gentleman, into my room, unless entitled by age and long acquaintance—it is now past 9 o'clock and I cease to write but to dream of thee—Miss P is beside me as usual and sends you abundance of love and fills up the blank with Cousin Isaac. Tuesday morning. I was so entirely exhausted with my short ride of yesterday that the Doctor thinks I had better be still today, and I shall be helped down stairs to see my acquaintance, Doctor and Mrs: Rush called after I had bid you adieu last night, and left word they must see me this morning—I have been interrupted with company—Mr: Baldwin, Dr: Physic, Dr: Logan and General Tourreau. The General seems to have forgotten his English, I could not understand when he intends going to Washington, or what he was about here— he said he had been afflicted with every thing this summer but yellow fever. Mr: Baldwin is waiting the arrival of his sister Mrs: Barlow and her husband. Mr: Patton has just called to say I must sell my horses and take a pair he is acquainted with they are very fine and handsome—I told him I would consult you directly. I must again leave you as I am down in the parlor and surrounded with visitors, tell Mrs: Thornton that I am having a model of a bonnet made for her, the new ones are just coming in. Write to thy ever affectionate

Dolley.

Tr (MCR-S: Mary Estelle Elizabeth Cutts Papers). Tr made by Mary Cutts.
    1. Revolutionary War general Stephen Moylan rented DPM's Philadelphia house (*PJM* 16:353 n. 1).

From James Madison

WASHINGTON Ocr. 31. [1805]

Your second letter my dearest of the 26. continued on the 28. is this moment recd; and flatters my anxious wishes & hopes for your perfect recovery, and your *safe* return to Washington. I am glad to find you so determined in your adherence to the Drs. prescriptions. Be assured that he will give none that are not indispensable, & that you will not rejoice in having strictly observed.

I had not the pleasure of seeing Dr. P. & his daugr. till this morning. They intended to set out for Philada. this afternoon. I had therefore no opportuny of shewing them some attention which I wished. They will tell their own story of Washington the Races &c. Mrs. Randolph is expected by the Presidt. but he does not consider her coming as absolutely certain. My last informed you that I had written to Bishop Carrol with respect to Payne. He was so good as to lose not a moment in attending to the contents of it. I inclose his answer. I am sorry for the delay; but a birth seems at last to be secured for our son, & I hope it will prove a fortunate one. Tell me whether there be any steps in the mean time that you wish to be taken. We are all well. Inclosed are a letter from Mrs. Washington & another sent in by Mrs. Thornton. I believe I have already referred to Bishop Carroll's to me also inclosed. I can give you no acct of the races nor of the Theatre, having not been at either. The excess of business formed an objection, which was not combated by the slightest inclination. I repeat my kisses to Miss P. I wish I could give her more substantial ones than can be put on paper. She shall know the difference between them the moment she presents her sweet lips in Washington—after I have sett the example on those of another person whose name I flatter myself you will not find it difficult to guess. I shall comply with all the commands in your letter. With unalterable love I remain Yrs.

James Madison

Our worthy old friend Judge Jones death is published from Fredg.

RC (NjP).

To James Madison

PHILADELPHIA Novr: 1st: [1805]

I have great pleasure, my beloved in repeating to you what the Doctor has just now said, that the knee would be well in one day more and in two or three I might begin to ride—so that I may reasonably hope that a fortnight more will be the extent of my stay in Philadelphia. I am so impatient to be restored to you.

I wish you would indulge me with some information respecting the war with Spain and disagreement with England, as it is so generally expected here that I am at a loss what to surmise—You know I am not much of a politician but I am extremely anxious to hear (as far as you may think proper) what is going forward in the Cabinet—on this subject, I beleive you would not desire your wife the active partizan, such as her neighbor Mrs: L, nor will there be the slightest danger whilst she is conscious of her want of talents, and her diffidence in expressing her opinions always imperfectly understood by her sex—In my last I told you every thing the state of my finances &c &c. I have sent Peter to the office for letters and I hope to hear from you and to receive some account of Anna. I expect to see her every day.

Kiss my child for me and remember me to my friends. Could you speak a word to General Dearborn in favor of poor Mrs: Jackson—the Doctor's widow who used to supply so well the soldiers—adieu, my dear husband, Peter brings me no letters which really unfits me for writing more to any one, your ever affectionate

D.

Tr (MCR-S: Mary Estelle Elizabeth Cutts Papers). Tr made by Mary Cutts.

To James Madison

Saturday 4OClock [2 November 1805?]

Your charming letter My beloved, has revived my Spirit, & made me feel like another being—so much does my health peace, & every thing else, depend on your Affection & goodness. I am very greatful for the prospect you have opened for our child, & shall now look forward to his Manhood, when he will bless—and do honour to his guardians. I wrote you yesterday & have but a moment now—as the 2 hours since I reced: yours, has been devoted to the inclosed. Pray take as much relaxation, & pleasure as you can. All together, business will not agree with you, & unless you amuse yourself as usual I may travel too soon.

Betsy P. is almost frantic with the prospect of seeing W. & says she feels already your sweet kisses. What must some body else do. Farewell til tomorrow. Your own

D

Please to put a wafer in Lucys Letter & send it without delay.

RC (Occidental College Library: The Elizabeth and Stuart Chevalier Autograph Collection).

From James Madison

[ca. 2 November 1805]

The last mail brought me, my dearest yours of the 30 Ocr. I am happy to find you able to walk about. I hope that will help to restore your appetite & strength, and that it will not be long before you will be able to undertake a journey hither; tho' anxiously as I sigh for it, I can not wish it to be precipitated agst. the fullest approbation of Dr. P. I inclose a letter from the President and another from Mr. Jackson. I have one from the latter but it says nothing except as to Lovells land. I find that the letter from Mrs. Pichon was brought by the black maid who went with her, and that a little box remains in her hands, containing probably the trinket referred to. If you wish it to be procured & forwarded, say so. Payne is well, and I am endeavoring to keep him in some sort of attention to his books. All my affection embraces you

J. M.

A Carte blanche to Miss P.
Inclosed. $300.

RC (ViU).

From James Madison

[6 November 1805]

Yours of the 1st. instant, my dearest gives me much happiness, but it can not be compleat till I have you again secure with me. Let me know the moment you can of the time you will set out that I may make arrangements for paying the Dr &c. My Tobo. has been sold in Richd; but unfortunately the bills are not yet come on, and are on N. York at 60 days, so that some negotiation will be necessary. I did not expect you wd. receive much from your Tenants. Don't forget to do something as to insuring the Buildings. Your question as to our situation in regard to Spain & England is puzzling. As one gets into ill humor it is possible the other may change her circumstance. If a general war takes place in Europe Spain will probably be less disposed to insult us; and England less sparing of her insults. Whether a war will be forced by either is more than can be foreseen. It certainly will not if they consult their interest. The power however of deciding questions of war and providing measures that will make or meet it, lies with Congress, and that is always our answer to newsmongers. Madam Turreau is here. The Genl. not. Your friends are all well: except Capt. Tingey who has been in extreme danger but is mending. Mrs. Tingey also has been unwell. I inclose a letter from Payne, and one from Mrs. K. Miss P's postscript makes my mouth water. Cousin Isaac's would too, if he had ever had the taste which I have had. Your ever affec.

J. M.

I have written to Gooch to hurry on with the waggon, & to bring the Carpet if it can be secured agst. injury from the greasy & dirty companions it will have

RC (NcGG: Dolley Madison Memorial Association).

To James Madison

PHILA: Novr: 12th: 1805

I received yours containing Payne's letter yesterday, my best beloved, which gave me great pleasure, and immediately after was surprised and pleased by a visit from our brother John, he says his anxiety to see me was so great that he could not control it and I only regret that he should have indulged it without informing you. He travelled in the mail and had not slept for 3 nights—and now my darling I must tell you that our poor horse is considered incurable and that Mr: Patten has so interested himself as to procure one of the finest pairs of Sorrel, he knows them perfectly and gives ours in exchange with three hundred and fifty dollars difference. I told him I was extremely averse to the purchase until I could hear from you, but he insists on paying for them, himself taking an order on Mr: Lewis, as he knows the opportunity will be lost.

I wish I could now appoint a day for returning, tho' my knee is perfectly healed and gains strength I am unable to ride two days together a few days without sinking under fatigue—but as I am well I shall expect to be quite ready for Mr: Cutts and Anna about the 20th. No tongue can express my anxiety to be with *you,* at home. The Doctor is much concerned at the idea of my journey, as I have freely told him I would wish every thing to join you, he says he hopes it will be sufficiently firm by that time to travel with great care. Adieu for the present my dear husband your

D.

Tr (MCR-S: Mary Estelle Elizabeth Cutts Papers). Tr made by Mary Cutts.

To James Madison

My darling,   PHILADELPHIA 12th: November 1805.

I have just parted with Col: Patton who is well satisfied with the term of payment for the horses and congratulated me on possessing them, our own poor grey being on a meadow, but not any change in him for the better. I have been this morning to make several visits and on my return found Anthony Morris, who had come with a petition from his wife that I would let him wait upon me to her house; I was not strong enough to go directly, but wish greatly to visit this old and dear friend, if the Doctor should think well of my going for two days. I expect Anna next Sunday, and as soon as your arrangements are made from New York, I will set out with or without her.

I see that Jackson's paper[1] has announced the Declaration of War from Spain against us, and that the Marquis d'Yruho has requested his passport. He was here the other evening with other company, Mrs: Steward enquired of him if this was true, he was terribly angry and declared it was "a lie." Teaureau is ill, but goes abroad—the impression of him in Philadelphia is a sad one—he is recollected as the cruel commander at *La Vendé,* and the fighting husband—and tho Morris's company went to salute him with their drums and fife, he says, that the Americans hate him.

13th: The doctor says I must not go to Molly Morris's so that I must think no more of it.

I am about to put up the articles for the President and will enclose a note for him, to you farewell, my beloved.

Tr (MCR-S: Mary Estelle Elizabeth Cutts Papers). Tr made by Mary Cutts.
  1. The newspaper to which JM was referring was *The Political and Commercial Register,* published by William Jackson in Philadelphia from 1804 to 1820 (Clarence S. Brigham, *History and Bibliography of American Newspapers, 1690–1820* [2 vols.; Worcester, Mass., 1947], 2:945–46).

To James Madison

PHILA: 15th: November 1805

I was so unwell yesterday, my dearest husband, that I omitted writing. Dr: Physic has been ill for two days and so surrounded by young students, who attend his lectures that I have not ventured to send for his bill—I will do it however—I was persuaded to take a social dinner yesterday with Mrs: Dallas and on my return found your short letter of the 13th.

17th: I am much better this morning, my dear husband, and should take a short ride but for unfavorable weather, tomorrow I propose to call on as many as I can, as one preperation for my journey to you—that is the object to which my wishes all tend. I have yet seen little of the city—the Museum &c I hope to peep into Monday morning.

Mr: Cutts and Anna arrived last evening, my beloved, and so pleased and agitated was I that I could not sleep—We leave Monday, if I am quite strong enough—but I must wait a little for your commands.

I have received visits and invitations from the Lewis's, and am to dine with them on Thursday and at the Governor's on Wednesday—tomorrow at Dr: Bache's, all my engagements are made conditionally and with the approbation of the Doctor. Mrs: Wingate will have called to tell you about us. Your own

D.

Tr (MCR-S: Mary Estelle Elizabeth Cutts Papers). Tr made by Mary Cutts.

From James Madison

WASHINGTON Novr. 15. 1805

I was not disappointed my dearest, in my expectation of a letter by the last mail, which continues to give me favorable reports of your returning health &

strength. I hope by this time Mrs. Cutts will have joined you and that the event will accelerate that of your setting out. Proceed nevertheless with all the caution the Dr. may recommend. The inclosed letter came by yesterdays mail. I have no news for you; unless you wish to know that Col. Hawkins with his Indians is about leaving us,[1] that Mr. Skipwith is just arrived from France, and that the Tunisian Ambassador is expected soon from Norfolk.[2] I have but just seen Mr. S. and had no time to enquire of your friend Mrs. Pichon &c. Mr. Livingston went off yesterday. I can give you no city news. The wedding at Mr Simmons' has produced a round of parties; but I have not attended one of them. I send a letter by the mail which came inclosed to me for Mr Barlow. It is addressed to Philada. which you may mention to Mr Baldwin if you have an oppy. Give Miss P. a kiss for me & accept a thousand for yourself. Why don't you send on the other vols. of Dallas.[3] Yr. affte. husband

James Madison

RC (owned by Charles M. Storey, Boston, Mass., 1961).

1. Benjamin Hawkins, U.S. agent to the southern Indians, accompanied a delegation of Creek and Cherokee Indians to Washington in the fall of 1805, at which time a treaty was concluded (C. L. Grant, ed., *Letters, Journals, and Writings of Benjamin Hawkins* [2 vols.; Savannah, 1980], 2:406, 458–59).

2. Sidi Suleiman Melli Melli.

3. JM here refers to the first three volumes of Alexander James Dallas, *Reports of Cases Ruled and Adjudged in the Several Courts of the United States, and of Pennsylvania* (4 vols.; Philadelphia, 1790–1807).

From James Madison

Wednesday Tuesday [19–20] Novr. 1805

I have recd. my dearest yours begun on the 15. & continued on the 16th. The low spirits which pervade it affects mine. I sho⟨uld⟩ be still more affected, if you did not tell me that your knee grew better and stronger. I am much consoled by that information, and think you ought to be also, as your knee has been the source of both our disquietudes. I hope your next will manifest better spirits, and be a cordial to mine. I hope also that the company of your sister will prove a good medicine to you, and accelerate all the requisites to our reunion, my anxiety for which you can better feel I trust than I can express. I have been exerting myself to provide a remittance for you, but shall not be able to get it ready before the mail of thursday. In the mean time I hope to learn something particular as to the Drs. Charge, and thence to estimate the better, the sum necessary. Should there be time however after you receive this, to let me know how much would be serviceable to you for your Philada. purposes, let me know without reserve, and I will do all I can in that as in all cases, to evince the happiness I feel in giving proofs of my unlimited affection & confidence—Gooch tells me he has hopes of making up nearly our quota of Bacon, & in general gives a favorable acct. of things—Your friends here are all well. Tingey is recovering from a tedious & dangerous attack. I send inclosed a letter from Mrs. Washington. Col. Burr & Genl Dayton are here from the Western Country. They were at Clarksburg, and speak highly of Mrs. Jackson's blooming resurrection from the puerperal bed. She was to set out the day after they left her, accompanied by Capt Washington whose health was also much improved. I inclose also $60 from the President to replace your advances. The things arrived safe. I hope you have not been unmindful of the civilities recd. from your friends, and among them the particular attentions of Mrs. Leiper. I inclose a specimen of Capt. W's Tobo. Present it to Mr. L. and tell him with my complts. I wish to have his judgmt. of it. Payne is well. I endeavor to keep him a little in the path of the Student; but the close employment of my time, at this juncture leaves much to his own disposition. I have not yet heard from Mr Dulany. As I hope soon to see Miss P. and settle all ballces. with her, I will pay her no more at 2d. hand, reserving to myself the payment & receipt of all kisses on both sides of the acct. Accept my dearest love the warmest affections of your

J. M.

RC (NjP). Addressed to DPM "at Mrs. Wood's Philada."

From James Madison

Novr. 21. [1805]

I mentioned in my last my dearest that I should put into the mail today the remittance promised you. Having failed to sell the bill on N. York. I was obliged to enter into an arrangement with the Bank here bottomed on the Credit of that Bill. It has enabled me to forward you the enclosed part note which I hope will arrive safe, and remove all pecuniary obstacles to your setting out. Should it be insufficient, you will be able doubtless to get credit till I can make a further remittance which can be done on your return to Washington. The Horses I understand are to be paid for some time hence. I think your brother to blame to precipitate a sale of lands. He can not be so pressed as to require it, I shd. imagine, and the moment is certainly not favorable to such a transaction. Mrs. Randolph is not arrived nor does the President know the precise time that she will. I have nothing to add to my last but repeated expressions of my anxiety to have you safe with me, and with best regards & respects to Dr. Physic & love to our Sister & Miss P. assurances of the truest affection of Yr.

J. M.

RC (owned by Mr. Gilbert S. McClintock, Wilkes-Barre, Pa., 1962).

To James Madison

Saturday 23d. Novr. [1805]

The letters of my beloved Husband are allways a cordial to my heart—particularly the one reccd. yesterday which breaths that affection so precious that I wept over it in joy—I thought to have written in reply by the last night's post but dined at Mr. Lewises where I saw a very large party of the first inhabitants in point of rank, among them the Bishop—I sent the Tobaco with a note to Mrs. Leaper, for whose civilitys I have been careful to make every return she expected—& I have call'd at the doors generally of those who visited me— they all seem satisfied with my ⟨. . .⟩ at acknowledgments—M Morris has been ⟨. . .⟩. Yours containing the Check ⟨has?⟩ arrived this moment which will be quite ⟨suff⟩icient for the Docr. & every other purpose & I will make my preparations to sett of on monday. The weather for 3 days has been bad for the roads but hope to get along as far as Chester the first night & by small stages, for as long as I can bear until I am safely lodged in your arms.

I go to Gilpins to dinner & must make an abreviation in the Vol. I could write you—for the Horses—we pay 3 months here—I could have had of Anna what mony I wanted, & regret that you should have the slightest uneasiness about it—pray take care of your health & keep up your spirits & when we are again together I hope never more to lose sight of you—I will say more tomorrow til then farewell my best love.

Anna Mr C. & Betsy with old Amey offer their kindest affection to you.

RC (DLC: DPM Papers). Torn by removal of seal.

From James Madison

WASHINGTON Monday Novr: [1805]

I have recd. my dearest your letter by the last mail. As the Horses have been bought, the bargain must not only be maintained but Mr. Patton must understand that I am particularly indebted to him for his kindness on that as

77

well as on other occasions. I inclose a note from Mr. Ker relating to the Cook. It implies that she was hired for a year and must be paid for accordingly. Let me know what answer is to be given; and what deductions are to be made for Cloaths &c. I inclose also the little bundle from Miss Wheeler. Cousin Isaac was only reminded of the reward in store for his share in the trust. Mrs. Forrest has also just sent in a letter to be inclosed, to which Payne adds another. I wish it were possible for you to get nearly at the Dr's Bill. Why might you not request it in order to be forwarded to me? I forgot to mention that the 2 other Vols. of Dallas might follow the 1st. in the same channel. Mr. Livingston arrived here last night. We are to have as a guest an Ambassador from Tunis who is on board one of the Frigates arrived from the Mediterranean.

I am rejoiced to hear that your knee remains perfectly healed. Take care of it I beseech you, till it can defy ordinary exercise, and that you may the sooner undertake your journey home. Being obliged to write in a hurry, I can only add my best love to you, with a little smack for your fair friend, who has a sweet lip, tho' I fear a sour face for me.

J. M.

RC (NjP).

From James Madison

[November 1805]

This is the last mail My Dearest that will be likely to find you in Philada. and I am not without some hope that this will be too late. I take the chance however for inclosing a few letters which as they will be returned in case of your previous departure, you will receive them as soon as if they were kept here. I am desirous that you shd. get Mr Carrol, before you arrive in Baltimore. You will see that Payne is admissible the 1st. of next month. I hope to learn this evening from your wish as to the arrangemt. & time for his being in Baltimore. I write this in haste, being sent for to dine with the P. at the moment of my picking up the pen, and it will be too late to write after I get home from dinner. Consoling myself now with the expectation of soon having you with me, I conclude with best regards to Mr. & Mrs. C. and Miss P. who I hope will not fail to be a travelling companion, and with the ardent affection which I know I feel Yours &c

Say every thing to Dr. Physic that can express my gratitude esteem & regard

RC (MHi).

From George Davis

NORFOLK July 12th: 06

By my actions let me be judged, altho they must even fall short of the attachment, I sincerely feel for your family—I receive John as a Brother, and feel most confident, that his new situation however unimportant in itself, will at least call forth those energies of mind, which have been cramped for a want of action; and open an extensive field for advancement.

You may rest assured his Interest and happiness is very dear to me; to hasten the one, & secure the other, will be the Ambition of those friends you have committed him to; who in thanking you for this mark of confidence, reciprocate unfeignedly, the prayers you have offered for their well being—With great respect your mo: ob: St.

George Davis

P:S: John, arrived while we were at Mr. Pennocks country seat, & has taken up his quarters at Mr. Calverts, with Mrs: P. I consent to this on one ⟨condition only . . .⟩ in Norfolk, he stays altogether at our Retreat—Mrs. D. is too unwell to write you, by this Mail. G.D: we Sail 1st. of August.

RC (MCR-S: Mary Estelle Elizabeth Cutts Papers). Words lost in fold.

To Mary Payne

To Mrs: M. Payne   August 4th: [1806]

Expressions are wanting, my dearest mother, to convey to you my feelings! I have not been well since the first letter from my dear afflicted Mary, and a part of the time have kept my bed—the second, makes me think I shall never feel as I have done, so deep is the sorrow which takes possession of my mind— Dolley Lucy, both gone![1] They are now angels! and can never know evil or misery—ought we not to console ourselves with this reflection! I trust, my beloved mother, whose trials have been so many, will exercise her fortitude which is to preserve her for those that are left of us! I wrote thee by last post. I have written repeatedly to John, but received only the letters enclosed. I have no doubt of his having sailed with Davis, I shall now look out for vessels going to the Mediteranean to write by them to him, thine for him, thee wilt inclose to me.

We expect to leave Washington tomorrow or the next day. Thy next must be directed to Orange, I believe it will be best to send them first to this city and Wagner will forward them, until we can judge which is the most expeditious way of getting them. Payne is to follow in the stage on the 14th. This day I shall look for a letter to cheer me with the news of thy health.

Farewell, I shall write the first post after reaching home. Thy ever affectionate daughter

D. P. Madison

Tr (MCR-S: Mary Estelle Elizabeth Cutts Papers). Tr made by Mary Cutts.
1. The Dolley and Lucy referred to here were the daughters of DPM's sister Mary and her husband, John G. Jackson (Dorothy Davis, *John George Jackson* [Parsons, W.Va., 1976], 117, 118).

To Thomas Parke

10 Feb. 1807

If I was a politician I would collect for you a great deal of news—as it is, I will send you the little scrap which I have this moment listened to. Colo. Burr had arrived on the 12th. Jany. within 40 miles of Natches from whence he announced, in a letter to the Governor the innocence of his purposes which ware agricultrial & warning him not to interupt them—intimating that the use of force *might* produce a civil war.[1] The Governor had his Militia ready, & was determined if possible, to take him prisoner—this information was communicated to Congress this morng. by the President. My Mother & Husband beg to join me in affectinate salutations to yourself & daughter.

D. P. Madison

Printed extract (offered for sale in Christie's Sale Catalogue [14 May 1992], item 20).
1. The events to which DPM is referring were part of what became known as the Burr Conspiracy. To this day historians are unsure whether Aaron Burr intended to commit treason by separating the Trans-Appalachian West from the United States and creating a southwestern empire (Mary-Jo Kline et al., eds., *Political Correspondence and Public Papers of Aaron Burr* [2 vols.; Princeton, N.J., 1983], 2:919–25).

To Anna Cutts

27th. March [1807]

I am greaved & surprised my dear Anna at not receiving a line from you since you left us. What can be the matter? If the precious children engrossed your time surely my good Brother would think to releave my anxiety by writeing himself. This is the 12 day of your absence & I know not where to direct to you, but shall venture this to Phia. as the P. Master will forward it, should you

be gone. I have reccd. 3 letters from our dear Mother, who yealded to Mr. Jacksons wishes & went on with them after a single day, at G. W——s it rained &
snowed on their way, but they got safe to Clerksburge & are all perfectly well.
Mama expresses great anxiety for you & wishes to hear from you very much.
I hope in my next to be able to give a good acct. of you & yours. Mr. M is very
unwell with a cold but is able to go to the office. We see no certain prospect
of going to Orange. The President has a sick headake every day, so that he
is obliged to retire to a dark room at 9 o clock in the morg. He will not leave
this until the 6th. of Aprel. I suppose you have heared that Coll. Burr is re-
taken & on his way to Richmond for trial. This is all I know about him.
Mrs. Tingy & Miss Clinton continue as low as possible. Poor Nancy Crawford
is dead. Many are sick, & some dead in our 2 Towns, since you left us. We are
pretty quiet, but few parties. We went to the weding feast of Miss Stodart. We
dined last saturday at Mr. Erskine's, with Mr Mrs. Krags Taylor's Capt Lewis
Cousin Isaac & ourselves. Mrs. Merry pass'd thro Toun, staid 2 nights at Taylors. I went to see her. She was quite polite &c. She goes on to N. York to embark. I think I have given you all the news in my *little* way, except that Wheaton
has bought & is going to live in Stevensons House opposite to us. I hope you
have seen Mrs. Waddell & some other's of my friends, & that I shall get a
letter soon, full of yourself & them. Mr. M & Dolley join me in best love to
Brother & yourself & the sweet boys. Write write. I gave Mr. Deblois the 12
dols. from Mr Cutts & sent your roses to the Packet. I hope you'l get all your
things safe. Adeiu for the present. Yours ever

DPM

RC (ViU).

To Anna Cutts

My dearest Anna   18th. June [1807]
    I have had a pain in my face for several days which has prevented my write-
ing—it is now nearly well & I have taken the pen to write without haveing
much that is new to tell you—I rejoice at your being so happily fixed in your
own house with your precious Husband & children & have only to regret that
I cannot be with you—tell my sweet boy that I dont like the story he tells on
me & that I'l give him another to lern—Aunt D. will come & take me to see
the Seals dance on the rocks & then cary me, her little son, to her home, to go
a guning with cousin Payne—he shall add what else his fancy may sugest—

how I long to hug your children & to hear M talk—Oh Anna 'tis a sad thing to feel myself so far from you—I have late letters from our Mother & sisters, all well but poor dear Polly, who has been ill & not yet recover'd. Mama says she is as thin as possible & complains of a pain in her side—I am very uneasy when I think of her—Lucy writes in her usial good spirits—G. W. was going to the Sweet Springs but was as usial in his health—we get only Official letters from John who was doing well—we hope to visit orange in july, but cant say at what time in the Month—Mr. M has just inclosed to Brother R¹ the last Richmond paper includeing the trial of B so far—the arrival &c. of Genl. Wilkenson—B—s party fight hard but it is the general oppinion that he will be convicted—he had the assurance you see to summons the President Genl. Dearborn & R Smith, but they will not go—Mrs. Duvall has return'd, & likes Washington best she says, after all—Mrs Latrobe is here, she told me she had lately been at a grand entertainment given by the Marquis & that in the midst of supper she fainted away—not a Lady rose, but she was left to the care of some Spanairds—mortified enuf was she—cousin Isaac I wrote you had return'd violently in love with B Boardly & indeed I think he has caught the delectable manners of that stiff sett, for you know they allways ware in high stile—he took no pains to be acquainted with the Marchoness of cource, as he thought he was with all that could be perfect—I think I have seen him 3 or 4 times since his return about 5 weeks—I told you of Eppes disappointment after geting his weding garment to marry Miss Fashie. I had a letter the other day from Becky Coles—sombody, I dont know who, is coarting her—one also from Mrs. Decatur—whose husband you see is a witness against Burr— Latrobe has also gone to R on that arrand—I hear often from Cousin Dolley, they are all well & the poor child is frantick to be back with me—Mrs. Forrest is very large & very glad, I sold her our traveling carriage & she rides about nobly in it for her health—The Dulanys are still in the same House & often give parties—other neighbours two, so that we are tolerably gay.

Your Tenant promises fair that before we depart he will pay—I shall be very happy to transmit your money—next week will set of Genl. Mrs. Dearborn & Peggy Tingy for Main—they promise themselves great pleasure in seeing you at your own house. They will take the stage, stop a while in Pha. & N. York—Mrs. Wingate is to meet them, I forget where—we have Dubourg to dine with us, he says Payne does us honour &c. I have never had courage to leave M to make him a visit but expect him to pass 5 weeks with us in Augus[t] & Sepr. Adeiu my dear sister. Ms love to you both & the boys with mine— your acquaintance here all enquire after you with great interest. Miss Clinton is still here; but her Father has sent for a vessel & intends sailing with her for

N. Y. in a few days—she cant walk yet. Mrs. Beckly was to set of to day for Pha. with her brother—write soon.

RC (MCR-S: Mary Estelle Elizabeth Cutts Papers).
1. Richard Cutts.

To an Unidentified Correspondent

Novr. 7th. 1807.

Deep affliction my dear friend has for some time past arrested my pen! My beloved & tender Mother left us forever, on the 20th. of October last—she was in Virgia with my youngest sister, where she died, without suffering or re- gret—The loss is only ours, & for that only ought we, her children, to mourn!

Mr. Madison unites with me in best wishes, & regard for you & yours

D P Madison

I can have no doubt but that Fitzgerald's statement is proper—& the balance due to us will perhaps answer for a new Ensurance, if you will have the good- ness to apply it.

RC (PHi). Probably to Thomas Parke.

From Martha Jefferson Randolph

EDGE HILL Jan 15, 1808

A hope of being able through your medium to serve an unfortunate family reduced to absolute want, has induced me to write to you My Dear Mrs Madi- son as the only person to whom I could with propriety apply in the present emergency. You have no doubt heard of the total ruin of David M. Randolph. He is himself gone to England upon a scheme so little likely to succeed, that nothing but dispair could have suggested it. His family in the mean time are entirely destitute, but my Sister with an energy that does her honour resolved to open a boarding house in Richmond by which means she will I hope be en- abled to suport her self and younger children. Her eldest son is also provided for for the present, there remains only Beverly the immediate subject of this letter. Their object is to obtain for him, if possible, an under clerkship in one of the offices; in Mr Madison's would be the wish of his friends, but if not in his, in any other that could be obtained. You were never backward in the cause of humanity, in the present case, My Dear friend, I must beg you to end the suspence in which the poor youth is kept, as soon as possible, that if he should be dissappointed, his friends may see what else can be done for him.[1]

I wish I had a *right* to complain of your withholding from a friend in solitude, so great a source of amusement as your letters but *I* deserve to do pennance for my sins, and *you* have been spared the *ennui* of reading letters dull, as the surounding scenery mountains covered with snow are not calculated to inspire or amuse the fancy. Mine seldom wanders from my own fire side unless it is to pay you a little visit occasionally, from which however, I am soon recalled to decide upon the merits of a misshapen letter or assist in the labours of the grammar or spelling book. Your boy is a very fine one in his mother's eyes.[2] I am sorry he will not have it in his power this winter to challenge Master Cutts and the ragged boys in F street to a game of marbles. Give my best affections to Mrs Cutts and believe me my Dear Mrs M. yours sincerely

Randolph

RC (MCR-S: Mary Estelle Elizabeth Cutts Papers). Docketed "Mrs. Randolph of Monticello."
    1. William Beverley Randolph did receive a position in the federal government in 1808. In 1816 he was a clerk in the Register's Office of the Treasury Department (Mary Randolph to DPM, 10 Feb. 1808; *ASP, Misc.* 2:309).
    2. James Madison Randolph was born 17 January 1806.

From Mary Randolph

My dear Madam   Richmond Febry 10 1808.

I cannot express the gratitude I feel for your very friendly attention in procuring so eligible a situation for my Son. He is at present on a visit to my Brother, but I shall direct him to go immediately to Washington and place himself under your patronage; he is young and will need the advice, which I am certain Yourself and my excellent friend Mr Madison will be good enough to offer him, I trust he will not prove unworthy of it. Be pleased to present my affectionate regards to Mr M. and believe me with cordial esteem Yours

M Randolph.

RC (MCR-S: Mary Estelle Elizabeth Cutts Papers).

To Eliza Collins Lee

26th. Feby. 1808

The testimony of your justice & your love, my ever dear friend, was as balm to my afflictions—you, who knew my tender & lamented Mother, from your

84

infancy—you whom she valued & caressed, will drop the tear of comesiration for her child—whose heart is bursting with grief whilst she tells you that the grave of her beloved Polly is within the same inclosure! Oh God! We must bow our heads to thy decrees however awful—we cannot change or avert them—Eliza, I cannot write—tho I wish to communicate every thing to you; when I trace the sad events that have occured to me, I feel as if I should die two—My Husband is nearly well & I have exerted all my fortitude, all my religion, in order to live for him & my son. Alass! My friend, I used to think that I could not survive the loss of my Mother & my Sisters yet am I still here; & in all the bitterness of mourning striveing to reconcile my heart to the greatest misfortune! Farewell my precious Eliza, Mr. M & Anna join me in love to you & yours

DPM

RC (DLC: DPM Papers).

From John G. Jackson

CLARKSBURG 8th May 1808

I write you again from Clarksburg my dear Sister—from the abode of death & misery unutterable—the silence which reigns throughout the House adds to the gloom which is no longer penetrated by the voice of a living soul: even the lisping tongue of our sweet Mary is not heard soothing her father, with "dont cry papa *Ma* will come back again."

I am so distracted by recurring to the past & present that I have not even contemplated my future destiny perhaps the scene will be soon closed & I shall be rid of the painful reflection—I know your kind enquiries lead to a knowledge of my situation—I am alone—I retrace the scenes & visit the places where we walked—we sat—& talked—while Our little lambs were playing around us—from thence I repair to the Orchard the depository of my beloved family—I weep over the grave of my incomparable Wife—I pray fervently for death & a reunion with her—but, Ah, my sister, God has been deaf to all my prayers life & death are denied me when I ask for either—with bursting heart I return to the house. I fling myself on the bed & sigh out the nights of misery—this is my journal except once a day for half an hour I call down to see my sister Williams she is sick. Her child who was born in April lived only a few days—except her I have not a single relative remaining: & when they go should I still live—there will be nothing to disturb my melancholy.

Tomorrow's Mail will bring letters from you. They will tell me that there are still a few friends who interest themselves in my fate. I wish I were worthy their regard—with kindest wishes for my dear friend M. your Affect Brother

J G Jackson

RC (ViU: Breckenridge-Watts Papers). Docketed by JM.

To Anna Cutts

3d. of june [1808]

I have reced. your letters my dear sister one from Boston, in which my dear Brother adds his mite of amusement for M & myself with one from your own House—I rejoiced more in the last the former frighten'd me *a little* but we hope from the public prints that we shall not be quite *out done* by the Feds. this time—we are still in Orange & shall not leave it before the 9th. or 10th. I have been very ill since I wrote you last, with the Inflamitory Rumatism— never had I more extream sickness & pain—Doct. Willis bled me & gave me medicin—Nelly & Mother M nursed & waited on me with great attention & kindness—but Anna—no language can give you an Idea of the poignancy of my misery when I recollected the loss of my dearest friends after fainting in the arms of strangers—for at that time Madison had rode out. I was never before in such a situation & therefore had never anticipated such a one—Alass! I Allways thought it would be my greatest misfortune to be seperated from you that I loved most—for what in this world can compensate for the sympathy & confidence of a Mother & a sister—nothing but that tye that binds us to a good Husband—such are ours, & we aught to be satisfied.

We have had a continuel round of company—which has been burthen-some tho I have taken no kind of trouble with them—the day I was most sick 15. or 20, dined here of the family & connection but I did not quit my bed or know any thing about them—I have a long letter from Lucy, they are all well. Jackson as usial—Hariot & Parks have broke up in B & gone to spend the Summer & fall there. It teazes Lucy greatly & she & George regret it & say it shall not be so.

I told you in my last from this place that I had a short letter from John dated a year ago—he was well &c.

Kiss the dear precious boys for their aunt—I will write you from W about the 13th. or 14th.

Adeiu I embrace you both—I could not move my right arm an inch until today & now tis painful to write so long—Payne is well.

RC (ViU). Unsigned. Addressed to Mrs. Cutts at Saco.

To Anna Cutts

28th. August [1808]

With heartfelt joy my beloved Sister did I recce. the short letter of my brother giveing the good tidings of your 3d. Son & promising health—Mr. M Lucy George & Payne ware with me & we all claped our hands in triumph— The post did not come here for a week after the letter or I should have written you directly & since that we have passed nearly a week at Monticello. Mrs. R. has just left her confinement with her 3d son likewise—she calls him Benja- min Franklin & hopes tis her last—Anna is to be married on the 15. Sepr. & I left them busy in preparations—I did not see much company there. Mr. Hay & his daughter spent a day—the Monroes ware at their Seat near but I did not see one of them—the Colo. himself is in Kentucky. Lucy left me on the 24th. George was in the same low way & poor dear little Mary was ill all most the whole time she staid, & went away sick with the ague & fever. I fear the pre- diction of her Father, who thinks she will not live to be a woman—he writes me often but all in his old stile of melancholy—we expect to go back to the city on the last of Sepr. which is sooner than we expected—because of public business—The President & M have been greatly perplexed at the remon- strances from so many Towns to remove the Embargo—you see they refer to Congress—& the evading it, also, by our people is a terrible thing—so they say—in short every thing seems to call them back to the seat of Govt. where I shall be sorry to go so soon—the prospect of meeting you my dear Anna is cheaf sweetner to my prospect. Lucy intends to come to us in the winter. We dined & staid all night at Colo. Walkers. They ware the same affectinate people & sent a thousand loves to you—I expect a large party from thence next week of Carters Nelsons &c. I wish it was over their visit, as I am sick of so much company. I have A. More with me as Housekeeper but she is far from perfec- tion & I hope I shall get clear of her on my return—This family is just as last year—all kindness & attention, & a great deal with me—Unkles family have been two sick to admit of their comeing—Patsy & Eleck have been at the point of death—but all are now geting well—our Post days are twice a week, some- times once so that I have fewer opptys of writeing than ever—this can not be sent for 3 days to come which greaves me. I will add whatever seems to inter- est us—I often hear from Mrs. Forrest Mrs. Thornton &c. All is dull they say & Mrs. F's little girl is threatened with another riseing on her side which I fear will be its death. We have expected Mr & Mrs Barlow for a week past & now I begin to hope they will not come as it grows preserving & pickling time.

Sept. 1t.   Last night I was regaled with my dear Brother's 2d. letter—do not talk of our correspondence ending for tho our beloved Anna resumes the pen you must continue to favor your sister sometimes—& now let me tell you that when you come to the traveling you will find our sweet Walter less trouble than pleasure. I know he will be very good on his way to his Aunty who longs to embrace him—I am charm'd with the name. Walter was that, of our only Unkle, who was every thing that was amiable.

RC (MCR-S: Mary Estelle Elizabeth Cutts Papers).

To Anna Maria Thornton

1t. Sepr. [1808]

You allways write charming letters my dear Mrs. T. & when I profit by them as I have done by your last I lament my inability to return you *the same.* For tho the world may be dull with us, yet *you,* are in or near a Toun—I am absolutely in the County where the people I see are nearly all unknown to you— This, of course must make me lack the pleasing incident—We return'd from Montecello after passing a week with the inhabitants—Mrs. Randolph looks fat & chearful—her new son is a fine one but cross as you could wish any thing to be. Ann was most truly occupied in making dresses &c &c for her wedding which is to take place on the 15t. of this month. They wished us to be there on the occation, but that was out of the question—The President had a good deal of company—among them was Mr. Hay who is to mary Miss Monroe, Mr. Wert the author of the British Spy &c. I did not see Mrs. Monroe or Mr. Trist, who ware in the neighbourhood. On our return, we spent a day & night at Colo. Walkers—they enquire affectionately after you—your Mama & the Docr. Mrs. Nelson reminded me of past times when playing on her delightful Organ—I expect the whole family in a day or so to pay me a visit— We have some company lately arrived; from the upper country. They tell me they saw Mr & Mrs. R Smith near Bath in Berkley—so I suppose they have changed their rout from the ⟨?⟩ to the Virga. springs—I am glad to find that you have gay partys now & then—& hope they will continue as I hope to join in your bustle by & by—I should like to see a good Play once more but fear they will not stay with you long enuf. We have not fixed on the day of returning, but suppose the last in this month, may bring us up—I am oblidged to leave you, without saying half I wish, as I am in the midst of mirth & confusion. I am greaved to hear of the sickness in the city—is it in our neighbourhood? We shall not have a good Bunch of grapes this season—all withered—

Have you heared of a Barrel of Slips Mrs. Cathcart sent me? I fear they will be spoil'd unless buried in the Earth. Adeiu Mr. M. & Payne beg to add their best regard & wishes, with mine for you & yours.

RC (DLC: Thornton Papers). Unsigned. Addressed to Mrs. Thornton at F Street.

From John G. Jackson

My Dear Sister.   HAREWOOD Octr. 8th 1808

I reached this place yesterday where I found my precious Child,[1] with Lucy & little George all very ill with a billious fever—Lucy was alarmingly so last night—Great God! When shall sickness & death cease to terrify & distract me?—here I counted on being saluted with smiles of healthy countenances & all is sallow pale & emaciated—I was 4 days at Winchester on business at Court where I found more political warmth than for many months past the feds have a story by the handle which they wield most dexterously it is that Sec. Smith declared at Martinsburg that the President & M urged the embargo against the opinion of his great self Gallatin & Co[2]—I have written the whole matter to the President by this day's mail—depend on it those little great men are filled with venom & Gall at the idea of Ms. being taken from among them to preside over them—no wonder poor man jealous vain & ambitious, he envies those talents & virtues in a rival that he cannot equal; & is the last of his race to discover his own inferiority—farewell, love to my dear M, & my *dearest* sister

J G Jackson

RC (DLC). Docketed by JM.

    1. This was Mary Elizabeth Payne Jackson, the daughter of Mary and John G. Jackson. In 1824 she married John J. Allen, a Virginia lawyer who later became a state judge.

    2. The story retailed by the Federalists, as reported here by Jackson, reflected the power of the embargo issue to polarize the country. Jackson's comment is also an early reference to the struggle between Robert Smith and Albert Gallatin that later would split JM's cabinet (Ketcham, *James Madison*, 468–69; Joseph Gales Jr., "Recollections of the Civil History of the War of 1812. By a Contemporary," *Historical Magazine*, 3d ser., 3 [1874–75]: 154).

The Politics
of War

1809-1817

A NEW SENSE OF EXCITEMENT STIRRED WASHINGTON AT THE START OF 1809. James Madison had been elected president of the United States. A flurry of expectations blew around town, born more from a feeling that Dolley Madison would alter society than that her husband would transform politics. He, after all, was Thomas Jefferson's old friend and adviser; he had been secretary of state for the previous eight years. She, on the other hand, would occupy a brand-new place. She would be the first First Lady to preside over the new national capital.

Her duties progressively absorbed her time, and she found fewer moments to sit and write to her friends. Her correspondence took on a new tone. Her notes became more disjointed and fragmentary. No longer did her letters reflect the life of an ordinary woman during the early years of the new republic, or even that of a woman who was a member of the ruling elite. For the next eight years, the most important thing about her would be her extraofficial position. While her mail as a young woman in Philadelphia and as the wife and then widow of a retired president in Virginia presents a strictly personal view, her correspondence for the years when she presided over official Washington has a different import. The journeys between Montpelier and Washington, the joys and sorrows of her family, or the importance of an illness become background events, overshadowed by the activities and impact of her public life. While her husband served as president, she was the "queen," as both admirers and detractors called her, of the new nation.

Her correspondence from the very beginning of James Madison's administration demonstrates that everyone understood the change. Old friends and new acquaintances began increasingly to write to her, drawn by their assumption that she now had the power to grant them favors: pardons and advancements, positions and clemency, invitations and status. Offers of help arrived, gifts of a kind she had never received before. "I have been endeavoring without effect to search out a good Coachman for you," John Tayloe, the richest man in the city, smoothly proffered, with just a hint of the obsequious. "It would give me *infinite pleasure* to execute at any time any commands of which you may think me trustworthy." Ruth Hooper Dalton Deblois, the wife of the local merchant Louis Deblois, dispatched a kerchief, in the hope that Mrs. Madison would "some times throw it across your shoulders," thereby greatly honoring Mrs. Deblois. George Watterston, a local playwright, novelist, and literatus-about-town, sent her a brand-new comedy he had written—a ploy to introduce himself and to acquire her favor.[1] All of these transactions demonstrate not only her new importance and standing; they mark a shift in the nature of her mail. Her letters during these years, at least those that have been preserved, are not on the whole personal. Few record her activities, and many were meant to be passed on to her husband. Such correspondence often hints at the larger political context: a sentence about "the Henry affair," an account of the progress of a ship called the *Hornet*, a comment on how her friend Ruth Barlow, wife of the U.S. minister to France, was doing. Dolley Madison's letters of this period are filled with political gossip and thus should be read differently from the way her other letters are read.

Outstanding among these letters is one written on 2 March 1809 by her friend Eliza Collins Lee. The two women had known each other since they were girls growing up in Quaker Philadelphia; both had married out of the faith by wedding Virginia politicians. Lee's words reflect the importance of Dolley Madison's new role and the influence she gained as First Lady. "'Tis but on events most productive of Great pain, or pleasure to you," she wrote, perhaps remembering many of their shared joys and sorrows, "that I am induced to intrude upon your time. . . . Allow me then to offer my congratulations at a time when you are about to fill the character the most dignified and respectable in society." Lee understood her friend well; she went on to detail the very strengths that Dolley Madison would bring to her new post. Lee recognized that the First Lady's greatness would come out of "the mind, temper, and manners of my Philadelphia Quaker friend," whom she described as "peculiarly fitted for the station, where hospitality and graciousness of deportment, will appear conspicuously charming & conciliating." Thus Lee, among all of Mrs. Madison's correspondents, introduces the major theme of this section. Why is Dolley Madison considered one of the most important nineteenth-century American women and the greatest First Lady until Eleanor Roosevelt assumed the position in 1933? To find the answer requires looking in these letters for references to ceremony and society, how she dressed and behaved, the way she decorated the White House, and those whom she helped obtain favors. In sum, these letters reveal the unofficial power she created through her station and, as Eliza Collins Lee put it, through her "hospitality and graciousness of deportment."

Between 1801 and 1809 Dolley Madison had become well acquainted with Washington society and politics. She had been there at the creation, perfectly positioned to acquire the knowledge she would need to assume the role of First Lady. She had matured, learned about national politics and the national capital, and acquired the lexicon of the official language. She added this education to what she had learned in Philadelphia, where as a young woman she had gained a firsthand education in political and international relations, as well as a sense of what was most fashionable in dress, design, and display. By March 1809 she was ready to take over the role of First Lady, to define and refine the position.[2]

She began to do so from the very moment of her husband's inauguration. Both Madisons understood that her role would be new, not only because Jefferson had been a widower, not only because Dolley was a charismatic person in her own right, but also because her social and ceremonial activities would bear political implications. Jefferson's extreme republican practices simply would not do for the Madison administration.

Thus the Madisons—meaning, in practice, Dolley Madison—would have to invent new ceremonial forms. As the reigning heads of state, they could neither continue Jefferson's radical habits nor revert to Federalist conventions. As president, James Madison required his wife to make sure that politics and diplomacy flowed as smoothly as it was in her power to ensure. This need grew as international hostilities and domestic animosities mushroomed. Both Dolley and James needed to find ways to negotiate these tensions, to create social conditions under which both Federalist and Republican leaders— as well as their wives and daughters—could gather at White House functions. This would be Dolley Madison's job. From the very beginning of her term, she fulfilled her role through her choice of fashion, her selection of White House decor, her definition of official entertainment, and the warmth of her personality.

She started on the day of the inauguration. The Madisons were the first presidential couple to close the day's ceremonies with an inaugural ball. Four hundred guests were invited. During the day Mrs. Madison wore "a plain cambrick" dress with a long train, "plain round the neck without any hand-kerchief, and [a] beautiful bonnet of purple velvet, and white satin with white plumes," while the new president wore a dark brown suit that had been spe-cially made for him from the wool of Merino sheep raised on the Hudson River valley farm of Robert R. Livingston.[3] In both cases the presidential couple made a statement of simple taste and practical values. But hers showed a love of fashion that became fully evident in her attire that evening. For the ball Dolley chose a pale buff-colored velvet gown "made plain, with a very long train, but not the least trimming, and beautiful pearl necklace, earrings, and bracelets" and "a matching turban with white satin and feather plumes."[4]

In choosing her inaugural ball outfits, Dolley selected a garment that was light in color but not the white that was fashionable in Europe. Stylishly low-cut but not indiscreetly décolleté, it was neither made of sheer muslin, such as a French leader of fashion might wear, nor elaborately trimmed with the wo-ven satin or cotton that a British aristocrat might choose. And it displayed nei-ther French artificial lightness nor British heavy opulence. Velvet, moreover, is a heavy fabric that provided a degree of modesty conforming to American notions of appropriate decorum.[5]

Dolley wore pearls where a European woman at court would have worn di-amonds, as many as possible. When Elizabeth Merry, wife of the British min-ister Anthony Merry, appeared in Washington dressed in a white satin dress in 1803, she had "her hair bound tight to her head with a diamond crescent be-fore and a diamond comb behind, diamond earrings and necklace displayed on her bare bosom."[6] Even if the Madisons had been able to afford diamonds, they would not have done so. The First Lady would never have chosen to be "monarchical" or opulent in her dress. Pearls denoted taste, elegance, and vir-tue. Though many Americans called Dolley Madison "queenly," her dress would not have been adequate to the fashion demands of any European court. Her inaugural ball gown was her opening shot, a signal that she would walk a line between European-influenced finery that expressed American power and abundance and a republican modesty that demonstrated adherence to the po-litical principles of the new nation. It showed how Dolley approached her job: not only with energy and flair but with care and caution. Her dress declared that the presidential mansion was not the court of a monarch but the residence of the American executive.[7]

The White House needed work. Jefferson had applied federal funds toward improving the exterior of the building, but the Madisons had much to do on the inside. As early as mid-February, therefore, President-elect Madison authorized the redecoration of the presidential mansion and ordered that it be done in conjunction with the wishes of his wife. The logical choice for architect-cum-decorator was Benjamin Henry Latrobe, the British-born Philadelphia architect whom Jefferson had appointed surveyor of public buildings in 1803 and who had already done much to beautify the executive mansion's exterior. His wife, Mary Elizabeth Hazlehurst Latrobe, was a Philadelphia Quaker who had known Dolley in the 1780s. The Latrobes and the Madisons were personal friends, dining at each other's houses and sharing political gossip and friends. Latrobe wrote to his brother in December 1808 of the new president: "I have been for many years on an intimate footing with him. Mary had known his excellent and amiable wife from a child."[8]

By mid-March the three were already working as a team, designing a new carriage and ordering items to fill the new rooms. They undertook the important downstairs rooms in sequence: first Mrs. Madison's sitting room; then the Oval Room, which was to be the most formal entertaining area; and finally the dining room.[9] Dolley and the Latrobes created a uniquely American and republican flavor by ensuring that all of the furniture would be supplied by American craftsmen, artisans, and business people. The design of the furniture, moreover, was aesthetically complex and overtly political. Latrobe drew up plans for the furniture himself, pursuing a pure republican ideal through the imitation of Greek and Roman patterns and following the latest European architectural style. His object was to portray the United States as a new Greece located in the American forest. As Latrobe argued, "Greece was free: in Greece every citizen felt himself an important part of his republic." Thus the mansion's decor, he believed, should represent a culture worthy of the new republic and its place in history. The imitation of antiquity through his designs promised a marriage of perfect beauty and austere patriotism.[10]

Dolley approached their task of creating the interior of the White House as a symbol of the new republic with attention to detail, care, and caution. Her drawing room was the first piece of the decorating project to be completed. When she began Wednesday evening entertainments in May 1809, Washingtonians flocked to a room upholstered in canary yellow satin with matching damask curtains and appointed with a piano and guitar for music. Latrobe wrote to a friend: "Mrs. Madison gives drawing rooms every Wednesday. The first one was very numerously attended by none but respectable people. The Second, La la," by which he meant that the assembled crowd was of only middling rank. And "the last by a perfect rabble in beards and boots."[11]

The drawing-room evenings were a political necessity.[12] Unlike a monarch, the president had to be accessible to anyone who wanted to see him. But if there were no schedule, he could be constantly interrupted. George Washington had inaugurated a schedule of weekly social events to make himself and his wife available to the public. So Dolley began her weekly affairs as quickly as she could, carefully changing the nomenclature from the Federalist "levee" to the more republican "drawing room" and reducing the formality of the occasion. She placed announcements in the newspaper and deliberately invited as broad a range of people as possible. Her parties were very well attended; they soon became known as "squeezes." Mary Boardman Crowninshield, wife of Madison's final secretary of the navy, wrote in 1816: "Such a crowd I was never in. It took us ten minutes to push and shove ourselves through the dining room; at the upper part of it stood the President and his lady, all standing, and a continual moving in and out."[13]

Her "entertainments" were varyingly received, according to the politics of the guest. Alexander Dick, a member of the British legation in Washington, described his first "drawing room" in his journal in June 1809: "We went this Evening & found a Crowd of Ladies and Gentlemen Walking through the Apartments which were all thrown open & a band of Military Music playing." He found the food too simple and complained that there was neither dancing nor cards, but he added that "in a place like Washington where there are Scarcely any public places at all, Such a Meeting seems to be much relished, & there is the honor of Seeing the President & his Lady."[14]

At the other end of the political spectrum, Jonathan Roberts, a Republican congressman from Pennsylvania, wrote his brother that he was having difficulty deciding whether or not to attend a presidential party. "It is not pleasant to encounter new scenes where it is not easy to be prepar'd for all that passes & where embarrassments may arise that may subject one to the sneers of the narrow minded," he complained. But he decided to risk his country manners, and once there, he "found Mrs. Madison & her widowed sister Washington & perhaps [eight] or ten gentlemen." He approached Mrs. Madison and her sister, bowed, and retreated to sit down, and after about thirty minutes the meal was served. He survived the ordeal—and thereafter returned to the Wednesday drawing rooms. On those occasions, Roberts wrote, some men put on their best suits of "superfine-blue-cloth" with trimmings of silver vellum lace, pleated buttons, and white pantaloons in the summer, or a black coat, silk waistcoat, cravat, and black velvet pantaloons in the winter. This attire seemed elegant and even monarchical to Roberts, although it would have been too plain and provincial for a European court. Yet even this level of dress was not required. "Those who aspire to distinguished gallantry do not appear in boots," he explained. But he for one did not approve of such airs and went attired in good republican footwear: leather boots. He concluded, "Mrs. Madison . . . is a democrat tho the world have strong doubts about it." [15]

Dolley Madison, working as the ceremonial head of state, created a path that threaded its way between the demands of Jonathan Roberts and the requirements of Alexander Dick. Perhaps she could not have done it had the city been larger and more established. As a Federalist congressman from Pennsylvania wrote his wife, "I have never yet been at an evening *party* except Mrs. Madison's." He described these parties as serving "to releive this oppressive tedium, arising from the continued sameness of our daily routine of engagements, wholly destitute as these are of that exhilarating variety and interest which my professional business and other avocations at home supply." [16]

Anecdotes of Dolley Madison's generosity and sociability abound. Margaret Bayard Smith wrote that she united "all the elegance and polish of fashion" with "the unadulterated simplicity, frankness, warmth, and friendliness of her native character and native state." William Winston Seaton of the *National Intelligencer* commented that it was "not her form, 'tis not her face, it is the woman altogether, whom I should wish you to see." The British minister Francis James Jackson was less generous when he described her as fat and forty, if not fair. Frances Few described her by saying that "it is impossible however to be with her and not be pleased," adding, "there is something very fascinating about her." And Augustus John Foster observed that "she rendered her husband's house as far as depended on her agreeable to all parties." In 1837 Anthony Morris recalled to Dolley's niece "the peculiar power she always possessd, of making & preserving friends, and of disarming Enemies." [17] But perhaps the last word here should be from the third letter in this section, in which the Washington writer George Watterston, asks Dolley for permission to dedicate to her his play *The Child of Feeling*. A long-standing admirer, he wrote in his novel *The Wanderer in Washington* that "Mrs. Madison seemed to have been qualified by nature for the situation she held."

> She spared no pains to please all who might visit her, and all were pleased from the most exalted to the most humble. She had a peculiar tact in ingratiating herself into the good opinion of her visitors, who never failed to admire, as much as they loved her. There was nothing in her manner that looked like condescension,

or bordered on haughtiness; everything she did had the appearance of real kindness, and seemed to spring from a sincere desire to oblige and to gratify those who came to see her. To strangers, and such as discovered any degree of diffidence and awkwardness, she was particularly assiduous in her attentions, and soon made them feel perfectly at ease. . . . She employed herself in entertaining the company in every possible variety of manner. Her memory was so tenacious, that after a single introduction she could, like Cato, name every gentleman and lady that had been introduced to her; and strangers have often been surprised at the facility with which she could address them by name, when they had no expectation of being known.

And thus, Watterston concluded, "Her feelings, like those of her husband, were altogether republican."[18]

Five years after the Madisons' retirement from Washington, Watterston wrote *The L—— Family in Washington; or, A Winter in the Metropolis*. In it Watterston lampooned Washington as a mecca for men who wanted office and women who sought well-connected husbands. Who did write to Dolley Madison for help, and how did she choose to exert her influence?[19] Was there, as Watterston has one of the characters in his novel proclaim, "a *petticoat influence*" on recommendations and appointments?

Many people did ask her for favors. Some, like Jane O'Bryan, wanted to secure clemency for members of their families. Anne Cary Morris wrote in order to spread her own version of a very public fight she had had with the Virginia congressman John Randolph of Roanoke, her first cousin. George W. Erving sent Dolley a letter in order that she might convey its contents to her husband. The letters written to Dolley asking for her help in obtaining jobs can be placed in a larger governmental context and reveal both something of what others expected of her and what she hoped to accomplish in response to these requests.

Even in a small federal government, and even though the personnel changes were few between the administrations of Jefferson and Madison, there were positions to be handed out. Postmasters and consuls, judges and military surgeons, territorial governors and Indian agents, ensigns and lieutenants, captains and midshipmen, surveyors and port collectors were needed, as well as permanent bureaucratic staff for the government offices in Washington, D.C. Much of the evidence is epistolary, anecdotal, and unquantifiable — notes passed along the corridors of power. But we do know several things. To begin with, the number of extant letters to Dolley is small when compared to the known number of appeals written to the president and members of his cabinet. And most of these positions were handed out as patronage to augment the power of the administration and the Republican Party.[20]

In 1809 Dolley Madison received letters of petition from four men: Thomas B. Johnson, Samuel Todd, Stephen Sayre, and Henry C. Lewis. She worked hard and consistently to help only one of these supplicants, however: Samuel Todd.[21] As far as we know, she did nothing to help Sayre, Lewis, or Johnson. Sayre and Johnson failed to obtain jobs or promotions in the Madison administration. Of Lewis we know nothing more.

Samuel Todd was her nephew by her first marriage. His father was James Todd, her former brother-in-law, whom the Philadelphia Bank had hired in 1803 to run its daily operations. Until November 1805, when he fled to Georgia, James Todd embezzled money from the bank, stealing over $3,000 in cash plus credit for an additional $1,500. He never returned, leaving his family in misery and humiliation.[22] Five years later Dolley took on the task of obtaining a job for Samuel Todd in the federal government. After several months of searching, she found him a clerkship in the Navy Department, where he remained until 1812, when he was promoted to a navy purser.[23]

Jobs could be very difficult to obtain, and congressional politics could work against the wishes of the administration. Dolley went out of her way in July 1811 to help her cousin Isaac Coles obtain a post as secretary to the legation in Paris, but in this she failed. She also tried to place her brother, John Coles Payne, with the U.S. legation in Paris. For her old and dear friend Anthony Morris, she searched for a spot in the diplomatic service, and when the British refused to let Morris go to Bermuda in 1812, James Madison sent him on an unofficial mission to Spain. She also helped James Taylor, her husband's relative, in April 1813.[24]

In all of these cases, Dolley Madison was combining a woman's commitment to family and close friends with her unique position in Washington politics. As a woman of property, she was concerned that her children, siblings, nieces, and nephews keep in touch with her and with each other, that they prosper, and that the family resources be brought to bear to help them all. This meant both moral and material support. It included the organization of an increasingly geographically dispersed family, as she developed and maintained her family network.[25]

Not only did Dolley Madison extend her help to the men of her family and circle, but she aided the women as well. At a time when a woman's most important career decision was her choice of a husband, Dolley invited these women to stay at the White House during the city's social season. William C. Preston wrote of his stay in the White House and his treatment by the two young women then living there, Sarah Coles and Maria Mayo: "They soon turned me to account; made me useful as an attendant; were entertained by my freshness—perhaps amused at my greenness. I rode with them, danced with them, waited on them." Two of Dolley's oldest friends, Anthony Morris and Mary Pemberton, married in 1790, and after Mary died in 1808, the two families drew even closer.[26] Dolley Madison took their daughter Phoebe under her wing, brought her to Washington to live in the executive mansion for extended periods of time, and treated her as a daughter. She saw to her introductions and her education in the rules of etiquette and refinement.

The White House was often a swirl of people. But amid the bustle and personalities, the delights of parties, and the exasperations of a too close confinement, there was a larger purpose behind Dolley's arrangements. She was cementing family, teaching the younger generation how to behave, and introducing young women to eligible young men.

Foreign affairs dominated the Madison administration from the day the new president took office. The fundamental problem was how to preserve America's neutral status during the Napoleonic Wars. The United States was caught between the two superpowers, France and Great Britain. Both nations sought to deny American trade to the other, leading them to seize American vessels and confiscate their cargoes. For the United States the economic consequences were serious, as were the political and psychological implications. A failure to vindicate the nation's interest would call into question the validity of independence itself, but too vigorous an assertion of American neutrality would risk war. James Madison wished to avoid both these unpalatable alternatives.

He had commenced his presidency with an apparent triumph: an understanding with the British minister, David Erskine, that his country would repeal its Orders in Council, a succession of decrees intended to control neutral trade with European ports. The British foreign secretary, George Canning, however, repudiated Erskine's agreement, after which the president attempted to return to a policy of nonintercourse, only to find that Congress would not support him. The passage of Macon's Bill No. 2 in April 1810 removed all restrictions on American foreign trade and allowed the president to reimpose them only if one of the European belligerents lifted its antineutral policies and the other failed to follow suit within an interval of three months. Pursuant to the American law, Napoleon offered to repeal his responses to Great Britain's naval blockade, the Berlin and Milan Decrees, by November 1810.[27] Madison chose to interpret this as a valid repeal, and he reimposed nonintercourse against Great Britain in March 1811, even though the French emperor continued to seize American vessels. Great Britain and the Federalists disputed both the expediency and the legitimacy of Madison's decision, but the president continued on his course. In July 1811 he summoned the Twelfth Congress a month early, and in November he asked it to prepare for war with Great Britain in response to that power's continued refusal to respect American neutral rights.

The British remained unyielding, and the administration began to split apart under the strain. Secretary of State Robert Smith broke openly with the president over his policy toward Great Britain, while the secretary's brother, Senator Samuel Smith of Maryland, and his supporters pursued their intense dislike of Madison's friend and secretary of the treasury, Albert Gallatin. As the Smiths mounted their campaign against the president, Madison removed Robert Smith from office and replaced him with James Monroe in July 1811. The Smiths therefore opposed Madison for reelection in 1812, and relations between the two competing Republican factions deteriorated, with a corresponding impact on social life. The anger between the factions dug deeper into politics and society, and after June 1812 the war against Great Britain increased the antagonism of the Federalists. Dolley Madison's letters are filled with allusions to these events and conflicts.

It was easy in Washington to get dragged into party politics, to be misquoted and misunderstood, and as First Lady, Dolley Madison needed to be gracious and entertaining, to talk to each guest, to charm everyone, all without becoming involved in political disputes. As in her choices of clothing and decor, she went about her tasks with a meticulous concern for details and with caution. She held Wednesday evening drawing rooms and circulated at these parties as much as she could. She walked around, moving among her guests, in direct contrast to the conventions of the Federalist-era levees. Martha and George Washington had sat on a raised platform. Guests came up to them, presented themselves, and then withdrew to mingle with the crowd. Martha Washington never had to find small talk to dispense to an evening's crowd; she sat above it all. When Mrs. Madison discarded that strategy, she made it imperative for the First Lady to be a more involved politician, to know everyone and to have an apt word for everybody.

She was often praised for her efforts. Joseph Dennie, a Federalist editor and publisher of the Philadelphia *Port Folio,* wrote of her: "She glided into a stream of conversation and accommodated herself to its endless variety. In the art of conversation she is said to be distinguished."[28] Dolley had a strategy by which she would always have something neutral to say: she walked about with a book in her hand, employing it both as a prop and as a barrier between her and the public. William Campbell Preston noted in his journal that when he asked her why she was carrying a copy of *Don Quixote*—whether she had time to read it, whether she enjoyed it—she responded, "I have this book in my hand . . . to have something not ungraceful to say, and, if need be, to supply a word of talk."[29] Anything she said or did could boomerang against her. She understood the importance of doing whatever she could at her parties—and at other entertainments around the city—to support her husband's policies. But she was cautious in her approach, albeit graceful and charming in her manner. After James Madison removed Robert Smith from the office of secretary of state, for example, Dolley became a target of the Smiths' anger. Edward Coles went on a trip to the northern states over the summer of 1811, passing through Baltimore, where the Smiths lived. "I was treated quite civilly by them all," Coles wrote Dolley on 10 June, "but their displeasure with the President and yourself was very apparent." After Robert Smith publicly attacked Madison in a pamphlet, relations grew increasingly bitter. With anger and sarcasm Dolley wrote her sister Anna on 20 June 1811, "We expect too Mr S—s book," his *Address to the People of the United States,* in which Smith described James Madison as weak and indecisive, "opening the eyes of the world on all our sins &. &."

Although Massachusetts congressman Josiah Quincy had written that his wife, during the one term she spent in Washington, "was admired for her manners and mind" and "was most kindly received by Mrs. Madison at the palace," Quincy was one of James Madison's most implacable foes. By 1813 he was prepared to use Dolley as ammunition for his assaults on the president and his policies. In the House of Representatives on 5 January 1813, Quincy rose to attack the bill to expand American military forces. He launched into a diatribe against Madison. No true Federalist could support this policy, he thundered. If the administration thought otherwise, it was listening to men "who come trooping to Washington for place, appointments, and emoluments, men who will say anything to please the ear." And then, reaching for the most hateful and personal attack he could make on the White House and the president, he directed his venom at the First Lady. Those "little men who sigh after great offices," he charged, are "toads that live upon the vapor of the palace [and] that swallow great men's spittle at the levees."[30]

Dolley Madison's drawing rooms did indeed provide opportunities for politics. But they were not occasions for the First Lady to design and plot her own or the administration's political course. Again and again in her letters Dolley Madison demonstrated how enraged she could be at politics and politicians. But she understood that politics created the environment in which she operated as First Lady. Her drawing-room parties became increasingly charged with partisan debate, and eventually the rancor of war could not be kept out. It became impossible even for the skilled Mrs. Madison not to be drawn into the fray. As her letters witness, she became increasingly angry with those who, like the Smiths, opposed her husband's policies. But she remained publicly calm and retained her sense of balance.

Washington was a very distinct environment. The social system of the new republic was fluid and unstructured. In a European court the roles men and women played were determined by their fixed places in a hierarchy: each was a king, a queen, bishop, knight, or pawn on the chessboard of drawing-room politics. In Europe a monarch never dined with visiting ministers; the social implications of everyone's position were known and prescribed. But the United States was a new and experimental republic. Congressmen floated in and out of "court," depending not upon the will of the president but on the desires of the electorate, and most did not bring their wives and families to Washington. All of this meant that there was no structured role for the First Lady to play. The game of power played so skillfully by both men and women in Europe had no reference points in Washington, no guideposts, no fixed rule. It was a fluid situation, and it played into people's fears—and hopes— about women and power in the Early Republic.

When Dolley took up the role of First Lady in Washington, she was, in a very significant way, the first "First Lady" of the new American nation. She was a blank slate upon which people could write their wishes and anxieties. Some adored her. Others loathed her. Many exaggerated her power.

Throughout her years as First Lady, Dolley continued to cherish her family, to do whatever she could for them, and to miss her sisters whenever they were not with her, whether in Washington or at Montpelier. In 1806 her son, John Payne Todd, enrolled at the new Catholic boys' school in Baltimore, Saint Mary's College. In 1809 her brother-in-law George Steptoe Washington died, leaving Lucy a wealthy widow with three children. Lucy spent much of the next few years living with the Madisons in the White House, until she married an associate Supreme Court justice from Kentucky, Thomas Todd, on 29 March 1812. It was the first wedding to be held in the White House, but it was a very small and private affair, in keeping with the practices of the period.

In September 1809 she heard from her brother John C. Payne for the first time in a year. Worried about his future in Tripoli, he seems to have been slowly falling apart, drinking and gambling. Reassuring him, she told him that she would do what she could and would even try to get him appointed as temporary consul, should George Davis decide to take a leave of a few months, so that Payne would "have a good standing with the Senate, who appoint all officers with the previous recomendation of the President." Two years later Payne's appointment in Tripoli had ended, and James Madison had tried to get him a post at the U.S. legation in France. But that effort failed, and in fact, Payne had run up such extraordinary debts abroad that he could not go to Paris. In 1811 he fled North Africa, leaving behind everything he owned, returned to the United States, where he was forced to sell all the property he had inherited from his mother, and arrived to live with the Madisons. Dolley was indeed distressed. "I wish often that he had been never in Tripola with Davis," she wrote her sister Anna. "He is now entirely dependent ... but let me stop—You are at a distance & so is Lucy." [31]

By the start of the war, Dolley had suffered still more family difficulties. Payne Todd had failed as the kind of student both she and James had hoped he would be, and it had become clear that they could never send him to the college at Princeton, James's alma mater. When Edward Coles was ill in 1813, Payne Todd served as James Madison's secretary. But mostly he attended Washington balls and dinners, becoming increasingly dissolute. The Madisons gave him a foreign appointment with Albert Gallatin's peace mission to Europe in 1814. But that solution too failed: the young Todd found himself treated by the European royals as a prince, and he became even more idle and foppish, mounting up debts for his parents to pay.[32] At the same time both of Dolley's sisters were away far more than she would have liked, especially after Lucy married Judge Todd and moved to Kentucky. Yet she kept the White House filled with friends and relations, including Phoebe Morris and William Campbell Preston, her cousin Sally Coles and the Richmond belle Maria Mayo.

In June 1812 the United States declared war against Great Britain. Dolley Madison supported the war from the beginning, even when the conflict was concentrated on the Canadian border. But when the British opened operations in the Chesapeake Bay in 1813, she came especially to despise Rear Admiral George Cockburn, who led these enemy forces. The summer of 1813 proved an especially difficult one. Edward Coles had left for Philadelphia to attend to his health. Strangers poured into Washington; company flocked to the president's mansion. And while the politics of war were being debated in Congress, James Madison grew gravely ill with a bilious fever. While congressmen stewed and argued, the president lay exhausted from his political battles, weakened by a constant fever. Republicans worried that he might die; the French minister wrote of this possibility as a national calamity. Madison's opponents, both Federalist and Republican, took every possible political advantage of his illness. But finally the fever broke. On 2 July Dolley wrote to her cousin Edward Coles of her relief: "It has been three weeks since I have nursed him night & day—sometimes in despair! but now that I see he will get well I feel as if I should die myself, with fatigue."

A year later, on 17 August 1814, a British fleet landed thirty-five miles from the capital. Enemy troops began to walk toward Washington, although at first they moved so slowly it was hard to believe they would ever reach the city. As late as 21 August, President Madison thought the British would not attack. But by the following day he had changed his mind, and he left the city to review the troops. Dolley Madison stayed on at the White House, ready to pack up the government papers if necessary and secure them from harm.

On 23 August the British continued to advance. Dolley prepared to evacuate the building, writing to her sister Lucy of her preparations. The next day Dolley was still guarding the gates of the executive mansion. She anxiously awaited the enemy's troops for hours, and by afternoon the British were advancing too fast to be ignored. She ordered a wagon filled with official papers, silver, and valuables and sent it off to the Bank of Maryland. Then, as she informed her sister, she decided that she had one more task to accomplish: "I insist on waiting until the large picture of Gen. Washington is secured, and it requires to be unscrewed from the wall. This process was found too tedious for these perilous moments; I have ordered the frame to be broken, and the canvass taken out it is done, and the precious portrait placed in the hands of two gentlemen of New York, for safe keeping. And now, dear sister, I must leave this house." The British would otherwise have taken her captive. She fled to Virginia, and the British torched the White House. Never again would the Madisons live there.

When they returned to Washington, the Madisons moved into John Tayloe's Octagon House, the second largest residence in the city. They remained there for less than a year, moving in August 1815 to Nineteenth Street and Pennsylvania Avenue, to a corner house in a group of townhouses known as the "Seven Buildings." Mrs. Madison continued to entertain with great energy and style, but a new note of worry crept into her correspondence. The new house was empty, and their furniture had been destroyed. She had to outfit the new residence with almost no money. Their own funds were being stretched both to support the Cutts family and to pay off Payne Todd's debts. Dolley bought what she could secondhand through members of the American

THE POLITICS OF WAR, 1809–1817

legation in France and purchased furniture from the house the Gallatins were closing up in Washington.

And yet this was also a period of triumph and glory. The partisan venom was gone, replaced by a national feeling of goodwill and success. In early May 1815 the Madisons paid a visit to Annapolis, where they inspected the 74-gun warship *Washington*.[33] It was a lovely trip, marked by good company and a sense of well-being.

Dolley Madison had succeeded in establishing herself as the first First Lady of the land and in so doing had set a model for her successors to follow. "My dear friend," Eliza Collins Lee wrote in March 1817, "On this day eight years ago I wrote . . . to congratulate you on the joyful event that placed you in the highest station our country can bestow. . . . How much greater cause have I to congratulate you, at this period for having so filled it as to render yourself more enviable this day, than your successor, as it is more difficult to deserve the gratitude and thanks of the community than their congratulations. *You* have deservedly received of all."[34]

1. John Tayloe to DPM, 29 Dec. 1808, and Mrs. Deblois to DPM, 18 Feb. 1809, DLC: DPM Papers; George Watterston to DPM, 10 March 1809.

2. For the most recent study of Dolley Madison as First Lady, see Allgor, *Parlor Politics*.

3. Gaillard Hunt, "The First Inaugural Ball," *Century Magazine* 69 (1905): 757; Smith, *First Forty Years*, 58. Cambric can be made of either fine white linen cloth or fine cotton, but in 1809 it would probably have been linen; plain in weave, it was suitable for daytime wear. George Washington "had initiated the custom of inaugural clothing of native manufacture" (Lucia C. Stanton, "Sheep for the President," in *Fall Dinner at Monticello, November 3, 2000* [pamphlet, Thomas Jefferson Memorial Foundation, Charlottesville, Va., 2000], 9).

4. Smith, *First Forty Years*, 62. See also James Laver, *Costume and Fashion* (New York, 1995); Nigel Arch and Joanna Marschner, *Splendour at Court: Dressing for Royal Occasions since 1700* (London, 1987); Wendy A. Nicholson, "Making the Private Public: Anne Willing Bingham's Role as a Leader of Philadelphia's Social Elite in the Late Eighteenth Century" (M.A. thesis, Univ. of Delaware, 1988); Carson, *Ambitious Appetites*; Branson, *These Fiery Frenchified Dames*.

5. Dolley Madison may have liked to wear velvet—which she seems repeatedly to have done for dress occasions—precisely because it was distinctive. Her portraits indicate that she developed a kind of signature clothing. Thus she continued to wear turbans long after they had gone out of style; and for the rest of her life she wore the shawls that became à la mode in the 1790s and early 1800s in large measure because Europe was too cold for flimsy muslin dresses (Jean Starobinski, *Revolution in Fashion: European Clothing, 1715–1815* [New York, 1989], 116).

6. Elisabeth McClellan, *Historic Dress in America* (New York, 1910), 56. See also Diana Scarisbrick, *Jewelry* (London, 1984). Even Martha Washington owned a large collection of gem jewelry (Starobinski, *Revolution in Fashion*, 135).

7. See Allgor, *Parlor Politics*, 91–94. See also Arch and Marschner, *Splendour at Court*; Robert Ralph Davis Jr., "Diplomatic Plumage: American Court Dress in the National Period," *American Quarterly* 20 (1968): 164–79.

8. John C. Van Horne and Lee W. Formwalt, eds., *The Correspondence and Miscellaneous Papers of Benjamin Henry Latrobe* (3 vols.; New Haven, 1984–88), 2:705–7; Latrobe quoted in

R. L. Raley, "Interior Designs by Benjamin Henry Latrobe for the President's House," *Antiquities* 75 (June 1959): 568.

9. See Hunt-Jones, *Dolley and the "Great Little Madison"*; Raley, "Interior Designs"; Betty C. Monkman, *The White House* (New York, 2000); Margaret Klapthor, "Benjamin Latrobe and Dolley Madison Decorate the White House, 1809–1811," *Contributions from the Museum of History and Technology*, paper 49 (1965). Historians have also noted that Dolley's taste was deeply influenced by the French style in furniture, that James Monroe sent the Madisons furniture and porcelain from Paris, and that she longed for all things she considered elegant and stylish (see Monkman, *White House*, 43).

10. Raley, "Interior Designs," 569; Richard L. Bushman, "Introduction," in Wendy Cooper, *Classical Taste in America, 1800–1840* (Baltimore, 1993), 16. Latrobe's work was itself derivative; he was profoundly influenced by the British designer Thomas Hope, who had introduced French style and design to Britain, determined to reform English furniture and interior decoration. See David Watkins, *Thomas Hope, 1769–1831, and the Neo-Classical Idea* (London, 1968).

11. Latrobe to George Harrison, 30 June 1809, quoted in Talbot Hamlin, *Benjamin Henry Latrobe* (New York, 1955), 311. See also Gaillard Hunt, "Mrs. Madison's First Drawing-Room," *Harper's Monthly Magazine* 121 (June 1910): 141–48.

12. For another discussion of DPM and Washington society, see Allgor, *Parlor Politics*, 70–75.

13. Francis Boardman Crowninshield, ed., *Letters of Mary Boardman Crowninshield, 1815–1816* (Cambridge, Mass., 1905), 35.

14. Carson, *Ambitious Appetites*, 159–60.

15. John S. Stone, *A Memoir of the Life of James Milnor* (New York, 1849), 49; Jonathan Roberts to Matthew Roberts, 2 Dec. 1811, *PJM-PS* 4:44 n. 1. For the legislators' lives without their families, see Young, *The Washington Community*.

16. Stone, *Memoir of the Life of James Milnor*, 49, 58.

17. Smith, *First Forty Years*, 82; William Winston Seaton, *A Biographical Sketch* (Boston, 1871), 85; Ketcham, *James Madison*, 496; Noble Cunningham Jr., ed., "Diary of Frances Few," *Journal of Southern History* 29 (1963): 351–52; Foster, *Jeffersonian America*, 155; Anthony Morris to Anna Payne, 26 June 1837, National Society of the Colonial Dames of America.

18. George Watterston, *A Wanderer in Washington* (Washington, D.C., 1827), 61–62.

19. The editors have chosen here to consider only those letters that petition Mrs. Madison for help in securing federal appointments. There were other requests, which generally fall into the following categories: letters of introduction, letters requesting relief from pecuniary or other distress, and other appeals for aid. Examples of these kinds of letters can be found in this volume.

20. We can count heads in two places. The first is the record of appointments that required Senate approval, only a fraction of all federal positions. The second is the collection of Letters of Application and Recommendation retained by the State Department and now filed in the National Archives, RG 59. In 1809 JM nominated 76 men whose jobs required the Senate's advice and consent, 77 men seeking jobs either wrote letters themselves or had others write letters for them that are filed in RG 59. Six names appear on both lists, so the total number of names in the two lists combined is 147 applicants and nominees.

21. For an alternative view of the role women played in the public power structure of Washington, see Lewis, "Politics and the Ambivalence of the Private Sphere," and Teute, "Roman Matron on the Banks of Tiber Creek." For a different perspective on the role DPM played in the process of appointments, see Allgor, "'A Lady Will Have More Influence': Women and Patronage in Early Washington City," in *Women and the Unstable State in Nineteenth-Century America*, ed. Alison M. Parker (College Station, Tex., 2000), 37–60.

22. *Heads of Families at the First Census of the United States Taken in the Year 1790 . . . Pennsylvania* (Washington, D.C., 1908), 224; Nicholas B. Wainwright, *History of the Philadelphia National*

Bank (Philadelphia, 1953), 8, 18–19; Van Horne and Formwalt, *Correspondence of Latrobe* 1: 551–52.

23. Samuel Todd's brother, John N. Todd, was also a purser in the navy (Christopher McKee, *A Gentlemanly and Honorable Profession: The Creation of the U.S. Naval Officer Corps, 1794–1815* [Annapolis, 1991], 21, 526).

24. DPM to Anna Cutts, 15 July 1811; Isaac A. Coles to DPM, 28 July 1811, ICHi; DPM to Phoebe P. Morris, 24 April 1813; James Taylor to DPM, 13 April 1813, owned by Walter N. Eastburn, East Orange, N.J., 1961.

25. We are indebted to Scott Taylor for introducing us to David W. Sabean, *Kinship in Neckerhausen, 1700–1870* (Cambridge, 1998). See also Lorri Glover, *All Our Relations: Blood Ties and Emotional Bonds among the Early South Carolina Gentry* (Baltimore, 2000), and Sidney H. Aronson, *Status and Kinship in the Higher Civil Service: Standards of Selection in the Administrations of John Adams, Thomas Jefferson, and Andrew Jackson* (Cambridge, Mass., 1964).

26. William C. Preston in his autobiography, quoted in Ellet, *Court Circles of the Republic*, 85; Virginia Armentrout, ed., *Castles in Spain: Anthony Morris' Letters to His Children, 1813–1817* (Philadelphia, 1982), vii.

27. See Leigh Whaley, "Orders in Council," James Edward Scanlon, "Macon's Bill No. 2," and Frederick C. Drake, "Milan Decree," in *Encyclopedia of the War of 1812*, ed. David S. and Jeanne T. Heidler (Santa Barbara, Calif., 1997), 394–95, 313–14, 348–49.

28. Ethel Stephens Arnett, *Mrs. James Madison: The Incomparable Dolley* (Greensboro, N.C., 1972), 119.

29. Ellet, *Court Circles of the Republic*, 86.

30. Edmund Quincy, *Life of Josiah Quincy of Massachusetts* (Boston, 1869), 204; *Annals of Congress*, 12th Cong., 2d sess., 549–50. For Quincy's rhetorical style, see James Milnor to Ellen Milnor, 16 Jan. 1813, in Stone, *Memoir of the Life of James Milnor*, 49.

31. DPM to Anna Cutts, 15 July 1811.

32. Ketcham, *James Madison*, 552.

33. Brant, *Madison* 6:406–7.

34. Eliza Collins Lee to DPM, 4 March 1817.

From Eliza Collins Lee

My dear friend   March 2d. 1809

'Tis but on events most productive of Great pain, or pleasure to you that I am induced to intrude upon your time, sensible that from the retirements of my life I could neither affoard you information or amusement.

Allow me then to offer my congratulations at a moment when you are about to fill a character the most dignified and respectable in society. And I assure you I feel no small degree of exultation in knowing that the mind, temper, and manners of my Philadelphia Quaker friend, are peculiarly fitted for the station, where hospitality and graciousness of deportment, will appear conspicuously charming & conciliating—And I feel still greater sattisfaction in believing that in the Husband of this friend we have a Man whose Abilities and principles justly elect him to a seat which he will fill with equal dignity and justice. Offer him if you please my congratulations and respects—To your Son and Sister my affectionate love—And believe me tho' for family reasons *only* I have not been able to meet you Personally—there is nothing can make me forgetful of your happiness, or unmindful of your Friendship in which no one more sincerely participates than Your truly Affecte friend

Eliza Lee

RC (MCR-S: Mary Estelle Elizabeth Cutts Papers). Docketed by DPM.

From John G. Jackson

Sunday Morning [5 March 1809]

Farewell my dear Sister & say good bye for me to my beloved friend Madison. He carries with him into the Presidency the most affectionate good wishes of my heart: produced by an intimate acquaintance with his public & private virtues for nine years past; & I can say with great truth that not one single act of his life during the period I speak of, has excited a momentary doubt as to its justice. If he does not guide the helm successfully, the requisite qualifications for that station cannot be found on earth. I salute you my dear Sister with the tenderest regards.

J G Jackson

RC (ViU: Breckenridge-Watts Papers).

From George Watterston

Madam!   CITY OF WASHINGTON March 10th [1809]

A youth, as but little known to fame, and as little known to you; presumes to tresspass for a few moments, on your attention. Your generosity will pardon his presumption; & your goodness will, I trust, gratify the desire which induces me to address you.

Having been early smitten, with a love of the muses, & having devoted some portion of his time to their servise: he has been enabled to produce a *Comedy,* a baggatelle of fancy, which, with your approbation, he desires to dedicate to you. Your character, ma'am! is not unknown to him. Of the qualities of your heart, he has heard much; but of the faculties of your mind, he has heard more. Always an admirer of intellectual worth, & mental excellence, he woud experience an unspeakable gratifycation, in having an opportunity to evince the admiration he feels for your character, by a permission to dedicate, to you, this humble offspring of his mind; in expectation that under your patronage, it will survive the nipping blasts [of] criticism, & outlive the noisy storms of malignity.

That this proposition, ma'am, may, therefore, meet with your approbation, is the most anxcious wish of, Your most obedient Huml. sert.

Geo. Watterston

P.S. An answer is expected.

RC (ViU: Coles Collection).

From Thomas B. Johnson

Madam, NEW-ORLEANS 11 March 1809

Were I addressing myself to any person less distinguished than yourself for indulgence to the errors of others, it would cost me an effort little compatible with my feelings thus to arrogate, even in appearance a privilege unsanctioned by your permission—The motives however which induce me to obtrude myself on your notice, will exonerate me I doubt not, when fully understood from what alone I should shrink to incurr, the charge of presumption; while to the violation of rigid etiquette which may be urged against me I shall offer no extenuation, trusting solely to your clemency to pardon or overlook it.

Impelled by a sense of obligation for the favor conferred on me by Mr. Madison, when he furnished me with letters to Govr. Claiborn, I was preparing to address you one of thanks in return, for your friendly interference in obtaining them for me, when an event took place which decided me to embrace the opportunity it presented, of offering to you the assurance of my gratitude for former obligations & of making it at the same time the instrument of solicitation for a fresh one—I could have wished to avoid the appearance which it doubtless must carry of encroaching on your goodness, but the urgency of an early intimation of my hopes, will I am sure with you absolve me from so distressing an accusation—Without further intrusion on your time I will proceed to state the object of this letter—By the death of Mr. Guley lately killed in a duel, the particulars of which will probably have reached you before this letter arrives, the place which he held under the Government of the United States of Commissioner & Register of the land office becomes vacant—Its emoluments are a handsome provision & it's duties I believe exact not qualification of a more exclusive description than to such as on experiment I flatter myself I might be found entitled fully to prettend— backed as they would be by such attention & industry in their discharge as it would be no less my ambition than my wish to exert. With pretensions to your recommendation, much as I fear you will regard these, & with a power to defer them as inadequate as I consciously confess it, I would have spared you the trouble of this application, had I not been certain that your knowledge of the family to which I belong, upon whom unmerited misfortune has fallen most heavily, & who fondly look forward to my advancement for their restoration to the respectable station in life they once filled, had I not known I repeat it My dear Madam that these circumstances would interest you in my behalf, while they added to the claims which I aspire to be sanctioned by your approbation—Should this representation of my wishes induce you to lend me your friendly aid in the prosecution of them, will you add to the favor of interesting Mr. Madison in my behalf, that of instructing my Mother in the proper method of stating to the President the object of my wishes, & of gaining his approbation of my suit? While I live it will be acknowledged with gratitude, the assurance of which, with that of my regret at being reduced to the necessity of thus importuning you, I beg leave most respectfully to tender I remain Madam your most Obliged & Obedt. Sert.

Thos. B. Johnson

RC (MCR-S: Mary Estelle Elizabeth Cutts Papers).

To Samuel P. Todd

My dear Samuel,   March 16th. 1809
I have reccd. & read with particular interest yours of the 13th. & beg you to be assured that nothing would gratify me more than to be of use in promoteing your wishes & your good—Independant of my love for your Mother & every individuel of your family I feel truly anxious for the wellfare of you all. As to yourself, I will make every exertion to procure you some eligable employment—& the best I can do, shall be yours.

I greave at the hint you give me on the situation of your affairs—but as I understand you have been an excellent son I hope it will still be your good fortune to smooth the way of your Parent & dear sister's—I deliver'd your letter to Mr Madison who is fully disposed to be your friend—he desired me to tell you That the Consuls only on the Barbary Coast are allowed Salerys; & we understand, that every Frigate in the Ports of N. York &

Washington are supli'd with Pursers. Indeed, there are so few places of emolument, ever vacant or unengaged that I dont know what to advise at this moment—If you would accept a Clerkship in one of the Offices, for the present, write me accordingly, & I will apply to the Heads of the Depts. to obtain one for you.

Your Cousin J. P. Todd is still at Colledge, & I hope you will know & love each other. Adeiu dear Samuel beleive me your sincear friend & Aunt

D P Madison

RC (DLC: DPM Papers). Addressed to Samuel P. Todd in Philadelphia.

From Benjamin Henry Latrobe

Madam,   PHILADELPHIA, March 22d 1809
I had yesterday the honor of your letter of the 20th. inst.—I had already written to you on the subject of your carriages; & transmitted two patterns of English Lace, the only handsome ones which I could find in the city of that kind. When you have made your choice, it will not be necessary to send back the patterns as I shall understand which you mean, by your mentioning the *broadest* or *narrowest* of them.

I now beg you to determine on the following points. Do you wish the quarters of your Chariot to be open that is, to have blinds & Glasses, or to be close quartered with a plated sham joint. I have expressed the opening in dotts. I recommend close quarters as the handsomest by far, as well as most fashionable, & the only inducement to have open quarters would be that the Carriage might be more airy. It will be soon necessary to know what arms or cypher should be put on the carriage & in a few days I will transmit to you drawings for that purpose—The fashion requires them to be painted which can be done here very elegantly—Carriages are no longer made so very round & bulging as formerly. The body of the Summer carriage was sent yesterday to the painters, ⟨Mr.⟩ Harvey having run the risk of putting it in hand as soon as I left Philadelphia the last time. I have ordered harness for 4 horses. Will you have separate plain harness for the Coachee or keep that you now have? What shall the Coachee be lined with? Cloth, or cotton Velvet? I have also considered what sort of a *close moveable* front you should have, & have *invented* one, (for which I do not want a patent) which is I think better than the usual front & much more close (besides being cheaper, it being an extra Charge). It will have two Glasses, & can be taken out & put away in a few minutes. Will you leave this to me?

There is no Silk Damask to be had either in New York or Philadelphia, & I am therefore forced to give you crimson Velvet curtains, of which I can get plenty & which to my astonishment will not be dearer than Damask.

I have already bought most of the articles in the small way & Mrs. Latrobe is so good as to runabout for me & aid me with her taste & judgment in those articles which she understands better than I.

The Guitar will be bought as soon as she finds one she likes. You know she has the reputation of being a good player on that in[s]trument.

I bought yesterday 4 Chimney pieces of Pennsylvania Marble. They are handsome & cheap & may be immediately put up. Hand[1] who is now here, will bring round a number of things for you.

If you will do my Son Henry the honor to inform him of any thing you wish to communicate & which is not worthy of your own pen, he will immediately write to me.

With mine & Mrs. Latrobe's best respects to you & Mr & Mrs. Cutts, & my sincere assurances to the president that I shall keep in view the ideas impressed upon me by him in the execution of my duty I am Your obedt hble Servt.

B H Latrobe

If the President will do me the honor to forward the list of books he wants I shall be happy to look out for them.

PS. Since writing the within I have bought a set of Scarlet Japanned waiters of the largest Size. They are sold in sets of 3, one 32 inches, the other 31, & the least 29 inches long. They are the largest I have ever seen. Also 2 dozen very elegant white[2] handled knives & forks 2 dozen desert ditto, 2 steels, 2 Carving knifes & forks & a Cheese knife being a compleat set—Also, 4 plated Chamber candlesticks, snuffers, & extinguishers. I could not get any with very broad bottoms, in any of the shops. I have not yet been able to find any double or treble Wine Coasters, but hope still to succeed.

To show you what a scandalous city this is since you left it, I will tell you that I was this day very seriously asked what Post Mr. Jefferson had refused me, after having promised it, under the plea of having forgotten it; & whether it was true that having complained of this treatment to Mr. Madison, *who at the time was poking the fire,* he had turned round & *swore* that that was nothing to the treatment he had received from Mr. Jefferson. On insisting on knowing the author of the report, I was told that it has been mentioned in a company of 2 or 300 & nobody could tell whence the story arose, but it was considered as very true notwithstanding!

RC (NHi: Misc. Mss). Docketed by JM. Printed in *PJM-PS* 1:73–75.

1. John Hand Sr. was master of the sloop *Sally,* which delivered goods from Philadelphia (ibid., 88 n. 2).

2. Latrobe wrote "ivory" above this word.

From Benjamin Henry Latrobe

Madam,   PHILA. March 29h. 1809

Your very obliging & kind letter was received by Mrs. Latrobe yesterday, & I had also your commands on business which I beg leave to answer concisely today & to write more at large tomorrow.

Your directions as to the liveries shall be obeyed. The patterns of colors on Glass met with an accident. They were broken & shall be sent on, *repainted,* tomorrow.

The sketch of the Chariot in my letter was merely to explain the *sham-joint,* but not to show the form of the carriage. But the *extreme* Bulges, top, bottom, & sides, are entirely out of fashion I assure you. However your carriage will have a little smattering of the bulging taste about it: just enough to give it an air not entirely different from other carriages, *fashionable here.*

I have ordered the articles agreed on of *Liberty Browne* namely 2 Sugar dishes, 2 Cream Ewers 1 doz. fren⟨ch⟩ forks, 2 do. desert, 6 *Skewers* from 18 inches to 7 in.

I fear the damask Tablecloths & napkins are bought at New York. There is nothing of the kind here. I have written to countermand them, and shall write to Mr. Johnston to send his on. I know him.

I have sought a G[u]itar in vain as yet, but think we are on the track of one.

I shall get Col. Preston's belt lengthened one foot. It will cost about 15$. After much hunting I found a Man who could embroider on *Leather.* There are plenty who work on Cloth. There is no real gold Perl in the city, & no gold thread of any kind, but I thnk we can make out so as to match the old work tolerably, but not as well as I expected. I fear no 3 Bottle coasters can be had. Plated ware begins to be scarce. By Capt. Hand I send knives forks & ⟨spoons?⟩ Yours most respectfully

B Henry Latrobe

RC (NHi: Misc. Mss). Printed in *PJM-PS* 1:87–88.

To Samuel P. Todd

31st. March 1809.

I have delayed writeing to you my dear Samuel for some days until the new Secretarys should arrive, with whom I hope to place you. They have not yet made their appearance tho daily expected.

I trust you will be patient, under this delay, & rely on my assurance of a sincear & affectinate interest, which, shall not be inactive—The place I have in view at present, is a clerkship at 7. or 800$ pr. year—perhaps more, & the advantage of your being in this place, will be considerable towards your obtaining something better.

You will not resign your situation in the Bank until the other is secure. With best love to your Mother & sisters—yours truly

D P Madison

RC (DLC: DPM Papers). Franked by JM.

From Mary E. Latrobe

PHILADELPHIA April 12th [1809]

I have sate down at a late hour my dear Mrs Madison to reply to your Letter of the 10th: in which you acknowledge the arrival of the *Wig*. I am releived from some anxiety concerning it, as it ought to have been with you many days sooner.

Respecting the Colour of your Carriage Mr Latrobe and myself approve your choice of the *Red Brown*. There were several shades of it among the patterns, but he says the glass has a little decieved you. It is very fashionable and will suit well with a fawn Coloured Lining and the lace you chose. The Carriages will now go on rapidly—Mr. Rae has been fortunate in procuring a Sufficient Quantity of Velvet for the drawing room Curtains sopha's, chairs & *all* and they will certainly be very elegant.

The dinner sett of China we have decided upon this Morning I was out in pursuit of it at eight Oclock—But there is a Miserable choice here at present—The dinner sett is "India Stone china," blue & white, the dessert sett is the same colour but *Nankin china* gilt handsomely. We must have taken this, or none, and I am sure you are in immediate want of it. The two setts will cost about 400$ or perhaps rather less. We have at once orderd them pack'd and wait now the arrival of Capt Hand.

I wrote to you the impossibility of procuring french China, but in setts. There is no such thing as Cups & saucers alone. And you know the setts are very small, what will you do? I can send you some very handsome Nankin china Cups & saucers (blue & white) by the dozen—the Coffee Cups of the shape of the Sèvre china and also the saucers. The tea Cups of the old shape— The Coffee Cup & Saucers 15$ pr doz. The tea cups 10$. There is one sett of beautiful french china in town Containing one doz. of Coffee & one doz. tea Cups and saucers to each, tea pot, bowl sugar dish and (I believe) a plate. The Colour is a pea green richly gilt at the edge—price 70$—This is realy the only thing worth looking at in the way of a tea sett—The late situation of the Country I imagine is the Cause of great deficiency in the stores throughout the City, for many articles are not to be had for Love or Money—I enclose you a list of the China we send, and beg you to believe we have used every exertion to get the best we could.

Tomorrow you will recieve your Box containing the hat & Turban, I ought to have been more of a Merchant than to have neglected to acknowledge the reciept of your Remittance—which I have done in the Letter that accompanies the Box.

Write to me soon respecting the tea china, for it is probable we may leave Philadelphia the middle of next week—Our little Julié[1] was quite pleased with your kind remembrance of her and begs I will send you a kiss in my Letter. She does not forget the many sweet *Cakes* she has rece[i]ved from you.

Mr Latrobe will not write by this post he is particularly busy this evening and has commissiond me to write you quite a Letter of business—which I am sure I have faithfully performed—Believe me always yours most Affly

Mary E Latrobe

It is now eleven at night which will excuse my miserable writing I am half asleep.

RC (ViHi: Dolley Madison Papers). Printed in *PJM-PS* 1:112–13.
  1. This was Juliana Latrobe, born in 1804.

From Benjamin Henry Latrobe

Madam   PHILADELPHIA, April 21st. 1809.

Your letter of the 19th: has just been received. Permit me in the first place to thank You for the excellent political News which concludes it. The interruption of the friendly intercourse thus restored, has cost you individually many an odd dollar extraordinary. For instance: I could not find in the whole city among the merchants a Yard of cloth fit to line your carriage, & have at last been obliged to a Taylor (McAlpin) for the quantity required, at 11$ ₩ Yard. There was not enough for the travelling carriage, & I have been obliged to have recourse to second cloth of somewhat a darker tint, but of the same character of color. The color of your carriage will be a very beautiful reddish brown according to your wish. Your taste in this respect agrees with the fashion. The travelling carriage has its first coat, & with favorable weather, there is no doubt of your getting it in time. The Chariot is a very neat thing, the most so I recollect to have seen for a long time. I have chosen to-day the springs, & call almost everyday to keep them agoing—My stay here is lengthened by a great variety of business relative to Washington. I hope every day to see it concluded, but the hurry of every body in this enormous & encreasing city is such that without daily inspection, every thing is put off. Today I was so fortunate as to get on board Captain Hand, 4 Chimney pieces, 2 for your dining room, 1 for the Antichamber & one for the drawing room.

I am sorry to have counteracted any wish of yours as to Genl Washington's picture. The dining room is properly the picture room, and in speaking to the president as to the furniture of the room, I understood it to be arranged that not only the Genl.—but the succeeding Presidents should have a place there. I therefore intended him to occupy either the place at the West end of the room between the Windows, or the fire place at the East end. Over the drawing room Chimney piece, I intended my best looking glass. Opposite to the door, & over the fire place (that is to be) of the dining room my *squarest* Glass, to repeat the Landscape through the Center windows.

But if you have the slightest wish to the contrary remember that the Motto of my family—of my art—& of my duty, is *tutto si fa*—tout se fait. Mr Bridport, the decorator to whom I have committed this business, is a man of great taste & talents & the first line of his instructions is, do as Mr & Mrs. Madison wish.

The curtains! Oh the terrible velvet curtains! Their effect will ruin me entirely, so brilliant will they be.

I shall certainly not be here another week. Your liveries are now the only things in my department not accomplished, and they are attended & tomorrow I report upon them. With the highest respect I have the honor to be Your obedt. hble Servt.

B H Latrob⟨e⟩

⟨Dear⟩ madam

I am sorry the Wig does not *exactly* fit. But I beg you to return it & I will send you another at the same time send me the size of your sisters head, & any alterations it may want. I shall be here a few days longer, and can give orders to have it sent after me if I do not get it done in time to bring it. Yrs Sincerely

ME LT.

RC (NN: James Madison Papers). Postscript in the hand of Mary E. Latrobe. Docketed by JM. Printed in *PJM-PS* 1:130–31.

To Phoebe P. Morris

2d May 1809

Remembrance wakes with all her busy Train
Swells at my breast, & turns the past to pain!

How forcibly did thy precious letter beloved Phebe, bring to my recollection that sainted friend, whom I loved with more tenderness—more enthusiasm, than can be told—Alass! I have every reason to sympathise with thee, her estimable child for our intimacy began in the morning of her days; when her friendship was my happiness and pride—nor had I ever cause to beleive, otherwise, than that thy Mother was the most perfect of human beings![1]

My sweet Girl will pardon me for dwelling on this affecting subject when I assert, that not *one* ever loved her Parents more than myself. I rejoice that you spend your time with my ever dear Betsy,[2] she is worthy be assured, of every attention from her Cousin. In a short time, I hope to have a little Picture for my dear Phebe, which I shall ask her to wear, or to keep, as an assurance of my affectinate esteem—& I must entreat that if it is ever in her power to visit me that she will do so. Perhaps her cousin & her Father may be persuaided to bring her to Washington, where I shall receve them with heart-felt pleasure. My Husband desires me to salute you for him, & to present him to your Father.

D. P. Madison

RC (ViHi: Hunton-Payne Papers). Docketed as received 4 May.
 1. Anthony and Mary Pemberton Morris had four children, Phoebe, Rebecca, James, and Louisa, before Mary's death in 1808 (Armentrout, *Castles in Spain*, vii).
 2. Betsy Pemberton was a cousin of Mary Pemberton Morris.

To Samuel P. Todd

5th. May 1809.

I have just now reccd. your's of the 2d. dear Samuel, & hasten to tell you that I have the best ground to assure you of a good place—the positive promises of the Secy of State for the first vacancy that shall occur—As yet there has not been *one,* but one or two are expected to take place soon. I beleive you cannot have felt more anxiety than I have, on this subject—as I have been expecting every week since I wrote you, to be able to Invite you to our City—this greatly desired day, must soon arrive, when I shall rejoice to see you placed in a situable [*sic*] at once profitable & agreable. Adeiu dear Samuel present me to your Mother & Sisters & be persuaided that this delay will not be unfavorable to you in the end. Your Affec. Aunt

DPM

RC (DLC: DPM Papers). Franked by JM.

From Benjamin Henry Latrobe

Dear Madam,   BALTIMORE May 7h. 1809.
    I am here & expected to have been tomorrow in Washington. It is however necessary, I find that I should see Mr Finlay, who is making the Chairs & Sofas for your Drawing room in his Shop, & therefore I shall stay tomorrow & arrive in the city on Tuesday—Your Chariot is in great forwardness, & will be one of the handsomest things Philadelphia has produced. The Coachee has its last Coat of paint on, & the Cypher very elegantly managed. I have attended closely to this business & think you will not be disappointed. I am with high respect Yr. obedient humble Servt.

B Henry Latrobe.

RC (NN: James Madison Papers). Docketed by JM. Printed in *PJM-PS* 1:174.

To Phoebe P. Morris

June 15th. 1809.
    You will accept my beloved Phebe The inclosed resemblance of your "Parents friend," that tender friend, who loves & admires you—I should have sent you a Picture long ere this, but those in my possesion ware *too young,* & I waited to procure my *present self.*
    Will you pardon *the appearance* of neglect, in regard to your last charming letter? When *tranquility* shall resume its reign, I will repay you with a Vol. I

shall write by this post, to our ever dear Eliza. W. Who I trust is yet, your peculiar care. Adeiu sweet one!

D. P. Madison

RC (DNCD: Morris Papers).

From Benjamin Henry Latrobe

Madam   WASHINGTON, July 4th. 1809

I am more mortified than I can express at the conduct of the Coachmaker, I have had the misfortune to employ in your service, in furnishing to you a Carriage, which even before it has been used is discovered to be so extremely faulty. I am the more irritated and disappointed, as he has in every other instance in which I have employed or recommended him, done himself so much credit, as to have gained the character of being one of the most honest & faithful workmen in Philadelphia. Mr Harvie, has built for me 5 Carriages of different sorts for my own use, all of which have done me most excellent service, & were universally admired. My present carriage has undergone every possible hardship for 3 Years, & so well is it built, that the first Wheels have now their third tire. Still as in your particular case, he has so entirely forgotten what is due to You & to his own interest & reputation as regards the Coachee, I cannot help thinking that it would be just to throw the Chariot upon his hands, especially as there is ample time to get another built before winter. I am sufficiently punished for my own indiscreet zeal by the mortification I suffer, and would much rather have been mulcted in the whole price of the carriage than have occasioned you so much vexation & disappointment.

I shall by the Mail of this evening write to Mr. Harvie what is proper on the subject, and if you will please to order the deficiencies to be made good, I have the means of throwing the expense of the repair upon his hands. Some small articles are usually required to be altered or amended in every new carriage after the first trial, but no hurry in which this has been built, (it being not yet quite 3 Months since it was ordered) not even the very unfavorable weather for painting it, which has continued nearly the whole of that time can be an excuse for so total a neglect as he seems to have been guilty of, in your opinion.

I hope you will have the goodness to believe that want of judgement on my part, not of the most anxious desire to procure for you a good carriage has led me into the mortifying predicament in which I am.

As to the price (which Mr. Cutts informs me is also thought extravagant) I beg to assure you, that it is below that, which has been given for inferior carriages to Fielding & other fashionable builders, by many of my acquaintance whom I could name. With the sincerest respect I am Madam Your obedt hble Servt

B H Latrobe

PS. If you can spare half an hour tomorrow, to ascertain the deficiencies, I will exert myself to have them repaired before you go.

RC (NN: James Madison Papers). Docketed by DPM.

From Phoebe P. Morris

Dear Madam,   July. 22d. 1809.

When I reflect on your amiable condescention, in conferring on me the elegant representation of your present Self I am at a loss how to thank you sufficiently—Mr & Mrs Cadwalader who have lately seen its lovely & greatly beloved original at Washington, both pronounce it to be as correct a resemblance as the painters art can pourtray—Indeed I cannot express the variety, nor the degree of pleasure & pride it affords to myself & all my Friends, Those who formerly enjoyed the pleasure of your acquaintance, retrace the lines, features and expressions of a face and form on which they once gazed with delight; & those who have not been so favored gratify an anxious and amiable curiosity, in beholding a just resemblance of Her, in whose virtues they also claim an interest, as the dignified representative of our Sex in every female virtue adorned with all her sex's beauty, grace & loveliness—It is now with us, about five miles from Bristol, at Bolton, a patrimonial Estate, where we pass away the sultry summer months; it accompanies a small portrait of my Sainted Mother, and I pay as much honor to them, as the ancients did to any of their household Gods—As neither Papa nor ourselves could reconcile the idea of indiscriminate interrment in the City, we have consecrated here a little spot of Ground, where her dear reliques lie; a little family Repository—there is something consolatory in the idea of being with those you love, even in the Grave.

But now, my dear Mrs. Madison, I must confess this beautiful Portrait has originated, or rather confirmed another want in my little panting heart; it wants most anxiously to embrace the dear original; if it is not among the secrets of state, do tell me whether you cannot persuade the President to make a Tour to Philadelphia this Summer or Autumn; Papa says every body would hail his arrival with the greatest joy, all Parties & all Persons; & indeed, I think the Sovereign People ought to be gratified sometimes with a sight of Those, who rule over them; Oh! could I only behold you my dearest Madam, I think I should be completely happy—They tell me that every President makes the tour of the States, so that sooner or later I expect to be gratified—Adieu my dearest Mrs Madison, when I write to you, I forget myself in so delightful an employment; even now I lay down my pen with reluctance. Believe me your most obliged, devoted & affectionate

Phebe P. Morris

RC (DLC: DPM Papers). Docketed by DPM.

From James Madison

My dearest,   WASHINGTON August 7th. 1809

We reached the end of our journey yesterday at one o'clock; without interruption of any sort on the road—Mr. Coles had been here sometime, one, if not two of the expected dispatch vessels of England, had just arrived, and Mr. Gilston[1] after a short passage from France, entered Washington about the moment I did. You may guess therefore the volumes of papers before us. I am but just dipping into them; and have seen no one as yet except Mr. Smith for a few minutes last evening. What number of days I may be detained here it is impossible to say. The period you may be sure will be shortened as much as possible. Every thing around and within reminds me that you are absent, and makes me anxious to quit the solitude. In my next I hope I shall be able to say when I shall have this gratification; perhaps also to say something of the intelligence just brought us. I send the paper of this morning which has something on the subject. I hope the communications of Gilston will be found more favorable than is stated. Those from England can scarcely be favorable, when such men hold the riens as we have latterly had to do with. Mr. and Mrs. Erskine are here. His successor had not sailed on the 20th: of June. God bless you and be assured of My constant affection

J. Madison

Tr (NjP: Crane Collection). Printed in *PJM-PS* 1:318–19.
    1. Maltby Gelston, son of New York port collector David Gelston, had carried dispatches to John Armstrong, U.S. minister at Paris (JM to Thomas Jefferson, 1 May 1809, ibid., 149, 150 n. 1).

From James Madison

[9 August 1809]

I hope you recced., my dearest, a letter written by the last Mail. I write this in haste just to tell you that P.[1] & myself are well; & that I am making exertions to get thro' the necessary business, with a hope of setting out on my return tomorrow. It is very possible however that I may be detained till friday Morning. I send you all the foreign news in the inclosed papers. That from France has a better complexion than preceding accts. of her temper towards the U.S. The tone of Cannings speech also is a little different from the arrogance of his instructions to Mr. Erskine. Payne writes. I must refer to his letter for what I am prevented from adding, relative to Capt. Coles &c &c.

RC (PHi). Signature clipped. Printed in *PJM-PS* 1:320.
    1. John Payne Todd.

From Harriet Hackley

My Dear Madam,   CADIZ August 10th. 1809.

Relying on your goodness I have taken the liberty to introduce to *you particularly* Mrs: Onis Lady of the Minister plenipotentiary & Envoy extraordinary of Spain, whose excellence I am sure will gain on you each time that you are in her company; I feel myself so much interested in her forming a favourable opinion of our Country, that I have recommended her to your friendship, well aware that your amiable manners will impress her (as they must do every one) highly in favour of our Country women. The Lady whom I have the honour to present to you has the polish of the European, added to the genuine qualities of an *American,* & I am happy to have it in my power to make you acquainted with by far the most charming family I have met with in this Kingdom. I remain my dear Madam with every assurance of esteem, & respect your most sincere well wisher & admirer

                                                      Harriet Hackley.

RC (MCR-S: Mary Estelle Elizabeth Cutts Papers).

From Anna Maria Thornton

My dear Mrs. Madison   CITY OF WASN: Augt 21. 1809

As I understand that you are overwhelmed with Company, I fear my letter may be an intrusion, & indeed not having had any encouragement, verbal or written to adress you I do not know whether I ought to take the liberty to do so, but I feel loth to relinquish all my ancient privileges and pleasures—I fear I cannot even afford you any information that you have not had already, for all the little news of our place I suppose you receive regularly, and you are at the fountainhead of great & public news, so I fear I can have no chance of entertaining you for a moment, and write only to remind you of one who wou'd be much hurt at a discontinuance of your remembrance & good will.

We rode out yesterday to see Mrs S. H Smith, who (as from my own experience I had no doubt she wou'd be) is much delighted with her excursion, she seems to admire your situation more than Mr Jefferson's, & indeed I think myself it is capable of much greater embellishment, as the land lies, in a more extended & varied position. I am very sorry to hear of Mrs: Bankhead's loss & Mrs. Randolph's little boy's illness. Do you think of going to Monticello before your return? Do you not my dear Mrs Madison feel for our amiable acquaintance Mr & Mrs Erskine, what a stroke it must have been when they first heard the sad news! They now appear in good Spirits & conduct themselves as they always have done with the greatest propriety—I sincerely regret their recall & fear that in that situation we ne'er shall see their like again—They are I suppose (independent of the mortification of being so recalled) happy at returning, they go to their children & dear friends—with an elegant Seat to retreat to, and the prospect of spending their winter months in London, as there is little doubt of his getting into Parliament—I always thought they had every reason to be happy & most truly do I hope they may always continue to be so, for they are most estimable people.[1]

Mrs Wharton & little daughter are both very sick—Capt Tingey & Sally will set off about Thursday next for Boston, their relations Mrs Swears and Daughter will stay here till their return. Mrs Buchannan has lost her infant & is now better after having been very ill. The New Bank is begun on the Capitol Hill, & the Subscription is to be opened the 2d Wednesday in next month[2]— Do you not think of taking some shares in it for your Son—Mr Carroll is to be the president, it is said, & I imagine it will be an advantageous and profitable institution.

I suppose you have had fires, it has been almost cool enough to wish for them, now we begin to feel a little of the August & Septr burning Sun.

Mr Cutts did not do us the favr. to call tho' I heard he was in the neighborhood. I hope Mrs Cutts & children are well please[d] to remember us kindly to her—& tell her I hope her wishes may be gratified in the next stranger she introduces to our acquaintance.

I suppose we must not expect the pleasure to see you all in the City till the beginning of october. We I believe shall remain quietly here, we did talk of a little excursion, but I do not know whether we shall have resolution to put it into Effect—Home I think after all, is the most desirable place in hot weather.

Mrs: Willis has given us up I find, which I am very sorry for, as I had expected to have a very agreable neighbor in her—Will you do me the favor to give my love to her when you see her. And our Compts to any persons who may have been kind enough to remember us.

Mama & Dr. T. join me in best regards to you & respects to the President & remembrance to Payne. In hopes of having the gratification to hear that you are all well & that you now & then cast a thought to this side of F. Street, I remain my dear Mrs Madison your sincere & respectful friend

A M Thornton

RC (PPPrHi: Shane Collection, RG 196, folder 16, box 19). Docketed by DPM.

    1. In 1809 David Erskine, British minister to the U.S., in a bid to close the growing rift in Anglo-American relations, offered to rescind the British Orders in Council in exchange for the exemption of British ships from the Nonintercourse Act. On 10 June 1809 JM reopened Anglo-American trade on the assumption that the Erskine agreement had been acceptable to both sides, and in July the Madisons left for Montpelier. The British government, however, repudiated the agreement, recalled Erskine, and replaced him that fall with Francis James Jackson (Ketcham, *James Madison*, 492–95).

    2. The Bank of Washington opened its doors to business on 1 Dec. 1809 with Daniel Carroll as president. It was capitalized at $1 million, and each share cost $40; it was oversubscribed the first day the subscription books were opened (Bryan, *History of the National Capital* 1:535; Charles E. Howe, "The Financial Institutions of Washington City in Its Early Days," *Records of the Columbia Historical Society* 8 [1905]: 1–42).

From Benjamin Henry Latrobe

Madam,   WASHINGTON, Septr. 8th. 1809

Immediately after your departure I went to the President's house in order to forward every part of the work which it was necessary to compleat before your return.

I was however stopped in my intentions untill it could be ascertained whether the building fund would afford to pay for these operations. After this was ascertained, in order to strengthen the fund, I bought the two Chimney pieces intended for the dining room, for the Capitol, and immediately after the departure of the President, after his short visit to the city, I set our people to work.

Parlor. The Marble Chimney piece is set, and in a few days the papering of the room will be finished.

The Chamber door, ordered on the North side is opened.

The Kitchen stairs under the great stairs leading to the turning closet, are in great forwardness.

The Coach houses are finished.

The Pump may be put into the Well on that side of the house in a few days.

So far I could proceed boldly as Surveyor of the public Buildings. But in my other capacity of *Upholsterer,* as I am called in the Newspapers, I found that I could not be as useful as I wished.

Having been informed by you that Mrs. Swiney would attend to a variety of business in her line with which you had made her acquainted, I sent for her, and independently of general instructions to attend to & obey all your orders, I desired her to examine the curtains, to take down such as required it, that is *all* that required Washing, or belonged to bed chambers which were in use, & would harbor bugs, to get them washed, and to have them laid up, ready to be put up, on the approach of your return by Mr Labille. I found that this order was not obeyed, and having again sent for Mrs. Swiney, I enquired into the reason. She was embarrassed but at last told me, that on attempting to obey me she was informed, that you are so displeased with my conduct especially with my long absence in February and April that you intended I should do nothing more for you.

As this information could only come from your servants, I ought to presume that it was false. It was completely contradicted by yourself in the whole of your conduct towards me, and it would be an insult to you to suppose it possible that such intelligence would be conveyed to a man of character, and a public officer, at second hand, by a servant. Having however received two anonymous letters to the same effect, I have not presumed to interfere beyond my duties as surveyor of the public buildings, and have refrained from going into the house more than that duty required. Mr. Lenox having informed me, on behalf of your Steward that you are expected in a shorter time than you originally intended, I have had the necessary conversation with Labille, & have ordered the repairs to be done in the Kitchen which were pointed out by the Cook, and such other things to be done as your Steward thought necessary.

The furniture of the drawing room, as far as depended on Mr. Rae has been finished since the beginning of July. But Mr. Findlay of Baltimore who has the Chairs & Sofas in hand, appears not to have been equally attentive. I therefore went to Baltimore in July, and fou⟨nd⟩ all the Chairs ready, and such as I wished them, but the Sofas were unfinished. I said every thing to urge their completion & applied to Genl. Smith who had recommended him to me, to urge him on. But the General, it seems, had also reason to be dissatisfied himself. However a⟨s⟩ all the Chairs are finished, the Drawing-room may be furnished thus far. About 10 days ago I wrote another pressing letter to Find-lay, but receiving no answer, I have written to Rae, and desired him to come on immediately with his part of the furniture and to stop at Baltimore for Findlay's. I now expect Rae within a week, and shall send a conveyance to Baltimore as soon as I find the things are ready. My wish is not to put them up till just before your arrival, otherwise the croud of visitors who will press to see them, will give great trouble & perhaps do injury.

There is in Philadelphia a Carpet, for which I gave directions in London for Mrs. Waln (formerly Mary Wilcocks). It would exactly suit in style & colors the Curtains of your drawing room, and as Mrs. Waln is in a very distressing state of health, & her drawing room will not be furnished this winter I can obtain the Carpet for you, if there is enough of it. Rae will bring on a piece.

If there is any thing in my power to execute for you, I hope *still* to receive your commands. I have the honor to be with true respect Yrs.

B H Latrobe.

P.S. The public business of which it was my duty to apprize You is contained in the preceding pages. *Personally*, permit me to say, I cannot possibly suppose the information I have received to be correct. You *have reason* to be dissatisfied with your carriage. I am more than sufficiently punished already by my misfortune in employing a man of universally good character, but who deceived me; and I hope you have pardoned me that error. As to my long stay in Phila., it has been in the first place, productive of not a single omission in my duties here, and besides, if it had, it must be enquired whether my *duties* there could have been neglected, before I am condemned. When you see the Marble colonnade of the Senate Chamber alone, you will agree that *in Six Weeks*, I must have been very industrious to have designed it, and got the whole of it into the hands of the Workmen. Besides this, I had to design, & even lay out in the frame, the whole of the furniture of your drawing room, *also a public concern*. Workmen require constant watching in the commencement of work which is new to them. They must be taught like Children. Altho' the papers have said that I staid to attend to my splendid buildings, it is not true; for the only one I have lately built, was finished last Year, and Mr. Markoe's house has been begun since my return.[1]

But if I had had no public business, is my salary such as to preclude me from visiting my family once a Year? and only for a few weeks. I carried Mrs. Latrobe to Phila, the end of Feby. staid a few days with her, & returned on the 4h. of March. I remained here 3 Weeks, & went back to Phila, the end of March. I left Pha. the 2d. of May. Nothing sufferred during my absence, &

many things were forwarded *there;* which must otherwise have been given up. I leave my cause in your hands. It is humiliating to me to have to defend it; but I know it is a good one.

RC (NIC). Docketed by DPM. Printed in *PJM-PS* 1:365–68.
    1. In 1807 John Markoe (1781–1834) had asked Latrobe to design a house at the corner of Chestnut and Ninth Streets in Philadelphia (Van Horne and Formwalt, *Correspondence of Latrobe* 2:646 n.).

To Benjamin Henry Latrobe

⟨Mr. La⟩trobe   Sept: 12th. 1809.
    Incredulous, indeed must be the ear that receives, without belief the "Varnished tale"—but most happy would it be, for you, could you listen *without* emotion, to the variety of falsehoods, framed but to play, on your sensibility—The letter I have this moment recd. from you, gives me uneasiness; because I find my conduct, which always contradicted any opinion, or expression against you, has been insufficient to assure your judgment, that I would, at least—be consistent—In the first place my affection for Mrs. Latrobe would in itself prevent my doing injustice to her Husband—& in the next, I always knew, that *I* had no right to animadvert on his journeys, or conduct, as a Public officer—(& as it is one of my sources of happiness, never to desire a knowledge of other peoples business). Thirdly, I never for a moment doubted your taste or honour, in the direction of public buildings, or even in the building of our *Little* Carriage. The moment we examined the latter, we declared *you* had been deceived by the Maker.
    Mrs Sweny is a woman of many words—I have never talk'd to her, or before her, but of her work—In your absence, she would reherse to the Household *terrible tales of dis-affection,* from the Capitol—which I lamented for your sake—I can account for Mrs Sweny's mis-information to you, only by supposing her offended at my leaving her but little to do, in the house.
    Not knowing how far I could incur additio⟨n⟩al ⟨expense,⟩ I therefore ordered, that she should merely repair the beds. I shall be strict in my examination of the servants, when I return, as I wish to know those, who have taken the liberty to mis-represent me. I will say little of the anonymous letters, but that you excite my surprise at suffering *them* to have the slightest effect on your spirits, or transactions. Allow me again, to thank you, with all my heart, for the trouble you have taken, in many instances, to oblige and accommodate

me, and tho' our enemies may strive to throw around me ungrateful appearances I shall take a pleasure in counteracting their designs.

D. P. Madison

RC (DCHi).

To John C. Payne

ORANGE Septr. 21st. 1809

Yesterday I received your letter, My beloved Brother, dated July the 4th. I grieve more than I can express, to find you did not get my letters, be assured, I have written you vols. since your departure, and directed them all to Doctr. Davis for security—believing that with Dispatches from Government they would reach your hands—I have now no doubt but they are lost—& the many & sad changes in your family, you are yet to weep over—Alas! my Dear John nearly two years have elapsed since the loss of our beloved & sainted mother! Our tender & amiable sister, Polly remained but a few weeks after! Mama was ill but a few days—Polly appeared to be in a decline for some months—she left only one child, little Mary who has been alternately with Lucy & myself. George Washington died last Jany. in Georgia where he had gone for his health. He left three sons well provided for & a rich widow. Lucy spent two months with me in the City this spring—Anna, Mr. Cutts & their three fine boys went with us to the President's House, where you know we now reside, & have remained with us ever since, & where I wish you my Dear Brother was also a resident.

You promised to return to us long before this, & I hope & trust that if you are disappointed in your prospects where you are, that you will not suffer those weak ref[l]ections, on yourself, which affect me, in your letter, to stay you one moment from my arms & heart, that are open to receive you. You would return to sisters and Brothers that love you & whose happiness it would be to do every thing for you, if you required it, but our Mother has left you all she possessed in this World, a respectable independence if properly managed, for this purpose you had better send me power of Attorney to sell your Kentucky lands & other property which ought to be turned into Money, also a power to collect any & all debts due to Mama, now your own. I will write you as soon as I return to the City, the last of this month, & inclose you a copy of the Will, where you will see that Washington Boyde & John G. Jackson are named as Executors—Mr. Boyde did not chuse to act, & I got Mr. Jackson to have it proved &c. Mr. J. is your debtor for some 2 or 300$, I forget which I hold his bond for your orders—I saw Doctr. Ridgly & received his note for a horse you owed him—I immediately purchased a very fine one of Genl. Dearborn at 250$ & paid to him, with which he was highly pleased—those left at Black Meadow not being worth 20$—I have taken up several small notes of yours, & will take every care of your interest as much as if it was my own son's, who is by the bye, a fine fellow, & who remembers & talks of you with the tenderest affection—& indeed so do all your old acquaintances, many of them have written to you, & I truly believe that you left no enemy behind you— Adieu my ever Dear John for the present—I will write you on the subject of your continuance at Tripoli, & the capacity you speak of the instant I can. Mr. M. who you *must know,* is President of the U.S. is now over his head in Dispatches from Europe, & when he gets through them I will consult him— We have had within a fortnight Mr. Erskine recalled & Mr. Jackson his successor arrived in Washington—The British having disavowed the treaty made by Erskine Mr. M. has the trouble to negotiate anew. You perhaps have already seen that after removing the Embargo of many months standing & letting our vessels go out &c &c. for merely a few weeks we have to stop the intercourse again, from the treachery of England.

Anna will write you by this opportunity—Aunt and Uncle Winston & al their family are well. They always enquire after you & sigh to see you again. I shall remind Mr. Forest of this opportunity who will no doubt write you— Pray write to me by all vessels likely to come & tell more particularly your situation & what I shall send you.

I am assured that if Doctr. Davis returns he will leave you in his place to act as Consul & that no person will be appointed for a considerable time, in order that you may so act, as to have a good standing with the Senate, who appoint all officers with the previous recomendation of the President, you will of course receive the salary of Consul & make the best of your situation And in case of an appointment being made contrary to my hopes, you shall have with him, the choice of remaining or not, in the place you now hold— Assure Doctr. and Mrs. Davis of my affectionate remembrance—Mr. & Mrs. Howard—Mother M. & old Aunt Taylor beg me to present you their love & best wishes. The salaries of the Consuls & secretaries stand on the same footing as when you left us—further efforts will be made in their favour, I am informed—Payne is in Baltimore—or he would write you—Ever your own & affectionate sister.

D. P. Madison

P.S. If I receive your power of Attorney to collect your money & sell your land I will either transmit it to you or appropriate it here according to your order.

Madison who has just had the pleasure of being his Aunt's amanuensis & who perhaps has long since been forgotten avails himself of this opportunity of sending Mr. Payne his best respects & warmest wishes for his welfare.

RC (owned by Nathaniel E. Stein, New York, N.Y., 1961). Marked "Duplicate"; in the hand of Alfred Madison, signed by DPM. Addressed to John C. Payne at Tripoli.

From John G. Jackson

MONTE ALTO October 23rd. 1809

Why, my dear Sister, do you distress yourself on my account & allow alarms of danger & of Duels to reach you? Know you not that I live *now* only for my Country, & if, in subserving its interest *they* cross my path shall your Brother pusillanimously skulk into a corner?[1] You must say no, my dear Sister, for I should be unworthy of the title you bestow on me if I acted thus.

Sometimes it happens when I set out in writing upon a topic out of the usual course of epistolary communica⟨tion⟩ for the life of me I can not get set to rights unless I begin again. It is so now, perhaps my head runs too much on the party to be given me to-morrow in the neighborhood; preparatory to our military exercises which commence next day & last the whole week—when they have ended & I do well—for I am a sad correspondent when I am sick— I will write you a long letter & tell you with what sincerity I am & shall be as long as I live my dear Sister yours affectionately

J G Jackson

The Snuff arrived sound & good & I now take a pinch (in imagination) with you.

RC (ViU: Breckenridge-Watts Papers).
1. Jackson referred to controversy between himself and North Carolina Federalist Joseph Pearson, who had attacked the motives of the administration in a debate in the House of Representatives in June. Jackson rose to defend Jefferson and JM in intemperate language, and over the summer the two men engaged in personal attacks on each other. The affair culminated in a duel fought on 4 Dec. 1809. Jackson was wounded in the hip and nearly died; his lameness thereafter led him to resign his House seat in September 1810 (Brown, *Voice of the New West*, 85–93).

To Samuel Stanhope Smith

WASHINGTON Jany. 10th. [18]10.

I have been favored with your letter of the 31t. Decr. and with feelings of regret I found it was too late to make the proposal you desired, a nomination haveing been made to the Senate some days before.[1]

On the subject of the Govr: of N. O. I can say nothing, as he has given no intimation of his intention to resign.

I hope you will beleive Sir, that my Husband feels for you the highest regard, & that I shall always cherish those sentements of affection and interest, which are so entirely due to you, and your amiable daughter.

D. P. Madison

RC (NjP: Crane Collection). Addressed to Smith at "Prince Town."

1. Reverend Samuel Smith, president of the College of New Jersey at Princeton and an old friend of JM, had written to the president in April 1809 for help in reinstating his son, John W. Smith, as clerk for the superior court at New Orleans. He wrote JM again six months later asking for an appointment for his son, and evidently wrote DPM as well (*PJM-PS* 1:115–16, 2:30–31).

From Harriet Hackley

PHILADELPHIA April 27th. 1810.

Your kind, & welcome letter my dear Madam reach'd me only a few days before I was under the disagreeable necessity of quitting my home, my Husband, & part of my little family to cross the Ocean; without a protector, seeking in the bosoms of my natural friends, & my beloved Country an assylum from the horrors of war:[1] under such circumstances I know the excellence of your heart will induce you to pardon my not having sooner return'd you my gratefull acknowledgements, not only for your friendly mode of addressing me, but for the disposition you shew'd on a *former* & *most important* occasion to serve me, & mine; believe me my dear Mrs: Maddison you have excited the warmest feelings of gratitude in (not unworthy hearts). I expect to be in Washington in a few days, when I hope to have the satisfaction of expressing to you in person my sentiments. Tomorrow I leave this in the Packet for Baltimore where I shall not remain more than one night as my time is limitted, you will think me possess'd of a good stock of courage to undertake a journey from this place to Monticello with four children, & the prospect of a fifth the latter end of the ensuing month, indeed I tremble at the thought, but must at least attempt it, so great is my anxiety to be with my dear friends.

I have seen Mr. Onis, he is enchanted with your conduct to him, & speaks of you in the most exalted terms, he also expresses the highest satisfaction at the personal marks of attention he recieved from the President as well as the heads of Department under his mortifying circumstances; Poor Man I am sorry for him; he is deserving of good fortune.[2]

Adieu my dear Madam, permit me I beg to assure you of my unbounded esteem, & respect, yours

H. Hackley.

RC (MCR-S: Mary Estelle Elizabeth Cutts Papers). Docketed by DPM.

1. Harriet Randolph Hackley and her husband, U.S. vice consul Richard S. Hackley, had been living in Cádiz, Spain, then under siege by French troops. Mrs. Hackley, pregnant with her fifth child, had returned to the United States with her children to make her home at Monticello with her brother and sister-in-law Thomas Mann and Martha Jefferson Randolph (*Report of the Select Committee in the Case of Richard S. Hackley, Accompanied with a Bill for His Relief,* 11 April 1820 [Washington, D.C., 1820; Shaw and Shoemaker 4035]; Betts and Bear, *Family Letters,* 397–98).

2. JM's refusal to recognize Onís as the accredited Spanish minister on his arrival in Washington in October 1809 stemmed from the political situation in Spain. At that time there were two governments—a monarchy backed by France and an insurgent government backed by Great Britain. As a neutral, the United States could not receive diplomats from either Spanish government. In the meantime, however, upon an accidental meeting with the Madisons at the horse races, British minister Francis James Jackson introduced Onís informally, and DPM felt compelled by social convention to invite Onís to the President's Mansion for a reception. It is probably to this event that Harriet Hackley is referring (Brant, *Madison* 5:99).

From John B. Colvin

WASHINGTON CITY, June 26: 1810.

The sketch of Mr Madison's Life, which has appeared in a volume called a Biographical Dictionary, published at Baltimore by a Mr. Kingston, was not written by me.[1] I think it necessary to state this fact to you, and to assure you that I should have furnished a sketch for the work in question, had I not early discovered that its execution by Mr. Kingston, would be feeble and faultering. I have too just an esteem for the President's character—his intellectual powers—his political qualities—his amenity of manners—to paint his likeness for a wretched Gallery, where the miserable portraits will not answer even for foils to superior excellence.

Having turned my attention to the particulars of the President's Life, however, I shall, in a neat form of about twelve duodecima pages, in the course of this aproaching autumn, publish, without my name, a biographical sketch of Mr. Madison. Upon this composition I shall bestow all the art I possess—it will, nevertheless, be no further *art,* than to place *truth* in the best points of view. This performance, together with my other literary pledge to you, will be forthcoming in good time and season. I have the honor to be, Madam, Very respectfully, Your most obt. sert.

John B. Colvin.

RC (DLC). Docketed by JM.
1. DPM must have complained to Colvin about the essay on JM in John Kingston's *The New American Biographical Dictionary* (Baltimore, 1810).

To James Taylor

Novr. 10th. [18]10.

I reccd: your kind letter dear friend, of Octor., as well as that from the Springs, for which at this late hour you must accept my best thanks. I rejoiced at the account you gave me of your amiable Wife & family—may they long continue to make your happiness & you theirs.

On our return to the City we found some few of our acquaintance sick, Cousin Edward & our Steward ware threaten'd with a bilious fever, but Doctr. Elzy has restore[d] them to gaiety again. The Hornet has just return'd from France & brings us nothing contradictory of the *affectinate* intentions of Napolian I know, however, by the intense study of Mr M & his constant devotion to the Cabinet, that affairs, are troublesome & difficult—You see the English are stuborn yet, but we anticipate their yealding before long—in short, the Proclamation gives you the state of things *now*.[1] Genl. Armstrong is, hourly expected—no successor yet decided on. I am much mortified, that Genl. Mason has not had an oppty. to send your boxes &c & he hope's for one every week & is to let me know of it. Your China && has not arrived, but I hope you will not loose your patience, the Waters & the Winds will not be commanded by us—My Brother & Sister Cutts are detain'd by a snow storm in Main which we all regret—They will, however come on as soon as they can. Lucy is with me & offers Mrs. Taylor & yourself a great deal of Love but not more than I can with great sincerity.

Our Mother & connections in Virga. are well Alfred Madison has been with us, & is now in Phila. with Doctor's Rush & Physic—poor fellow. I fear he can never be well again—I fancy the good impression you made on Simmons will never be effaced—all the long list of your acquaintance here speak of you with high regard & I have sometimes flattered them & myself with a hope that you would yet bring Mrs. Taylor to visit us—tell her she has a cousin in your attatched friend

D P Madison

When any thing interesting occurs I will write you again in the mean time, let us hear from you. Govr. C. has return'd to N.O. he talks of seeing us again in the spring or summer but I doubt whether, on the same arrand, with Govr. H. altho *we* admire him, we are two selfish to wish him *success.*[2] Mrs. Eustis is a fine woman & the Doctr. a happy man.

RC (KyHi). Addressed by DPM to Col. James Taylor at "Belle Vue Kentucky."
    1. JM issued a proclamation on 2 Nov. 1810 imposing nonintercourse upon Great Britain and announcing the discontinuance of such restrictions "in relation to France and her dependencies" (*PJM-PS* 2:612–13).
    2. "Govr. C" is William C. C. Claiborne, the governor of Orleans Territory; "Govr. H." is David Holmes, governor of the Mississippi Territory.

From Jane O'Bryan

Madam   NEW YORK Jany the 27th 1811

Permit me to solicit you to pardon the temerity apparent in my thus obtruding myself on your notice, to whom I must be entirely unknown; what nothing could induce me to be guilty of but a desire to ingage in my favour an exertion of that active humanity and benevolence that your immediate friends and common fame proclaim you to possess in an eminent degree.

Convinced that you, Madam, can, and will sympathise with the miserable and unfortunate, I am emboldened to apply to you in the moment that complicated distress and anguish unutterable overwhelm me, and supplicate from you that consolation and relief that is elswhere denied.[1]

To justify you in affording the succour I implore; I take leave [to] state to you the source of the deep and heartfelt sorrows that wring from me this application. I am Madam the wife of John O'Bryan of this City, a man whose general demeanour among men made him esteemed, while his endearing conduct to me as an husband has rivetted every affection of my heart to him; which a number of Children, the sweet pledges of our happy union, has so closely intertwined as to render his happiness essential to my existence; and happy indeed we have been, for tho' neither opulent, nor affluent, we, through his professional labours were so independant, as by being above want, to be completely content, and thus loving and beloved our days glided happily by, my husband universally revered, and my darling Children admired and beloved.

But Madam those halcion days are flown, never, I fear to return; for my husband, a plain Sailor, unaquainted with law, was by designing men basely seduced into the unintentional commission of a breach of the Embargo laws, for which he has been eighteen months and upward a prisoner, and still remains confined on the limits of the prison of this City, whither I have brought my family and immured myself that I might in person minister to his wants, alleviate his afflictions, and soothe his anguish, and, where want and misery has so accumulated around us as to have broken our spirit effectually, and render my situation pitiable in the extreme; for while an earnest desire to save my adored husbands feelings and if possible rescue him from the most gloomy despondence, I am compelled to conceal a breaking heart. The little property the fruits of my husbands labours that we once possessed, being entirely exhausted in the supporting for such a length of time, ourselves and ten young and helpless Children, we are now dependent on loans from, and the benevolent contributions of a few friends, which supply is so precarious and humiliating, and pity and charity are so short lived and cold, that the relief afforded for our wants in this inclement climate and season is scanty indeed.

Beleive me Madam that the picture I have above exhibited of my situation and distress, is a faithfull one, nor would I presume to offer any other even to awaken your compassion for myself and family. It is (Madam) a plain and honest narative of facts that without the knowledge of my suffering husband, I have presumed to make known to you, from an humble but sanguine hope that you would feel so far interested for an unhappy wife and mother as to patronise a petition forwarded by my husband to both houses of Congress praying for releif, which I hope and fervently pray to my God, may be speedily granted; as the confining an industrious man for a debt he is utterly unable to pay, is inutile; and which if done will restore my husband to his labours and myself and Children, of course to those comforts we enjoyed before this fell blast of adversity so fatally blighted our prospects.

Should we Madam owe this happiness, this unspeakable felicity to your interposition and good offices, The Prayers of myself and innocent little family shall dayly ascend to the throne of mercy to implore Blessings on our patroness and Benefacttress. With the greatest respect and deference I have the honor to subscribe myself Madam Your Most afflicted & Devoted, Humble Servant

Jane O'Bryan

RC (DLC: Madison Miscellany). Docketed by JM.

1. John O'Bryan was in debtors' prison for failure to pay a fine of $4,000 imposed on him in May 1809 for violating the embargo laws. While Jane O'Bryan wrote DPM, John O'Bryan sent a petition to his congressman, Samuel Latham Mitchill, who delivered it to JM with a note on 26 Feb. 1811. Two months after her initial letter, Mrs. O'Bryan once again wrote DPM,

enclosing additional papers for the president to examine, noting that "the good and humane Doctor Mitchill . . . stated to us the warm interest you had taken in our situation and your wish to alleviate our miseries and distresses." On 30 March JM pardoned O'Bryan (*PJM-PS* 3:187 and n. 1; Jane O'Bryan to DPM, 25 March 1811, DLC: Madison Miscellany).

To David Bailie Warden

8th. March [18]11

Mrs. Madison presents her respects to Mr Warden & requests the favor of him to hasten the inclosed letter to her Brother.

She also begs Mr Warden will have the goodness to write to John C. Payne at Tripola after his arrival, & by a different oppertunity, lest her letter should not reach him. Mr & Mrs. M are extreamly anxious that the circumstance of their Brother's appointment as Seccy. to Mr Barlow, should be known to him, in order that he should, immediately repair to Paris. It is for *this* purpose, they would trouble ⟨Mr.⟩ W. to drop him a few lines, & his attention ⟨to⟩ the object will be highly appreciated by them.

Mrs. M will add the Memom. of her sister & her ⟨. . .⟩ but as she is ignorent of the best method of ⟨ge⟩ting him mony, she will enqu[i]re of Mr Barlow ⟨to se⟩nd it by him. Mr. Warden will accept the assurances of our best wishes & friendship.

RC (MdHi: Warden Papers). Ms torn.

To James Taylor

13th. March [1811]

I had flattered myself, that after so long a silence on my part, my amiable friend that I should be able to compensate you by a agreable inteligence of every sort; particularly on the subject of your China & Glass—I am sadly disappointed—Mr Cutts assured me that he wrote instantly, to his Agent, but that he has reccd: neither the articles, or an answer to his order. At present, the Non-intercourse law will prevent their comeing unless shiped before the 2d. Feby. What shall we do in the case? & what shall I do with your mony? Mr C. will not take it until the things arrive—give me your direction, & I will adhear to it.

You have seen by the N. Papers the present state of things—*we* have no further insight at this moment. Vessels are expected hourly & the state of our Relations in Europe will decide whether an extra Session will be necessary— *some very wicked, & silly doings at home.*[1]

My brother & Sister C. will set of for Main as soon as the roads permit— Lucy talks of Hairwood & I shall be the only companion of my Husband in a short time, as cousin Ned intends to visit Boston in May—We had the pleasure of seeing Govr. Howard & his fair Bride last week—They talk of going immediately to St. Louis—We all think, & talk of you, with affection my kind friend, & should rejoice to see & know our kinswoman Mrs. Taylor, with all her sweet little ones—*I* look forward to the time. I have sent a small box with the seed you left with me & a few books—If I have the oppty. I will certainly add to the No. I have been engaged all the Session, without an hour's leasure, & have still, a weight of cares. Adeiu for the present, I will soon write again.

D P M

Genl. Mason sends the box.

RC (KyHi).

1. In early March 1811 the Madison administration was as much beset with internal turmoil as with external threat. Criticism of JM's foreign policy came not only from Federalists but from Republicans as well, especially Robert and Samuel Smith and their allies. The Philadelphia *Aurora General Advertiser* went so far as to accuse Gallatin of being an agent of British influence and the Baltimore *Whig* described JM as without the requisite energy to run the country. The situation was at such a pass that Gallatin offered the president his resignation (*PJM-PS* 3:209 n. 1; J. C. A. Stagg, *Mr. Madison's War: Politics, Diplomacy, and Warfare in the Early American Republic, 1783–1830* [Princeton, N.J., 1983], 48–64).

To John G. Jackson

10th. Apl. [18]11.

Our precious Mary was right my dear Brother, when she answered for her Aunt Ds love to the little stranger. I sincerely congratulate you & the sister of my adoption, on this pleasing adition & I pray that they may both be well & happy—as I think you have reason to be on many accounts[1]—You must feel more tha[n] ever, your independence & peace after knowing the turbulence & miseries of a publick life. The last Winter has *convinced me.* You know before this that Govr. Monroe is Secry of State & that R. S. *does not go to Russia.* Just so—he has retired (the papers state) to what he was wont to be. Duane & &. take a *few liberties* with M on the subject tho they do not deny *his right* to make a Secry to *suit him* & the Office. I could tell you many curious things my brother, but as *people say I have my oppinions* & &. I must not trust my pen—Mr Barlow Mintr. to France takes my brother John to reside with him as Secry. at two thousand $ p. Year a place of all others, I prefer for him—I will send your letter to Aunt by next post, & wish I may be able to aid you in the Suit, because I know that in Justice Coles Hill belongs to John & Mary—I dont remember how the property came but allways was impressed with the idea that my GrandMother was rich when she married last, & that my Grand-Father had but little—Aunt can tell exactly—The Dispatch Vessel, Essex, is detain'd to bring Pinckney from England—Foster comes as their Minister—the last accts. state, that our negociations are broken off at St. James's & that we have nothing to expect from them—that France has repealed her decrees & & & will do us all favours. When we know further, I will tell you. Adeiu for the present—this is D. Room night & I write badly from haste as we have still, great crouds—The New french Minister[2] is quite a polished modest man the Russians are all the rage & Moorea [Morier] in the background—Monroe has taken ⟨rooms?⟩ at Suters[3] where I have just sent lime to white wash them—Mr. M will write you Lucy too intends it—Anna & Cutts are now in N York. L talks of Hair Wood—kisses for you all—ever Your sister

DPM

RC (IU: Jackson Collection).

    1. John G. Jackson had married Mary Sophia Meigs on 19 July 1810. Mary bore their first child, a daughter, in late March or early April 1811 (Brown, *Voice of the New West,* 100, 143).

    2. The new French minister was Louis-Barbé-Charles Sérurier.

    3. Suter's boardinghouse was located at the corner of Fifteenth and F Streets (Bryan, *History of the National Capital* 1:518).

From Phoebe P. Morris

WILMINGTON May 6th. 1811.

After the requisite delight of a reception so sincere and so affectionate, as to revive in my Heart even the long lost but never forgotten extacy of maternal embraces, the only consolation I am capable of feeling is in the effort to express my love, my gratitude, & my duty, to you, my dearest & tenderest Friend, who having so well known my Sainted Mother, were best qualified to revive in a Daughter's bosom, for a few fleeting hours, the dear the delicate delusion: how pure must be the source from whence flowed those tears of tenderness, when in the Daughter's arms was revived the recollection of her Mother's love! In this sense, I feel indeed that "Love is Heaven & Heaven is Love"—To *my honored President* I would also endeavor to express the gratitude I feel, for his kind, his condescending, his elegant hospitality, his interesting & improving society: but though I cannot communicate to you my feelings, you will both, I am sure believe them to be such as ought to be excited in a youthful heart susceptible of the strongest impressions from causes so justly calculated to excite them.

Your united cordiality, with the amiable, & animated endearments, of my dear Mrs. Washington, added to the fascinating charms of society, & scenery, even brightened with smiles the countenance of my dearest Father, whose heart has been long a stranger to joy, though his face sometimes borrows the Veil of Serenity. For your creation of all these delights how sincerely could I wish to make some return more suitable than the artless effusions of my heart! Oh Madam! Believe me when I declare that I can love no person (besides my dear Parents) as I now love you—In the moment of my separation from you, tears were my only language—My affection for you is a sensation new to my heart; it differs from *that love* I feel for many of my young Friends, it is more pure, it is more refined, it approaches more nearly to the purity of Filial veneration! Oh never can this sentiment be enfeebled, I feel that absence will add new force to an attachment so ardent & so tender; and you will I know indulge me in expressing it without fear or restraint, as the compensation for an absence, which must, I fear be permanent; how sad the idea! Papa says he shall be obliged to apply to the President for the mission to Russia, to temper the ardor of his feelings towards the fair Lady of Harewood, but I remind him that

"His hair is grey, his limbs are old
  His heart is dead, his veins are cold"
that "He may not, must not, sing of Love."

What may I say to you of the polite visit of Mr. Todd to us at Baltimore— it is my duty to tell you he was well, it is my delight, to know, that he inherits your engaging affability, & it shall be my prayer to Heaven, that he may add to the great blessings you possess, in the society of the best of Husbands, every source of joy and consolation which a Parents Heart can feel—Excuse my solicitation of one short note of remembrance in reply that I may know you are well, that my honored President is well, & that you will always love your most tenderly affectionate

Phebe P. Morris

RC (ViU: Nourse Family Papers). Docketed by DPM.

To Phoebe P. Morris

My ever dear & precious Phebe   10th. May [18]11.

I have wept over your charming letter—which proves, that I love, & regret you. Alass! why did you leave me? Lucy too has gone! and your friend may wander thro the appartments you enlivened, with solitude in her heart! I never will ceace to love & thank your Father for that short visit, until he forgets his promis to come again in a few months, with the same & an aditional daughter. Yes, I *will* know your sweet sisters, & *you shall* stay longer with me next Winter. Now, must I chide thee love for misapplying as you have done the Minstrell's sad strain—Tho eligantly quoted, it is inapplicable. Your estimable Parent, is but, in the prime of life—& his appearance, in every respect, corresponds with that age, when perfection of mind, & inteligence, interest's most, both the old & the young & tho I *would* prefer, his "sneaking up the Baltic" to his mariage, with any one (*except the lass in question*) I will not allow him, changed, from the being I admired twenty years ago. My Husband loves & admires you both, my dear Phebe, *just as* I hoped he would, my tenderest & earliest friend—in truth I cannot tell you half he says of you among the rest, he wonders I did not prevail on you to pass the summer with me. Thus, have you made, a bright impression; *where,* your warm heart has given *too much credit,* for the half express'd feelings, they cherish for you.

The Count's return'd on Sunday, & on Wednesday Eveg. they delighted me with an account of your person & accomplishments, given them, by the French Minister & *Little Carramin.* They regretted the advantage, their absence had given, to *three* Beaux, but hope, *to see you* in Phila. The Citizens appear to sympathise in my losse's, & determined that I shall not pass one hour alone. Since the day you left me I have been sorounded, or I should, at least, have given Mr Morris, a *Chapter* from *Horace* instead of a *Verse which,* I hope will induce him to reperuse the whole ode. It is, as follows—

Happy the man, and he alone,
Who master of himself can say,
Today at least hath been my own,
For I have clearly liv'd to day;
Then let to-morrow's clouds arise,
Or purer suns o'erspread the chearful skies.[1]

I am glad you like my son & I hope he will, by & by, reconcile you to his name.

The heart can never a transport know[2]—do you recollect the rest? Farewell—continue to write me & present a kiss to your sisters from your ever affect. friend

D P Madison

RC (DNCD: Morris Papers). Docketed as received 13 May.
 1. See Horace, *Odes and Epodes,* Loeb Classical Library (rept., Cambridge, Mass., 1995), 275–76.
 2. "Alas! by some degree of woe / We every bliss must gain: / The heart can ne'er a transport know, / That never feels a pain" (Lord Lyttleton, "Song: Say, Myra, what is gentle love," *Poems by the Right Honourable the Late Lord Lyttleton* [Glasgow, 1777], 58).

To Anna Cutts

8th. June [1811]

Yesterday I reccd. yours my dearest sister which tells me of the continued absence of my dear Brother—I knew he was at N York & I hope when you get this, he will be by your side—I wrote you since my recovery from a dangerious & severe illness, & I beleive Mrs. Custis wrote you also—she nursed me faithfully, as did Mrs. Galletin & others—I hope you have reccd. your bacon & your biscuit—Latrobe has not return'd yet when he does I will make the bargain, & send you the Instrument. Deblois promises it shall reach you in a few days—The little Frock is about—I waited until I could get pritty triming & now I have it—My expected articles, are yet in France (so Lee tells me). The Essex not yet come that we hear of & nothing new presents itself for me to amuse you with—We have a large dinner party today & are makeing ready for Orange directly after the 4h. july—I hear often from Lucy, she is well & promises to come to O. We hear nothi[n]g of Clairborn or of our Brother Jno. Barlows will not sail til this long expected arrival—how I long to be with you & your dear boys at this particular time but I hope Heaven will preserve you—take care not to be without good assistance allways at a moments call—remember this[1]—Docr. Sim & his wife who now live in the 6 buildings, calld to see me today—They made many enquiries after you—all your acquaintance here think of you a great deal & are anxious for you—Mrs. Mason Galletin & Eustis beged me to write their love to you—I rather expect that Congress will meet in Octr. or Novr. but all is yet uncertain—When I hear further I will write you—farewell my dear Anna for the present. I will write in a day or 2 again—keep up your spirits & kiss dear little Dick & the others for their ever affectinat Aunt

RC (MCR-S: Mary Estelle Elizabeth Cutts Papers).
1. Anna Cutts was eight months pregnant. She gave birth to Dolley Cutts on 13 July 1811 (Coles, *Coles Family of Virginia*, 179).

From Edward Coles

My Dear Cousin   NEW YORK June 10th 1811

Before I left Washington you had flattered me into the belief that I should soon have had the pleasure of receiving a letter from you. But for the expectation, and the occupation and bustle of Phia, I certainly should have complyed with my promise of writing you long before this, were it for no other purpose but to express to you how often I think of you, and the gratification I derive from holding converse with you, even thro' the formal & restrictd channel of a letter, at the distance of 250 miles.

It is impossible to comply with my promise in writing you every thing that interests me, as every hour presents something either amusing or instructive, every town abounds in hospitality, the country smiles with the highest state of cultivation, in short every thing seems to contribute to make my tour as delightful as possible.

As you expressed some curiousity to know how the Smiths &c would treat me, I requested Payne, who told me he was about to write, to inform you that I was treated quite civilly by them all, but that their displeasure with the President and yourself was very apparent. Not having heard that Miss Nicholas had left Baltimore, I concluded she was still there, and waited on Mr. & Mrs. R. Smith (who were living with old Mr Smith) with the expectation of meeting with her. She had just left Baltimore for Va. Mr. & Mrs. Smith received us very civilly, and after conversing some short time we rose to take leave, when Mrs. Smith asked me if I had been to see Gen. Smiths family, on my answering in the negative, she said she would go with me to shew me the way. We met with the same kind of reception at Gen. Smiths. Our visits were the next day returned. We dined & were twice invited to take tea at Gen Smiths. None of them made any enquiries after you, or the President, except Mrs. Gen. S., who ask[ed] after *your* health. I was quite diverted at the caution & sameness of the enquiries of Gen., and Mr. & Mrs. R. Smith "I hope you left our friends well in Washington" said they. The Smiths are said not directly to vent their spleen, but to spur on their relations & friends, many of whom are extremely abusive of the President & Col. Monroe As a proof of which, it is only necessary to tell the President that those abusive & scurrilous pieces signed Timolian, that made there appearance some time since in the Whig, are now publicly known (indeed he boasts of being the author), to be from the pen of George Stevenson, the son-in-law of P. Carr, & the nephew of the Smith who lives in the counting room of Gen. Smith.[1] I believe I have said too much about this little clan, whose vanity or weakness is such, as to make them believe that they can make & unmak[e] any administration; but you will excuse me for having written so much when I tell you that *you* are somewhat a *favourite* with them, for on meeting in the St. Dr. Leib, who is one of their leaders in Phia., he made no other enquiry but after *your* health.

We were treated with great hospitality in Phia., where we remained ten days, and frequently had the pleasure of answering the enquiries made after you by your numerous friends. We arrived here four days ago, and have, if possible, been treated with more civility than in Phia. We expect to leave this in four or five days to pass through Connecticut & Rhode Island to Boston and from thence to the District of Maine. Mr. Cutts has no doubt informed you of his having been in N. York. I regret very much I did not reach this one day sooner, as he left town the day I arrived.

I congratulate you on the safe arrival of your Brother John. The pleasure of seeing him must have been much enhanced from its having been unexpected. Present my respects to him, as well as to the President, for whom permit me to say, I feel a filial attachment, and accept for yourself the assurance of the same, with the addition of the affection of a cousin.

Edward Coles

P.S. While I was in Phia., some of the friends of B. C. Wilcocks, with whom I became slightly acquainted, requested me to recommend him as a fit person to be made consul for Canton in China. Not knowing any thing of his character or qualifications I wished to have declined it, but being pressed to say something, I promised to name him to the President as a person anxious to obtain the above appointment. I have no doubt but what he has furnished letters of recommendation, but in order to comply with my promise, I wish you to name this to the President.

E. C.

RC (NN: James Madison Papers).

1. In 1810 and 1811 the Baltimore *Whig* published a series of essays under the signature of Timoleon, the fourth century B.C. liberator of Sicily, which criticized JM and various members of the administration, in particular, Gallatin and Monroe (*PJM-PS* 3:337–38 n. 2).

To Edward Coles

15th. June [18]11.

I have had the pleasure to recce. your Welcome letter, my amiable cousin & *should* have many apoligies to make for my silence, but that I have been extreamly ill. I am just now recovering from a three weeks confinement during, which, I was most carefully nursed by some of your favorites—Mrs. Galletin Mrs Custis &. &. I am delighted to find that you have been amused & instructed—I knew it could not be otherwise when you visited those interesting places & people—The farther you proceed, the greater will be your gratification—Cousin John two, I hope is equally pleased. I think there is some danger of your both geting married before you return; if it should be so, give *me* timely notis, that I may strew roses about our Mountain paths and augment, all I can, the Enchantments that await my *new* cousins. Payne gave me the *little* account you directed, & I exult in my heart at the full indemnification we have for all their Malice,[1] in Colo. Monroe's talents & virtue.

It seems that my dear Brother was landed at Cape Henry—from thence, we suppose he went to Norfolk—I am watching every Carriage with impatience to see him arrive. I am impatient also for the arrival of the Essex on many accounts first, it would have enabled me to enliven this letter with *all* the news, that could possibly interest you & secondly, it would enable us to visit Orange—but alass it seems that *it* will never come—& we are precisely in the state of suspens[e] that you left us as it regards European affairs. The Vessel, in which, Mr. Lee *put* our Watches, was still in France, a Month ago—I regret their detention, more than I can express—The Barlows Lee & Warden are still *in waiting.* I heared the other day that your Mother & her family ware all well, but I have reccd. no letter from that quarter. Lucy writes me often & is anxious to be with us again; she hopes to meet *you* in Orange on your return home (she says) and "to be inform'd of all your adventures."

Miss Diggs is to be married next week—Docr. May & Miss Slakum, tomorrow—McGruder brought home his bride (Miss Goodwin) a few days ago—Mr & Mrs Giles are expected here in a day or two—The Miss Hamiltons are our greatest Belles—They have dances very often. We had a breackfast at the French Ministers which was quite pleasant—a small party, & profusion of Fruit—I hope you will soon see my dear Anna & her family—Tell her to hasten her preperations for Washington as *I* have no doubt, but that Congress will be call'd before Novr.[2] Farewell dear Cousin remember me allways, as your affectinate friend.

DPM

If any thing should occur, worth your knowing, & in time, I will write to you at Saco. Mr Ms best wishes, & regard, I promised to send you.

RC (MCR-S: Mary Estelle Elizabeth Cutts Papers).

    1. DPM referred here to the Smith family of Baltimore. Tensions between Secretary of State Robert Smith and JM grew to such a degree that the president removed him in 1811 and replaced him with James Monroe.

    2. DPM's message to Anna implied that JM believed that talks with the new British minister, Augustus John Foster, would fail and that Congress would convene earlier than usual to prepare for war with Great Britain. Two other messages were implicit in this one: that Coles, the president's secretary, should return before Congress met and that Anna's husband, Congressman Richard Cutts, would be needed in Washington to support the administration (Stagg, *Mr. Madison's War*, 68–69).

To Anna Cutts

20th. June [1811]

Joy Joy! to you my beloved brother & to you oh my dearest Anna—but are you sure it is a girl? Now do not hum me, because you know I have set my heart on haveing a girl, & I tell you plump, that I shall be sick if, in your haste to write, you have mistaken.[1] Every one of you[r] little rascalls are nocked up now—Why did you not tell the colour of her ⟨hair⟩ or has she any?

Yes Mad Tom Dick & Wat—Sweet as you are, stand aside, that I may kiss & squeeze the cherub—Dolley—Lucy—Ann—Mary—Julia, or what ever else she may be named, I claim her as my pet, my darling daughter—I wish Payne could marry her at once to put it out of doubt—her being my own— Last night we had a very full D. Room, where I anounced in great triumph my daughter's arrival, & had many, many Joys ⟨wi⟩shed to her & me. Mr & Mrs. Giles, with many other strangers appeared, in all their charms—This Morg. Mr. M has a short letter from John at Drummond Town near the Capes of Virga. He has been unwell there but promises to "be with us in a few days when he will explain the causes of his sudden return &. &." When he comes I will write you every thing—We look out for Pinkney & Foster every hour Mr. M haveing accts. of their being *on the way*—I mean at sea[2]—We expect too *Mr S—s book opening the eyes of the world on all our sins*[3] &. &. but I am now in great ⟨has⟩te to dispatch this scribble. ⟨I⟩ reccd. your's at 4 oClock yesterday—& am looking anxiously for another bullitin—Your own

RC (owned by Charles M. Storey, Boston, Mass., 1961). Unsigned.

    1. DPM refers to the birth of Dolley Payne Madison Cutts (1811–1838).

    2. William Pinkney was returning to the United States after six years as minister to Great

Britain. Augustus John Foster was the new British minister to the United States (JM to Jefferson, 3 May 1811, *PJM-PS* 3:296–97, 344, 374 n. 3).

3. In the last week of June, Robert Smith published his pamphlet *Address to the People of the United States*, which attacked JM personally and characterized the foreign policy of the administration as weak and indecisive (ibid., xxxii).

From Lucy Payne Washington

[July 1811]

my heart to see your dear hand on the back. I sent to the office in fear and trembling, if you had not written you wou'd have seen me, before you see this letter—I almost wish you had let my dear brother send for me—'twou'd have been a good excuse to come to you again—indeed, I have been as usual on the stool of repentance for leaving you before the fourth of July—but I am a bit of a fool, always was, and I fear always will be—or rather shall be— I hope you will take the greatest care of your precious self hereafter—and guard against colds—yes I shall be pretty certain to meet you in Orange my belov'd—and as early as you please, for I am almost kill'd here with *ennui*— yet there are some exertions to please—I shall go to a party in sheppherds Town tomorrow—and Saturday Doctr. Wood has made a ⟨. . .⟩ to complain of—I got a long ⟨. . .⟩ letter from our brother John G J[1]—he says he has calld his daughter expressly after me—he added Ann to the name he says not out of any reference to Anna—but merely that it might not be the same exactly of the dear angel that he lost[2]—he says that he loves me better than any body in the world, longs to see me, and hopes next year to come—poor Warden[3] I joked him so much about the two widows, that you think he fancied the third—but his sighing at me is all conceit—tell him I have engaged him to Mrs Crawfurd and he must not prove false hearted—but take her to france and *finish* her education—she wants a little of what the french call *Je ne se quoi*—The poor French Minister[4]—If I disliked him for speaking bad english—he ought to have hated me for speaking no french—but we'll make the matter up in Orange. Edward Coles promis'd to write and tell me all the news of Philada., but I expect he is like a goslin let loose out of a pen, and so wonder struck at all he sees that he thinks of nothing—Jack too with his scally nose and wide mouth—have you heard any thing further of the *flower* and his *gander plot*—and no news I suppose of my old *ram*—mind thats to be the name hereafter—I scarcely expect our things will ever reach America—there surely must be a fatallity attending them—I am sorry indeed our affairs over the water shou'd wear so unfavorable an aspect—but still hope we shall not be reduced to war—fighting is as much my aversion as ever it was Jeffersons. You despair too soon about our ticket—tis no bad sign being still in the wheel—I have great expectations from it yet, no doubt 'twill come out ⟨a⟩ thumping prize[5]—you must give my love to the good ladies who were attentive to you, and ⟨th⟩ank them in my name—tho' I begrudg'd them ⟨th⟩eir office—tell Miss Ann Lee—he must write me a long letter—I know he has ingenuity and wit at his fingers end—and tell me all the scandal of the City—if he does not I shall give him a rub about Mrs. Sweeney and many other little affairs of the *like kind*—Mrs. Custis must wait a bit I will answer her letter shortly. Give my love to Payne & tell him I wish he woud come here directly after the fourth of July and go with me to Orange. Poor Dolly is as big with child as she can go, I may thank your Jem for that I expect[6]—I'm sure I dont know what I shall do for a maid—I cant keep one so long—give much love to my dear brot⟨her⟩[7] and tell him I expect to make twenty barrels of corn to the acre and that the worms have not meddled with it, as he *prognosticated*—take care my darling sister of your precious self, and write often and long—long letters—Your own

Washington

The boys are at school I will give yr. love to them when they come home—poor fellows I intend taking them to germantown this fall.

RC (MCR-S: Mary Estelle Elizabeth Cutts Papers). Tops of first two pages torn.
   1. John G. Jackson.
   2. Mary Payne Jackson had given birth to a daughter named Lucy in 1803 who died three years later. In 1810 John G. Jackson married Mary Meigs, who a year later gave birth to a daughter, also named Lucy, who evidently lived but for a short time (Brown, *Voice of the New West*, 143).
   3. David Bailie Warden.
   4. Louis-Barbé-Charles Sérurier.
   5. Lucy was here referring to the election of 1812, in which DeWitt Clinton ran against JM.
   6. Dolley and Jem were slaves of Lucy Washington and the Madisons, respectively.
   7. James Madison.

To Anna Cutts

15th. July [1811]

I reccd. your last, my dear Sister & find you had yet two letters on the road from me. I hope you have them safe by this time as they treated, cheifly on the subject of our Brother—I rejoice that you continue well with the sweet girl, & have no doubt but her precious foot will be well enuf by the time she wants it. John *will not* go with Barlow—he has returnd in greater difficulties than he went, being oblidged as he thought to borrow money at Malta & if he went to france without *it,* he would be liable to arrest there—he stays, to sell his lands, arrange his debts of *all sort* here, & then he intends to go into some Business Heaven only knows what—I shall take him to O, & if possible stimulate him to this undertakeing that he may be once unembarrassed—he left in Tripola every thing worth bringing home, oweing to his illness. I have pd. 100$ for him since he got home & advanced 50$ for his current expences. Alass! I wish often that he had been never in Tripola with Davis—I know not what to wish— for the past, more than that he had allways been prudent & wise. He is now entirely dependent even if he sells his lands to advantage—but let me stop— you are at a distance & so is Lucy. We are still here waiting for M—publick business engrosses him—I cant tell how it will go—you ask me if we laughed over the Smith Pamphlet. Mr. M did, but I did not—It was too impertinent to exite any other feeling in me than anger—he will be sick of his attempt when he reads all that will be replyed to it. Cousins E. & I. have been with you no doubt—I hope Ed. got my letter at Boston—I mention'd his Brother I. A. C.[1] to Mr Barlow for his Secy but I dont know the result. We have some hope of geting of in 4 or 5 days—continue to write me & tell me your thoughts on Jno. his affairs &c.—He borrowed of More Consul at Malta 3 or 4 thousand dols. & this man *wrote* about *him* to D. We have had plays here for some time. M & myself have been 3 or 4 times—last night we went to Fennels benifit,[2] Lear, twas well acted & deep—great riot & confusion on comeing home our Horses got frightend & on one of ⟨t⟩hem jumping out of the harness, we walked home at one oClock in the morg. The city is gayer than I ever knew it in Summer—John & Payne dined at the Fr. Ministers yesterday & brought him to the Play with ⟨us.⟩ The⟨y⟩ go to Eustises to day & have numereous invitations—Apropo—Eustis declared against Smiths Pamphlet, as soon as he saw the Book. Hamilton is enraged, & writes, or intends it on the subject you may guess how the other Secys feel & speak—in short, the Smiths are down whatever harm they may have done to M—My Picture, which she sent to Paris for seating, I saw the other day in the hands of the Messenger—elegantly sett, & *he* pd. 40$ for the Copy by an artist in Paris. I expect it will be returned on my hands, at least I hope so—We wrote for Payne to go with us to O. He sends his best love to his Unkle & Aunt with kisses to his sweetheart the little Puss—My most affectinate love for my Brother & boys—I have little else to add there being no news of any sort, & I cant tell the state of negotiation with Foster—he enquir'd after you &. &. He has taken Hillens house,[3] & intends to give Balls—I have seen little of him—farewell my dear Sister—John is out,

& you know his stile of forgeting home, & neglecting to write—I told you the Hamiltons had visited Lucy—I hear little of Govr. C. he cant leave his station for months to come.

RC (MCR-S: Mary Estelle Elizabeth Cutts Papers). Unsigned.
   1. Edward Coles was traveling with his cousin Isaac Coles (1777–1820) of Springwood in Halifax County. Edward Coles also had a brother named Isaac (1780–1841), who lived at Enniscorthy in Albemarle County, Va., and added "A." as a middle initial to distinguish himself from his slightly older cousin (Coles, *Coles Family of Virginia*, 52, 63, 95).
   2. James Fennell (1766–1816) was a London-born actor who had been working in the United States since 1793. Three of his performances were advertised in the *National Intelligencer* in July 1811 (Van Horne and Formwalt, *Correspondence of Latrobe* 2:933 n. 9).
   3. Foster rented a house on the northwest corner of Pennsylvania Avenue and Nineteenth Street (Charles O. Paullin, "Early British Diplomats in Washington," *Records of the Columbia Historical Society* 44–45 [1942–43]: 249).

To Anna Cutts

August 19th. [1811]

I have this moment reccd. yours my beloved in which you tell me of your poor breast—Would to heaven I could releave you in any way—Alass we cannot assist each other even in the sweet consolations of sympathy so far apart— I trust before this you have got well—The Milk & bread I am told, will cure, of itself—especially after lanceing—but your precious daughter—What shall we do? when you are able, come on, & stop with Dr Physick—many, many, have been made perfect by [his] care, & why may we not hope that *her* dr. foot will be streighten'd with care—Yes I am sure it will—Neither Lucy or John are with me—tho the House is now full of ⟨th⟩e family—Wm. Ms wife Children & &. &. I have scarcly a momme[n]t to breath—they ⟨a⟩re here for some days—Lucy is well—has ⟨h⟩ad the Hamiltons & Eustises to visit her—is ⟨di⟩spleased at John for not going for her & I question whether she will come this summer—John was to follow us directly—but 3 weeks gone by & he not come—you may guess at my anxiety—he set out of from W. several day[s] ago for O but he lingers I know not where—We have had Mr & Mrs. Basset 2 days—expect Mr & Mrs Eustis—Mrs. Page & family every day—& all these people, with a Miss Homerzill of Richmond are here—but Mitchell is with us & we have 4 aditional chambers, but my head is turned—my heart oppressed. I am miserable for John, & anxious for you—We shall be in W early in Octor. Pray get well & come to me—I have only time to add that I wrote you last week, & told you every thing I could think of—Kiss the dear boys for me &

present my best affection to my dear Brother—farewell my dear sister—try to keep up your spirits for all our sakes.

RC (MCR-S: Mary Estelle Elizabeth Cutts Papers).

To Ruth Barlow

Ever dear & Valued friends   Novr. 15th. 1811.

Your short Notes, which gave us an account of your progress on the Water, were grateful indeed—but the news of your safe arrival in France, infinitely more so. Many, many are the questions that rise to my lips—such as how did you bear the Voyage? how is our precious Clara, Mr Barlow, Mr Lee? I hope soon to know these things, which I confess interests *me* more than all the success of your Mission of which few have a doubt—even the Enemies of *our* Minister admit his talents & Virtue, how then, can any of *them* doubt?

We passed two Months on our mountain in health & peace—return'd the 1st. Octor to a sick & afflicted city—The unfinished Canal[1] caused a bilious fever to prevail almost, thro' all its streets—many died & Congress conven'd, in some dread of contagion—Happily all fears are, now, over & public business engrosses them. Jno. R——h is the only one (as yet) who seems hostile to a quiet House. They have before them the Nomination of Colo. M & some lesser appointments.[2] I believe they are in a disposition to do as they are advised.

The Judges are not yet made—Mr Duvall is thought of for Maryland, & Mr Adams haveing declin'd, to return or accept, gives an oppertny for G—— to try again.[3] I am sorry to tell you of the translation of the Pahlens to Rio Janiro—Mr. Dashcoff takes their place—The French Minister is still delighted with Calirama, & takes pleasure in beautifying the grounds[4]— Mrs. Baldwin, who came to see me, & whom I visited, was well & chearful a few days ago—She will write you a Vol. no doubt, & she will tell you of the health of your little Dog—Many others will write you my dear friend & leave me but little to inform you of. Mr M is writeing also he will tell you, that he has settled the business of the Chesapeak with Mr Foster & &.[5]

Tell our estimable Lee that —— conduct has not injured him here, on the contrary, it ex[c]ited a horror of the persicutor & we trust that Heaven will prosper him & his family[6]—I have not yet begun *my Jurnal* as I had nothing remarkable to narrate—Mr Barlow knows the disposition of *our World* better than I do, & from all *I lern* good sense & principle will prevail over *Intrigue* & *vanity*—The instance of Mr R. S. is strikeing.[7] The poor man is down! even his Brother professes to have borne no part, & comes *here* as usial—Madame Bon——e too, who has been some weeks in Toun, says *she is on our side*. You will see that Colvin declares himself the author of the *boasted* letters—some think this a finishing stroke—but I, absolutely pity him for "he has fallen, fallen—from his high Estate"! We have new Members in abundance—their wives daughters &. &. and I, never felt the entertainment of company, oppressive until now—Oh! I wish I was in France with you, for a little relaxation—My Sister Washington is with me, but never will forgive me refuseing to let her go with you—but I know it is better for her to remain with me. My poor Brother has been ill ever since you left us, until now. As you have every thing that is beautiful; & we have nothing—I will ask the favor of you to send me by safe Vessels—large Headdresses a few Flowers, Feathers, gloves & stockings (Black & White) or any other pritty thing, suitable to an Economist & draw on my Husband for the Amt.

We have a House full of visitors & I must conclude with love & prayers for you all, my best friends.

D. P. Madison

Present my respects, & best wishes to Mr Warden

RC (CSmH).

1. A canal to connect Tiber Creek to the Anacostia River, linking the eastern and western parts of the capital, was part of the original plan of the city. Congress first chartered a canal company in 1802, but it was not until the Washington Canal Company's charter was granted in 1809 that subscriptions were filled, with construction beginning in 1810. Work progressed by fits and starts, with the canal finally opening in the fall of 1815 (Van Horne and Formwalt, *Correspondence of Latrobe* 2:821–24).

2. DPM refers here to John Randolph of Roanoke and JM's nomination of James Monroe to be secretary of state.

3. The death of Associate Justice Samuel Chase in June had left a seat vacant on the Supreme Court. Despite Gideon Granger's desire for a seat on the court, JM offered it to Gabriel Duvall (*PJM-PS* 3:31 and n., 264 n. 13).

4. The Barlows had rented their estate, Kalorama, to the French minister Sérurier.

5. On 22 June 1807 the British naval ship *Leopard*, after demanding the return of deserters and meeting refusal, fired on the U.S. frigate *Chesapeake* off Hampton Roads, Va. Unprepared for battle, the *Chesapeake* soon surrendered, with three Americans killed and eighteen wounded. Public response in the United States was angry and indignant, with many calling for war. The issue remained unresolved until November 1811 (Spencer C. Tucker, "Chesapeake-Leopard Affair," in Heidler and Heidler, *Encyclopedia of the War of 1812*, 96–97).

6. The persecutor of William Lee was probably John Armstrong (*PJM-PS* 4:23 n. 11).

7. Robert Smith.

From Joel Barlow

Dear Mrs Madison   PARIS 21 Dec 1811.

I send you the oddest present that you will recieve from France if not of the least value. It is a beetroot, of that sort that they make so much noise about as cultivated for sugar. This root weighs about 14½ pounds our weight. The man who gave it me said he could give me a hundred from his garden that would weigh a thousand pounds. Put it in your garden for seed, not that I think it worth our while to make sugar of them, but to eat & feed our sheep & cattle. It is the same as our common beet, but the seed taken from more vigorous plants may produce more vigorous ones. Our girls will write you about Courts & fashions & finery. For my part, tho I have got to be a prodigious fine gentleman & a perfect cortier, I dont like to talk about it. I have been here three months at work very hard for our blessed country yet I am afraid I shall have produced but little effect, & the president may think I have been idle. If he should approve my conduct I wish you would let me know it. For you cannot reallize how much I am attached to him & his administration. It is therefore natural that I should be anxious to merit his approbation.

The greatest Sin I have committed is detaining the frigate so long. I have endeavored to explain this both in my official dispatch to the Secy of State & in my private letter to Mr. Madison, sent yesterday by way of England.[1] I ought to add that the Emperor, who assumed such an air of goodness to me at the first audience & every time since, desired expressly that I would detain her for the ministers answer to my great note. This answer, he assured me with his own mouth at the audience would be satisfactory. And as I was told repeatedly not only by the duke but by every one else that came near the emperor, that he was very much struck with my note & was probably changing his system relative to the U. States, I thought I could not with a decent respect to him, & ought not for the inter[e]st of our govt. to send off the frigate under such circumstances.

I still believe he is changing his system & that I shall have the result in a day or two. We wrote you from mid ocean ten days out—We dont know whether you got the letter—Yr. obt. St.

                                                    J. Barlow

You cannot think how my precious wife has renewed her life since her terrible fever of last winter. She has not known so much health before in 20 years as within the last six months. We found our own convenient & elegant house vacant, & so we have moved into it. It is well situated airy & handsome, & the garden, now grown up to a thicket, is more interesting to us from having been planted by our own hands.

RC (DLC: DPM Papers). Docketed by DPM "You must send this back to me."

1. In his private letter to JM of 19 Dec., Barlow described Napoleon's reaction to a note the U.S. minister had presented to Hugues-Bernard Maret, duc de Bassano, Napoleon's foreign minister, and conveyed to JM the hope that he would soon be able to negotiate a full and satisfactory adjustment of Franco-American difficulties, including commercial restrictions that had bedeviled U.S. trade (*PJM-PS* 4:76–77 and nn.).

To Anna Cutts

My dearest Sister   22 Decr. [1811]

I reccd. your short letter of the 7th. & before this I trust you have the arrears of my letters to you—26th. I have rarely had such a treat my beloved, as on the last night—it was the recct. of yours of the 19th. & being longer & fuller than the preceeding letters, it raised my spirits—which had been low for some time, occation'd by sore ears & deafness—The deafness continues, & distresses me beyond any thing that ever ail'd me—it may be cold still, & I may throw it of—the dear precious Children—how I long to kiss them—It is indeed gratifying to my heart to be loved & rememberd by your precious boys whom I love as my own—The darling daughter I have yet to make an interest in—Tell Madison Thomas Walter & Ricd. that I send them a thousand kisses & that I have taken care of their Waggon Cradle & all their little things to restore to them, with many others—No Constitution heard of yet—The Hornet went to take dispatches & to let *them know* our ⟨determination⟩ to fight for our rights. I expect very little by the return of these Vessels because Lee was the only one I commissiond & he told me he could get nothing without the *mony*.[1] I made up *as much* as I could 200$ & *gave* it to him with a small Memo. He read the one we made jointly, & said the articles would amt. to 600$ the sum was so far beyond what I had calculated & what I could give him that, I made a new one & trusted to another oppty. which I have not had again—The Barlows did not seem the sort of People to commission & I gave them none at all—I wrote by the Hornet to Mrs. B & beged her to send me any thing that she thought would suit me & draw on Mr M for the Amt. I'm affraid that I shall not obtain a new fashion'd Pattern for you—but I will make your Cap which is very much worn here, & look for a M. dress to copy—

your shoes are safe here from Mrs. Burke. I have nothing new this winter but the Lyons silk ⟨. . .⟩ Black Velvet—2 bonits made by ⟨. . .⟩ very smart & becoming ⟨. . .⟩ out this winter ⟨. . .⟩ evg.— once sleighing to Alexa. for an hour in Taylors Sleigh Foster Miss Caton P Morris Lucy Jno. & a whole dozen more—We have had the coldest weather ever felt here, & since yours which I hope & trust you found not more trying than we did—I am rejoiced that you dress warm & take care of you[r]selves—I hope also that my dear Brothers Sholde[r] has got well as you do not speak of it—Lucy wrote you a long letter which I enclosed & you [ha]ve by this time I tru[s]t—Fosters party took place the other night all went but me it was Elegant & on the Queens birth night.[2] The F Min[i]ster gives another tomorrow night. They all go again—not I— The Intrigu[e]s for P. & Vice P. go on but I expect it may terminate as the last did—The Clintons Smiths Snyders—Armstrongs are all in the field—I believe there will be War as M see's no end to our perplexities without it— they are going on with the preperations to [g]reat extent—Genl. Dearborn you know is nominated to command—I told you these things ⟨in⟩ my last— what do *you* think of them? We had another shock of Earth Quake on Wednesdy Night & Thursday Morg—Jno. will go into the army if he can get a commission & no doubt he will get one—he has *taken up* a good deal by my persuasion. I have dressed him & forced him to change bad for good society—In the spring I hope he'l go to see after his Lands &c. Congress have talked (some of them) of adjourning for 2 months, but it is mearly talk I beleive & I expect they will sit til May—before then I trust you will be able to come on, as the roads will be good in April—I sent to know the fate of your Ticket but Millegan was gone to Baltimore & the young man could not tell, I will go myself in a day or 2 & write you the result. I hope you will have better fortune than I had & *all of this* house—our friends are well in Virg. I expect ⟨Jim?⟩ in a few days—Thornton is better & our neighbours are going on as usial—Becky Coles was to be married on the 20th. Cousin I. went to her Weeding after waiting here 2 or 3 weeks for ⟨his comm⟩ission in the Army, which was not yet ⟨. . .⟩ & their Ladies go on pritty well—they ⟨have g⟩iven no Evg. parties ⟨. . .⟩ Granger is ⟨. . .⟩ thing . . .

RC (MCR-S: Mary Estelle Elizabeth Cutts Papers). Bottom of pages torn.

    1. DPM had commissioned William Lee, U.S. commercial agent at Bordeaux, to purchase various items for her.

    2. Foster wrote to his mother that he had given a ball for the queen's birthday, adding, "I am afraid my rooms will burst" (Parr, "Foster," 325).

From Clara Baldwin

PARIS 1 January 1812

I wish you a happy new year my dear Mrs Madison & that it may be the happiest of your life & may every succeeding one be the same.

Pray do not be angry with me dear madam for writing another letter—it is a long time since I wrote the first. I believed then that the frigate would sail immediately which is my apology for its ancient date. It is so pleasant to complain to those we love, & whom we know love us, that I can not refrain from telling you that these french surgeons are almost as spiteful as I found Dr Worthington, in Washington, not quite how ever, for the former only confines me to my room, & the latter confined me to my bed—was ever any thing so cruel—in Paris too—for this month at least I am completely secluded & tho we have been here three months I have seen nobody or nothing—one thing they cannot deprive me of, contentment—tho they shut out the world they cannot happiness—I read write sew, sing, make rhimes, & am as happy as the day is long—I have no one to please & amuse but myself & that I can always do—only write me now & then, say you think of me some times, & love me a little, & I shall envy no one.

I am sure you will be pleased with Lees purchases, we think them chosen with a great deal of taste & judgment—never a poor fellow worked harder or took more pains to endevour to give satisfaction—he has done nothing else this two months but waddle round Paris & cull from the magazines of fashion—he ought to thank you for it, for it has reduced him to quite a decent size, he can trot about now like a youngish man & even stoop upon extraordinary occasions.

Kind & respectful remembrance to Mr. Madison your sisters Mrs Nourse—Duval & all the dear ladies of W—— who still remember me with esteem & affection ever yours

C Baldwin

I forget every word I wrote in my first letter if there is any treason against this government please to suppress it.

RC (DLC: DPM Papers).

From Ruth Barlow

My dear Madam   PARIS 4. March. 1812

As it is uncertain whether the Neptune, which is to take this will not be taken into England I shall write a few lines only—first, to thank you for your very kind letter by the Hornet, & for all your goodness to us—& then, to request a good Portrait of our excellent President, which is so often asked for. I am mortified not to have it hanging up in our drawing room—if I dare, would ask for yours the same size to hang beside it. I hope you will be able to gratify us. Will you let sister Washington come & pass next winter with us? I fear she has not forgiven me for not insisting more on her coming. It would indeed have given me great pleasure to have her with us but I saw you did not wish it. I now ask your permission—before I ask her to come. I think however she will be married before next winter & so give us the slip—tell her to wait a little she may perhaps break a few more hearts here[1]—poor Clara is obliged to reserve her Man slaughter for next winter. She has been confined three Months with her knee. The Surgeons (of which we have the first) say she must be very quiet & she will get well—We are very glad to hear there is such a spirit of union in public affairs—we hope things will yet go right here & that good may come out of evil—My health continues better than I expected, it has supported a vast deal of fatigue of every kind—if we can serve our country & do any thing which may add to the honor & prosperity of the present Administration we shall esteem ourselves most happy—We are lamenting over the sad news from Richmond[2]—it must have caused you a melancholly winter. My husband will I believe add something to this letter—& I hope make it better—I want to send you some pretty things in embroidery which are the high style here, gold & silfer, with silk done on Mul—Mr. Lee has sent you so much of every kind of dress, & it is so dificult to send to the Port, & then to get any one to take charge of valuable things, that I shall send nothing. Be so good my dear Madam as to tell me what you would like—if you wish things assorted here— China, or any thing else, nothing can give us so much pleasure as to [be] able [to] serve you. Forever your Obld. & affectinate frd.

                                                              R. Barlow

RC (ViU); Tr (MH). RC docketed by DPM.

1. After her husband George Steptoe Washington died in 1808, DPM's sister Lucy often lived at the White House and was considered a great belle in Washington society. She married Supreme Court associate justice Thomas Todd on 29 March 1812 (Ketcham, *James Madison,* 519).

2. On the evening of 26 Dec. 1811, a fire burned down the Richmond Theatre, killing a hundred people and injuring many more (John G. Jackson to JM, 27 Dec. 1811, *PJM-PS* 4:94–95 and n. 1).

To Anna Cutts

My beloved sister   20th March [1812]

Be⟨fore⟩ this reaches you Lucy will be ⟨mar⟩ried to Judge Todd of Kentucky! Yes—sudden as it is, we *must* be reconciled to it from her choice of a Man of the most estimable character, best principles, & high talents—he is a widower with five child⟨ren,⟩ one daughter married, the others provided ⟨for and⟩ not to live with them—residence, in Lexington, very near our old fd. Taylor, where there is fine society good schools for her Children, in short my dear Anna, tho it breaks my heart to find myself left far from my sister I rejoice at the Husband ⟨she⟩ will have, & the Brother we shall acquire. As a Supreme Judge he is oblidged to come h⟨ere⟩ for 2 months every winter & he binds himself to bring her to her fds. when she pleases to come—They have appointed tomorrow week to be married & to go of for Hairwood next day, stay a week & with the Children, proceed to Lexington—Lucy is in deep distress & you may suppose that my greaf is not slight—My nights are miserable & so are my days—Jno. is still in his old habits, & will do nothing for himself. ⟨. . .⟩ do nothing but cry—& I can scar⟨cely⟩ refrain ⟨from?⟩ or can I realize the event, it has been so expidiceously effected—I can say little else to you at this moment—all is bustle here—Electioneering yet. De Wit &. &. & The Smiths & I know not who all, intend to break us down—The Federalists affront⟨ed to a⟩ Man—not one (I mean of the 2 houses of ⟨Cong⟩ress) will enter Ms door since the communication of (Henry) to Congress[1]—except Le Roy Livingston who *considers* him self attatched by his appt. of Colo. to the Gov. Genl. Dearborn has had a fall which, tho not serious, confines him ⟨to⟩ his house— I wish you were here ⟨at⟩ this mome[n]t—P M[2] is still waiting for her Father—Adeiu—I will send you something in a day or 2 & save you shoes & other things from france—I will say little about the extravigan⟨ce⟩ of Mr. Lee—the duties charges &&.

RC (ViU); Tr (MCR-S: Mary Estelle Elizabeth Cutts Papers). RC torn by removal of seal. Words in angle brackets supplied from Tr made by Mary Cutts.

1. John Henry was an Irishman who in 1808 had been employed by the British to gath information on political disaffection in New England. In 1812 he sold his letters and report to the Madison administration for the staggering sum of $50,000. JM forwarded these letters to

Congress, presumably to bring Anglo-American relations to the point of rupture while tarring the Federalists with disaffection and bolstering his own administration. Although at first the maneuver seemed to work, by the third week in March JM was greatly embarrassed as it became known that he had paid for the documents without being able to identify any potential traitors in New England. Both the Federalists and the factions in his own party led by Dewitt Clinton and Robert and Samuel Smith took great glee in JM's discomfort (Stagg, *Mr. Madison's War*, 93–99).

2. Phoebe Morris.

To Anna Cutts

[ca. 27 March 1812]

The Vice P lies dangeriously ill—Ele[c]tioneering for his office goes on beyond all description. The World seems runing Mad, what with one thing & another—The Feds. as I told you, ware all affronted with M, refused to dine or come but they have changed their *tack*—last *night* & the *night* before, our rooms ware crouded with republicans, & such a ralying of our party has alarm'd them into a *return*. They came in a large party last night also & are continuelly calling—Even D. R. Will⟨iams⟩ who is a fine fellow, came last night. The old & the young Muster'd—The War business goes on slowly—but I fear twill be sure—Where is Mr Cs vessells? Why dont he get them in? What can be done for him?

Lucy intends to write you before she goes & we have persuaded Jno. to go with—he has to buy a Horse cloaths & many &c &c. I am mending & fixing his wardrobe, & trust in Heaven twill be for his good—I. Coles is here—made a Major & is waiting to be groomsman—so you will immagin & partake of my cares—as well as of my regrets. Cant you come on this Spring & go with us to Orange? Write me what you wish & intend to ⟨do.⟩ Congress will sit til may—perhaps longer

RC (MCR-S: Mary Estelle Elizabeth Cutts Papers). Probably one page of a longer letter.

To Anna Cutts

[8 April 1812]

I have just now reccd. yours of the 30th. March my beloved sister—It cause's me more greaf than I can speak—your constant indisposition your low spirits—every thing that disturbs you never fails to vibrate thro all my heart—I flattered myself that you ware healthy & happy—Without health we enjoy nothing—Your estimable Husband, lovely children fail to yeald you that sweet peace which we aught only to seek for in this world. Try to get ready & come to me—I think you would soon be well if you once set of on your jurney to your sister who longs to fold you to her heart & to restore your system to its naturel strength by her cares—May will soon be here lock up your property & leave it—I wrote you two letters to prepare you for Lucys Marriage— the Night she was married I inclosed one from her—since that I wrote you of her departure, & that of Jno. 3 days after to join her—I now enclose you the first letter she has written. I have not yet heared from Jno. but have no doubt of his being at Hairwood & doing well with *them*—It is not worth while to tell you the particulars of his *last* frolick, or the sum he spent on it. *I refixed* him, with *my all even* my *credit,* & set him of in a Hack, with his frd. Green, whose expenses I also pd., in order to secure his retreat *from this den of Theaves.* Miss Ms visit of 3 weeks terminates in ⟨. . . ⟩. ⟨We are a little⟩ more calm as to Politicks, or rather I hear less about it—the Vice P. is like to get well—Congress talk of adjourning in a few days but I cant tell yet, whether they will or not— I wrote you that the Embargo was to take place—but I fear they intercept my letters—you dont speak of them—did you get my Childs Necklace & earings? Why will you talk of not wanting pretty things my dear Anna, & how can you think I would, or could, wear mine, unless you partook—dont give way to such notions but remember we have a goodly prospect before us of injoying together, the blessings an approveing Heaven has already bestowed upon us—I told you how amiable & respectable Judge Todd is—how wise Lucy was to chuse him in preferance to the gay flirts who coarted her—yes—my regrets are all selfish—not for her, but myself I am sorry—she will be here in Jany. next to stay 2 or 3 months, & every winter the same—perhaps the 7 supreme Judges will be obligded to live at or near the seat of Govt. M thinks it will come to that—I shall save you a white sattin, a white crape, 6 or 8 pr. shoes dito stockings—Flowers, gloves p. Hankerchifs, a pritty comb—a necklace of false pearls &. &. You inquired some time ago, what was to *pay* with Davis[1]— I will ⟨. . .⟩ he & Granger had, *had* some confidential *confab* but Davis came here few days ago & explaind all, when I found he had acted like a friend, & Mr Granger like a *feind*—so that as you know what G. has been, & what he has *done,* years ago, I should tell you nothing new when I repeated his *conduct* & his *communications* to Davis—It is all beneath our notis tho, G. is not below our contempt & hatred—I *have* all the *corrispondenc[e]* in my keeping for you when we meet[2]—Green has this moment returnd from Hairwood where he left Jno. Lucy & all well & gay & preparing to set out for K——y.

My dr Anna frd. Little is in Baltimo—but I wish & seriously advise the

simple weak french brandy & Water for your Eyes and ears—dont take phis-
ick, unless a little cream of tarter, as a drink, & Magnesia now & then—tis
weakness that continues thy sad complaint so long I am fully persuaided—remember that Dr. Honyman cured my eyes, in this simple way—& I allwa[y]s
have continued the practice, & know the eutility of the system—I will watch
for Fd. Little & write you the mome[n]t she comes—adeiu for the present—
with love & kisses for you all, & I am join'd by Mr. M. Ed. Payne & Phebe your
own Sister

RC and Tr (MCR-S: Mary Estelle Elizabeth Cutts Papers). RC undated; date assigned from Tr.
The tops of the second and third pages of the RC have been clipped. Letters and words in angle
brackets have been supplied, where possible, by the Tr.
    1. This was probably George Davis, although it could also be his brother, Matthew L.
Davis. The latter was active in Republican Party circles in New York. John C. Payne had served
as George Davis's secretary in the consulate at Tripoli.
    2. DPM loathed longtime postmaster general Gideon Granger. Besides his conflicts with
JM—he had supported George Clinton for the presidency in 1808, greatly resented being
passed over for an appointment to the Supreme Court in 1810, and opposed the war with
Great Britain—Granger seemed to have acted in a particularly offensive way toward DPM
and her sister Anna Cutts. By 1814, during the patronage fight that would ultimately lead to his
firing, Granger was not above threatening to revive rumors of the sisters' unchastity
(Ketcham, *James Madison*, 521, 569).

To Anna Cutts

[ca. 15 April 1812]
⟨I wrote you⟩ that the Embargo would ta⟨ke place⟩ 3 or 4 days before
it did, & I had a ⟨better right⟩ to do so than the Fedl. Member. Genl Dea⟨r-
born⟩ will leave this in a few days—I went to Mrs. Eustis last sunday night
with Mr & M⟨rs⟩ M. Mrs. Mason—Mm Bon——e Miss Spear, ⟨Mrs.⟩ Custis
& myself ware the ladies. Foster ⟨Ser⟩urier Genl Dearborn D. Brent & 2 or 3
other men—but dull—Mrs. Hamilton & Mrs. Eus⟨tis⟩ have had parties, no
other of the *Heads*—Mrs. Rush is liveing in the House Graham left near
Pahlens—she looks like dea⟨th⟩ & is seldom out—qu[i]te big again—but
elsew⟨ays⟩ as usial. Congress will not adjourn *I believe*, ⟨tho⟩ it has been much
spoken of, the intention, is on the decline, from an idea that it will ha⟨ve⟩ a bad
impression, both in & out of our count⟨ry⟩—So now my dear Anna May will
smi⟨le⟩ on your journey, & if you take it, you wi⟨ll⟩ be the better in all respects
I trust—wi⟨ll you⟩ tell me when & how, you'l set out—did you get L⟨ucy's⟩
Letter written the day of her wedding? Kiss the dear boy⟨s⟩ ⟨. . .⟩ wish I ⟨. . .⟩
constantly painting to myself ⟨. . .⟩ in Dolley—Mr. M gives me some ⟨pa⟩pers

to enclose—farewell my dr sister ⟨&⟩ Brother ever yours—M, Payne Ed. Phebe send you kisses & love—I recd. ⟨a⟩ letter by a ship—3 days ago from Mrs Barlow which I intended to send but canot ⟨fi⟩nd it—she says the Hornet will sail ⟨in⟩ a few days, that Mr. B detains it to bring a Treaty of Comerce & &. That every prospect is fair in that quarter & & &. Mrs. Baldwin confined for 3 months, with her knee.

RC and partial Tr (MCR-S: Mary Estelle Elizabeth Cutts Papers). RC unsigned. Ms incomplete and torn. Words and letters in angle brackets supplied from the Tr.

From Lucy Washington Todd

PITSBURG April 18th. 1812.

We have just arriv'd my best darling, at this smoky place—after a delightful trip—you are amazed that I shou'd say so no doubt—for never surely was a journey more dreaded but I hope my account being so favorable will almost induce you to *visit* us—the weather except the last two days was very fine—the roads one thousand times better than yours from Washington to MontPelier—indeed you have no conception how very good they are—I dont feel the least fatigued myself, the children bore the journey astonishingly. My dear husband who insisted on riding in the Carriage all the way says he is a little sore about the *elbows*—I'm sure he must have had by far the worst of it, gentlemen in general not being fond of close Carriages—we had four good horses and did sail along to my amazement—Seven days brought us here, the accomidation too was delightful—good beds and excellent fare—the Waggon with our furniture and things from HareWood arriv'd yesterday so that we are almost ready to take the boat for our sail down the Ohio—I have the pleasure to tell you my dearest sister that John is pleased with his trip has behav'd quite correct and appears in much better health than when he arriv'd at the Wood—tho' he amused us on the road with complaints of the loss of his *hide,* he rode the Judges horse so that his expenses have been no great deal, and his spirits are better than I have known them for some time—I hope by kindness and attention he may be brought to reason yet—your dear darling letter has arriv'd. O my best belov'd sister I cant describe my sensations when I read it—My tears blinded me—but they were tears of joy to know that you were well and often thinking of us indeed If I had not reciev'd a letter from you at this place I shou'd have pined my very life out—yes no doubt there were plenty of *observers*—as well as *enquirers*—at the drawing room—I feel greatly flatter'd at

161

the regret of my friends and acquaintence, the Verses you sent were very good indeed and caused us a hearty laugh and me a *kiss extra*—tho' I cant complain of a *scarcity at any time*—My dear husband Says the Wine shall be kept sacred for you and he hopes indeed you will pledge him in Many a glass. ⟨He got⟩ quite warm on the subject and almost swore he would bring you out next Spring, O that we cou'd; O pray that hope be realized. I'm in extacy at the Idea—the reality wou'd run me wild I expect—poor Anthony, and poor Phebe—I wish indeed you cou'd be reliev'd of their *agreeable* company—for it must have arriv'd to a trying point. I expected cousin Edward & herself wou'd scarcely part without blows—they were very near it when I left them—her letter was very amusing. I have not perform'd my promise of writing to her—indeed I shall write so often to you that my time and *talents* will be monopolized. I feel very much provoked at that old hag Mrs. Duval—yet I scarcely think her worth your notice every body knows her disposition to venom and no body loves or respects her—tho if I had her head here I'd box her ears—I have been taking a view of this place in company with Mrs. HollingsWorth a lady of the judges acquaintance it improves on inspection we went to the glass house to choose some ware—the glass made here is very tasty indeed we selected what we wanted and bought a little snuff to comfort us in our sail down the river—poor Anna she must have been surprised at my sudden exit—I hope when she arrives you may find comfort in her society—yet *I hope still she may scarcely fill the void I have left*—dont think me selfish dear sister—you know I always was jealous of you because I wish to be first in your affections—I will do all in my power towards our poor dear brothers reformation, and am not without hope that he may return to you an alter'd Man—I cannot believe that with his heart and understanding he will prove incorrigible—I have written to Jackson to let him know—*Who I am*—how is my dear brother James—tell him I hope he Misses me at Meals and takes his usual walk to and fro in the little sitting room in the even'g—oh! and when he Kisses you—he was always so fearful of making my *mouth water*—*tell him I get kisses now that wou'd make his mouth run over*—tell cousin Ned not to forget his promise of writing to me—I will write to him as soon as I reach home—who cou'd have been so very busy as to say Russell did not pay *his devoirs at my shrine* but as you justly observe tis beneath our notice—I suppose Payne has return'd to Baltimore—Phebe says he was a gallant of the first *water*—when you write give much love to him from me—and give my love to Mrs. Gallatin—the Hamiltons Mrs. Eustis—tell Mrs. Eustis to write me all the news of W—— how Mrs Custis and the Count *progress in their loves*—and what little *Boney* and Spear are doing—If Mrs. Clay should not have started before this reaches you—I wish you cou'd send me a handsome fashionable Spring hat or Bonnet and trust me till I see you—I shou'd like right well to attend your summer session—tho' I do declare my love that you are the only inducement now—for my happiness, and pleasure, run in a different channel to what, they were wont to do. Phebes comparing the judge to still champaign—was an error in judgment—as you may tell by his postscript—tho I hope you wont credit the half of it—*he* is only in *hopes it* may be so—hurry off the Wine my dear sister the journey w⟨ill⟩ improve it greatly—and I hope induce brother to come & taste it with you, and *us* next spring—and now my sweetest let me hope (and disappoint me not) that you will write eve⟨ry⟩ Mail and tell me every thing, let me tho far distant, still share thy joys—and sorrows if any thou shou'dst have but heaven I hope will avert all grief from thee my be⟨st⟩ belov'd Sister, Adieu—from Lexington I shall write aga⟨in⟩ ever thine, with constancy and truth.

L W Todd

RC (MCR-S: Mary Estelle Elizabeth Cutts Papers).

To Ruth Barlow

[ca. 19 April 1812]

This unexpected oppertunity, & short notis scarcely gives me time to embrace you, round my beloved friends—still I do it, with my whole heart. I have reccd. *all* your valuable letters—Mr Barlows—my dear Clara's—& Mr Lee's by the Constitution, with one from Mr Warden, all which I would answer now; but that the dispatches close in one hour—& I can only return, to each individuel, my best thanks, for their goodness & friendship. Before this, you know of our Embargo—to be followed by War!! Yes—that terrible event is at hand, & yet England wants faith! Our appointments for the purpose are generally made, & the Recruiting business goes on with alackrity—The Major Gens. are H. Dearborn Th——s Pinkney—S.C.—Brigr. Genl. Joseph Bloomfield, N.Y. Js Winchester Tenee. Wm. Polk, N.C. Wm. Hull Mitchn. Territory— Quarter Master Genl. Morgan Lewis—&.&. You will have an acct. of our political situation in all its shades, by this Vessel—We anticipate *some little* contention among ourselves, on the death of the Vice President, whose Physians give out, that he cannot live til morning![1] The sentiment is, at present, in favor of Jno. Langdon as his successor. Congress will remain in session perhaps, til July—If not, full powers to declare War, will be vested in the President. Your letters by the Neptune ware particularly acceptable as we had been

163

annoyed by a report, that the Emperor had *seazed* The Hornet &. &. and as I *promised* to write you things, you aught to know you will pardon me when I say *aught*, that gives you pain—I am prepareing you, for the disappobation, express'd at Mr Barlow's haveing *told* the state of his *Negociation*, to Mr. *Granger* who directly gave it circulation & a place in the N. Papers—In the *detail* of objections to *this* communication is—"that you may yet be disappointed"—That "the anticipation of such a Treaty, might cause *improper speculations*—That Mr G. was not a proper chanel" &. &. All this is from the *people*, not from the Cabinet—yet you know every thing *vibrates* there.[2] Tell Mr Lee, that I shall be ever greatful for the fatigue & trouble he must have experienced for my sake, in procureing the valuable collection he sent me—His bill was paid immediately, but he will be astonished at the whole amt. duties &. &. two thousand dollars—I am affraid that I never shall send for any thing more—The dresses, & every other article, indeed, is beautiful—The head's I could not get on, being two tight around—Their price was so high, that the Ladies of my acquaintance would neither buy or swap one, so that I shall lay them by for next Winter, & then enlarge & make them fit. My shoes ware just a size two short, but the flowers, trimings & ornaments, are enchanting. I wish I could gratify you my dear friend, with the Portraits you mention, but I see little prospect of doing so. Steward is far from us & we have no Painter of skill in this quarter—be assured if an oppertunity occurs, I will employ it to send you such, as you shall approve.

You have kindly recollected my dear Lucy—she was maried on the 30th. of March to Judge Todd, & left me the next day for Lexington in Kentucky—I have been fill'd with *selfish* regrets. Her union is a most happy one & met our entire approbation—her Husband is of the supreme court, & oblidged to pass a great deal of time here, which lessens *my* misfortune—he is amiable, inteligent, in short, he is all that I could wish in a brother. John has gone with them, & you now see *me*, the *very* shadow of my Husband. My sister Cutts did not visit us the last winter, but she will soon be here to console me, so that as ever, my prospect is tinctured with hope!

My precious Clary—I cannot exp[r]ess my sorrow at your confinement—pray sit still & charm me with a *journal;* your letters deserve & shall be fully requited, by the first Dispatch that I can *find out* in time, to shew you my sense of the obligation—You know that I love you as my sister, & if you cannot be such, you shall allways have that place in my affe[c]tion. You must write, some one of you, *continuelly,* you cant Immagin the impatience that is *felt here,* when *you are silent.* Your own

DPM.

RC (CSmH).

1. George Clinton (1739–1812) of New York served as vice president from March 1804 until his death on 20 April 1812.

2. Joel Barlow had written Gideon Granger, an old friend from Connecticut and Yale, that he was negotiating a commercial treaty with France. Granger leaked this information to the newspapers, which caused something of a public stir. Although Secretary of State Monroe sent an official letter to Barlow, pointing out where Barlow had exceeded his instructions, JM did not, preferring, as DPM was writing to Ruth Barlow at this time, to issue a gentle reprimand through her (*PJM-PS* 4:347 n. 4; James Woodress, *A Yankee's Odyssey: The Life of Joel Barlow* [Philadelphia, 1958], 260, 291).

To Anna Cutts

My dear Sister,   May 1812

John Randolph has been firing away at the House, this morning against the declaration of War, but we suppose it will have little effect—I told you of the Hornet and all the news it brought, we have nothing among ourselves worth repeating—it seems Count Crillon, is an imposter, but that we do not care for—Lucy writes often and is still delighted with Kentucky, our friends in Virginia are well, but we do not know when we shall see them. My dear husband is overpowered with business but is very well, I am always sighing to see you and the precious little ones. We have parties in town now for Mrs: Ogle—she dines here tomorrow.

We had to dinner yesterday all the Heads of departments and their wives, Tayloes and Mrs: Ogle, Mr: and Mrs: Halsey from Providence, some officers &c. Mrs: Rush has come to beg me to go to a small party at her house tomorrow and I beleive I shall gratify her—she longs to see you—I enclose Lucy's last and Mrs Bomford's you may burn Ls and return the latter, just say you have received all mine and no more, I do not expect you to write much now your hands are so full—You must be consoled for a short seperation from your husband and friends it may be for the best. I shall embrace you this fall if we live and I hope and trust we shall be indemnified for all troubles, if you had good and trusty domestics I should not be half so anxious, as I know the amusements and pleasures inseperable from such charming and promising children as yours, tho' blended with care will make the time glide by—I will write you every day that I can take up the pen and I will prepare a room for and pay every sisterly attention to your good husband, so that I hope with our joint letters you will have nothing to complain of—You may rely upon it, if Mr. Cutts does not come it will be a disadvantage to him as well as to his party—some of them have reproached him already, but he will be here, we hope, just in time—not a moment too soon, it is supposed, to give his vote for War—however, this may be a mistake and the epoch may yet be a greater distance than a week. You may remember Catharine Coles's son Walter, he is here now and made a Lieutenant in the Army—he looks just as he did when you and I staid with him in Chestnut St. Payne is in Baltimore yet and as much admired and respected as you could wish, he writes me that Mrs: Patterson and Mrs: Bonaparte are very attentive to him and he is invited to all the great houses there—except the Smiths—We intend to send him in a few months to Princeton—Your acquaintance are all anxious to see you, they are as usual—Mrs: Forrest gave a great party two nights since—Edward was there and said it was very pleasant. Kiss the sweet girl and boys for me and sleep in peace my dear Sister, heaven will preserve you and yours as you trust in its great power! Ever your own

D.

Tr (MCR-S: Mary Estelle Elizabeth Cutts Papers). Tr made by Mary Cutts.

From Sally McKean Yrujo

My Dear Mrs Madison   BALTIMORE June 20th. 1812.

I arrived here about ten days ago & had a strong desire of writing to you the same moment of my arrival, but the state of affairs suggested me the idea that it was more prudent to suspend it, until they took a decisive turn lest some ex-alted patriot might suspect our innocent correspondence treasonable under existing circumstances: this motive haveing at present ceased, I dont loose a moment to write to you;[1] It would delight me to be able to spend a day with you, and press you to my heart, but I am obliged to set off for Philameclink[2] to-morrow, or next day at farthest; but I will not leave America without see-ing you. On account of the Marquis's begining to be affected by the bad cli-mate of the Brazils, he requested to be recalled, & we were about embarking in a Spanish 74 for Spain, when fortunately for me the opportunity of a fine Ship for this port offered—& I prevailed on the Marquis to return by the way of my dear native Country, on condition that we are to depart for Cadiz in Oc-tober, but I will not go before next Spring if I can possibly help it, for I am tired of so many sea voyages. Your Son Paine has been twice to see me but un-fortunately I was out both times—the Marquis saw him & says he is a fine young man, grown very tall, & very much improved, I shall make an effort to see him to day and intend to ask him if he remembers when he was a little fel-low, his pulling off Genl. Van Courtlands wig at the very moment he was makeing me a flourishing compliment, to his no small mortification, what has become of the old beaux?

The Ladies, & gentleman of this place have been very polite to us—all my acquaintances have been to see me, I have scarcely dined at my lodgeings—except it was three days that I was obliged to keep my bed owing to a cholick occasion'd by eating too much fruit, & then drinking ice water; yesterday I was able to go out again, & last night met with the *amiable*—honarable Miss Lucretia Mac Tab—who is as charming & as satirical as ever—& spoke of haveing the intention to have some interest in a schooner that is fitting out to go a privateering—which is to be commanded by Barney,[3] in fact she was so taken up by politicks there was no possibility of being heard: I have been highly amused by reading a piece of poetry relative to a scene they say past in Washington last winter in which the famous Count de Crillon cut a figure, as well as some Ladies—&c. I am told that last winter was really very dashing in your City—I am sorry the Counts Palings have left this before I arrived as they say so many fine things in their praise: I find Madame Bonaparte a good deal changed, she is not by a good deal so pretty as she was—we heard in Rio Janeiro she had the title of Dutches & a salary of 50,000 pounds a year. I find many changes have taken place in my absence—among others that Mrs Law—is Miss Custis, & exchanged her military spirit—to one quite the reverse—I think I can now see her drest in riding dress, dirk, & immense soldier feather, standing an end ¾ of a yd high—shooting at a mark—as she used to do when she was my neighbour; I am told Eliza has grown a fine girl— I hope she may in no way suffer for the folly of her parents. I verrily think if I was to see you & Anne once more, I should have as much to tell you of what I have seen, & heard abroad as would keep me talking for three days, & I am morally certain I should make you laugh & your good Husband into the bargain—I am almost as giddy, & as full of spirits as ever, I am for the french principal never to let any thing trouble me much, as it never does any good. Your sister Lucy is again married—I find—but am sorry she has gone so far off, I am told she has been a great belle, & as lively, & amiable as ever: I request you to remember me affectionately to her when you write to her next, I find Anne has not been idle in my absence—but increase & multiply is the order of the day—there is my brother Tom too, married & with two children—tell Anna I say she may go as far as ten & then she must possitively stop. Tell me if you received a letter from me dated Rio de Janeiro by a Mr Clagget of this place—as I never received an answer: they tell me here in answer to a thousand enquiries I have made about you—that you never look'd so well in your life—& that you give & have given universal satisfaction to all your friends & visitors which is indeed a very dificult matter to please every body, but you always possest so much goodness, & sweetness of manner as has made every body your friends, I have heard many things indeed in your praise from all the American Gentlemen who have been in the Brazil where you may be sure I have ask'd a hundred questions about you all. My two dear children (only two, you see how pretty I behave) are well & grown so much you would not know them & speak English; Spanish, & Portugeese fluently & will very soon— french—I cant now say a word in that language they do not understand— give my most affectionate love to Anne & tell her when she has a moments leisure, she must write to me & tell me the names of all her children: give my love (aye—love) to Mr Madison & ask him if he remembers old times—& remember me to Mr Cutts & all enquiring friends not forgetting the good, talkative Mrs Duval, & the first time you write to Mr Jeffersons daughter Mrs Randolph pray remember me very particularly to her—she is a sweet woman I have a particular regard for her—The Marquis desires his best compli(ments) to yourself, Mrs Cutts, & Mr Madison & Mr Cutts & believe me my Dear Mrs Madison your old—& affectionate friend.

Sally Yrujo

RC and Tr (MCR-S: Mary Estelle Elizabeth Cutts Papers).
1. Congress had been debating the issue of peace or war since JM's war message of 1 June 1812, finally declaring war on Great Britain on 18 June (*PJM-PS* 4:432–39, 489–90).
2. Presumably Philadelphia.
3. In June 1812 Joshua Barney accepted command of a private armed vessel, the *Rossie,* which had been purchased and outfitted by Baltimore merchants and furnished with a privateer's commission (Hulbert Footner, *Sailor of Fortune: The Life and Adventures of Commodore Barney, U.S.N.* [New York, 1940], 250–51).

From Anthony Morris

My honord Friend,   BOLTON FARM July 20. 1812.
I have by this Mail written to the President relative to an appointment,[1] which involves in its consequencies (should they at any time be such as I wish) so much of the fate of our darling Phoebe, that I should from this consideration only, be inexcusable in not mentioning it to you; while I anticipate the probability, that from various causes my views may not now be attainable, I indulge the belief that neither the personal wishes of the President or yourself will be among the number; I shall therefore easily reconcile myself to a disappointment, which will come with healing on its Wings.
I yet feel most sensibly and almost constantly my honord friend, the necessity of a total change of Scene to my health, my feelings, and my Interests;

I wish to try a new heaven, and a new Earth; thro' every Clime, I should carry with me, the recollections of those Friends, which have been ever my most endearing consolations, from the enchanting days of youth & Joy, to the maturity of meredion Life, Hope would still flatter me with a return to them, and to my native Land regenerated, and restord to feelings, without which, Life, is only a duty to be endured; while mine lasts, among its principal pleasures, will be the remembrance of your early and uninterrupted friendship; the terms of your last grateful Evidence of flattering attention, in the sanction of Miss Dupont's introduction; I shall ever cherish with particular pride and pleasure; the Sensations which both these Sources of gratification confer, I shall always Experience with those of the present Esteem & Gratitude, while I am permitted to subscribe myself yr truly Sincere & faithful St

A

P. S. Among the little embarrassments to which the honor of an intercourse with the palace subjects Me are the Solicitations for Letters of recommendation, introduction &c &c to the President, to the President's Lady, or to some of the Household; I evade all that are possible declaring that I have no pretensions which would justify my writing any such letters, one, which I have written this Morning of introduction to the President, (and wh I hope he will Excuse) is at the Request of my Friend Mr. Saml Mifflin whose object is the very appointment within alluded to, without his having the least Idea of my application, for I do not wish it known to any. I could not refuse the letter of introduction, as Mr. M. is really a Gentleman who has all the recommendations it enumerates, but I wrote to him, that as to the appointment, I could not mention it in his behalf to the President.

RC (DLC: DPM Papers); FC (DNCD). RC docketed by DPM.

　　1. Morris requested of JM "an appointment to some Southern port of Europe, or South America, in which commercial advantages might be probably connected with a change of Climate and Scene, which I have some years past been advis'd to try the efficacy of" (Morris to JM, 20 July 1812, DLC).

To Phoebe P. Morris

29th. July 1812

Your illness has given me great unesiness my dearest Phebe—& perhaps from sympathy, I have suffered also.

For the last 10 days I have been very sick, so much so, that I could not write or do any thing but nurse myself—I am yet in my chamber—I have reccd yours of the 17th. with one from your dear Father for which, I am impatient to thank you and to assure him of our attention to his wishes, & constant interest & affection.

We have little prospect of leaveing the City this Summer—If we do it will be but for a few days—Two weeks ago we spoke of visiting Phila. & spending a month at Jerman Toun, but that pleasant prospect is over, as my Husband found it would be inconvenient to leave the Offices, at a time like this, when—
——. We have had several mariages Mr Todd, Mr Cutts—& Mr. Cambell your old lover found, consolation for your frowns in the smiles of Miss Stodard, whom you have often seen here with her sister Euwell—Miss Southall & Mrs. Todd I saw married, but could not go to Bladensburg to a 3d weding—Lucy wrote me from the Toun in which Cambell lives & desired me to discribe his House & the preperations he was makeing to receive you, but as he has sealed his destiny, I will withold her long string of remarks—she tells me to say she loves you sincearly & hopes you'l take a Kentucky Beau she has in reserve for you—What then will become of Payne? I will send him to bring me your sweet Rebecca—I will so—I see that your Cousin John has obtained Miss C. & I rejoice at it—but my love you have never told me any thing of Mrs. Waddell who I am affraid is offended with me, as I wrote her before we parted (you & I) & have had no reply—Have you seen the Marchioness? Mrs Gallitin two was in hopes of meeting you in the City where she has been for some days—I am affraid Bolton is unhealthy, if so you aught not to remain there & a prospect of your visiting Europe before the end of the War would not be eligable or agreable. There is *nothing* to be *done*—in such times as these! Mr M is anxio⟨us⟩ to employ your Papa in some good place, entirely within his own gift, when *we* would not be subject to the political or personal objections of a capricious Senate (allmost treason my dear) but it is really true that M has but a small voice, at present, in appointments that go into the House. I am so unwel my darling, that I write terribly so burn this, & continue to speak to your

Mother

RC (DNCD: Morris Papers). Docketed as received 4 Aug.

To Phoebe P. Morris

16th. August. [1812]

This day, the letters of my most dear friends ware reccd. I rejoice at the good health of both & long to see them, & *this same* Bolton where I could embrace all the children, & set myself down amidst those who ever, & will allways hold the first place in my heart. Since I wrote you my Phebe, I reccd. a very kind letter from your Cousin Mrs W[1] who tells me of her fine son, & that our Handsome Garnet is devoted to Miss de Gouge! *How soon some people can forget impressions*—I saw the Hamiltons yesterday, & from the love Eliza express'd for you, immagin'd she wrote you a great deal. A few days ago We had 29 Indians to dinner with us, attended by 5 Interpretors & the Heads of Depts. makeing 40 persons.[2] At 5 oClock Mrs. Eustis Mrs. Rush, the Hamiltons & many other's came in the Band was playing, & danceing succeeded—We sent off their red *children* however, before we began & had a frolick that would have delighted you. Another set of the same terrifick Kings & Princes have arrived since, & we shall have the same seen again, tomorrow. I pray you join us, my sweetest— bring Papa, James, Rebeca & My little Louisa—You shall have choice of partners my darling for Payne will not be here—he has gone to the sweet Springs—not that he was much out of health, but because he was very thin, & his Papa thought it would do him good. Do you remember the beautiful goats, at which you & I so often laughed? Well, they march up, every now & then to divert me, & make Edward angry—but what a digression! The Major, my dear, has become a Colonel—ah—& he looks more like Lochinvar than ever—he is station'd at Richmond but is under orders to march.[3] War is indeed, a melancholy business but we hope ours, will soon blow over. The orders in Council are removed & *negociation* must follow[4]—every disposition to meet an honorable peace is *here*—We go to our Seat in Orange on friday or Saturday next, mearly to breath the air & see our Mother for two or three weeks, at most.

Write to me when you can, & If you meet with poor Mrs. Custis remember her misfortunes—she is at present in Jerman Toun near her daughter, & intends to some of your Watering places, & is anxious to see *you*—every body speaks of you & loves you in this quarter—Next Year I intend to pick up my Husband & bring him your way—Tell your dear Father that I will write to him soon, when if possible, I will let him know how precious is his friendship! how valuable his letters.

DPM

RC (DNCD: Morris Papers).

1. This was Elizabeth (Betsy) Pemberton Waddell, a cousin of Phoebe Morris and an old friend of DPM.

2. JM received two Indian delegations during August 1812, which included leaders of the Sac, Fox, Osage, and Sioux Indians (Brant, *Madison* 6:68–70).

3. In 1809 Isaac A. Coles was appointed a captain in the U.S. Army. He was promoted to major in March 1812 and to colonel a year later (*Senate Exec. Proceedings* 2:94, 221, 289, 276).

4. The British Orders in Council, restricting neutral trade, inflicted great losses on American commerce. Their imposition was a leading cause of the War of 1812. They were repealed on 16 June 1812, too late to prevent the U.S. declaration of war.

To Edward Coles

31t. August [1812]

Here we are, my dear Cousin (I will not say still) but again! We had reached Dumfries on friday Evg. on our way home, when an Express overtook us, with the melancholy tidings, that Genl. Hull had surrender'd Detroit, *himself* & the whole Army to the British! Do you not tremble with resentment, at this treacherous act?[1] Yet, we must not judge the Man until we are in possesion of his reasons—they have not arrived, but all we *have* hear'd is unfavorable to his honor. Mr. M found it necessary to return to the City, in order to repair our misfortunes by ——. We hope to get off again tomorrow, at any rate, we shall be at home this week. I will enclose you some papers, & I wish I could give you good news—In great haste, but sincere affection for you all—yours

D P M

RC (MiD).

1. Gen. William Hull's surrender of the Northwest Army on 16 Aug. 1812 proved demoralizing and politically divisive and hurt the popularity of the president and his administration (Brant, *Madison* 6:73–81).

To Phoebe P. Morris

[ca. 17 October 1812]

I think of you often my dearest Phebe, tho I am a delinquent correspondent. Your enlighten'd mind, & affectinate heart, forms many an apology for me, & augments my love, & gratitude. For what is there more affecting, than the patient forbearance of friendship? but for this—Your dear Father & yourself must have given *me* up, in such *perilous times as these!* Your last letter was the more welcome for its good account of your health. I was glad to see you at the Prince Toun Ball, & I hope you have preserved your sprightly temper, which allways delighted, & allways will. You thought Miss Mayo less beautiful than Miss Caton—I think, *she* has rather the advantage in this, but Miss C. excells in grace. I expect Miss M to pass a few days with me next month, when our routine of gaiety commences—indeed the Races & D. Room will give a begining about the 27th. of this—I wish you my beloved, could join, in all good things with me, & I flatter myself that I shall some time, or other, have you again—We spent *one week* at our Seat in Orange, this Summer, the rest, where you left us—in the midst of business & namely—anxious for the fate of the War, *only*—knowing that if success crouned our arms, prosperity & happiness would attend our Country. The disgraceful conduct of Hull has been repaired—& the Brave Harrison, will soon finish a contest forced upon us, by every sort of oppress⟨ion.⟩[1] At this moment, my dear, I am *full of hope*—In a few days I shall embrace my sister Cutts & her children. I expect they are now at Phila. where I wish you may see them—Lucy, our darling, will be with us in Jany. Payne is now studying with his Papa, & acting for poor Edward, who has been ill in Virga & not yet return'd. Your acquaintances here, are well. The Miss Hamiltons had a Ball given them at the Navy Yard last night, where they *danced* til Morng. Miss Hay is to be in the City soon, as well as Made. Boneparte, & a multitude of Beauties—The F Mintr is paveing his road & intends to *frolick continually*—How is James, & your dear sisters? allways tell me something about them when you write. I do not hear further of Mr. Garnet—Soon I hope to write a good postscript for my valued friend, who will be assured, as well as my Phebe, that I am forever their Affectinate

DPM

RC (DNCD: Morris Papers). Docketed as received 20 Oct.

1. In August 1812 William Henry Harrison was appointed to command a special force of Kentucky volunteers. Asserting that he had "an army competent in numbers, and in spirit," he moved to relieve Fort Wayne with the intention of retaking Detroit (Stagg, *Mr. Madison's War*, 212–17; Ketcham, *James Madison*, 542).

To Phoebe P. Morris

My dearest Phebe.   14th. Jany. [18]13.

Mr. Milnor has just left me delighted, with your charming present. All the House hasten'd around me to read, & admire the ingenuiety of our little darling—Miss Mayo said she was very jealous of you, Miss Coles longed to embrace you & Payne told them, "it was nothing to what you *could* do so entirely accomplished was Miss M.["] We have a large party with us—besides the young ladies, my sister & her family Mr Ms nephew & Payne stay with us so that when I have been well enuf to write you my love, I have found no retired moment for this pleasant duty. Our dear Lucy does not come this winter. You have heared of the changes in our circle; I was truly attatched to the families & have felt it with sorrow[1]—Mrs. Eustis wrote me from Phia. where I am affraid she did not see you. Mr Pemberton staid but two days in Washington he gave me the ⟨lined?⟩ box which is beautiful—All these things my dear child are very precious to us, & remind us of that attatchment which we hope will last with our lives.

The city is more dissipated than I ever knew it, the week is two short for parties. The mornings are devoted to Congress, where *all* delight to listen, to the violence of evil spirits—I stay quietly at home—as quietly as one can be, who has so much to feel at the *expression, for & against their conduct.* Tell your dear Papa that all will *end* well at last, the pure intentions of his friends must meet the reward, so much wished & expected—I will write you soon more fully at this moment I can only add that I love you all most dearly.

D P M

Read this, if you please to Papa but let no one see the sad scrawl, for your frds sake.

RC (DNCD: Morris Papers).
    1. In December 1812 the secretary of war, William Eustis, and the secretary of the navy, Paul Hamilton, resigned their offices. They were replaced by John Armstrong and William Jones, respectively.

To Phoebe P. Morris

March 6th. [18]13.

Can you forgive me beloved Phebe for my long silence? Even after that kind letter from your dear Father? Pray do my darling, & beleive—If I had been *blessed* with one hour's leisure or *quiet,* It should have been devoted to you, for whom I am very anxious, as well as for dear James. Mrs. Garnet tells me this day, that you were both sick. Tho I do not appear to deserve it I shall be uneasy, until I hear from your own hand that you are well. Mrs. Garnet is a sweet creature—she arrived in time for the 4 of *March Ball* where I met her. The next day she came to visit me; she said, she should write you that *I* would be in Phia. this summer, & I hope it may be the case, but this sad summer Session, breaks up all my plans, unless it is made short by the fear of our unfinished Canal or some other source of evil. The charming girls, who have passed the winter with are about to leave Washington after haveing their heads turn'd with gaiety beaux &.&. Last night we were *all* at the R. Ministers party, which was briliant, & *pleasant.* Several couple[s] danced the Waltz among whom Mrs. Pederson appeared to great advantage as an eligant & graceful lady. Miss Coles & Miss Mayo have often regretted that they did not know you—if they had been even slightly acquainted with my Phebe, she would have reccd. fine descriptions of *high seenes* from Washington. You remember

174

the Judges. They have been some time amongst us, & are as agreable as ever. They talk of you continually particularly Story. All but Judge Todd who has remain'd with My dear Lucy to nurse their young daughter of whom they are very proud. It is call'd Madisonia Dolley. The last name I am determin'd shall be left out when they come to me next Summer.

7th. This day seems devoted to *leave-taking,* a hundred adeiu's have been bid & reccd. & the sombre contenance takes place of the sprightly air of yesterday. Thus my love, will the bitter & sweets of life, alternately be felt. "For tho the Sun may rise & see us unbless'd & siting, leave us in misery—Yet on its return it may behold us changed, & the face, which was yesterday clouded with tears, will tomorrow brighten into smiles." I hope to send you a great deal by Judge Story who will see you on his return. I embrace you all with true affection my dearest Phebe

D P M

RC (DNCD: Morris Papers).

To Phoebe P. Morris

Wednesday 24th. Apl. [1813]

I hope my dearest Phebe will not fail to go with her amiable Father whose peace would be incompleat without her. The climate of Burmuda is of all others perhaps, the best for rhumatic complaints. In truth my love, you would *all* find a short residence there, both beneficial & pleasant.[1] Mr. M & myself, have reccd. my dear friends last letters—*he* will answer as soon as some arrangements are concluded on, & *I* would as I aught, write a great deal, but that I am most *anxiously* prepareing Payne for his voyage to Russia! Yes—I have consented to his going as one of Mr. Gallatins Seceys. on this *Mission of peace.*[2] I hope Payne will see you in Phila. on this day week—he has been sick & is still so, which will detain him here until allmost, the last day, as the Ship is expected to sail on the 29th. Be of good chear beloved friends Heaven will restore you to health & your country when we shall meet—with unabated affection—forever your

D P M

RC (DNCD: Morris Papers). Docketed as received and answered 24 April.

1. The Madisons had hoped to accommodate Anthony Morris's request for a diplomatic appointment by sending him to Bermuda, but his passage there was refused by British vice admiral Sir John Borlase Warren (Morris to JM, 29 April 1813 [DLC]).

2. Albert and James Gallatin and John Payne Todd were preparing to sail on a peace mission to Russia.

To Edward Coles

May 13th. [18]13.

Your letter caused me great affliction My dear Cousin. The continuation of your illness & Paynes reluctance at leaving America, left me not fortitude to write you *until* now, that I have reccd. a letter from my Son on Ship-board, in which he expresses satisfaction at all arround him & seen Mr Swertchkoff, who assures me, *you* will soon be well, in *spite* of *yourself.*[1]

We indulge this pleasing hope, in adition to that of your remaining with us, to the last—not that I would, for the World, retard any plan for your prosperity; but that I flatter myself the Western country *may* be given up for something more consonant with your happiness & that of your conections. Among them there are none, who feel a more affectinate interest for you than Mr. Madison & myself. I hope you will beleive, that such is our regard & esteem for you, that we should consider your leaving us, a misfortune. Mr M can do very well without a Seccy. until your heath is re-established. The winter is not a Season for emigration—so that next Spring or Summer you will be better able to make your election—*to go, or not to go.* & now, if I could, I would describe to you the fears & alarms, that circulate around me. For the last week all the City & G. Toun (except the Cabinet) have expected a visit from the Enimy, & ware not lacking in their expressions of terror & reproach. Yesterday an express anounced the pause of a Frigate at the mouth of the Potomack, the Commander sent his boats to examin a Swedish Ship that lay near, but our informer did not wait to know further. We are makeing considerable efforts for defence. The Fort is repairing, & 500 Militia, with perhaps as many regulars are; & *to be,* stationd on the green near the *Wind Mill,* or rather, near Majr. Tayloes. The 20 Tents, allready look well, in My eyes as I have allways been an advocate for fighting when *assailed,* tho *a Quaker.* I therefore keep the old Tunesian Sabre within my reach. One of our Generals has discovered a plan of the British. It is to land as many chosen *Rogues* as they can about 14 miles below Alexa. in the night, who may arrive before day & set fire to the offices & Presidents House when, if opposed, they are to surrender themselves as prisoners. I do not tremble at this, but feel *affronted* that the Admiral (of Havre-de Grace memory) should send me notis that he would make his bow at my Drawing room *soon.*[2] Mrs. Bonaparte & Miss Spear return'd to their House 4 days ago to secure their Wardrobe, but I question whether they leave us again, as strangers & Members are flocking in. I presented you to the Monroes. They dined with us yesterday in a large party given to Mrs. Jones & &. Mr. Hay was with them—he comes to galant Mrs. M to Richmond on a visit of 3 weeks to her daughters. Cousin Sally is still in S. Carolina, & Miss Mayo is as gay as ever. Mr. Cutts has rented Mrs. Pollocks House & it is repairing for him. Anna has been very unwell of late, & her children are sick with the Measles, I confine myself with them. Lucy writes in her usial sprightly strain, says she will come to us in Novr. from Noxville. Be careful of your self dear Cousin & return as soon as you can to your anxious friends

D P M

RC (Henry Ford Museum, Dearborn, Michigan).

1. On 21 March, Edward Coles left Washington to seek the medical care of Dr. Philip Syng Physick in Philadelphia for an attack of hemorrhoids. By May he was no better and wrote JM that he wished to be relieved of his duties as the president's private secretary. JM refused this request, and Coles returned to Washington in the fall of 1813 (Coles to John Coles, 28 March, and to Mrs. Coles, 19 May 1813, PHi: Coles Collection).

2. On 3 May 1813 the British under the command of Rear Admiral Sir George Cockburn attacked Havre de Grace, Md., at the head of Chesapeake Bay. The British burned nearly two-thirds of the town, including the Cecil Company cannon foundry (Heidler and Heidler, *Encyclopedia of the War of 1812*, 235).

To Edward Coles

2d. july [18]13.

I have the happiness to assure you my dear Cousin that Mr. Madison recovers. For the last 3 days, his fever has been so slight as to permit him to take bark every hour, & with good effect. It has been three weeks since I have nursed him night & day—sometimes in despair! but now that I see he will get well I feel as if I should die myself, with fatigue. Adieu ever yours

D.

RC (NjP: Edward Coles Papers).

From Sarah Coles

ENNISCORTHY July 19th. [18]13.

Your more than welcome letter my dearest Cousin made me the happiest of the happy; it releived me from a state of the most painful solicitude, and from all the tortures that suspense and anxiety could inflict; Rumour with her hundred tongues had circulated at least an hundred reports about your dear Husband, all calculated to afflict those who know and love him for his virtues: imagine then my delight when impatiently seizing the news papers with the hope that they might dissipate my fears your letter met my eye—it was a blessed moment indeed—and most fervently do I thank Heaven for granting to our prayers one who is not only necessary to the happiness of those who "love him best" but to the prosperity and welfare of his Country—long, very long may you my beloved and excellent Mrs. Madison, continue to enjoy the blessings you have so well deserved. If it were possible I would love you better than ever for bestowing a thought on your little Cousin at a time when your whole soul was absorbed by so dear an object, but you are ever the same benevolent being, always attentive to the happiness of others.

I am grieved to hear of Cousin Anna's misfortune, but flatter myself Montpellier will soon restore health to both herself and Mr. Madison. Tell her, if you please, I thank her for her postscript, tho' short, it was very sweet for it assured me I still retain a place in her remembrance yet I should have cherished that hope even without such an assurance; I trust dear little Dolly has not been sick—pray give her a kiss for me.

You can form no idea of the spirit that has been excited in Virginia by the late invasion[1]—it transformed all our young men into Hero's. They waited not for the "spirit stiring drum"[2] to call them to their duty. This neighborhood alone organized a company of between 50 and 60 Volunteer's, in the short space of two days, my brothers were among the number, brother John had the honor to kill one horse in the service, but no other honors decked his brow, the Governor dismissed them with a *speech,* the alarm having subsided. Nothing, it is said, could exceed the confusion and dismay which reigned in Richmond while an attack was expected, old men bowed down with age were seen taking their places in the ranks, and little boys formed themselves into companies with the same spirit that animated their Fathers. They will find it no easy task to conquer Virginian's, even the ladies shew a spartan courage. But I forget how many cares you have to occupy you at this time, soon may they be dispeled by the perfect restoration of your Husband's health, yet I shall not be entirely at ease untill he is released from his public duties, and is breathing the pure air of Montpellier. Would to Heaven my dear Edward was with you, he writes us that he is rather better.

Good Night, my more than Friend, may I behold you in the "dreams of my rest" as I was wont to do, radiant with smiles of joy and happiness. Your Own

Sarah Coles

RC (MCR-S: Mary Estelle Elizabeth Cutts Papers). Docketed by JM.

1. The British navy attacked Norfolk, Va., on 22 June 1813. Beaten back by the Americans, they successfully attacked Hampton three days later (Roger Morriss, *Cockburn and the British Navy in Transition* [Exeter, Eng., 1997], 94–95).

2. Shakespeare, *Othello* 3.3.352 (*Riverside*).

To Hannah Gallatin

29th. July [18]13.

I cannot allow Mr Astor to leave us without his bearing a few lines, from me, to you, my beloved friend: You to whom my heart has often addressed itself, since our seperation and constantly sympathised with, on the subject of our dear Voagers. You have heared no doubt, of the illness of my Husband but can have no idea of its extent, and the dispair, in which I attended his bed for nearly five weeks! Even now, I watch over him, as I would an infant, so precarious is his convalessence—added to this, the disappointments & vexations, heaped upon him by party spirit. Nothing however has borne so hard, as the conduct of the Senate in regard to Mr Gallatin—Mr A will tell you many particulars, that *I aught not* to *write*, of the desertion of some whose support we had a right to expect; & of the *maneauvering* of others, allways hostile to superior merit. We console ourselves with the hope of *its* terminating both in the Public good, and Mr. Gallatins honorable triumph.[1] Anna, Mr. M & Mr Cutts join me in affectinate love & wishes for you—Anna will go with us to Orange, where we often wish we could have you & your precious Francis, in order, that we might do our part, to console you for the absence, of the best of friends—Heaven send, we may soon have good accounts from him. Adeiu my darling, beleive me—ever yours

D. P. Madison

RC (NHi: Gallatin Papers, 1813, no. 102). Addressed to Mrs. Gallatin at New York.

1. On 24 May the special session of Congress, which had been called by JM on 23 Feb., met to raise revenue to prosecute the war and to confirm the nominations of Gallatin, John Quincy Adams, and James A. Bayard as U.S. commissioners to negotiate peace with Great Britain within the framework of the offered Russian mediation. The session proved extremely divisive and acrimonious and resulted in the rejection of Gallatin's nomination (Stagg, *Mr. Madison's War*, 304–16).

From Anthony Morris

ON BOARD THE BRIG, CHRISTIAN HENDRICK,
My Excellent Friend   HARBOUR OF NEW HAVEN Sunday Aug 1. 1813.

We are now on our passage to Lisbon, that I have not been able earlier to communicate this to you has not been for want of my best Exertions: James is with Me, with the view to send him to Paris for the completion of his education; I dont know why, but I cherish an agreeable Expectation, that he may in the course of the Year meet Payne there; you will no doubt have been informd how satisfactorily, I trust very advantageously I have arrang'd a little Establishment for your favorite Phoebe, with Rebecca, & Louisa, in the new institution of the Misses Lyman, where the instruction of Louisa, and in some branches Rebecca, will be aided by the superintendance & Society of their Sister: I found the times too perilous, and the difficulties too great, or I should have preferd taking them all with Me; I have leas'd Bolton for three years, when James will be of age; in the interim, I shall hope to hover about him in some Shape, that when he returns, he may be able to say, how much he owes to Heaven, & you.[1] I cannot omit this last opportunity of repeating how sincerely I rejoice in the restoration of the Prest to his family & Country; and how unwearied shall be my efforts to accomplish all his Views, which my Situation may enable me to be accessory to. You will remember I am Sure, as our ministering Angel, the happiness you confer on Phoebe by the occasional correspondence you favor her with, and how greatly its continuance will increase the obligations of your most Sincere, obligd, & ever grateful Friend

Anthony Morris

RC (DLC: DPM Papers). Docketed by DPM.

    1. JM had appointed Morris special agent to Spain in May 1813. While his son James accompanied him across the Atlantic to finish his education in Scotland, Morris arranged for his three daughters—Phoebe, Rebecca, and Louisa—to attend Miss Jerushia Lyman's Ladies' Seminary in Philadelphia. Bolton was the family farm in Bucks County, Pa. (Armentrout, *Castles in Spain*, vii-viii).

From Hannah Gallatin

New York August 15th: 1813

I have seen by the Newspapers that you have my dear friend left Washington. I hope it is to enjoy a little peace after the turmoil & bustle you have lately experienced, and that your beloved husband by breathing his pure native air may be restored to perfect health. How often did I think of you during his illness & what a comfort it was to me to think that you had your Sister & Mr. Cutts with you, but I did not know how very ill the President had been until he was better. Your feelings must have been agony in the extreme alas! what you must have suffered.

At this time I am all anxiety to hear of the safe arrival of our dear *Voyagers*. I have been so miserable about my dear husband that I think I did very wrong not to accompany him, and if it pleases Heaven ever to restore him to me, I think it must be the last time of separation. His enemies have triumphed over him in his absence, but that is a trifle he is much happier than they are for he has a self approving conscience and his peace is within his own breast while theirs are torn with every black and malevolent passion, and if he is the means of restoring peace to our beloved Country, that will be suffic[i]ent reward to him, and the greatest cause of regret is that the Presidents feelings have been so tortured at a time too when it was so necessary for him to enjoy repose. I hope our Country will not suffer by their wickedness.

Write to me again soon my dear friend. I love to receive your letters, they comfort me I have been a good deal affected lately by the death of our young friend Col. Chrystie, such a young man was a loss to his Country as well as his friends, for he was every thing that was noble & generous. There had been a long attachment between him & my niece Frances Few, and it would make your heart ache to see her distress.

Remember me affectionately to Mr. Madison & Mr. & Mrs. Cutts, and believe me unalterably your sincere & grateful friend

H Gallatin

Will you make my best respects to old Mrs. Madison.

RC (ViU). Addressed to DPM at Montpelier.

To Hannah Gallatin

MONTPELIER 30th. August. [18]13.

It has been some days since I reccd: yours my beloved friend, & tho I have been impatient to write you I have found it impossible, oweing to the croud of company with which our house has been fill'd ever since our return to it— I have this morning turned all off to my sister Cutts, determined to congratulate you on the safe arrival of our treasur's at Gottenburg—Thank Heaven they are so far safe, & I suppose their passage has been reasonably short. I am constantly cheared with the sweet hope of their safe & early return, when you will find your dear Husband standing higher than ever in his countrys estimation & attattment; for Mr. Madison says, that tho his Enimies *immagin* they have prevailed in a *degree* against him, their machinations will treble his friends & shew him to the world as he really is, one of the best, as well as one of the greatest men.

I pray that you may cherish fortitude & banish all regrets, & that we may be re-united before the winter, in Washington—I cannot express my longing to see you, or the drearyness of my feelings when you are absent from our circle.

I was greaved to hear of the death of Colo. Chrystie! he was an honor to his country & is lamented by it. I suppose you have seen Mr. Cutts, as he intended to visit you, if he could stay an hour—Genl. Armstrong too, told me he would see you—Colo. Coles left us 2 or 3 days ago, & will be soon on his march to the Lines, when he will call on you. Mother Madison my Husband & Anna charge me to present them, with great affection to you. I have nothing interesting to tell you, in the way of news, as the Papers contain all *we know;* & those you see. I expect Mrs. Randolph with her Father, to visit us in a few days—she is miserable at parting with Mr R who leaves her for the army—I was pleased to see David R. Williams on *his way to it.*

We left Mrs. Wilkenson & her sister in Washington, they are very pleasing women, but I fear *me,* they will be tired of that place before long, as they meet so few persons at this season, who speak French & *they* speak no English, but live at Docr. Blakes, *in a warm situation*—Seccy. Jones has taken Madame B——s house—Mr Lear, that of Goldsborough so that our neighbourhood will be much changed—The F. Minister will come into it if he can. He tells a foolish story about Mrs. Barlows being on the eve of marriage with some young french man; but I will not beleive it. The Latrobe's are on the wing for Pittsburge, & Walter Jones to their house. We hear that Gales is to mary the pritty little Miss Lee of Virga. whom you have seen at our house, & Weightman, Serena Hanson. I have made a sad letter of this my darling, but have no time to copy or correct it—you will receive, I know, with kindness & charity from your ever affectinate

D P M

My love to Mr. Astor—Kiss sister Holdon & Francis for me. We shall stay here til Octor if we can—but Colo. Monroe is very sick & Mr. Jones impatient for Mr. Ms return—Mr. M is now perfectly well but will be the better for another Month on the Mountain.

RC (NHi: Gallatin Papers, 1813, no. 123).

To Martha Jefferson Randolph

9th. Jany. [18]14.

To write to you, & to think of you my beloved friend, is one of the greatest pleasures of my life—You will immagin then my gratification at seeing, & receiving from Captn. Peyton your letter, & the good acct. of your whole family. As much as I desired to see Colo. Randolph I should have admired him less, if he had *paused* to visit any being, when on the wing to his precious wife & children—May this find you *safe* & well! & blessed with the adition you expected. If so—& you could possibly spare Ellen, it would delight us to receive her[1]— S. Coles (who is a lovely girl) would be her companion, & together they would enjoy a large & enlighten'd society—We have Ladies from almost every State in the Union, & the City was never known so thronged with strangers—Thus, it is a pleasing & instructive scene for the young & gay. The members of Congress seem a good deal occupied at *present* in dispute about French Influence some of them desire to Impeach the President, in order that he may come forward & manifest his innocence of the charge—They have a report among them that your dear Father has consented again, to tempt the Ocian for the great object of makeing a peice.[2] Colo. Jno. Nicholas, who is here is to be of the party—It would be weak in me to tell & tiresome to you, to hear our *particular occupation* in this Great City, I will then only add that we are looking anxiously for Mr. Gallatin & my son. Should Mr. G. remain with Mr. Byard[3] he would still make the 3d. negotiator. My sisters Todd & Cutts are with me & send you their most affectinate remembrance. Present me to all at Montecello & know me ever your

DPM

RC (owned by Dolly L. Maass, White Plains, N.Y., 1961).
    1. Martha Jefferson Randolph's daughter Septimia Anne was born on 3 Jan. 1814. Ellen Wayles Randolph was another of her daughters (Malone, *Jefferson and His Time* 6: app. 1).
    2. Though by late December 1813 Washington was rife with reports of British peace proposals, there was no thought of sending Jefferson as a peace negotiator. Nor was there a move in Congress to impeach JM.
    3. James A. Bayard.

To Hannah Gallatin

21st. Jany. [1814]

I rejoice with you my beloved friend, on hearing from Mr Gallatin—& I have the pleasure to tell you that a letter dated on the 15th. Septr. from Payne, has reached me, containing a good account of the whole party—He says—"If you should see Mrs. Gallatin, or the families of any of our party, inform them that we are *all* perfectly well—James has been a little indisposed, but has recovered. Of politics & many other things, I must not speak tho it is now the 15th. Sept. & no answer reccd. respecting the 2d. offer of mediation!"

He says also "That our friend" (meaning your estimable Husband) *"does not care* for *machinations* &c &c" & apologises for writing obscurely, "but as this letter is written, *some time* after those of the Mission, he hopes it will be a consolation to *you.*"

Be consoled then, my precious friend in the knowledge, that your Husband & son are safe & well. Mr. Madison has looked, with anxiety & impatience for Mr. Gs arrival, & does not at *this moment* give up the *hope* of *seeing him notwithstanding the uncertainty* expressed in his letter to you—but for this hope, Mr. M would have taken advantage of his talents, to form the *new* treaty; & *will* yet propose him to the Senate, if he *should* hear that Mr. G. *will pass the* winter in Europe. Oh that we could hear, *decidedly* whether he came home or not. For you, & for myself, I pray that he may return directly, & re-ocupy his place in the Treasury, restore you, our valued & dear friend to us who love you more than you immagin.

Mr. M has *counseled* Mr. Granger to appoint R. Bache as post Master—It would indeed be an insult to *us* all, to give it to *the other.*[1] I long to see you, & trust you will yet have the *best occation* to come to Washington this Winter. My Sisters, Miss Coles, Mr. M, & all our house offer you best wishes & love. Present me affectinately to Mr & Mrs. Dallas & burn this scrawl—It is written in haste & in company *but only* for your eye. Your own ever

DPM

RC (NHi: Gallatin Papers, 1814, no. 7). Addressed to Mrs. Gallatin at "Mr. Dallas's Philadelphia."

1. In January 1814 Postmaster General Gideon Granger—a longtime opponent of JM's within the Republican Party—made it known that he intended to appoint the bitterly anti-Madison senator Michael Leib to the postmastership of Philadelphia. This incensed Republicans loyal to JM who announced their support of Benjamin Franklin's grandson Richard Bache. Granger went ahead and appointed Leib, but was forced out of office on 17 March 1814, when JM nominated Return Jonathan Meigs Jr. as postmaster general. When the Senate confirmed Meigs, Granger retired to upstate New York (Ketcham, *James Madison,* 569; Arthur S. Hamlin, *Gideon Granger* [Canandaigua, N.Y., 1982], 46–50).

From Hannah Gallatin

NEW YORK May 15th. 1814

I have this day my dear friend received a letter from Mr Gallatin dated *Amsterdam March the 9th.* and of which I will give you an extract as he seems to wish that you & the President should be informed of his proceedings.[1]

"We left St Petersburgh the 25th: of January and after a tedious journey of 1500 miles by way of Riga, Konigsburg and Berlin, arrived here without accident on the 4th: instant. Previous to our leaving St. Petersburgh, we had directed Capt. Jones then at Gottenburgh to proceed with the Neptune to this place. She has not yet arrived & I apprehend that on account of the severity of the winter she may be detained at Gottenburgh by the ice till the middle of this month. It is not possible therefore that we can embark & sail from Europe prior to the first of April. James, myself & our two blacks will certainly return in the Neptune. Mr. Bayard goes on his mission to Gottenburgh. Todd & Milligan left St. Petersburgh two weeks before us & proceeded by way of Sweden to Gottenburgh, where they were to embark either on board the Neptune for Holland, or in a British packet for England. They have not yet arrived and indeed it is impossible they should, not a single vessel having arrived for seven weeks from Gottenburgh, the outer harbour of which (where Capt. Jones wintered) being frozen contrary to custom & our expectation. Had we anticipated the revolution in Holland, we would have sent him to winter here & gained one month. But we did all that was in our power, having sent her to the neutral port in the north seas farthest from us & least liable to ice. Write all this to Mrs. Madison, both on account of her Son, & to show that I have lost no time.

The newspaper account of the rejection of my nomination did not reach me till late in October after Capt. Jones's departure. I could not indeed have then taken the Neptune from Mr. Bayard & I had no other means of returning to America. I never received any official accounts of the rejection of my nomination, nor a line from the Dep. of State later than 23d. June. I concluded to wait for Mr. Bayard, and we finally departed without having been officially informed that the mediation was rejected by Great Britain. We found the account here in the Presidents message and a letter from Mr. Monroe to Mr. Bayard of 8th. January last. The messenger who brought this we fortunately met here.["] He adds "But now once more on the Shores of the Atlantic I think all difficulties are over & that I am almost home. I do not know whether Dallas, Todd or Milligan intend returning with me.["]

What do you think of this letter my dear friend? Am I to expect to see my dear husband & child every moment, or am I again to be disappointed, My prayers night and day are that he will have left Europe before the news of his new appointment can possibly reach him. If the President should know or hear any thing further about him, you will I know have the goodness to communicate it to me. Although I have received such late information yet my anxiety & suspense is not entirely removed. I have not written to you in a great while, I have been too miserable. Will you write to me soon. I have not heard whether or not you have returned to Washington. Remember me to the

President & Mr. & Mrs. Cutts. and believe me with unalterable affection Your sincere friend

H Gallatin

When Mr. Gallatin returns I mean to accompany him to Washington, to bid you adieu, before we fix at our home.

HG.

RC (ViU).

1. In 1813 JM had appointed Albert Gallatin as one of three peace commissioners charged with arranging the neutral mediation offered by the Russian czar. After Gallatin left for St. Petersburg, the Senate rejected his nomination. Gallatin learned of this through John Payne Todd, a member of the commission staff, in October 1813. With the collapse of the Russian mediation in the winter of 1814, Gallatin left Russia for London. In Great Britain he learned that the Senate had approved his nomination as one of the commissioners to negotiate peace with the British (Stagg, *Mr. Madison's War*, 316, 370; Raymond Walters Jr., *Albert Gallatin* [New York, 1957], 266–75).

To Hannah Gallatin

ORANGE May 22d. 1814.

Not until this Morning, did I recce. yours of the 15th. my ever dear friend oweing to the high waters, which in our county often impede the arrival of letters—The day before yesterday Mr Madison reccd. the Dispatches from Colo Monroe, containing one letter from Mr Byard dated 17th. march saying "that he should shortly proseed to Gottenburge." Mr. Gallatin had not then, any knowledge of his re-appointment nor does Mr. B. say more of him, than that they ware together at Amsterdam—This day Mr. M has a communication from Mr. Beasly in London, dated 20th. March he *had just dispatched*, to Mr. Gallatin the official information of his appointment & Mr M *thinks* the *Ministers* are *now all together* in Gottenburge—I greave for your disappointment—your long & anxous trials—yet I trust, your fortitude my beloved, will support you a little longer—It may be, that your good Husband, will have sailed for America before Mr Ms letters could reach him—still it is not probable. The Negotiations will not last more than a month, when the chance for propitious Gales will be augmented & July or August will bring back your happiness—I am distressed at Paynes leaveing Mr. Gallatin—What could have lead him to do so? Nothing but anxiety to get home I hope. All the Winter I looked for you—sighing for the visit you promised me. I cannot dwell on a seperation from you, but in deep regret—May the prospect of continueing to see you whilst I live, brighten when we meet at Washington this summer. We shall set out on our return in three or four days, as the time M. intended to stay here, has expired. If I had reccd. any information (or if Mr. M possessed any) likely to gratify you I should have written to you oftener—Accept our united Affection & think of me your ever constant friend

D P M

The post has waited for this, which has caused me to abridge, & badly express the little I could say—love for Francis & Mr. Astor.

RC (NHi: Gallatin Papers, 1814, no. 70).

From Sarah Coles

Enniscorthy June 28th. [18]14

The day that Edward left us I received your thrice welcome letter, my beloved Cousin, for which I return you a thousand thanks. I have yet scarcely done wondering at the information it contained, and which the news-papers have since confirmed—On how slender a thread hangs all worldly prosperity that Bonaparte who but a short time ago was the terror of all Europe, to have become a pensioner on the bounty of his Enemies! what a pity that he did not die under the walls of Paris, it would have been a glorious close of his political career.[1]

I should like to know how Madame Bonaparte bears the extinction of all her hopes of future greatness. Jerome they say is coming to America. Madame I dare say will not receive him *now* with much kindness—Mr: Jefferson was here the other day, and gave us a very interesting account of the Bourbons. You know he was personally acquainted with them when in Europe. He says the King is scarcely one degree removed from idiotism, a perfect child in intellect, & extremely corpulent, and unweildly in his person; (his wife was a *great drunkard*, but for the honor of France died some years ago. The King's brother is the greatest *Gamester* in the World and has very little more understanding than his August Majesty, the King).[2] The poor Empress! I am sorry for her, to be *married* and *seperated* against her inclination is a hard destiny indeed, for I take it for granted *she* could not [in] *reality* wish for an alliance with Bonaparte; altho' she might like to be an Empress I cannot forbear smiling when I look back on all I have writen about Kings and Emperor's, but who is it that does not feel interested in this great and surprising revolution: so important to our own Country. May it give us the blessings of Peace.

187

I forgot to mention to you that when I passed through Alexandria Mrs Hopkins again mentioned Miss Lomax poems, and her intention of sending you double the number for which you subscribed. I gave her to understand as *modestly* and as *delicately* as I could that *I suspected* this would not be agreeable to you. I believe she took the hint.

You say nothing of Cousin Anna or dear little Richard. I flatter myself from your silence on the subject he is getting well. Lynch the Husband of Polly told me he had seen her and that she was very well, and had been very kind to his Wife, her benevolence was never excited by a more worthy object than this poor Girl who is one of the best most faithful and trusty creatures in the world.

I wish you would tell me *honestly* how you like the ruffle as I intend if you are pleased with it to work you another, and it shall be *superlatively* elegant if I can procure the right sort of lace for letting in. Tell cousin Anna her stockings for my darling Doll shall be forth-coming by and bye, if she will assure me that she has left of Coquetting now that I am come away, and continues to bestow on me the epithet of "my Sally"—pray dont you deliver any message in answer to all this for I am determined to get a letter from Cousin Anna in return for the long one I sent her about a month ago.

And now my dear Cousin I must thank *you* for ⟨. . .⟩ civil things Madame Serurier says of me—if this is her Ladiship's opinion it will be good policy in me to keep away from her, as the sight of me will prove how erroneous it is— but what flattered me infinitely more than any thing this Lady could say of me was the assurance that I am necessary to your happiness, this makes me very, very proud.

I thank you my more than Friend for the wish you express for my spending the next Winter with you—but I dare not hope, or think about it.

What a long letter I have writen you, and could scribble a great deal more if I were not afraid of boring you—Your friends here desire to be affectionately remembered to you and yours & to your Husband present *my* cordial love, for in truth my dear Cousin I do love him dearly. When you see Mrs Rush, pray make her remember me for it would give me concern to be forgotten by her— Adieu, my own Friend

Sarah Coles

RC (MCR-S: Mary Estelle Elizabeth Cutts Papers). Damaged by removal of seal.

1. Napoleon Bonaparte had abdicated on 4 April 1814.

2. Louis XVIII (1755–1824) ruled 1814–15 and again 1815–24, his reign being temporarily interrupted by the reappearance of Napoleon during the Hundred Days. In 1824 his brother Charles X (1757–1836) acceded to the throne.

To Hannah Gallatin

July 28th. [18]14.

Forgive my long silence beloved friend I have been waiting for acceptable news to communicate to you—but alass we have nothing from Europe except from the News-papers. This does not prevent our hopes of peace, & the spedy return of your dear Husband with our sons.

I ardently hope you are more composed more resigned, than when you wrote last as the time, is nearer at hand when your anxieties will end. I wish I could see you, at your new lodgings—or indeed any where in this world. We have been in a state of purturbation here, for a long time—The depredations of the Enemy approaching within 20 miles of the City & the disaffected, makeing incessant difficulties for the Government. Such a place as this has become I can not discribe it—I wish (for my own part) *we ware* at Phila. The people here do not deserve that *I* should prefer it—among other exclamations & threats they say if Mr. M. attempts to move from *this House,* in case of an atack, they will *stop him* & that he shall *fall with it*—I am not the least alarmed at these things, but entirely disgusted, & determined to stay with him. Our preperations for defence by some means or other, is constantly retarded but the small force the British have on the Bay will never venture nearer that at present 23 miles—I desired Mr. Astor to tell you the strange story they made, about your haveing reccd. a letter from Mr. G. full of alarming information, such, as his haveing no prospect of makeing peace & urgeing you for your personal safety to quit N. York & reside in Phila. It had a distressing effect on our Loan & threw many into consternation for a while but we ware able to contradict & soften consequences. I was rejoiced at your last letter containing the acct. of my precious Payne's going to France from England—I have written him by Mr Carraman to return only with Mr. Gallatin & James—be that when it may—I hope we shall see our Sons highly benifitted by their Tour— How is your dear Francis? Miss Morris tell's me you are near her—Lucy writes me that Mrs. Clay is quite well & busy, in prepareing a fine Gardin &c &c. for her Husband—They will elect him again in Kentucky for Congress—Anna is very *large,* & complaining, but her genl. health better than when you saw her last—Richd. who has been long afflicted, is geting well now—I have often thought of your Furniture my dear friend, in these frightful times, & have wished it was sold for your sake—Madame Bs went off very well, & the anxiety for its safety is over, *with her,* when in other hands—However, I hope now, the worst is over & that I shall yet see you siting in your own Sopha in *our own* circle—Adeiu for the present.

30th. For the 2 last days a distressing rise in the rivers has prevented our sending the mail—Tis uncertain whether it can go to day—Nothing has occured since I began this—I am told Dispatches will go directly to France—should you desire to write perhaps from hence, it would be best to send your letters. I hope soon to hear from you—accept our united affections ever your own friend

D P M

RC (NHi: Gallatin Papers, 1814, no. 113).

To John Payne Todd

6th. August [18]14.

Early in July I wrote you my dearest P. by Mr. Carraman—I hope you have the letter by this day—I wrote also by Mr Hughes & Mr Carrol. Not a line from you has reached us since you left St. P———.[1] How impatient I am, you *aught* to immagin—I am consoled for your absence & your silence by the impression that you are engrossed by the variety of objects in Europe which are to enlighten & benifit you the rest of your life. Mr. G.[2] wrote his wife, that you had left England for France, which at such a time must gratify you in many respects. Mr. Boyde[3] will hand you this, if he can, if not, it will be sent to you—I hope however, you will meet him, as he is an estimable man & a friend who can tell you all about your family &&. Nothing has occured either publick or private worth writeing, since my last—The British on our shore's are stealing & destroying private property, rarely comeing to battle but when they do, are allways beaten—You will hear by this oppy. of the briliant affair by Genls. Brown & Scott.[4] If the War should last 6 months longer the U.S. will conquer her Enimies. Robert is better & very anxious to go abroad[5]—all well in Orange & every one anxious to see you—Your P. & you[r] Mother in good health sighing to hear from you—& looking forward to the fall with anxious hope that you will return to them. Ed. Coles is now on a visit to Balls Town[6] he wrote you by Mr. Carraman—farewell May Heaven bless, & protect you!

RC (Macculloch Hall Historical Museum, Morristown, N.J.).
1. St. Petersburg, Russia.
2. Albert Gallatin.

3. George Boyd.

4. The "briliant affair" to which DPM refers here was probably the Battle of Chippewa, 5 July 1814, fought along the Canadian frontier near Niagara. It was followed by the Battle of Lundy's Lane on 25 July. These battles "marked the first occasion in the war when American regulars had met and beaten British regulars on anything like equal terms" (Stagg, *Mr. Madison's War*, 401–2).

5. Robert L. Madison, JM's nephew.

6. Balls Town (present-day Ballston Spa) was a mineral-spring resort in upstate New York.

To Hannah Gallatin

17th. August [1814]

I have been waiting to see Genl Mason my dear friend, in order to urge the security of your plate, before I answer'd your last—The Genl. did not know that it had been removed, but assures me he will attend to it & have it sent to a proper place—so that you may be easy on the subject—I hope you have reccd. letters by the D. Minister before this—They, if written as lately, as the official one to Mr. M. will tell you, that Mr. Gallatin was in London on the 2d. of June—he tells Mr. M that Mr. Byard had gone to Flanders, & that *he should* also go there in a few days to negociate for Peace. Mr M says, this is all sd. letter contained, which would interest you—he joines us in praying for the success, & safe return of our ever valued Mr. Gallatin—Be of good chear my precious—your reward will be ample for the sorrow & anxieties, you have suffered in this seperation—Yours, ever affectinate

D P M

RC (NHi: Gallatin Papers, 1814, no. 127).

To Hannah Gallatin

Saturday August [1814]

A short Official letter from Mr. Gallatin was reccd. yesterday—dated London 1st of June—he says nothing of Payne of course, but perhaps in your's my dear friend, I can be favored with some acct. of him—This suspence is distressing—but you have known, & felt so much that I aught not to complain— Tell me something of your prospects now—Is there hope of their return soon? or can the expectation of peace be cherished still(?) In case of peace would you like to be in Europe, as *Minister?* Oh that I could see you my beloved friend, that I might tell you, & hear from you many things—We are still without an idea of going from hence. Tell me, in case of the Reinforcement of the British & their comeing here, whether you have an active agent to take care of your furniture—If you have not, I will have it secured for you most assuredly—I wrote to you last week & told you of an oppty. to write to your Husband—In a very few days, will go a Messenger, tho tis necessary to say nothing about it least the British be informed also—If you should see Mrs. Custis please to tell her if she wishes to write to france she must do it directly, & send to the Office of State. I write you in the greatest haste, as we have a large party to dine & they are now collecting—pray say a word to me directly & burn this scrall—yours ever & affectinately

D

RC (NHi: Gallatin Papers, 1814, no. 131).

From James Madison

MR. WILLIAM'S ABOUT 6 OR 7 MILES FROM WASHINGTON

My dearest   Tuesday Aug. 23. [1814]

We reached our quarters last evening at the Camp between 8 & 9 o'c. and made out very well. I have passed the forenoon among the troops, who are in high spirits & make a good appearance. The reports as to the enemy have varied every hour. The last & probably truest information is that they are not very strong, and are without cavilry and artillery, and of course that they are not in a condition to strike at Washington. It is believed also that they are not about to move from Marlbro unless it be from an apprehension of our gathering force and on a retreat to their ships. It is possible, however they may have a greater force or expect one, than has been represented or that their timerity may be greater than their strength. I sent you a message last night by Col. M. and one today by messenger of Genl. Winder who set out at a moment when it was impossible to write. I have retained Shorter that I might give you by him some final & certain information. We expect every hour to have something further from the camp concerning the Enemy. If it should be a matter ⟨?⟩ to make it advisable to return to the Camp; you will not see me this morning; otherwise I hope I shall be with you in the course of . . . perhaps later in the evening. Your devoted husband

J.M.

Printed extract (Frederick B. McGuire—Madison Catalogue [26 Feb. 1917], item 91).

To Lucy Payne Washington Todd

Dear Sister   Tuesday Augt. 23d. 1814.

My husband left me yesterday morng. to join Gen. Winder. He enquired anxiously whether I had courage, or firmness to remain in the President's house until his return, on the morrow, or succeeding day, and on my assurance that I had no fear but for him and the success of our army, he left me, beseeching me to take care of myself, and of the cabinet papers, public and private. I have since recd. two despatches from him, written with a pencil; the last is alarming, because he desires I should be ready at a moment's warning to enter my carriage and leave the city; that the enemy seemed stronger than had been reported and that it might happen that they would reach the city, with intention to destroy it. . . . I am accordingly ready; I have pressed as many cabinet papers into trunks as to fill one carriage; our private property must be sacrificed, as it is impossible to procure wagons for its transportation. I am determined not to go myself until I see Mr Madison safe, and he can accompany me, as I hear of much hostility towards him, . . . disaffection stalks around us. . . . My friends and acquaintances are all gone; Even Col. C[1] with his hundred men, who were stationed as a guard in the enclosure . . . French John (a faithful domestic,) with his usual activity and resolution, offers to spike the cannon at the gate, and to lay a train of powder which would blow up the British, should they enter the house. To the last proposition I positively object, without being able, however, to make him understand why all advantages in war may not be taken.

Wednesday morng., twelve o'clock. Since sunrise I have been turning my spy glass in every direction and watching with unwearied anxiety, hoping to discern the approach of my dear husband and his friends, but, alas, I can descry only groups of military wandering in all directions, as if there was a lack of arms, or of spirit to fight for their own firesides!

Three O'clock. Will you believe it, my Sister? We have had a battle or skirmish near Bladensburg, and I am still here within sound of the cannon! Mr. Madison comes not; may God protect him! Two messengers covered with dust, come to bid me fly; but I wait for him. . . . At this late hour a wagon has been procured, I have had it filled with the plate and most valuable portable articles belonging to the house; whether it will reach its destination; the Bank of Maryland, or fall into the hands of British soldiery, events must determine.

Our kind friend, Mr. Carroll,[2] has come to hasten my departure, and is in a very bad humor with me because I insist on waiting until the large picture of Gen. Washington is secured, and it requires to be unscrewed from the wall. This process was found too tedious for these perilous moments; I have ordered the frame to be broken, and the canvass taken out it is done, and the precious portrait placed in the hands of two gentlemen of New York,[3] for safe keeping. And now, dear sister, I must leave this house, or the retreating army will make me a prisoner in it, by filling up the road I am directed to take. When I shall again write you, or where I shall be tomorrow, I cannot tell!!

Tr (DLC: DPM Papers). Marked at top "Extract from a letter to my Sister published in the sketch of my life written for the 'National Portrait Gallery.'"
1. This probably refers to Col. Henry Carberry (1757–1822) of the U.S. Army (William M. Marine, *The British Invasion of Maryland, 1812–1815* [Baltimore, 1913], 87–89, 238–39).
2. Charles Carroll of Bellevue.
3. Robert Gilbert Livingston DePeyster and Jacob Barker.

From Anna Cutts

My Sister—   [ca. 23 August 1814]
    Tell me for gods sake where you are and what [you are] going to do—I have only time to ask Mr. C. to take out the fore part of the carriage—put in the piano—and any thing he can get in there, or in a wagon if the British are coming—We can hear nothing but what is horrible here—I know not who to send this to—and will say but little—

                                                              A Cutts

RC (owned by Mrs. Ronald T. Lyman, Charleston, S.C., 2001).

From James Madison

My dearest   BROOKVILLE Aug. 27. 10 OC. [1814]
    Finding that our army had left Montgomery Court House we pushed on to this place, with a view to join it, or proceed to the City as further information might prescribe. I have just recd. a line from Col. Monroe, saying that the Enemy were out of Washington, & on the retreat to their Ships & advising our immediate return to Washington. We shall accordingly set out thither immediately. You will all of course take the same resolution. I know not where we are in the first instance to hide our heads; but shall look for a place on my arrival. Mr Rush offers his house in the six buildings and the offer claims attention. Perhaps I may fall in with Mr. Cutts, and have the aid of his advice. I saw Mr. Bradley[1] at Montgomery Ct. H. who told me that Mrs Cutts

was well. Jamey will give you some particulars wch. I have not time to write. Truly yours

J. Madison

Since the above it is found necessary to detain Jamey, & sent a Trooper

RC (DLC).

1. This was probably Abraham Bradley (d. 1838), the first assistant postmaster general (Charles S. Bradley, "The Bradley Family and the Times in Which They Lived," *Records of the Columbia Historical Society* 6 [1903]: 123–42).

From James Madison

[28 August 1814]

and I cannot yet learn what has been the result. Should the fort have been taken, the British Ships with their barges will be able to throw the City again into alarm, and you may be again compelled to retire from it, which I find would have a disagreeable effect. Should the Ships have failed in their attack, you cannot return too soon. ⟨I will⟩ keep Freeman till the question is decided, and then lose no time in sending him to you. In the mean time it will be best for you to remain in your present quarters. I wrote you yesterday morning by express from Brookeville, and at the same time to the Secy. of the Navy,[1] supposing you all to be together. It is possible the separation may have prevented your receiving the letter. I returned to the City yesterday, in company with Mr. Monroe, Mr. Rush &c. and have summoned the Heads of Dept to meet here without delay. Inclosed is a letter from Mr Cutts. My next will be by Freeman & as soon as I can decide the point of your coming on. Every [*sic*] & most affy Yours

J. M.

RC (DLC). First page missing.
1. William Jones.

From Anne Cary Morris

Dear Madam   [ca. December 1814–January 1815]

I hope you will pardon the liberty I take—my fee[l]ings are too much wounded to consult my husband on the propriety of the measure. I pray you to shew the enclosed, to every Virginian, in Washington, who possesses honour—My beloved husband was informed of Jack Randolph's *insinuations* respecting me—and suppressed them—nothing but insinuation was heard—he avoided being brought to the test—Yesterday I received the anonymous letter in a strange hand—containing his hideous charges—it came from the post office. I have sent it to a Friend in Virginia—Merciful God I knew not how Base he was till now. I am, dear Madam, respectfully Yrs

Ann C. Morris.[1]

[ENCLOSURE]

A Southern Friend of mine, who witnessed Jack Randolph's frantic conduct, at not being sent minister to Great Briton, will soon furnish from that quarter a sketch of his baseness as a politician—his constituents (at least, those who once were) must be deranged if they ever reelect this malignant madman—He hates Colonel Monroe—because he is under obligations to that Gentleman—his Deaf and dumb nephew[2] was befriended by Col. M's family—his Savage heart cannot forgive kindness—his other nephew was thrown on the bounty of a relative who had been turned out without Shelter by Jack Randolph and his "amiable" Sister in Law—This young man wrote from Cambridge early last Spring (then in bad health) to borrow money from his relation—it was sent without delay—In a *style suited* to Mr. *John Randolph's* pride this nephew with a Carriage—three horses and a Servant—was thrown on the *bounty* of a relative (whom providence had protected) on the fourth of last August—his physician pronounced him on the borders of incurable disease—he remained in total dependance even for wages to answer the demands of his Servant—twelve weeks—a heavy tax on the time—the health—and purse of his relation until her health was destroyed. Mr. Randolph wrote long letters filled with highly coloured accts. of his "illustrious Ancestry"—but they must have lain unopened if this relation had not paid the postage—they contained no mention of supplies—The Gentleman's mother wrote him of the Uncle's neglect, and the generosity of the Grandpapa (a most excellent man) in lending her money to bring her to the Son who was continually relapsing—Mr. Jack Randolph's return for all the kindness and liberality shewn his nephew Tudor has been conveyed to the benefactress in an anonymous letter accusing her of crimes which her Soul abhors—This lady was engaged at an early period of life to the second brother of John Randolph.[3] She imparted to John Randolph the extent of their relative situations, in a confidential letter—on leaving Virginia never to return—with no refuge from suffering in view, except the Grave—John Randolph is afraid the Law may lay hold of him.

Mr. Jack Randolph causes to be asserted in New York (he has cautiously avoided prosecution as yet) that Miss Randolph (now Mrs. Morris) lived as the wife of one of her Father's black Gardener's from the age of nineteen until she gained a living by prostitution in Richmond—that—as she made much money in this way—she refused his assistance—that she murdered her brother-in-law[4] because he knew she had killed a black child which she had—that her son is no Morris—that she is in the habit of committing forgery.

Merciful God—can such a Man be Countenanced!—by any one professing honour—justice, or the least regard to Truth.

RC (MCR-S: Mary Estelle Elizabeth Cutts Papers).

1. Anne Cary (Nancy) Randolph Morris was the center of a major scandal in Virginia in 1792–93, having been accused of having an affair with her brother-in-law Richard Randolph, eldest brother of John Randolph of Roanoke, and of infanticide. Though the charges were dismissed, John Randolph threw her out of his home, Bizarre, in 1805, and for the next four years she lived in poverty in Richmond and New York City. In 1809 she married the wealthy New York patrician Gouverneur Morris and in 1814 was comfortably established at Morrisania, her husband's estate. That year, however, one of her nephews, Tudor Randolph, a consumptive college student, paid a lengthy visit to the Morrises. At one point during the visit, he became very ill, and John Randolph came to Morrisania to visit him. After that meeting Nancy Morris received a letter from Randolph and two months later an anonymous letter, charging her with crimes of murder, prostitution, miscegenation, and adultery. Her response was to begin a campaign to refute his charges and to destroy his reputation. This letter to DPM was very likely an attempt to convince the First Lady to lead an effort to ostracize John Randolph (Alan Pell Crawford, *Unwise Passions* [New York, 2000]).

2. John St. George Randolph, son of Judith and Richard Randolph.

3. Theodorick Randolph.

4. Richard Randolph, who died in 1796.

To Hannah Gallatin

14th. Jany. [18]15.

I understand my dear friend, that you wish to sell your Furniture, & as I shall soon move into an *empty house,* may I ask the favor of you to let me have 2 or 3 beds, the 2 *Eustis* Chairs, & some other articles? I will name *nothing* else until you tell me whether it would be agreable to you that I should see, & purchase what I want of any agent you may appoint. Things of *this* sort are scarce & dear, yet at Octions, they are often sacrificed—We hear nothing from Mr. Gallatin, but expect every day, some arrival. Our anxieties cannot be expressed—The fate of N. Orleans will be known to day—on which so much depends—We have had a frightful fever in Alxa. & Washington, but it abates & our spirits are re-newed. Mr Rush is still very low but hopes are entertain'd that he will recover soon—Anna has had a sick family all the Winter as well as myself—Miss Coles[1] is with me & begs to be affectinately remembered to you, as does the whole of our house. Adeiu my dear friend I am ever truly yours

DPM

RC (NHi: Gallatin Papers, 1815, no. 8).
1. DPM's cousin Sarah Coles.

From Hannah Gallatin

My dear friend,   PHILADELPHIA January 18th. 1815

I did not receive your letter dated the 14th. untill this day. I presume it must be owing to the badness of the roads.

I hasten to tell you that you may have what you may want of my furniture, at the same time I wish it could suit you to take all that is in the house at Washington. I have written to Mr. Cazenove to have the things valued, he is our agent, and will give you all the necessary information about them.

What would I give my dear friend could I enjoy the happiness of an hour's conversation with you, it would be worth all the letters I could write. How often do I think of you, & how much have I felt for you, what trials you have passed through in the last six months. Capt. Jones has told me some details, that I had no idea of. I hope you may never witness such scenes again.

I wish we could hear from Europe. I am all anxiety also about the fate of New Orleans. Heaven grant that we may have good tidings soon.

Remember me to Mr. Madison to Mr. & Mrs. Cutts, Miss Coles & Cousin Edward and believe me ever your sincere friend

H Gallatin

RC (ViU). Docketed by JM.

To Hannah Gallatin

[5 March 1815]

I have been silent my dear friend but I have thought of you continually— I have rejoiced *with* you & for you—our glorious Peace. The prospect of seeing objects most dear to us in Aprl. has fill'd me with gratitude to Heaven & again—I trust you are pleased with Mr. G——s appointment to France.[1] You know I enquired of you long ago how you would like it, since which many circumstances have occured to render more agreable to your Husband, a residence at that Coart. How I should like to go with you! Tell me how you feel—what Albert & Francis think of it. I'm told that James is so improved that we shall scarcely know him & that he is delighted with Europe. I had indulged some hope of seeing you in Phila this Spring—dureing the Winter, but now I see plainly that I decievd myself—Washington & Orange, forever rise up to impede my *fairer prospects*—How then am I ever to see you again? You must come here indeed—The roads will mend, & when Mr. Gallatin arrives you must accompany him to the City—We shall move in 10 days[2] & if you will give me leave, I will take to my house the Eustis Chares until you come or make other arrangements on the subject of your Furniture which has been injured from disuse. Mrs. Knapp sent me your letter, or I should have taken many things after the Apraisment proposed by Mr. Caznauf.[3] Do you know of any easy french Chairs to be sold in Phila. for a reasonable price? second hand sophas Carpits—or in short any handsome furniture that would answer for us—give my best love to Mrs. Dallas, & her daughters & hasten to tell me something of yourself my dear friend—Congress adjourn'd last night, still our house is crouded with company—in truth ever since the peace my brain has been turn'd with noise & bustle. Such over flowing rooms I never saw before—I sigh for repose, & for the removal of the Treasury, when I may get into the *sun-shine*, tho nearly *bereft* of furniture & cloaths—Anna Cousins Sally & Edd. join me in best wishes & affection for you—ever yours

DPM

RC (NHi: Gallatin Papers, 1815, no. 10). Conjectural date assigned on the basis of internal evidence and the postmark.

1. JM offered Gallatin the position of U.S. minister to France while the latter was still negotiating the peace at Ghent. On 22 July 1815 Gallatin set sail for the United States with his son James, Henry Clay, and John Payne Todd. He returned to Europe with his family in June 1816 (Walters, *Albert Gallatin*, 290–98).

2. The Madisons moved from the Octagon House to the Seven Buildings, located on the corner of Nineteenth Street and Pennsylvania Avenue.

3. Anthony-Charles Cazenove.

To Hannah Gallatin

19th. March [1815]

I am on the wing for Orange my dear friend, & have just time to tell you that Mr M thinks (indeed is sure) that Mr Gallatin will return to you before he visits Paris as Minister, because in the first place it was not in his power to let Mr. G. know his intention to appoint him, before the moment would arrive to exicute it. The Dispatches, which woud have given him the earliest inteligence & might have saved him the voage home—ware sent too late for the *Favorite* & I beleive are still in this Country, if not in the Office of State. Yes you will soon see them all—about the 10 or 15th. of may you will embrace your estimable Husband & son—but when shall *I* see you? It will be the last of May before we return to W—even then I trust I shall not be too late to see you once more—I have not courage to write about it—Alass! how many things occur in this world to afflict us—For the first time I leave Washington with sorrow because it lessens my chance of seeing you, & retards my meeting with Payne. I hope you will write me from time to time, because you know that I love you as my sister—farewell for the present. Mr. M & Anna join me in best affection for you—Cousins S. & Ed. left us 3 days ago—love to Mrs. Dallas—P. Morris—& respects &c &c &c. for Mrs. Kantzou & daughters—Mr. and Mrs. Hughes dine with us to day—I expect Mrs Bonoparte will try to go over with you in preferance to—Yours ever

DPM

RC (NHi: Gallatin Papers, 1815, no. 12).

From Abigail Adams

Dear Madam   QUINCY May 14th. 1815

My Grandson William Stuben Smith, having returnd from abroad, declines the honour which I have been informd, was intended him by the president, as secretary of Legation, to the Mission to England. His brother, John Adams Smith, has written to me to request of the president, the appointment, if he should deem it proper to grant it to him.

As Congress do not allow a private Secretary to their Foreign Ministers, they are placed in rather a dissagreable Situation; if a Secretary of Legation is appointed, who is a Stranger to them, and in whom they may not be able to place a confidence.

Mr. Smith who will have the honour to deliver you this Letter, has been Educated to the Bar, is a young Gentleman of correct principles, and by no means addicted to dissipation.

Unaccustomed to ask favours of this nature for Friends or connections—I have the rather addrest you Madam, than the president, altho I have never had the pleasure of a personal accquaintance with you—that I may thus introduce myself to you: and embrace the opportunity of expressing my esteem for your Character, and respect for the president, and with these Sentiments I Subscribe myself Your Humble Servant

Abigail Adams

RC (ICN).

From Sarah Coles

ENNISCORTHY June 17th 1815

I am quite provoked that the edging will not hold out to do the collar, but the circumference of the Vandyke is so great that it has taken all except the little peice enclosed: I wished to have completed it so that you would have nothing to do but to throw it over your neck, tho' I dare say it will be prettier with richer lace on the collar—my design was to sew two rows about the width of that around it, upright on the collar, with a little fullness.

The papers announce your safe arrival in Washington and Cousin Anna has no doubt greeted you with the most heart-felt joy: I have heard nothing of her plans for the Summer, whether she has relinquished all idea of the Springs.

I suppose you are in daily expectation of Cousin Payne's arrival. I trust that pleasant gales are now wafting him to you and that a very few days will bless you with a sight of him—sad and spiritless as I feel at this moment, I can still rejoice at the prospect of happiness to you—Thine own affectionate

Sarah Coles

RC (MCR-S: Mary Estelle Elizabeth Cutts Papers). Docketed by DPM.

From Sarah Coles

ENNISCORTHY July 31st. 1815.

I can scarcely beleive it possible that two weeks have elapsed since I received the sweetest kindest letter that ever charmed the friendly heart—and the beautiful trimming too! For both, accept my thanks, my dearest best Cousin, and believe that I could not have delayed my acknowledgements thus long, but for the want of one little minute to make them: Rebecca[1] and her family arrived soon after, and the house has been cro[w]ded with visitors ever since a Mr Taylor of South Carolina,[2] Miss Robertson, Cousin Walter[3] &c &c and

201

you know how difficult it is to steal a moment from visitors in the Country. I see from the papers of yesterday that you have returned to Orange, and without Cousin Payne,[4] yet I will still hope that a very short time will bring him to you, we are told that "tis expectation makes a blessing dear"[5] how dear, how very dear, then will be the sight of your darling son—Cousin Anna[6] I hope has returned with you, tell her I dispair now of having her company to the Springs, as we leave this next Monday and I hear nothing from her—I regret very much that I shall not see you while you are at Montpelier but it is impossible, without giving up my trip to the Springs and I should be very unwilling to let sister Carter[7] go alo⟨ne.⟩ Helen[8] is also going for her health, which has and still is so delicate as to alarm the apprehensive tenderness of her husband, but her stay will be very short, and her movements too irregular for sister Carter. The latter is much disappointed at not having Cousin Anna's company—offer my affectionate love to her and tell her if she had given me an opportunity I should have made myself so *amiable* that she would have loved me better than she *ever* did in her life.

I saw Mrs Randolph and Ellen a short time since they were well, and in fine spirits. Little Sep[9] had been very sick, but is now quite recovered—The Nicholas's and Smith's[10] were here the other day in all their splendor—and amused themselves in uttering the severest philippics I ever heard against our good old Col Munroe. I was shocked to hear from the lips of a lady such vindictive language—Excuse this scrawl, I am in the midst of preparation for our intended excursion.

May Heaven ever bless you—my dear and precious Friend, and sheild you from every harm is the ardent prayer of thine own

S. Coles

RC (MCR-S: Mary Estelle Elizabeth Cutts Papers).

1. Rebecca Coles Singleton.

2. This may have been Thomas Taylor (1743–1833) of Columbia, S.C., whose son married into the Coles family.

3. Walter Coles.

4. John Payne Todd.

5. "Tis expectation makes a blessing dear; / Heaven were not heaven if we knew what it were" (Sir John Suckling, "Against Fruition," in *The Works of Sir John Suckling in Prose and Verse,* ed. A. Hamilton Thompson [London, 1910], 18).

6. Anna Payne Cutts.

7. Mary Eliza Coles Carter, wife of Robert Carter.

8. Helen Skipwith Coles.

9. Septimia Anne Randolph, daughter of Martha Jefferson and Thomas Mann Randolph. Ellen Wayles Randolph was one of her sisters.

10. This was probably a reference to the families of Wilson Cary Nicholas and Samuel and Robert Smith.

To Hannah Gallatin

[ca. 7 August 1815]

I am so miserable & so astonished at the entire silence of Mr Crawford, after his haveing left our best friends, without their knowledge or consent[1]— that I am induced to make enquiries of you my beloved Mrs. Gallatin—It is said one of your servants has return'd in the Neptune with Baggage—can he tell you in what Vessel *they* will return, or when? whether they ware well & likly to make the Treaty?[2] Mr M has expected every day to recce. some inteligence from Mr. C. but to this moment he is ignorent on eviry point, & so are the News Papers (except that Mr. G. & Mr. Clay are left behind without knowing of Capn. Jone's departure—Mr. Dallas supposes (as was naturel) that *we* had known something more but no—we are kept in painful suspence—Will you have the goodness to ask the favor of Capt. Jones to send to Washington my dear Paynes Cloaths, & a variety of articles he has collected in Europe for us— I am affraid they ware placed carlessly on board the Neptune without direction, or security, as he expected to come with them, & may be lost, without the particular attention of Capt. Jones—I feel deeply for you my dear friend as your trials seem to continue beyond the term of human patience—present me affectinately to Mrs. Dallas & beleive me ever yours

DPM

Write me a few lines & let *no one* see this hasty scrawl.

Orange *Monday 7th. August.* & after the Mail from Washington—Anna & her six children are with us—greatly improved in their health & spirits.

RC (NHi: Gallatin Papers, 1815, no. 73).

1. William Harris Crawford was U.S. minister to France 1813–15. Having originally intended to return to the United States with the members of the Ghent Peace Commission, Crawford and commissioner James A. Bayard hurriedly left from London in June after Bayard became dangerously ill, bringing with them Gallatin's and Clay's baggage and one of Gallatin's servants. Bayard died within days of his arrival in Delaware. Crawford did, in fact, visit Montpelier later that month, on his way home to Georgia (Walters, *Albert Gallatin*, 291–94; Ketcham, *James Madison*, 601).

2. After the Treaty of Ghent was signed, Gallatin, Henry Clay, and John Quincy Adams went to London, where they negotiated a commercial treaty, completing their work on 3 July. John Payne Todd, traveling with the Gallatins, left Liverpool for the United States on 22 July and arrived in New York on 1 Sept. (Walters, *Albert Gallatin*, 291–94).

To Hannah Gallatin

My dear friend   12th. August. [18]15.

I wrote you on the 7th. to Phila. asking *information* & your interest with Capn. Jones, on the subject of my sons baggage on board the Nepturn—on the 9th. I reccd. a letter from Payne dated London & about the time of *this* Vessel's sailing—I will give you his own words, as they contain (Mr Madison says) the only satisfactory information we have. "Messrs. Gallatin & Clay, in consequence of an interview with Commissioners from the board of trade have been induced to delay their departure somewhat longer—Mr Adams has joined them. Messrs. Robertson,[1] of the Admiralty, Goulbourn & Docr. Adams, two of the late Bth. Ministers at Gent, have been appointed by their Govt. Comms to negociate a commertial treaty with Mr Gallatin Clay & Adams—They have had several meetings, & the project on a treaty has been given by *our Ministers* who await a counter project, & after it is reccd. if it should appear expediant to remain longer than next week, at most, they will decide on sending the Neptern home without them. A disadvantagious Treaty will not be signed—tho I apprehend there is not much room to hope for a happy settlement of the question of *Impressment.* The existance of this Negotiation is not made public here. It is best, therefore, not to mention it until one of our Ministers shall write. We are all perfectly well & hope *still* to embrace you in *all July*—We have a great deal for you on board the Neptern with Mr. G. & Mr C—s baggage."

I would inclose you the precious letter my dear friend, but that I find the above is all that interests you particularly we may surely, expect them *this* month & my ardent prayer is for their safe return! poor Byard—& his poor wife! how I greave for her! I hear you have left Phila. for N. York but where ever you are my affections will follow you. Let me hear from you—& before long I will hope to see you. This hasty letter is for your eye alone.

DPM

RC (NHi: Gallatin Papers, 1815, no. 75).
1. Frederick John Robinson.

From Hannah Gallatin

NEW YORK August 13th. 1815

Ah! my dear friend what misery are we enduring. How can Mr. Crawford be so unfeeling, I thought you had certainly received every information about your beloved Payne, and was in hopes from day to day that it would come to Mr. C's recollection also, what my feelings must be, but alas, not one word from him. William Nicholson (whom you may remember lived with us), tells me that Mr. Crawford wrote to Mr. Gallatin that the Ship could not be detained on account of Mr. Bayard and that Mr. Gallatin answered it was impossible for them to be at Plymouth before the 24th. of June, that they sailed immediately, without waiting for any further information from them. It is proved to be sure that there was no time to be lost for poor Mr. Bayard, he died the sixth day after their arrival, but Mr. Crawford I cannot forgive for not attending a little to our feelings. Oh what anguish there is in disappointed hope.

Our Servant Harry has arrived in the Neptune with all Mr. Gallatin's & James's baggage. I have written to Capt. Jones to send them on to me here with Harry who is a faithful excellent creature, his family live in Washington, and I presume he will be anxious to go & see them, I will when he returns through Philaa. get him to take charge of all the things that belong to Payne & yourself and take them to Washington. Harry was I am told very much distressed at the Ship sailing without his master as he calls Mr. Gallatin. If you approve of this arrangement I will give him a letter to Capt. Jones with the directions.

I have seen in the Newspaper that a Vessel had arrived at Boston, direct from London, left there the 26th. June. The Captn. says that he was to have brought out Messrs. Clay Gallatin & suite, but afterwards they had concluded to sail from Liverpool, I presume from this that they had finished the treaty & that we may expect them every moment. I think they wil come to New York. The instant they arrive I will my dear friend let you know of it. You & I can best feel for one another. In the mean time if Mr. Crawford should give you any information about them do let me know, at all events write to me my dear friend. I do not think you have any cause to feel uneasy about the things you have on board the Neptune. I believe the Capt. is very careful, and I think it probable Harry has attended to this too. What a disappointment to those left behind, all the cloaths that they were to wear at sea every thing has come in the Ship, and worst of all for my poor husband who is distressedly sick at sea. Harry was his Nurse. I do assure you I feel almost broken hearted. I can neither, sleep nor eat. After all my anxiety about the Neptune that she should arrive without my husband & child, it is indeed distressing beyond what I could conceive, and I feel afraid to expect them. I dread another disappointment.

It is a comfort to you to have Mrs. Cutts with you and it is a pleasure to me to hear she & her children are well. Remember me to her, also to Mr. Madison, who I hope has quite recovered his health. Heaven bless you ever your affectionate friend

H Gallatin

It is four weeks since I left Philadelphia for this place.

RC (owned by Charles M. Storey, Boston, Mass., 1961).

To Edward Coles

March 6th. 1816.

Your letter from Mr Singletons has been greatfully reccd. my dr. Cousin and I hasten to apprize you of your being an *unjust* man. For all our anxieties—our sighs, & regrets after you, you reward us by doubts of our constancy!!! but, with what is of infinate value to our hearts—your affection & friendship—among the many proofs of this, are your welcome letters—all of which have been answered by my Husband & son. Their last, ware sent to N. Orlians, & I trust will still be in your possession. I am truly glad to hear of Cousin Singleton's doing so well, she deserves to be the happiest as she is the best of women. Yesterday I had a letter from Enniscorthy—they are all well—People say that Cousin S. is to mary a man who is very highly spoken of, & I allmost hope it is true, for her sake.[1] As to the abominable story of Mrs. *Morse* of Paynes engagement, no one could beleive it—In truth I am affraid he will become as difficult to please, or to fall in love as *yourself,* & *consequently become a rover*—Mrs. Baldwin is soon to be united to Colo. Bumford, but no truth in the report (as yet) of Mrs. Barlow. Poor Mrs. Custis has been shocked, by the account of DeGraffs haveing cut his own throat in Paris two or 3 months ago—Miss Swan is in the city as beautiful as ever—Thornton, her devoted, is also here, but I hear nothing of their marriage. She speaks of you with apparently the same interest she used to do—If the world was not so full of deception I should think Miss Swan loved & prefer'd you to all others, but as it is, I would not answer for her—poor Ringold[2] has fallen in his fortune entirely—his young & amiable wife behaves well on the occation—He has sold to his creditors the fine House, & they have rented it to Mr Baker for his Minister[3]—I wish you could be here now, to try your *sensability* we count one hundred young ladies in the city—not 10 of them belong to the place—some of them are really fine & handsome—Miss Law—two Miss Byards—Miss Tallmadge & Eliza Carter I think, have most beauty—many of the others are prefered. Our Virga. Belles for instance, Miss Randolph & Misses Barbour &

Robertson—We have also an unusual numr. of young men from every direction—in short, we never had so busy a winter because the city was never before so full of respectable strangers—You may have heared of the visit to us, of Marshall Groushe,[4] so celebrated for his talents milatary, his mildness & the dangers he has passed—I saw him several times & like him much, poor old man! I am writeing in my worst stile my cousin, because I have a bad pen & ink, & am excessively hurried—This is D. Room evg—& we have such throngs, *you never saw.*

The Judge & Lucy, as well as all the rest of us rejoice in your return. They leave us in 3 weeks—Congress have yet done nothing with Mr. C's office[5]—but *they,* as well as most of the Politicians are busy forming the next President me & mine still adhear to Colo. M[6] as the best deserveing on every point. Mr. Crawford has many friends & few *open* enimies—Colo. M many of the last descreption. Govr. Tompkins too, devides the republican interest but, I *think,* however the storm may rage for a time our estimable country man will gain the *prize* (*as they think*)—Mr. M has been very well since you saw him—his spirits are fine, & nothing can surpass the sweetness of his temper—whilst these blessings are continued you[r] cousin can look with calmness, if not with pleasure to the day, when she is to give place to one more worthy than herself. Have you heard that Mr Pinkney goes to Russia—Mr. Gallatin to France?

I hope we shall soon see you either here or in Orange, & if you are able to read this pray make every allowance, & burn it—Mr M & Payne will surely write you but I must be beforehand with them. Ever your sincere friend

DPM

RC (NjP: Edward Coles Papers).
1. Sarah Coles married Andrew Stevenson on 8 Oct. 1816.
2. Tench Ringgold.
3. Anthony St. John Baker and Charles Bagot.
4. Emmanuel Grouchy.
5. Richard Cutts.
6. James Monroe.

To Hannah Gallatin

20th. Apl. 16.

All my hopes of seeing you again, in Washington have fled! Yet, I cannot doubt my dear friend but that you will be the happier for the decision you have made. I pray that it may be so. I have nothing amuseing or new to tell you my

motive for this hasty letter is rather to express my affection for you & yours—
& to say that, whilst I live I shall feel the warmest interest in all that concerns
you, & to express my hope's that you will some times write me, & when you
return that you will visit me in Virga. A few days ago I was ernestly requested
by Mrs. Patterson[1] & Miss Caton to enquire whether it would be agreable
to you that they, with Mr. Patterson should go in your Ship with you to
France—However unreasonable I was oblidged to promis I would mention
their wishes, & convey to them your answer—Say no, if you please—or yes—
they are not to take it a miss or be at all disappointed. If you are so good as to
tell me directly there will be an end to solicitation of *more* than *these,* at the
same time—Kiss Mr. Gallatin & Francis for me, & accept from your old &
faithful friend, her best love & wishes.

DPM

RC (NHi: Gallatin Papers, 1816, no. 43).
    1. Dorcas Spear Patterson was the mother of Elizabeth Patterson Bonaparte.

To Hannah Gallatin

26th. May 16.

I reccd. your kind letter my beloved friend, & am now about to accept the
favor you offer me of makeing purchases for me. I will confine myself to a very
few—Mr Madison has proposed that I ask you to chuse for me three Curtains
suited to a Country Drawing room of silk, trimed, & with cornishes—*all* of
reasonable price—our 3 windows are near together & form 3 door's—The
colour I leave to you—with eighteen Chairs & two small sophas suited to the
Curtains, & of *cheap price.* Two cheap cambrick ⟨worwked?⟩ morng. Caps one
dito Spencer, for myself (by your own size) or a little larger—with the largest
& ha[n]dsomest thread lace Vail you can get for 40. or 50$—any other little
cheap & beautiful thing you may send shall be greatfully paid for, whenever
Mr. Gallatin pleases—*My* mony would be good for nothing to you or I would
inclose—A Vessel arrived in W. lately from france with all sorts of fine work
&. &—but so dear that I could not buy—We have had a very pleasant visit
of a week, to Annapolis—where we saw the 74[1]—Mr. & Mrs. Pinkney, &
many other interesting people. Mrs. P. hopes to see you at Paris before she
returns—The Dallass family have all left us (he will return for 4 months) a
report has *return'd* from Phila. that *They despise Washington* & &. which I
do not believe, but which makes the whole Town *affronted with them*—so
different is the impression you have left that they mourn for the loss of a

friend—for my part I should have been too happy to live in *this* same *Washington* with you both—My dear friend I know too well what your situation will be on your arrival at Paris to expect you to shop but you will find Mr. Barnet or some other *knowing* American who will get at Oaction or at stores the inclosed list of articles on good terms, & send them to Alexa. Washington or Norfolk this summer or by the fall—present me affectinately to Madame Patterson Her Brother, with the Miss Catons, ware to sail for England this day— Mrs. Rush & Mrs. Lourd, went with me to the ship & beg me to offer their best regard to you—Kiss Mr. G., Francis & your sons for me. Accept from Mr. M. Payne & Anna & your ever affectinate friend their assurances of unalterable attatchment.

DPM.

RC (NHi: Gallatin Papers, 1816, no. 45).

    1. The *Washington,* a seventy-four-gun ship-of-the-line authorized by Congress in 1813 and commissioned in 1815, arrived in Annapolis, Md., on 15 May 1816. Over the next few days, a number of distinguished citizens, including the Madisons, visited the ship (Brant, *Madison* 6:406).

To Anna Cutts

My dear Anna,   Sunday Morng. [ca. May 1816]

    We got here quite well on the 3d. day to dinner, & found all pleasant—Jno. & Clary[1] joined us next day which was yesterday—with their fine little girl— Jno. is quite altered—sober, thin & industrious his wife in the same way— they will stay a few days this time, & I must send them home in the Carriage— Aunt & Unkle are well & going to live near Stephensburg on a place for Dolley[2]—Payne got up safe last night or rather at 5 oClock yesterday—I wish you & yours could enjoy this fine air &c—for the summer heats—I shall be allways anxious about you, & trust Heaven will preserve you allways particularly in the absence of your Husband, whose efforts for his family's good, I pray God to prosper & smile upon—I am all bustle, setling my House—I shall write per Freeman hereafter, who I told to call on you for information when & how he should come. I hope the Vessel we expected, will soon come & I will write you on the subject when I get the mans list of articles brought for me, so that they may be devided for the two places Washington & this—but I will write you often & you will I hope do the same—give my love to Mr. Cutts & the children & to my frends whom you may see—I think you had bette[r] not buy the Veil as I am almost sure I sent for one by Lantrings—& I shant want it.

Fare well for the present take care of yourself in all respects yours ever

I got a letter from Mrs. Gallatin yesterday she sails next Wednsday.[3]

RC (MCR-S: Mary Estelle Elizabeth Cutts Papers).
    1. John Coles Payne and his wife, Clara Wilcox Payne.
    2. The aunt and uncle mentioned here are probably Isaac and Lucy Coles Winston, who lived in Culpeper County, Va.; one of their daughters was Dolley Winston.
    3. The Gallatins sailed for France on 11 June 1816 (Walters, *Albert Gallatin*, 298).

From Hannah Gallatin

NEW YORK 2d. June 1816

I shall certainly my dear friend attend to the commission you have given me to make your purchases when I arrive in Paris, we shall have to get furniture of the same kind that you want for ourselves and it shall be done altogether. As to the cheap part, I fear, for it seems to be well understood in this place, that every thing is monstrous dear in Paris—and that cheap and handsome cannot be united, but we will promise to do our best.

We expect to embark on Wednesday. There seems to be a great *talk* about our being sent in a Sloop of War, while Mr. Pinckney has a 74 to await his orders. I am asked "why this marked difference." I answer to go in the Peacock was Mr. Gallatin's own request. I have been mortified several times, but you know there are some, that love to throw the Apple of discord.

I hope I shall hear from you when I am in Paris, I shall be glad to hear of my dear friends in Washington, there are many there that I take great interest in.

Mr. Gallatin writes with me in affectionate remembrance to Mr. Madison, Mr. & Mrs. Cutts, and to our good friend Payne. And believe me, dear Mrs. Madison ever & Affectionately yours,

H Gallatin

RC (ViU).

To Edward Coles

[1 July] 1816

I have recieved your letter my kind friend and have spoken to Mr Madison according to your request, on the subject of a Consulate for you. He is sincerely disposed to favor your interest and refers you to the Secy: of State, & in case of a failure, to the Secy: of War, for an Indian Agency—The choice of a Secy: of Legation to England, depends on Mr Adams—Why have you not expressed your wishes to *him?* I cannot doubt his acquiescence in them. I am in hopes that the Lamps Mr. Hughs speaks of are for me, as I repeatedly wrote to Mr. Lee for such. If you can obtain them, therefore I shall be greatly acco-modated. I have written to my sister Cutts to consult you on the advantage of purchasing Drawing Room Chairs Sofa's &c in Baltimore.

Draft (ViU). Incomplete. Docketed by DPM "To Ed. Coles. 1816."

From Hannah Gallatin

My dear Mrs. Madison,   PARIS August 12th. 1816

I send you by Mr. Vail, the small articles you requested me to get for you consisting of a cambric muslin Spencer, a lace Veil & two muslin caps, I hope you will like them, as I was limited as to price, they are not quite as elegant as they might otherwise have been, but indeed every thing is very high here, quite as much so as in New York. The furniture we are making enquiries about, but not able to get them for this opportunity.

I am very much pleased with every thing I see in this wonderful place. The Palaces and Hotels more splended than you can imagine. We moved the day before Yesterday into a Hotel that belongs and was formerly occupied by Cambaceres. It is furnished, and just as he left it when he was exiled. It is very handsome, we have taken it for a Year and get it reasonable.

I am to be presented to the King this evening. It is a parade that I wish was over. I have many things to do previous, which is my apology my dear friend for not writing you a longer letter this time, but I will write again soon & give you some more particulars. Make my best respects to the President, love to Mrs. Cutts and all our dear friends. Ever & Affectionately Yours

H Gallatin

a cap	36 francs	
a do	30	"
a cambc. muslin spencer	40	"
a lace veil	230	"
a cartoon	2	"

francs   338.

18 arm chairs & 2 sophas (silk) will cost 1800 to 2000 francs

Note 3 curtains do 800 to 1200 do—
But the length of the curtains should be known—how high is the ceiling?

RC (NHi: Gallatin Papers, box 82, no. 64).

From George Boyd

My dear Madam   WASHINGTON Septr 2d. 1816.
    In obedience to your wishes, expressed thro' Mr. Cutts, my vouchers
for furniture &c. have been presented to the Treasury—with a deficit of
$349.41—which you will have the goodness to furnish me as soon as con-
venient—as all the funds belonging to that account have been placed in
your hands, & for which I have received receipted bills, except In the above
amount—The Account, however, in its present shape, will not be taken up by
the Treasury—as there are bills paid, & included in it, for *repairs* of the President's House, amounting to $733 $^{40}/_{100}$—This amount can at once be drawn
by the President from the sum of $3,550—appropriated by the act of the 16 of
April 1816, for House rent, & repairs of the House occupied by the President
since the 24 Augt. 1814. The whole amount of this fund remains undrawn on
the Books of the Treasury. When this money is received by me it will be placed
to the Credit of the Furniture fund—& the bills paid by me from the funds of
the furniture account, deposited in the treasury, as debits to the fund for repairs. In the event of my going to Europe, I shall place this money, together
with a complete statement of the whole business, in the hands of Mr. Caldwell
and by his attention to it—as I by no means wish to appear a defaulter with
the Government, when, in reality, all public monies entrusted to me, have
been long since fully & faithfully accounted for. On the opposite side, is a list
of the bills belonging to the fund for repairs &c, & paid out of the furniture
fund. With every sentiment of respect & attachment to Yourself & the President, I have the honor to remain, My dear Madam, Your most obedient &
Humble Servant

George Boyd
Agent for the President's Furniture fund

RC and enclosure (ViU). Enclosed is a one-page account listing seventeen charges amounting to $753.40.

From Caroline L. Eustis

My dear Madam,   HAGUE October 6. 1816.

My last letter to you was dated early in July, for the enormous length of which an apology I fear is necessary—but I am sure your goodness will permit the garrulity of true affection—and if I again fall into the same error you will be indulgent—We hear this morning that a Vessel is on the point of sailing for Bal[t]imore, so direct an opportunity I cannot resist, believing at all times that you are pleased to hear of our health and happiness—our letters must go to Amsterdam this Evg. therefore I have but a moment, and shall be obliged to *curtail* my communications—At present we are very much in the same state as when I last wrote—the fêtes over, which have been very splendid and very fatiguing—the new princess, her Imperial Highness,[1] is not handsome, but very much admired—resembling her mother, the Queen of Holland, in her amiable affability which never fails to charme every one who is presented—her pregnancy has been announced in the Churches—the situation does not prevent her going to Bruxelles, where she is to be confined—her Brother, the Emperor of Russia has presented a rich marriage present, the most costly jewels & plate, and the most splended furniture which could be found in India, France & England for *40* rooms—The King of Holland has presented them a Palace in the Hague—and there is another building in Gilderland where the King has a Country palace and the Government is preparing another at Bruxelles for them—We have received the formal communication that the King & Queen depart for Bruxelles the present week. It is left to the convenience of the Corps diplomatique *when to follow*—they generally depart the next week, as going to B. implys taking a house for 6 months. Mr: Eustis thinks of defering our departure a few weeks thinking he may hear from our Government. A fortnight since we received a very friendly letter from Mr. Gallatin, and we hear of them frequently through our countrymen who pass this way to England. Mr. Bourne our Consul at Amsterdam spent the last week with us—poor Man! he is out of health—he wants something from Government what it is I do not know—He says the other Consuls receive an allowance, and he does not—he made me promise to mention his name to you believing the Ladies had great influence, and that I could interest you in his cause, which I hope will be my apology—it is unpleasant to me to trouble you on subjects of this nature knowing your disposition to quiet every discontent, and the pain it gives you when you find it impossible.

Mr: Eustis respectfully joins me in best remberances to yourself & the President—likewise we pray you to present us affectionately to your Sisters & their husbands and believe us ever sincerely Yours

C. L. Eustis

RC (Society for the Preservation of New England Antiquities).

1. The prince of the Netherlands, the future William II, married Anna Pavlovna Romanov, daughter of Czar Alexander I of Russia, in 1816. The year before, the Congress of Vienna had confirmed the unification of Holland and Belgium as the kingdom of the United Netherlands, with William I as king.

From Eliza Collins Lee

My dear friend,   WASHINGTON 4th. March 1817

On this day eight years ago I wrote from the retirement of Sully—to congratulate you on the joyful event that placed you in the highest station our country can bestow. I then enjoyed the proudest feelings—that *my friend*—the friend of my youth, who never had forsaken me, should be thus distinguished and so peculiarly fitted to fill it.

How much greater cause have I to congratulate you, at this period for having so filled it as to render yourself more enviable this day, than your successor, as it is more difficult to deserve the gratitude and thanks of the community than their congratulations—*You* have deservedly received of all.

Being deprived, by the sickness of my child from joining the multitude today in paying my respects to where they are due, I feel the sweetest consolation in devoting myself entirely to you.

My heart clings to you, my beloved friend and has done so for the last fortnight, with a selfishness that produces the keenest feelings of regret. And tho' my domestic habits, more than inclination, have prevented my taking advantage of your kind invitations to be more with you—yet I feel a security and pleasure in being so near you, and a confidence in your affection, that constituted my chief pride, as a citizen I assure you. But the period has at length arrived, when we must again part. You will retire from the tumult and fatigue of public life to your favorite retreat in Orange, and will carry with you principles and manners not to be put off with the robe of state, having been drawn from maternal breasts, and nurtured from the example of those dear pious parents, to whom you ever resigned yourself with such filial obedience and devotion as to bring their blessings on your head.

Talents such as yours were never intended to remain inactive on retiring from public life, you will form a more fortunate arrangement of your time, be able to display them in the more noble and interesting walks of life—you will cherish them, my dear friend, in a more native soil, they will constitute the chief felicity of your dear venerated husband, and descend in full perfection to your son. I remember at this moment in my last conversation with my venerable Uncle Parrish, your father's friend, he said of you "She will hold out to the end, she was a dutiful daughter and never turned her back on an old friend, and was charitable to the poor."

Thus the blessing of this good old man went with you, better even, we are taught to beleive, than the sounding trumpet of fame!

Will you do me the favor, my dear friend, for it is near my heart that you should, to take advantage of some leisure moment, to say something for me to your highly respected husband. In the fullness of my gratitude I can express nothing, but shall ever hold in sacred remembrance the highly valued friendship and confidence he has shewn my husband.[1]

I rejoice to hear, that you do not leave the city very soon. I may hope to enjoy your society, tho' I presume your engagements are many. I shall reserve myself to meet you on a future occasion.

I must ask your pardon for thrusting such an epistle at you, but it relieved my heart and will not I trust wound yours—it demands no other acknowledgment at present than a cordial reception. It grows dark, and you shall have this tonight. Beleive me truly yours

Eliza Lee.

Tr (MCR-S: Mary Estelle Elizabeth Cutts Papers). Tr made by Mary Cutts.

    1. At a time of severe financial hardship for the Lees, President Madison had appointed Richard Bland Lee commissioner of claims. The office carried an annual salary of $2,000.

A Well-Deserved Retirement

1817-1836

THE MADISON ADMINISTRATION ENDED IN A WHIRL OF PARTIES AND farewell celebrations that lasted a month beyond the 4 March 1817 inaugural of James Monroe as president. The festivities, including a ball in Georgetown given in Dolley Madison's honor on 13 March, celebrated the Madisons' well-deserved retirement from "the tumult and fatigue of public life," as Eliza Collins Lee put it.[1] Eight years of Wednesday night "squeezes," formal dinners, and the anxieties and uncertainties of war had come to an end. As Dolley occupied herself packing up her entire household, final visits were made and returned, farewell notes written and received, and arrangements made to travel to Montpelier not for the usual summer vacation but for good.

No extant record tells how Dolley Madison felt about leaving social Washington for the plantation life of the Virginia Piedmont. On the steamboat voyage down the Potomac to Aquia Creek, where the Madisons would meet their carriage for the rest of the journey, her husband, "freed from the cares of Public Life . . . was as playful as a child; talked and jested with every body on board," reminding James K. Paulding of "a school Boy on a long vacation."[2] Whether Mrs. Madison shared that sense of relief is unknown. She had lived at Montpelier for only short stretches during the previous sixteen years.

Before that she had been a young bride in the home of her in-laws: certainly in no sense then had she been the mistress of Montpelier. Washington had been her home; it was where her friends and many of her family were and where she had presided over a social nexus of importance and complexity. Now what had once been a summer retreat and calm haven from the political storms of the nation's capital would become her permanent home.

The Montpelier to which the Madisons returned in 1817 was a large estate of over two thousand acres with an imposing house described by one British visitor as bearing "a great resemblance to an English nobleman's mansion." When Charles Ingersoll visited the Madisons in 1836, though time had taken its toll on the structure, its essential lines were still commanding:

> You enter his outer gate from the woods, and at once get into something like a park, with his well-looking house about a mile off: the whole cleared and improved, with trees in clumps and other signs of ornamental agriculture. The house is a two story brick mansion, with wings and colonnades front and back, in good design, but decayed and in need of inconsiderable repairs, which, at a trifling expense, would make a great difference in favor of the first impression of the residence. . . . The view from the front of the house is very picturesque, bounded by the blue ridge, which begins about eighteen miles off, seeming to be close by.

Many visitors found the setting equally impressive. Mary Bagot, the wife of the British minister, noted in 1817 that Montpelier was "wildly situated—surrounded by forest & with the blue ridge before it," and John Latrobe described the view from the house as "a very delightful undulating country."[3]

The Madisons shared their home with James's mother, Nelly Conway Madison, who occupied one-half of the main house with her servants and kept to her own daily schedule. Little is known about the relationship between Dolley and "Mother" Madison, though it seems to have been an affectionate one.[4] The many letters the two women exchanged over the years of the Madisons' residence in Washington presumably were destroyed during the retirement years, along with many others, as private and therefore of little public interest.

The estate was a working plantation made up of four farms, with a village of slave cabins situated on each farm. Tobacco and wheat were grown as cash crops; corn and pork were staples of the diet. Beef cattle and sheep were also raised. Of those who made this life possible—the Montpelier slaves—there are only rare, if telling, glimpses in these letters. Among the over one hundred slaves, both named and unnamed, living on the property during the Madisons' tenure were skilled artisans: blacksmiths, carpenters, wheelwrights, spinners, and weavers.[5] Other prized servants were domestics—including Mrs. Madison's maid, Sucky, and various cooks—and gardeners, whose efforts provided a steady stream of vegetables and fruit to Montpelier's table.

The Madisons rarely lacked company at Montpelier. That first summer, and for many summers thereafter, scores of neighbors, old friends, new acquaintances, and family, especially Anna Cutts and her children, made lengthy visits there. In addition to these "connections," the Madisons, practicing traditional Virginia hospitality, opened their doors to the many strangers who found themselves traveling through the area.[6] Orange Court House sat astride one of the routes from Washington to the Virginia springs—a complex of warm and hot mineral springs in and around Bath County, Virginia—which had become a center for the upper crust of the eastern seaboard. Swarms of the curious and well-to-do found it de rigueur to stop and pay homage to the former president and First Lady. More than once Dolley would excuse herself to a correspondent, as she did to Richard Cutts in December 1818, by writing, "The house is full of company & oblidges me to say thus little to you." Dinners at which twenty people sat down to table were not unusual. Nor did the flow of visitors abate as time went on and James grew too ill to leave his bed. In the year before his death, Dolley would still complain to Mary Cutts of "a house full of company relations connections, neighbors and strangers."[7]

Food for these dinners was "not only abundantly, but handsomely provided; good soups, flesh, fish and vegetables, well cooked—desert and excellent wines of various kinds." Congressman George Ticknor noted after a visit in 1825, "The table is very ample and elegant, and somewhat luxurious; it is evidently a serious item in the account of Mr. M's happiness, and it seems to be his habit to pass about an hour, after the cloth is removed, with a variety of wines of no mean quality."[8] On grand occasions Dolley could call forth all the art and organizing skills that had served her so well in the White House. When Lafayette paused at Montpelier for a few days in November 1824 on his grand tour of the United States, he was the honored guest at a reception attended by hundreds of county citizens and at a somewhat smaller formal dinner hosted by the Madisons. Perhaps no banquet during the Madisons' retirement matched the Fourth of July feast of 1816, at which more than eighty gentlemen and a few ladies celebrated the day at one table set out on Montpelier's back lawn, but the continuous round of summer entertainments and company provided plenty of opportunities for gaiety and distraction.[9]

In the spring of 1817, the Madisons settled into a rhythm of life largely determined by the seasons and the management of their plantation. Aside from short visits to neighboring estates, trips to Charlottesville for meetings of the University of Virginia Board of Visitors, and an annual stay at Monticello, the first twelve years of their retirement found them always at Montpelier. The letters from these years are replete with references to the blossoming of spring flowers, the first appearance of asparagus and cherries, "grapes and figs in abundance," the packing of pork, and the curing of bacon. "I am too busy a House keeper to become a poetess in my solitude," Dolley wrote in December 1826, during one of James's rare absences. In fact, in these letters there are only a few mentions of what must have been for Dolley a time-consuming and rigorous task: the planning and management of the Madison household. It was, all in all, a busy and enviable retirement, and a happy one too, at least to all outward appearances. Writing in March 1819, Eliza Collins Lee reported that a friend who had recently visited Montpelier had told her, "Mr M. is the picture of happiness they look like Adam and eve in Paradise."[10]

Some private concerns, however, cast shadows over this Edenic picture. After the end of the wars in Europe, demand for U.S. grain had declined, leading to a steep reduction in the price of wheat. That, coupled with a long series of dreadful tobacco and wheat harvests in the 1820s, left Virginia farmers strapped for cash. With no alternative but the sale of land or slaves, whole families joined a vast tide of emigration to virgin fields in the Deep South and the Southwest. Land prices fell, and debts remained unpaid. Now that he was without a government salary, all of James's income necessarily came from the sale of tobacco and wheat produced on the plantation. Given the vagaries of commodity prices, the Madisons' lavish hospitality, the support of a large establishment, including over a hundred slaves, and the Madisons' appetite for books, fine wines, and other luxuries, what had once provided for high living within comfortable margins now supplied less than what was needed to maintain the life of a country planter. By the late 1820s even careful and "scientific" planters like James Madison were, as he put it, "living very much throughout on borrowed means." Dolley's frustration with tobacco prices was apparent in a letter to her son in July 1832, when she burst out that she would rather work for a salary "than depend on a plantation for *pin* money."[11]

Nor was the failure of Virginia agriculture the only drain on the Madisons' fortune. Mrs. Madison's son, John Payne Todd, who had made a Continental tour during the presidential years, had developed a taste for European art, luxury, and dissipation, all of which he continued to enjoy during the Madisons' retirement years. Charming, willing, but weak, Payne Todd, between short visits at Montpelier, drank and gambled his way from Washington to Philadelphia, to New York, and back again, leaving a trail of debt in his wake. For long periods he disappeared altogether, the only indication of his movements being dunning letters from creditors to James Madison.[12] Despite his mother's repeated pleas to write or to come home, Todd spent most of his time in drunken carousings or chasing various pipe dreams: wooing an unwilling belle, promoting a gold mine, quarrying marble, planning a railroad, and later, making improvements to the estate James Madison gave him, which he called Toddsberth.

By the winter of 1827, Todd's "strange and distressing career" was undeniably burdensome on the Madisons.[13] James had provided his stepson with a note for nearly $4,000 to pay outstanding debts but had heard nothing from him. He feared that Todd had simply spent the money. This was all of JM's ready cash; he had tried to raise more by the sale of land but had found no purchasers. He refused to sell any of his slaves, calling that sacrifice "the last which I could prevail on myself to resort to." (James was finally reduced to a sale of sixteen slaves to a Louisiana relative in 1834 in order to repay a large loan.)[14] In all, James Madison spent approximately $40,000 to pay off Todd's debts, at least half of which he paid without Dolley Madison's knowledge, "to ensure her tranquility by concealing from her the ruinous extravagance of her son."[15]

Though James attempted to conceal Todd's behavior, he admitted to Edward Coles that "his mother has known eno' to make her wretched the whole time of his strange absence & misterious silence." It was about this time that Mrs. Madison noted in her commonplace book, in an effort to buoy her own spirits, "Trouble not yourself with wishes that things may be just as you would have them, but be well pleased they should be just as they are, and then you will live easy." JM pleaded with Coles to help bring Todd home, but Coles was unsuccessful. By the summer of 1829, John Payne Todd was residing in debtor's prison in Philadelphia, a circumstance that dealt a crushing blow to his mother. "My pride—my sensibility, & every feeling of my soul is wounded," she wrote to her sister Anna. A year later Todd was still in Philadelphia, where a cousin reported that he was "very intemperate, and unless he be forced to leave this place, all hope of reclaiming him will be lost." The reason for this latest bender? "Mrs. Madison has sent to her son 130$, this has been the cause of his absenting himself so long, & depend upon it, he will not return untill every cent is gone."[16] Perhaps even more painful than the constant drain on the Madisons' finances was the eclipse of Mrs. Madison's hope that Payne Todd would marry and settle down to a life worthy of respect, not just as the stepson of James Madison but in his own right.

There had been another blow to the family's fortunes earlier, when Dolley Madison's brother-in-law Richard Cutts had to declare bankruptcy. Cutts, a

former Massachusetts congressman, had lost a small fortune in mercantile activities during the War of 1812 and compounded his misfortunes by ill-advised
investments thereafter. Part of the money he lost belonged to the Madisons.
Though as president James Madison had appointed Cutts to a salaried position in the government, this was not enough to keep him afloat. Shortly after
the Panic of 1819 struck, Cutts was hounded by creditors and forced to sell his
remaining investments, including his house. At Dolley Madison's behest her
husband purchased the Cutts house on Lafayette Square and allowed Anna
Cutts and her family to continue residing there. Mrs. Madison's anxieties for
this sister, to whom she had always been extraordinarily close, grew to near
hysteria at times during this period.

Another of Dolley Madison's family for whom she shouldered the greatest
share of responsibility was her brother, John C. Payne. Despite the brightest
prospects of advancement while James was secretary of state and president,
Payne had disappointed his sister time and time again with his gambling and
bouts of insobriety. Shipped off to Tripoli as an aide to the U.S. consul in 1806,
he came home in an even more hopeless condition and heavily in debt. Once
again Dolley cleaned him up, dried him out, and put his financial affairs in order. By 1816, after his marriage to Clara Wilcox and the birth of his first child,
he seemed to have found himself. The couple settled first on a plantation in
Louisa County, Virginia, and then, when financial difficulties ensued, moved
to a farm adjacent to Montpelier, where they lived well enough to support a
half-dozen children.[17] Still, because of his alcoholism, John could never be relied on for even the simplest tasks away from the supervision of his sister.[18]

The intensity of Dolley Madison's emotions about her family can be partly
explained by the failures of her son, her brother, and her brother-in-law and
her anxieties about the future of her nieces and nephews. Accustomed as she
was to a leading role in the finest society America had to offer, accustomed too
to helping deserving young men and women take their rightful places among
the successful, she must have resented the weakness and lack of achievement
in her own family. Opportunities there had been aplenty, but they had not
been seized. Defeatism had gained a toehold even within her nephews' generation, and the definitive judgment on the whole family, as James Madison
Cutts explained in 1835, was "young & old, it almost seems we cannot get a
start."[19]

Much as Dolley may have loved Montpelier, part of her intense feelings of
anxiety for her family was due to her sense of isolation in the Virginia piedmont. As early as April 1818 she would write to her sister Anna that the lovely
Montpelier spring only reminded her of "the many happy scenes I have

passed, never I fear, to return," and a year later, in writing to her friend Eliza Collins Lee, she would complain, "I am without subjects that could entertain you. ... Our amusements in this region, are confined to books and rural ocu-pations." She longed for political news and gossip and read with a jealous eye of Anna's delighted movements in Washington society. She begged, often querulously, her nieces Dolley and Mary Cutts to write her, assuring the latter in January 1825, "You do not know how acceptable the news from Washing-ton is to us—a far off." [20]

With spring, summer, and fall given over to supervising the planting, tend-ing, and harvesting of crops and to hosting a constant stream of visitors, win-ter was a time of quiet pleasures: chess, reading, and conversation. Few, if any, visitors came as the snow—or more often, cold rain—made a quagmire of the roads. Dolley Madison filled much of the time reading plays, poems, and novels. She tried her hand at writing poetry, leaving snippets of verse scattered throughout her papers. But her taste ran more to novels of romance and ad-venture—by James Fenimore Cooper and Sir Walter Scott—and she went to great lengths to acquire the latest offerings from Philadelphia and New York.

In the first winter after his return to Montpelier, James Madison, with the help of his wife and later John C. Payne, began to edit his papers, especially the notes he had taken during the Constitutional Convention in 1787. Filing, copying, and retrieving letters from his correspondents was an exhausting and time-consuming task, as Dolley's comments demonstrate. After three winters of work, she complained to her Albemarle County cousin Sarah Coles Steven-son that "the business appears to accumalate as he proceeds—so that I calcu-late its out-lasting my patience." Seven years later they were still engaged in the project; James told a friend that owing to the escalating demands on his time, he had "yet to put a final hand to the digest and arrangement" of his papers. [21]

But Dolley Madison understood the importance of the project both for her husband and for the nation. "I cannot press him to forsake a duty so impor-tant, or find it in my heart to leave him during its fulfilment," she wrote in reply to an invitation to visit Mrs. Stevenson. [22] For James Madison these pa-pers were a legacy to his country that would also provide financial support for his wife should she survive him. So confident was he of the ultimate profitabil-ity of their posthumous publication, that in his will he tied to them the pay-ment of a number of legacies to nieces and nephews, charitable organizations, and colleges and universities. For Dolley the end result of all those long—and somewhat tedious—winters should have been financial security and a feeling of great responsibility well discharged.

If time hung heavily in winter in the Virginia countryside, there were other grounds for restlessness. Winter was the social season in Washington, a time of balls, parties, and elegant drawing rooms. Mrs. Madison longed to partake in them again. Some of her letters to her nieces Dolley and Mary Cutts sound grumpy and dictatorial, evincing a mixture of sharpness, jealousy, and rue. After Andrew Jackson's election to the presidency in 1828, however, the Margaret Eaton affair made the Washington social scene so bitter and divisive that Dolley, though eager as ever to hear the latest gossip, was glad of her distance from the capital. Washington had changed, and not for the better. As she wrote to Dolley Cutts in 1830, "In Washington I had most *old* acquaintances and if they were now as they used to be in *those* times, my old partialities would still be felt."[23]

That they were not was partly due to the warm hospitality she had enjoyed in Richmond over the winter of 1829–30. James Madison had been elected as a delegate to the Virginia constitutional convention held there that winter, and Dolley profited from the occasion by renewing old friendships and forging new ones. The sojourn was liberating, especially after the close confinement of the past years and the death of James's mother in February 1829 at the age of ninety-eight. The Madisons stayed with Dolley's cousin Sarah Coles Stevenson and her husband Andrew and enjoyed a full social season.

Back at Montpelier, the tide of visitors continued to flow from spring through fall and to ebb in the winter, but now under more trying circumstances. James endured the first of a series of rheumatic attacks in 1830, and intermittent "bilious fevers" over the next few years left him weak and confined to his bed for months at a time. By March 1832 Dolley wrote her friend Frances Lear that she had become her husband's constant nurse: "I never leave him, more than a few minuts at a time, and have not left the enclosure around our house for the last eight months." As her husband's condition worsened, Dolley clung ever more tightly to the wide correspondence with friends and family she had maintained in her retirement. This circle was reduced by one in August 1832 with the death of her beloved sister Anna Cutts. "What should we do without you!" Mrs. Madison had written her sister just days before her death.[24]

If her husband's illness and her sister's death taxed her severely, it was hardly apparent to the casual observer. George Shattuck Jr., visiting in 1835, remarked that "Mrs. Madison is a fine looking woman, tall, large, of very captivating manners . . . [who] shows no marks of age." In an earlier sojourn at Montpelier, John Latrobe, who had seen Dolley Madison during her husband's presidency, noted: "When she entered the room it seemed to me as though I had parted with her only yesterday—so little has time been able to change her personal appearance—not a wrinkle, no alteration in her complexion, no difference in her walk. She had escaped, unscathed, as the spoiler passed."[25] And in truth, Dolley had escaped—with the exception of eye trouble—all but the usual bouts of influenza during this period.

Enfeebled though he was in those last years, James Madison enjoyed the many visitors who made their way to Montpelier, Jared Sparks, President Jackson, Henry Clay, Fanny Wright, James Maury, Harriet Martineau, George Ticknor, and Charles Ingersoll among them. With Dolley's constant attendance and her service as occasional amanuensis, James continued his own correspondence. From time to time he would rally, but never long enough to hazard the trip to the Virginia springs that his doctors had prescribed and that no doubt would have had a beneficial effect on Mrs. Madison as well. By 1834 James was bedridden, and the next year Dolley reported to her niece Dolley, "*My days* are devoted to nursing and comforting my *patient,* who walks only from the bed in which he breakfasts, to one in the little chamber." An April 1835 attack of what was "first supposed to be Erysipelas in its burning, Itching and feverish character," which left "a distressing Eruption all over him," was particularly debilitating.[26] Each new onslaught left James weaker and Dolley more attentive to his needs, until, more than a year later, on 28 June 1836, James Madison drew his last breath.

Her marriage to James Madison was a union she had described forty-two years earlier as ensuring for her "every thing that is soothing and greatful in prospect."[27] It had been all that and more. She had found not only economic security but also a larger role to play. She had discovered great talents within herself and displayed them on a national stage. In return, she had been a faithful, supportive, and loving companion. Now, a widow once again, she would have to undertake a different role and, in many ways, a much more difficult one.

1. Eliza Collins Lee to DPM, 4 March 1817, MCR-S: Mary Estelle Elizabeth Cutts Papers.

2. Ralph L. Ketcham, ed., "An Unpublished Sketch of James Madison by James K. Paulding," *VMHB* 67 (1959): 432–37.

3. John Finch, *Travel in the United States of America and Canada* (London, 1833), 243–44; Charles Ingersoll, "Visit to Mr. Madison," Washington *Globe,* 12 Aug. 1836; David Hosford, ed., "Exile in Yankeeland: The Journal of Mary Bagot, 1816–1819," *Records of the Columbia Historical Society* 51 (1984): 47; John E. Semmes, *John H. B. Latrobe and His Times* (Baltimore, 1917), 239–45.

4. Ketcham, *James Madison,* 619–20.

5. Foster, *Jeffersonian America,* 141–42; John T. Schlotterbeck, "Plantation and Farm: Social and Economic Change in Orange and Greene Counties, Virginia, 1716 to 1860" (Ph.D. diss., Johns Hopkins Univ., 1980), 67–70.

6. Rhys Isaac, *The Transformation of Virginia, 1740–1790* (Chapel Hill, N.C., 1982), 70–71.

7. DPM to Richard Cutts, 9 Dec. 1818, and to Mary E. E. Cutts, 18 May 1835, MCR-S: Mary Estelle Elizabeth Cutts Papers.

8. Ingersoll, "Visit to Mr. Madison"; George Ticknor, *Life, Letters, and Journals of George Ticknor* (2 vols.; Boston, 1876), 1:347.

9. DPM to Anna Cutts, 5 July 1816.

10. DPM to JM, 5 Dec. 1826, St. Johns Seminary, Camarillo, Calif.; Eliza Collins Lee to DPM, 30 March 1819, DLC: DPM Papers.

11. Schlotterbeck, "Plantation and Farm," 68–71; JM to Thomas Jefferson, 24 Feb. 1826, in Gaillard Hunt, ed., *The Writings of James Madison* (9 vols.; New York, 1900–1910), 9:244; DPM to John Payne Todd, 20 July 1832, MCR-S: Mary Estelle Elizabeth Cutts Papers.

12. See, for example, Levett Harris to JM, 21 March 1826, ViU, regarding $5,000 John Payne Todd owed to Harris.

13. See JM to Edward Coles, 23 Feb. 1827, NjP: Edward Coles Papers.

14. Drew R. McCoy, *Last of the Fathers: James Madison and the Republican Legacy* (Cambridge, 1989), 255–60.

15. John C. Payne to James Madison Cutts, 1 Sept. 1849, owned by Mrs. J. M. Cutts III, Chevy Chase, Md., 1959.

16. JM to Edward Coles, 23 Feb. 1827, NjP: Edward Coles Papers; DPM note, 14 Sept. 1827, DLC; DPM to Anna Cutts, 6 June 1829, MCR-S: Mary Estelle Elizabeth Cutts Papers; Rebecca A. Todd to Anna Cutts, 4 June 1830, owned by Charles M. Storey, Boston, Mass., 1961.

17. John C. Payne to Mary E. P. Jackson Allen, 6 June 1825, owned by Mary Allen Cassady, Fincastle, Va., 2000.

18. See, for example, DPM's fear that John could not travel to Fredericksburg to meet Anna without falling into temptation (DPM to Anna Cutts, 18 May 1825).

19. James Madison Cutts to DPM, 4 Sept. 1835, NHi: Misc. Mss.

20. DPM to Anna Cutts, 3 April 1818, owned by Charles M. Storey, Boston, Mass., 1961; to Eliza Collins Lee, 21 April 1819, DLC: DPM Papers; to Mary Cutts, 22 Jan. 1825, MCR-S: Mary Estelle Elizabeth Cutts Papers.

21. DPM to Sarah Coles Stevenson, February 1820, owned by Richard J. Hooker, Chicago, 1957; JM to Robert Walsh Jr., 22 Dec. 1827, DLC.

22. DPM to Sarah Coles Stevenson, February 1820, owned by Richard J. Hooker, Chicago, 1957.

23. DPM to Dolley Cutts, 10 March 1830, MCR-S: Mary Estelle Elizabeth Cutts Papers.

24. DPM to Frances Lear, March 1832, DLC: J. Henley Smith Papers; DPM to Anna Cutts, 4 Aug. 1832, MCR-S: Mary Estelle Elizabeth Cutts Papers.

25. George C. Shattuck Jr. to Dr. George C. Shattuck, 24 Jan. 1835, MHi; Semmes, *Latrobe and His Times,* 244–45.

26. DPM to Dolley Cutts, 11 May 1835, MCR-S: Mary Estelle Elizabeth Cutts Papers; DPM to Edward Coles, 16 April 1834, NjP: Coles Papers.

27. DPM to Eliza Collins Lee, 16 Sept. 1794.

From William Johnson Jr.

WASHINGTON Sunday [16 March] 1817

I am this moment on the eve of leaving Washington, and shall leave it without a parting interview with one whom I must be indulged in the liberty of comprising among the most respected and most cherished of my friends.

But you, Madam, cannot mistake the feelings which dictate to me this mode of making you an humble tender of a most affectionate Adieu.

You are now about to enter upon the enjoyment of the most enviable state which can fall to the lot of mankind. To carry with you to your retirement the blessings of all who ever knew you. Think not, madam, that I address to you the language of flattery. It is what no one, but yourself would hesitate at conceding. And be assured that all who have ever enjoyed the honor of your acquaintance, will long remember, that polite condescension which never failed to encourage the diffident, that suavity of manner which tempted the morose or thoughtful to be cheerful, or that benevolence of aspect which suffered no one to turn from you without an emotion of gratitude.

Permit, Madam, one who has shared his due proportion of your attentions, to make you a sincere tender of the most heartfelt gratitude and respect and to wish that you may long enjoy every blessing that heaven dispenses to the meritorious.

Do me the favor to tender to Mr: Madison also, a respectful Adieu and a cordial and sincerely friendly one to your Son. Very respectfully

William Johnson Jr.

Tr (MCR-S: Mary Estelle Elizabeth Cutts Papers). Conjectural date based on the closing of the Supreme Court session on 15 March 1817.

From Eliza Collins Lee

My beloved friend   WASHINGTON June 29. 1817
I did not intend your Sister should have left the City without a letter from me acknowledging the receipt of those precious testimonies of your Friendship and confidence, lately finished by Wood. At no other period of our lives could they have been so acceptable.

The likeness of your dear Husband almost breaths, and expresses much of the serenity of his feelings at the moment it was taken. In short it is, *himself,* and most valuable to us.

Your likness my dear friend is not so sattisfactory to *me.* To a common observer, it is sufficient, and instantly recognized. But I lament the absence of that expression of your eye, which speaks *from,* and *to,* the Heart—the want of which robs your countenance of its richest treasure. And tho' whilst memory lasts, I shall always be able to supply to myself the deficiency, yet I regret I cannot paint it to my children—Wood however, has promised to try his skill again when we meet in Washington.

Your dear Payne, who is now here, on his way to join you, will soon complete the happy family in Orange, where methinks I see you more enviable— more exalted—and more bless'd, than I have ever traced you! because, now indeed you are at *Home*. You will now be uninterupted in your duties, and enjoyments—I shall long to witness the effect of your domestic life, and endearments on those who derive their chief happiness therefrom.

The aged Parent of your dear Madison: how will she rejoice in those filial cares and attentions so greatful to her declining years—I really flatter myself that in the course of another summer I may rouse up to such enjoyment, and make one of your party.

Will you my dear friend, Present my Husband & myself with the most respectful affection to Mr Madison.

The Girls beg to join me in love to you and Anna—Payne waits for my letter. I never saw him look so well—I need not remind you how acceptable a letter from you will be—I have had every consideration for you as yet, knowing it must take some time to fix you in your leisure arrangements—when I hope to come in for a full share of your recollection. Adieu God bless you all affy

Eliza Lee

RC (DLC: DPM Papers). Docketed by DPM.

From Sarah Coles Stevenson

ENNISCORTHY Novbr 5th 1817

I cannot let Edward depart without bearing to you something from my daughter[1]—who seems by her quiet placid looks to be conscious to whom the gift is to be made, I regret that it does not resemble more the raven locks of the beloved Friend who is so dear to the heart of her Mother—the name of *Mother* sounds strangely in my ear, yet it fills my heart with such new & delightful emotions that I feel I would not have it otherwise for the world. Edward will tell you that I am yet scarcely emancipated from my thraldom Mamma has kept me close prisoner for a month & seems inclined to continue it yet longer; contrary to my expectations when I saw you, she prevailed on me to remain with her, & I now rejoice that I consented to do so—altho' I have been sadly disappointed in not seeing you *here*—how happy it would make me if I could flatter myself with the hope of embracing you this winter in Richmond—I have used my eyes so little for the last four weeks that I find it painful to write by candle light, & am forced to bid you an abrupt Adieu. Offer to Mr: Madison my Affectionate love, & when you write to Cousin Anna say to her all that is affectionate & kind, tell her my little girl will I hope be almost as pretty as Dolly—Good-Night my ever dear Cousin & think of me always as your sincerely attached

Sarah C. Stevenson

RC (MCR-S: Mary Estelle Elizabeth Cutts Papers). Docketed by JM.

1. Frances Arnett Stevenson, the couple's only child, was born on 5 Oct. 1817 (Francis Fry Wayland, *Andrew Stevenson: Democrat and Diplomat, 1785–1857* [Philadelphia, 1949], 41–42).

To Anna Cutts

3d. April. [18]18

I have written twice to you My dear Sister since I reccd. your last letter, & begin to be anxious to know how you all are. We are just as I told you in my last—The Old lady is quite well—& comes to dinner as usial—Payne has not been well & has not fixed on the day to leave us—I told you Ed. had been here for a day & 2 nights—The spring advances—The flowers are blooming—the trees changeing to green & yet my heart is solitary! All things—even the cooing of the Doves remind me of you my Sisters! and the many happy scenes I have passed, never I fear, to return! My eyes overflow with tears, as I look around on the beauties of nature & reflect that my sisters are far from me—That their tender words, their fond looks cannot bless me in sickness or in health! & yet I blame myself for this frailty—this foolish repineing—foolish because it is vain, & I become ungreatful towards a wise & merciful Providence whilst I indulge a murmor, & forget to thank him for so many blessings bestowed! Jno. & his little family are quite well he writes me. I had a letter from Lucy whilst the Judge was here—She & the children well—I beleive I told you this before. Tomorrow is post day & I hope to rece. a letter from you—I shall tell you all I can by *Payne* next week, as he will see you in the course of it—I hope & trust Walter has been with you on his way to Williamsburg—I am uneasy on acct. of that affair—as I fear Walter is capricious, & will injure Miss P[age]. & infinately more, himself, If he should not act honorably—not that I wish the match, from any other motive than that—I know she is good enuf for him or any other young man—I expect now that your gaiety is drawing to a close—You have been to *one* D. R. this winter & no more I think—you'l see Ed. soon on his way to the West—he's a great fidget, & is hard to mary—I'm thinking Payne will be the same—& they are both in the right—tho I should like a fine daughte[r] much—Maria Scott has a girl—Mrs. Bagot I suppose will go a jaunting this summer—& all the rest of your agreable people—Has the P. got well. You have the hopeful Hay in W. now—

Adeiu you see I have not much to say, tho I cannot bear a week, or a post should go without a letter for you—Love & kisses for all my precious children!

RC (owned by Charles M. Storey, Boston, Mass., 1961).

From Lucia Alice von Kantzow

My dear Madam   STOCKHOLM the 26th. June 1818
    That I should ever forget America, its happiness diffused unto so many, its many advantages over many an other part of the globe, the friends I made there, the kindness I recieved, and the happiness I found, in making your acquaintance, with the respect & gratitude I feel, towards you, and your Husband, is impossible. I therefore take the pen in hand with lively recollections, not one single twitch at my conscience, and with a heart no ways frozen, altho' I have past a long winter in Sweden. It is 13 months, since I wrote to you my farewell, from good Philadelphia, it is some time since, I had the pleasure to recieve your kind answer of the 20th. Octor. Long ere this, I would have told you we continued in the Land of the living, had not I thought that this summer we returned to the united States; when we go now, is not yet fixed, and in fact our plans are quite in the air, and all is in embryo, till the King settles if Mr. de Kantzou leaves Sweden, returns to the other Hemisphere, or what is very common for a deplomate, to be sent on an other mission—what is certain, none will produce to us more real satisfaction, open more our eyes, enlarge our ideas, experience more the delight of natural, easy kind deeds, and kind ways, than what charmed us, in your flourishing, prosperous and fortunate country—If I do not go, the longer I live, the steadier I will be, in my admiration of your many virtues, and the gigantic strides your Republic makes to rival the best parts of Europe. You must not think my dear Mrs. Madison, that because I was born in Portugal, (perhaps an hypocritical country) or that because I have been a great traveller, and now living, in the focus, of a ceremonious, ettiquettish, poorish, proudish, gay, lively, courtious, polished court, I am become a complimenter, and that what I said over leaf, were mere words, and that my thoughts and heart, were there, for nothing— you would wrong me very much, had you such an opinion of me—and least you question my sincerity, I will be as honest as any in your liberal, free-thinking, America—and tell you there are draw backs in my own mind, towards wishing to pay you a second visit—I must seperate for very far off, from all my own connections and family, but my husband, with whom, I will jog on to

229

the Antipodes, if necessary—my next objection, is, that on the other side of the water, they do not like old people, & that I have not the virtue of Hocus pocus, to regenerate, and become young and agreeable—and the worst joke of all is, that to enjoy your country, I must again cross the atlantic and next to Mr. Short, I believe no one hates the Sea, or suffers more, than I do—but be assured if Kantzou is dispatched there, sink or Swim, his old wife, will buffet the waves too—as a little recompense, let me claim the renewal of your obliging and flattering offer to go and see you and Mr. Madison at Mont Pelier, if I do not find you at Washington, or some other, nearer city—I fancy you now there, and sincerely do I hope enjoying perfect health; He, deriving Balsum to his Soul with the persuasion, that whilst first in his Nation, he was fore most towards its aggrandizement and prosperity, both at Peace and War, and that his memory will ever be cherished and respected whilst an independent people appreciate their constitution and laws. You my dear Madam had a less skillful game to play, but your cards were so well delt, in that you had friends among both parties, and as Mrs. Madison, you were loved by all your country men and country women, and as the Wife of their President, you honored his elevated post, and were respected for your judicious conduct, and affable kind manners—I have come nearly to the end of my sheet, and I find I am still in america—judge of the cordiality of my thoughts! Before I transport my self here again, let me beg of you to give my very kind compts. to your Son & Sisters—and if any of my acquaintance are with you at your estate, and that you find they yet honor me with their recollection, to assure them, that ⟨. . .⟩ fresh as a rose—I hope among some of your visiters may be Mr. Coreia, & the de Caturs, to get, my friendly message.

Here we have had much variety, after a still greater variety of events, both by land & sea, through various countries, since I left yours, upwards of a year ago—winter & summer is a great contrast, in these regions, now we enjoy heavenly weather—and for bad, I must say the Sweeds are masters, to guard against the cold, or being beset, by the blue Divils, for there are no want of amusements at Stockholm—and my girls have danced and laughed here, comme partout ailleurs—if they have kept their hearts free, I cannot tell all I see, are many beauxs fluttering about, and what I know is, that they are very good girls and make us very happy, as such, their respectful compts. I hope will be accepted by you & Mr. Madison, along with Mr. de Kantzou's & mine, uniting every sentiment of sincere regard for you & yours—the King has created my Husband one of his Chamberlains and made him Knight of the order of the polar Star—in Europe this has a sound, and tickles the ear, with you, I know it answers neither for profit nor pleasure—let him therefore in America keep the reputation he had the good luck to obtain there, of an honest well informed good man and that title will make me very proud, remaining ever dear Mrs. Madison your obliged humble Servant & very sincere friend

L. de Kantzou

RC (ViU). Words obscured by fold.

To Anna Cutts

[ca. 23 July 1818]

I am sorry to find the dear children yet sick by yours of Saturday this morg reccd. We have felt the heat most sensibly here & not far from us, has prevail'd the Disentary—I reccd. a letter from Jno. a few days ago by one of his men, *whom he sent up to me*—he had been sick with it, & so had little Lucy—but ware both on the recoverry—I thought Paulding would see you & give you an acct. of us—but suppose he was poorly—poor Mrs. Bagot! Carrols is not a lucky place for her to visit at, it seems—I'm affraid I shant see Mrs. M as my Husband Wrote here, he should be from home next Tuesday,[1] & I don't hear of his leaveing W. or being ready to do so—as Graham & & are now with you—When you pay Goldsborough & the Washerwoman we shall be even— I dont wish for any snuff or beans, can do well without—Payne forgot to settle with the woman—I like the China & price well & should not return it—the difference between W. & Richmond was allways the same—Mother M is very sick again & Fanny here nursing her—I hope your Woman will turn out well—I'd try to attatch her to me & my children, now that she is your own— Sucky has made so many depridations on every thing, in every part of the house that, I sent her to black Meadow last week but find it terribly inconvenient to do without her, & suppose I shall take her again, as I feel too old to undertake to bring up another—so I must even let her steal from me, to keep from labour myself—more than my strength will permit—I would buy a maid but good ones are rare & as high as 8 & 900$—I should like to know what you gave for yours—We have this moment reced. a note from Mr & Mrs. Dade to say they will dine wi[t]h us tomorrow with a large party—so that I must stir my self to fix for them—as at present we have Fanny & her daughter with Dr. Taylors & Mrs ⟨Jirdons?⟩ Daughters Wm. M[2] &—here since yesterday Morg—I have nothing new to tell you—Was in great hopes you could have come with the children by this time—I have not decided yet whether to go to the Springs—dont like to be left nor do I wish to go—If you ware with me should be happier at home—but will write you next post.

Thursday Evg.

If I could allways know you & yours ware well I should not be so unreasonable as to ask you to give your time or attention to writeing to me—as I see plainly by the little of late that it is a task—I neither blame or wonder at it, for I am ⟨a⟩ poor dull creature, & at such a distance that I must submit & live along as well as I can detatched from others—but while I live I shall be your Affectinate & anxious Sister—& frd. in all cares—I sent Jno. all he wanted for the present.

RC (MCR-S: Mary Estelle Elizabeth Cutts Papers). Conjectural date based on internal evidence and JM to Paulding, 23 July 1818.
  1. JM attended a meeting at Rockfish Gap, Va., as a commissioner to determine the site for a state university. He was absent from home from 29 July to 5 August. "Mrs. M" is Elizabeth Kortright Monroe, wife of the president.
  2. William Madison.

From James Madison

My dearest   Monticello Thursday morning [30 July 1818]

We arrived here about half an hour by sun.[1] We had a hot ride, but have not suffered from it. The ladies enquired affectionately after you, and recd. the message with which you charged me. None of the deputies were with Mr. Jefferson. We set out this forenoon for Mr. Divers, with whom we shall dine & pass the night, and tomorrow morning proceed for Rockfish Gap. I fear I shall not have an opportunity for some days of writing, and this will not reach O. C. House till saturday. I shall however embrace every oppy. I can as yet make no guess of the time we shall be detained. I hope it will not be many days; and I shall not lose a moment in getting home. The situation in which I left my mother & sister Rose would hasten me, if other motives were wanting than my anxiety [to] be again with you. Your devoted husband

J. Madison

I find by a Letter from the President to Mr Jefferson of same date with the one to me, that he expected to leave Washington abt. Friday for Loudon, and to come on thence to Albermarle—*with his family.*

RC (ICHi).
  1. "By sun": before sunset.

232

From Anne-Marguérite-Henriette Hyde de Neuville

Madam,   WASHINGTON tuesday 22. of october. [1818]

I follow yours orders in Writing to you in english, and I hope that your goodness Will excuse my numerous blunders, if it was as easy to express her Sentimens as to feel them, the gratitude and respect that you and Monsieur Madison know so well inspire Shall be very Well explained our Journey was very happy, and We arrive here Saturday Night by the Steam Boat of frederik-Burg, favored With a Very charming Day. We found your amiable Sister and her familly in perfect health, and your numerous friends Very happy to hear good News of you and Monsieur Madison, Very gratful of your remembrance, and Wishing the Pleasure to See you.

Will you Madam accept the Respects of Mr de Neuville for you and Monsieur Madison and receive the assurance of the Sentiments of high Regard of your devoted Servant

h. h. de Neuville

P.S. Permettez Madame que Monsieur Votre fils trouve ici nos plus emprésser Compliments, nous avons fait sa Petite commition et je vous enverrai les recettes que vous avez désirées *for the french Salad* and *fish,* aussi-tôt que Je les aurai reçues de notre ancien Cuisinier, votre Prévoyante bonté, en remplissant la voiture de Pain et D'Excellent vin a rendu nos repas d'auberge très *confortable.*[1]

RC (NjP).

1. "Your son finds here our most willing attentions; we have done his little errand and I will send you the recipes that you desired for the French salad and the fish, as soon as I can get them from our old cook. Your foresight and goodness, in filling our carriage with bread and excellent wine, made our dinner at the inn very comfortable" (editors' translation).

To Caroline L. Eustis

MONTPELLEIR 22d. Jany. 1819.

Not until this day, my beloved friend did I receive your kind letter of the 14th. It rejoiced my heart, to find you, and dear Doctr. Eustis well, and so hapily situated, in the midst of enlightened and amiable people.[1] Would to Heaven we could join you there or any where—so highly do we value your friendship and society. I have been intimately acquainted with Mrs. Page for many years, and know her to be one of the most estimable woman [sic] in the world, other ladies in Williamsburge I admire and respect and could not doubt, the pleasure and advantage arriseing to them, from your sojourning amongst them. Every week brings me a letter from my sister Cutts, she speak[s] of you, with that interest and affection you deserve from her—but you must not persuaide her to go further from me—Boston! alass I should dispair of her ever comeing (with her little flock) to Montpellier, if she lived in Boston! She tells me of parties and exibitions in the City, but of *fewer social meetings* than *formerly.* She had seen Mrs. Genl. Smith and Miss Spear, who had left our little Bonaparte well, & in Baltimore.

By the post of this day, I have a letter from Mrs. Deblois, who says, *your relations are well, and impatient for your return. She* mourn's the departure of Com: & Mr⟨s⟩ Hull, who are now in Washington &c &c. They ware very good and kind to poor Mrs. Deblois and she is greatful for every attention, which, I think, all the family deserve, from society—How we wish my dear friends, you had remained with us this winter—it has been so mild— & for the last ten days, the weather has been, that of May—how selfish!— we have had three dishes of Asparagus & our Lalacks are in bud! Wonder not then, at my sighs—when I supposed you wandered, mearly in serch of a moderate climate. Please to present me particularly to Mrs. Page & daughter—Mrs. Tucker & the Judge. And that we may meet again My ever precious friend, is the prayer of your affectinate Sister!

D P Madison

RC (Society for the Preservation of New England Antiquities).
1. After a December visit with the Madisons at Montpelier, William and Caroline Eustis passed some time at Williamsburg, Va. (Eustis to JM, 27 Dec. 1818).

From Eliza Collins Lee

My belov'd friend   March 30th. 1819.
I am this moment informed by my Son that your Nephew will dine with us to day—he leaves the city in the morning and will no doubt see you in a day or two—nor must he leave my House without a renew'd assurance of my love & friendship—Forget you! I never could Yet whilst those highly valued resemblances of yourself and Husband remind me daily of the dear friends I boast of, they also remind me that I omit the only intercourse that remains of keeping myself alive in their remembrance—permit me then my belov'd friend to renew my intreaties still to hold that place in your heart—the gift of youthfull affection and friendship and which I trust has never been forfieted.

So little belongs to me that is pleasing or interesting to speak of myself or family that I shall not attempt it in this hurried moment save that I am peculiarly fortunate and happy in having for my neighbour and friend that dear little unassuming woman who with her noble generous Husband I found on board the steam boat waiting to take a last look and bid Adieu to you the day you left us, and to whom you recommended my further acquaintance[1]—tis strange my dear Dolly as fortunate—that since that period which again seperated me from a dear and long known friend—I have found in these very people the kindest consolation with souls truely congenial with our own—almost daily does the greatful generous Commodore make his bow to your resemblance when his fine eyes express the noble feelings of his heart.

I saw your Sister yesterday she was then writing to you. I regret that our truely domestic habits prevent our more frequent interviews but we have promised better.

Do you know? or do not know my belov'd Dolly that your absence from this City is more and more lamented. That the urbanity, benevolence, and chearfulness that was defused through the circles over which *you* presided will be long sought for *in vain*[2]—But *you* are happier—and Oh! that I could witness that superior happiness you enjoy in bestowing those talents and virtues on the dear objects that alone claim them—Truely did I enjoy the picture painted by the pen of Mrs. Miller in a letter a few days since, as original as herself—she says—"I spent 2 days with Mr & Mrs. Madison—they enquir'd kindly after you. Her soul is as big as ever and her boddy has not decreased Mr M. is the picture of happiness they look like Adam and eve in Paradise."

I am call'd to dinner and will only beg you to present Mr Lee and myself in the most respectful terms to your Husband—and I take the liberty to offer to the dear venerable Mother of Mr Madison the love and respect of *your* friend

E Lee

P.S. I must not omit to present the respects of Comr. & Mrs. Rodgers to Mr M & yourself in haste Adieu

E Lee

RC (DLC: DPM Papers). Docketed by DPM.

1. Commodore John Rodgers (1773–1838) and his wife, Minerva Denison Rodgers (1784–1877), were friends of the Madisons and lived at Greenleaf Point, and later on Lafayette Square, in Washington, D.C. (Charles Oscar Paullin, *Commodore John Rodgers* [1910; rept. Annapolis, Md., 1967], 367, 381–82, 403).

2. Elizabeth Monroe's more formal and reserved manner and her decision not to make or return calls provoked resentment in the highest Washington social circles and sparked an etiquette war which even the president and his cabinet could not quell (Harry Ammon, *James Monroe: The Quest for National Identity* [New York, 1971], 396–402).

To Eliza Collins Lee

MONTPELLIER 21t. Apl. [18]19.

Our Nephew presented your welcome letter my beloved friend, two weeks *after* its date. I cannot express the delight it afforded me to find myself still, affectinately remembered by you! still recollected with kindness by our noble Comodore, his dear wife, and others! It was a gratification next, to seeing them, and you! To say that I sigh to see you, would be a feble mode of expressing my wishes! Two years absence from Washington has not deminished my attachment to it—you will immagin then, with what pleasure I received, the kind and good hearted Mrs. Millar, who could tell me of *you,* of Mr Lee, of your amiable children and of many, in whom I shall ever, feel interested! You aught not to consider a *short* hundred miles an insurmountable difficulty, but persuaide Mr Lee to bring you to Montpellier about the first of June—Mr & Mrs. Cutts would come with you Comodore and Mrs. Rodgers, also (I hope) when we would feast you with *cheries,* and give you the heartiest welcome. Indeed if I do not see you all here, I shall be *oblidged* to visit Wn *before long.* I expect soon to have my sister Todd and family, to spend some months with me, and we *talk* of visiting our dear Anna together.

We understand the agreable foreigners are about to leave your city. I regret it for your sake's, and wish you may be as happy in their successors—I am without subjects that could entertain you, my precious friend—Our amusements in this region, are confined to books and rural ocupations—our society strangers all, to you—I can only tell you of myself—my Husband and son, who are perfectly well, and love and respect you—my atatchment to you is that of a tender sister!

D. P. Madison

RC (DLC: DPM Papers).

From Ellen W. Randolph

MONTICELLO Oct. 15th 1819

When Mama and myself parted from you my dear Mrs Madison, it was under the impression that in a few days we should meet again, and at your own house, but the time destined for a visit which would have given us so much pleasure has been occupied by a close attendance upon my dear Grandfather, who after a sudden and violent attack, has been within this last two days, declared, by his Physycians, entirely out of danger. Although relieved from all present apprehensions on his account we cannot expect that at his age his recovery will be a very rapid one; some time must elapse before he regains his usual health & he has decided to give up all thoughts of a visit to Bedford for this season. His complaint was a violent and obstinate cholic lasting about thirty hours.

A Physician in whom we have great confidence, (Dr Watkins) has engaged that if Grandpapa will only stay at home and *take care of himself,* during this winter, that the return of warm weather, shall find him restored to the health he enjoyed, before his unfortunate visit to the Warm Springs.[1] The first part of the prescription is practicable enough, but I much fear that he does not know how, to *take care of himself,* to be very attentive to his diet, to use less exercise, and to avoid all fatigue of body or mind & especially to give up letter-writing, are the points on which the doctor most insists.

And now that our anxiety on a subject of much importance to us is giving place to other feelings, we are becoming sensible of the disappointment which GrandPapa's illness, has caused us, but so much is my heart set on the intended visit that I have not yet relinquished all hope of seeing you before the roads become impracticable; if we find this gratification within our reach you shall hear from me again; in the mean time, my dear Mrs Madison, Mama unites with me in respectfull compliments to Mr Madison and Mr Todd, and in the hope that for yourself no fresh assurance of our affection is necessary. Aunt Randolph's absence, alone prevents her from joining in the expression of these sentiments, and on this occasion you will permit her to be represented by your friend

Ellen W. Randolph

RC (MCR-S: Mary Estelle Elizabeth Cutts Papers).

1. After the Rockfish Gap meeting in August 1818, Jefferson made a visit to Warm Springs where he hoped the baths would ease his rheumatism. He picked up a staphylococcus infection instead, which resulted in a series of boils on his posterior (Malone, *Jefferson and His Time* 6:279 and n. 48).

From Ellen W. Randolph

MONTICELLO Jan. 17h. [18]20

On my return from a visit to Aunt Cary, I found ⟨yo⟩ur letter of the 10th, my dear Mrs Madison, waiting for me at ⟨M⟩onticello. We should have experienced no sort of inconvenience ⟨. . .⟩ you detained the books the whole winter, for we have all read them. A long absence from home must plead my excuse for not having returned the Volumes of La Harpe's Cours de Literature[1] lent me by Mr Todd, and as I have not yet had an opportunity of reading them, he will pardon me, I hope, for keeping them a little longer. I accompanied Aunt Randolph to Fluvanna, where she proposes to spend the winter, and she did not take leave of me without repeated charges, to remember her most particularly to you, whenever I should write.

The Turban you were so good as to make for Lady Randolph excited the admiration, and gratitude of the *Thespian Society*. Under its magic influence a gawky school-boy became a beautifull, nay, an elegant woman, and the talismanic head-dress appeared to possess the power of communicating to another, some portion of the graces borrowed from its former mistress.

Mama has determined not to go to Richmond this winter, and the girls & myself are staying quietly at home with her. She desires me to say that she is even now experiencing the renovating effects of her visit to Montpellier. Her health has been uniformly good since she left you. She joins me in the hope that Mr Madison and yourself will not ⟨postpone?⟩ your wanted visit, beyond the return of good roads & settled weather, & that Mr Todd in compliance with his promise will make Monticello his first stage on leaving home.

Adieu my dear Mrs Madison. Mama writes in the assurances of affection offered by your friend

Ellen Randolph

Mama begs that you will tell Mrs Reuben Conway, that the Multiflora Rose, which she promised her has been stuck and is very flourishing.

RC (MCR-S: Mary Estelle Elizabeth Cutts Papers). Ms torn. Docketed by DPM.
    1. This was probably Jean-François de La Harpe, *Lycée, ou Cours de litterature ancienne et moderne*.

To Sarah Coles Stevenson

[ca. February 1820]

I have just now reccd. by post your welcome letter my ever dear cousin, and cannot express my anxiety to embrace you once more! But a spell rests upon me and withholds me from those I love best in this world—not a mile can I go from home—and in no way can I account for it, but that my Husband is also fixed there. This is the third winter in which he has been engaged in the arrangement of papers, and the business appears to accumalate as he proceeds—so that I calculate its out-lasting my patience and yet I cannot press him to forsake a duty so important, or find it in my heart to leave him during its fulfilment. We very often speak of you, and the many causes of our admiration of you—and conclude by assureing *one another, that if we* could leave home this winter, it should be only to visit you and Mr. Stevenson. Allow us then my beloved to retain the priviledge you so kindly give us of our room & little stand, where you shall some day see us. I greave to find that you have lately been sick and weak—and I pray that you may be now entirely restored! This fall I had the pleasure to recce. a visit of a week from Mrs. Randolph her sister Mrs. D. M.[1] & Ellen. They told me you had been indisposed—and from your long silence, I was afraid you had not recovered! I suppose you will soon have this estimable family in your city, tho' Ellen writes me, they do not go down this winter.

I cannot help rejoicing with you, that your brothers decline going to the Western country. We hope to see cousin Edward on his return from Phla. and to hear, that he too, gives it up.

I recce. letters every week from my sister Cutts—she is in a round of pleasant society, and tho devoted as ever, to her children, takes time to enjoy a dance. Mrs. Brown whom you remember has rented a house near her, and gives splendid parties. Mrs. Adams, Mrs. Crawford & many others keep up the fashion of dissipation. Made. Neuvilles return to Washington was a source of pleasure to Anna—they live near each other & are intimate. It is uncertain when I shall see her, tho I flatter myself ⟨again?⟩

RC (owned by Richard J. Hooker, Chicago, Ill., 1957). Ms incomplete.

1. This was Mary Randolph, wife of David Meade Randolph.

From Phoebe P. Morris

My dear Mrs. Madison   BOLTON FARM March 22 1820.

I heard yesterday & I assure you with much anxiety, that you had not for some time enjoyed your usual good health, & that Mr. M also was indisposed; this rumour, altho' I have no reason to believe it, immediately recalled to my mind all the past parental attentions for which more than to any, or to all other persons out of my own house, I am so much indebted to you both, & it is the immediate object of this letter to know from yourself the truth, or as I hope the f⟨alsity of?⟩ the report; I think my dearest friend I have every reason to believe it false; if it were true, you would I think have found means to tell me so, that I might offer my assistance to cheer & to comfort you, & that I might practise some of the lessons I have learned in the chambers of sickness for the benefit of those to whom I am most sincerely & tenderly devoted—

indeed my dear Mrs. M—when I review those incidents in my life which will ever appear to me among the most important in its varied character I always trace your hand in their origin; & shall always ascribe to it an influence which shall ever be gratefully acknowledged as to my good & guardian Genius. When life was new, & gaiety & fashion, & perhaps folly, were my favorite pursuits you guided my steps thro' the giddy dance, at a time too, when the dignity & brilliancy of your station, while they confer'd favor on every object of its selection might well have divided & distracted your choice. To the delicacy of your attentions then, & since, I have never been insensible; & will never permit myself to think that I am not among the first who ought to be selected to smooth the pillow of sickness when it may assail you, or to assist you in every office of affection when it may be useful for my ever lov'd & honor'd friend Mrs. M. I hope most sincerely the rumor I have accidentally heard will prove unfounded—& that you wont accept my proffered services, which are only made on the condition of your being indisposed, if assured of this & they will be acceptable, I will immediately attend you. Since my movements in Europe we have all been very tranquil & stationary & seldom leaving home, but on some particular occasion. Papa & Louisa unite in all effusions of heart towards Mr. Madison & yourself. He entirely approves of my tender of services, & Louisa requests that she may be equally considered as always at your disposition—She has had indeed more experience in the sick chambers of her friends than myself. While you were as I understood in the summer, well & happy & gay & surrounded by your friends, it scarcely occur'd to me that you had not answered my last letter. I shall always cheerfully reconcile myself even to your temporary forgetfulness, while its cause is the overflow of your cup of happiness, but when sorrow or sickness (& long very long may they be far from you both) shall assail you, then always rely on all the affection & all the attention of your ever faithful & most affecte frnd.

P. P. Morris

Please to address to the Post Office Bristol Penna.

RC (DLC: DPM Papers).

From Anthony Morris

Dr Madam   BOLTON, NEAR BRISTOL PENNA. July. 14. 1820.

Phœbe had delayd so long a reply to your most wellcome letter of April in the daily expectation of seeing Mr Todd, that She was about concluding him a false Knight, and was actually preparing a denunciation of him to you, when he suddenly appeard at Bolton to speak for himself, which he has done so amiably and satisfactorily that he has silencd all censure, and made the most favorab[l]e impressions on our hearts, indeed my excellent friend I cant convey to you the pleasure his company afforded to us all, we have receivd from him the most acceptable accounts of your health, & Mr Madisons, and seem to know more of your goings on at Mt.Pelier than We ever did before, what particularly pleasd us was his assurance that you really sometimes talk of a Northern tour, which he thinks you will undertake some future Year, a change of place & scene is often serviceab[l]e, even from those which abound less with blessings & beauties than those we leave; I need not repeat how happy some stay with Us would make the family at Bolton; I have committed to Mr Todd my most respectful remembrances to Mr. Madison; Phœbe is preparing for a ride with him to Bristol, and has made Me her Secy. to assure you of her most affe wishes, and her intention soon to write to You; My Daughters Rosa & Louisa also request Me to present to you theirs with every most respectful Sentiment of Esteem & Friendship, from Yr Most devoted Friend

A Morris

RC (DLC: DPM Papers).

From Catherine E. Rush

My dear Mrs Madison   LONDON November 24th 1820

I heard with great delight by a letter which Mr Rush had the pleasure to recieve from Mr Madison that you had been good enough to write to me. Allow me to return my grateful thanks for this mark of friendship. Among my omissions for the last three years, I recal with pain that of never having written to you; but I hope my dear Madam that you will attribute my silence to the novelty of a London life, and the distractions of a large family. This is the real cause and I must throw myself on your goodness to excuse me.

After living two years in London we fancied it would be very delightful to take our children to a pretty little English Cottage surrounded by neat Shrubberies and quiet hay fields. The Cottage was procured, and away we went, rejoicing to leave the smoke and fogs of London—But alas! every situation has its alloys. Our Cottage was very pretty, but rather too small, and we encountered a thousand inconveniences, as unexpected as they were annoying. My husband too had his troubles, and after a years repentence, such perhaps as

241

frequently falls to the lot of those who seek "Love in a Cottage"[1] we are very glad to return to the very house we quitted a year ago, and are quite willing to encounter to [sic] minor miseries of smoke fog and noisy streets.

The town has lately presented quite a festive scene. Illuminations, transparencies, Squits, and crakers, in honour of the Queen's triumph.[2] I am heartily glad it is all over, for in truth it was an apalling sight, to see crouds of Men & boys going through the streets with lighted torches, and various odd contrivances to disturb those, who from Loyalty or disinclination did not choose to join in this outward display of Joy—Blind-mans buff, appears to be a favourite amusement among royal personages. Col Wilkes, the Governor of St Helena at the time Buonapartte was taken there, told me the Ex Emperor was particularly fond of this pastime, and would play with the little school girls of the Island. It is among the *Crimes imputed* to Queen Caroline, that she frequently played blindmans buff with her Servants in Italy. And yet it is a fact which I have had from high authority, that "her Majesty" has often played the same game at Black-Heath with the *Kings Servants,* (Sir William Scott and others) without the slightest imputation of impropriety.

The gay Season has not yet begun. Dinner parties however are allways going on. We dined in company yesterday with Lord Erskine, who really kept the table in an uproar with his Witty annecdotes. He is full of annimation and uses very decided language upon all subjects—We were dining at the house of a Friend near Hampstead one of the most beautiful villages near London at which place his Lordship has a Villa. Something was said as to the Sterility of the Soil—Yes! it is indeed a poor Soil Said Lord E. My Grand father was buried there An Earl, a hundred years ago—and has since only sprouted up a "poor Baron"—I put a monument he added to mark the spot. But, said one of the company, his Wife was burried by his side, why has she no stone. Oh! he replied ["]she was his second Wife, and not my Grand mother. She may lie there and be d—md, before I will put any stone, she must find her way up as she can."

He paid some high compliments to Burke's Genius, but added, Burke was the *very worst* man I ever knew—I do think the Almighty will be puzzled to find any place bad enough for him. He was very sarcastic on the late proceedings in the house of Lords; but I should not do him justice to repeat his invectives unaccompanied by his annimated manner.

I often think of you my dear Mrs Madison; and the very agreeable hours I have spent with you at Washington. One of my first pleasures on my return home after meeting my dear Mother and Sister will be to visit Montpelier. To Mr Madison may I beg you to present my remembrance. I am much obliged to him, for having the goodness to mention me, in the gratifying letters which Mr Rush has had the good fortune to recieve from him.

Mrs Cutts I hope is quite well. I do not forget the happy hours I have spent with her under your hospitable roof in F Street, and the agreeable acquaintances I formed under your auspices—Among them I always rank "Cousin Isaac" and if he has not forgotten me, I must beg you to present my regards to him. Mr Rush charges me to present his kind compliments to you and we both beg to be presented to Mr Todd.

Sir Charles and Lady Bagot were quite well at St Petersburgh last summer, They both often spoke of the agreeable visit they made to Orange. I am in daily hopes of recieving your letter. Really Mr Astor makes a provokingly long visit to Paris, but I shall be in such a good humour with him for bringing me your letter, that he will find me quite delighted to see him—I have not heard from Mrs Gallatin for some time—The last accounts said all were well.

Adieu My dear Madam I am intruding sadly on your valuable time, but really having taken up the pen, I cannot put it down—My little flock are well, and our two girls very great pets. Your God-son Richard is a fine little fellow and is just learning to ride—He often boasts of his God Mother, and says he will write a letter to his dear God Mamma as soon as he gets *out of strokes* to tell her what funny things Punch says and does.

I remain my dear Madam very sincerely and affectionately yours.

Cath E Rush

RC (PHi).

1. "Love in a Cottage": a euphemistic expression for marriage with insufficient means (*OED*).

2. In 1820 a bill was introduced in the House of Lords to strip Queen Caroline of her titles and dissolve her marriage with George IV because of her adulterous behaviour. The sensational public inquiry ended in the bill's abandonment, resulting in three days of celebrations and illuminations (Christopher Hibbert, *George IV, Regent and King, 1811–1830* [London, 1973], 154–87).

To Anna Cutts

[June 1820?]

This is friday, & yours of Sunday last my beloved sister came safe to hand on wednesday was read in secret & bur[n]t, as you desired & as it aught to be—but my Sister—no words can convey an idea of the agony with which I read—& now recollect, some expressions in that letter—That you, who have been since your birth, the darling—the friend & the Sister that lived most in

my thoughts & affections should be sick & unhappy—& I at a distance unable
to sooth, nurse or comfort you! Alass I cant bear it much longer, & if you come
not—I will see you where ever you are. I will leave my husband & run all risks
to see you. I know it would be best for you to leave your home & the provoca-
tions of it, bringing with you my dear children, to breath another air, & to receve into your hearts the welcome of M & me here, & I will send Sam with my
Carriage to Fredricksburg or ⟨. . .⟩ as soon as you will prepare ⟨. . .⟩ the day, to
bring you all up ⟨. . .⟩ get all the mony I can ⟨. . .⟩ & return you to W. So let me
hear from you directly—that you'l come or you shall see me bounce in upon
you some night from the boat, to force you all on board next day for Montpelleir, as I could not stay from my Husband, & the heat of summer comeing
on—last Tuesday our Merchant Davis set off for Baltimore & promis'd to
hand you a small package it contain a few lines with a knotted muslin for
your dress I hope you have it. I shd. have sent a plain one two but was in such
haste & uncertainty—I'l keep it for you—My dear Payne wrote me that he
wd. have been with me the 1t. of this week but could not collect his mony to
bring him—I hope to hear from or see him tomorrow—or wd. write him
again. Since I wrote the foregoing—My good M came in, & I consulted him
about sending mony to P. he directly drew an order & told me to inclose it to
you, which I must beg you to send to him directly if you can—*hire* a messenger—do so—as I know your difficulties. I inclose you 20$ to help out for your
comeing—& you'l tell me what the expenses are for I have been at home so
long that I forget all about traveling—Adeiu—a thousand kisses for the sweet
Dick & all the others—Mr. M bids me tell you that you shall come & that I
must tell ⟨. . .⟩ to see him ⟨. . .⟩

RC (ViU). Torn at bottom of both pages.

To John Payne Todd

24th. May. [18]21.

I was glad to recce. the few lines from you at Baltimore my dearest Payne
and can have no doubt that you have good reasons for remaining there—I am
sorry & disappointed at my letters not reaching your hands—I wrote you at
W. at Phila. & at Baltimore, those for the last place ware enclosed to your Aunt
C. who, I desired would keep the last one until she saw you. It was short, & in
my great alarm, it contain a request that you wd. come to me, as I had a wish
to travel a distance from home on acct. of the Typhus fever—but that fear, has

been dissipated for the present, by the children in the house geting well, & the negros also. I trust therefore that you will not leave your business unfinished on my Account—tho I cannot express my anxiety to see you. Your Unkle Jno. & family came up to visit us—Mr. M. & myself went to meet them, & staid with them at Nellys & Mrs Howards 3 days, & then sent them home without their comeing here on acct. of the danger—We have nothing new in the neighbourhood—Dr. Shepherd sent me word that he saw you well in B. I have not reccd. the boxes—I mention it not that I want them to come, but that you may know in case you put them in the Post—I got the Snuff last sent, as well as some time ago. Adeiu my son—may Heaven bless thee. Your Papa sends his love to you

RC (DLC: DPM Papers). Addressed to Todd care of Mrs. Cutts at Washington. Docketed by Todd.

To John Payne Todd

Monday May 29 [1821]

This moment I reccd. your 2 letters my dearest Payne & should make you a remittance in *this letter* but for the uncertainty of your being in W—you must write directly if you reccd it & say if you'l wait for your mony & how much you'l have—don't fail to do so—We are all well here now, & you will finish your business 'ere you leave a place which you may not find it convenient to return to directly—that is, if it shd. not promis to detain you too long more than another week. Your allways afte

M

RC (owned by Lone Star Autographs, Kaufman, Tex., 1993). Docketed by Payne Todd "From my Mother May 29th. 1821."

From James Madison

My dearest   MONTICELLO Friday Morning [30 November 1821]

I snatch a moment and a very bad pen to tell you that we ended our journey in good time that is before it was dark. The roads, with a little exception, were better than was expected. We found every body well, much regretting that you could not join in the visit. It was well that I did not decline it, for there would not have been a Quorum without me, Gen'l. Taylor &

Mr. Breckinridge, not being heard from & Mr. Cabell sick in Williamsburg. Genl. Cocke arrived just before me, himself imperfectly recd. from his late illness. To-day we shall make a Quorum with the aid of Mr. Johnson who is in the neighbourhood on his way to Richmond & will be sent for to meet us at the University. It seems that yesterday was the day requiring me to be *there*, instead of at Monticello; so that if others had attended I should have been a day after the fair. I hope the business will be over today & that tomorrow evening I may be again with you or the morning after at farthest, unless I shd. be obliged to stop at Col: Lindsay, or the weather shd. embargo us. Yrs most affectly.

James Madison

RC (owned by Harry J. Sonneborn, Theodore, Ala., 1968).

From Ellen W. Randolph

[ca. 30 September 1822]

Mr Middleton leaves us this morning, my dear Mrs Madison, but is so polite as to wait until I can write one line to intreat in Mama's name, in my own, in that of the whole family, that you will not disappoint us in the pleasure of seeing you with Mr Madison in the course of the present week. The meeting of the Visiters takes place on the 7th Oct. but we hope you will come some days previous to that time, in order to give us as much of your society as you can afford to bestow upon us. We are all considerably mortified that Mrs Cutts should have returned to Washington without paying us her promised visit, do not, I pray you, be influenced by her example, but come and cheer us with your presence which diffuses pleasure wherever it is felt.

Mr Middleton has been spending a few days with us, gloomy ones, I fear they proved to *him*, for it has been raining incessantly almost ever since his arrival. The weather cleared up yesterday in time to allow him to visit our University. He came to us from Enniscorthy, and brought the first accounts of the deplorable loss Mrs Stevenson has met with—it curdled my blood to hear the tale—and I can scarcely bear to think of it now.[1]

Adieu my dear Mrs Madison—we shall *certainly* expect you in a few days with Mr Madison, do not disappoint us, and if Mr Todd has no more agreable engagement, I hope he does not require to be assured of the pleasure his company will give to us all. Mama joins in what I have said and in the love with which I remain your own

Ellen

RC (MCR-S: Mary Estelle Elizabeth Cutts Papers). Docketed by DPM.

1. Frances Arnett Stevenson died of burns suffered when she fell into the fire in her nursery (Wayland, *Andrew Stevenson*, 41-42).

To John G. Jackson

29th. Novr. 1822

I have been apprehensive for a long time my dear brother, that you and Mrs. Jackson had totally forgotten me—and that my beloved Mary was unconcious of the fond affection, which her Aunt has ever cherished for her. Your letter however of the 17th. reccd: this day, revives my hopes that our friendship may not pass away, like the fabrick of a vision[1]—and that I may yet be so happy as to embrace you all three at Montpellier.

It would be of service to my dear Mrs. Jackson and her little ones, to accompany you & Mary on a visit to us—and no where, could you be welcomed with more sincerity—this Winter—Spring, or any time—the sooner the better—You must no longer disappoint me in bringing them, but write & tell me when you will come.

I greave for the misfortunes of Mr Cutts—and fear, & feel more for his family! I had no idea that you would be injured by him—my sister & 4 of her children ware with us last summer, when they flattered themselves with the prospect of a rise in city property & B. Stock & that they would have been able to pay all, & save a fortune—but *she* was entirely ignorent of the extent of his embarisments, or the individuals who would suffer by her Husbands losses—Their furniture was sold at Auction & a part of it secured to her, by my Agent. Mr M. purchased their new house, with a hope that he may here after be able to re-purchase *that home* for his wife & children. Judge Todd has been to visit us several times—but our dear Lucy has been so engrossed with her children & grand-children, that we have not seen her for seven years! She writes me constantly, & *now vows* to visit me next spring, or summer. Payne has been at home with us, for the last eighteen months, but left us for Washington last week. He often speaks of you & talked of going with Ed. Coles to see you this fall, when something occured to prevent him. With affecte. wishes & salutations for you & yours, from Your Sister & friend

DPM

Mr. M will write you.

RC (InU: Jackson Collection). Addressed to Jackson at Clarksburg.

1. Shakespeare, *The Tempest* 4.1.151 (*Riverside*).

To Lucy Winston

March 10th. 1823

This—My ever beloved Aunt, is the 2d letter I have written you since the return of John just before Xmass—to thank my dear cousin Dolley for that kind letter which releaved my heart of great trouble about you, as well as my dear cousin Patsy & her whole family, who we had understood ware all afflicted with severe illness—Oh I cannot describe the sorrow I feel when I think of your being, where I can no longer see you, & so seldom hear from you! I heard lately from Culpeper, that your children ware all well with the exception of cousin Susan whose health was delicate still, but I have not seen one of them since you left us—I wish much to visit them, but I scarsly ever leave home. The Old lady (our Mother) is quite well, & Mr. M & myself stay at home a good deal on her account—Nothing meterial has happened amongst us of late—Anna & 4 of her little ones made us a visit last summer but the promised visit from our dear Lucy is yet to come—she says now—that next fall she will be with me, & I think she will, as her son Walter proposes to settle at Hair Wood—Payne spent the winter in Washington & has lately gone from thence to Phila. We missed him dureing the dreary months, but now spring opens, & I shall be amused without him in my garden & woods, tho I never cease to wish for his company— Oh that I could have you & my cousins also, to enjoy the beauties of nature around me. Those about *you* may be as briliant but I cannot see them *with you.* John & his family are thriveing near us—His fifth child is a lovely one, & called Mary Coles—Mr. A. ⟨Fontaine?⟩[1] has consented to pay about half value of the land, lost by his bad advice, but nothing has yet been received for it by my brother—he is industrious however, & has not wanted it as yet—My darling Dolly's recovery was a source of joy to me, I hope she will be more healthy after that frightfull illness! May Heaven preserve you my best of Aunts & comfort you for all deprivations, in the dutifull affection & prosperity of your children! I know so well that your life & happiness depends on your daughters that I must ever love them the better for prolonging it—my amiable & dear cousin Peter too—farewell! Could I *once* know that you received my letters safe, I would write you volum's. Mr. M sends affectinate love to you & every individual of your family—The old lady also— your own neice

D P M

My dear cousins Patsy & Dolley write to me for your Mother when she is tired.

RC (THi). Addressed to Mrs. Lucy Winston "at Mr. P. Armistead near Florence Alabama."
    1. Aaron Fontaine (1753–1823) of Louisa County moved to Kentucky by 1802 (*PJM* 15: 479 n. 1).

To John Payne Todd

12th. Apl. [18]23.

I had the pleasure to receive yours of the 4 my dear Son the day after I wrote you—I trust indeed, your heath is good—& that you will be carefull of it—I told you in mine, that Las Case's journal had reached us, & we are much amused with the perusial[1]—I also mention'd our haveing made a visit to Montecello. I hear'd there that Colo. Isaac Coles had gone to Norfolk to be married to Miss Neverson & that Judge Nelsons son whom you saw here with his mother, was to be married in a few days to Miss Page. We had a visit from Mr Dodge of Marseilles (Consul) Your Papa gave him a commission to send us some good Claret, Hermitage,[2] Oil, some other light wines, & some Mackeroni—which is better than giveing you the trouble to purchase at Phila. I will therefore confine my wants, in that place to a few pds. of Dicks highest sented Macua.[3] which you can have packed in a canester or lead paper, & bring it home in your trunk—Bottles wd. certainly break. I have lately hear'd from my sisters—Lucy is well & gay—sanguine in her hopes of visiting me, & seeing her favorite candidate succeed—Mr. Clay. Anna has been & ⟨is?⟩ still very sick. We have all been well ⟨. . .⟩ thro the winter, except poor old Cuffee who died yesterday.

I enclosed you Genl Taylors letter wherein he mentions his intention of paying you out of the proceeds of Horses, sent or to be sent to Virga. I mention this least you may not get *that letter*—I reccd. from Mr Gray Scotts last Novel[4]—I tell you *this,* in order that you may not purchase it—tho if you meet with Molier's plays translated, I shd. be glad ⟨to⟩ have them. Your Unkle Jno. has received no mony from Fountain,[5] tho he wrote the Judge to *take whatever* he could get for the debt—*Our* debtors also, hold back, for better times, I suppose. Your Papa tells me to remind you of the debt for papers to Mr. Walsh & the Franklin Gazett,[6] the latter he did not wa⟨nt⟩ continued, but as it has been sent he wishes to pay for ⟨it.⟩ I hope you will write me *all* you can, as it is n⟨ext⟩ best consolation to hear from you in your absence, ⟨which⟩ I flatter myself will not be too long—tho I wish, only for your benefit & happiness. It is reported that Jane Smith is to be united to Mr. Morton, & Elisabeth John⟨son?⟩ to a young man from below, I forget his name. Robert is rideing about anxiously soliciting votes[7]—Thus, have I given you all the news within my small circle. Cant you repay me with some, of the fine girls & agreable people of Phi⟨la.⟩ How goes on ⟨. . .⟩ & his wife—we see & hear so much of the Prel. candidates that I am as tired of them as I was of Monroes Tour.[8] Adeiu my dearest Son allways your Affecte.

M

If you have not reccd. mine of the 9th. enquire for it at the P. Office—it was directed there by Mr M.

RC (DLC: DPM Papers). Ms torn.

1. DPM probably referred to Emmanuel, comte de Las Cases, *Mémorial de Sainte Hélène: Journal of the Private Life and Conversations of the Emperor Napoleon at Saint Helena* (Philadelphia, 1823; Shaw and Shoemaker 13049).

2. Hermitage is a wine from the Rhone region in France.

3. Macouba: a kind of snuff.

4. This was probably Sir Walter Scott's *Fortunes of Nigel,* published in Edinburgh in May 1822 and in Albany, N.Y., that same year.

5. Probably Aaron Fontaine.

6. The *Franklin Gazette* was a Philadelphia newspaper owned by Richard Bache and John Norvell (Brigham, *History and Bibliography of American Newspapers* 2:907).

7. This was Robert L. Madison, son of Gen. William Madison and JM's nephew, who served two terms in the House of Delegates as a representative for Madison County, 1821–23 (Earl G. Swem and John W. Williams, eds., *A Register of the General Assembly of Virginia, 1776– 1918* [Richmond, 1918], 106, 109).

8. In the summer of 1817, President Monroe toured the northern states in an effort to build goodwill for his administration. His travels, covered exhaustively by the newspapers, met with great enthusiasm and ceremonial receptions everywhere. In 1819 he made a similar tour of the southern states (Ammon, *Monroe,* 372–79).

From Phoebe P. Morris

My dear Friend   Monday Morng. June 2. [1823]

As you had made me promise to detail the result of my Fathers affairs here[1] I must begin with the interview he had this morning with the Pres. The greatest men are not always in the greatest good humor, & a President has certainly many apologies for being sometimes a little *sour;* Papa thought that even Mr Monroe was this morning not in his best manner—He said after the usual compliments, that he wuld not be pressed & that the account must take its usual course, & go back to the Secretary of State, as *he* had already declined positively from motives of delicacy. Papa resisted this re-reference. The President then renewed his suggestion of Mr. Madison, and said expressly, "if He would say in writing, that he thought the account should be balanced, *that* should be done"—Much more was said of references of the whole subject to the other Secretaries—to Mr Irving—to Mr Forsyth—to most of whom no particular objection could be made—but new delays—those who have felt that sickness of heart which arises from hope deferred can only conceive disappointments thus unnecessarily created—My Father has already waited seven years—& the President talks of *griping*.

I shall leave Washington in a few days with a very heavy heart, in which I am sure you will sympathize.

Adieu, my dearest Mrs Madison present me most affectionately to Mr M. and believe me in all circumstances, unalterably yours.

Phebe P. Morris

RC (DLC: DPM Papers). Docketed by DPM.

    1. Anthony Morris was trying to settle his accounts for contingent expenses as special agent to Spain during the Madison administration (see Joseph Nourse to JM, 16 April 1823, DLC).

From Phoebe P. Morris

My dearest Mrs Madison,   WASHINGTON Jany 19th. 1824.

I have been in Washington about a fortnight, where every thing reminds me of you, but alas! sometimes painfully, for so many scenes of joy and sorrow have passed since the happy period of my early youth which was rendered more joyous by your protecting care. I have every reason to be most grateful to heaven for our present situation—my dear Father is well in health and in excellent Spirits. Major Nourse is still somewhat of an invalid, but with much care and attention he looks & feels at times tolerably well. We are very comfortably established alltogether at the six buildings—I often think of you and my dear Mr Madison alone at Montpelier, as you have told me the Winter is not your season of visiting. I know all your motions & ways so well, that at any hour of the day I can represent to myself what you are doing—What do you think of the probability of having the Marquis de la Fayette for a visitor? for surely he will go to Montpelier, should he visit the United States. The Secretary of the Navy says he shall have one of the first & best manned vessels in the service to convey him hither, if Mr Mitchell's resolution is carried, and *he chuses to come*, which does not appear as yet quite decided.[1]

Mr Monroe is really going to have a drawing Room on Wednesday. You have no doubt seen the description of *Mrs Hay's* personal elegance of deportment & costume in one of the late papers—Written I suppose by some native

THE SELECTED LETTERS OF DOLLEY PAYNE MADISON

after his first appearance at any levée. We all attended at Mrs Adams on the 8th. It was really a very brilliant party & admirably well arranged. The ladies climbed the cha⟨irs⟩ & benches to see Genl. Jackson, & Mrs Adams very gracefully took his arm, & walked through the apartment with him, which gratified the general curiosity—It is said there were 1400 cards issued, & about 800 supposed to be present.[2]

I wish to hear something of my favorite Miss Willis; whenever I feel a little romantic, & think of some pure & innocent being sheltered from the storms of life & lovely in the bosom of retreat, my imagination turns to that sweet & interesting girl. I beg you will remember me to her affectionately, my ⟨dear⟩est Friend, also to her excellent Mother, & to Mrs Conway.

How is Mrs Madison, does she still continue cheerful & in as good health as when I was with you. If she has not forgotten me, pray give my respectful love to her—Papa & Major Nourse beg me to remember their fervent wishes for yours & Mr Madison's health & happiness. Adieu! my dearest & best Friend believe me as ever your own affectionate

Phebe P. Morris

RC (MCR-S: Mary Estelle Elizabeth Cutts Papers). Docketed by DPM.

1. On 12 Jan. 1824 George E. Mitchell of Maryland submitted in the House of Representatives a joint resolution of the House and Senate inviting the marquis de Lafayette to visit the United States. The House passed it on 21 Jan., and the Senate on 26 Jan. (*Annals of Congress*, 18th Cong., 1st sess., 143–46, 988, 1127).

2. In 1824, on the anniversary of the Battle of New Orleans, Louisa Catherine Adams and her husband, John Quincy Adams, the secretary of state, gave a memorable ball for Andrew Jackson (Allgor, *Parlor Politics*, 176–82).

From Eliza Collins Lee

Feby. 12. 1824

The moment my beloved friend you recognise the hand that addresses you—you will, I trust, acknowledge the claims my heart has on your remembrance—neither time or circumstance can change its feelings towards you and tho' the habits of many years have somewhat check'd the indulgence of its dearest recollections they have I find, neither impaired nor blunted them.

In my more frequent visits to your dear Sister, drawn to her by her indisposition, I have ask'd myself who is there amongst the many friends who daily visit her that is called by so sacred an obligation to give her their attentions as I am? Who is their now near her, that can enter into the vicissitudes of her life and from *experience,* feel them too, as I can? Is there amongst the correspondents of her Sister one to whome she has such a right to look for faithful accounts of her situation and for every material care and feeling towards her? Under such conviction my dear friend I take up my pen to offer myself. It will be unnecessary I presume for me at this late period to give you any information of her situation heretofore.

You well know her excellent constitution—you know also the advantage she has taken of it, her habits of self denial in every thing like self indulgence— and while every thing is to be hoped & expected from the former—to the latter may be attributed in great degree her protracted confinement and sickness—at this moment however every thing is to be gained by her feeling the necessity of the strictest care and nursing—she is still unwill⟨ing⟩ to think herself as seriously indisposed as her friends think her and feels a little irritable on that subject—she tells me she fears that your correspondents will unnecesarily alarm you—above all she dreads they may excite your feelings which might determine you to come and see for yourself—Cordially do I join her in feeling that to induce, or allow, you to leave your Husband and aged Mother and your own Comfortable arrangments to encounter all the diffi-⟨cu⟩lties of such an undertaking would greatly add to her distress than alleviate it—It has pleased God my beloved friend thus to separate you and even should he see fit to bring our dear Ann lower much lower—I know your trust is in his wisdom and mercy—Your Situation is peculiarly your own. You have those depending on your presence and your care—even dearer than a Sister—I know your anxiety at this moment, and I would soothe not augment it nor do I mean to deceive you. I saw your Sister day before yesterday—she had taken fresh col⟨d⟩ and was more oppress'd than I have seen her, her cough of course ⟨was⟩ deeply distressing. She was in her parlor and as cheerful as her feelings would permit, more so than is good for her, but you know her spirits—her feet & legs much swolen no fever, which she says leaves her after she leaves her room and returns again in the evening—she complain'd of great soreness and pain in her limbs. She had been bled that day and felt s⟨ome⟩ relief in the chest—was to take calomel that night—I sent yesterday—the effects of which, of course, made her very sick. My Servant has this moment returned (not being able to go myself) you have her own words. "I am much better to day yesterday was ill in bed all day in consequence of the medicine the Doctor has ordered me to be kept quiet—but I chuse to answer your note to Dolly myself" &c &c—I had indeed determind differently well knowing how necesary *quiet* is for her—I hope to see her tomorrow and really find her much better—If this long letter and detail implies to you more anxiety & fear than I intended you know how to pardon it—my chief purpose is to assure you of the interest I must ever take in every member of your dear family my best and earliest friends—and to beg you to put the fullest confidence in me at all times.

I must now beg the favour of you to present me & my Husband most respectfully, and greatfully to your dear husband—my children offer you their love—till we hear from you and command me and you will add to the many obligations confer'd on your friend

Eliza Lee

P.S. excuse incorrect⟨ness?⟩

RC (DLC: DPM Papers). Docketed by DPM.

From Eliza Collins Lee

April 5. 1824

I have defered acknowledging your most acceptable letter my belov'd friend much longer than I intended though I never meant to urge your correspondence believing there was many claims on your pen; yet I certainly should have sooner offered my aid also, as well in relieving as in exciteing your feelings on account of the health of your dear Sister and more particularly so as I fear my letter breathed more of fears, and forebodeing, than of hope and comfort. I certainly felt some anxiety, and some fear for the state she was there, & more than I intended to express at that time. I now feel free and happy to have it in my power to say that I believe that her good constitution and great care will carry her through wonderfully, every unfavourable symptom has subsided—she only waits for better weather to enable her to take exercise—which will prepare her for the Journey that takes her to the arms and care of the dearest Sister, where she will breath in new life & strength and where forgetful of every past pain, and care, she will enjoy a privilege and blessing that falls not to the lot of one Sister in a thousand.

She spent the day with me with her dear children 18 days ago—she look'd and *was* quite herself. I have not heard from her some days but so put ⟨. . .⟩ little back by ten days most unfavour⟨. . .⟩.

I pause—for other matters that might ⟨. . .⟩ and feel my insignificance—but you know I ⟨. . .⟩ obliged, or thought so, to keep myself so much in the ⟨back⟩ ground of the scene that you used so much to enjoy when here—and am now so unknown to that society in which you moved so happily, that I am unfit to give you any thing pleasing or amusing—I know you blame me and I feel that if for neglect of former blessings or the too great indulgence of former ambition, I must be made more & more sensible of the wants of some of the former, and more & more humbled for the vanity & presumption of the latter—I must not complain.

But believe me my dear friend when I tell you one truth—that had I even dared to promise to myself some great gratification, some delightful *treat,* within these last eight years, it would have been in seating myself beside you at Montpellier—how often have my poor children urged me to this enjoyment: would to God I could now, even at this moment, say it should be reallised—should it ever, it will answer the first wish of your friend—my children beg to be presented to you. Mr. Lee and myself with all respect to dear Mr. Madison and you well know how much is offered to you by your truely affte. friend

E Lee

RC (DLC: DPM Papers). Ms torn. Docketed by DPM.

Trust Agreement for Anna Cutts

[12 June 1824]

We James Madison & Dolly P. Madison have received and promise to hold in trust for the use of Mrs. Anna P. Cutts, or in case of her death, any surplus remaining, for that of her two daughters or the survivor of them, the sum of twelve hundred dollars consisting of monies furnished by her sister Lucy P. Todd and others of her kindred & friends, for the said purposes. Given under our hands this twelfth day of June in the year eighteen hundred & twenty four.

Printed copy (*The Splendid Library of the Late Mr. and Mrs. William A. Read* [American Art Association, Anderson Galleries, 1936], item 272, 170).

From James Madison

Monticello

Friday morning 7 OC. [5 November 1824]

We arrived about sunset: just as they were commencing their Desert. The Genl.[1] had arrived about 3 OC. with his son & Secrety. the last so sick that he went to bed instead of Dinner. I have not heard how he is this morning. I found here only the General & his family, Col. Campbel & Wm. Roane of the Council, who will attend him till he goes out of the State, and a few of the

THE SELECTED LETTERS OF DOLLEY PAYNE MADISON

family connection. I may add Mr. Coolidge just from Boston. A large crowd had been here, including the indviduals appointed to receive the Guest from Fluvanna, and the party escorting him: but they did not remain, even Genl. Cocke to dinner. The Genl. does not say yet how many days he stays here. He declines a visit to Staunton, and will divide the time not required for the road & the appointed festivities, between Mr Jefferson & myself. It is probable he will not be with us till near or quite the middle of next week. He will have with him besides his son & Secy. the 2 Councillors, and such of the Company of Orange meeting & conducting him as may chuse to stop at Montpellier. The Miss Wrights are expected here tomorrow of Mrs. Douglas & her daughters the family here have no notice. The Genl. thinks they may make a call as a morning visit only. They travel it seems with the Miss Wrights, but whether they will preceede them in the visit to us is unknown, nor can I learn whether the Miss Wrights will precede or accompany or follow the Genl. I may learn more to day, but not in time to write you. The Genl. on finding I had a letter for them proposed to take charge of it, and it was given him of course. My old friend embraced me with great warmth. He is in fine health & spirits but so much increased in bulk & changed in aspect that I should not have known him. They are doing their *possible* at the University to do him honor. We shall set out thither about 9 OC. I can not decide till the evening when I shall return. I am not without hope that it may be tomm[or]ow.

With devoted affection

J.M.

I just hear that Mr Vosin is better. I am hastening Paul to the post office, that the letter may be in no danger of failing, & that he may be back by 9 OC.

RC (WHi: Gratz Collection).
    1. In 1824 Congress invited the marquis de Lafayette to return to the United States for a visit. In a yearlong triumphal progress throughout the nation, Lafayette, along with his son, George Washington Lafayette, and his secretary, Auguste Levasseur, visited the Madisons at Montpelier twice, in November 1824 and August 1825 (Ketcham, *James Madison,* 664–65).

To John G. Jackson

Nover. 27th. 1824.

I reccd. by the last post, your kind letter my dear Brother, giving me the interesting account of our beloved Mary's marriage[1]—May every happiness attend her—and her estimable companion. It would afford us heartfelt pleasure to see them here—you, also, with my dear Mrs. Jackson. We looked for you all—long after your last letter giveing me hopes of seeing you with Mary—I answered it, without delay, & have often feared, you never received it, as from that time to the present, you have been silent. I sincerely regret your want of health & hope you will soon be well again.

Mr. Madison & myself have been favored with fine health since our residence at Montpelleir, & tho we have not been far from home within 8 years, we have had the satisfaction of seeing many of our friends from a distance. Our dear Lucy has promised to come every fall, but such has been her increase of cares, with children & grand-children, that she has not yet, reached us. Anna & her little ones have been with us every summer, whilst Mr Cutts remain'd in Washington, we have never seen Mr. C. since his misfortune's, & are perfectly unacquainted with the state of his affairs—but we understand his anxiety to pay, is great, & his expectations considerable.

We have lately had a visit from Genl. La Fayette & family of a few days— the former, you know, was an old friend of Mr M——s. I was charmed with his society—& never witnessed so much enthusism as his appearance occationed here and at our court house, where hundreds of both sexes collected together, to hail & welcome him—He has promised to spend some time with us again, before he leaves this country. I hope to hear from you again soon & must beg you to enclose Jno Payne's Deeds for his Harison &c Lands under cover to Mr Madison, as it appears nothing has been done with them there; he lives near us with a large family & in poor circumstances—& we have some hope of turning the land to acct. for his helpless family. With affectinate love & wishes for you all, in which Mr M cordially joines, I am dear Brother truly yours

D P Madison

RC (InU).
    1. Mary E. P. Jackson married John James Allen.

To John Payne Todd

Decr. 2d. 1824.

I have reccd. your's my dearest Payne of the 23d & 24th Novr. & was impatient to answer them yesterday (the day of their reaching me) but oweing to the winter establishment for the Male, no post leaves this until tomorrow morg. Mr Clay with 2 members of congress left us yesterday after passing 2 days—Mr. C. enquired affectinately after you, as, does all your old acquaintance whom I see—but my dear son it seems to be the wonder of them all that you shd. stay so long from us! & now I am ashamed to tell, when asked, how long my only child has been absent from the home of his mother! Your Papa & myself entreat you to come to us—to arrange your business with those concern'd to return to them when necessary, & let us see you here, as soon as possible with your interest & convenience. Your Papa thinks as I do, that it would be best for your reputation & happiness, as well as ours, that you shd have the appearance of consulting your parents, on subjects of deep acct. to you & that you wd. find it so in *returning* to Phila. when you appointed, or choose to do so. I have said in my late letters, as well as this, all that *I thought sufficient* to influence you—I must now, put my trust in God alone! If the young lady you have followed so long, has not yet been won, I fear she ⟨hasn't⟩ the character to form your happiness here after, tho others might be found, who would. I enclose you 30$ instead of 20 which you mentiond, & tho I am sure 'tis insufficient for the jurney, I am unable to add to the sum to day—I recently pd. Holoway $200, on your note, with interest for 2 years—The other small debts in this quarter I settled long ago with funds of yours in my hands. I hope you will write me the moment you get this, that I may *know certainly* your determinations & make up my own. I can add no news that is likely to interest you except that poor Judge Todd is likely to die & that Ellen R——h[1] is to be married to Mr. Coolledge. ⟨As to the⟩ "occurance" you elude to, I hope is propicious & if it ware for your good, we might rejoice in your immediate union—provided it brought you spedily to our arms, who love with inexpressible tenderness & constancy. Your own—Mother.

RC (NjP).
    1. Ellen Wayles Randolph.

To Richard D. Cutts

Dear Sir   [ca. 1824]

Your Unkle has reccd. your Elegant & lerned Epistle, & his finger being a little sore at present he desires me to answer it for him. He says your loop of Tobaco turned out as well as could be expected considering the dryness of weather—he does not dispare that it will weigh 3 ounces—he wants to know whether you'l have it shiped or sold in the country—every body who has seen it admires it very much—& wants to know what is the sort—some think it little Frederick—others are at a loss whether it is thick joint or Shoe String—the prevailing, is that it's bull ⟨fire?⟩. They will be glad to know the oppinion of such an experienced planter as yourself of what is the best kind for Cultivation—perhap you may chuse to have your Tobaco manufactured—you must say in that case—whether you prefer its being made into pig tail or twist for chewing—or if you think it best to make it into snuff—you must decide between Rappee Maccua—or No 9. He guesses, you wd. prefer the Blackgaurd—He incloses a remittance by way of advance & is sorry he could not send you small change instead of it—He is very glad to hear you intend to make him a visit, & says you must bring with you among your other frds. Miss Modesty—her sister tacciturnity & above all, their cousin good humour—you need not take the trouble to bring your appetite for bacon & chicken—nor for Warffle Butter, Custard nor hony—particularly you'd better leave behind, your relish for grapes figs & waterMellons—All your friends White Yellow & black send complimts. to you—Dr Dick—your Unkle sat by me & dictated this letter & inclosed a *Cent*—I add these a few words of my own & inclose you six peices to prepare you for his jokes & your jurney—From

Aunt D.

RC (MCR-S: Mary Estelle Elizabeth Cutts Papers). Addressed to "Richard Cutts Tobaco planter Washington."

To John G. Jackson

Jany. 4th. 1825.

I thank you dear Brother for your last kind letter and the trouble you have taken to find the Deeds you sent me—I hope you will not doubt my wishes to be equally prompt in serveing you, when ever it is in my power. I am extreamly sorry—and so is Mr Madison, for the loss and difficulties, you are suffering by Mr Cutts—but you are under a mistake in regard to his furniture as well as some other property sold in the city—The furniture was sold for its full value, about 7 or 800$ for a Boston debt, and paid for with mony, which was never his. The House & lots attatched to it, ware sold by the Bank to pay a Bank debt, for an appraised value, between 5 & 6 thousand dolls. as *they ware bought* by Mr M and the family remaining in the house—some seem to suppose, that thro him, the property was settled on Mrs. Cutts or her children—but the property is as absolutely Mr M——s as any he holds—without any claim or condition whatever, in favor of them or any body else. It has been 6 or 7 years since we saw Mr. Cutts and we have never had any communication from him on the general state of his affairs—From what we have heared lately, we fear that his unpaid debts are beyond any idea, heretofore entertained, and hold out a gloomy prospect for my sister her children, and his many creditors,

& you may suppose, that in such a situation he will be *influenced only* by the necessity of it.

I beg you to present us most affectinately to Mrs. Jackson—and say to my beloved Mary that, we shall hope to see her with Mr Allen in the spring—nor shall we give up the pleasing expectation of yet seeing Mrs. J & yourself at Montpellier.

John has desired me to say that Marys portion of the Louisa land[1] was safe for her—but I will get him to be more particular on the subject when I see him.

He says also, that if you will be so good as to let him know the amt. of taxes due from him, that he will inclose the mony to you for immediate payment of it. Allways sincearly & affectinately Your Sister

D P Madison

Mr. Madison & Payne offer to you and yours their best regard & wishes.

RC (ViU: Breckenridge-Watts Papers).

1. This was land once owned by DPM's brother Walter Payne in Louisa County, Va., which John C. Payne sold in 1822, reserving a sixth of the proceeds for Mary E. P. Jackson Allen (John C. Payne to Mary E. P. Allen, 6 June 1825, Mary Allen Black Collection, Fincastle, Va.).

To Mary E. E. Cutts

MONTPELIER 22d. Jany. 1825

Must I fill this pretty paper, with your good pen, my sweetest of daughters! What if your Aunt is scarce of amusing materials—would you not be sorry and weary, to read a long letter, but you are reasonable and ask only for a "little letter" which you shall have—Your Uncle and cousins are all well and think highly of you and love you accordingly—Dolley P. prefers plaiting straw to learning her book, still I think her taste will improve by and bye. Kiss Dolley[1] for me and tell her I hope and trust, she will be a fine accomplished girl, if she yields implicit obedience to her dear Mother, her best friend and councellor! I long to hear good news from my favorite Walter and hope to see him a good man and a great captain—Tell Madison that I hope he is quite well, that his Uncle John talks of writing to him for new books &c. We have had two weeks of spring like weather, when the birds came out with their summer song and I went to gardening. We dismissed our gardener as soon as possible after you left, and called in three black men, who understood the business—and we hope to have from them as many good things as usual. I go but little from home, except to ride for exercise and can therefore tell you but little of those you know in this quarter. I suppose you see Cornelia Barbour sometimes, or at least you know to what her studies are directed: Present me to Mrs. Bomford. What has become of Miss Vail, remember me to her and to Caroline Crawford and Mrs. Nurse, Mr. Morris and Mrs. Whitcroft, if you ever see her, and when you write me, my darling, get a large paper and place it where you can go and write, as you recollect things, and as you find you can tell me something of these I mention, and all others of my old acquaintance, as well as the new people, what they say and do—There is a task for you—my excuse for asking as much is a persuasion that it would improve you to express yourself freely to me, my darling, and if you tell me all the secrets of the nation, they shall be sacred. You do not know how acceptable the news from Washington is to us—a far off—in two weeks more you will make a new president and go to the Coronation; in the mean time people will think freely and act under some restraint. Your Grandmamma and *Nelly* enquire about you every post day, and seem to cherish a friendship for you all. I enclose you a few lines, in imitation of the Scottish Bards, which are good enough for your book or mine. Adieu, my dearest Mary, Always your affectionate Aunt and friend

D. P. Madison

Tr (MCR-S: Mary Estelle Elizabeth Cutts Papers). Tr made by Mary Cutts.
    1. Dolley Payne was the daughter of John C. Payne. Mary and her sister, Dolley Cutts, were the daughters of Anna Cutts.

To Anna Cutts

Wednesday 18th. May [1825?]

Yours of the 6th. my dear Sister distresses me very much—It bore the W——n Post mark of the 15th. May, & I flatter myself Dolleys was written after it, & that you have got better—nearly *well* again. I pray that this may find you so much in health, as to be ready in your affairs & mind, to set off for a safe haven—I wish I could send Jno. for you—but am affraid—he might distress you by intemperance, tho his kind & tender care of you wd. be great—If he went *alone* to Fredrickg. for you, he might be tempted (& wd. be) to go into bad habits, & you might not see him. If you could arrive there before night from the Boat, you wd. be safe, & every body wd. befriend & take care of you. Can't Madison come with you it wd. be a pleasant thing for him, to come, if but for one week, to see his Mother & Sisters safe—If Phil Barbour, or any other man of your acquaintance was comeing, it might superscede the necessity of Ms being with you, if inconvenient to him to leave the office.[1] I'm more affraid of your being in the night air than any thing else—If the Steam boat setts off early & *arrives early,* you'd have nothing to fear or if the House at the landing was fit for you to stay all night, so that no exposure shd. befall you— You *must not* travel in the night—it wd. throw you back into agues & destroy you. Oh that I could come for & take care of you myself. We must make the best of existing circumstances, & you'l find your spirits rise with your health, as soon as you leave care & trouble behind, & think only of re-creation & tranquility—In your present state, I do not like to give you commissions, to perplex, & fatigue you—& if I do name any thing that I want, remember that tis of no consequence & that you are not to get it, unless it shd. be a pleasure to you when rideing to do so.

My Messenger has not retur[n]'d from Richd. with the black silk dress I sent for, tho I hope he'l bring it; I sent however, to an utter stranger to get it for me, & he may not do it—so that I shd. like one of the figur'd blacks you sent me at 84½ cents if *you* think it gentele & pretty 8 yds—I thought a various colour'd plaid silk wd. bind full, & dress my white chip,[2] & if you think well of it bring 4 yds. for that purpose & a skarf—I leave it to your judgement.

RC (ViU).
    1. James Madison Cutts was a clerk in the office of his father, Richard Cutts, the second comptroller of the treasury (*A Register of All Officers and Agents, Civil, Military, and Naval, in the Service of the United States* [Washington, D.C., 1828], 18).
    2. Chip: a hat (*OED*).

From Sally McKean Yrujo

My Dear Mrs Madison.   MADRID. July 11. 1825.
    I cannot let pass so good an opportunity as the return of Mr Nelson to the United States without having the pleasure of writing, to assure you of my unalterable affection and friendship, beleive me my dear friend that altho' such a length of time has elapsed since we have seen each other, and such an immense distance seperates us, I have never ceased to think of you, and love you, the remembrance of those happy hours we have spent together in our younger days I still reflect upon with pleasure.

    I suppose you must have heard some time ago of the terrible loss I have had, in that of a tender and affectionate husband whose memory I honor and cherish; it has been a heavy blow for me my friend, a female, & a stranger— to say more is useless you have only to reflect a moment—you will readily conceive the *Anguish* I have suffered; but the Almighty has been very kind in makeing my two dear children all that a fond Mother could wish. My Narcisa is what the world calls pretty, she is very like what the Marquis was when we were first married, she is still single but I do not know if she will remain so long, as there are two gentleman solicitous for her hand. My son Charles who is very like me in the face, is makeing a rapid progress in the diplomatick career, he is Secretary of Embassy in Paris, and during 7 months that the Ambassador was absent, he was chargé des Affaires: his career will cause him to be made a minister in the course of a year or two, very probably to the United States in case of such an event I shall go once more to visit my native country and fold my dear Mrs Madison once more to my heart—such an idea alone makes me feel happy. The bearer of this appears to be an excellent Man, he told me he lived not far from Orange, you may suppose how many questions I asked him about you; and how happy I was to hear you was so well, and looking equally so, and that you had proposed writing to me by him and he apoligized to me for having come away without letting you know, as some unforseen event had prevented him. Pray write to me soon and let me know how you are, give me news of your Sister Lucy, and how many children she has, also of Anna, what number she has & if she lives in Washington: Mrs Gallatin and myself often talked together about you all when we were in Paris together: I hear that Frances has been married since their return to America.[1] As to my situation, independent of my property I have the pension of widow of Minister of State as long as I live which is 2000 dollars A year, myself and daughter live together I have a pretty house, keep my coach, am respected, and keep the first Society in Madrid: but since I have had the misfortune to loose my husband I have seen but little company: Mr Nelson can give you news of me—you see I have also been particular in informing you of my situation and that of my children, knowing the interest you take in us. My Dear Narcisa unites with me in being affectionately remembered to you, and I request you to remember me particularly to Mr Madison and give my best love and affectionate remembrance to your Sisters Lucy, and Anne and beleive me to remain your My dear Madam sincere and affectionate Friend—

Sarah Maria Terisa Marchioness of the House of Yrujo.
P.S. Pray dont forget to write to me soon & give me news of yourself,[2] and also how your Son Payne is, and if he is married yet. I have been so little in the habit of writing in english for some years back, that you must pardon any faults: I forgot to tell you that I saw Betsy Patterson (Madame Buonaparte) in Paris, I thought she looked very much broke in her whole appearance. I send you one of my Charles passports to see ⟨given'd?⟩ by him at the age of 22 years, as you allmost saw him born I may say.

RC (MdHi).

1. Frances Gallatin married Byam Kerby Stevens in 1830.

2. On 7 May 1827 Sally Yrujo wrote to Anna Cutts, "As for your Sister Madison I suspect she has forgotten me altogether: for altho' I have written to her at different times, I have never received a single scrape of a pen from her; If she knew the interest I have allways had for her, she would not have acted thus; I give you the commission to tell her so from me, and if you like give her a scolding for me" (MCR-S: Mary Estelle Elizabeth Cutts Papers).

To Lydia H. Sigourney

Septr. 16th. 1825.

I have lately received your kind and flattering letter my dear Madam, and whilst I thank you for it, I must also express our admiration of the poetry, which so eloquently augments the beauties of Montpellier[1]—as well as the merits of its inhabitants, who cannot be diverted, by all the love and respect with which you inspired them, from the feeling—that they owe to your benevolent and fruitful fancy, many of the flowers with which you have decorated them.

In the "Traits of the Aborigines," for which I repeat my thanks,[2] a grateful banquet has been furnished us by your happy pencil.

I should most gladly have introduced you to our aged Mother, but that she was a little indisposed during the warm weather, when you favored us with a short visit. Our mutual friend Mr Hatch, with his family, enjoy good health, and the high esteem they justly merit. Will you allow us to hope for a longer visit from Mr Segourney and yourself, should you be led at any time, to repeat your tour to Virginia? In this, Mr Madison joins me as well, as in all the good wishes, with which I salute you.

D P Madison

RC (CtHi).

1. "Montpelier" was published in Sigourney's volume entitled *Poems* (Philadelphia, 1834), 37–38.

2. Sigourney's *Traits of the Aborigines* (Cambridge, Mass., 1822), a 284-page collection of Indian tales in blank verse, with copious notes, was published anonymously.

To John Payne Todd

July 6 [18]26

These few lines my dear son (if they reach you) will inform you that Mr. Jefferson died on the 4th—about 12 or 1 o'clock. Mr. M feels his departure deeply, as no doubt his family must.

I wrote you immediately after your last requesting the letters of introduction & enclosed one for the Marchioness W——y & one for Madame Preshon with mony. I should like to know that you rec'd them & to know whether Hariot embarked & took them. In truth I sh'd be gratified to hear from & to communicate with you, if it was possible.

I shall add mearly, that I had a message from Lynch, saying that he expected & hoped I w'd have sent for your horse last summer. Your Aunt Todd writes me that George got home safe. All love ones as usual Your aff'te

Mother

If you can hear what the people of N. York & other Cities intend to do in the mony business, as it regards Mr. J's fund, pray let me know[1]—& if convenient send me a paper of fine snuff.

Printed extract (offered for sale in Paul C. Richards Autographs, Catalogue 271, item 5).

1. In January 1826 Jefferson had asked the Virginia legislature for permission to hold a lottery to dispose of enough property to meet his indebtedness. Once the lottery was approved, some friends floated a plan whereby lottery tickets would be sold and then burned on the Fourth of July, with the money presented as a gift to Jefferson. Much hinged on the success of the plan in New York and other cities in the North, but Jefferson's death put an end to the lottery's prospects (Malone, *Jefferson and His Time* 6:473–81, 495–96).

From James Madison

MR. CONWAY'S UNIVERSITY

My dearest   Monday night Decr. 4. 1826

Here we are snug in a warm room consoling ourselves on our escape from the Storm, by our safe arrival, mine about 2 O.C. yesterday, Mr. Monroe's last night. We found the road so good that it was difficult to avoid getting to Mr Nelson's too soon. We found them well except young Mrs. N. whose indisposition tho' not serious, suspended, if nothing more, the trip below. Mr. Monroe set out before breakfast in order to call on his brother in Milton leaving me to follow at leisure directly to the University. At Everettsville, he learnt that his brother had died the day before.[1] We are as yet without a Board. Mr. Cabell alone having joined us. He left Enniscorthy this morning travelling the whole way with this snow & hail in his face. He can give no particular account of Mrs. Stephenson, who he understood had gone to S. C. in bad health. He says there had been no sale nor final arrangement of the old family seat. He answered my enquiry as to Mrs. Carter that he believed she was pretty well. It seems uncertain whether we shall make a Board at all; Genl. Cocke is detained by a sick son and we hear nothing of either of the other Visitors. I have seen all the professors, particularly Dungleson Tucker Blatterman Key & Lomax &

Bonnycastle. The first question from them was whether you were with me; followed by regret at my answer: We have been present at the examinations today and shall continue to attend. They will not be over till wednesday in next week and I fear we shall find it difficult to get away before the end of them. Mr. Trist got down thro' the snow this afternoon. I have had but little opportunity of conversing with him. He says they are all well, and in their new Quarters. Mr. J. T. R.[2] is gone to Washington with some view to his great object. Their last accts. from Mrs Randolph continued to be favorable. Col. R is expected to set out soon on his Southern Mission.[3] The mail brought me nothing to day, so that there has been some mistake at our post office or some accident in the case. Yours always

J.M.

RC (ViU).
    1. Andrew Monroe.
    2. Thomas Jefferson Randolph.
    3. In the wake of Jefferson's death, Martha Jefferson Randolph went to Boston to visit her daughter Ellen Coolidge. Thomas Mann Randolph was appointed to the boundary commission authorized to settle a dispute between Georgia and the Florida Territory (William H. Gaines Jr., *Thomas Mann Randolph* [Baton Rouge, La., 1966], 166–67).

To James Madison

Tuesday Eveg. [5 December 1826]

The four days passed without you my beloved, seem so many weeks. I am now expecting a letter from you, which I know will console me, especially if it tells me you are well. Sister Macon dined with me until this day, when she went home with her son M &c. Mr. S⟨laughter?⟩ came to dinner (as usial) but to do him justice, he was ignorent of your absence. Mama is quite well. Jno. & Clary spent Sunday with me, & I keep Dolley to sleep in your place. I have not reccd. a letter from Payne or Anna & not until this Evg. the letter from Mrs. Blaterman, which I wish to answer & inclose to you, if I have time, tomorrow.

The snow storm has put an end to my hopes of rideing, tho not to my attention to the Blankets—& preperation for Pork which will come in from Black Meadow & Eddens in 2 days—in truth, I am too busy a House keeper to become a poetess in my solitude.

Wednesday 2 oClock

Sam has just return'd with yours of Monday night, & I rejoice that you are safe my dear Husband, & will be subject to no risk whatever, from exposure to the weather, or forgetfulness of me. I would have written you by our old friend Long, but that he left this directly after breakfast & did not give me time—he will tell you that we continue well. I am surprised at your not getting papers & letters by the Sundays post as I gave written directions at the P. Office to that effect—Paul shd. go to both offices for them. I will enquire into the cause tomorrow. Gales's paper[1] was sent me, as you desired, but it contains nothing new except the arrival of Members—so that I can tell *you nothing new*—the expression of my tender, & devoted affection, does not come under *that* head. Please to present me to the ladies around you—as well as to Montecello family thro Mr. Trist, & send Paul for my books, lent to Mary & Ellen B.[2] I'm sorry for Mr. Monroes troubles, of any sort—& hope that you will get *thro* yours, at the examination on Wednesday next, & inform me how soon after, I may expect you, as well as what figure the youth's make, in their exibition. If the inclosed is not to the purpose, please to return it to me *what* it aught to be, when you shall *have* it *improved.* I must bid you adeiu—or become troublesome, as some others of your long winded corrispondents, who love to write you, because it pleases themselves. Forever your own

DPM

Seal the lady's letter 'ere tis sent.

RC (St. John's Seminary, Camarillo, Calif., 1957).

1. The *National Intelligencer* (Washington, D.C.), published by Joseph Gales and William W. Seaton.

2. This was probably Mary Jefferson Randolph, daughter of Martha Jefferson and Thomas Mann Randolph, and her cousin Ellen Wayles Bankhead.

From James Madison

My dearest   [ca. 8 December 1826]

My last was so full that it has left me little to add. General Cocke joined on tuesday afternoon which makes up a board, but we are chiefly engaged with the Examinations, which go on very well. I fear that it will be impossible to get away before the middle of next week. I need not say how anxious I am to be with you. We have dined every day from home since we arrived except the first & are engaged for every day to come till tuesday next. As the dinners are all male parties, except that of Mr. Blatterman, and the weather &c. prevent ordinary visits I have not yet seen any of the ladies of your acquaintance. I must if I can catch opportunities of calling on them before I leave the University. I have recd. the packet from O. C. House, and shall look for another tomorrow which I hope will bring a line from you, which I hope will tell me that you are well and that nothing amiss has occurred. Ever & most affectionately yours

J. M.

RC (DLC).

From James Madison

UNIVERSITY Decr. 14. (thursday morning) [1826]

I wrote you my beloved by the mail of tuesday, and hoped it would be the last from this place, with fears however that overbalanced hope. It appears now not to be certain that I shall be able to get away even tomorrow (friday). Every exertion however will be made to effect it. The Examinations, did not close till last night, and our attendance on them left the other business undone during that long period: and it is found to [be] of greater amount, and importance than was at first apparent. The mail of yesterday brought me the inclosed letter, & I send with it a few of the papers recd. at the same time. I can not express my anxiety to be with you; I hope never again to be so long from you, being with devoted affection ever yours.

J. M.

RC (PCarlD).

To Anna Cutts

My dear Sister   Mondy 23d Apl. [1827]

I began a letter to you directly after the rect of yours dated Sunday night on thursday *last*—but was too sick to go on—after that company came & prevented my finishing yesterday. I now begin a new one alltogether as yours of Thursday reached me yesterday telling me of the bonit sent by Mrs. D[1]—I must thank you sincearly for it—tho I regret the trouble you have had with it—I hope you'l send me the acct. that I may aid in *replacing* one upon *your* head. I have looked for Mrs. D. every day so long, that I supposed she had changed her mind—I observe my dr. Sister that you are silent on the *subjects,* in several of my late letters—I am very *anxious* to know if you got *one* soon after you went to the *Island weeding*[2]—speaking of my *dream*—t'was a silly letter enuf, but being allways a dreamer you know—I cannot be reconciled to think another has sight of my folly in writeing them—one also in which I told you of Mrs. Randolphs letter to me. The book you sent Jno. he says, is very good but more suited to further advanced schollars—The *book* recd. yesterday he took home to read first, & I will take care to return it safe with the 2d Vol. when it comes. I shd. have rejoiced to see Dolley, Mary or Richard, with Mrs. D. but they are yours—& you know what is best for them—I'm affraid Mrs. D.'s procrastination will not be so well, as if she had begun her visit at the time she threatened. Mrs Randolph & her family from Montecello are to meet here in May early, with some others. Secy B. & son in-law[3] passed Saturday & yesterday here—*He* is more altered than any body I have ever seen, in so short a time, & appears so full of care, that I was sorry for him. The Election is going on today at our C. House where young J—s B.[4] is to be left *out,* the people say. The Secy has gone to see—his wife is sick, & his daughter come up to lay in. Cornelia left with Miss Vail til Augt. The report is—that Miss Livermore is to be at BarboursVille for some time & there to preach to us all—I wish she may—I for one wd. go listen to her in serch of light—but is she of the pure in spirit? fill'd with true religion without alloy or does worldly ambition for éclat, tarnish the perfection of Soul she professes—Edward has not yet been to see us—his sister S——[5] is very low in health at Richd. Few expect her to survive! I have recd two letters from P——[6] since Edward left Phia. P says he was not *prepared* to accompany E. but will come to me ere long—I cant acct. for Lucys silence, the last month—I hope she is not sick, as she was when I heard last from her. I will continue this, tomorrow—Jno. & his *are as usial*—no doubt of the things you send being highly acceptable—let them be what they may—the Children Increasing in No. & size, makes a great difference *with us*—I hope Madison got my note with the last Vol. I left it so that you could read it first—you will tell me—did you get a specimin of D. P—s[7] writing? By that I might know you had mine that enclosed it. It rains here, & of cource no Mrs. D til fair weather. Eveg—The Election is over & J—s. B. left out—to his great dismay—haveing treated the people at a high rate—I suppose tis best to say *nothing*—I'm affraid the licence people take with their tongues & pens, will blast the good of the country—& display all sorts of evil traits of character that can mark a selfish & Savage Race—Under the cloak of Politicks our Country Men come out—not like Romans, but Goths & Vandals—dont you think so or are you affraid to say. I suppose Mrs. Adams has got pretty well as she goes to parties—& I hope Mrs. Mason is happy in the marriage of her children this Summer. Adeiu my dear nothing has occured since I begun this, to add amusement & interest to my letter—I seldom feel quite well & walk badly from rhumatism in my ankle. I want you to send me half a pd. more of the same Coars Rappee Snuff that you sent me last. Yours allways—Il write you when D comes—& ask the same favor of you

RC (MCR-S: Mary Estelle Elizabeth Cutts Papers).
    1. Susan Decatur.
    2. This was probably the 1827 wedding of Sarah Maria Mason, the daughter of John and Anna Marie Murray Mason, and Samuel Cooper (1798–1876) at the Masons' home on Analostan Island in the Potomac River at Washington. Cooper served as adjutant general of the Confederate armies during the Civil War.
    3. James Barbour and John Taliaferro.
    4. James Barbour Jr. had represented Orange County in the Virginia House of Delegates in the 1826–27 session (Swem and Williams, *Register*, 120).
    5. Sarah Coles Stevenson.
    6. John Payne Todd.
    7. Dolley Payne, daughter of John C. Payne.

From James Madison

My dearest,   UNIVERSITY. July 11. 1827

    We made out to get to Mr. Goodwins by 5 OC. where we luckily fell in with Genl. Cocke. After consultation as to our lodging &c at the University, he was left to make the arrangements on his arrival, which would be that evening. On our reaching the University the morning after, we found, much to our satisfaction that he had provided by treaty with Mr. Brokenborough, that we shd. all lodge in the Pavilion evacuated by Mr. Key, and be there supplied with a table & every other accomodation requisite. Our situation is thus made as convenient as possible, all the Visitors being together and able to proceed on their business, at every interval left by the Examinations. These commence at 5 OC. in the morning, are resumed at half after 8 OC. & continued till Eleven; & after an interval of half an hour are again continued till one OC. At three we dine and at five, are again at the Examinations till 8 OC. I have seen Mrs. Blatterman and Mrs. Conway, and said to them what you would wish. I shall call on Mrs. D.[1] & the other Ladies of your acquaintance as I can. Mr. Trist says they are all well at Tuffton, except Mr. J. Randolph; who is not so. Late accts. from Mrs. R. are favorable. Every body is full of expressed regrets that you did not come with me. Mr. Monroe was a little indisposed yesterday forenoon, but I hope is again well. By not getting off early from Mr. Goodwin's, I lost the opportunity of writing by the last post. The mail of this morning brought me nothing, which is explained by what Mr. Chapman mentioned to you. We are not without hopes that the examination will be closed on the 18th. instead of the 20th. Mean time be assured of my greatest anxiety to hasten the moment of being where my heart always is.

Mr. Cabell saw Mrs. Stephenson on his way, and was desired to let her know whether you were here, intending, with her sister, to come to you. He has got her word that you were not. She is low, but rides about.

RC (DLC).
    1. Harriette Leadam Dunglison, wife of Robley Dunglison.

To James Madison

My Beloved   Monday, 9. oclock [16 July 1827]

I trust in God that you are well again, as your letters assure me you are. How bitterly I regret not being with you! Yours of "friday Midday" did not reach me til *last evig.* I felt so full of fear that you might relapse that I hasten'd to pack a few cloaths, & give orders for the Carriage to be ready; & the post waited for this morg. Happily, the messenger has return'd with your letter of yesterday which revives my heart, & leads me to hope you will be safe at home on Wednesday night, with your own affectionate nurse. If business shd. detain you longer or you shd feel unwell again, let me come for you. Mama & all are well, here. I enclose you this letter. the only one recd. by yesterdays post, with two latest papers, to read on your journey back. I hope you recd my last of Thursday containing letters & papers. My mind is so anxiously occupied about you, that I cannot write. May angels guard thee my dear best friend

D

RC (NjP: Crane Collection). Addressed to JM at "University" and "Tuesday morg."

From James Madison

[17 July 1827]

I recd yesterday morning, your welcome letter of Saturday evening. I hope you recd. in due time my two last, the latter of which will have dissipated any doubts as to the degree of my indisposition. As I hoped, my health has continued to strengthen. I joined the Board yesterday, and am well enough today for the ride home if the business were over. But this is not the case and I fear a detention till friday. I shall as you may be sure not lose a moment, after I am liberated, from hastening to you. Genl. Dade is here & I have made with him the best arrangement the case admitted for neutralizing what passed on the 4th. of July.[1] On Dr. T.s letter we will communicate as soon as I get home. It will be well to impress on P. the inexpediency of waiting for the recovery of a doubtful debt, at a certain expence that must soon exceed it in amount if recovered. Paul tells me he saw John Carter from whom he learned that Mrs. Stephenson would not make the promised visit to us for a week or two. This may be occasioned by the visit of Mr. S. to Washington. Mrs. Dungleson, the Docr. tells me had at one time a trip over the mountain in view, but will be kept at home by a cause well understood by married Ladies. I understand that the movement intended by Mr. Bonnycastle's family may be retarded if not prevented by an attack on health of Miss ⟨Tate?⟩, who has called on Dr. D. Mr. Key may *perhaps* be with us on saturday on his way to N.Y where he embarks with his family for England. Being in a hurry to join my Colleagues, I add only that I am ever yours most devotedly.

J. M.

Let no mail be forwarded to me after this arrives.

RC (NN: Richard John Levy and Sally Waldman Sweet Collection). Date assigned on the basis of the postmark.

1. JM participated in a Fourth of July celebration at Orange Court House, giving a toast and making a few remarks in memory of his old friend John Page. JM was disturbed, however, by the political partisanship of the managers of the dinner, who included Virginia state senator Lawrence T. Dade, and thought that his attendance had been used for party, not national, purposes in the run-up to the bitterly contested election of 1828 (Dade to JM, 5 July, and JM to Dade, 7 July 1827, DLC).

To Richard D. Cutts

[ca. 1827–29]

I was as much pleased with your letter my dear Richard as your young cousins ware with your *loving presents*—they have all set down to answer you—& I hope they will superceede the necessity of my expressing for them, the great delight they felt at hearing from you. Your Unkle's JM & Jo. P. desire me to assure you that they wd. be very glad to see you & to witness your improvement in Latin & all other things—they know you are a kind hearted, & feeling gentleman, & estimate you accordingly. In your next, I hope you will tell us something of dear Walter as well as of the city news.

Do not fail to come to us this summer with your Mama & sisters—& be assured my dear Richd. of the love of all here—your Grandmama Nelly[,] Barret—& even the black faces—all offer you their remembrance.

Your Aunt D.

P.S. The girls say They "cant finish their letters to their minds" for this post. I'l send.

RC (MCR-S: Mary Estelle Elizabeth Cutts Papers).

To Christopher Hughes

MONTPELLIER March 20th. 1828.

Your very interesting letter of Novr. 8th. my estimable friend reached me only yesterday—and I hasten to acknowledge it with thankful feelings. I cannot recollect haveing at the Presidents house, the picture you describe. There ware upon the Walls two or three Engravings, by Edwin of Mr Madison and myself, with large Portraits of both, by Stewart—the latter, were removed before the British entered, and the former, we understood, were taken by the destroyers of the building. Several of my family, and friends had small pictures and miniatures of me, but I am not aware of their haveing lost one. The one, which has caused you so much trouble, must have belonged to another than myself, and can be of too little consequence to Captain Gardner, or any one else, to deserve your further care.

I am sincerly glad that Mrs. Hughes and your little ones, are so well and happy at Brussels—and I wish you had the augmentation of Salery which we all know you deserve, and it seems would be found so convenient. I am sure, if it had depended on Mr. Madison, he would not have been disinclined to a full measure of proper allowance. Whilst you are glancing at a supposed inattention, in the case, his liberality is undergoing a scrutiny in Congress. The handsome names of your son and daughter are a sufficient evidence of the merit of those characters, for whose sake they bear them—and I hope to see them some day, with their parents at Montpellier, where I beg to assure Mrs. Hughes she would be received with as much pleasure, as I used to feel at seeing her when a blooming and amiable girl.

Our residence is at so great a distance from your friends and acquaintance, that I cannot give you as much information about them as you doubtless receive directly from them.

My sister Cutts often speaks of Genl. & Mrs. Smith, & Miss Spear who ware lately in good health at Washington. Your friend Payne is at present in Philadelphia which place, I beleive, he prefers to all others in the world. In politicks you know, I was never an Adept—I therefore will only observe, that our Country seems now to be entirly of Mr. Laws opinion that "Agitation and excitement are happiness."[1] I hope some, of the scenes got up in the House of Representatives, *never* reach you as in that case, they would exite even more regret among the considerate here, than they now do.

Mr Madison unites with me in every good wish for Mrs. Hughes and yourself, as well as in assurances to Lord & Lady Bagot of our affectinate remembrance. Have the goodness also, when you see Mr. de Cabre, to tell him, that he is remembered by us with constant friendship.

D P Madison.

RC (MiU-C). Docketed by Hughes and postmarked "Le Havre 23 July."

1. Amid the general frenzy and heated rhetoric of an election-year congressional session, the passage of the Tariff of Abominations threw some sections of the country into an uproar (George Dangerfield, *The Awakening of American Nationalism, 1815–1828* [New York, 1965], 279–87).

To John Payne Todd

Apl. 27th. 1828.

Since yours of the 5th. my dearest Son I have not heard from yourself—the state of your health, and hurt—tho Mr. M had a short letter from Ed. Coles of the 13th. in which he says, you had nearly ⟨re⟩covered your strength, but was still in the country.[1] I trust you ⟨are⟩ entirely well, & that you stay out ⟨. . .⟩ from choice, at this ⟨se⟩ason, when "the Landscape gazed on ⟨. . .⟩ eyes, is ever bathed in sun-shine." Such would be the case, even with me, if *you* ware with me—and *happy at being so.* The freshness of spring would rest upon my spirits in your presence, now, "tis odour fled as soon as shed; Tis mornings winged dream."[2]

I find there is a change of Post Master at Phia. & for your residence may not be known to him—my letters in consequence may remain on hand unless you apply for them. You will find three to be notised—that of the 2d. Apl. contained 10$ the one of the 4th. 20$—the 3d. was to enounce these. The Mail of this day may chear me by your own good acct. of yourself. I told you we ware well fixed & pleased with speckls. tho I made a mistake in saying No. 10 wd. suit the Eye Glass—I found, since I sent it back to you, & since I wrote on the subject, that No. 36 was best, to see across the room or to a greater distance. You are surprized that your Papa shd. be best suited with glasses that answered for me, but so it is—since his illness last summer he has read with my glasses, & the long & short sight which was peculiar to him, I beleive, no longer exists—I do not pretend to account for the change. From letters I have lately reccd. from Mrs. Randolph & Mrs. Coolledge I shall look soon for the former on her return to Montecello where her husband & children are now living—I often hear from my sisters—your Aunt Todd talks of comeing to see me some time this summer—Anna is engrossed amongst the fashionables of the day—her Husband paying too slowly his debt to Mr. M. About half the price of the house is yet to be given in to the Bank & in his last letter he promises to close that acct. by the end of this year. I have written to request as a favor, that he will remit me two or three hundred dollars on the sum he owes me, & if I shd. be so happy as to prevail on him to do so—you shall have it—but alass I do not—or da⟨re not⟩ flatter myself that he will do so, if it shd. be in his power.

Many ⟨. . .⟩ taken place around, since you le⟨ft⟩ tho none sufficiently interesting to speak of now. I shall write you in a day or two perhaps—especially if I hear from you or have any thing worth communicateing. I suppose, you have seen Mr. Tucker Coles & lady—& with them Sally Carter, a very sweet little girl. Does Mrs. Scott go to Europe this spring? Adeiu—my dear Son

Your M

RC (NN: Lee Kohns Memorial Collection). Ms torn. Addressed to Todd at Philadelphia.

1. On 29 March, Edward Coles had written JM with the news of John Payne Todd's accident. He had fallen while taking a walk near the Philadelphia waterworks and injured his leg severely enough to be confined to a tavern lodging for two weeks (Coles to JM, 29 March, 13 April 1828 [DLC]).

2. These lines are taken from "Love's Young Dream," a poem published in one of the many editions of Thomas Moore's *Irish Melodies* (Philadelphia, 1816; Shaw and Shoemaker 38279).

From Judith Page Rives

WASHINGTON January 26th 1829

You were so kind my dear Mrs Madison as to say when I was last with you, that it would give you pleasure to hear from us during our sojourn in the city—I have been wishing to avail myself of your permission to write to you ever since my arrival here, but immediately after I came, an attack of a sort of Influenza—prevalent in the city so completely stupified me, that I could not *in conscience* inflict upon you a letter so dull and dismal, and spiritless, as one written under its influence would have been. Being now relieved from this troublesome visitant, I will proceed to give you, as far as I can, the news of the *beau monde.*

For some time after my arrival here, Washington was unusually dull, and a "waveless calm"[1] appeared to pervade the fashionable, as well as the political world, and my indisposition prevented me from participating in the few scenes of mirth which were then going on; the spirit of dissipation, however, appears now to be reviving, and there is some danger of the torrent, swelling to such magnitude before the season is over, as to draw those into the vortex who are now only standing on the brink. This last modest position would be quite accordant with my taste, but I have been drawn into the current this week, having an engagement for every evening in it. There is some pleasure in attending the dining parties, which are uncommonly agreeable, but the *soirées* have not the same attraction. Such a multitude of people are present at all of them that it is quite oppressive, and there are so many strangers here that it is almost in vain to look for the face of a friend amid such a crowd.

We went last night to a wedding—the marriage of Miss McLean, where *every body* went. There were said to be a thousand people invited—certainly there were twice as many asked as the house would hold. Every body appeared in fine humour, and finer dress, but alas, such crushing of flowers, feathers, silks, satins, crapes &c. never was witnessed before, and I am sure the rooms after the route was over must have resembled a tournament after the knights had departed. My inducement for going was to look at the Bride who is really a very beautiful creature. But even her loveliness hardly compensated for the trouble of getting through the crowd to look at her. I had the pleasure of seeing there your sister and Mrs. Rush who were both well and in good spirits. I have yet, seen your sister but at these crowded parties, though she has been so good as to call several times to see me, when I have been absent, and I have returned her visits with no better success—When the parties become less frequent I shall endeavour to catch her at home and spend an evening with her *sans ceremonie.* Our situation this winter will admit of visits of that sort, to, and from our friends, which renders it much more agreeable than our remote position on the capitol hill—I hope before the session is over to see our mutual Friends much oftener, and to be able to tell you all the news.

Amid the crowd of strange people here, there are but few, I am sure, in whom you would take any interest. The south, is however, much better represented than the north, and the most distinguished ladies are from that quarter. Mrs. Calhoun, Mrs Stevenson, Mrs Hayne, Mrs Johnson, Mrs Mclane, and *last and least your humble servant,* are but feebly opposed by Mrs Everett,

Mrs Ingersoll, and Mrs Dickenson, who are the only Northern ladies here of any distinction. The utmost harmony, however, prevails among us, and the keenest observer would hardly detect any remains of party spirit even among the politicians, and certainly not the least shadow of it among the ladies. An idea may be formed of the good spirit now prevalent among us, from the circumstances which attended our visit to the president on new years day, when every body goes to make their respects and to offer the compliments of the season to the *King & queen*. Mrs Stevenson and I went together escorted by two of the leaders of the administration, Mr Everett and Gen. Van Rensselaer. I believe the good people who were there stared a little, but I very willingly attributed their astonishment to a famous dress which I paraded there, being quite *en militaire*, wanting only a pair of epaulettes to make it complete, and finished off by a hat partaking of the same spirit—turned up on one side with a most knowing air, and surmounted by a plume that would have done honour to the chapeau of a *general*. There were but two untoward circumstances that I observed there—one was, that the drawing room was so dark that it was almost impossible to distinguish one person from another, and a *dog* unfortunately assisted in the reception of the company, at which some of the Jackson ladies were greatly scandalized, thinking that it was designed for their benefit. Mrs S. & myself took the liberty of making a few remarks and *comparisons* after we made our escape which were not very complimentary to the *present* inhabitants of the palace, but at which I think some of our revered and absent Friends would not have had cause to be offended—The next day we were invited to dine there, but as I had a very bad cold which I feared to increase by a *chilling reception*, we declined going. Had Mr. and Mrs. Madison been there, I should have set the cold at defiance and felt assured of an alleviation of my indisposition from the benignant influence of a cordial and graceful reception and a circle of charming Friends. From what I afterwards heard, there was not much to regret.

The British minister[2] was my beau the other day at a dining party, and he made so many enquiries about you, that if he should pay a visit to Virginia I must take the liberty of putting Mr. Madison on his guard against so formidable a personage. He is already much elated by a piece somebody put into the newspapers about him, accusing all the ladies of being in love with him.

I hope my dear Mrs Madison that I shall not incure the imputation of disrespect by writing to you about these "trifles light as air"[3]—in the hope of beguiling a few leisure moments I have offered them, and hope you will not think me very saucy.

Mr Rives desires me to make his best respects acceptable to you, and unites with me in asking you to present our most respectful and cordial regards to Mr Madison. I remain, with sincere affection, yours

J P Rives

RC (PPRF).
1. Virgil, *Aeneid* 10.103.
2. Sir Charles Vaughan.
3. Shakespeare, *Othello* 3.3.322 (*Riverside*).

To Anna Cutts

6th June [18]29

Yours of 31st may, I recd. in due time my dear sister—but in the first place I have the consolation to tell you that Mr. M is getting well fast—We rode over to John's yesterday, the first time either of us had been out of the yard since the 7th. of may, the day of that Funeral—*which, was near, causing another.*[1] I trust he will be again strong & well. Your letter previous to the last—& all—have come safe—so be easy on that subject. The conduct of the P. & his cabinet, is indeed astonishing, & exibits a melancholy perspective, as well as re-trospect to our country—but I doubt not of *impeachments,* by & by, if they go on in this *lawless,* & unfeeling manner. A pretty state of society—when Mrs. M *will visit* Mrs E.[2] I'm glad *you did not,* as you had nothing to loose by *her.*

I wrote you 3 days ago that Jn. had a son a few days old—they intend to call it after Mr. M. Clary is doing well, & the famaly also. I told you of Lucy's let-ter—that she wd. come by to see you, & be with us early in july on her way to K. I hope you recd. the letter—I think of Mr. Stevensons neglect as well as of R's as you do—The latter, I know was in great haste. The former, I cannot acct. for *his* coldness—*Mr. C. must be the cause.* I regret deeply, that your af-fairs are in such a state that you fear to leave them—but indeed I dont see that it wd. be better to stay a month longer with *them,* as at the end of that time, you may find the same objections exist—Mr. C. must certainly have lost his senses—no effort yet to get business—& his sons office uncertain—we shd. not be surprized if M——n was removed, for what will J——n not do?[3] I told you of my recg. a letter from M Randolph who says T. has taken a house for her near Mr. Rushes—do you know it? And that Brouse T. was to live with them[4] & I think you replyed very properly to Mrs. S. H. S[5]—she is a *curious* body—& tho she appears affectinate & frank, I think she is *dangerious.* Poor old Mrs. Nourse! But I feel for so many that I can scarsly tell, for which I'm most sorry. Tis astonishing Pleasanton & Hagner are still retaind—but some must stay to teach others, for their accomodation & *then* go. It will become a reproach to hold an office under the present sett. I wd. *my self* rather be my own cook & keep a respectable boarding house than have the Dept. of State under Genl. J——n because I think there wd. be more honor & independence in it. How then can Mr C. reconcile himself to loiter in his neighborhood? But we know sometimes, that all efforts are in vain to obtain business—if such was his case at W——n he ought to get to the East where he has naturel friends who might exert themselves to place him in Mercantile or other business—all this sort of neglect, however is not so unworthy as the conduct towards his wife—his daughters—Alass that I could but help—& save them! but what am I—a poor one indeed! If you wish it, I will get from Mr M the *Interest* in advance til fall, for your jurney here or any thing else. I enquired of you if you had heared from or of my dear Child—you say nothing & since that letter, I recd. one from him in which he tells me that he was boarding within Prison bounds! for a debt of 2—or 300$ he has submitted to this horrid— horrid situation. It allmost breaks my heart to think of it ⟨and⟩ that Mr Cutts owed him more than this, of the mony P. entrusted to him, to place in the Bank—but he owes you even more I know, still *that* is not to the purpose. I dont know that I shall send you this letter—in truth I feel as if I could not write a letter—my pride—my sensibility, & every feeling of my soul is wounded. Yet *we* shall do something—what or when, depends on Mr Ms health, & strength, to do business—his anxiety, & wish to aid, & benefit P. is as great as a Father's—but his ability to command mony in this country, is not greater than that of others—I loath the idea of going to Rchd. but if M goes, so I must—something may occur to cause us to decline the invitation of the G——.[6] I wish it may. I begin at last to feel a dislike to the whole race—& the continued professions, towards *me* seem to contribute to my disgust—something must be wrong, between us—perhaps on both sides—I must pray, without ceasing for fortitude from above, as well as for the devine gift of Humility—& charity towards all.

June 8th. I ⟨fee⟩l the past days are changed & I had to wait to the 3d day after I began this letter before it could be sent. Mr M continues to mend—at Johns well. I inclose this in one from Mr M to Mr C which contains an order on Wm Allen—Fredrg for 150$ to finish paying for the house & the release of Charles Nourse's name which he was so good as to lend for our accomodation.

Adeiu dr Sister—answer this soon, & say If you'l want the Interest til fall to bring you here & every thing, you can think of. I shall enclose you soon for a sett of new & fashionable curls. Did you send a box of oranges, & some figs?[7]

You did not tell me so but spoke of a box by R. Taylor. I reccd. it but too long on the way so that the oranges rotted all to ⟨. . .⟩ Pray burn this & all such.

RC (MCR-S: Mary Estelle Elizabeth Cutts Papers).

1. On 11 Feb. 1829 JM's mother, Nelly Conway Madison, died at the age of ninety-seven. After the funeral JM came down with a serious case of influenza from which he struggled to recover throughout the summer of 1829.

2. DPM is referring here to a visit made by Catherine Milligan McLane to Margaret Eaton, the wife of John Eaton, secretary of war. Mrs. Eaton was being ostracized by the women of Washington society, including President Jackson's niece, Emily Donelson, despite Jackson's passionate defense of her character. The social imbroglio had political consequences, splitting the Democrats into Van Buren and Calhoun parties, and eventually resulted in the resignation of Jackson's entire cabinet. For a thorough treatment of the Eaton affair, see John F. Marszalek, *The Petticoat Affair: Manners, Mutiny, and Sex in Andrew Jackson's White House* (New York, 1997).

3. President Jackson removed Richard Cutts from his position as second comptroller of the U.S. Treasury in March 1829. James Madison Cutts was employed in the federal bureaucracy (Washington *United States Telegraph,* 20 March 1829).

4. Nicholas P. Trist had married Virginia Jefferson Randolph, daughter of Thomas Mann and Martha Jefferson Randolph, who made her home with them after the death of her father and her husband. Hore Browse Trist was Nicholas's brother.

5. Margaret Bayard Smith, wife of Samuel Harrison Smith.

6. The governor of Virginia, William B. Giles, a longtime antagonist of JM, had invited the Madisons to stay at the governor's mansion during the constitutional convention scheduled for December 1829. The Madisons courteously declined (Giles to JM, 10 Aug., and JM to Giles, 15 Aug. 1829, DLC).

7. The oranges and figs were sent by Nicholas P. Trist (see Trist to JM, 5 June 1829, ViHi).

To John C. Payne

My dear Brother   [4 December 1829]

I recd. yours of 27th. & greave ab⟨out⟩ your eyes—It seems to me that I have mentiond 3 tim⟨es⟩ at least that Sister Wn might have 20 wt wool if there was enuf—If not & the Merino is plenty let her have that—either in reels or not—Im affraid some of my hurried scrawls misscary—& that wd be bad as I have scarsly time to write such as I do. The longer we stay the more attention we rece [1]—until they are too numerous to be convenient—Indeed, I feel that there is a *short* interval allowed me in which I ought to be happy—⟨. . .⟩ as *such* a situation alltogether, is rare, & gratifying—but m⟨y son?⟩ comes not—nor do I hear from him, which covers me with sadness in the midst of pleasantness—Paul is much oblig⟨ed⟩ by news from his wife & children—& when oppty offer⟨s to⟩ send he woud to write him—& Sarahs husband too. Sarah has got into better health *tell him* & wants to hear from him—Sam is well & sober so his wife may also be regaled by the *news*—Tell Ralph his mother sends her love to him & says shel bring him something—Now for ourselves—I recd yesterday 3d. of Decr. yours enclosing Tallys—He is a *Nepolian* born Man to be sure—As to the butter it wd. not be good I fear—& moreover we did not ex⟨pect⟩ to be gone so long when I gave orders for them to keep all except what you wanted he ought therefore to act according to circumstances—it will be the first of next month at nearest before we reach home, & we can spare 40. wt. butter & 10 Turkeys, & the mony wd. be an accomodation ⟨. . .⟩ or to me—but do as you please abt it. Keep Turkeys fo⟨r your⟩ Table & if none ⟨. . .⟩ can tell him so & also that Mr M & myself wish him ⟨. . .⟩ to pay the 5$ for Pork than wait for the bacon as these people dont cure it as well as we wish to have it at home—I insist on Hariots weaving for you—or Amey's doing it whichever you like best. I've just got a letter from Anna all well—none from Lucy yet I wrote her again—Anna sends love to you & Clary & children as I do heartily, & Mr M too. Mr M made a speach yesterdy which you'l see in a paper of tomorrow[2]—A fd. told me that the whole house rose & all that could get near him crouded round until it look'd ⟨. . .⟩fully. I was not there tho he told me he wd. try ⟨. . .⟩. It will have its affect some say—tho men had ⟨co⟩mmitted themselves much, before he brought himself ⟨to the⟩ point. There will be compromises but impossible yet to say, to what extent. Mr M is not yet well of his Influenza ⟨. . .⟩ better & goes every day to convention, just a little walk but they are to move, I beleive to a Church a little further off to give place to the Assembly whose room they occupy now. Alfred Anderson call'd just now to see us—he's here from curiosity he sa⟨ys.⟩ I dont find in Allens letter to Mr M, that he notises the Draft for P. but suppose it must have been recd. & gotten the one he spoke ⟨. . .⟩ was the 50$ in favor of Colo Peyton. Let Ben get abt. 3 pd. saltpetre ⟨. . .⟩ pr. gal. molasses, for the meat, & do you get a jug full or more if you ⟨. . .⟩ it for the Children. I'l write soon again—was prevented last post. Ever your dear Sister. This will be put in post tomorrow in order to suit *our* mail—I *think tis the 4th.*

5th Decr. I send you the book & no more writeing now but love for all.

RC (owned by Mrs. Dolly L. Maass, White Plains, N.Y., 1961). Ms torn.

1. The Madisons spent the winter of 1829 in Richmond, where JM was a delegate to the state constitutional convention.

2. JM's speech on 2 Dec. advocated the acceptance of the three-fifths ratio for the apportionment of representatives to the Virginia House of Delegates, a compromise between eastern interests, which wished to count all slaves, and the western part of the state, which wanted to count only white inhabitants. Instead, the eastern part of the state maintained a majority in both houses of the legislature through an arbitrary apportionment of seats (Ketcham, *James Madison*, 638–40).

To Anna Cutts

Monday 28th Decr. [1829]

I am greaved beloved Sister to learn from Mary & Richard that you are sick—What made you so? Mary says ⟨you?⟩ came from the Barons sick—I fear you expose yourself too much ⟨to the⟩ night air—all Richd. allmost, has been afflicted with Influenza ⟨and your⟩ indisposition is perhaps the same—I trust nothing worse & that by ⟨Spring⟩ you are well again—but you *must* take great care of yourself.

The Convention seems impatient for a close of its labour⟨s. I⟩ think it will not sit more than a week longer—I had a letter ⟨. . .⟩ yesterday who was well with his family—The Stevensons will ha⟨. . .⟩ the city when you get this—they have been passing Xmass in Fredri⟨cksburg⟩.

Colo. I.[1] got here a day or 2 ago on his way to Phila—by ⟨. . .⟩ where Ed. is, & from whence, I hope soon to see my dear Son. My mind ⟨is⟩ now, all turn'd towards home—not that I'm tired of Richd. indeed I shd. like ⟨to stay⟩ til April, but that I know we must go & I long to have the jurney ⟨over with.⟩

I must now tell you of the curious reports that have reach'd ⟨. . .⟩ or rather some of them—Tis sd. that the Baron gave his Ball ⟨for the⟩ purpose of rec-oncileing the ladies of the Cabinet & of W——— to Mrs. E———[2] ⟨& that only⟩ one wd. speak to her there—The wonder is who is that one—pray tell me if Mrs Stevenson visits her—If she does it will be odd after what I have heard & &—another is, that Mr V. B.[3] is the favorite with you all for the next Pt. & that Mr. Kalhoon[4] is a little in the wane. That you are to have no Drawing Room because it is thought that ought to be reform'd.

That Mrs Decatur is comeing to the City, to be Mrs. J———n.[5] & to patron-ize Mrs. E. When you are well enuf tell me the news. Mrs. R.[6] & family have steped at once into the fashionable vortex I suppose. I have not heard from Lucy since I enclosed hers to you & hope she will not go to Ky. before she see's us again.

Give my affec. love to the girls & Richd. & tell Mary her book is safe & shall be return'd to her soon, but that I have no prospect of getting the *great* mans writing which she name'd—Jno. R———h[7] is too *capricious to ask,* Mr. Mon-roe still confined to his bed tho a little better than he has been—I have seen Mrs. Hay but once, she refused all others, admittance—Now my dear Sister make haste to be well & tell me so—I really am miserable until I hear from yourself.

I wd. write to the Girls & Richd. at this time, but company waits for me in the next room. We dined at Major Gibbon's on Xmass day, & Betsy had a large party in the Evg. The night before I had been at a party at Mr. Myers where abt. a douzn Masks appeared in Characters danced, & caused a deal of amusemt. One of the Masks personated Rob Roy & acted it with one or 2 others very well—Mrs. Mayo was there & all the ton of Rd. (allmost) I went with Mrs Conway the Govrs. daughter & son, as Mr. M did not want to go—tho he has generally gone to parties with me, I staid only til 10 oClock. Mrs. Conway is very cleaver & affte—She'l be in W——n next month—perhaps at Turners but I don't know.

I was never at any exibition with young Dickens—except a party at Rodgers's when he went as B. Coles beau—he's modest & cleaver & brought an introduction to Mr M & me from his Father—B. C.[8] is with her sister—If you see them give my love & remembrance to them as from one much in theirs & Mr Stevensons debt, for every kindness—I will write you again—adeiu my dr. Sister ever yours

RC (MCR-S: Mary Estelle Elizabeth Cutts Papers). Ms torn.
   1. Isaac Coles.
   2. If Baron Von Krüdener's ball was held in order to reconcile the ladies of Washington society, it was not a success. It merely alienated the Dutch minister's wife and included the diplomatic corps among those who snubbed Margaret Eaton (Marszalek, *Petticoat Affair*, 112–14).
   3. Martin Van Buren.
   4. John C. Calhoun.
   5. Andrew Jackson's wife Rachel had died before his inauguration in March 1829. He had banished his niece, Emily Donelson, to Tennessee for her refusal to socialize with Margaret Eaton. Thus, he had no one to act as hostess at the White House (Marszalek, *Petticoat Affair*, 20, 135–36).
   6. Martha Jefferson Randolph.
   7. John Randolph of Roanoke.
   8. Elizabeth (Betsy) Coles.

To Anna Cutts

25th. Jany. 30.
We have been six days at home my dear Sister, but not a line has reached me from you since our return, & for a long time before we left Richd. What is the matter? I trust you *have continued* well since you wrote me that you had recovered. I wrote you twice after that from Richd. & I sent Marys book but am uncertain of its fate, or of any thing that regards you, or yours! I had high hopes of meeting my dear P.[1] at Montpellier or seeing him arrive soon after us, but am disappointed, nor can I hear where or how he is, since his letter of a month ago! I heared thro Mrs. Rutherford that Betsy Coles had seen you, &

I suppose Mrs. S——n[2] also had been to return your call, but dont know—They are very gay there I *presume*, & have it all to *themselves*—Mrs. Eaton, I understand, did not mix with the other heads—but all this is of little importance to me. We had a very pleasant visit of 3 months & more & in the present state of society in W——n I wd. prefer Richd. for a residence. I met many of your old acquaintan[c]e—Among others Mrs Morgan of Shepherds-Town who spoke affety of you & Lucy—sd. she had call'd once, to see you in W——n. We saw Mr. Allen often, he told me that our dear Mary had been threatened with consumption, & that the climate of Clerksburge was not suited to her *constitution* & that he had thoughts of moveing to Stanton or some where else—he promised to come to see us on his way home from the Assembly—It could not have been him, tho it might have been his brother, who spoke so harshly of Mr. Cutts—He talk'd to me abt. Jacksons affairs, sd. they were left in sad confusion & that he had remaind at Clarksburge to try to save something for the last wifes children, that *he could make enuf* for himself & Mary—that he had been trying to obtain from the Bank of W——n a part of the debt from Mr. C to J——n[3] but I could not understand whether he expected to succeed—I suppose you saw Mr. Monroe & Mrs. Hay—I mention'd in my last that Mrs. Hay was just the same minded person that she used to be—but I know not that you *got that letter*—I hope to hear this day, as the post comes—If you have seen any one from Pha. who has seen P. you will tell me—& if you see Mrs. Stevenson tell her I wd. write her, but that I know she's too much engaged to read. I find myself over head in business here—as usial—& could allmost wish myself back in Richd. surrounded as I *was* by the kindest, & most agreable people—Mrs. Mayo was as kind as she could be as was her daughter Cabell & all their connections—I can never forget them! our old acquaintance Mrs. Chevalier was like—nothing that I

RC (ViU). Incomplete.
   1. John Payne Todd.
   2. Sarah Coles Stevenson.
   3. John G. Jackson.

To Dolley P. Madison Cutts

MONTPELIER 10th. March 1830

I am now seated pen in hand to write you, my sweet girl, tho' in very bad humor for the success I desire, in producing an amusing letter—such *should* mine be, in answer to your short, tho kind one.

Imagine if you can, a greater trial of patience than seeing the destruction of a *radiant patch* of green peas, by frost! It came last night on the skirts of a storm, and while I was lamenting that our dear midshipman, should ever be exposed in such wailing winds, my young adventurers were wrecked off their moorings! but away with complaints, other patches will arise, and I will mourn no longer, over a mess of peas or of pottage, but would rather meet you at the next party, where I hope you intend to go — or if you espy me not, by the side of your *favorite,* be assured I am unavoidably detained at home, from whence I shall breathe many wishes for your happiness there, and wherever else you go. I had indeed, my "quantum sufficit" of gaity in Richmond, but what I enjoyed most was the quiet hospitality of the inhabitants, among whom I should like to spend my winters. In Washington I had most *old* acquaintances and if they were now as they used to be in *those* times, my old partialities would still be felt. But I confess I do not admire the contention of parties, political or civil, tho' in my quiet retreat I am anxious to know all the manoeuverings of both, the one and the other, so, be not timid in laying their claims before me, no one shall see statements but myself. I hope you become acquainted with Miss Preston, she is very large of her age, and a most amiable woman, should her father and herself be still in the city, present them my best love. I wish that circumstances would have permitted you to have accepted Mr. V. B.s[1] invitation, but I cannot doubt that you had good reasons for declining. You know that I saw him and his sons in Richmond. By the bye — do you never get hold of a clever novel, new or old that you could lend me? I bought Cooper's last,[2] but did not like it, because the story was too full of horrors.

Adieu! my precious D. Think of me as your own friend and Aunt, and write often as you can.

Tr (MCR-S: Mary Estelle Elizabeth Cutts Papers). Tr made by Mary Cutts.
1. Martin Van Buren.
2. DPM probably referred to James Fenimore Cooper's *The Wept of Wish-ton Wish* (1829). The novel was set in Puritan New England at the time of King Philip's War.

From Sally McKean Yrujo

My dear friend,   MADRID November 16. 1830

A safe opportunity offering, which seldom occurs, I cannot let it pass without having the satisfaction of writing to you; in the latter part of December last, I wrote you a long letter in answer to yours brought by Mrs: Ousely, which I gave to a young Englishman a Mr: Wheaton, who left this to return to Gibralter.

I have been filled with indignation at the manner in which some of my old friends have been treated: but to tell the truth I was apprehensive of some excesses of that nature from the *strong* character of the one who commands. I can assure you that I greatly admire many of the just and generous customs in Monarchial Governments—one of the first of which is that a man who has served his country faithfully and uprightly is *never* neglected or *forgotten,* if by chance he is removed from office, he is allowed a pension for life equivolent to one half his salary, if by death his widow gets it; and this is fair and honorable, so make the comparison.

The present American Minister here,[1] his wife and family are all Jacksonites; you have no idea of any thing like it; he has adopted a sort of uniform, very singular indeed, which is a bottle green coat with a black cape and two very large silver stars fixed on the two ends of the cape, he goes to Court with his secretary and his son, dressed alike—they all ask me if this is a new fashion in the United States, for the American Ministers heretofore have had pretty neat uniforms resembling those worn by other diplomatists.

How years slip over our heads, time flies imperceptably, what changes in this fickle world, I suspect if we were to meet by chance without knowing it, we should never recognize each other. I have grown very fat, and altho' I have good health to boast of, cannot say so much for my sight: I have to use spectacles. I often sit down to think of the days that are gone—and what changes have taken place in my family! It is nineteen years since I left my native country, and think I should be puzzled to recollect the streets of Philadelphia.

What singular events have happened in Europe within this year past, scarcely to be credited, France is at present quiet, the Dey of Algiers safe in Naples, with his fifty wives. The Duke of Brunswick in England, as is also the Ex King of France, along with the duke and Dutchess of Angulême, Dutchess of Berry and her children, living in retirement; I again repeat, what a fickle world is this! Seven years ago when my husband was Ambassador in Paris they were in the splendor of their glory, I could but gaze and wonder; now, the reverse, the Duke of Orleans, in their place, a great and powerful King,[2] you must also remember him as well as myself, when he lived in old Viar's remarkably small house in 4th. street, just above the chapel—when for several months he had not wherewithal to pay his rent, and glad he used to be, the days my husband would invite him to dinner, and you as well as myself have danced with him: but to tell you the truth, when we were in Paris, he was very grateful for past attentions, and shewed us a great deal and always praised the United States.

I have written so much about this side of the Atlantick, that I fear you will be tired—therefore mean to conclude by telling you they are making great improvements *here*—such as iron rail roads, new invented stage coaches, introducing horse racing &c &c but I think nothing will induce them to give up their *beloved* and cruel bull fights.

Now for a little news about myself and family, my son and daughter live with me, Narcisa was engaged to be married some months ago, to a well looking and rich man, the wedding dresses were made, his house taken and elegantly furnished, a carriage and four fine horses bought by him, in fact every thing prepared with even luxury, the bands had also been published—when a terrible truth came to light about him—thanks to my penetration and activity, I discovered it in time; I immediately broke off the match, & saying, my daughter, it is true, might be highly established, but she beyond doubt would be *unhappy,* and that no earthly consideration should make me consent to her being so: at present, there is another suitor, time will shew how it is to be. My son Charles has been named Minister to the Court of Saxony, but he will not go for some months yet, as he has been recently appointed Director of the Bank of St. Fernando, the only bank there is in Spain; he will remain but some few months when he goes on his mission.

God bless you! Keep up your spirits and hope for the best, there is no such thing as real happiness in this world; at all events we must do for the best; often things take a turn for the best when least expected.

Excuse all the defects in my letter, so little accustomed to write in English. I fear there are many. Your unalterably attached friend,

The Marchioness de Casa Yrujo

Tr (MCR-S: Mary Estelle Elizabeth Cutts Papers). Tr made by Mary Cutts.

1. Cornelius Peter Van Ness, a native New Yorker who moved to Vermont in 1806, was governor of that state 1823–25 and U.S. minister to Spain 1829–37 (James F. Hopkins et al., eds., *The Papers of Henry Clay* [11 vols. to date; Lexington, Ky., 1959—], 3:188 n. 18).

2. Louis-Philippe (1773–1850) reigned in France from 1830 to 1848. He spent the years 1796–1800 traveling in the United States, with Philadelphia as his headquarters.

From James Taylor

Washington 2d Jany 1831

The compliments of the season to yourself & my good friend Mr Madison, & may you both enjoy them many years.

I am sorry to inform you that Mrs Cutts has been ill, but I saw Mr C yesterdy at the drawing room & am glad to learn from him that she is recovering. I was at the house two days ago to learn how she was.

There was much fashion beauty &c. at the White house yesterdy, but no Lady to preside & I understand there will be none this winter for Majr Donoldson told me a day or two ago, that his Lady would not be on this season.

⟨On dits⟩ of the City. It is said there is not the greatest cordiality, between the P. & the Majr owing to the conduct of Mrs D. toward Mrs. E.[1] report say that there is a breach between the P. & V. P. that some information reached the former, of a hostile course by the latter during the last Session, that the P addressed the V. P. a letter, that after some time a long answer was returned, that it was sent back saying the explanation was not satisfactory.[2] The V. P. did not attend the drawing room yesterday. He is at this house (Gadsbys). I saw Majr D. in his room new years night. From expressions I have hear[d] myself I do not think there is much good feeling by certain members of the Cabinet save Mr V. B. W T Barry toward the Secy of the Navy & arising it is supposed principally from Gen. B. & family refusing to hold intercourse with Mrs. E. Mr Governeur is here urging the claim of P. Monroe. I wish it could be allowed. I am throwing in my little aid. I really feel for the situation of the good old man.[3]

I think Walkers paper is taken at Montpelier, if so you have seen the depos. of Genl S. Smith & Bayard in relation to the Contest between Mr J & B. I fear T. J. Randolph has been imprudent in making public certain letters memos of Mr. Jefferson.[4] I make the following communication in confidence. You must recollect M. L. Davis of N.Y. He is here & in the same house, he told me of the publication before I saw it, that the seal under which these depos. were taken was a ficticious one, between two of his clerks & placed in the docket of the Court in N.Y. on an alledged bet about the election. That this authord him to obtain a Commission to take these depositions, that both Bayard & Smith at first refused to give evidence, that Burr wrote them a tart note demanding on what ground or right they refused to give evidence in a Case where his honor was implicated. Bayard & Smith consulted & thought they had better comply or they would be challenged—They consulted & thought it best to harmonize as near as possible & gave the testimony which was sided up of Course & directed to the Clk of the Court. Davis called at the office. The clerk opened them in his presence, he demanded them as his papers the clerk gave them up to him & he has the originals now. He said he gave, Genl. R G. Harper & Mr. Bradly copies of them that the Sons of Mr Bayard applied to him for Copies, he referred them to the reps of those gentlemen, & I understood him Mr. D that he supposes they got copies of them from Genl B. ⟨Roper?⟩ or from him before his death. I understood distinctly the object of the suit was to obtain those depos & to perpetuate their testimony & to endeavor to shew that Col. B. did not intrigue for the office & that Mr J. did. B. was no doubt at the bottom of the Matter and planed it. D. told me it was never intended to have the suit tried.

You know my good old father, myself & most of our friends were great admirers of the great & worthy Jefferson. I have thought it my duty to give you this information, every word of which I would testify to or to the substance if necessary but only in case it was deemed indispensably necessary, to guard the honor of one of the best & greatest men that ever lived in my opinion.

In the part I took against Col B. conduct in 1806. 7 I brought on me the enmity of several, actually recd two challenges, one from Col. J. H. Daviess & one from John Smith, & some thing like one from Col. Carbury, all growing out of the affairs of Burr and Smith. I am now getting old & wish to keep out of contention as far as possible but if the reputation of so great & good a man as Jefferson can be saved from stigma by any thing I can do or say, & in the opinion of —— you know who, I should think I would be wanting in nerve courage not to be willing to stand forward & say what I have heard on this subject. I have understood Mr J said to Mr M "you have been my friend in life, take care of me after I am dead." I have called to see Mrs. Randolph twice since her return from Boston. She was at the Presidents yesterday she looks very well. I also called to see Mr Adams yesterday, he appears to be in fine health. Mrs As health is somewhat delicate. I did not see her.

There are a number of candidates for the Senate of the U.S. in Ohio. Gen. Harrison, Col. King, J. C. Wright, Gov: Trimble, Gen Vance, of the Clay party. Lucas Judge Campbell & I think one or two others of the Amn party. Gov: Morrow is also spoken of. If would consent to serve he could succeed, it is thot in preference to any of them, he is of the Clay party. It is said the election will take place about the 15th. inst.[5]

There is much difficulty also as to the Senator in Ky. Candidates on the Adn. side. Rowan, Jno S. Smith, Co Rid. Johnson between them it is thot. here it will lay between the two latter candidates if one of that party suceed this can only be by certain pledged men, adhering to promises, it is said they have made: & I am induced to believe there is more in thear pledges than had appeared. On the other side, Crittindon Ben: Hardin I understand C. can be elected if he will vote for himself which it is said he will not do. The same is said of Hardin it is said he has no scruples of this kind. Some mention is made of the postponement of the election til an other session, but I rather think it will come in about the midst of this month.[6] Judge Bibb has got on, his wrist

& fingers have mended so far as to be got to write. Rowan has not got on, nor is he expected before the election takes place. It is thot. he cannot be reelected.

Judge Parks trial I presume will commence again tomorrow. My own impression is that he will not loose his office but his conduct is considered very outrageously tyranical.

I could not get off so as to be at the Fed. Ct in Ohio & as I have much of my land business to arrange yet so as to obtain my patents, have been devoting my attention to that subject. I think I shall get off in about 2 weeks.

My family & friends were well lately. Health happiness & prosperity attend you Mr M. & all my friends to whom I offer my best salutation

James Taylor

Excuse rough Paper & haste

RC (DLC). Docketed by JM.

1. The breach between President Jackson and his nephew and private secretary, Andrew Jackson Donelson, over Emily Donelson's refusal to visit Margaret Eaton had widened to such a degree that although they both lived at the White House, they communicated only in writing (Marszalek, *Petticoat Affair,* 139–42).

2. Throughout 1830 Jackson and his vice president, John C. Calhoun, had been feuding over Calhoun's role in the Monroe administration's censure of Jackson's invasion of Florida in 1818. The feud became public in February 1831 when Calhoun published their correspondence (Robert V. Remini, *Andrew Jackson and the Course of American Freedom, 1822–1832* [New York, 1981], 240–47, 306–10).

3. Samuel L. Gouverneur was in Washington lobbying Congress on behalf of the claims of his father-in-law, James Monroe. Congress made a grant of $30,000 to the former president in February 1831 (Ammon, *James Monroe,* 569–70).

4. Taylor is referring here to depositions taken from Samuel Smith and James A. Bayard in 1806 about the election of 1800. Bayard claimed to have sought assurances from Thomas Jefferson through Smith that in the event of Jefferson's election, the president would abide by certain policies. Bayard claimed to have received such assurances and withdrew his opposition to Jefferson's election. Although these depositions were not publicized at the time, Jefferson noted down their details, and these notes were published in the first edition of his papers, compiled by his grandson Thomas Jefferson Randolph in 1829. The depositions, along with other papers, were published by Bayard's son, Richard H. Bayard, in the Philadelphia *National Gazette and Literary Register* in December 1830. See Kline et al., *Correspondence of Aaron Burr* 2:964–67.

5. Thomas Ewing (1789–1871) was elected U.S. senator from Ohio and served from 1831 to 1837.

6. Henry Clay replaced John Rowan as U.S. senator from Kentucky after his election in 1831.

To Mary E. E. Cutts

MONTPELIER 5th. January 1831

Yours ending on the 2d. of January came to releive my oppressed heart with the tidings of your beloved mother's recovery, from that extreme illness under which I knew or feared she was laboring. I had written a week ago, this day, to D.[1] and one to you, enclosed to your father, which, I fear you have not received or you would have told me so—and you would have yielded to my pleadings for that single line by every post, which would tell me your mamma is better, and has a prospect of entire health. To secure this, my dear girls, you must keep her room quiet and herself from the slightest agitation or uneasiness—that nervousness of which Dr. Sim speaks, must be attended to with all your delicacy of thought and conduct—her sufferings have caused it, now, let no one approach her, who is not sensible of the importance of smiles and comfort to one who has been so near the grave! May heaven sustain and support her long, to bless you both with her protecting love! "The Oxonians" are enclosed,[2] I could not read while my heart was oppressed with fears for you, you will speak of their safety. All here are well—Adieu—your own Aunt.

Tr (MCR-S: Mary Estelle Elizabeth Cutts Papers). Tr made by Mary Cutts.
1. Dolley Cutts.
2. Samuel Beazley's *The Oxonians: A Glance at Society* (2 vols.; New York, 1830) might not have appealed to DPM in any event, since it describes in detail the lives of a group of Oxford graduates who spend their time in drinking, gambling, and games of seduction, not unlike DPM's son, John Payne Todd.

To Elizabeth Coles

Apl. 8th. 1831.

A thousand thanks my dear cousin for the book, and many more for your acceptable letter—which I should not have kept a day unanswered, but for indisposition.

But how comes it that you require an excuse to write to your own friend? Yet I will not enquire too closely—lest I discover that you have found me wanting, in some attribute of character, consistent with your idea of what I ought to be. Ah, I am sensible that you could not fail to do so, but be assured, I am not lacking in that affectionate attatchmt. which I have felt for you, ever since you were a little girl. This *last*, Norwegian Winter, has proved too cold for me. I am but now recovering from Influenza, of two months continuance. My Husband's cold lasted three or four weeks, and has left him entirely, whilst the effects of mine are still felt—so you see, how much younger & stronger he is, than I am.

I am glad to hear of the good health & acquisition of Colo. Isaac & his Lady, and I expect you will find it difficult to deny their wishes for your return with them, to Eniscorthy—provided you can leave our precious Sisters Sally &

Emily. Cousin Edward's long stay in New York *must* have brought him nearer, to the Rock of his hope, I trust so however, & that he now makes his farewell visit to Illinois.

I am flattered by the remembrance of my estimable acquaintances in Richmond, and I certainly reciprocate all their kind feelings, tho I cannot expect to see them again in their fair city. Poor dear Mrs. Mayo—I am truly sorry to hear of her long confinement, as well as of Mrs. Wickham's affliction!

We have now beautiful weather, & our garden and grove begin to charm me with musick & flowers—I wish we could enjoy them together, after the quiet winter you speak of, on which, if we could compare notes, I think a balance would *remain* in favor of Montpelr. where "We three met"[1] to read & write, to play at chess &—caugh.

I hope you will rece. the books with this letter, & if you are in possession of More's life of Byron[2] I should be gratified to see it. I had read the one you offer me, as well as Separation.[3] I wish I could now speak to you of the unfortunate relation who has so excited my sympathy and astonishment—but I know too little of the affair to form a just opinion of his conduct—I have not seen him since the proper dismission he recd.[4] His Father was with us soon after, & evidently without the smallest suspicion of his son's honor—Heaven send the result may justify his hopes, that calumny alone, has exagerated, some imprudence, into crime, & that we may apply the observation to John that rectitude of mind, & innate goodness, are such celestial & endureing gifts that however overpower'd for a time, by falsehood, they cannot be entirely destroyed. Be this as it will, I pray that it may never effect the peace of that lovely girl who, deserves to be happy & fortunate, in her choice, of a partner thro' life.

Mr. Madison charges me with many affectionate messages to you, but I must cheat you out of some of them, or miss the post. With our best love to cousin Emily & Mr. Rutherford we are yours most truly,

D. P. Madison

RC (owned by Charles M. Storey, Boston, Mass., 1961).

1. DPM is probably referring to the opening line of Shakespeare's *Macbeth* (*Riverside*, 1312).

2. In 1830 Harper's published a two-volume edition of the *Letters and Journals of Lord Byron: with Notices of His Life*, by Thomas Moore.

3. DPM probably referred to *The Separation: A Novel*, by Charlotte Campbell, Lady Bury (London, 1830).

4. This was probably JM's great-nephew John Willis, who was expelled from the University of Virginia in July 1830.

To Mary E. E. Cutts

My sweet Mary,   MONTPELIER 16th. September [1831]

I hasten to answer your kind letter, in order that I may the better obtain your forgiveness in the case of having mislaid your letter to Louisa! I can neither find nor trace it, after much search and I think it has been put into the fire by Miss Becky whose hurry to kindle a little fire for her master, made her collect every thing like paper on or about my table this rainy morning. It was a short letter and I hope you will recollect enough of it to write over and add more, for your amiable correspondant, to whom give my assurance of love. I am grieved that your Mamma is unwell, but trust it proceeds from fatigue, do persuade her to go to Mrs. Bomford, and not to worry herself with household or any business. I hope the bustle and alarm of *Insurrections* are over in the city—tho' I hope all will be on guard ever after this.[1] I am quiet, knowing little about it and that I cannot help myself if I am in danger. I beleive there is none at present.

Tell Mr. Trist I send *him* a few leaves from the Cape Jessamine if not the whole flower of his dear lady who is now blooming, when all her contemporaries have changed color and are passing away! emblematic of her good heart and disposition, whose fragrance will last until the end! You will find enclosed a leaf from each of the flowers named—as follows, Monsieur and Madame Serurier and two sons, Mrs. Cutts, and Mrs Madison—the bride and groom Lear, Mrs. Lear—Dolley and yourself with Mrs. Trist's.

Your uncle Madison still wears the bead ring you placed on his finger, I see him look at it every now and then—My eyes are very weak, still I am writing you a deal of nonsense. I have notes that tomorrow will bring with it, to me, a large party from Richmond and the lower country, Mayos &c Payne is on the wing to his mine with three gentlemen in his train. Adieu! ever yours

D. P. Madison

Tr (MCR-S: Mary Estelle Elizabeth Cutts Papers). Tr made by Mary Cutts.

1. On 21 Aug. 1831 Nat Turner, a slave preacher on a plantation in Southampton County, Va., led a slave uprising that killed fifty-one white persons and spread alarm throughout the South. Turner was later apprehended and executed, along with sixteen of his followers.

To Frances D. Lear

[March 1832]

I hasten to thank you beloved friend (as well as very sore eyes will permit me) for your interesting letter of the 26th—in which you tell me my dear Sister is on the recovery—I pray that it may be the case, and that she may be long spared to her family and to me! I have as you suppose, been miserable about her, and tho the girls have been good in writing, and she also when able, I have found all communications too slow for my constant anxiety. My dear Husband is still confined to his bed—In addition to a disabling Rheumatism throughout the winter, he has had a bilious fever, which has reduced him so much that he can only walk from one bed to another. I never leave him, more than a few minuts at a time, and have not left the enclosure around our house for the last eight months, on account of his continued indisposition, concerning which, friends at a distance, have recd. but too favorable reports. Our Physians have advised the warm Springs for Mr. Madison, and we hoped to have taken him there, but as he could not travel unless conveyed on his bed, we dare not think of it at present.

Now my precious friend I would express my deep regret that any obstacle should exist to our enjoyment of your society this summer. No persons should I be more delighted to see here, than yourself, your son & daughter, and I will still indulge the hope, that my Husband will be well enough for this gratification, & my sister sufficiently recovered to come with you, before the Winter throws its barriers between us.

I must ever love the kind friends of my Sister yourself Mrs. Bomford, Mrs. Clay—have been as Sisters to her—and some others also, of whom she speaks with great sensibility Doctr. Sim are enroll'd by me on a grateful memory! We hear at a distance of the Alarming Cholera, but as yet, no report of its existence in our State. Be pleased to present my affectinate love to Mrs. Randolph & Mrs. Trist, & tell them I shall be proud of my new cousin Ellen.

Accept Mr. Madisons best wishes—& my son's best respects, with the long, & sincere attatchment, of your

D. P. Madison

RC (DLC: J. Henley Smith Papers).

To Anna Cutts

My dear Sister,   [ca. 15 May 1832]

Your handwriting on the box was a cordial to me. I shewed it to my Husband who sd., "Yes—I will eat of the jelly for her dear sake." He is still confined entirely to his bed—too feeble to sit up but to have it made. His fever has abated within 3 days, & he seems better in some respects—I find however that no one at W——n knows how much has been, or is the matter with him, which is a *disadvantage* to him. He reces. letters, & visitors as if he was made of Iron—to his great disadvantage & mine. I have just finished a letter from him to Mr. Trist & will inclose this & Lucys in it—on sunday Morg. my last to you, left the C. House & you aught to have recd. it on Monday—I was in such haste that I inclosed it unsealed to Mr Cutts which I trust did not prevent your getting it—Tell dear Mary I will write to her for all hers as soon as I can, & say the same to my dr Dolley—I recd. by Mrs. Ballard the Curls & Silk & think the Curls by far the handsomest I have seen—The Silk will answer me very well—Payne had gone to the GoldMine for a day or he wd. have written the letter to Mr. T.[1] & our brother is confined at his home with Rheumatism—D. & Anna[2] are with me—Mary says the Livingstons[3] are comeing here on their way to the Springs—I am sick at the very idea of seeing *such* strangers, in our condition, but no more abt. it. I wd. not add a word to cause you uneasiness—You must let the girls pay for my silk & Curls, & I'l send you more mony than the little in your hands to make it up—I'm sorry you took any trouble abt. the Emboss'd Green or Crimson Cambrick, & I wrote to that amt. several times—I can get something here, I dare say, if ever I ride out again, & if I do not, shall not want it—so dont think abt. it now—I wd. rather wait until you look into stores yourself. In great haste I close this for the oppy. thro Mr. T. as Mr. M can scarsly frank. Your own & ever My dr Sister

Tell me if you see Mrs Willis who has gone to Alexa. to Convention with Mr. Cole & Jno. Willis—all going over to see you—They know you are sick & cant Entertain but go from frdship.

RC (ViU). Undated. Date assigned on the basis of internal evidence and JM to Nicholas P. Trist, 15 May 1832 (DLC: Nicholas P. Trist Papers).

  1. Nicholas P. Trist.
  2. Dolley and Anna Payne.
  3. This was probably Edward Livingston, the secretary of state, and his family.

To John Payne Todd

20th. July 1832.

Yours, dearest, came safe. I was glad mine with the enclosure had reached you—you will tell me when you mean to return &c &c that I may be au fait on the subjects interesting to us both—Messrs. Patton and Rives dined with us on the 12th—they enquired for you and said they hoped to have seen you at the party as "a Jackson man"—Genl. Madison came with them, looking gay and happy.

Mr. Madison is better—a few days ago he was ill, & I now hope he will soon be well enough for me to leave him on an expedition to the Court House. It would be quite an event, for me to go there—5 miles from home! The last tobacco both of Mr Madisons and John's was a failure, the first sold at 5$—the last at 7$—when 17 was expected—so it goes with planters—I would rather earn, or *receive* the salary of one of A. Ds daughters, than depend on a plantation for *pin* money.

Yesterday came Mr. J. Randall of Phila. with his daughter and niece—they remained to dinner—he told me that he had a glimpse of you in W——n —that he was fixing his baggage and about to pursue you, but that he lost sight of you. D. and M. wrote me yesterday that you were popular in the City—I should like to be with you to witness it—as the respect and love shewn my son would be the highest gratification the world could bestow upon me. We have seen but few strangers since you left home—Mr. Barney of Baltimore on his way to the Springs—and of course we know little of the great world—I suppose you see Madame *Serurier*. If you can, see Mrs. Lear give my best love to her and tell her she must come from the springs to visit me.

Adieu my son—may Heaven preserve & protect you.

(P. S.) Mr. and Mrs. Forsyth were old friends of mine, as well as Govr. Cass— present me to them kindly also to the Tayloes and others whom I had reason to like.

Tr (MCR-S: Mary Estelle Elizabeth Cutts Papers). Tr made by Mary Cutts.

To Anna Cutts

[ca. 4 August 1832]

Yours, beloved sister, came last night, the account of your great and many sufferings fall heavily on my heart, but I will hope the last attack was the crisis of your disorder and that good spirits and a quiet mind will soon restore you to us—I am sure the kindness of your many friends will prove as it ought to do, a charm and cordial against vexations which otherwise might have an influence on your health—strive to be happy and well, my dear sister for my sake and for your childrens! What should we do without you! As soon as my eyes are well I will write to dear Mrs. Bomford, in the mean time offer her my love and thanks for all her goodness to you. My husband is not as well as he was two ⟨. . .⟩ confined to his bed. I will write and tell ⟨. . .⟩ Mr. Madison sends you his affectionate ⟨. . .⟩ best hopes that you are getting well. Adieu my dear ever and always

Your sister D.

Tr (MCR-S: Mary Estelle Elizabeth Cutts Papers). Ms torn.

To Richard Cutts

Dear Brother,   6th. Augt. 1832.

The heart of your miserable sister mourns with you, with your precious daughters, with your sons![1] Come to us as soon as you can, & bring them with you. I feel deeply interested in all that concerned my sister & her children—I wish to know her Will, & where you have deposited her remains!

I wish to present my self with gratitude & love to Mrs. Bomford Mrs. Mason, and to one & all, of those excellent friends, who have, to the end, extended their kindness & consolations to my lamented sister! Mr Madison partakes in our sorrows, & in my wish to see you all here. Shew this to Dolley and Mary as, I cannot write to them at this moment—I recd. yours yesterday Evg. Yours affly

D P M

RC (MCR-S: Mary Estelle Elizabeth Cutts Papers).
   1. Anna had been gravely ill for months and died on 4 Aug. 1832.

To Mary E. E. Cutts

Dearest Mary,   MONTPELIER March 10th. 33

Yours acknowledging mine came safe, but I have not been well enough to write you since. I took a bad cold which still adheres to me, and your Uncle has not been so well as he was in the winter, so, that I have been prevented from writing, except to copy for him. I felt disappointed when Mr. and Mrs. Rives passed the Court House, without bringing me any thing from any of you, it was a good opportunity to send books, letters accounts of fashions &c. What has become of the house Mr. Trist left? Who takes it now? Have you called on Mrs. Preston? So Mrs. —— is one of your sett. It is in her power to be kind and perhaps useful to you, but if she is ever offended in any way she is *bitter*. It is best for us my dear, to beware of "most every body"—as I have often said. Mr. —— is an elegant and accomplished person, but—be perfectly respectful to him and ready to receive the instruction which lurks forever in his conversation—and now I wish you to tell me about certain parties now at peace. Has there been a good treaty made, not to be broken, or will it resemble scratches on agate, which a wet sponge apparently wipes away for ever, but which come back when the stone is dry?

Tr (MCR-S: Mary Estelle Elizabeth Cutts Papers).

To Mary E. E. Cutts

13th. March [1833]

Yours of the 2d. my beloved Mary gave me more than common pleasure, because it express'd love, & care for me, as well as for your Unkle M.

I had written to you on the same day yours was dated, which you recd. no doubt, as your Father & Sister acknowledged the[i]rs, from the same enclosure.

I had several times mentiond my indisposition, but continued to write to you notwithstanding—I now feel quite well except an inflamed Eye.

I answered the letter from your Papa to which you refered—I wish he wd. *shew* you the corrispondence, for tho' you have little to do with the subject, I think you shd. be acquainted with all things, that consern you, even, in the least. You say nothing from M——n but I will not tease you—I wish I could amuse you, rather. I *asked too* many questions in my last—did I not? Yes—but you are very good & amiable my dear to write me as much as you do, & I value you accordingly tho' I may complain a little now & then at your not answering questions—by the by—I hope my ever dear Mrs Lear is not offended with me—she says nothing, even thro' you—but she never wd. forget me if she knew how my heart clings to her. What has become of Mrs Decatur? I was very sorry her Claim on Congress was not allowed,[1] but trust it will yet, be. My dear Payne has had—& has now, an allarming Caugh, which makes me melancholy to hear—As I told you, I hear nothing more of his *likeing,* to the young lady, report gave him for a wife & I'm sorry for it. I hope you witnessed the Inauguration—& have seen Mrs Johnson—Is Mr. Jno. Randolph with you yet & *how is he?* Mr. Trists family are not as much with you as formerly—I mean the Miss R——s.[2] We suppose the Livingstons will not go to France yet a while from the Ps. arrangements—how do you like Made. Pagiot. We hear the Old Minister of Rusia return'd—suppose you sett your Cap or Curls, at him—he has been in love once in this country, & I see no objection to your becomeing *Baroness* de ——.[3] I hope dear Walter is off to Sea—& that you'l see Thomas & wife, some time soon. I am highly pleased with Ds sentiments abt. Mr. A. She has too much sense to encourage any man to her disadvantage, If I judge rightly of her mind—still a kind sister who is a looker on, will be able to give the best advise, & *I will* help her—I was affraid W. Willis wd. anoy you all he's a good hearted *ignoramus*—a report here that he was stabed at school—but suppose he's *well of it,* or you wd. have mentiond—I dont know his family, but hear they are good & respectable—but I wanted to know whether you had promised your *cousin* Wm Washington to go there, & to Bath with his wife &c—I wish you had sent the Shauls we spoke of, as I've had to buy for the girls, & wd. rather have sent you the mony, a thousand times. When spring goods reach you—I'l ask—what you see

RC (MCR-S: Mary Estelle Elizabeth Cutts Papers).

1. In December 1832 Susan Decatur, widow of the naval captain Stephen Decatur, unsuccessfully petitioned Congress to be paid prize money for the 1804 destruction of the *Philadelphia.* She renewed her petition to each subsequent Congress until her claim was granted in 1837 (*Digested Summary and Alphabetical List of Private Claims . . . Presented to the House of Representatives* [3 vols.; Washington, D.C., 1853], 1:476–77).

2. The Miss Randolphs, that is, the unmarried daughters of Martha Jefferson and Thomas Mann Randolph.

3. Baron Paul Von Krüdener, Russian minister to the United States.

To Mary E. E. Cutts

MONTPELIER August 1st. 1833

May your fortune, dearest Mary, be even better than the Sybil's predictions. There is a secret she did not tell you, however, it is, that we have all, a great hand in the formation of our own destiny. We must press on, that intricate path, leading to perfection and happiness, by doing all that is good and handsome before we can be taken under the silver wing of our rewarding angel.

This, I cannot doubt you will aim at and succeed in. I need not re-capitulate all the virtues necessary to render us worthy and deserving of good fortune, because, you know them "at your fingers ends."

I received your last letter, just a week after the inside date, tho' the envelope was marked 26th. July. Be assured all you write me is *sacred*. I hope you received my last enclosing the Lady's Book,[1] and that you are ready to set out on your visit to Cousin William, present me affectionately to him Margaret and Louisa. I should delight in going to see them all, I heard lately from their dear mother, at Frankfort (Ky) she was well, tho' surrounded by Cholera! Your Uncle John talks of going to the West this fall, but I trust he will not as his house is now commodious, and his crops the last year encouraging. Your Uncle Madison mends in his health but often relapses. We have had more company this summer than *I* can describe and I have been more indisposed than usual this morning I could not go to breakfast with a party of eight, two ladies among them, on account of illness, but I have taken a ride with my husband and shall join them at dinner. Anna is at school, doing well. Present me affectionately to Dolley, your brothers and Father—I hope Madame Serurier will soon recover and return. I hear nothing of Mrs. Johnson, but suppose she will be entirely retired for a time. Adieu, ever my own dear, ever your faithful friend

Tr (MCR-S: Mary Estelle Elizabeth Cutts Papers).

1. The *Lady's Book* was first published in 1830 in Philadelphia by Louis Antoine Godey in imitation of a British magazine for women which combined articles, fiction, music, and fashion. It soon enjoyed a wide circulation.

To Richard Cutts

Dear brother   Mon Augt. 11. 1833.

Yours of the 4th. was recd duly & its contents 30$ handed to Mr M—You will scarsly credit me when I tell you that every moment of my time has been so occupied as to prevent my answering you before this day—My Husband tho better, requires more of my attention every day—& my most effecient House servant Sucky lies very ill with billious fever. The rest of us, including Jno. & family are well. Your statement of accts. no doubt, is just & proper— Did you get my last letter enclosing one to Mary, sent the 5th. Augt.? I am glad the Girls have gone with Richd because I think it will be an advantage to them to see other characters, than those they are confined to, in W———n—You know it expands the minds of Men & women to look into the varieties of this world, to a certain degree. If my prayers for them may have effect, they will be happy in their Husbands & fortune & make their Father so.

Dont forget your promise to write me often—whatever you hear from D & M as well as about yourself your dr Sons, & every thing else.

When you see Mrs. Randolph & Mrs. Lear & dr. Mrs. Bomford present me to them—your's allways

D P M

Do they sell 2d hand Carpets—or Carpetting at Oction cheap? at what price?

RC (owned by Charles M. Storey, Boston, Mass., 1961).

To Mary E. E. Cutts

MONTPELIER Novr. 4 1833

I have just now received yours, dearest Mary, and feel quite sorry that *you* have *not* called on Madame Serurier—surely Dolley and yourself know better the etiquette near courts, where ambassadors and ministers reside, than to expect the ladies of either to call "on you" *first*—unless, indeed, from a particular courtesy—I pray you not to let *this mistaken idea* deprive you of the *acquaintance* and friendship of Madame Serurier—if you have gone to visit at any house go *there* immediately, or you will never see her at yours—As I lived sixteen years in the midst of *ceremonies* in Washington I can tell you, that you and Dolley, as young ladies—are to visit our own ministers and Foreign Ministers ladies first, if you desire their acquaintance! I was also four years in Philadelphia, where Mrs Washington presided, and intimate with the heads of Departments and Ministers from Europe and I never knew their ladies to visit young girls first—indeed! I know they made a point of *not doing so,* and in my humble opinion they were in the right—When they or you take a journey the first call must be made by you.

I am grateful for the mats but sorry you should spend money on my account—as I fear the steamboat will ⟨not⟩ stop and I should have no other chance of getting them—I would rather have the pretty dress for turban than all ⟨the⟩ mats in town.

Adieu my dear child, May heaven protect you both the children of my most beloved sister!

D. P. Madison

Tr (MCR-S: Mary Estelle Elizabeth Cutts Papers).

From Sarah Coles Stevenson

My dear friend   RICHMOND Novr. 22d 1833

I wrote you about a week since informing you of our safe arrival &c. and now I write again, not because I have any thing to say, but because I wish to get you so deeply in my debt that you will be obliged to make me some return, and afford me the satisfaction of hearing of dear Mr Madison's health, about which I feel anxious on the approach of cold weather—I heard yesterday from our friends in Philadelphia, poor Betsy has been ill,[1] with a *rheumatism* of the *muscles,* and had had Dr. Chapman in constant attendance for a fortnight when she last wrote, she seems much out of spirits, & if she continues ill Emily or myself will go on to her, brother Tucker has also been suffering a good deal but both are now much better—Edward will be married on the 28th. next Thursday, *or* the 2d of December, the tuesday after. They leave Philadelphia on the day after their marriage for Virginia, so you may look out for the blum-ing bride, and happy *brides-groom.* Betsy writes she is very handsome, and modest, and looks amiable—Tell cousin Payne if a grey headed old fellow can do such things, what ought he to do, without a grey hair in his head. I have re-ceived but one letter from Edward filled with praises of his fair one—How delightful it is to be always *young!* I do verily believe he has found the elixir of life somewhere, and takes a dose every now & then—No news, the City ve[r]y dull, & I more so—for my husband leaves me on Sunday—Heigho! I feel more *desolate* than Robinson Crusoe on his Island—I dont know what is to become of me this winter, and wish my husband was a *plain comfortable Farmer* in the Country.[2] The dye is cast—& I must try to be *content,* but dont be surprised if you hear of me some of these days, as "*strayed* or *stolen.*" God bless you all—prays your own

                                                        S C Stevenson

P.S. I return Mr Madison Colo. Taylor's Speech on the carriage tax, according to promise![3] I made two efforts to get at Mr. Randolphs papers, but without success! Mr Daniel has none of Mr R. papers, & does not know what has be-come of them! I have written to Mr. Meade on the subject, & hope soon to hear from him! I send for Mr Payne the auditor's letter about his land; I did not get it until yesterday! I find on reference to my *agricultural memoranda's,* that I was right in my conjecture about the Devon's sent to Mr Patterson! In 1817, June, Mr W. Patterson imported from Mr Coke M. P. the celebrated *Tor-rance* & his mate, (Devon Short Horn) from which all his stock have sprung!

He has lent none since I am sure; These fine calves of Mrs. M's ought to be traced, & the quantity of Devon blood ascertained![4] I am on the wing for Washington, & go with a heavy heart! For the next six months I had as lief be any where else, & especially if I am to go to the Chr; as I fear I shall be forced to do! What a fiery ordeal he shall have—I shudder when I think of it, & wish most sincerely, I was snug in the Country for the winter, at least! My affc regards & best wishes attend you all my dr. friends.

A S.

RC (MCR-S: Mary Estelle Elizabeth Cutts Papers).

1. Elizabeth (Betsy) Coles.

2. Andrew Stevenson was a U.S. congressman from 1821 to 1834, and Speaker of the House of Representatives for the last seven of those years.

3. Stevenson referred to John Taylor of Caroline, *An Argument respecting the Constitutionality of the Carriage Tax* (Richmond, 1795; Evans 29606).

4. William Patterson of Baltimore had presented DPM with a pair of Devon Shorthorn calves in the fall of 1833 (JM to William Allen, 15 Sept. 1833, DLC).

To Mary E. P. Allen

My precious dear Mary   MONTPELLIER Feby. 25. 1834.

I have just recd. your welcome letter, and thank you for it—especially for the interesting account you give me, of yourself and family—We should indeed rejoice to see you, your estimable husband, and little ones here, where I have so long sighed to embrace you. You will not I trust, allow "the candid lady's" description of us all, to prejudice you against relations, who are tenderly attatched to you tho' so long, & so far, seperated from you. Mrs. Clay was truly kind to my lamented sister Cutts, for which I shall always & gratefully remember her.

Your Unkle ⟨J⟩no. Payne resides within a mile & a half of us—is an honorable & industrious man, with Eight children: Three of six daughters are nearly grown, Dolley, Lucy, & Anna, the last, lives entirely with me & the others are much with me also. They are very amiable girls, rather pretty, & so far, have good plain educations. The names of the three younger, are Mary, Louisa & Susan. The boys are William Temple & James Madison.

Your Cousins of Washington often visit us in the summer—Dolley & Mary Cutts are well educated sensible girls, full of gaiety & fashion. Madison's wife is very pretty & amiable and I hope the time approaches when you will be able to judge all these characters for yourself, with others of your kindred, whom I would fain introduce to your acquaintance & regard.

When we met Mr. Allen in Richmond he was so good as to promise us a visit on his journey home, and that he would some time, before long bring you to Montpellier—I looked anxiously for him after the adjournment when I intended to have written you a long letter at least. Since that period my dear Husband has been in very bad health—and is still confined to the house with feebleness—resulting from a painful and diffusive Rheumatism—I have never left him half an hour, for the last two years—so deep is the interest, & sympathy, I feel for him! I look forward, however with hope, to the genial season so near—for his restoration, when he will be able to take exercise in his Carriage in the open air—which was serviceable to him last summer—tho' not sufficiently, so, to enable us to go to the Springs—which I the more regretted when our cousin Stevenson told me that you were there.

I recd a letter this morg. from your Aunt Todd dated 10. days ago when she was quite well—her Sons Johnson & J—s M. Todd are at College. Madisonia, her only daughter, is with her in Frankfort—she is a dutiful & attentive daughter, but unfortunately nervous.

Your poor cousin's Walter & George Washington died in rapid Consumption! Their brother William (I am told) is a robust & hearty man. I trust Heaven will prolong your life & health beloved Mary—& that I may have the happiness to witness it—Your Unkle Madison & my son, Payne Todd, unite with me, in this hope.

Present me to Mrs. Jackson & tell her, if her son should come to the University of Virga. that we should take great pleasure in seeing him, & rendering any service for her's & his Father's sake.

Govr. Coles brought his handsome Bride to visit me in Decr. She is of Phila. & tho' not rich, is of a wealthy family—I think he was very fortunate in obtaining so fine a woman; for whom, it is likely he will abandon the Western country, as she is most partial to her own neighbourhood.

I must now beg my dear Neice to excuse a delinquent correspondent—& to be assured of the true love of her Aunt

D P Madison

RC (ViHi: Allen Family Papers). Addressed to Mrs. Allen at Clarksburg, Harrison County, Va.

To Edward Coles

MONTPELLIER April 16. 1834.

I should have replied to your kind letter dear cousin, which accompanied the beautiful Chintz, before this day, but for the increased indisposition of my dear Husband, who has had a distressing Eruption all over him for the last three weeks—It was at first supposed to be Erysipelas in its burning, Itching and feverish character, but his Physicians concluded that it was not exactly that, and seem at a loss for its proper name. It is now very slowly mending, and I trust when it disappears, that he will be the better for present sufferings. In addition to this cause for my silence I have been sick also—a violent cold affected my eyes so badly that I have been unable to write until within a few days. I now try my pen as I am impatient to thank you and my amiable Cousin Sally for remembering my wishes, and for your kindness in anticipating my Commission.

We sincerely hope you will both enjoy the long journey you propose to take this spring—escaping dangers of every sort, and returning to your friends in Virginia, and Philadelphia, with increased health and happiness.

I am sorry that I cannot tell you something of our relations in this quarter, but it has been long, since I heard from them—and I regret that my anxious, and confined situation, at this time will permit me only to assure you, and your precious Wife, that we are ever, and affectionately Yours

D. P. Madison

RC (NjP: Edward Coles Papers).

To Margaret Bayard Smith

MONTPELLIER Augt. 31st. 1834.

I have received with due sensibility my dear friend your kind letter of the 29th. and can assure you that if a Biographical Sketch must be taken, its accomplishment by your pen, would be more agreeable to me than by any other to which such a task could be committed, being persuaided not only of its competency, but of the just dispositions by which it would be guided.

Dolley and Mary are now with us, but if I had known your wish as it regards my letters to them, and some of mine to their Mother—I should have directed them to shew them to you without scruple—not ⟨. . .⟩ have thrown light on the early occurrences of my life but that they contain my unvarnished

305

opinions and feelings on different subjects. As it is I will have them sent here, when the Girls return to the city, in order that I may select those at all worthy of your attention.

My family are all Virginians except myself, who was born in N. Carolina whilst my Parents were there on a visit of one year, to an Uncle. Their families on both sides, were among the most respectable and they, becoming members of the society of friends soon after their Marriage—Manumitted their Slaves, and left this state for that of Pennsylvania, bearing with them their children to be educated in their religion. I beleive my age at that time was 11. or 12 years— I was educated in Philadelphia where I was married to Mr Todd in 1790, and to Mr. Madison in 94, when I returned with him to the soil of my Father, and to Washington, where you have already traced me with the kindness of a sister. In the year 91, and after the death of my Father, my Mother received into her house some Gentlemen as boarders—and in 93 she left Philadelphia to reside with her daughter Washington—afterwards, with my Sister Jackson—and occasionally with me. I am sensible that this, is but a general answer to yours. Should any particular information be desired, I will endeaver to furnish it.

I am sorry to add that Mr. Madisons health has not been and is not now so advanced as might be inferred from occasional references to it in the News papers. The effect of his severe and protracted Rheumatism has been increased by other indispositions—one of which is still hanging on him—he is happily however, exempt from much pain, and every favourable change in him brightens my hope of his recovery. He unites with me in every good wish and affectionate remembrance for yourself Mr. Smith and your daughters. Your constant friend

D. P. M.

RC (DLC: J. Henley Smith Papers). Ms torn.

To Mary E. E. Cutts

2d. Decr. 34.

Be assured sweet Mary that when I am silent to D, & you, it is because I cannot write. At this moment my eyes are half closed—cold, added to their habitual weakness, has made me thus long in replying to your acceptable letters—I recd. them safe, & must ever think highly of your heart (as I always have done) when I recollect how much you have done for that dr brother, who has hitherto been unfortunate, but who, I trust will now flourish in defiance of all *sorts* of enimies—I recd. your bonit pattern & have cut, & made one by it of black Velvet—Give my kind love to Mrs. Smith & tell her It wd. give me pleasure to do what she recommends, & that I hope it will not be long before I make the effort, tho' I can not promise much, as I cannot give her anything of importance *in my own Eyes*. I have other letters beside the one the extract was taken from—which continues the *little* history of War times, & *my especial difficulties;* but egotism is so repugnant to my nature that I *shrink* from recording my own feelings, acts or doings. You can *repeat this* to Mrs. S. whom I consider a kind friend, & amiable lady.

Have you seen Mrs. Lucy Cutts? I recd. a long handsome letter from her the other day & answered it—it was a pathetic letter speaking of the sad situation of her husband self & children—She wanted letters to the President secys &c—in order to get in to some humble office & I wish it had been in my power to assist her—as I think Mr C. Cutts is an amiable & honorable man, tho' sd. to be unfortunate in his habits—but all *this* is between ourselves, you must not breath it, because it is enough that I can do nothing for her, without wounding her feelings by speaking of them—You need not buy the calico, as I had to send some time ago for it to Fredricksbg. & obtained a whole piece 30. yards, at one shilling, very much like the pattern you sent—I have dress'd Anna for home & as far as it will go the little family. Docr. Rose has gone to Phila. & Sally A is as you left her—We have a dull neighbourhood & I can not amuse you, *out of it.* Adeiu my beloved for the present—hope my eyes will permit me to say more, & *better* soon. I have not heard lately from your Aunt Lucy—has Mary Allen come to W. She wrote me, you know, that she'd be here this fall, so tell me if she is with you, or whether her husband has left her at home—You have all the world with you now & will soon be gay—Present my respects good wishes & thanks to Mr Wise & tell him we recd. his handsome box of excellent Pruens safe in 2 days after they were sent. Anna will write you. Dont fail to give my love to Ellen & a kiss to my great Neice. What's its name?

Will you tell Madison with my love, that the beer is safe & very good & acceptable & that he must write me the price &c—I wd. write *him* but cant see—*so burn this.*

I keep Mrs. Smiths note to you a little longer I wish you'd both visit her, as she invites &c &c.

Tell me if Mrs White has returnd with her husband & if they have brought me anything—whats become of Mrs Hay—The 5$ in Ds, folded up with this will pay all—I have this moment recd. yours enclosing dear Thomas's & beg you to send him my affte love, & to his wife & daughter when you write again—more soon from your ever

Tr (MCR-S: Mary Estelle Elizabeth Cutts Papers).

To Margaret Bayard Smith

MONTPELLIER Jany. 17. 1835.

Be assured my dear friend that we reciprocate all the good wishes which your letter has so kindly conveyed to us this day—for yourself Mr Smith and your amiable family and truly, your observations on new acquaintances accord also, with my feelings on the subject—my experience teaches, that our hearts recur and cling to early attachments, as the most happy of our lives. I ought now to offer many apologies for my silence, and if I was not acquainted with your goodness and forbearance—I should despair of forgiveness—but I trust in a simple statement of facts to shew you that my delinquency has not proceeded from want of love, and confidence in your friendship, nor am I without explanations, which will at least mitigate it. My letters to my Sister Todd at the closing scenes of the War, happen to be with her in Kentucky, and I was unwilling to have them exposed to the Mail, if I had been sure of their arrival in time, and that they contained any thing worthy of being extracted. I might plead also my constant engagements of different sorts at home, which have not permitted me to search over papers, and bring my mind to the revisal of scenes or circumstances that might possibly throw a faint interest over a recital of them, and lastly I must in candour say, that I have felt more than a mere reluctance in being a judge and witness, of incidents if existing, that might be worthy of the use to be made of them.

Your enquiries after my dear Husband will be partially answered by himself. He is better in health than he was two months ago, tho' still feeble and confined to his rooms—we trust however, that with great care against the cold of this Winter, he will be able to take exercise in his Carriage when the Spring season shall cheer us again.

I have been afflicted for the last two weeks with Influenza, the violence of which seems slowly passing away, altho' the cough continues.

I send you an Engraving from Stuarts Portrait which tho' indifferently executed, is a better likeness than Mr Wood's, which I would send also but that the *Stage* has ceased to run from Orange C. House for a few days, on account of bad roads.

I hope the efforts of our friend Mr. Clay, in his interesting Report, to keep "sweet peace" without a loss of honour, may prove successful.[1] A War between the United States and France that would cost both so much, for a cause apparently so insignificant, would be a *spectacle* truly deplorable, in the present state of the World. Ever affectionately yours

D. P Madison

I am very thankful, my kind friend, for the interest you take in my health. It is not good, and at my age, nature can afford little of the medical aid she exerts on younger patients. I have indeed got through the most painful stages of my principal malady, a diffusive & obstinate Rheumatism, but I feel its crippling effects on my limbs, particularly my hands & fingers, as this little effort of the pen will shew. I owe my thanks to Dr Smith also for the friendly lines which accompanied your former letter to Mrs. M. and the good wishes conveyed in your last. Assure him of the continuance of my great esteem & cordial regards. May you both long enjoy the blessing of health, with every other necesary to fill the measure of your happiness

James Madison

RC (DLC: J. Henley Smith Papers).
1. Henry Clay's report, written as chairman of the Senate Committee on Foreign Affairs, was an attempt to defuse a growing controversy over U.S. spoliation claims against France that, through the intemperate remarks of President Jackson, threatened to ignite a war between the two countries (Robert V. Remini, *Henry Clay: Statesman for the Union* [New York, 1991], 474–76).

To Dolley P. Madison Cutts

MONTPELIER 10th Feby. 1835

You worry yourself too much, my dear Dolley, when you say, you cannot write well (or to that amount) when beleive me I think few can write better or more handsomely than you do, whenever you please, But what is this you tell me of your having personated a *sorceress* covered with reptiles! Had I been near you I would have persuaded you to appear in a more feminine and congenial character—If I could see to express myself with these eyes of mine, I might fill a volume in favor of *always sustaining* a sweet and gentle character— You tell me, you hear of my inviting persons to spend the summer here, indeed, my love there must be a mistake somewhere—As I should be quite unhappy to think I should be confined at home to receive company during the next and only season of the year when your sick uncle could go out at all, no, we both hope to visit some Springs, or at least to be at liberty to travel about for our health's sake. I say *our* health, because mine has been worse than his since December owing to Influenza.

Can you tell me what has become of Mrs. Hay and Mrs. White. A gentleman lately visited us, who had seen Mrs. White in Paris and elsewhere, last year as well as Mrs. Hay. My love and admiration to Mrs. Ogle Tayloe, I am attached to all that family—Mr. Madison wants an engraving from your Quaker Cap Miniature of me, but knows not how he will get it. Your affecte:

D. P. Madison

Tr (MCR-S: Mary Estelle Elizabeth Cutts Papers).

To Mary E. E. Cutts

MONTPELIER 10th. March 1835

I rejoiced at the pleasant visit you made to Kalarama, dearest Mary, as well as at hearing of the health and enjoyments of my dear Dolley and yourself during the *hard* winter. I was anxious to write and tell you of Miss Martineau's visit, and how much we were pleased with her enlightened conversation and unassuming manners—her lively little friend Miss Jeffrys also, but weak eyes! even now, I can scarcely write five minutes together, so that I must hasten to say as much as I can now, and do more when they are better. Dear good Mrs. Smith will have so few incidents to make her Biography interesting that I ought to *tremble* for it (between you and I).

I have no idea of the new dance or its motions but approve of your declining to learn it, if disapproved of by society—*Our sex* are ever loosers, when they stem the torrent of public opinion. Baron Krudner's parties must be piquant, but if Sir Charles Vaughn leaves what will the city do. What has become of Lewis Randolph's marriage? I see he has a handsome appointment—best love and kisses to his dear mother, Mrs. Cooledge and Mrs. Trist—Murry Mason is a fine young man and Miss Forsyth a handsome girl, I hear. I send Dolley all the love I can express, tell her the English ladies observed that Mr. Pitt Adams would be greatly missed in the city, and that he was a fine fellow—has he gone? I was sure *you* had *made* acquaintance with Miss Martineau and Miss Jeffery's and of course enquired after you, but "they has not been favored with your attentions." Adieu, for the present, precious Mary—

Your Uncle is still in his room, but I think him better, and hope to make him much more so when the season advances, for exercise abroad, he nor I could ever be quite well again if we remained stationary, as we have been for many years past.

Tr (MCR-S: Mary Estelle Elizabeth Cutts Papers).

To Dolley P. Madison Cutts

Dearest Dolché   MONTPELIER May 11th. 1835
    Yesterday morning Payne met with your interesting friend Mr. Hodgson at Orange C. House, and brought him home to dinner with his two cousins— We were much pleased with his society as well as with the account he gave of you and Mary. He told me of your pleasant party and how much he admired and regarded you both, but not half as much about you as I desired to know, indeed, how could he, when my love for you makes me wish to trace your every word and deed throughout the year. He gave me your welcome letter and beautiful gloves, for both I thank you. He told us of Commodores Patterson, Porter &c and many other great personages—but what was my grief to receive only one Music box? The box I prized most, the one you and Mary gave me was missing! I will hope, however, that by some mistake it was left with you and that I shall hear it again in these deep shades.

    Your inquiries after your Uncle, and how we pass our time can be more accurately answered—*My days* are devoted to nursing and comforting my *patient,* who walks only from the bed in which he breakfasts, to one in the little chamber, where you *left* him. Anna who is a sterling girl stays much at home with me and sleeps beside my bed ever since the illness of Mr. Madison in April, of which I wrote you in a letter to Mary—he is better now but not yet well enough to walk across the two rooms or decide on entering a carriage to go to any springs or even to the road. Should I be so happy as to see him well enough, and decided to visit a watering place I will hasten to tell you, in order that you Mary and I may meet "at Phillippi."

    I saw the compliment to Mr. Adams in the Globe and other papers. I can tell you nothing of our neighbours which would amuse you.

    I hope as "Septimia was singing" that my dear friend Mrs. Randolph has got well. In my last to Mary I told her of Mrs. Gryme's visit to me, she is delighted at her daughter's marriage and expects to see her in New York in July, she sent Rozine for her young children and is going next week to meet them in New York—She seemed to have hopes of seeing you at New York the North, where she said she was ordered to go by her physicians "to keep cool," she is amusing and affectionate.

Adieu, for the present, my darling, soon, I write again and on more agreeable topics. My best love to Mary, tell her I will write her I answered her last with a few lines to your father. Your own Aunt

Dolley P. Madison

Tr (MCR-S: Mary Estelle Elizabeth Cutts Papers).

From James Madison Cutts

Dear Aunt. WASHINGTON CITY Sep: 4th 1835.

If you had almost forgotten me I should perhaps have deserved it, from not having written before tho' from no forgetfulness of Montpelier of which Ellen & myself daily speak in terms of fond recollection.

I am loth to refer to my last letter—it has been some time ago—a month perhaps—since I wrote so will tell you all our proceedings for the time past.

I have been closely confined to my office & was therefore unable to do more than escort Ellen & the infant to her Uncle's—Jno: Hamilton Esqr. of Chas: Co: Maryland where she spent six weeks with much advantage to her own & child's health. Mr Hamilton is a widower with handsome property & devotedly fond of Ellen. Tho' his estate is not in a very gay neighborhood Ellen had around her much to enjoy—unlimited command of a large house & household. I saw her there for the first time in the character of a housewife— & well did she become it. Her Uncle would willingly have detained her— whom he sincerely loves & more that she would leave him to his servants entirely alone as he has no children left. He is yet young tho' twice married—but I could spare her no longer. Since her return she has been not only unwell for a time herself but anxious as to her infant who has been quite sick tho' now almost in robust health—the Dr (Hunt) says she has escaped well as we might have feared an attack of some more serious nature.

We are very domestic—tho' failing not to visit many kind friends, whom we see quite in a sociable way—a mode I greatly prefer. A day or two ago— we went up to see Mrs Lear, in hopes she had returned—she was represented by Mrs Hendly with whom we spent a pleasant evening & concluded among us that Mrs Lear was doing the same with you. We are informed that in a very few days Mrs. Louisa Lear will be married to Mr Derby of Boston where they go immediately after a rather private ceremony, & that their projected trip to Europe is abandoned. The gentleman I saw this morning on his way to Kalorama—it is undoubtedly "une affaire arrangée."

Ellen will write you of news, which the ladies best gather—of the fashionables—of probable marriages &c among the young daughters of your old acquaintances &c.

Our mobocratic spirit is here quelled & I hope may never recur again. Of politicks I hear & meddle in little or none—To-day's newspapers have nothing in them of interest & we have no private rumours. In fact—we, at the Seat of Gov't. hear from abroad of measures & men before, it is noised here.

Richard has written you, as I know, & perhaps explained his plans—tho' I cannot believe he has formed any definite ones—Physic he dislikes—Law is averse to & as a merchant, my father is I believe unwilling he should commence life—He wants capital for a farmer. My plan is for him to study surveying, engineering &c. when perfected in it—to visit the west, under such auspices as he may be able to look out for in the mean time, & there invest such capital, in land, as he may scrape together—rise with the growth of the west & flourish with its strength.

A recent letter from my brother Thomas informs us of his intention to visit us about October—He writes in good spirits.

I am often disheartened—here having ⟨sacr⟩ificed years of my life, perhaps the most ⟨. . .⟩ I am not one iota advanced towards independence. Ellen urges me to no despondence—nor do I give way when I can possibly stem it—but rather wish to keep my attention turned to every chance of bettering my fortunes. I have so often repeated it, that, at length I come to the belief that "better times will come."

Will Uncle John go westward? my best wishes attend him—young & old, it almost seems we cannot get a start—give my love to him & his. I want Dolley or Lucy to write Ellen—that it may not be, we should speak more of Anna, who does write, than of others whom we love alike. I shall make up a package of books for them & you—"Richard of York"[1] Ellen speaks enthusiastically of—this I hope you have not already read, meaning to enclose it in a day or two, with some other work to be obtained from my library.

Ellen sends much love in which she will never fail—from her constant reference to your name in our private converse—I feel this. She speaks too of cousin Payne & bade me not forget him when I wrote, & remind him of her promised autographs from ⟨. . .⟩—his notes of invitation—letters &c—when in Europe. Remember me to him—& most affectionately to my honored uncle, on whose & your head may heaven dispense its blessings.

My sister D. has been staying for a few days past with Mrs Featherstone-haugh at her boarding house, in Georgetown—& all are well at home.

I do not know that it was of any consequence but I certainly was negligent in regard to Hayman—the day after the receipt of your last letter I met him in the street & told him to send his bill, as I was led to pay it—he did not do so & I have had to go after him—The Ale has always been charged to me—as you will see by the inclosed rect. I have written such a letter as to ask of you to learn it, reserving many things to write of hereafter—tho' I cannot but repeat the substance of my previous communications—*We are barely vegetating.* With all love yr Nephew,

J. M. Cutts

RC (NHi: Misc. Mss). Docketed by DPM. Damaged by removal of seal.
1. *Richard of York; or, "The White Rose of England,"* by Caroline S. Norton (1808–1877), was published in London in 1832 and in New York in 1835.

To Richard D. Cutts

My dear Richard   23d Octr. 35.

I feel melancholy at the idea of your departure for a country so far from us as Kety! but I approve of it at the same time—and so does your Uncle, believing that you can push your fortunes, in that quarter more surely & with more expedition than in this. Your reasons for going too, are the best—pray write me fully when ever you can, and let me hope to see you soon return to us, rich, and as good as you are now. May the blessings of Heaven be showered upon you! Your affectionate friend & Aunt

D. P Madison

Please say to your dear Sisters that I wrote to them last week, & will soon do so again.

RC (owned by Charles E. Feinberg, Detroit, Mich., 1961); Tr (MCR-S: Mary Estelle Elizabeth Cutts Papers).

To Lucy Payne Washington Todd

Beloved Sister   Octor. 23d. 1835.

This will I hope be handed to you by our Nephew Richard D. Cutts, to whom you are in some measure a stranger, not having seen him since his infancy—Those who know him best, can tell you, that he is an honor to his relations and to himself. He has conducted himself through his short life, with propriety in all respects, and his heart is made up of the sterling virtues. This brief account, I know will gratify you, and induce you to shew him the kindness of an affectionate aunt, as you are.

I have now a house full of visitors and dear Richard begins his journey so soon, that I can only add a world of love to you & yours, from Mr. Madison—who joins me in this recommendation.

I have received your letter of the 10th. and will soon answer it fully. Your own & ever

D. P Madison

RC (MCR-S: Mary Estelle Elizabeth Cutts Papers). Addressed to Mrs. Todd at Frankfort, Ky.

To Mary E. E. Cutts

Octor. [1835]

I had indeed waited with impatience for an acknowledgement of my letter & 45$ by Mrs. R. or rather by Mrs. Cooledge who knew the money was Enclosed as she read it on the outside—but 'tis past & safe in your hands. Now dearest I must call your attention to a few points after congratulating Madisons Ellen on the birth of their fine daughter, with my best wishes for their all doing well, so tell them, both from me. In the first place—I *fear* that you have not given Mrs. Smith the extract of a letter I wrote my sister, finished, the day of the destruction of the Ps. House. If you have lost it, or omitted to give it to her, it *will be* much to my injury, as the original is nearly torn to *bits* by the mice with several others, describing what followed—2d. did you rece. the residue of my letters to you & Dolley & lend them to Mrs. Smith for her perusal? I *pray* you to do these things. You do not tell me whether Mr. Trist has gone, or not, to Cuba, or what has become of the Grymes's—the last went on to N. York instead of coming here. I want to know every thing of the Randolph family that you can possibly tell me. Whether Lewis is to be married, or any others of them—I love them very much & feel that sort of interest in them, that seeks to know all is well with each individual. To Dolley I wrote last & will write again—tell her so with my love—She & yourself must send a small rect. to please your Uncle for the Interest by Mr R. He was anxious to pay you the Principle but the sale he made of his Negroes who wanted to go with Taylor, did not enable him to do so, & fell short of paying—several thousand dollrs.—so that he still talks of the last resort, "the *House in Washington.*" By mistake you did not rece 5 gallons of very large chesnuts I put up for you—A Hack Man took them else where, which I regretted as I picked them from bushels of others to give you the largest—Sucky had nothing to do with any of them I assure you—Arora will soon write—Your Aunt L. remarks on the youth of the lovers, but likes it very much—still I am of opinion that changes may take place in Anna's mind, on the subject—she thinks nothing about it now—You will hasten to write me abt. the *letters for Mrs. S. & what she says.* I am miserable to think that I have not written to her, & know not when I can do so—love to her & dr Mrs. Lear. Did you ask Mrs Lear if she got my letter. I told you of Mrs. Featherstons which I answered. Please to look around you & tell me all you *see*—Dolley too—If you could find an oppty. to send me a whole peice of pritty 12½ cent calico—I wd. pay for it directly—It wd. be to cover *those* who want it sadly—Now burn this, & all like it—In greater haste than ever—Your Uncle is very poorly—Your own & ever—The persons you enquire after are well & good for nothing.

Tr (MCR-S: Mary Estelle Elizabeth Cutts Papers).

Washington Widow

1836-1849

IN THE IMMEDIATE AFTERMATH OF HER HUSBAND'S DEATH IN JUNE 1836, Dolley Madison gave "way to the grief and dejected spirit which could not at first be restrained." But some weeks later, surrounded by family and friends—Anna Payne, Mary Cutts, and Martha Jefferson Randolph and three of her daughters among them—she appeared to be "striving to be composed, if not cheerful, as Uncle Madison begged and entreated her to be."[1] Though hampered by rheumatism in her right arm and hand, which prevented her from writing, she began to attend to the formidable business of settling James Madison's estate, running the Montpelier plantation, and providing for the publication of her husband's papers.

James Madison's bequests—to his nieces and nephews, the College of New Jersey at Princeton, the University of Virginia, and the American Colonization Society—amounted to nearly $15,000. The payment of that sum depended on the proceeds of the publication of his papers, a project that he had been led to believe would garner at least $100,000, easily paying his bequests and also providing a comfortable income for his widow.[2] Clearly Dolley's first order of business was to pay the legacies and open negotiations with publishers in Philadelphia and New York.

Though she was without experience at this kind of task, Dolley did have friends and acquaintances on whom she could rely. From Montpelier a stream of letters flowed to Edward Coles, George Tucker, William Cabell Rives, Charles J. Ingersoll, and many others. All these men had experience in the publishing world or had contacts who could provide information about it. In addition, she set her brother, John C. Payne, to work at Montpelier supervising a number of secretaries engaged in making fair copies of James's manuscripts for publication, and she sent Payne Todd to Philadelphia and New York to negotiate with publishing houses on her behalf.[3] This last was a mistake, as almost anyone who knew Todd could have told her. James Kirke Paulding, a New York writer and friend of the Madisons, wrote to historian and editor Jared Sparks in September, asking for the "particulars of your agreement with the Publishers of the Washington Papers" in order to advise Payne Todd in his negotiations. As to Todd, Paulding went on, "if you are acquainted with him, you need not be told that he is the last man in the world to compass such a business."[4] By the fall of 1836, Payne Todd had been in touch with, and had alienated, the major publishers of Philadelphia and New York as well as a number of Dolley's friends.[5]

James Madison, with the help of his wife and brother-in-law, had spent a good deal of his retirement collecting, editing, and otherwise preparing his papers for publication after his death. His first priority had been to make public the notes he had taken during the Constitutional Convention of 1787, together with those made of the debates in the Confederation Congress of 1782, 1783, and 1787. To these notes he had added "selections" from his letters, "narrating the proceedings of that Body during the periods of his service in it." It was these three volumes that Dolley sought to publish privately, in both the United States and Great Britain.[6]

By early fall, however, it was clear that Dolley would not be able to make satisfactory arrangements with any publishing house. Those who had made offers—like John S. Littell of Philadelphia and the New England firm of Marsh, Capen, and Lyon—were small businesses with little or no record of successful publications. The only large firm that had made an offer, Harper and Brothers of New York, had done so on terms—half the risk, half the profits—unsuitable for Mrs. Madison's financial situation.

The prospect of a delay in or full stop to the publication of the papers plunged Dolley into a full physical and mental collapse. The accumulated stress of years of nursing her husband, his death, the unsuccessful struggle to find a publisher for his papers, the absence of Payne Todd and her anxieties about his well-being, all combined to bring her world to a stand. In

September she began to suffer from "a painful inflammation of the eyes, which brought on chills and fevers, and her general health became so bad and so enfeebled that she could not walk alone." What made it still worse, wrote Anna Payne, was "the consciousness that the world has expected the publication of the works, and the fear that her friends would consider their appearance tardy, after every effort having been made on her part to finish the copies for the press, and to obtain a responsible publisher having failed to prevent this appearance."[7]

It was all too much. For years Dolley Madison had been the pillar that supported her family, just as James had provided a secure foundation for her. It was to her that her sisters Anna and Lucy looked for financial and moral support during the crises of their lives. It was to her that her brother John looked to straighten out the various tangles in which he found himself. And it was to her that her son, Payne Todd, looked to bail him out of debtor's prison and provide a haven from creditors and the bottle. After James's death there was no one to whom she could turn, no one who would look out for her in any real sense, except her niece Anna Payne, whose kind ministrations could only go so far. The important decisions—business decisions—had to be made by her alone.

That fall, with Payne Todd incommunicado in New York or Philadelphia, John C. Payne writing of his desire to leave Virginia for the free soil of Illinois, and herself sick in both body and soul, Dolley eagerly grasped an idea floated by her friends in Washington to sell the first three manuscript volumes to Congress. Various plans were projected and discussed over the succeeding months of greater or lesser advantage to her, but by the end of March 1837, Congress had passed a bill purchasing these three volumes of James Madison's manuscripts for $30,000. The volumes were published in 1840 under the direction of Henry D. Gilpin, solicitor of the U.S. Treasury and later attorney general of the United States.[8]

Once Dolley had agreed to the congressional plan in early January 1837, her health slowly began to improve. With the exception of the condition of her eyes, which continued to flare up at times, and the usual bouts of fever and influenza that were common to all in this period, Dolley enjoyed relatively robust health until the end of her life. She began once again to handle her own correspondence and immediately took steps to pay James's bequests, which were all fulfilled within the next few months.[9]

With that difficult business finished, Dolley began to give thought to how she might best organize her life. As she took stock of her situation, she may well have looked back to happier times—her Washington years—and thought of how she might recapture them. She had always enjoyed her summer vacations at Montpelier and the gay social season during the Washington winters. And so began the pattern of her widowhood. After a two-week stay at White Sulphur Springs in Bath County, Virginia, in August, she made arrangements to move back to her house on President's Square in Washington, where by November 1837 she was happily settled.[10]

That winter Dolley Madison was swept along in the tide of Washington society as if she had never stepped outside its current. She made sixty-five social visits in December 1837 alone and quickly became a fixture at parties, teas, and balls. She dined at the homes and messes of the prominent—twice at the White House at the invitation of President Van Buren, at Henry Clay's mess, at the Poinsetts', and at the Van Nesses', among many others.[11] The next winter, after she spent a late summer and early fall at Montpelier, continued much the same.

Any rough measure of Dolley Madison's status in Washington society would have to take into consideration the many letters she received requesting help in obtaining government appointments, the flood of letters she received from all over the United States asking for her autograph, and the petitions from aspiring poets, playwrights, and novelists for permission to dedicate volumes to her. "I have now more letters piled upon my table than I can answer," she wrote one winter's day in 1842, "and more engagements at home and abroad that I can perform."[12] While these requests clearly placed demands on her time and energy, they also testified to the fact that she mattered—that she had become a fixture of Washington life. No doubt a good deal of respect attached to her as the relict of James Madison, but there were many who remembered or had heard stories of her own celebrity.

Something of Dolley Madison's manner and enjoyment of life at this time can be gleaned from a description by William Kemble of a dinner party given by the Pauldings in January 1839. Kemble sat next to Dolley at table and reported, "The old lady is a very hearty, good looking woman of about 75.— Soon after we were seated, we became on the most friendly terms & I paid her the same attentions I should have done a girl of 15—which seemed to suit her fancy very well and after eating about 20 plates—each with the smallest slice of something on it & drinking as many glasses of wine, the company rose & we adjourned to the drawing room for Coffee."[13] This was living in high style indeed.

Yet looming over such happy occasions was the prospect of harder times to come. The country had been mired in a depression since the spring of 1837, when a series of mercantile and banking failures triggered a credit squeeze and the suspension of specie payments at the banks.[14] With money tight, lenders called for the repayment of outstanding loans, while borrowers increasingly were unable to pay both interest and principle, or sometimes either. The already straitened circumstances of Virginia planters were further pinched as business slowdowns and unemployment dampened demand for agricultural products.

Dolley was caught in this credit squeeze, and it was a significant factor in her decision to remain at Montpelier during 1840 and 1841. Though she put a cheerful face on it, what kept her in Virginia was a lack of cash and, in particular, the "false promises of payment to me of considerable sums." She owed her niece Mary Cutts and the Bank of the Metropolis over $3,000 which she was unable to repay due to the delinquency of her debtors. By staying at Montpelier she could avoid the expenses of Washington and rent out her home there.[15] She could also pay stricter attention to the farming operation on the plantation, which had suffered in her absence.

Montpelier, never profitable during James's retirement, was now further reduced by land sales he had made in the years before his death. The same slave force that had worked four large farms was now concentrated in a smaller area, too numerous to be efficiently employed in raising tobacco and wheat. Moreover, in Dolley's absence, her overseer had taken advantage of her, working the property on his own behalf. While Dolley and her extensive "family" could exist on the produce from the farm, little or no cash was generated to pay taxes or the interest on an accumulating debt. Not only did she lack a reliable farm manager, but she was further burdened with the nursing of her sister Lucy, who had arrived in the summer of 1840 with "her health . . . broken by many afflictions." Lucy seems to have suffered a stroke, for after more than a year at Montpelier, Dolley reported that she was "improving in health and spirits—her memory too, and that almost lost faculty of expressing her thoughts." By the winter of 1841, Dolley described herself as "sick and overwhelmed with business," with little prospect of returning to Washington.[16]

Nor could she turn to her son, John Payne Todd, for any real help. He was, as he had always been, a drain on both her emotional and financial resources. She had always indulged him in his eccentricities and dissipations, providing him with money whenever he fell short, covering his debts, and welcoming him home when he finally ran out of cash. Her friends could see it, even if she was blind to the problem. After Congress bought her husband's papers in 1837, one friend worried that as Payne Todd's "intimates are the Blacklegs and Gamblers of Washington . . . this money will in all likelihood be lost to Mrs. Madison if he has any power over it."[17] Because Dolley often made Todd her agent in financial dealings, it is quite likely that as much of the balance remaining after the legacies had been paid was frittered away by him as was used for her support. By the winter of 1841, even Dolley must have realized that she was enabling Todd's irresponsible behavior, and she rewrote her will, placing all her assets in a trust and naming several close friends as trustees for Todd in the event of her death. The new will also provided some incentives for Todd to marry and start a family. But Dolley's desperate and transparent effort to change his life was unsuccessful.[18]

For the moment, Dolley needed cash. Casting about for assets she might convert, she considered a number of options. Land and slaves she had aplenty, but there were no buyers, or rather, no buyers to whom she would sell.[19] She considered a plan to rent out half of the Montpelier mansion and share the immediate grounds. But almost immediately she turned again to the idea of selling the second part of her husband's papers.

Her failure to publish the four additional volumes of papers James had collected and edited for that purpose came as a shock to Dolley. As early as the spring of 1837, after the sale to Congress of the first lot of papers had been consummated, Dolley had offered the second lot—two volumes of James's letters from before 1801, one volume of papers from the Washington years, and a fourth consisting of documents on constitutional topics—to various publishing houses. She finally arranged an option with Harper and Brothers in New York to print the four volumes, beginning with the fourth, the appearance of which she hoped would coincide with the congressional publication. But by 1840 that volume still had not appeared, and Dolley wrote to her nephew Richard: "The other volumes are in my hands still waiting a favorable opportunity to issue them such as a purchaser, or partner in the expensive business of publication, which many of my friends have advised me *not* to undertake, of myself. I may add that my anxiety to have all these writings before the public is intense, and has been so for the last two years but disappointing impediments have occured." By the spring of 1842, when Dolley visited New York, in part to check on its progress, the fourth volume was in page proofs; two years later the volume lacked only a preface and title page. Yet it never appeared.[20]

On Dolley's return from New York and Philadelphia in April—after making eighty-two social visits at the latter place alone—she consulted her friends about what she should do with the remaining Madison papers. President John Tyler advised her to sell the collection to Congress. This she determined to do, but she decided she needed to be in Washington to lobby for the measure.[21]

Affairs in Orange County pressed, however, and she returned to Virginia in September 1842.

For immediate cash and to pay taxes and at least the interest on her debts in Washington, Dolley had arranged a loan of $3,000 from John Jacob Astor before she left, giving as security her President's Square home. She also rented that house to Congressman James J. Roosevelt and his family to raise a little more cash. Back at Montpelier for the next year and still involved in a thicket of debt suits in Orange County court, she sold 750 acres to Henry W. Moncure, a Richmond merchant, in December 1842. With all these efforts she tried to bring order to her financial affairs, and with the help of her nephew William Temple Payne, she worked to bring order to the plantation. As she explained to her friend Judith Page Rives in the summer of 1843, on her return home, "finding my little Territory run *wild,* I became a reformer, and ere success crowned my *humble* attempt, I fell ill with Influenza, or violent cold, which lasted me two or three months. . . . I am now well, but must tell you, that I have not passed the enclosure of my lawn since I came back to it." [22]

Sometime in the summer of 1843, besieged by debt and unable any longer to shoulder the responsibilities of her plantation, Dolley opened negotiations with Henry W. Moncure for the conditional sale of Montpelier. For an unnamed sum she relinquished title to the house, land, slaves, animals, furniture, farm utensils, and other personal property. The condition was that she might repay the sum along with the amount of any improvements within five years and reclaim the property. Though she returned to Washington for good in December 1843, it took her until August 1844 to bring herself to execute the sale. As she wrote to Moncure, "No one I think, can appreciate my feeling of grief and dismay at the necessity of transferring to another a beloved home." [23]

And what of the Montpelier slave community, whose roots went back to James's grandfather Ambrose Madison's move to the piedmont in the 1720s? We can only imagine its collective "grief and dismay" at the change in ownership. To the chagrin of some, like Edward Coles, James Madison made no provision to free his slaves but willed them with his other property to Dolley. [24] In the summer of 1836, as Coles noted, "Reports had gotten around that she (Mrs. Madison) wished to sell many of them (her slaves) & every day or two (while I was at her house in Aug:) a Negro trader would make his appearance, & was permitted to examine the Negroes." "It was like the hawk among the pigeons." At that time, Dolley sold at least a few slaves to neighbors and connections; how many, we do not know. [25]

For the next several years the plantation was run by an overseer, with

Dolley intervening from time to time. By the summer of 1844, however, she faced a financial crisis that directly involved her slaves. In 1837, according to Anna Payne, Dolley had been coerced into signing an obligation to her brother-in-law William Madison for $2,000 that he claimed was owed him by James for settling the estate of their father.[26] This note, which William Madison never attempted to have paid, was included in the settlement of his estate when he died in 1843, and his executors filed suit against Dolley for its payment. When judgment was made against her in 1844, a number of her slaves were lodged in the Orange County jail to be sold for the note's payment. She countersued and effected a stay of the judgment, and at the same time she deeded over forty of her slaves to her son, Payne Todd. Thereafter, those slaves were divided between her home in Washington and his at Toddsberth; the rest of the slaves were deeded to Moncure with the Montpelier property.

The case of *Madison* v. *Madison* ran on for several years. In fact, it became John Payne Todd's lifework to represent Dolley and himself in various court suits for debt. No sum was too small to be pursued. "I have promised to make them suffer," he wrote his mother about his antagonists, "& I will redeem my pledge."[27] His life became a perpetual dun, as he begged loans in one quarter while fending off demands for repayment in another. In the years before the sale to Moncure was finalized, Todd pillaged the Montpelier mansion of books, furniture, manuscripts, and slaves to raise cash, taking off to Toddsberth what he could not sell immediately.

Some of this booty was, of course, meant to help support his mother, who also depended on borrowed funds while she waited for Congress to buy the second collection of her husband's papers. Though the plan was unsuccessful in the 1843–44 session, when it was first projected, and for several subsequent sessions, Congress finally bought the papers in May 1848, giving Dolley $5,000 outright and the income from $20,000 in trust. The news of the purchase, far from giving her ease, unleashed a flood of requests for Dolley to repay her debts, which by this time totaled nearly $11,000. Still strapped for cash, she began to make plans to sell valuable paintings and other furnishings by either raffle or auction.[28]

Yet even if her private affairs wore a grim cast, she turned a smiling face to the public, attending private parties and presidential receptions alike, enlivening with her presence the social scene of Washington. She became a regular worshiper at St. John's Episcopal Church, eventually being confirmed on 15 July 1845. In September of that year, she greeted the Surviving Defenders of September 1814, who marched by her home in commemoration of the Washington and Baltimore campaigns of 1814. Invited to participate in the laying of the cornerstone of the Washington Monument in July 1848, she watched from the White House the "immense audience" that attended. And she maintained the tradition of hosting an open-house reception on New Year's Day each year. Her old friends—Eliza Collins Lee and Frances D. Lear, among others—remained close and no doubt provided many evenings of pleasant recollection.[29]

By the spring of 1849, however, Dolley began "failing in strength & health." She fell into periods of sickness and a prolonged decline. In June she was visited by Payne Todd, who drew up a will that she signed in which she made him the executor of her estate and bequeathed all her possessions to him alone. On 8 July she was "forced by weakness and suffering" to take to her bed; the next day doctors were sent for. They dosed her with opium, and a stream of "devoted relatives & hosts of untiring friends" provided "comfort and solace" in her last hours. Among her visitors were her oldest friend, Eliza Collins Lee, and her nephew James Madison Cutts. Cutts drew up another will, one which divided Dolley's congressional trust equally between Payne Todd and Anna Payne. Having signed it, "she expired without a struggle or apparent pain, at a quarter past ten o'clock at night Thursday the 12th instant, at peace with her maker, & with all the world & it with her."[30]

Her funeral took place four days after her death. It was a state occasion. Hundreds of visitors paid respect to her remains at St. John's Episcopal Church, and following a service before an overflowing congregation, a procession began, led by the president of the United States and including members of his cabinet, Congress, and the diplomatic corps, judges of the federal courts, army and navy officers, and scores of "citizens and strangers." They took her body to be temporarily interred in a vault at the Congressional Cemetery. Three years later her niece Anna Payne and Anna's new husband, Dr. James H. Causten, removed the casket to a private vault, where it stayed until 1858, when they finally obtained permission to bury her next to her husband at Montpelier, the family estate she had been forced to sell in 1844.

Soon after John Payne Todd learned of his mother's last will, he began contesting it. Todd refused to share the $20,000 with his cousin and filed suit in court. The case was finally heard in the spring of 1850 and settled in Anna's favor. The two continued to battle over Dolley's remaining artifacts, including books and silverware, but with Dolley's burial at Montpelier, a measure of peace was achieved.

John Payne Todd died on a snowy, stormy day in January 1852, still profligate, still unmarried. In his will he manumitted his slaves, gave each $200, and left the residue of his estate to the American Colonization Society, but it is doubtful what came of these bequests, given his debt-ridden finances. Even the silver forks Anna Payne Causten had kept, then put into a bank for safe-keeping, were taken to pay debts owed by Payne Todd's estate. With the settlement of the estate, John C. Payne began making claims on his daughter's inheritance, but whether or not Anna distributed her money among her family there is no record. On 9 November 1852 Anna Payne Causten died too. Within three years of Mrs. Madison's death, all traces of the household on Lafayette Square were gone, her house's contents auctioned off and scattered, and her dependents dead.

1. Anna Payne to Frances D. Lear, 16 July 1836, DLC: J. Henley Smith Papers.

2. Will of James Madison, 19 April 1835, in Hunt, *Writings of Madison* 9:549–50; John C. Payne to William Cabell Rives, 14, 15, and 24 Dec. 1836, DLC: Rives Papers.

3. Anna Payne to Frances D. Lear, 16 July 1836, DLC: J. Henley Smith Papers; John C. Payne to George Tucker, 20 July 1836, DLC.

4. Paulding to Jared Sparks, 11 Sept. 1836, in Ralph M. Aderman, ed., *The Letters of James Kirke Paulding* (Madison, Wis., 1962), 182–83.

5. See George Tucker to DPM, 23 Aug. 1836, and Edward Coles to DPM, 7 Nov. 1836.

6. *PJM* 1:xvi–xviii; John C. Payne to Richard Rush, 21 Aug. 1836, DLC.

7. Anna Payne to Edward Coles, 23 Oct. 1836, NjP: Edward Coles Papers.

8. John C. Payne to John Payne Todd, 12 Oct. 1836, owned by Gary Hendershott, Little Rock, Ark., 1993; John C. Payne to Edward Coles, 28 Feb. 1837, NjP: Edward Coles Papers; John C. Payne to William Cabell Rives, 20 Oct. 1836, DLC: Rives Papers; DPM to Henry Clay, 8 Nov. 1836; *PJM* 1:xviii.

9. DPM to William Cabell Rives and Judith P. Rives, 4 April 1837; DPM to William Cabell Rives, 10 April 1837, DLC: Rives Papers.

10. DPM to Richard D. Cutts, October 1837; DPM to Frances D. Lear, 20 Nov. 1837, DLC: J. Henley Smith Papers.

11. List of dinners attended, November 1837–March 1838, and list of visits made, December 1837, DLC: DPM Papers.

12. DPM to Richard D. Cutts, 25 Feb. 1842, CoCCC. For requests for appointments, see DPM to Lucy H. Conway, 2 Feb. 1839, ViU, and Joel Poinsett to DPM, 28 March 1839, NHi; for autograph seekers, see letters to DPM from C. A. Davison, 18 Jan., Bushrod W. Herbert, 31 Jan., T. R. Beck Jones, 30 May, L. S. Thomas, 8 June, and Henry A. Brady, 18 Oct., 1842, DLC: DPM Papers; for a literary dedication to DPM, see William Emmons to DPM, 6 April 1838, ViHi.

13. William Kemble to William Kemble Jr., 26 Jan. 1839, in Aderman, *Letters of James Kirke Paulding,* 243 n. 1.

14. John Niven, *Martin Van Buren: The Romantic Age of American Politics* (Oxford, 1983), 412–24; Samuel Rezneck, "The Social History of an American Depression, 1837–1843," *American Historical Review* 40 (1935): 662–87.

15. DPM to Richard D. Cutts, 2 Feb. 1840, NjP: Crane Collection. DPM owed $1,500 to Mary Cutts and $1,600 to the Bank of the Metropolis (DPM to Richard D. Cutts, 2 Feb. 1840, to Richard Smith, 25 Dec. 1839). The Prestons rented the house on President's Square for $70 a month for a period during 1840–41 (see William C. Preston to DPM, 1 March 1840 and ca. January 1841 [NN]).

16. DPM to Frances D. Lear, 7 Feb. 1841, 25 Dec. 1840, to Edward Coles, 6 Sept. 1841, to Richard D. Cutts, 27 Feb. 1841.

17. George W. Featherstonehaugh to William Cabell Rives, 6 April 1837, DLC: Rives Papers.

18. Will of Dolley Payne Madison, 1 Feb. 1841.

19. DPM to Richard D. Cutts, 12 May 1840.

20. Ibid., 20 April 1840; *PJM* 1:xviii-xx.

21. Visits returned in Philadelphia, April 1842, DLC: DPM Papers; DPM to John Payne Todd, 1 Sept. 1842, to James K. Paulding, 10 Jan. 1844.

22. DPM to John Payne Todd, 1 Sept. 1842, to John Jacob Astor, 12 Sept. 1842; DPM to Cornelia Van Ness Roosevelt, 1 Jan. 1843, DLC: Misc. Manuscripts; Henry W. Moncure to DPM, 17 Dec. 1842; DPM to Judith Page Rives, 1 July 1843, DLC: Rives Papers.

23. Proposed indenture for the sale of Montpelier, 1843; DPM to Henry W. Moncure, 12 Aug. 1844.

24. For JM's views on slavery, see McCoy, *The Last of the Fathers,* 253–322.

25. Edward Coles to Sarah Coles Stevenson, 12 Nov. 1836, *WMQ,* 2d ser., 7 (1927): 108–9.

26. The depositions and correspondence in the case of *Madison* v. *Madison* are filed in DLC: DPM Papers.

27. John Payne Todd to DPM, 26 Nov. 1844, DLC: DPM Papers.

28. See, for example, William W. Corcoran to DPM, 17 June 1848, D. M. Trice to John Payne Todd, 19 Oct. 1848, Eloxins Simms to DPM, 7 Feb. 1849, William A. Borren to DPM, 9 March 1849, and list of debts compiled by DPM, June 1848, DLC: DPM Papers.

29. Certificate of confirmation, 15 July 1845, ibid.; Donald B. Cole and John J. McDonough, eds., *Benjamin Brown French: Witness to the Young Republic* (Hanover, N.H., 1989), 181; DPM to the Committee of Arrangements, 3 July 1848, DNA: RG 42, Washington National Monument Society; Herbert Weaver et al., eds., *Correspondence of James K. Polk* (9 vols. to date; Nashville, 1969—), 9:6.

30. James Madison Cutts to William Cabell Rives, 17 July 1849, DLC: Rives Papers; T. E. Mason to John Y. Mason, 19 July 1849, ViHi.

From Martha Jefferson Randolph

WASHINGTON July 1st. 1836

I heard yesterday, my very dear friend, of a misfortune, that I beleive we were both but too well prepared to expect. I would if possible be with you immediately, but shall be detained here some days by circumstances over which I have no control. Friday evening probably, I shall be at the Court House and if you can send your carriage for me next morning, Cornelia and myself will go to you, if however, you should have consented to withdraw yourself for a time from scenes of so much former happiness and present Sorrow, tell me frankly, my dear friend, and we will delay our visit until you return home. One line left at the Court House will inform me of your present plan and determine mine. God bless and support you dear friend, under your present affliction, prays yours most affectionately and unalterably

M. Randolph.

Tr (MCR-S: Mary Estelle Elizabeth Cutts Papers).

From Louisa Catherine Adams

WASHINGTON 2d July 1836

At a moment of deep interest to the whole American Nation, whose sympathies will be offered to you in the sincerity of deep regret; permit me, my dear Madam, to express the sentiment of respect, and veneration which I have ever entertainted [sic], for the departed, one of the *greatest men;* whose name will adorn the annals of his Country, in the proudest days of her existence, and deck the page of history with an honoured fame.

It is but a small tribute, offered by an humble individual to his living worth which will remain indelibly engraved on the hearts of a family, who knew him only to receive from him, and yourself, the unremitted proofs of personal kindness—all of whom unite with me in condolence with you on your recent bereavement; and request me to assure you of their profound regard, esteem, and gratitude through the medium of their Sister and your sympathizing friend

Louisa Catherine Adams

Draft (MHi: Adams Papers).

To Richard Cutts

MONTPELIER, July 5th, 1836.

I could never doubt your sympathy, dear brother, and require it much now. When can you come and see me? I hope it will be soon, relying on that hearty welcome always in store for you, and each one of your dear children, who have been ever as my own. . . .

I would write more, dear Richard, but have no power over my confused and oppressed mind to speak fully of the enduring goodness of my beloved husband. He left me many pledges of his confidence and love. Especially do I value all his writings. Adieu, with love,

Dolley P. Madison.

Printed copy (*Records of the Columbia Historical Society* 3 [1900]: 46).

From Andrew Jackson

Madam,   WASHINGTON, July 9th. 1836.

It appearing to have been the intention of Congress ⟨to⟩ make me the organ of assuring you of the profound respect ⟨en⟩tertained by both its branches for your person ⟨an⟩d character, and of their sincere condolence in the late afflicting dis⟨pe⟩nsation of Providence which has at once deprived you of ⟨a be⟩loved companion and your Country of one of its most ⟨valu⟩ed citizens; I perform that duty, by transmitting the ⟨senti⟩ments herewith enclosed.

No expression of my own sensibility at the loss ⟨sustai⟩ned by yourself and the Nation could add to the ⟨consola⟩tion to be derived from these high evidences of the ⟨Nation's⟩ sympathy. Be assured, Madam, that there is not ⟨one of⟩ our Countrymen who feels more poignantly the stroke ⟨that⟩ has fallen upon you, or who will cherish with a more ⟨endear⟩ing constancy the memory of the virtues, the services ⟨and th⟩e purity of the illustrious man whose glorious and ⟨patrioti⟩c life has been just terminated by a tranquil ⟨death.⟩ I have the honor to be, Madam, Your most Obedient Servant,

Andrew Jackson

RC (owned by Charles M. Storey, Boston, Mass., 1961); Tr (DNA: RG 59, ML). RC in a clerk's hand, signed by Jackson. Words and letters in angle brackets supplied from Tr.

To Eliza Collins Lee

My ever dear friend   MONTPELLIER July 26. 1836.

Your acceptable letter has been some days with me, tho' I had not the power to tell you how highly I valued your kind sympathy, and how much I needed it! Indeed I have been as one in a troubled dream since my irreparable loss of him, for whom my affection was perfect, as was his character and conduct thro' life—the remembrance of this arouses me at times, to a sense of what I owe to his wishes—that I should be calm, and strive to live long after him—that I should proceed to fulfil the trust he reposed in me, of many things—especially in finishing the little left to be done, in copying his writings before their publication. Accordingly I strive to give my mind to business, as far as my anxious friends will allow me, who have generally thought I ought first to recruit myself by riding every day; an exercise which I have not felt the want of; for the last four years. In thus speaking of myself, I feel that I leave a subject of infinite interest—but my spirit seems to appeal to you still, for that indulgence so kind—so uniformly extended to me from our early years—How shall I thank you beloved friend—May I not yet hope to see you here? to shew you how precious is the remembrance of those days—and the continuance to this, of your love and good opinion.

DP Madison

RC (DLC: DPM Papers). Addressed to Mrs. Lee at Buckland, Prince William County, Va.

To John Forsyth

MONTPELLIER August 20. 1836.

Mrs Madison has received the note of the Secretary of State dated July 8th. transmitting an act of the last session of Congress, giving her the franking privelege;[1] for which she returns the grateful acknowledgments due for this distinguished evidence of consideration for her lamented Husband so generously accorded to her. She highly appreciates the kind terms with which Mr. Forsyth accompanied the documents, and with her regard and esteem for him, she begs to offer her affectionate remembrance to Mrs. Meigs and Mrs. Forsyth.

Be pleased to deliver the enclosed to the President.[2]

RC (ViU).
    1. "An Act to extend the privilege of franking letters and packages to Dolly P. Madison," 2 July 1836, *U.S. Statutes at Large* 5:107.
    2. DPM to Andrew Jackson, 20 Aug. 1836.

To Andrew Jackson

[20 August 1836]

I received, Sir, in due time, the communication from Congress, made more grateful to me by the kind expression of your sympathy, which accompanied it.

The high and just estimation of my Husband, by my countrymen and friends, and their generous participation in the sorrow occasioned by our irretrievable loss (expressed through its supreme authoritys, and otherwise) is the only solace of which my heart is susceptible, on the departure of him who had never lost sight of that consistency, symmetry and beauty of character, in all its parts, which rendered his, transcendent as a whole, and worthy of the best aspirations.

I am now preparing to execute the trust his confidence reposed in me—that of placing before Congress and the World, what his pen had prepared for their use, and with the importance of this Legacy, I am deeply impressed. With great respect &c. &c.

D P Madison

Draft (DCHi). Docketed "1st. Rough Copy."

From George Tucker

My dear Madam,   PHILADELPHIA. Aug. 23. 1836

Your letter of the 4th. inst. having arrived at New york after I had left it, did not reach me until the 19th when I was on my return home. I however immediately called on the Harpers, and on sounding them, found that they would be very glad to publish the work, but were not inclined to make any specific bid for an edition of it—On pressing them however they stated, that is the only one of the partners I was able to see, that they would be willing to publish the book on your & their joint account—each party to bear half the expense, & to divide the profits—thus estimating their services in selling the work as equivalent to the authorship. I told them that the offer was less liberal than I thought it ought to be—and that the whole expense of printing &c. should be advanced by them—In reply they said that as the paper would be bought on 6 ms. credit most of the expense would be reimbursed before actual payment was required. I informed them that I would communicate their offer to you—without any expectation however that it would be acceded to—but should you approve of the terms you would so inform them. The cost per vol: of the book, in case you had it printed on your account would be about 80 cents per volume—The precise sum being greater or less according to the quality of the paper, style of printing & binding. They further requested that if you declined their proposal you would name the terms on which you would dispose of an edition of 4000 or 5000 copies. As I mentioned to you before—there is no bookseller who has either capital or credit but would gladly publish the work—and I think it is clearly in your power to obtain a fair price per copy, when I think the intrinsic value of the work will ensure a sale that will make it very profitable. It may not however be advisable for you to bargain with the person who makes the most liberal offer, for it is not an uncommon thing for booksellers to make contracts which they are not able to comply with, & in some cases, which they never meant to comply with at the moment they were made. Were it my case I would endeavour to limit my negotiations to those who were of fair character & in responsible circumstances.

On the day that I had the pleasure of writing you before, I accidentelly met with Mr. Todd, in the street, and on my mentioning that I had written to you on the subject, as I had promised, he informed me that he had come on for the purpose of ascertaining the views of booksellers with regard to the work— and as he had no further communication with me on the subject, I thought that any further efforts on my part were unnecessary, & my continued inquiries were consequently suspended, until I received your letter. I regret that the neccessity for my immediate return to this place prevented me from communicating with other booksellers, for I was of opinion that the price for which the book could be extensively sold would enable the bookseller to give you a dollar a volume for any edition he chose to publish—and I am still of that opinion, if the work does not exceed 2 vols.—but the greater the no. of volumes the smaller will be the no. of copies sold. Would it not be better to publish the volume you propose to add separately? *Most* people who bought the debates, would like also to buy the other—yet some might like to buy one & not the other—besides there are not a few who will lay out six dollars in a book who will hesitate, & at last delay laying out 9$. It would be far better for you to take 75 cents a vol: for each copy printed than to *accept the ⟨demode?⟩ offer of the Harpers.* Perhaps your best course would be to authorize some person—*Mr Payne for instance*—to write to such booksellers as you have confidence in—with a specific offer—say one dollar a volume for an edition not less than 4000 or 5000, and as many more as he pleases—and if none of them accept this offer, you will be able to learn from their answers who you can most advantageously bargain with. Mrs Tucker offers her respects & best wishes in which she is cordially joined by your obedt. Servant

George Tucker

RC (NN: James Madison Papers). Docketed by DPM.

To Charles J. Ingersoll

MONTPELLIER Augt. 29th. 1836.
I ought long since dear Sir, to have acknowleged your valued letter of July 31t.[1] and I hope you will pardon an omission arising from many causes—

the first of which was a constant attention to the preparation of Manuscripts, which you are aware should be soon published—and which tho' left in a perfect state for the press, requires the vigilant care of one whose highest aspiration is to fulfil the sacred trust by judicious selections.

You have analyzed truly my grief on the bereavement I have suffered, and you apply to it the purest source of consolation in the remembrance "of a just man gradually and with all his bright mind unclouded to the last, in the course of nature made perfect."

As a proof of Mr Madison's personal feelings towards yourself as well as the interest he took in the subject of the enclosed,[2] he had it copied for your use, but the omission to send it arose from the appropriate time having passed, as it should have gone with a letter to you which it was better adapted to accompany than to have been sent in a more isolated manner. The original appears to have been intended for the press at the period it was written, but it was not published, nor the reference filled up. It is now given, more as a memento of a friendly intention than an expectation of present usefulness.

Should you travel into Virginia I hope you will perform your promise of a visit to Montpellier and be assured of the great pleasure it would afford me to see you—and Miss Ingersoll, to whom I offer as well as to yourself sincere regard and respect.

May I ask the favor of you to ascertain and to apprize me confidentially of the character of Mr. John S. Littell as to his capacity and integrity.[3] This liberty finds its apology in my want of sufficient acquaintance with this gentleman to enable me to decide on a proposition he has made to become the publisher of Mr. Madison's writings. He proposes to advance the necessary funds for stereotyping them and after deducting the expences, paying over to me the profits, at intervals of three or six months—and undertaking the superintendence of every thing connected with the execution of the whole business for a compensation of 10 p cent.

D P Madison

RC (PHi).

1. Ingersoll had made a visit to Montpelier in May 1836. His letter of condolence is at the New York Public Library.

2. Document not identified, but it is likely to have been a copy of JM's "Autobiography," a short sketch of his life JM wrote for James Kirke Paulding sometime in 1831. Paulding had intended to write a biography of JM (Charles J. Ingersoll to DPM, 9 June 1836, NN; Douglass Adair, ed., "James Madison's Autobiography," WMQ, 3d ser., 2 [1945]: 191–209).

3. Ingersoll answered DPM's request on 2 Sept., describing Littell as "a man of good character but not of good circumstances" (ViU).

To Ann Maury

My dear friend,   MONTPELLIER Sept: 7th. 1836.

I intended to have answered fully your letter of July 2d., but urgent demands on my attention at the moment deprived me of the pleasure, and when your second arrived I was confined with a painful inflammation of my eyes, and I am even now compelled to employ the pen of my niece as I continue unable to use my own longer than to sign my name. Allow me, with Anna's pen to express my gratitude for the contents of both. In the first you offer that sympathy so precious which I knew you would extend to me when I required it so much; and in your last, sweet friend there is a tempting proposal. I have not anticipated the necessity of being in New York, but should it prove so it would be but for a short visit during which time I should delight in seeing as much of you and your dear father as might be in my power.

My Son has not yet entered into an engagement for me with any of the publishers, and I am so distant from the scene of business that I cannot understand which of them are disposed to make the most reasonable arrangements. I hope soon however to have from him and others information that may allay my anxiety on this subject. The writings left me by my lamented husband engross my attention. I have been engaged with others in copying and preparing them for the press, and my aspirations for the fulfilment of his wishes are supported against the difficulties to be encountered by a conciousness of their importance. I can only add to this imperfect letter my constant affection.

D P Madison

RC (ViU). In Anna Payne's hand, signed by DPM.

To the Beneficiaries of James Madison

Sir,   MONTPELLIER Oct: 4th: 1836

By the will of Mr. Madison his widow is directed to deposit $9000 in the Bank of Virginia within three years after his death "to be equally divided between all my nephews and nieces which shall at that time be living, and in case of any of them being dead leaving issue at that time living then such issue shall take the place of its or their deceased parent."

As one of the legatees under this clause of Mr. Madison's will you are hereby

WASHINGTON WIDOW, 1836–1849

notified that the deposite has been made, and the Bank having declined the task of distribution I will as Executrix check for the separate amounts due; but a question having arisen among some of the legatees as to the construction of the clause I will as legally advised limit the amount to be paid to each to the share produced by a division of the whole sum among the 31 nephews and nieces including those not living and those who are dead leaving issue now living; but the payments to the latter will be suspended until the decision of the Chancery Court is had whether they are entitled to the money or not, and measures have been taken to obtain it.

When personal application for the check is inconvenient it should be made by formal power of Attorney, legally authenticated.

Be pleased to acknowledge the receipt of this.

Tr (DLC). Marked "(Copy.)" and "(Circular)." In an unidentified hand.

To Ann Maury

MONTPELLIER October 9th. 1836.

I wish indeed I was with you in New York dear Cousin, where my Son had pressed me to come before this distressing malady of the eyes had arrived at such a degree as to make it impossible—he continues to send the advice of your best occulists, with books and engravings on the subject to instruct my Doctor's here. I can only write my name yet—the pain from the inflamed eyes and lids calls for continual bathing with milk & water—sassafras tea &c. thereby I derive the only ease that I can experience. Our physicians have applied leeches and blisters—given some little medecine and now and then a more decided lotion, but the affliction continues, not quite so bad as two or three weeks ago. My general health has suffered much since I wrote you, it forbids me even to think of a shorter journey I intended taking as far as Washington on the affair I mentioned.

I do not propose yielding to the propositions of the *New Yorker,* or any other for half the expense, and half the profits [1]—and fear that all must be delayed until I am well enough to follow your excellent advice of having a voice, and view, for myself in my all important business.

I thank you many times as well as your dear father for the kind feelings you extend to me, and for your valued invitation. Should I ever be with you my little Anna would be by my side in every position, as she is now writing for me to you, which she will soon do again to tell you how I progress. She adds to mine, hers and Dolley's constant love for you.

D P Madison

RC (ViU). In the hand of Anna Payne, signed by DPM.
    1. This was probably the offer of Harper and Brothers (see George Tucker to DPM, 23 Aug. 1836).

From Edward Coles

My dear Cousin: PHILADELPHIA Nov: 7. 1836.
    While in Virginia I recd. information which led me to fear that a draft for about $2000. which had been sent me by mail from St. Louis had been lost on the way or in the Post-office here; and I also recd. notice about the same time that the Girard House, which I had applied to rent, and which was to have been finished in October, would not be finished until January, but I was called on to say whether I would take it or not; and I was further informed that it was very difficult to procure a House in the City on any terms. These two circumstances made it necessary for us to hasten back here as soon as possible. I am happy to say I have since received my money from St. Louis; but I regret to say I have not had equal good luck in procuring a house. The plastering of some of the Girard Houses is not even yet completed, and there is no hope of any of them being finished sooner than Jany: certainly, & more probable Feb:[1] Mrs. Coles situation, the difficulties & inconveniences attending buying furniture & getting fixed in mid winter, the disagreeableness & hazard of removing to a damp & freshly painted house, and the impossibility of procuring comfortable apartments in an agreeable boarding house where we could remain until we could move to our new house, all conspired to make us do all we could to procure another and more suitable House. I have been incessantly imployed every day since I returned looking for a house but without success—and I now almost despair of it. No one can recollect the time when houses were so scarce, & so much in demand, & when they commanded such high prices. But for Mrs. C. expecting to be confined early in the spring, I should leave this City & seek lodging in some place where there was more room. As it is I fear we shall be compelled to wait for the Girard house, & encounter all the inconvenience & danger from removing in mid winter to a newly finished residence. I am still however making a daily tour around the City in every direction, in search of a house. I am the more impatient as we have gotten into a private boarding house where our dear little Mary & her

nurse sleep two stories above us in not a very spacious or suitable room. But for this we should be quite agreeably lodged.

I was much concerned to hear from Cousin Anna's letter (which was not recd. until long after its date, in consequence of the negligent Post Master here having sent it *back* to Va.) how much you had suffered. I had not been aware that you had suffered from any other cause but sore eyes, & was therefore the more surprised & concerned to learn that you had been so very unwell. Before I left you you were suffering from your eyes, & I had supposed they had become worse, but had no idea of your having had "chills & fevers," & had been so much afflicted & had been so reduced as Cousin Anna describes. If I had known you were so very unwell I should have run the further risk of losing my money & my house, by stoping for a day at the Court house, & paying you a visit. But as it was, not knowing of your being more afflicted than with sore eyes, & thinking it very important to save my money & house by hurrying on here as soon as I could, I not only passed you, but traveled the whole (except from 10 to 2 oclock) of one of the darkest & most rainy & stormy nights I ever experienced, at the great risk of our lives over one of the worse roads I ever traveled. It was indeed a most disagreeable night, & we ran great risk, as well of taking cold as of upsetting, and deemed ourselves most fortunate in escaping both, & reaching this safe & well. As the traveling on that route was then arranged we reached Washington at 7 at night, & must leave that at 2 in the morning, or 3½ oclock in the afternoon. The former we were too much fatigued to do — so next day we employed ourselves by paying my Taxes — looking at my Lots — & visiting the Cutt's — with whom we set an hour & found them busy preparing for your reception — reached Baltimore that night, & the next evening this place.

Soon after my return from Va. I called on Messrs. Carey & Lea — the former was in Jersey, the latter & myself had a long conversation, in which I found they had not answered your communication, and were evidently estranged, if not displeased, by what had passed between them & Mr. Tucker, & what they had been informed Payne had been doing in New York. Mr. Lea said they had been at first willing to have undertaken the publication, but they were not now. He said they had told Mr. Tucker every thing very frankly; and after what had passed between them he seemed not to like what they had heard Payne had been doing in N.Y. — & then on the back of all the receipt of your *"Circular."*[2] He called it screwing, to get the proposals of one Bookseller & then going to another & seeing if a better bargain could not be gotten out of him — of inducing one to bid against the other — that you had too exalted an idea of the value of the publication — that you would be disappointed & would probably blame the publisher &c &c &c. I said all I could to explain your conduct, & to remove his impressions, & to induce him to reply to your communication—which he promised to do. As the impressions left on my mind were not agreeable, I lost no time in seeing Mr. Carey on his return to the City, & was sorry to find his impressions and views were very similar to those of Mr. Lea—I soon after saw them a 2d time & repeated my enquiry about his answer to you, & my desire that they would make it as soon as they could— which they again promised. On the receipt of your Brother Johns letter of Nov: 2, which came to hand on Saturday (the day before yesterday) I called again on Messrs. Carey & Lea, found them both alone, & had a long talk with them, and could not avoid feeling a little nettled at hearing them repeat the same language. I could not understand exactly what they had heard Payne had been doing. Lea said "Mr Todds proposition to McCarvell was the strangest one that had ever been made"—he seemed to catch himself, & waved telling me what it was. In this conversation I repeated & enlarged on my former remarks explanatory of your conduct, told them I had advised the circular, contended, as I conceived in an unanswerable manner, that your course had been correct, & insisted that they were bound as Gentlemen to reply respectfully to your communication. If they did not choose to undertake the publication say so—if they thought proper to make any suggestions or give any advice do so. They expressed a wish that I would make some suggestions *as coming from them,* I said no when you have your pen in hand make them yourselves. I must confess I cannot understand the conduct of Messrs. Carey & Lea. They certainly must be very strange men, or they must have been grossly misinformed, or I am very ignorant of the subject— of what has been done, and what ought to have been done. I was so positive that my advise about the *Circular* was correct, & so anxious to remove all wrong impressions on that subject, that I took to the "Wistar party"[3] on Saturday night, where I expected to meet Carey & Lea, Mr. Sparks letter to me in which he advises, that "proposals should be sent to the principal publishers in Phila. New York & Boston & get their terms—then close with the best offer"—that he had consulted with Judge Story whose "sentiments accorded entirely with those which I (Sparks) have above expressed." In showing this letter to Mr. Lea (Mr. Carey was not there) I observed I was anxious to remove from him the least remnant of an idea that there had been in the course you had pursued any dispostion to jew, screw, or make a hard bargain—but that you had acted as you had been advised, not only by me, but by men of far more experience, such men as Sparks, Story, Rives, Tucker & others. Sparks letter evidently made a salutary impression on him. He said he should write you on Monday (this day) and expressed regret at its having been so long delayed. These details perhaps were not worth giving to you. But as there appears to me to be some mystery about Carey & Leas conduct, I thought it was possible it might be best to give them to you, as you might understand the matter better than I do. Carey & Lea do not seem to me to have treated you well, but I would not notice them, or worry myself about them. I am satisfied there are others who will do your business on more reasonable & accommodating terms.

If I were you I should still continue my efforts and endeavour to have published as soon as I could a specified number of copies for individual distribution—reserving the right of supplying Congress & the State Legislatures with as many copies as they wanted. The more I hear & the more I reflect on the subject the more I am convinced your best plan is to contract for a specified number—say 5 or 10 thousand—at so much, say one dollar per volume. This I believe can be done without difficulty, if not here, certainly in New York & Boston—the latter I suspect would be the best place, & the publishers of Washingtons papers the best persons.

Immediately on receiving Cousin Johns letter on Saturday, I turned out & took the rounds, & enquired at some 10 or 12 public houses where I thought it was most likely I should hear of your Son, if he were in the City; and also called on several persons who I thought would be most likely to have seen or heard of him—And I also renewed my enquiries that night at the Wistar party—but I could hear nothing of him, & am led to believe he is not here, nor has not passed through this city. I shall be particularly gratified to see him, not only to hear what he has been doing in N.Y., but to impart to him information about Harris which may be of value to him. When you write to him let him know I am in a Boarding house (Mrs. Prevost) No. 215 Walnut Street.

My thanks are especially due to my sweet young Cousin Anna for the letter which she address[ed] to me for you. It is a letter which does her great credit, & shows she has been more industrious, & made more proficiency in her education than most young Ladies of her age.

My last letter from my sister Stevenson was dated Sep: 6. They were both well. She informed me she had written to you, & that Mr. S. would write you soon about the publication of Mr. Madisons papers, in reply to my letter from Newport. I hope you may have recd. it.

My Wife & child are enjoying their usual good health. Mine has become much better, & I am much cheered by finding the cold weather does me no harm—on the contrary cold *dry* weather seems to agree with me best. If we could only get fixed in a dry comfortable House we should feel greatly relieved.

I fear you will consider me a bad correspondent for one who has weak eyes. But I could not well write you a shorter letter, & hope that you have been prudent enough to get Cousin Anna to read this to you. I trust you will soon be well, and be able to reach Washington before the cold weather sets in. I pray you may have good weather for your journey, & find the road to Fredburg. in better order than we did. I forgot to mention in the proper place, as a further reason for passing you without stoping even for a day, was the great number of travellers that were then on the road, wh: made it necessary for us to take in common with others an extra stage in Charlottesville, which if we had stoped at Orange C. H. we might & probable [*sic*] would have been detained some days before we could again procure *three* seats to Fredericksburg.

With our prayers for your speedy restoration to your wonted health, we add the assurances of our unalterable regard—& good wishes to you & all under your roof

Ed: Coles

RC (PHi). Docketed by DPM.

1. Before his death in 1831, Stephen Girard had begun to build homes and stores in the Chestnut-Market Streets square. The twenty houses on the south side of Girard Street were completed in December 1835; those on the north side were not finished until 1838 (McMaster, *Life and Times of Stephen Girard* 2:460–61).

2. A draft of a circular offering JM's writings for publication is in DLC: Madison Papers, with this notation: "(Original of intended Circular) not sent but one from Littell's letters made out & sent Sept. 1836."

3. The "Wistar party" was an intellectual salon begun by Dr. Caspar Wistar in 1800 and continued by the Wistar Association after his death in 1818 (Nicholas B. Wainwright, ed., *A Philadelphia Perspective: The Diary of Sidney George Fisher, 1834–1871* [Philadelphia, 1967], 10 n. 3).

To Henry Clay

MONTPELLIER Nov: 8th. 1836.

The continued and very severe affection [*sic*] of my eyes not permitting but with much difficulty even the signature of my name, has deferred, dear friend, the acknowledgments due for your very kind and acceptable letter of August 18th. I should sooner have resorted for this purpose to the pen of an amanuensis but that the failure of my general health combining equal, and sometimes greater suffering, rendered dictation very painful, and hope still flattered me that I might yet use my own. So much time however having elapsed with but little improvement in my situation, I can submit to no longer delay in offering this explanation of my silence; nor omit the expression of my deep sensibility to that pure and true sympathy which I am conscious I receive from such highly valued friends as Mrs: Clay and yourself.

The sources of consolation in my bereavement which you suggest, are those which my heart can most truly appreciate. The reflected rays of his virtues still linger around me, and my mind now dwells with calmer feelings on their mellowed tints. He left me too a charge, dear and sacred; and deeply impressed with its value to his fame, and its usefulness to his country, the important trust ⟨has⟩ sustained me under the heavy pressure of recent loss, and formed an oasis to the desert it created in my feelings.

In fulfilment of his wishes I have therefore devoted myself to the object of having prepared for the press the productions of his own pen—it will form the surest evidence of his claim to the gratitude of his country and the world.

With the aid of my brother who had prepared copies of the Debates in the Revolutionary Congress and in the Convention under Mr. Madison's eye, triplicates have been completed for publication here and abroad. My Son went in July as far as New-York and remained there for the purpose of negotiating with the most eminent publishers, and I have had communication with those in other Cities, but no offer has been made by any entitled to confidence, which would free me from heavy and inconvenient pecuniary advances and the risk of impositions and eventual loss. Under these circumstances I have been advised by a friend to offer the work to the patronage of Congress[1] asking their aid so far as to relieve the work from the charges upon it, principally for literary and other benevolent purposes, and, after their use by Congress, to give me the stereotype plates. This would at once allow me to throw them into general circulation on a scale that would remunerate me more in accordance with the expectations entertained by their author, and would also allow the price to be so graduated as to ensure their general diffusion.

As this plan was suggested by one favorable to the administration he advised also that the channel of his friends, as the majority of those who were to decide on the proposition, should be employed in making it, and pledged their support. This work being a record only of what passed preceding the existence of present parties, cannot associate the name of Mr: Madison with either, and therefore its introduction and advocacy by the one can be no bar to the favor of the other. On your part, I am sure that, in my yielding to it this direction, you will perceive no deviation from the high respect and friendly regard I entertain towards yourself; but approving an adoption of this course, as most conducive to success, you will, with your friends, ensure it on the merits of the work alone, uninfluenced by adversary feelings towards the source from whence the measure originated.

It was my intention to have gone to Washington principally with a view to obtain in personal conference the advice of my best friends, but my protracted ill health and the approach of an inclement season I fear may prevent the journey.

In addition to the three volumes of Debates (near 600 pages each), now ready for the press, matter enough for another volume is expected, and nearly 400 pages copied, of writings and letters on Constitutional subjects—considerable selections have also been made from his early correspondence which may form a volume on the legislative proceedings of Virginia and historical letters of the period from 1780 up to the commencement of the new Government. His Congressional and Executive career may furnish two more. His writings already in print as "Political observations" a pamphlet in 1795, "Examination of the British doctrine" &c. it is thought should be embodied with his other works for more permanent preservation.

It is important that these manuscripts should be prepared and committed to the press as early as they can follow the Debates, and the success of the latter will much facilitate the publication of the former, even if Congress should decline a like patronage to them, a mode which would be much preferred.

The near approach of the time which will call you to your senatorial duties rendering it uncertain whether this would reach you ere your departure from home, I deem it safest to address it to Washington, whence I hope, on your safe arrival, you will favor me with an acknowledgment of its receipt and any suggestions your friendship may offer.

Accept for Mrs. Clay and yourself my affectionate respects.

D P Madison

RC (IU); draft (DLC). RC in the hand of Anna Payne, signed by DPM.

1. Nicholas P. Trist was one of several friends to propose that DPM offer to sell JM's papers to Congress. For his plan, see his letters to DPM, 27 Sept. and 12 Oct. 1836, ViHi.

To Edward Coles

MONTPELLIER Jany. 7th. 1837

How shall I thank you my best cousin for all you have done to alleviate my sufferings? as well as for your care in representing them to our dear Doctor Physic. How I wish that I could be set down at his gate, where I might have the consolation of seeing one whom I have long regarded so much, as well as to receive the benefit of his observation, which I am persuaded would relieve the most distressing malady I ever experienced—he enquires whether the inside of the lids of my eyes are inflamed.[1] I cannot doubt it from the feeling of heat and itching, allayed for the moment only by the application of milk and water or cream, and sometimes with fresh butter.

There is still ¼ of the ointment left which I have had mixed with fresh lard and will use it as directed. At present the soreness is so much increased by it that I have paused in its use till it is lessened, as well as to recover the strength of my sight, which has been considerably weakened within a few days past. The discharge has increased and seems equally thick and difficult to free itself, and a slight sensation of twisting interior to the muscles of the upper lids occasionally returns, which attended, in a greater degree, the previous use of the ointment. The lids and around them seem a little swollen, more so since the use of the ointment, and a soreness to the touch has accompanied it. My diet is abstemious tho' not equally so with the rule first observed which was considered by my physicians too rigid. It is seldom that I resort to medecine. They have not attempted to examine the internal surface of the lids, possibly from the pain which exposing them would occasion, and therefore I judge only by the sensation—the outer sides, particularly of the lower lids, have always had an excoriated streak, attributed to the acridness of the discharge coming in contact with them to a distance which partook of the inflammation—it is narrow and no other external inflammation has shewn itself on them—Some of the eye-lashes came out but a fresh growth has succeeded.

I hastened to prepare the Elder water, and will tell you the effects of it in my next—I will also strive to cherish patience and resignation, so properly recommended to me.

I seldom see the Doctors who I employed—and cannot say much of their present opinions, and as it is distressing for me to dictate a letter I must salute Dr. Physic, yourself and cousin Sally with every affectionate wish & remembrance.

D P Madison

RC (NjP).

1. While diagnosis of medical conditions across the centuries is fraught with uncertainty, DPM's eye problems might have been a case of severe chronic blepharitis, that is, a chronic inflammation of the eyelids, which even today is difficult to treat (note from Brian P. Conway, Professor and Chair, Department of Opthalmology, University of Virginia Medical School, to the editors, 4 Oct. 2001).

From Edward Coles

My dear Cousin: PHILADELPHIA Jany: 11. 1837.

Just as I was setting out today on my daily round in pursuit of the delinquent & faithless mechanicks of this good City, I had the pleasure to receive your letter of the 7th., with Cousin Johns addition dated the 8th instant. I put it in my pocket & in my round made it my business to call & show it to

Dr Physick—or rather *read* it to the good old Doctor, who I found suffering with head ache. I hasten to apprise you that there has been a most extraordinary mistake or misconception on the part of the Doctor, or some of us. He ment not to recommend a wash of *Elder* but *Sassafras.* I hope there has no bad consequences resulted from this error. The Doctor expressed more than once a similar hope, & said he did not know what would be the effect of Elder—he never knew it applied in that way to the eyes—he feared it was too astringent for your eyes—but still thought it probable it had done no great injury. But he begs you will lose no time in procuring the *pith* of *Sassafras* from the twiggs of the last years growth, & make a wash in the way I described in my last letter—taking great care to strain it so thoroughly as to leave not the smallest mote or particle of the fibres of the Sassafras pith in the wash—and to wash your eyes as I have already informed you. He wishes you not to use the ointment any more—but for the present to make no other application to your eyes but the Sassafras wash. He told me today, he had taken up an impression from what he had heard that the disease of your eyes from its long duration had become somewhat chronick, & that it was under this impression he had recommended the ointment; but that he was disposed to think now that it was more inflammatory & acute than he first supposed—and under this impression he wished her to use nothing of an alterative or severe character, but of the most mild & soothing nature—& that the Sassafras wash was of this description. In furtherance of the same views, & to allay the excitement & inflammation he recommended she shd. be Leeched on the temples & all around the eyes—taking care not to let the Leeches touch the eye balls—he said she had better get the Doctor or some skilful persons to apply the Leeches, as there was some danger of their injuring her eyes if improperly or carelessly applied. He also recommended that she should refrain from all stimulating drinks or rich food—nay that she should eat no meat or very little indeed, & live on rice, potatoes, tea & bread &c &c—The Doctor expressed over & over again the embarrassment he felt in prescribing for so delicate an organ as the eye without being able to see it—& said emphatically nothing but his great regard for you, and his great desire to relieve you, had induced him to venture to take such a responsible step when he felt himself so much in the dark. He desired me to make this known to you, & at the same time to convey to you his Kindest regards & sympathies, and also the anxiety he felt not only to relieve you, but to hear from time to time of your situation—and beged I would call on him as soon as I should hear again from you—which I promised to do promptly.

I[n] pursuance of your request, made known to me through your Brother, that I should pay for the National Gazette to the end of the year of your subscription, and then to direct it to be discontinued, I paid yesterday ten dollars for two years subscription to *April 5. 1837,* & had it entered in their Books that the paper was then to be discontinued. Enclosed I send you the Receipt.

We moved into our House on the 3d. before we got our furniture in the house—and have ever since & are still excessively busy in getting it in, & making our arrangements & completing our fixtures. We have been & are still daily much worried by the want of punctuality and bad treatment of the different Mechanicks we have employed. Our expectation was to have gotten into our house by the 20th of Dec: at least that was the day fixed for the completion of our furniture—& yet here is the 11th of Jany: & much of it is not even yet done. The sin⟨gle?⟩ delay would not have been so annoying if they had not promised repeatedly to have the articles in a day or two—nay in some cases in an hour or two—& then not to attend to their promises. This has kept us going & sending in the most tantalising & provoking manner—& compelled us to sleep the first night without a bedstead on the floor.

It is to my being so incessantly occupied that you must attribute all the faults of this hasty scrawl. I hope soon to hear from you—in the mean time accept our affectionate greetings & best wishes for your speedy restoration.

Ed: Coles

I shall attend to your enquiries about the insurance of yr. House as soon as I can. I am glad to hear your prospects are so good before Congress. Excuse my great haste & consequent errors.

RC (ICHi). Docketed by DPM "ansd. by J.C.P. on the 16th."

To William C. Rives

Dear Sir: MONTPELLIER Jan: 15th. 1837.

I have received your favor of the 12th. enclosing the result of the deliberations of the Joint Committee of the Library on my application to Congress.

It was never contemplated by me that, in the offer of the manuscripts brought to their consideration, a relinquishment of my privelege over them, as proprietress in other countries than the United States, was to be included. In proof of my intention in this respect a copy was transmitted to Europe before the meeting of Congress, to be published at the proper moment; but which, if made necessary, may be withdrawn.

With this reservation therefore of my copy-right abroad as the representative of the Author, I empower you to assent on my part to the projected report of the Committee in favor of a full purchase by Congress, of the manuscripts mentioned in my letter to the President of November 15th. 1836,[1] for $30,000 the sum therein named. With great regard and respect

D P Madison

RC (DLC: William C. Rives Papers). In Anna Payne's hand, signed by DPM.
   1. In DPM's letter to President Jackson, she offered to Congress the notes JM had taken at the Constitutional Convention of 1787, along with notes taken at the Confederation Congresses of 1781–83 and 1787, as well as "selections made by himself and prepared under his eye from his letters narrating the proceedings of that Body during the periods of his service in it" (DNA: RG 59, ML).

To William C. and Judith P. Rives

My dear and good friends: MONTPELLIER April 4th. 1837.

I have had the pleasure to receive all your valued letters, particularly the last of the 28th. ultimo.

My general health is better, and encouraged yesterday by the same feeling and appearance in my eyes I wrote a long letter to my son, now in Washington, which has caused a relapse in them, and thrown me again on the exertions of my little Anna and back into a shaded chamber, when the beauties of Spring would lure me to my garden.

I rejoice at your safe return home, in the quiet of which, I hope you rest sweetly after those perplexities which appeared to me so frightful on paper.

My brother has had three volumes of letters copied for the press, and placed others in order to be done so. He is about to leave us with his family for his long intended removal to the west—a circumstance which gives me great sorrow.[1]

I am very grateful for your efficient exertions in my behalf and am sensible of the good fortune of having been attached to the great Bill. I have just now received a letter from the Secretary of State, enclosing an instrument for me to sign away my rights over the Debates, containing a clause with the observation that, there was no doubt that Congress would allow me, what they had forgotten in their haste—the privilege of printing them in Europe.

I hope soon to be able to see you both here and at Castle-Hill. I am now favored with a visit from Col: Isaac Coles and lady which prevents my farther dictation, but shall resume my pen in a few days.

D P Madison

RC (DLC: William C. Rives Papers). In Anna Payne's hand, signed by DPM.
   1. John C. Payne and his family, with the exception of his daughter Anna, moved to Illinois in the spring of 1837. His decision to settle there was driven in part at least by his aversion to African Americans. After a promising start Payne seems to have once again sunk into a state

of dissipation (Payne to Edward Coles, 28 Feb., 15 March 1837, NjP: Edward Coles Papers; George W. Spotswood to John Payne Todd, 15 Sept. 1841, ViU).

To Richard D. Cutts

Ever dear Richard   [ca. October 1837]

I trust you will continue to think as well of your aunt & cousin, as *circumstances* will allow—being always assured that you are an object of great interest with them. I wish with all my heart, *you* had come to pass your holiday with us—I thought you were detained in the City on Engineering business, all this time—and now, it is our intention to be in W——n before you leave it, which is near at hand. All the time I can take from other business we pass in packing, & arranging for my absence but the task is not easy—every mail brings occupation for the next day—Company too.

My house in W——n. will do very well no doubt. Madison is active & kind, & when I asked him to take the trouble, Payne had left it, & I knew it wd. be dissagreeable to your Father on many accts. to have more to do with it, & the girls would have found it too *dissagreable* to attend to—or where there was workmen. The colour of the walls was chosen by Payne for the sake of my eyes & I like it of course—I was charm'd with your letters from Baltimore & feel that I have every reason, both from pride in your talents & affection for you, to *entice* the continuance of them by punctual reply's—prevented only by weak eyes—they are apparently well, but reading & writing a little hurts them much—Anna is my only scribe in P—s absence, & you will see by *this* writg. that I *ought* to be *quiet.*

My best love for the dear girls, whose letters I will answer tomorrow— When you, or any of you communicate with Walter & Thomas, remember me, as also to your Father—To give you a naritive of our trip to the springs wd. be impossible for me; Anna must do that, & I will tell you in *whisper,* that my anxiety to get home before the expiration of *two weeks,* made me sick! You will laugh at the idea that such astonishing scenery could not charm & you wd. be mistaken. It charmed & astonished my sight but my spirit was not there—Yet I may go again—tempted by Mr Caldwell & his small comme. who waited on me to offer a pretty cottage *forever,* or call it by my name, if I wd. *accept,* & come.

Will you, or dr Mary thank Mrs. Thornton for the message she sent me from Made. N—— thro Mrs. Smith—if prefered. Yours ever

                                                                      D.

RC (MCR-S: Mary Estelle Elizabeth Cutts Papers).

To Caroline Hite

WASHINGTON Decr. 13th. 1838.

Two days ago beloved Caroline I received from Mr. Mason your beautiful slippers and valued letter—but I cannot express to you how highly I prize them, and most of all that precious regard which prompted you to send them to me.

I have been ten days in Washington after remaining from early in July till late in November at Montpellier, not leaving it a single night until I sat out for my return hither, where I found my poor dear Niece Dolley Cutts extremely ill with pleurisy which terminated her life yesterday, about 8 O'clock in the morning—leaving her family especially her only sister Mary, inconsolable!

The kind invitation of your dear parents and yourself is very tempting to me as well as to Anna and if we ever have it in our power we shall accept it be assured—and you know my sweet Girl how gratifying it would be to me to bear you off to the seat of your Ancestors so that if circumstances favor us we may yet see Guilford.

Anna loves you dearly and will write soon—we are both much occupied at this time with the afflicted! Ever your affectionate Aunt

D P Madison

RC (MoSHi).

From George A. Waggaman

Madam,   BALTIMORE 6th. Oct: 1839

I pray your excuse for the liberty I take in addressing you personally on a matter of business.

Last year in a conversation with your Son, Mr. Todd, he informed me, that he thought it probable, in order to rid yourself of the trouble of the management, you would be willing to dispose of the negroes on your Estate, in Virginia—Wishing to increase my stock of negroes in Louisiana, should you be inclined to dispose of yours, I have no doubt we might readily agree upon a transaction in relation to them—I shall be much obliged, if you will do me the honor to have an answer addressed to me at this City—With Sentiments of the greatest esteem I have the honor to be most respectfully Your obt Servt.

George A. Waggaman

RC (TxU-Hu).

To George A. Waggaman

MONTPELLIER October 10th. 1839.

I am favored this day Sir, with your letter of the 6th. and hasten to express my regret that I cannot at this time transfer my colored people to a gentleman for whom I have so great a respect. I had not at any period intended to part with more than half about fifty, owing to their reluctance to leave this place or its neighbourhood, added to which the Manager at Montpellier is now finishing a large and tedious crop of Tobacco and preparing for a similar one of wheat, Tobacco, &c. which seems to require them all except the children of which there is a full proportion.

Soon after my son conversed with you on the subject, I hoped to rent my land and negroes together, with the exception of my house and grounds around it, but finding much difficulty in the pursuance of this plan and having a rich and productive tract, I have concluded to keep them together yet longer. Be pleased to accept my good wishes

D P Madison

RC (MnHi: Ford Collection).

To Richard Smith

MONTPELLIER Decr. 25th. 1839.

I have yet to thank you my valued friend for your last note, which I hoped to have done in person some weeks ago—but yielding to the temptation of remaining at home *nearly* as long as the weather was fine I have been *taken in* by the unusual occurrence here, of winter early in December—At this time the snow is reported to be two feet deep and our roads impassable for carriages so that in the spirit of Philosophy Anna and I are contenting ourselves in the calm of Montpellier, rather than in vain resentment against the elements, and regrets for a communion with the interesting society of Washington.

I must now ask the favor of you to have my note renewed in Bank and to place the enclosed five hundred dollars to my credit, there being no private opportunity I venture to send it by Mail. Present our kind remembrances to Mrs. Smith and your daughters with our best wishes for yours, and their happy Christmas.

D P Madison

RC (NBuU).

To John Sioussat

MONTPELLIER Jany. 4th. 1840.

I thank you very sincerely for all the good wishes you have sent me, and hope you will accept the same from me for your own and family's prosperity. I have also to thank you for your efficient attention to my house, and the repairs in & about it. I am only sorry that you did not write me of your expenditures before, so that I might have re-imbursed you immediately—I did not know before the receipt of your letter that your son had been at work for me, or should gladly have paid him—be pleased to send me his Bill—The small sum from Mr. James was merely a token of my remembrance, at a time when I expected to be in Washington shortly after it—but the weather became so inclement that I was afraid to attempt a journey of fifty miles over bad roads, or the storms upon the water. I enclose you $50 in order that you may pay yourself and support the capricious cow, if you prefer to keep, rather than sell her. I hope and expect to see the City in the Spring or as soon as the weather permits me to travel.

The cavity you speak of, near the water hogshead, could be easily filled up with some earth from the enclosure after, or before the snow melts, if you will order it done, to save the kitchen from inundation—also a few pieces of slate put on the roof might repair the leak which probably may have been augmented by leaving the trap door open. Your obliged friend

D P Madison

RC (owned by Mrs. Aimee McCormick King, Mobile, Ala., 1957). Addressed to "Mr. Sioussa at the Bank of the Metropolis, Washington City."

To Richard D. Cutts

Dearest Richard— [2 February 1840]

I safely recd. both your late letters, and in that of the 19th. I followed you with my whole mind in pleasure & admiration of your talents—in your second of the 23d. I find food for grief & deep sympathy with you at my inability to comply with your just demand of the sum I owe Mary—*that* complete *inability* at this time—*which* has kept me *here*. My situation like your own, from false promises of payment to me of considerable sums in Novr. Decr. & Jany. has become doubly painful, as it deprives me of the joy I should experience in accommodating you with that which I proposed some months ago, to return to your Sister; and at this moment you find me from the delinquency of *friends* with 3 or 400$ in one Bank where I owe more.

What can I say or do in the case? The law would take months, and these debtors many more, if I attempted to coerce, but in consequence of my waiting, they are *moved* to exert themselves to pay me. When they do you shall have it—I have no other alternative—Alas not one, nor would I *tell this* to any body but yourself.

I write these lines in great haste as a post leaves directly, and hope you will speedily tell me that you can surmount these ills for a time at any rate.

RC (NjP: Crane Collection). Undated and unsigned; date assigned on the basis of Cutts's docket.

To Eliza Collins Lee

MONTPELLIER Feby. 19th 1840

Yes I can meet thee there dear friend on those "green spots" where we sported, the happiest of girls where a sisters love sprang up in my heart, which was cherished by you with a genuine goodness of soul which ever marked your character—Years have since rolled away but these feelings have never strayed from my early friend—When lately I found myself in the same City with you I was flattered by the hope that we might "live together" but the present disappointment has made me fear others in the vista—Our winter set in a month earlier than usual & before two marrages in our family, of great-neices & nephews could be consumated I was literally weather bound—they would not allow me to leave home before I had given them frolicks & partaken of others—then came & continued the storms of snow & rain until we determined to remain & enjoy the quiet of Montpellier—thus was my first disappointment & on this day vegetation is abroad with birds singing in the "ever breathing spring" my gardener busily planting in his ground all sorts of bu[l]bes for my taste & detention & our roads are abominably bad & that I may not be able to travel until May—Anna & Payne have been with me until a few weeks ago my son left me for Richmond to have sawed & polished there some specimens of fine marble of which he has a quarry—Anna has been reading & improving her self in many desirable things she offers you her respectful love. I cannot close this brief letter dearest friend without expressing

351

to you the pleasure & admiration I have felt in perusing the beautiful effusions of your son Z. C. Lee on the occasion of his public addresses[1]—his mother & wife must be justly proud to feel that his fine talents are in part their property in as much as the professor belongs to them. My eyes are generally well when I am *idle* & I must pay the penalty for such a disposition in them by ceasing to write more at this time. Adieu all health & happiness be with you & yours

D. P. Madison

Tr (DLC: DPM Papers).

   1. Lee's son Zaccheus Collins Lee, a Baltimore lawyer, spoke before the annual meeting of the Horticultural Society of Maryland on 6 June 1839 (Robert S. Gamble, *Sully: The Biography of a House* [Chantilly, Va., 1973], 54; *Address before the Horticultural Society of Maryland* [Baltimore, 1839], copy in NUC).

To Edward Coles

My ever dear cousin   MONTPELLIER March 3d. 1840.

Your letter of the 26th. was most welcome—it still breathes that constant friendship of which I was always proud, but of late fearful of having by some means diminished, which would have been a misfortune, as my heart clings with particular sensibility to my friends of long standing such as yourself and your family. I had failed in my promise to visit you, your precious wife, and little ones, as well as that of writing to you—the last, was occasioned by a propensity in my eyes to inflame whenever I wrote a letter, and I constantly intended to explain my silence, but the busy life I lead has been a bar to many of my favorite plans. I wish your letter had told me of your entire recovery—the contrary account has made me melancholy—united as it is, with the intelligence of our beloved Betsey, of whose illness I had not heard—Payne called at Mr. Rutherfoord's to deliver a message from me but did not see her, she was riding out and from this circumstance I trust she is getting well—I shall write to her tomorrow. I cannot give you an idea of my sorrow for the loss of Enniscorthy[1] but by referring to your own feelings—I hope your brother will build on the same spot where that venerated mansion stood.

The Manuscripts of which you speak are all in Bank at Washington in the safe keeping of Mr. Richard Smith, except the 4th. Volume in the hands of the Harpers, who were to give it to the world months ago by promise—and which will certainly be out soon.[2] The Debates are ready for the public I understand, but waiting the vote of those who may *please* to give—or sell—In a letter I received yesterday I'm told Judge Barbour was designated to bring me a copy—

it being too large for the mail. I intended to proceed in arrangements for the remaining Volumes last Winter, either to print or sell to Congress according to best advice—having been assured by some who *had published,* that it was a hazardous business for me. I shall go on perhaps this Spring and may be so happy as to converse with you—but do not *expect* until you see me, as uncertainty hovers over all the schemes of "mice and men" for instance, my own were set at nought this fall, by some nieces and nephews, who were in love with each other, and wanted me to see them married, and give them *frolics*— After yielding to them, and the temptation of remaining here as long as the weather was fine, we were taken in by the unusual occurrence of winter early in December and literally weather-bound—I could not believe in its continuance for more than a few days, until weeks elapsed of snow storms and rain, making our roads impassable, so that Anna and I, in the spirit of Philosophy determined to content ourselves in the calm of Montpellier, rather than indulge in vain resentment against the elements, or regrets for a communion with the interesting society of Washington, and now that the "incense breathing spring"[3] has broken in upon us, we would fain enjoy it here still longer, but my dear Sister is yet an invalid and I must go to her, and then to Washington without the intention of staying long in either place. We often hear from my brother and his family who are well—Dolley and Lucy both married some time—the elder to Dr. Thomas of Berlin and the second to Mr. Helm of New-port—in which both have pleased their parents as well as themselves. And now dear friend you see by my *expunging* that I cannot afford to rectify mistakes by writing over my letter, and I beg you will receive it with my most affectionate love to cousin Sally—my sweet Mary, & your fine boys—in which Anna & Payne most cordially unite. Pray tell me that you are well.

D P Madison

RC (NjP: Edward Coles Papers).

1. In December 1839 Enniscorthy, the home of Isaac A. Coles and the main home of the Coles family, was destroyed by fire (Elizabeth Langhorne, K. Edward Lay, and William D. Rieley, *A Virginia Family and Its Plantation Houses* [Charlottesville, Va., 1987], 142).

2. In addition to the manuscripts sold to Congress in 1838, JM had edited and DPM had copied enough documentary material to form four volumes of correspondence. The first three volumes of material were lodged in the bank safe. The fourth volume, largely touching on constitutional topics, was being prepared for publication by Harper and Brothers of New York (*PJM* 1:xvii–xx).

3. DPM may have been paraphrasing lines from William Collins's poem "A Song from Shakespeare's Cymbelyne": "To fair *Fidele's* grassy Tomb / Soft Maids and Village Hinds shall bring / Each op'ning Sweet, of earliest Bloom, / and rifle all the breathing Spring" (Richard Wendorf and Charles Ryskamp, eds., *The Works of William Collins* [Oxford, 1979], 21).

To Richard D. Cutts

My dear Richard   May 12th. 40.

The day on which I received yours I hastened to the Court-house where I had some hope of success in an appeal for one thousand dollars out of the three promised to me at the time you remember. I saw the gentleman, and saw, too soon, that I could not obtain it—nor could I extort another promise of it at any given time. It is all in vain for me to lament my disappointment or expect money here until "times (as they say) get better"—in the meantime, *I stay at home in waiting.* You, should not wait for, but receive your due if it was within my power. Here, is property in both land & negroes but they cannot command one hundred at this time, and I fear that I have not sufficient in Bank to pay my discount there—thus situated dear Richard I know not what to do—or would have *done it,* after knowing your necessity—but there was none to be loaned and, *thus they say now.* I will continue still to try and if I should happily succeed you shall know instantly as be assured I am even more miserable at my inability than any other on earth can be.

Be pleased to do me the favor to call & deliver this letter as directed, as it is important that hers to me should be answered—and this it is.

RC (NjP: Crane Collection). Docketed by Richard D. Cutts as received 16 May and with the notations: "being an answer to a letter of mine requesting the payment of the 1500$ due my sister Mary or such part of it as may be convenient to her—to be applied towards the payment of my debts with my sister's consent" and "including a letter to Mrs L. H. Cutts alluded to in the last paragraph."

To Frances D. Lear

MONTPELLIER Decr. 25th. 40.

Many thanks for your undeserved favor of the 14th. my beloved Friend. I have had so much to occupy me since I wrote you last that I must now approach you with apologies & *faith* in your forgiveness.

You know perhaps that your old acquaintance my dear Sister Lucy came to see me in the summer—her health had been broken by many afflictions, which her sojourn with us seems to ameliorate—but lately she has been indisposed—which added to the illness of Anna has engrossed me entirely. It has been six weeks since a bad cold has borne hard upon the latter, but she is now fast recovering, still, she may not be able to travel during the winter months, which we are all desirous of doing, in order to be again united to you, and other of our valued friends—*some* of whom, I *fear* to miss from our circle tho' the remembrance of their kindness will ever be with me.

Lucy will accompany us to the City on her way to her son Wm. Washington's whose very pretty daughter was married on the 10th. and much disappointed that her Grand Mama and ourselves were not present—The *burst* of winter having kept us secure from frolicking.

You enquire my plans dear Friend and I will give them to you as soon as I can believe that fruition will crown them—but you know when action depends on several persons, and as many circumstances, decisions are *difficult*.

You must tell me of our mutual acquaintance in Town—I have not written many letters lately for the reasons I give you, and therefore know less about them than I wish. Mary is so good as to write often but she is *imaginative* when I want real facts.

Please to offer my love to the Forsyths, Mrs. Rodgers & the Kanes, and to all around you, and accept with my best wishes for your health *another promise* of *another* letter. My sister and Anna send you love and desire for you also, many happy New Years. Ever yours

D P Madison

RC (DLC: J. Henley Smith Papers).

Will of Dolley Payne Madison

[1 February 1841]

I Dolley P. Madison widow of James Madison late President of the United States Do make this my last will and testament at Montpellier, this first day of February Anno Di. 1841. hereby revoking all wills by me heretofore made— From prudential considerations, and not from any want [of] affection for my dear Son John Payne Todd, I do Hereby give devise and bequeath all and every part of my estate real personal, and mixed, whatsoever and whensoever to my worthy friends, William C. Rives, Edward Coles and Philip P. Barbour their Heirs and assigns, and to the survi[v]or and Survi[v]ors of them and to the Executors and assigns of such survi[v]or, In trust nevertheless, and to and for the Sole and exclusive use benefit and behoof, of the person and persons respectively, and for the estate and estates herein after expressed.

I give and bequeath to my Son John P. Todd my house and lots in the City of Washington with the lands appertaining to the Montp[e]llier estate, except six hundred acres nearest the Mansion house, in fee simple, but if my Son

355

John P. Todd mary and have children, I then bequeath to the Said children the Said Mansion house and the six hundred of land to be divided equally, between them, if he should have none than one child; and if but one to that one child and its heirs forever, of this my bequeast. I give to my brother John Coles Payne one thousand dollars, to be laid out for his accommodation and comfort. I give to his sons William Temple and James Madison Payne three hundred dollars each, and I give to my neice Anna Payne, three thousand dollars, with my negro Woman and her children one third of my wearing apparel, my forte piano and the furniture of my chamber, with my private papers to *burn*. One hundred Volumes of my books and a likeness of Mr Madison and Myself. I give to my dear Sister Lucy P. Todd one negro girl of twelve or fifteen Years of age I give to my niece Mary E. P. Allen one negro girl of ten or twelve years of age—I give to my niece Mary E. E. Cutts one negro Girl of ten or twelve years of age, as Marks of my affection for them—I give to my Mulatto man Paul[1] his freedom—I give and bequeath to William C. Rives, John P. Todd and Edward Coles the Sum of five hundred dollars for the purpose of erecting a plain monument of White Marble over the remains of my dear Husband, and as it is my desire and request to be laid by his side, I give to the above three friends, the sum of five hundred dollars for the purpose of designating the latter place, in a maner they think proper.

I desire that all my just debts be paid out of my personal property after the legacies that are above and might be mentioned.

I hereby appoint James K. Paulding John P. Todd William C. Rives and Edward Coles, to have the management, direction and publication of the papers of my deceased Husband, as they were confided to me for the unfulfilled interests and purposes expressed in his will, as well as may desire that they shall appear without unnecessary delay to the upholding of our constitution, and friends of the writer. In witness whereof I have hereto signed my name and affixed my seal this first day of February anno Domini One thousand eight hundred and forty one

Witness   D. P. Madison

Lucy P. Todd

Anna Payne

L Pichot

True Copy Teste Ed. N. Roach Regl. wills

Jany. 27. 1849.

Tr (ViU).
1. Paul Jennings.

To Frances D. Lear

Feb. 7th. [1841]

Your last letter my beloved Friend was acceptable and precious to me— It was a proof of your kind partiality in the forgiveness of my silence—and it contained the best of wishes which must ever hover over my memory— "those consolations which this world can neither give nor take away"—May the amiable Sister who breathed this wish for me in like manner be blessed.

Finding on my return that the fortunes of an Absentee threatened me I determined to remain here "to direct the Storm" and have no doubt of an agreeable result—A pleasant family desire much to rent half the Montpellier house to which I may consent and dev⟨ulge?⟩ myself of cares and troubles—When this is consummated I will ⟨. . .⟩ to you—In the meantime I will often communicate with y⟨ou⟩ and always be near you in spirit, and in truth. Your affectionate

D P Madison

RC (DLC: J. Henley Smith Papers). Torn by removal of seal. Written on the third page of Anna Payne to Frances D. Lear of the same date.

To Richard D. Cutts

My dear Richard   MONTPELLIER Feby. 27th. 1841.

Your letter is before me and I congratulate you from my heart on your return to meet the smiles of hope which now illumine your path—You cannot doubt, as you say nor can one of your family doubt the delight I should feel at seeing prosperity cover the children of my sister, as well as their remaining parent. I have as yet no acquaintance with Genl. Harrison, tho' I desire it much, and expect hereafter to see and become known to him.[1] I mentioned this circumstance to my nephew Wm. Washington in a letter some time ago who was under a different impression—My Husband was attached to the General as one of our bravest and best men, so was I, but, *so* it happened *we* were personally *Strangers.* You will see therefore that it would be unbecoming in me to write to him, if I could write to any one. Give my love to Mr. Clay— shew him this, and he shall be the Umpire—He, whose wisdom, delicacy, and friendship I know well, and value accordingly—In *confidence* to him and you I will mention that dear Septimia entreats me from Cuba, to petition the

357

President elect in favor of Dr. Mickleham for a consulship—I have shrunk from the commission.

In truth dear Richard I am sick and overwhelmed with business, and pray you to excuse this short letter—I would tell you something of my prospects of returning to Washington but the time is not fixed or certain. Your Aunt Lucy is not well but anxious to accompany me when I go. I will write you again— Accept our love—Your affte. Aunt

D P Madison

RC (NjP: Crane Collection).

1. William Henry Harrison had recently been elected president of the United States. Harrison had served as a major general and commander of the U.S. Army of the Northwest in the War of 1812. He died one month after his inauguration in March 1841.

To Elizabeth Coles

Dearest Cousin   MONTPELLIER March 8th. 1841.

It would make me very unhappy to suppose that my last letter had not reached you—it was written in answer to your acceptable one, in which you told me of the views and intentions of our dear sister and brother Stevenson.[1] I sympathize in your affectionate and impatient wishes to see them on their own ground, where they will receive the greeting of thousands in that spirit of love and respect, which they have fairly earned, with its high reward.

I often hear from Washington having correspondents in both parties if indeed I may style those correspondents whose letters are not answered. Ex-President Van Buren was to remain with the Gilpins until this day the 8th.— but I hear less of Angelica than I wish, being anxious for her health and safety "she was however looking remarkably well at Mrs. Woodburys large party some few days ago." I had a very interesting letter from Mr. Paulding lately, giving me an account of his amiable Wife, whose illness continues in a lesser degree. Mr Preston and some other of your particular friends say they are in health and spirits of course—but such is not the case with me dear Coz, having heard on saturday that my son had lost his pleasant establishment at Todd's Birth,[2] by fire—he was absent in Richmond when it occurred, from the chamber of an inmate. Payne's favorite occupation had long been to improve and embelish his house, and grounds so that I feel the more sorrow at the disappointment which awaits his return—that of finding only, ashes— but the wind was tempered[3] it appears, as all his Out-houses which were very near, escaped—and his furniture was saved.

358

Anna is getting quite well again, and my sister Todd has greatly improved—they both offer you their love—I write this to-day to assure you of my constant attachment and my hopes that my next may be better worth your reading. To cousin Emily, Sally and Mr. Rutherfoord present me always as one who forgets them not.

D P Madison.

RC (owned by Charles M. Storey, Boston, Mass., 1961). Addressed to "Miss Betsy Coles Richmond Va."

1. DPM to Elizabeth Coles, 25 Dec. 1840, owned by Charles M. Storey, Boston, Mass., 1961. Andrew Stevenson, U.S. minister to Great Britain, had formally requested his recall in December 1840. He and his wife, Sarah Coles Stevenson, had resided in London since 1836 (Wayland, *Andrew Stevenson*, 112–13, 192–95).

2. Toddsberth, the home of John Payne Todd, was situated on nine acres about two miles southeast of the Montpelier estate. The "eccentric" complex contained a low two-story house and a complex of other buildings, including a library, a summerhouse, and a "Rotundo" intended as a ballroom (Ann L. Miller, "Historic Structure Report: Montpelier, Orange County, Virginia" [July 1990; copy at Papers of James Madison], 103, 108, 184–88).

3. "*God tempers the wind,* said Maria, *to the shorn lamb*" (Laurence Sterne, *A Sentimental Journey through France and Italy,* in *The Works of Laurence Sterne* [London, 1857], 472).

To John Payne Todd

[ca. 1 September 1842]

My dearest I waited for your advi⟨ce⟩ on the subject of Robertsons proposal to me for two Drafts on the Farmers Bk. of Fredbg Virga. for 600$ *and* 600$—making 1200—when I could do it with a prospect of repa⟨yment⟩ in 90 days for the 1t. & 4 months the 2d Draft—my negotiation with Mr Astor may give me the use of half the worth of this property—he "wd not have to do with Virga. property," he sd. "it was too distant he could not"—but I want that sum of this Morgage for my own particular necessities—I told you of taxes, & debts here which I must settle ere I left—I dont know from you yet your oppinon abt the Vol. Harper lost—whether you'd advise to have it recopied & sell it to him, or anyone else. The President has advised me to sell the other vols. to Congress next winter. I wish to be here on the occasion as he & others say it wd. be best—but I know not that I shd. have the means to be here—I wd. pay a part of my debt to Robertson if ⟨p⟩ossible somehow or other—even sooner than my other debt—you have not told me what we could do for the protested debt—Wd. it ⟨. . .⟩ to pay a part—would it mend the affair ⟨to⟩ pay 500$ or more if to be had, would it satisfy the Bk Directors? As to Overseers I'm glad you refused the 2 first Burnly & Shackleford—no whipper of Negros shd ever have our people or any others, to tirenize over. I thought better of Dr Ws recommendation—I suppose one must be employed because they will not work without but let it be a good & feeling honest one without much or any family, & very moderate demands $150 is eno' for any that offer to us—then they want less provision. I have always feared, & disliked the principles of that *troublesome correspondent* K M C—& can assure you that I wrote not a sentence to *compromise.* Il find if I can the copy of my *one* note which I sent it was very short & you might gather by his last enclosed you, that he could not cavil on a hair—there in I recd the check you intended for me but you did not say where Mr Pegram was, or in what Bank—I knew not on what to Bk to draw—the acceptance of the Morgage & deposit from N. York has not come yet—it was—as I wrote you to be for three thousand dolls. 6 pct. interest paid half yearly—Byard Smith drew it—had all done in form here as Astor desired, & I sent it thro Bumford—It was prudent to detain the Waggon under circumstances mention'd. I wish you to send in it half a doz pieces Bacon as I have been out a while & I shd. want after it got here for returg waggon & servants &c—I am out of all provisions—Here is what I propose; if I obtain the money A. to pay a part to Bk. *protest*—to Robertson & to pay taxes here—to pay fuel from Hercey my Baker Butcher Merchant— with several others—All amtg to $600. I'm obliged to pay a part to Mary of principle—& a years Int. Now hasten to give me your thoughts on each item here & tell me that the floors at you at the ⟨. . .⟩ & Montpr. are not hurt by the wheat—that it will be fit to pick. there in company in by the attention of servants in the orchard—lazy women—Your plan on the subject of Montpr. wd. not accord with mine if we could accomplish it—I wd. keep the house & 5 or 600. acres if obliged to part with the residue. Did you intend me to send Govr. Woods' certificate of the Lands, which you got in Rd. with a view to its redeption? If so; I will enclose to him—I have not a line from him for a long time, but the acct. was of much distress as could befall a poor family.

I enclose Mr Bs letter & wish you to say if I had not better sign his Notes sign'd on the Farmers Bk Fredricksburg and so you could see him & assure him that if possible I will pay him some part as soon as I can—A lady came to me the other day to buy the marble steps at Capola⟨?⟩ & sd. she wd give what the master of the public works decided they were worth. I told her have him value & let me know—in the mean time, I want your direction—Roland or some one of them said they were not worth much, & were of a acct. to them, on the buildings here

Draft (DLC: DPM Papers). Unsigned. Undated.

To John Jacob Astor

Dr. Sir.   MONT. Sept. 12th. 42.

In leaving Washington & travelling to Montpellier prevented me from recg. & acknowledging sooner your letter of the 8th. Your obliging loan came duly to hand thro' the attention of your son Wm. B. Astor in a check of $3,000 on the Bk. of the Metropolis, thereby made the more convenient to me, for which I am to express my acknowledgments to him.

I hope you are perfectly satisfied with the security—the tittle I believe to be unequivocal—its history is short—Mr. Cutts about the year 1815 bought Square 22.—sold lots to different individuals & among others to the Corporation of the Bank of the U.S. for their building which loaned him on the pledge of the House & Lots in question $3,000—He afterwards failing I induced Mr. Madison to buy it of him & pay the Bank. A suit was instituted by a creditor of Mr. Cutts when the District Court confirmed Mr. Madison's in the tittle, & it was given to me by Will of Record in Dept. of State, & I think Dist. Court to wit of record—and so it now stands with the addition of your Lein. With great esteem yr. fd. & servt.

Draft (DLC: DPM Papers). Unsigned. In an unknown hand.

To Edward Coles

MONTPELLIER Septr. 26th. 1842.

A few days ago my dear Friend I received your letter of the 13th. inst. containing the welcome intelligence of Cousin Sally's recovery, and the health of yourself and dear children. It found me in the midst of a sick colored family, whom I have nursed, and attended to ever since I came home, following the Physician's advice with great anxiety and fatigue—he having previously lost a man, and a woman Cook of great value to me—their disease generally, sore throat, which has been communicated to those I had at Washington leaving only one House servant in health. It has now been more than three weeks since my return, and this sickness still continues among the negroes here, and in the neighbourhood.

But, my cousin, if you had expressed *half* a wish to be at Montpellier when I saw you or afterwards, it would have been my highest pleasure to invite you to all that was pleasant there, for the summer, but I thought from your conversation, that your hearts were fixed on Schooley's Mountain[1]—as *mine was* on the prospect of seeing your beloved Sister Stevenson at my house on her way to the Springs—as before that period, and at that *time,* I expected to be there (in all June)—but when the month came I found that *business* kept me in Washington—I had a debt due me there, and I awaited the performance of promises of payment, to *enable* me *to return.* So now, you have the secret, which my *pride* has kept from all others—The debt was for money I had loaned to an "honorable gentleman" and it ended after a disagreeable detention of two months, in *non-payment!* Being however, a financier I, a few days after, travelled home, well and cheerfully—where other troubles awaited me as I have enumerated—and I fear fatigued you.

I would now make a short observation on Mr. Van Buren's communication to you.[2] I think he has been mistaken in it—he has confessed his forgetfulness in the *first* instance and in the *second* wherein he says "he was permitted to make copies and extracts as he pleased," I believe he did not remember that he expresed a wish to do so—and that the Manuscripts he was allowed to peruse were shewn him in strict *confidence*—without a farther privilege of any sort. I was aware of his request to P—— for perusal of some of the writings, but had no idea of the particular *letters* or part, he was curious to see, altho' I consented to his *seeing a very few of them.*

I have not heard from cousin Stevenson since she went to the White Sulphur, but look and long to see her on her return. Adieu! Be pleased to present my affectionate remembrances to your precious wife, her Mother, and Sisters. Ever yours

D P Madison

Anna's love to all—particularly to Sweet Mary—*Eddy* & *Robb.*

RC (NjP: Edward Coles Papers).

1. Schooley's Mountain in New Jersey was a mineral-water spa and a fashionable vacation resort (John T. Cunningham, *This Is New Jersey* [New Brunswick, N.J., 1968], 58–59).

2. Coles had complained in a letter to DPM of 13 Sept. that Martin Van Buren had been allowed to see some of the Coles-Madison correspondence that, according to Van Buren, was "designed to draw from him [JM] expressions of disapprobation of the course pursued by Gen: Jackson in the Admn: of the Govt:" Coles confronted Van Buren and later wrote to DPM that Payne Todd had "loaned him [Van Buren] the original correspondence in manuscript between Mr Madison & myself, & given him permission to take extracts from it, which he had done & had them now in his possession" (Coles to DPM, 26 Aug., 13 Sept. 1842, NjP: Coles Papers).

To Lucy Payne Washington Todd

My beloved Sister— Nov. 13th. 42.

I am glad to have a letter for you from our dear James,[1] and I trust in Heaven it will find you well and easy in mind on all subjects. I am now in excellent health tho' my eyes are *complaining* much, and have been so for many weeks preventing the use of my pen in a great measure—So that I require of Anna to give you an account of us and all else that can interest you.

I have no fixed prospect of going to Washington this winter, tho' the business of my papers ought to take me there. When I returned on the 1st. Sept. I found the Overseer had worked for himself and ruined my prospect of any sort of Crop—He was sent away & I am now without one—but Wm. Temple[2] being here I persuaded him to remain this Winter to superintend—and I hope we shall make something by & bye.

How is dear William & Margarette and precious Millisent with your sweet little pet?[3] I long to see you and them—and shall hope for it—My love to them but most to you my own sister.

DPM

RC (owned by John Tyler, Annapolis, Md., 1961).
    1. This was probably Lucy's youngest son, James Madison Todd.
    2. William Temple Payne, son of John C. Payne.
    3. Lucy's son William Washington, his wife Margaret, and their daughter Millicent.

From Henry W. Moncure

Respected dear Madam RICHMOND Decr 17th. 1842

Your polite note Post Marked the 13th. inst I recd, and to night I have that of Colo Todd dated yesterday, for both of these communications, I am indebted, and thank you for your kind invitation, to make you a visit, and more understandingly, make the arrangements, as proposed by Colo Todd; I have felt solicitous, before I entered on the terms of the negotiation with Colo Todd, to learn from you, how far the Plan, met your approbation. I rather infer from remarks, on this subject, that the proposed arrangement is not altogether Tasteful to your good self, if this be the Case I pray you my good Madam, to feel no farther solicitude about it; Should the weather permit I purpose to leave this on Monday the 26th inst, and if practicable the same day, to be with you & Colo Todd, and to enter into no engagement which does not meet with your entire approbation. I wish the Season promised the possibility of enabling Mrs Moncure to accompany me, we would both be most happy to make your valued Personal acquaintance, you are already most favourably known to us, thro the flattering recollections of Mrs Ambler with whom we now stay.

In regard to the Survey of "Sheen" I have to remark to Colo Todd, there has been much ado, for nothing, on the part of the Surveyor, for he surely must know, that deeds of Record, are unalterable Instruments, and that Surveys must be made, to comply with them, and not Deeds of Record altered, to suit Surveys; the Boundaries of the purchase, is described in the Deed supposed to contain 750 Acres, should there not be said quantity, within the boundaries called for by the deed, it was the understanding, that the deviding line should be so run, as to make up the quantity of 750 Acres. Should this prove to be the Case, in relation to the present Deed, a second Deed will be necessary, for whatever quantity, the first Deed may fall short. With this explanation a copy of the description of the first Deed, with the Original Plat of the Montpilier Farm, and a Copy of the Plat, attached to the first Deed, there is nothing to prevent the Surveyor, from running the dividing line so as to embrace the stipulated quantity of 750 Acres, should such dividing line embrace a portion more of land than 750 Acres and it be your wish and that of Colo Todd to convey it. I will promptly settle for such surplus, upon recpt of a sufficient Deed therefor; Should I have sufficient strength and the weather permit on the 26th inst I will be with you on that day and do myself the pleasure so to deport myself as satisfactorily and understandingly to close this negotiation which I fear has heretofore been distasteful to you, with my respectful regards to Colo Todd, and sentiments of high respect, for your goodness I am my dear Madam Your troublesome Ob H St

Henry W. Moncure

I take the liberty to write to Mr Clark to run his Survey according to your Deed and to confer with Colo Todd in running the line to embrace whatever may be defficient in the quantity of 750 Acres, with a request he will have the Plat and Survey with you by the 21st. inst and for this deficiency should there be any a Deed may be prepared and executed in conformity while I may be with you.

RC (ViU). With postscript addressed to Colo. Todd.

To Edward Coles

My dear Cousin—   MONTPELLIER Septr. 8th. 1843.

It has been some sad days since I received your kind letter, which I should have answered but for grief and sickness—My fine promising nephew Wm. Temple Payne died a fortnight ago, in a rapid decline. He was Anna's eldest brother—sensible—active and amiable—He had been with us for the last two years—and our deep interest in him cannot be exprest. His sister's heart was bound up in him and she has been inconsolable—Last week I thought it expedient to take her to Toddsberth for a few days, and hope it has been of service to her, tho' I have come home quite sick. I trust both cousin Sally and yourself, with brother Tucker, have entirely recovered, and that I shall have the happiness to see you in October—and if I know at what point to keep watch for you it will be a pleasure to send my carriage to meet you. Be pleased to present me with kindest love to your estimable brothers and sisters—whom I sigh to see once more. Adieu dear cousin—ever your constant and Affectionate friend

D P Madison

I was very proud of dear Mrs. Roberts' little note and hope soon to write to her. I should not have sent you the directions of the letters but that several of the seals stuck fast and in attempting to seperate the envelope I thought I might break open your letters. The postage marked on them was a mistake often made by the change of Post Masters but never required—so that I return your Bill.

RC (NjP: Edward Coles Papers). Addressed to Coles at "Garland's Store Albemarle County Virginia."

Proposed Indenture for the Sale of Montpelier

[1843]

This Indenture made this   day of   in the year One thousand eight hundred & forty-three between Dolley P. Madison of the County of Orange in the State of Virginia of the one part & Henry W. Moncure of the City of Richmond in the same State of the other part.

Whereas the said Dolley P Madison & Henry W. Moncure have treated for a conditional sale by the former and a conditional purchase by the latter of the property herein after mentioned and after fully contemplating each of them the value thereof have fixed upon   as the price of the same; and the real transactions of the parties being a sale on condition as distinguished from a loan of money and security therefor, the object of these presents, is to set forth the sale; the condition on which it is made, and the time within which that condition made be performed to make it available.

This indenture therefore witnesseth that the said Dolley P. Madison for and in consideration of the promises and of the sum of   to her in hand paid by the said Henry W. Moncure before the sealing and delivery of these presents, the receipt whereof is hereby acknowledged, hath given, granted, bargained and sold and, by their presents doth give, grant, bargain, sell and confirm unto the said Henry W. Moncure, the whole of the land in the County of Orange held by the said Dolley P. Madison under the Will of her late husband James Madison, Esq: and known by the name of Montpellier, except   acres heretofore sold & conveyed by the said Dolley P. Madison to   Newman and seven hundred and fifty acres heretofore sold & conveyed by her to the said Henry W. Moncure, which land now intended to be conveyed by these presents contain   acres be the same more or less, as bounded by the lands of   has on it the Montpellier dwelling house, springs, overseers house, sawmill and pond and plainly appears by the plat hereto annexed of a survey made by W. D. Clark of the seventeen hundred & sixty seven acres formerly constituting the Montpellier estate, the land hereby conveyed being all the land embraced in the said survey except the   acres conveyed to the said Newman which constitute a triangle at the Western corner denoted on the said plat by the letters U. J. T. and except the said 750 acres marked on the said plat as the said Henry W. Moncure's, together with all the buildings and other improvements on the said land hereby conveyed & the privileges & appurtenances of every kind thereunto belonging.

And the said Dolley P. Madison for the consideration aforesaid, hath given, granted, bargained and sold and by these presents doth give, grant, bargain and sell unto the said Henry W. Moncure, all the slaves, horses, cattle, sheep, hogs, furniture, farming utensils and personal property, of every description mentioned in the schedule hereunto annexed, signed by the said Dolley P. Madison: To have and to hold the said land hereby conveyed with all the buildings and other improvements thereon & the privileges & appurtenances of every kind, thereunto belonging unto the said Henry W. Moncure his heirs & assigns, to the only proper & behoof of the said Henry W. Moncure his heirs and assigns forever; and to have & to hold the said slaves, horses, cattle, sheep, hogs, furniture, farming utensils, personal property of every description unto the said Henry W. Moncure his executors, administrators & assigns forever. But upon this condition that if the said Dolley P. Madison, her heirs, executors, or administrators shall within five years from the date of these presents pay to the said Henry W. Moncure, his heirs, executors, administrators or assigns the sum of   without interest (the use profits of the property being put against interest, taxes & charges of insurance) & also within the same time pay to the said Henry W. Moncure, his heirs, executors, administrators or assigns   have expended for additional buildings, & repairs to the present buildings for pipes to convey water & for all the permanent improvements upon the premises including as such plaister & clover seed to improve the land, then upon such payments being made within the time aforesaid the estate hereby granted shall cease and determine. If however such payments be not made within the time aforesaid, then, from the expiration of that time this conditional sale & conveyance shall be absolute.

And the said Dolley P. Madison for herself, her heirs, executors & administrators covenants with the said Henry W. Moncure his heirs, administrators in manner following that is to say, that she has good right to convey all the said property unto the said Henry W. Moncure absolutely, that the same is free from any lien or incumbrance thereon, and that she and her heirs, executors & administrators will warrant and defend the same unto him the said Henry W. Moncure his heirs, executors, administrators and assigns forever against all claims & demands whatsoever.

In testimony whereof the said Dolley P. Madison has hereunto set her hand and affixed her seal on the same day and year first herein written.

Draft (DLC: DPM Papers). Blanks left in Ms.

From James K. Paulding

[NEW YORK 4 January 1844]

I did myself the pleasure to write You last winter, I think it was, on the subject of the selection from Mr Madison's Papers, the Proofs of which I corrected some Years ago at Washington, which have been long in Print, and are now ready for Publication, without any further expence on Your part. Nothing is wanting but a Preface and Title Page, which should be furnished by the person who made the selections. I am assured by the Messrs Harpers that nothing else is required, to enable them to give to the world, a series of Papers containing as I verily believe more political wisdom than any work ever written.

Permit me to suggest my dear Madam, that You owe it not only to the memory of Your Husband, but to the well-being of mankind that these Papers should be no longer withheld from the world.

Printed extract (offered for sale in McGuire-Madison Catalogue, 26 Feb. 1917, item 113). Original described as a two-page letter.

To the House of Representatives

WASHINGTON Jany. 9th. 1844.

Permit me to thank you Gentlemen, as the Committee on the part of the House of Representatives, for the great gratification you have conferred upon me this day by the delivery of the favor from that Honorable Body allowing me a seat within its Hall.[1] I shall be ever proud to recollect it, as a token of their remembrance, collectively and individually, of One who has gone before us!

FC (DLC: DPM Papers).
1. The resolution of the House, dated 8 Jan. 1844, assured DPM that "whenever it shall be her pleasure to visit the House that she be requested to take a seat within the Hall" (ViU).

To James K. Paulding

WASHINGTON January 10th. 1844.

I hope to be able dear Friend to answer your last kind letter in a few days, more satisfactorily than I can now do before the arrival of my son, with whom I came to the conclusion before we parted at Montpellier to offer the entire writings of Mr. Madison to Congress—including the 4th. Volume—this seems the only mode left for me to pursue, with my unabated wishes to place them before the world. I cannot at present accede in favor of your french friend for the same reason that my son is not here, to co-operate in my sincere wish to oblige you, and to act up to your opinions in all respects, as I can never forget either their wisdom or the kindness, which has made them of essential value to me. Yours most truly

D P Madison

RC (MB).

To John Payne Todd

WASHINGTON Jany: 22d. 44.

If you love me, my dear son, write to me—tell me when you will come to offer the papers to Congress, and to do something with the 4th: volume—we are without funds and those we owe are impatient—the time has arrived now when if lost or neglected will never return to us! Mr: Rives with whom *only* I have conversed,[1] assured me that if he could do any thing in it—we should chuse—but he had made himself so unpopular—that no *open* efforts of his would do any good to my interest and therefore some influential member of the lower house should be chosen and employed. Oh, my son! I am too unhappy not to have you with me, and not to have even your opinion and directions, what to do myself or what individuals to engage and at what time! Do not let this often repeated request offend or hurt you my son—but reflect on the miseries of your mother, when she sees that nothing but a happy and early result of this duty will give her bread or continue to her what is better a respectable standing before the world—but I will say little more—as it is not good for me to write.

You have no doubt seen in the papers a Resolution of Congress inviting me to a seat—and my answer—It is nothing in my eyes or my heart, nor would compliments even higher, unless you and myself were on safe ground with our creditors.

Astor's interest is due the 19th: of February—can you obtain it for me? Miss Legaré's best respects to you. Ever your affectionate mother

D P. Madison

Tr (MCR-S: Mary Estelle Elizabeth Cutts Papers).

1. On 28 Dec. 1843 DPM wrote Senator William C. Rives, asking his "opinion and advice . . . on the subject of the Manuscripts, which I wish Congress to purchase" (DLC: Rives Papers).

From Paul Jennings

Dear mistris   ORANGE April 23 [1844]

I write you A fiew line to let you Know that I arrive safe home with the horses an wagon Charley deserted me betwen Alaxandra an Auquan miles I hope he is at home I could not find doctor winstons becose it was night the peaple ar All well except stephen hariet is much better sary better milley was quite sic yesterday the little children ar all well. The peple ar goin on as well as thay can the lot is cleand up Every thing looks green an beautiful mr & mrs howards sends thair kindes love to you an miss Annay thay wer much to here from you. I found faney vary porley but she says she is better then she was in the winter mas payne is quite well an was at Courte on monday A greate in-quiaries Abute your helth mas payn wants me to do som painting at todds Burgh I Could not get Enney fish in fredrix mr Allen told me he would send them up as soon he got them by wagon. Mother is well sends her love to you fanney sends her love to you an miss anney an Elen faney is vary thankful to you for my Coming to see her[1] love to sukey Beckey henry Ralph Elen nick no more to say I Reman your servent

Paul Janning

RC (DLC: DPM Papers). Docketed by DPM.
    1. Paul Jenning's wife Fanny was very ill and died on 4 Aug. (Peter Walker to Becca, 1 May, Paul Jennings to Sukey, 13 May, John Payne Todd to DPM, 5 Aug. 1844, DLC: DPM Papers).

To John Payne Todd

WASHINGTON May 22d. 44.

    I wrote you my dear the day before yesterday—I again take the pen so soon after my last to tell you that our friends Drumgoole[1] & John Y. Mason came to me on yesterday about the papers saying that many were anxious to vote me the amount with which I would be satisfied could I name it—I was at a loss from delicacy & a want of knowledge what to name—They mentioned the sum for the Debates but I did not reply farther—hoping to obtain an answer from you to my late letters in which I wished you to advise—they wanted the letter explaining the reasons for the Veto on the Bank after adhering long to a contrary opinion[2]—Will you now tell me if I should let the Committee see that explanatory letter and what other letters I had best shew them as speci-mens of the writings—and the sum expected for them—Steriotype & all. What to say of Copyright—They & others advise that the sale of *these* papers should be consummated in my time and during this session. I have given no direct answer but told them I wanted you here to act for me, and to en-lighten me as to one more point whether they could have the letters or some of them *to Mr. M.* Now my dear Son will you say at once what you think best to these particular questions. They *seem* to dwell on the *$30,000* as if that was the proper sum, without *absolutely expressing* it—but I must speak *now,* as they are impatient to have some data. You know J. Y. Mason by character—he is kindly directed to my cause— Oh, that you my beloved were fixed in all things, to co-operate with me—I will not say to act solely, for me, because, I had become the object of interest, and less would be done without me.

This is one of the opportunities so seldom allowed, where in it is proper for persons to speak *well* of Themselves and I therefore, have & will repeat to you these facts as necessary to be taken into view.

I wait your reply a few days—five—Your last sd. nothing in answer to my 6 last—Captn. Smith applied thro Ballard—can you settle it—or can you remit any to me & when

RC (DLC: DPM Papers). In Anna Payne's hand, except for the last paragraph in DPM's hand.
    1. In a letter of 15 March 1844, George Drumgoole, a Virginia member of the House of Representatives, agreed to "cheerfully make the proposal to Congress in relation to the manuscript volumes of Mr. Madison's works" (ViU).
    2. On 25 June 1831 James Madison wrote Charles J. Ingersoll, explaining the apparent "inconsistency between my objection to the constitutionality of such a bank [a national bank] in 1791 and my assent in 1817" (James Madison, *Letters and Other Writings of James Madison* [4 vols.; Philadelphia, 1865], 4:183–87).

From John Payne Todd

My Dr Mother,   June 1st. 44.

    I have just recd your two letters of 22th. 27th and shall make a great exertion to come on immediately—The Books have been sent by Collins a print seller who stops on the Road only to sell—I have been Successful I think, as I wrote you in all your suits as I shall explain—I sent you Mr Roberts in answer to your enquiry of how much in the Bank & the note—I thought it was july instead of June it would fall due & I wished to correct Mr Allen—Mr Moncure I am still treating with I told you I had got him up to offer 1 or 2 thousand more than he or Ambler thought they should get it for. Mr. Mason a clever man has a limited influence. Mr Drumgoole is decidedly a constitutional lawyer—They might be indulged in their private perusals; but it is for political effect which should be managed the better to promote yr objects. Friend Rives the Same—It is the Constitutional & Revolutionary ⟨War?⟩ &c. papers to be sold only & shall try to get many letters to Mr M which will add to their value.

RC (DLC: DPM Papers).

Deed to John Payne Todd

[16 June 1844]

Know all men by these presents that I Dolley P. Madison late resident of the County of Orange and State of Virginia and now residing in the City of Washington District of Columbia, for value received, have bargained, sold and granted, and confirmed, and by these presents do grant bargain and sell and confirm unto John P. Todd a certain number of negro Slaves named Tydal of 65 yrs of age, Willoughby about 60 yrs do, John abt 40 yrs, Jerry abt 32 yrs. Matthew abt 45 yrs, Winny abt 45 yrs, Milly abt 40 yrs Sarah abt 50 yrs Caty and young children about 22 Charlotte abt 20 Raif Junr about 33 yrs, Joshua abt 22, Nicholas 36 yrs, Nicholas Junr abt 13 yrs, Gabriel abt 50 yrs and Charles abt 30 yrs with Sylvia and four children she abt 33 yrs old.

To have and to hold the said negroes in the above Schedule and their future increase, to the only proper use and behoof of the said John P. Todd his executors, administrators, and assigns forever. And I the said Dolley P. Madison for myself, my Executors, and Administrators, the said schedule of Negroes, and their future increase, to the Said John P. Todd, his Executors, administrators and assigns, against me, the Said Dolley P. Madison, my Executors, administrators and assigns, and against all and every other person and persons whatever, shall and will warrant, and forever defend, by these presents. In witness whereof, I have hereunto set my hand, and affixed my seal this sixteenth day of June in the year one thousand Eight hundred and forty four.

D P Madison

Signed & delivered in presence of
Anna Payne
Elizabeth Lee

Ms (ViU). In the hand of John Payne Todd, signed by DPM; docketed "Madison to Todd Deed May 19 1845. Filed in office." A month later DPM signed a second deed of gift to John Payne Todd and added the following slaves: "Lewis, Stephen, Ralf Junr., Gery, Randall, Ellick, Blind John as he is called, Sam, Tom, Ben Senr., Julia, Amy, Sucky, Harriet, Becca, Nancy, Fanny, Abraham, William, and Ellen" (ViU).

From Sarah Steward

My Misstress   ORANGE July 5th 1844

I don't like to send you bad news but the condition of all of us your servants is very bad, and we do not know whether you are acquainted with it. The sheriff has taken all of us and says he will sell us at next court unless something is done before to prevent it. We are afraid we shall be bought by what are called negro buyers and sent away from our husbands and wives. If we are obliged to be sold perhaps you could get neighbours to buy us that have husbands and wives, so as to save us some misery which will in a greater or less degree be sure to fall upon us at being seperated from you as well as from one & another. We are very sure you are sorry for this state of things and we do not like to trouble you with it but think my dear misstress what our sorrow must be. The sale is only a fortnight from next monday but perhaps you could make some bargain with some body by which we could be kept together. I get a young lady to write in my name but it is intended for us all. The husband of Caty is with you what is to be done with her and her children. Your dutiful servant

Sarah

RC (DLC: DPM Papers).

Articles of Agreement between DPM, John Payne Todd, and Henry W. Moncure

[8 August 1844]

To wit, It is agreed to sell Henry W. Moncure seven hundred and fifty acres of land a part of the Montpellier Tract in Orange at Thirteen dollars an acre. Five thousand dollars to be paid in Cash and the balance in two equal payments at six and twelve months from the date of the Deed of Conveyance for which bonds are to be given and to be paid at maturity (with the exception only that the Title to the land is made free from all encumbrances whatsoever). Secondly to rent for three years five cellar rooms, five rooms on first floor and passage of ten feet, and half the Peidement, Center Hall and Porticoes of the Montpellier Dwelling-House in common—An out-house or Kitchen containing four rooms, a smoke House, Stable and grounds; Grounds in common and attached garden and grounds, the numerous Pear, Apple, Cherry, Peach trees &c &c it is understood each are entitled to half.

Thirdly any servants or Slaves to be hired or bought at valuation at the pleasure of the parties.

Possession to be had during the month of April, in the meantime the exterior of the Dwelling, the wood-work to be repaired and Painted, the interior to be plastered and painted at least so far as occupied by the said Henry W. Moncure at the cost of the Proprietor. The rent to be Two hundred and fifty dollars a year, if possession is had by the said Moncure, if not occupied by him there is to be no obligation of Rent

(signed) Henry W. Moncure

Tr (DLC: DPM Papers).

To Henry W. Moncure

WASHINGTON Aug. 12th. 1844.

I have executed and send this day the Indenture &c. according to your request, my kind and respected Friend—the accuracy of which will I hope be found adequate to the occasion—I should have enclosed them to my Son a day or two before this but the Secretary of State and Chief Clerk were absent and I found a difficulty in having the seal annexed to them—It is now done and I trust a blessing will follow the transaction—to you and to myself—No one I think, can appreciate my feeling of grief and dismay at the necessity of transferring to another a beloved home.

I have expressed to Payne my readiness to return for a short time in order to assist in the arrangements of the household contents which must be in confusion some of which I wish to retain.

I have told him also that you and himself would place as much money to my credit in Banks as was consistent with the engagements you have mutually concluded—taking in view of course the sum you were so good as to loan me when I saw you last. I wish also to retain some few of the black people but cannot designate them at this time—I would write more in order to elicit more from you on this interesting subject which still troubles us but that I am yet very much indisposed. Annie offers you her affectionate remembrances and thanks for yours.

(Signed) D. P. Madison

Tr (DLC: DPM Papers).

From John Payne Todd

My Dr Mother.   Sunday TUR[N]PIKE ROAD Augt. 44

I am out on yr service not necessary just at this moment to go into long details about Commissions &c enough shortly will be given you—The Carriage I suppose you can keep to ride at less expence than hire—can come in it by short stages or send any servant at less expence than by the Steam

Conveyance—And sell it with the horses at 310$ or take 260$ for the three if opportunity presents which is a fair price. I want you to deliver to Mr Templeman the list of Books for himself and Mr Force to mark with approximate prices to be given & which is to be enclosed as soon as possible.[1] In answer to your enquiry whether you could dispose of a bad girl I have only to say that you are free to sell put in pledge or otherwise *any of the Slaves with you,* in Washn. or here, to neighbours who would take One or more as you please, & others if you were with me. As soon as I get back I will endeavour to enclose some funds & a paper by which you can raise immediately 200 & upwards of dollars. Tomorrow I wish you could come on at least for a time taking a servant male & female and leaving the rest to write of their disposition afterwards for I am trying my utmost to Save by arrangements as it would be desirable to you the Sale of Montpellier—Since the writing by Mr Moncure of the letter of the 5th of Augt, which I want, I have somewhat felt his pulse and it beats as I expected and there is no great advantage to be derived from him if he does not take other things at fair prices—I told you I had an individual ready to come to make offers the moment I said so under certain contingencies after an examination of the land. I hope you will be cautious in what you say to Mr Moncure who I suspect sent you the deed direct for another object than expediting the business that of getting you to say something to bear upon me towards his early acquirement of the purchase; but I should wish to talk—not put upon paper many things and thank God I have now but yourself first & Anny to try to take care of which trusting to my hopes of ample ability in a short time may God bless you.

RC (DLC: DPM Papers).
    1. Georgetown resident George Templeman purchased a number of books from DPM, including a twenty-one-volume set of *American State Papers* and a run of the *National Intelligencer* from 1801 to 1845 (DPM's letter of contract, 9 Dec. 1846, DLC: DPM Papers).

From John Payne Todd

My Dr Mother.   [August 1844]
    I enclose a letter just come to hand from Kentucky and another to put in the Post Office only at Washington simply for Cleveland Ohio—A few covers to Frank to save a penny. And an Offer from Mr Moncure for some furniture not accepted of course & referred to you—The Piano 75 is the only one I would wish to accept & a few thrown in to effect the sale of it with him. As I have no time to copy or for many other things I ask the return of this paper immediately before or after a copy be taken. Mr Moncure will write you that

he will cancel all bargains & for Montpellier particularly—acknowledge immediately the letter and say when you get a little better you will write him & more particularly as you will hear some detail of facts from me—You get little or no money as a Surplus for this Sale & it is not material in any respect that you or I take it back except for the chance of getting more and Keeping up credit the same I am persuaded can be got—Do not pay out your money fast & something pro rata for the present. Lend me back immediately the policy of insurance for if he does not take it I will return to be cashed by you as it may be necessary according to rules & regulations—I have not the laws of the District—How long a residence gives citizen ship? For I believe they Smith & Robinson would be defeated on the ground of bringing suit against you at the wrong place—Answer me please no matter what your inclinations are for information—God bless you—All that glitters, is not gold.

RC (DLC: DPM Papers).

To Henry W. Moncure

WASHINGTON Septr. 3d. 1844.

I have received dear Friend your generous and considerate proposals, and I thank you for them—I will not however take such latitude in the advantage you offer me, as to annul the arrangements you concluded with my Son—I had made up my mind to them, when I sent the Deed, and I hope that your mutual proceedings since, are satisfactory to you both as they appeared to myself so far as I understood the minutia of them—that I should be permitted to choose some few, of the Negroes, and some of the furniture—and to retain the family Burial Place. Pray excuse this brief answer to your last of   I am not well eno: to add more at present than my respectful regards, to which Anna's are cordially added.

D P M.

FC (DLC: DPM Papers).

From John Payne Todd

My Dr Mother.   [12 September 1844]

In consequence of receiving a letter from H W Moncure on 6th I came to Richmond and am nearly ready by business & recovery from indisposition to come *privately* to Washington to explain and go on with business—The sale to H. W. Moncure I consider a most unfortunate one and I would certainly wish it done away for he is the source of more difficulty than could have been apprehended; but more anon—I write by a small end of a Candle at 2 Oclock this morng—12 Sepr '44. which is burning out.

RC (DLC: DPM Papers).

From Henry W. Moncure

Respected Madam   Octo 5th. 1844
    I have been much disappointed, not to have recd a reply to my Letter giving to you the option, to cancel the Sale made to me by your Son of your Montpelier land, I was induced by the most respectful consideration to make you the offer, and that I had done so in the most unexceptionable terms, I certainly so intended.

    So long a Period has elapsed, since this Matter has been made subject to your control, that I now trespass on your Courtesy, to say by return Mail what is your conclusion, to confirm or to Cancel; should you confirm the Sale I will be obliged to you to transfer and send to me the Policy of Insurance for the House, that I may notify the Company of the change of Ownership, and then to you I will return the Amt on Deposit, as the yearly Quota for Insurance, awaiting your prompt decisive reply Ever yours Very Respty

Henry W. Moncure

RC (DLC: DPM Papers).

To Henry W. Moncure

WASHINGTON Oct. 7th. 1844.

    You have indeed apparent cause for displeasure my valued frd—yet is the appearance of neglect, on my part, groundless—I answered your letter in 2 or 3 days after its rect wherin you give me the option to cancel or not, the sale of Montpr. which offer as well as your manner, & motives were appreciated by me. I told you in my answer that I wd. abide by this sale, & that my mind was satisfied by a perfect confidence in your kind & honorable intentions towards me. I sent *this* letter to O. C house for my son to see & deliver to you, supposing you wd be there, but unfortunately he had gone to Richd. & proceedg.

from thence to W——n & N. York he was detained at the latter place & with me in the City more than a week with sickness, leavg. him just time to reach Orange for the Coart last week—he was directed & intended, to find Your letter at *that* post office & to deliver it without delay—I suppose however that the perplexities in that strange & troubled region of O. C. house has chained him to it from last Monday to this time—Mo[n]dy the 7th. of Octr.

I sent also the Policy of Insurance to Payne to be done with as you mutually thought proper—on all which I hope will be in your hands when you receive this explanation.

Draft (DLC: DPM Papers).

From John Payne Todd

My Dr. M.   [October 1844]

Yours of the 22d is just recd via Warrenton. I have attended to all your requests in regard to Furniture and Servants. The Mr H. W. Moncure have not the slightest authority over either furniture or Slaves except such as he bought some time ago none since I saw you. And I have only *rights* no favor or affection to ask from any of them. The tone of your letters would seem to give him authorities he never possessed and I think presumption which it will be my part to check if continued on business matters; personally we [are] all affability. Your papers were brought to Toddsberthe in the wooden desk or chest flat in the Waggon all safe & untouched in the same position & put away equally safe for you to open in the Spring—The waggon will be loaded after they all come here—All the books are at Toddsberthe safely placed on Shelves—Up stairs & cellar all cleared one new house finished & another in progress so therefore plenty of room & some perhaps for private entertainment. I am glad you have 134 from Mr Smith I do not fear of being able to place the 220 in Bank & indeed some time before due. I wrote once to day already. Let the Harpers as it would be useless & perhaps injurious.

RC (DLC: DPM Papers).

From John Payne Todd

My Dear Mother—   Sunday Novr. 1844

I have been travelling about for some time on business and could not conveniently write—Mr Nicholas Trist I met with at the Gordonsville depot on my return from Charlottesville, where I had proceeded to the fair with a view to expose and sell one or two full blooded Cattle in which I did not succeed in consequence of the political excitement preventing the attendance of the gentlemen and breaking up the fair. Mr Trist told me he would call I am on my way home now to answer all your enquiries—Pray try and get out of Sukey who was the father secretly of B⟨ecca?⟩ for it may be of an advantage in the Sale—As to Paul—⟨?⟩ of the question from Col⟨?⟩. Affy Yrs.

RC (DLC: DPM Papers). Damaged by ink smears.

To Richard Smith

June 2d. '45.

May I ask your opinion dear Friend, whether the Bank of the Metropolis would afford me the accommodation of one hundred dollars for a short time on my note, or otherwise. As often before, I am disappointed in receiving funds, expected last Saturday—and necessary on that day—Excuse me for troubling you thus.

D P Madison

RC (ViU).

To John Payne Todd

June 14th. 45.

What has been the matter with you and [where] have you been my beloved? It has been long since you wrote me, or acknowledged the receiving of one of my several letters—Your last spoke of Stevenson's call, and of Graham's letter to his lawyer here to whom I communicated your intention to settle with Graham but this morning I recd. another intimation from said lawyer Morfit in a letter from Graham—a copy of which Anne has made in haste whilst keeping to read. I answered that it was always my intention to pay any just debt of Mr. Graham, when I was myself paid money due me in Virga.—and that I shd. communicate with you on the subject—What they will do I know not— but I am anxious as I told you to hear your progress in the different business that is before you, as well as what I am to expect—I know your power is very limitted as regards money and will be so until my other resources are tried— It is not necessary to name them now, especially if you intend to act and to tell me in what manner. You know that I wished to come on to your house for a short time & to be enabled to do so I must pay money here and have it for traveling to you, first—'twould be difficult for you to get it without settling with Moncure. I have not been well for some time, oweing to want of exercise—I have been rideing with my friends sometimes—had a gratifying visit to Mount Vernon with the Pt. & Mrs. Polk &c. and with them also to Gen Hunters—but what can I do to forget misfortunes which overwhelm me at this moment . . . ⟨ga⟩ve Paul a pass to go to O. Ch. I have my fears of the ⟨. . .⟩ples & wish you wd. caution him about speaking of my ⟨. . .⟩ fond of ammusing persons who will listen to his fabrica⟨tions . . .⟩ knowing more than they do.

RC (ViU). Ms torn.

To Richard D. Cutts

My dear Richard.   WASHINGTON July 16th. 1845.

I have felt much satisfaction in the two letters received from our dear Mary who was in health and good spirits, tho' suffering a drawback to both, in the illness of her estimable friends, the Mrs. Adams'—both of whom she describes as ill in her last letter—the elder *habitually* sick—the younger threatened with deafness. Another, recd. this day announces herself at Nahant with the Crowninshields—How I should delight to keep her company there—my ancient and valued friends—kind and constant in love and in war—but I have been unable to leave the City as yet, and have suffered from the heat too much. The Ther: has been above 90 for many days. I hope you will as you anticipate, finish your business and get out of the way of sickness—and that you may arrive in *good heart* for the happy marriage.[1] Mary wrote me as I expected, that she was delighted with Martha. To speak of Farley's house—it would be a very pretty one for your purposes—more to my mind for you than the one you left—but persons are there at work and it looks as if the house was taken.

Our acquaintances here go on as usual—the Masons are still great favorites and we have seen much of the President & family and like them as we do the members of the Cabinet. I have postponed the pleasant trip we thought of, to my sweet friend Mrs. Wethered, but still hope to take it before the meeting of Congress. As to going to Virginia, I have hoped it so long that I do not know what to say about it now, farther than that I still intend it—to learn more of my business there than I possibly can without doing so.

And now my dear Richard I will tell you on what, our thoughts have dwelt a great deal—it was to become worthy of membership in the Church which I have attended for the last forty years—and which Anne has generally attended all her life—Yesterday this wish was consummated as far as confirmation extended[2]—Bishop Whittingham performed this ceremony, as well as that of Instituting Mr. Pyne our Rector. We had an excellent sermon from the Bishop of New Jersey—a fine preacher and beautiful champion for Charity which "suspects not, thinks no evil &c."

We have seen Madison every day since the absence of Ellen, who with the children are at Mrs. D. Young's.

Anne will finish my debt, for your last welcome letter, and I will write you again as soon as I can recover a little from a sad lassitude which a good rain might dispel. We spent an agreeable day at Brentwood last week—Mr. Ritchie is still here, and pleasant as usual—(not that he was there at all). Cousin Edward paid us a short visit ten days ago, on his way to the Green Mountain—with his wife and children. I have lately discovered that we have a relation (tho' not very near yet one I once knew well) ⟨. . .⟩ within a very short distance of me—Mrs. Swann, whose daughter married the Treasurer, Mr. Selden—and with whom she now stays on account [of] her little grand son. The family of Cabells, too are related—to whom you will be presented by & by. With all good wishes, your Aunt truly

D P Madison

I send Mary's letter for you to read—please return it for me to answer. Do you get the papers?

RC (NjP: Crane Collection). Addressed to Cutts at Havre de Grace, Md.

1. Richard D. Cutts married Martha Jefferson Hackley, the daughter of Richard and Harriet Randolph Hackley, on 16 Dec. 1845.

2. DPM's certificate of confirmation at St. John's Episcopal Church in Washington, D.C., 15 July 1845, is owned by Macculloch Hall Historical Museum, Morristown, N.J.

To John Payne Todd

My dear Son—   July 17th. 45.

I wish to say a few words on the subject of Paul—whom you have not mentioned since he left here for Orange. I hired him to the President, who (as well as myself) gave him the privilege of 2 or 3 weeks to visit his family—when he was to have returned & entered upon his duties again—It was of importance to me that he shd. have been punctual, but he has not appeared or written an apology—of course he will lose the best place and his mistress conveniant resources. I hope you recd. my last acknowledging the $30. I am waiting with impatience your next, by which I hope to know so much. Yours ever

M.

Printed copy (owned by Gary Hendershott, Little Rock, Ark., 1993).

To John Payne Todd

[19 February 1846]

I now write to you my beloved not that I have any thing very cheering to say, but that I wish to assure you of my constant thoughts, & prayers.

You have seen no doubt, that my ever dear Sister departed this life some days ago[1]—Wm wrote me that it was by apoplexy.

The writings of my Husband will be purchased by Congress, but no one can say at what time, as the Members are more interested in the acquiremt of Orregon, & other speculations. I have some attentive friends in the Committe who wish to benefit me, as do most of the Honble. body of Congress—by naming 25000$—the interest of which they will place at my command during life & desend as I like—They sujest that it will be more to my interest, that no interference from any other source shall be seen.

I lay this before you, that you may decide with me that our course is acquiesed when nothing better is to be

Draft (DLC: DPM Papers). Note "enclosing copy of Saunder's list."
1. Lucy Payne Washington Todd.

To John Payne Todd

My dearest   Apl. 23d. 46.

It has been too long since I was cheered with a line from you—what are you about, that prevents your communing with your Mother? You are taking special care of our mutual property of every sort, I trust—& my confidence in you to restore it to me is not diminished by the sad & tedious time in which I have been deprived of its use—a part of the furniture I wished to divide with you, & a part of it I desired to sell but I wished to be with you & together choose what best to dispose of. I take my pen *now* to say that by this post I send the notice for Mesrs. Booten & Walker & soon Annie's deposition shall follow in order that the cause shall not be ⟨dismissed?⟩ or lost[1]—I have recd. today a few polite lines from Mr Robertson (the one of) your counsil—saying to that in case it shd. not be in his power to see you in good time, he wd remind me of the vitel importance it was of in gaining the cause so I consulted Walter Jones about the manner & go by his directions in this. I must take time to say that nothing is done in regard to the papers more, than to place them in a sure state to be acted on some time or other—you saw in the N papers no doubt, the *report* of Mr Dromgoole[2]—& Mrs Hamiltons promised success by passing her petition to a third reading in the Senate. I hope to add the Deposition in full time for the first of May by sending it sooner—and have asked Mr. Hame to apply to the Clerk for a Commission for the taking of it. Anxious

Mother!

Draft (DLC: DPM Papers).

1. This was the case of *Madison* v. *Madison,* in which Richard C. Booten and James W. Walker, the executors of William Madison's estate, were suing for the payment of $2,000 alledgedly owed by James Madison to his brother for the settlement of their father's estate. William J. Robertson of Charlottesville was DPM's attorney.

2. George C. Dromgoole's report proposing the purchase of the remainder of JM's manuscript papers was made in the House of Representatives on 9 March (*Congressional Globe,* 29th Cong., 1st sess., 471).

From Sarah Steward

Dear Mistris   TODDSBERTH ORANGE CTY April 24th 1847

I write to let you know that I am better at time than I have been for some time past. You wished me to write to you as soon as I recd. your letter but I was verry unwell & could not attend to it Miss Ellen married a gentleman from Norfolk by the name of John Myers they were married at Doct. Slaughters & dined next day at her brother Thomas and then to Mrs Willis.s & then on the third day after they were maried they started for Norfolk. I believe the people in the naibourhood is generaly well Silvey was taken in labour last fryday & had Doct. Slaughter & Doct. Grymes with her but died last sunday morning at sunrise they could not deliver her. I have been very unwell and had to get some medison from Doct. Slaughter my love to Miss Anny and your self tell Susan that Rebecca has a fine daughter named Susan Ellen after her Mother give my love to Caty & Ralph & Mathew & tell him I should be glad to see him at home they are all well here & very buysey a planting of corn tell Susan that little Betty is verry unwell she has fitts verry bad & her son Thomas has bad risens on both of his armes give my love to catys three children & tell them I want to see them verry bad I must now conclude with my love & respects to all

Sarah Steward

NB. Winney is tolerable well and wishes to be rembered to Matthew and all the rest

RC (DLC: DPM Papers).

From John Payne Todd

My Dear Mother.   18th Sepr. 1847.

I left Washington knowing that you wanted money, and I have been trying to borrow or get it in any way; but can not succeed in this Country, & I have now since determined to return and renew my endeavours notherly. I shall now, early in Octr before the notes of the Bank falls due be enabled to come on and bring you some, & give Mr Harvey his 105$ at least, if not pay, if you can spare it, the Discount of 268$. The 100$ paid him & 12$ interest was for additional Coal & Wood subsequently obtained & this last bill is a continuation of accounts, preceding, & since my leaving Washington—I have been lately to Charlottesville where I saw Betsy Coles who looks as if she would live but a short time. Mrs Stevenson was in bed as it was early in the morning passing on to Mr W Robinson's the lawyer. With whom I wished to converse on legal business that is to come on (of Walker's) during next month. Hearing from Miss Betsy that Edward & family were at John Coles I went there & they the next Morning was going on their rout to Blenheim the new purchased place of Mr Stevenson where I saw him. John Tucker & Edward look as bad as Betsy, John Worse. There is no borrowing from this quarter. John has settled all his affairs for Death & expects it soon with apparent good Cause. The Homer & Gallery are safe I will look up & enclose. I had some motive to delay the letter drafted to young Mr Baldwin abt Interest. He recd I believe his portion from Madison Hite or his guardian & so one of these received the 1500$ left them &c but for any remnant unpaid I will ascertain as well as possible & write. You are I presume irresponsible for any of it—It lays with the two former or the Bank—I have been prevented from sending the Waggon of 2 horses old to the landing with things for you & for Suckey for want of funds to pay the expences—but in begginning of Oct I will come myself with all the money that will fall into my hands. In the mean time, I am full of taking depositions &c without money to pay for them. I labour under considerable disadvantages for little sums to advance your & my own interest occasionally. It is of great consequence in a pecuniary point of view to have, if could be procured, some Money, for a time for securityship. And if you could have succeeded with Mr Astor it would have afforded great advantage if the Amount was sufficient. I suppose Mr Bomford could not get a good opportunity to speak to him I should like to know for the sake of His Debt if he is likely to live.

I want to prepare a paper or deed for you to sign, thinking that it will defeat Moncure in the success of charges if on consultation it is judged expedient—Take care fore-ever of such men—he has an object of deception for 6¼ cts. By a proper suit damages could be recovered from him for his delays to many thousand dollars for his Conduct. He has sold 703 acres of his 1st purchase of 750$ to John Willis at 15$ he gave 13$. I am discontented & unhappy for many things altho Affcy yrs always

J. P. Todd

P. S. I sent the Bill of Walker for you to read to see the pretensions of delay of Moncure; but particularly to consult Mr Smith with a view only to know whether the Sheriff had actually come as implied or stated by which he learnt you had no goods as the bill sets forth. I alone can, & no lawyer, get the material for answer. I have duly recd the "Sun" newspapers & others sent for which I am much Obliged & would send as I have access to them Papers of this part, but no interest probably to you.

RC (DLC: DPM Papers).

To John Payne Todd

My beloved   Septr. 24th. 1847.

I am too sensible to all the troubles you encounter but I trust in Our Heavenly Father, who has in His Mercy supported us to this day—let your Faith be in Him, with Prayers for His continued goodness, to us, who are nothing without Him.

I entrusted the letters and some account of the Astor business, to Col. Bomford who promised his faithful attention—but I have recd. only verbal accts. from him, thro' his wife. He says he has made every effort to converse with *him* in vain—that he cannot *converse*—that his watchful friends do all that for him—and that the prospect of gaining on his former feelings *seems* hopeless—as he can neither listen nor reply. It is thought he will live but a short time, as he now lives on the milk of a wet nurse.

I am afraid the facility of borrowing money in the North could not be extended to our situation, when the same obstructions exist with a multitude of others.

I have borrowed as you *must* know, to live since and before we parted last, but now I am at a stand, until supplies come from you—I will as you advise take care of "*such men*"—whom I detest too much ever to hear their defence. I hope Mr Robinson & yourself will make wise & efficient conclusions in the case of Walker and every other in dispute—I take for granted that all will be granted with that immovable calmness of spirit which has ever been found the wisest.

I hope to see you in health and good prospects when you come to visit me in October—You will let me hear from you when you can. I send you some papers but object to your returning the like—I cannot think of any Deed being necessary for the purpose you mention. I have nothg. to convey away nor with which to benefit myself. My Eye rebels—adieu for this time.

Draft (DLC: DPM Papers).

Statement re: the Terms of Sale of the Madison Papers

[13 December 1847]

Whereas a proposition is now under consideration, in the House of Representatives, for the purchase of the papers and writings of my decd. Husband James Madison decd. the right whereof is vested in me by my said Husband's Will, and whereas, I am desirous of appropriating a portion of the purchase money to the payment of debts now due and owing by me, and of investing the balance in such mode, through the agency of a friend, that I may receive semi-annually the interest thereof during my life, without authority to touch the principal, and to convey the principal sum thereof remaining, to my devisees to be named in my Will—all which I will do by a more formal inst[r]ument when the said appropriation shall have been made—now in consideration of the love and affection I bear these persons, and of one dollar paid to me by my friend John Y. Mason, I hereby bind myself, by such conveyance as he may prepare legally to effect these objects, when the said appropriation shall have been made, after applying a sum not exceeding five thousand dollars to payment of debts now due and owing by me, to settle the residue of said appropriation on James Buchanan John Y. Mason and Richard Smith as trustees, so that during my life I shall receive the interest thereof, and at my death, the principal thereof shall go to the persons to be named in my Will as aforesaid. Witness my hand and seal this 13th. day of Decr. 1847.

D P Madison (seal)

Testor: Annie Payne

Draft (DLC: DPM Papers). Marked "Copy." Docketed "Copy of paper given by Mrs. D. P. Madison to the Hon. J. G. Crittendon for the Hon. J. Y. Mason."

To Robert G. L. De Peyster

Dear Sir: WASHINGTON, February 11th, 1848.

I did not receive your favor containing the newspapers, and therefore is my impatience to assure you of my gratitude for the interest you take in my defence in the little narrative of the picture rescue.

You will see by the enclosed what was said at the time. The impression that Mr. Carroll saved Stuart's portrait of Washington is erroneous. The paper which was to accompany your letter has not reached me, but I have heard that his family believed he rescued it. On the contrary, Mr. Carroll had left me to join Mr. Madison, when I directed my servants in what manner to remove it from the wall, remaining with them until it was done. I saw Mr. Barker and yourself (the two gentlemen alluded to) passing, and accepted your offer to assist me, in any way, by inviting you to help me to preserve this portrait, which you kindly carried, between you, to the humble but safe roof which sheltered it awhile. I acted thus because of my respect for General Washington—not that I felt a desire to gain laurels; but, should there be a merit in remaining an hour in danger of life and liberty to save the likeness of anything, the merit in this case belongs to me. Accept my respect and best wishes.

D. P. Madison

Printed copy (*Records of the Columbia Historical Society* 3 [1900]: 59).

To John Payne Todd

My dr. Son.   [24] Apl. 1848

I am very distressed at my failure to obtain for you the lawyer's opinion as you desired—because Mr. Jones was sick & B. Smith[1] too full of business to understand what was meant by the whole representation you made—I therefore rest my hopes on your & Mr. Green's powers, to have justice done in our case. If you can wait for a few days I hope to send you $100 which will put your clothes in order—by the sale of Ellen at $400—who is kept quietly in jail until she recovers from her 6 months dissipation—You have seen perhaps in the N. papers that she was taken in the vessel freighted for the North by Abolitionists[2]—I have not seen her, but heard a bad acct. of her morals & conduct—I wait as you suggest a quieter time for the Bill & sale of the girl—another week may bring it about, when I may act—now it is impossible—I'll write again to-morrow. This day they celebrate the French Revolution & nothing else can be done in the City.

Tr (DLC: DPM Papers). Marked "Copy." Date assigned on the basis of news reports of the Washington celebration of the French Revolution of February 1848 (*Daily Union,* 25 April 1848).

    1. J. Bayard Smith, son of Margaret Bayard Smith.

    2. On the night of 16 April 1848, a group of seventy-six African-American men, women, and children, most of them household slaves of families in Washington and Georgetown, boarded the schooner *Pearl* and attempted to sail to safe haven. That same day they were pursued and overtaken by a steamboat, whereupon the slaves were jailed for a time and later sold to a Baltimore slave dealer (Bryan, *History of the National Capital* 2:385–86).

From Thomas Ritchie

My dear Mrs. Madison—   [2 May 1848]

Mr. Brady of New York requests a line of introduction to you and I yield with great pleasure, for he is an Artist of eminent merit, the first, I understand, in his line in America. He is very desirous of daguerreotyping that face, which is so well known to so many of our countrymen, but which so many others are desirous of seeing, in some form or other. Let me join Mr. Brady in the request of persuading you to sit for him. He took Mrs. Polk, along with others in this city, but he cannot think his gallery complete without adding your face to his interesting collection. With true regard your friend and admirer

Thomas Ritchie

Printed copy (owned by Gary Hendershott, Little Rock, Ark., 1993).

To John Payne Todd

Sunday May 21st. 48.

You have seen by the Gazettes, my dear Son, that we had an alarm of fire in our house on last Saturday week[1]—At 4 O'clock in the morng. our chamber door was assailed by Ralph who begged Annie & myself to come down immediately, whilst the stairs remained—we did so, thro' a crackling fire—losing not a moment, we reached the garden ground—he returned and brought me down the trunks of papers—when our neighbours (just awakened) came to our assistance, and soon seperated the fire from the window frame, in which it had made great progress—It has been supposed to be the work of an incendiary and the Watch is nightly around the City. Yesterday Congress passed the Bill for the purchase of Mr. Madison's papers.[2] I will enclose you the newspapers—and beg you will tell me whether you have recd. my letter enclosing a $50 note[3]—also to say when you think you can come to me, and whether you have any papers to send me which you think would be better added to those I have—You promised me to be ready with the Harper directions—they are now wanting, as well as all other advice you can give or bring me—Your affectionate

Mother.

RC (DLC: DPM Papers).

1. "We learn that some miscreant attempted on Saturday morning to set fire to the dwelling of the venerable relict of ex-President Madison, situated near St. John's Church" (*National Intelligencer*, 15 May 1848).

2. "An Act to provide for the Purchase of the Manuscript Papers of the late James Madison, former President of the United States," 31 May 1848, *U.S. Statutes at Large* 9:235. The law provided for the purchase of all JM's manuscripts in DPM's possession for $25,000, of which $5,000 was to be paid directly to her and the balance held and invested by trustees James Buchanan, John Y. Mason, and Richard Smith, with the interest paid to her as it accrued. The principle was inalienable during her lifetime, "as a permanent fund for her maintenance, but subject to be disposed of as she may please by her last will and testament."

3. DPM to John Payne Todd, 9 May 1848, DLC: DPM Papers.

To John Payne Todd

My dear Son—   June 29th. 1848.

I sent on your trunk the morng. after you left, which I trust was safely recd. by you as such was the promise of the Captain. At this moment I am much distressed at the *conversations* you held, and the *determinations* you expressed, on the subject of bringing suit against my Trustees—and request the favor of you to make them easy and content, with you by the assurance that you abandon the idea, or that you never had any such intention. I say all this *for you* because I do not believe even *yourself* if you *declared* such an intention, which would at once ruin your fair ⟨fame?⟩—your mother would have no wish to live after her son issued such threats which would deprive her of her friends, who had no other view in taking the charge but pure friendship—This I do wish you to put at rest on the receipt of this, without losing a moment. Half as much as I have written will be sufficient.

Mr. Smith was Trustee and Executor to my sister's Will and he is now very infirm, scarcely able to live from day to day, but it is a deep trouble to him to believe that he is to be harassed with a suit which from every point of view would be unavailable to any one. Your affte. Mother

FC (DLC: DPM Papers).

To John Payne Todd

My dear Son.   July 10th. 1848.

I ardently hoped that you would have written me about our affairs before this, and that I should have some guide to lead from whelming darkness—but it is in vain to wait! I wish to tell you all that concerns us, but you are silent about your being at home or absent from it.

I have concluded to have a Raffle for the large painting with other pictures and some plate in order to be better *satisfied* &c. What ought the large painting and those of Washington and Jefferson by Stuart, to bring in a Raffle or sale? Those of Adams and Monroe also—please to give some guess and tell what estimate you place upon Columbus, Vespucius, Magellan, Cortez and the Bard of Ossian.

I wrote you a week ago but no answer has come to me tho' twas important I should have one. Your

M

FC (DLC: DPM Papers).

Elizabeth Collins Lee to Zaccheus Collins Lee

My dear Son   [1849]

You ask me wether my dear friend Mrs. Madison was conscious during her illness.

I was with her every day during her illness—Tho greatly prostrate from the first she lay quiet, with her eyes shut and when not disturbed by the *frequent attacks* of her disease appeard to suffer no pain and conscious when spoken to tho she spoke but very faintly.

When frequently requested to open her eyes by her Niece Annie Payne— she at length did so—and looking round on the Ladies around her Bed—*she* caught *my eye*—when I said to her do you know me.

She said with a ⟨distink'd?⟩ voice and a sweet smile—"Do I *know* you, my dear Betsey—Yes, and I love you"—extending her ⟨tiring?⟩ arms to imbrace me—This greatful recognition of an Old Frend reverting to our early days when she even call'd me *Betsey* is to me at least a greatful and conclusive evidence of her being in her sound mind.

RC (ViU).

Biographical Directory

Adams, Abigail Smith (1744–1818). Wife of John Adams and First Lady 1797–1801; the first First Lady to live in the executive mansion (White House).

Adams, Louisa Catherine Johnson (1775–1852). Wife of John Quincy Adams and First Lady 1825–29; lived in Washington 1803–8, 1817–29, and 1831–52.

Adams, William (1772–1851). British negotiator of the Treaty of Ghent.

Addison, Walter Dulaney (1769–1848). Episcopalian minister who established a school at Oxen Run, opposite Alexandria, in 1794, which John Payne Todd attended until 1805.

Allen, Mary Elizabeth Payne Jackson (1805—1881). Sole surviving daughter of DPM's sister Mary Payne Jackson and John G. Jackson. Spouse of John James Allen (1797–1871), judge of the Virginia Court of Appeals 1840–65.

Amy. A slave probably owned by the Payne family.

Armstrong, Alida Livingston (1761–1822). Daughter of Judge Robert R. and Margaret Beekman Livingston. In 1789 she married John Armstrong Jr. (1758–1843), soldier and politician from Pennsylvania, officer in the American Revolution, U.S. senator 1800–1802 and 1803–4, and minister to France 1804–10. JM appointed him brigadier general; he served as U.S. secretary of war 1813–14.

Astor, John Jacob (1763–1848). An American fur trader, merchant, and financier, Astor helped finance the War of 1812. In the 1840s DPM turned to him for financial help.

Astor, William Backhouse (1792–1875). Son of John Jacob Astor; real estate investor.

Bache, Richard (1794–1836). The son of Benjamin Franklin Bache, he was, after his widowed mother remarried, also the stepson of William Duane. He was a soldier and the author of a book of travels in South America published in the early 1820s.

Bagot, Mary (d. 1845). Wife of Sir Charles Bagot (1781–1843), British minister to the United States 1814–20, and niece of the duke of Wellington.

Baker, Anthony St. John (1785–1854). Secretary to the British legation in the United States 1810–13, he served as agent for British prisoners of war. After the war he was chargé d'affaires and then British consul general.

Baker, James (1796–1870). The brother of Anthony St. John Baker, he was a member of the British legation to the United States under Charles Bagot and acting consul general 1818–19. He married Catherine C. Tayloe, sister of Benjamin Ogle Tayloe, in 1824.

Baldwin, Clara. *See* Bomford, Clara Baldwin

Bankhead, Anne Cary Randolph (1791–1826). The eldest daughter of Martha Jefferson and Thomas Mann Randolph, she married Charles Lewis Bankhead in 1808.

Barbour, Lucy Johnson. Daughter of Benjamin Johnson of Orange County and wife of James Barbour (1775–1842), a plantation owner and neighbor of the Madisons. They had seven children, among them Lucy Maria (who married John Taliaferro), James Jr., Frances Cornelia, and Benjamin Johnson. James Barbour served multiple terms in the House of Delegates, was elected governor of Virginia in 1812, and represented that state in the U.S. Senate 1815–25. He was secretary of war 1825–28 and afterward minister to Great Britain.

Barbour, Philip Pendleton (1783–1841). Brother of James Barbour; practiced law and represented Orange County in the House of Delegates in 1812. Served in Congress 1814–24 (as Speaker of the House 1821–23) and 1827–30. Served as judge of the U.S. district court of eastern Virginia 1830–36; appointed to the U.S. Supreme Court in 1836.

Barker, Jacob (1779–1871). A financier who amassed and lost a number of fortunes over his lifetime, Barker helped finance the War of 1812. He and Robert De Peyster, at the behest of DPM, carried the Gilbert Stuart portrait of Washington from the White House in 1814. In 1834 Barker moved to New Orleans, where he became one of the South's leading capitalists.

Barlow, Joel (1754–1812). A writer, businessman, and diplomat, the Yale-educated Barlow first became known as an epic poet and a member of the Hartford Wits. Appointed minister to France in February 1811, he died in Poland in December 1812.

Barlow, Ruth Baldwin (1756–1818). Wife of Joel Barlow. The couple moved to Washington in 1808. She corresponded with DPM while she was in France and after her husband's death.

Barnet, Isaac Cox (b. 1773). A professional American diplomat who began his career in 1794; in 1816 JM appointed him consul to Paris.

Barney, Joshua (1759–1818). A Baltimore native and veteran of the American Revolutionary navy, Barney served as a commodore in the French navy in the 1790s. He reentered the U.S. Navy during the War of 1812.

Barry, William Taylor (1785–1835). A Virginia-born Kentuckian, he became a Democratic Party leader and lieutenant governor of Kentucky in 1821. He served as postmaster general 1829–35.

Bassett, Burwell (1764–1841). After multiple terms in the Virginia state legislature, Bassett served in the U.S. House of Representatives 1805–13, 1815–19, and 1821–29.

Bayard, James Ashton (1767–1815). Princeton-educated lawyer; served in the House 1797–1803 and in the Senate 1804–13. JM appointed him a member of the commission to negotiate peace with Great Britain. He signed the Treaty of Ghent in December 1814 but died shortly after JM nominated him minister to Russia in 1815.

Blaettermann, George. First professor of modern languages at the University of Virginia.

Blake, James H. In 1809 he set up a medical practice in the District of Columbia; in 1813 he became mayor of Washington.

Blicherolsen, Peder. Danish minister to the United States 1801–3.

Bomford, Clara Baldwin. Sister of Ruth Baldwin Barlow; married George Bomford in 1816. The couple bought Kalorama, the Barlow estate in Washington, D.C.

Bonaparte, Elizabeth Patterson (1785–1879). A famous beauty and socialite born into a wealthy Baltimore family, Betsy Patterson married Jerome Bonaparte (1784–1860), Napoleon's youngest brother, in 1803. Napoleon opposed the marriage, and it was annulled in 1806. Their son, Jerome-Napoleon Bonaparte (1805–1870), grandnephew of Margaret Spear Smith, married Susan May Williams of Baltimore in 1829.

Bonnycastle, Charles (1792–1840). English-born first professor of natural philosophy at the University of Virginia. In 1827 he became professor of mathematics, a position he held until his death.

Bourne, Sylvanus (1761–1817). U.S. consul at Amsterdam under Jefferson and JM.

Boyd, George (1779–1846). Secretary to the secretaries of war 1811–14 and Indian commissioner in Wisconsin 1818. Husband of Harriet Johnson Boyd, John Quincy Adams's sister-in-law.

Boyd, Washington. A native of the District of Columbia, Boyd was a federal city surveyor (1794), city tax collector (1801), city treasurer (1803), and U.S. marshal (1805).

Brady, Mathew B. (ca. 1823–1896). Photographer; made daguerreotype portraits of DPM.

Breckenridge, James (1763–1833). A veteran of the Revolutionary War and the War of 1812, Breckenridge served multiple terms in the Virginia House of Delegates and several terms in the U.S. House of Representatives. He was a member of the first Board of Visitors of the University of Virginia 1819–33.

Bridport, George (d. 1819). Decorative painter and draftsman.

Brockenbrough, Arthur S. Proctor of the University of Virginia who helped supervise its construction.

Brown, Jacob (1775–1828). Major general commanding in western New York. In 1814 he led the invasion of Canada. General in chief of the U.S. Army 1821–28.

Brown, Nancy Hart. Sister of Lucretia Hart Clay and wife of James Brown (1766–1835), U.S. senator from Louisiana 1813–17 and 1819–23 and minister to France 1823–29.

Buchanan, Mrs. Wife of James A. Buchanan, a partner in the Baltimore firm Smith and Buchanan, merchants and shipowners.

Buchanan, James (1791–1868). Representative from Pennsylvania in the U.S. Congress 1820–31, U.S. senator 1834–45, secretary of state 1844–48, president of the United States 1856–60.

Burke, Mrs. A member of a Washington theater family.

Burwell, William Armisted (1780–1821). A Virginian who served as private secretary to President Jefferson; he was a member of Congress 1806–21.

Cabell, Joseph Carrington (1778–1856). Served multiple terms in the Virginia House of Delegates and Senate, in particular promoting the creation and operation of the University of Virginia. He was a member of the university's original Board of Visitors and served in that capacity for thirty-seven years.

Cadwalader family. Gen. John Cadwalader (1742–1786) and his family belonged to Philadelphia society. A daughter, Frances, married David Erskine.

Caldwell, Elias Boudinot (1776–1825). Son of James Caldwell; adopted by Elias Boudinot. A Princeton-educated lawyer, he became clerk of the Supreme Court in 1800. During the War of 1812 he commanded a Maryland cavalry troop. Cofounded the American Colonization Society in 1816.

Calhoun, Floride Bouneau (b. 1792), a low-country heiress, married John C. Calhoun

(1782–1850), a Yale-educated South Carolina lawyer, in 1811. He served in Congress 1810–16, as secretary of war 1817–25, and as vice president 1825–32. In 1832 Calhoun resigned and was elected to the U.S. Senate (1832–43, 1845–50), from which platform he led the fight against the tariff and for the doctrine of nullification. He was secretary of state 1844–45.

Cambacérès, Jean-Jacques-Régis de (1753–1824). French government official during the Revolution and the Napoleonic era.

Campbell, Harriet Stoddert. Daughter of Federalist Benjamin Stoddert. In 1812 she married George Washington Campbell (1769–1848), who emigrated to North America from Scotland in 1772. He served in Congress as a Tennessee Republican 1803–9 and in the Senate 1809–14 and 1815–18. JM appointed him secretary of the treasury in 1814. He served as minister to Russia 1818–20.

Campbell, John W. (d. 1813). A Virginia-born soldier, he served in the U.S. Army during the War of 1812 and was killed in the Battle of Chippewa.

Campbell, Maria Dallas (b. 1793). Daughter of Alexander and Arabella Maria Dallas, she married Alexander Campbell, a Virginian, in 1813.

Canning, George (1770–1827). British foreign minister 1807–9.

Caraman, George de. Secretary of the French legation under Sérurier.

Carey and Lea. Philadelphia publishing business formed by Henry Carey and his brother-in-law, Isaac Lea, in 1822.

Carr, Peter (1770–1815). Nephew of Thomas Jefferson; married Hetty Smith Stevenson, sister of Samuel Smith of Baltimore.

Carroll, Charles (1767–1841). Charles Carroll of Bellevue, brother of Daniel Carroll of Duddington, was with DPM when the British were approaching on 23 Aug. 1814. A member of a wealthy Maryland Roman Catholic family, Charles Carroll moved to Washington in 1811. In 1813 he purchased Dumbarton House in Georgetown from Joseph Nourse. He was a member of the board of the Bank of Washington and a supporter of JM.

Carroll, Daniel (1764–1849). Daniel Carroll of Duddington, brother of Charles Carroll of Bellevue, was a real estate investor in the District of Columbia.

Carter, Mary Eliza Coles (1776–1856). Sister of Edward Coles and wife of Robert Carter of Redlands, Albemarle County, Va. Second cousin to DPM.

Cary, Jane Barbara Carr (1766–1840). Cousin of Martha Jefferson Randolph.

Caton, Miss. Richard and Mary Carroll Caton had four daughters, three of whom were known as "the three graces": Marianne, known as Mary (1778–1853); Elizabeth (1787–1862); and Louisa (1791–1874). Marianne married Robert Patterson. The other three married into British society.

Cazenove, Anthony-Charles (1775–1852). A Swiss-born merchant, Cazenove came to the United States in 1794 and settled in Alexandria, Va.

Chapman, Nathaniel (1778–1853). A student of Benjamin Rush, Chapman practiced medicine in Philadelphia and was the first president of the American Medical Association, in 1847.

Chevallie, Kitty Lyons. Daughter of Judge Peter Lyons of Hanover County, Va., and wife of John A. Chevallie of Richmond.

Christie, John (d. 1813). A New Yorker who served in the U.S. Army 1808–11. JM nominated him to the rank of lieutenant colonel in 1812. A year later he was promoted to colonel; he died on 22 July 1813.

Claiborne, William Charles Cole (1775–1817). Born in Sussex County, Va., he practiced law in Tennessee; was elected to Congress in 1797; and served as governor of the Mississippi Territory 1801–3, commissioner to oversee the transfer of the Louisiana Purchase 1803–4, governor of the Orleans Territory 1804–12, governor of Louisiana 1812–16, and U.S. senator from Louisiana 1817.

Clay, Henry (1777–1852). Representative, senator, secretary of state, and three-time candidate for president, Clay was both a supporter of the Madison administration and a long-standing friend of DPM.

Clay, Lucretia Hart (1781–1864). Daughter of Col. Thomas Hart of Lexington, Ky., and wife of Henry Clay.

Clifford, Rebecca. *See under* Pemberton, John

Clinton, DeWitt (1769–1828). A New York politician and a staunch Republican, Clinton was mayor of New York City. In 1807 he broke with the Republican Party over the Embargo Act and in 1812 ran for president against JM.

Clinton, George (1739–1812). Governor of New York 1777–95 and 1801–4 and two-term U.S. vice president 1805–12. He led the opposition to JM from within the Republican Party.

Cockburn, Admiral Sir George (1772–1853). Career British naval officer who in 1813 operated in Chesapeake Bay, attacking Havre de Grace, Md., in May and Hampton, Va., in June. In August 1814 he directed the destruction of Washington, D.C.

Cocke, John Hartwell (1780–1866). After studies at the College of William and Mary, Cocke settled at Bremo, his plantation in Fluvanna County, Va. He served as brigadier general of Virginia militia in the War of 1812. A leading force in such organizations as the American Colonization Society, American Temperance Union, and Bible and Sunday School Societies, Cocke served for thirty-three years as a member of the original Board of Visitors of the University of Virginia.

Coles, Catharine Thompson (1768–1848). Daughter of James and Catherine Walton Thompson; the second wife of DPM's uncle Isaac Coles; sister-in-law of Elbridge Gerry.

Coles, Edward (1786–1868). Son of John and Rebecca Elizabeth Tucker Coles. Brother of Isaac A., Mary Eliza, Sarah, Elizabeth, Rebecca Travis, and Tucker Coles. DPM's second cousin and a long-standing friend. He was private secretary to JM 1809–15 and later the second governor of Illinois. He married Sally Logan Roberts of Philadelphia.

Coles, Elizabeth (Betsy) (1791–1865). Daughter of John and Rebecca Elizabeth Tucker Coles; sister of Edward and other siblings; second cousin and friend of DPM.

Coles, Helen Skipwith (1789–1864). Wife of Tucker Coles (1782–1861), brother of Edward Coles and other siblings and owner of the plantation Tallwood in Albemarle County, Va.

Coles, Isaac A. (1780–1841). Private secretary to Presidents Jefferson and JM; brother of Edward and other siblings; DPM's second cousin. A veteran of the War of 1812. Married Louisa Nevison of Norfolk in 1823; she died in 1824. Coles married Julianna Stricker Rankin in 1830.

Coles, Mary Eliza. *See* Carter, Mary Eliza Coles

Coles, Rebecca Travis. *See* Singleton, Rebecca Travis Coles

Coles, Sarah. *See* Stevenson, Sarah Coles

Coles, Walter (1790–1857). Son of Catharine Thompson and Isaac Coles. A veteran of the War of 1812, he was a member of Congress 1835–45. In 1821 he married Lettice P. Carrington, daughter of Judge Paul Carrington. He was one of the founders of the states' rights movement.

Colvin, John B. (1778–1826). Editor and State Department clerk. Published the *Monitor,* a newspaper that supported JM for president in 1808.

Conway, Augusta Giles. Daughter of William B. Giles, governor of Virginia 1827–30; wife of Dr. James H. Conway.

Conway, Lucie Hartwell Macon (1794–1871). The daughter of Thomas Macon and JM's sister Sarah Catlett Madison Macon, she married Reuben Conway (1788–1838). The Conways lived at Greenwood, an estate in Orange County, Va.

Coolidge, Ellen Wayles Randolph (1796–1876). Daughter of Thomas Mann and Martha Jefferson Randolph; a granddaughter of Thomas Jefferson. Married Joseph Coolidge (1798–1879), a Boston merchant.

Correa da Serra, José Francisco (1750–1823). Portuguese botanist and diplomat. After his arrival in the United States in 1812, Correa da Serra lived in Philadelphia. He served as Portuguese minister in Washington 1816–20.

Crawford, Susanna Girardin. Wife of William Harris Crawford (1772–1834). Born in Virginia, he moved to Columbia County, Ga., in 1783. He served in that state's House of Representatives 1803–7 and in the U.S. Senate 1807–13. In 1813 JM asked Crawford to serve as secretary of war, but he declined. He was U.S. minister to France 1813–15, secretary of war after August 1815, and secretary of the treasury after October 1816. In 1824 he ran unsuccessfully for president. Caroline Crawford was their daughter.

Crillon, Eduoard de. A French confidence man whose real name was Paul-Émile Soubiron, Crillon arrived in the United States in 1811. In January 1812 he went to Washington, where he sold the John Henry correspondence, returning to France in May 1812.

Custis, Eliza Parke. *See* Law, Eliza Parke Custis

Cutts, Anna Payne (1779–1832). Younger sister of DPM. Married Richard Cutts in 1804. They had seven children: James Madison Cutts (1805–1863); Thomas Cutts (1806–1838), who married Hannah H. Irvine in 1833; Walter Coles Cutts (b. 1808), lost at sea; Richard Cutts; Dolley Payne Madison Cutts (1811–1838); Mary E. E. Cutts; and Richard Dominicus Cutts (1817–1883).

Cutts, Charles (1769–1846). A Harvard-educated New Hampshire Federalist, he served in the U.S. Senate 1810–13 and as its secretary 1814–25.

Cutts, Mary E. E. (1814–1856). Daughter of Anna Payne and Richard Cutts. She transcribed many of DPM's letters and wrote a memoir of her that was later used by Lucia B. Cutts in her *Memoirs and Letters of Dolly Madison.*

Cutts, Richard (1771–1845). Son of Thomas and Elizabeth Scammon Cutts of Maine and husband of Anna Payne Cutts. He served in Congress 1801–13 and was second auditor of the U.S. Treasury 1817–29.

Dallas, Arabella Maria Smith. Born and educated in England, in 1780 she married Alexander James Dallas (1759–1817). Born in Jamaica and educated in Great Britain, he came to the United States in 1783. He served as U.S. attorney for eastern Pennsylvania 1801–14, after which JM appointed him secretary of the treasury. Their daughter Maria married Alexander Campbell.

Dallas, Maria. *See* Campbell, Maria Dallas

Dalton, Tristram (1738–1817). A Massachusetts merchant and politician, Dalton served in the U.S. Senate 1789–91. He married Ruth Hooper (d. 1826), the daughter of a wealthy Massachusetts merchant, and moved to Washington, where he became a real estate investor.

Dashkov, Andrei Iakovlevich (1776–1831). Russian consul general and chargé d'affaires at Philadelphia 1809–11, then minister at Washington 1811–17.

Davis, George (1778–1818). Brother of Matthew Livingston Davis. A New Yorker and army surgeon commissioned into the U.S. Navy in 1799, he took temporary charge of affairs in Tunis in 1803. In 1806 JM sent DPM's brother John C. Payne to Tripoli as his secretary.

Davis, Matthew Livingston (1773–1850). A New York politician and supporter of JM. Brother of George Davis.

Dearborn, Henry (1751–1829). A Revolutionary War veteran and prominent New England Republican, Dearborn served in Congress 1793–97. He was secretary of war 1801–9, major general in the U.S. Army 1812, and minister to Portugal 1822–24. His son George served briefly as a clerk in the War Department until he went to sea in 1804; he died in the East Indies. Dorcas Osgood Marble Dearborn (d. 1811), Dearborn's second wife, lived most of the years 1801–9 in Washington and was a member of the city's society.

Deblois, Ruth Hooper Dalton (d. 1827) married Louis Deblois, a Washington merchant. He served as a director of the Bank of the United States 1806–11, and from 1808 to 1819 he was also agent and consul representing Portugal.

Decabre, Auguste. Secretary to the French minister to the United States, Gen. Louis-Marie Turreau de Garambouville, 1804–11.

Decatur, Susan Wheeler, daughter of Luke Wheeler, a wealthy merchant and mayor of Norfolk, Va. Married in 1806 to Stephen Decatur (1779–1820), a U.S. Navy officer who commanded the expedition that burned the captured *Philadelphia* in Tripoli harbor in 1804. He served in the War of 1812 with great distinction, in particular gaining victory over the *Macedonian*. He invested his prize money in Washington, D.C., real estate. He died from wounds received in a duel with James Barron in 1820. She lived across from DPM on President's Square.

De Gouge, Olympe Charlotte. *See* Garnett, Olympe Charlotte de Gouge

Delaplaine, Joseph (1777–1824). Philadelphia publisher of books and magazines, including *Delaplaine's Repository of the Lives and Portraits of Distinguished Americans*.

De Peyster, Robert Gilbert Livingston (b. 1795). The son of Capt. Frederic De Peyster and Helen Hake De Peyster, he was a New York merchant. He helped DPM remove the Washington portrait from the White House in August 1814.

Dickins, Asbury (1780–1861). A Philadelphia bookseller and editor, he was a clerk in the Treasury Department 1816–33, and chief clerk in the State Department 1833–36. His son Francis Asbury Dickins (1804–1879) clerked in the Treasury Department.

Divers, George. Along with his wife Martha, Divers lived at Farmington, a plantation near Charlottesville, Va.

Dodge, Joshua. Appointed consul at Marseilles by Monroe in 1820, he was a partner in the firm of Dodge and Oxnard.

Donelson, Emily Donelson (1798–1836). Niece of Andrew Jackson. In 1824 she married

Andrew Jackson Donelson (1799–1871), the ward of Andrew Jackson and a graduate of West Point. He served as Jackson's aide during the Seminole War and became Jackson's private secretary in the White House. She was hostess at the White House during Jackson's presidency with the exception of a period during which he banished her for joining Washington society in ostracizing Margaret Eaton.

Dromgoole, George Coke (1797–1847). Virginia representative in Congress 1835–41 and 1843–47.

Dubois, John (1764–1842). Dubois moved to the United States from France in 1791. In 1808 he moved to Emmitsburg, Md., where he and William Du Bourg began constructing Mount St. Mary's College. In 1826 Dubois became Roman Catholic bishop of New York.

Du Bourg, William Louis (1766–1833). A French Roman Catholic clergyman who in 1794 immigrated to the United States, he was president of Georgetown College 1796–98. Du Bourg moved to Baltimore, where he established St. Mary's College, a preparatory school that took in both Protestant and Roman Catholic boys. In 1812 Bishop Carroll appointed Du Bourg administrator-apostolic of the Louisiana and Florida dioceses, and he moved to New Orleans.

Dunglison, Robley (1798–1869). Born in England and educated at the Royal College of Surgeons in London, he was professor of medicine at the University of Virginia 1825–33, after which he taught at the University of Maryland and in Philadelphia. He married Harriette Leadam in 1824.

DuPont de Nemours, Victorine (b. 1792). Daughter of Eleuthère Irénée and Sophie DuPont de Nemours. She acted as her father's secretary during an 1812 trip to Washington.

Duvall, Gabriel (1752–1844). A U.S. congressman 1794–96, Maryland Supreme Court judge 1796–1802. Served as first comptroller of the treasury 1802–11; JM named him associate judge of the U.S. Supreme Court, and he served 1811–35.

Eaton, Margaret O'Neale Timberlake (1799–1879). Daughter of Rhoda and William O'Neale, a Washington tavern keeper. Soon after the death of her first husband, John Bowie Timberlake, she married John Henry Eaton, a friend of Andrew Jackson and secretary of war, to the scandal of Washington society. Jackson's insistence on befriending her sundered the cabinet in 1831.

Edwin, David (1776–1841). Came to the United States from England in 1797; worked as a stipple engraver for Philadelphia magazines.

Ellis, Billy. Slave carpenter with whom Anne Cary (Nancy) Randolph was accused of having an affair.

Ellzey, William. Washington physician. His wife was a member of a circle that regularly played cards with DPM.

Erskine, Frances Cadwalader (1781–1843). Daughter of John Cadwalader of Philadelphia and wife of David Montagu Erskine (1776–1855), British minister to the United States 1806–9. He was the son of Thomas Erskine, first Baron Erskine of Restormel (1750–1823), member of Parliament and lord chancellor.

Eustis, Caroline Langdon (1781–1865). A member of New Hampshire's leading Republican family, she was the niece of Gov. John Langdon and the wife of William Eustis (1753–1825), a physician and Massachusetts Republican. He served in Congress 1801–5 and 1818–23, as JM's secretary of war 1809–12, as minister to the Netherlands 1815–18, and as governor of Massachusetts 1823–25.

Everett, Edward (1794–1865). Harvard-educated clergyman; edited the *North American Review*. Married Charlotte Gray Brooks, the daughter of a wealthy Boston businessman, in 1822. Served in Congress 1825–35, as governor of Massachusetts 1836–39, as minister to Great Britain 1841–45, as secretary of state 1852–53, and in the U.S. Senate 1853–54.

Few, Frances (1789–1885). Niece of Hannah Gallatin; daughter of Catherine Nicholson and William Few. She kept a diary during a visit to Washington in 1808–9.

Finlay, John and Hugh. Baltimore cabinetmakers who built chairs for the White House and Montpelier.

Force, Peter (1790–1868). A Washington printer and newspaper editor who collected and published historical documents of the colonial and Revolutionary periods.

Forrest, Sarah Craufurd. Wife of Richard Forrest (d. 1828), son of Capt. Zachariah Forrest and nephew of Gen. Uriah Forrest, the postmaster of Georgetown 1797–99. He was a clerk in the Department of State 1801–28.

Forsyth, Clara Meigs. Daughter of Josiah Meigs, first president of Franklin College (later the University of Georgia); wife of John Forsyth (1780–1841), a Princeton-educated lawyer. He represented Georgia in the House of Representatives 1813–18 and 1823–27, where he was a supporter of JM, and in the U.S. Senate 1818 and 1829–34. He was secretary of state 1834–41. Their daughter Clara (b. 1810) married Murray Mason in 1837.

Gales, Sarah Juliana Maria Lee. Daughter of Theodorick Lee of Virginia, on 14 December 1813 she married Joseph Gales (1786–1860), a British-born newspaper editor who moved to Washington in 1807. In 1809 he formed a partnership with Samuel Harrison Smith of the *National Intelligencer*, in 1810 he became the paper's sole proprietor, and in 1812 he took as his new partner William W. Seaton.

Gallatin, Hannah Nicholson (1766–1849). Daughter of Commodore James Nicholson, a prominent New York leader and opponent of Alexander Hamilton, she was the second wife of Albert Gallatin (1761–1849). He served as a Pennsylvania congressman 1795–1801, secretary of the treasury 1801–13, member of the peace commission in Ghent 1814, minister to France 1816–23, and minister to Great Britain 1826–27. Their daughter Frances (b. 1803) married Byam Kerby Stevens, a New York merchant, in 1830.

Garnett, Olympe Charlotte de Gouge (1796–1856). The Paris-born daughter of Gen. Jean Pierre de Gouge, she was related to Olympe de Gouge, one of the leading feminists and pamphleteers of the French Revolution. In 1812 she married Robert Selden Garnett (1789–1840), son of Muscoe and Grace Garnett; brother of James Mercer Garnett. He served as a member of the Virginia House of Delegates 1816–17 and in Congress 1817–27 as a supporter of Andrew Jackson.

Gelston, Maltby (ca. 1773–1860). Son of David Gelston, the New York customs collector, he carried dispatches to France in May 1809. JM offered but Gelston declined a job as commercial agent to Buenos Aires in 1810. He was president of the Manhattan Company Bank 1830–40.

Gerry, Elbridge (1744–1814). Born in Massachusetts, he was a member of the Continental Congress, a signer of the Declaration of Independence, a member of Congress 1789–93, governor of Massachusetts 1810–12, and vice president during JM's second term.

Gibbon, James (1758–1835). Collector of customs at Richmond and a Revolutionary

War veteran, who led the charge of the left flank at the Battle of Stony Point (1779).

Giles, William Branch (1762–1830). Served as a representative from Virginia in the U.S. House 1790–98 and 1801–3, in the Senate 1804–15, and as governor of Virginia 1827–30.

Gilpin, Henry Dilworth (1801–1860). Philadelphia lawyer; U.S. attorney general 1840–41. Gilpin oversaw the publication of the first edition of JM's papers.

Gilpin, Joshua (1765–1841). A Philadelphia merchant from a distinguished Quaker family, Gilpin knew DPM from their youth.

Goldsborough, Charles W. (1777–1843). Chief clerk of the Navy Department.

Gooch, Gideon. JM employed Gooch as the plantation manager at Montpelier from 1804 through the presidential years.

Goulburn, Henry (1784–1856). One of the British negotiators of the Treaty of Ghent.

Gouverneur, Maria Hester Monroe (b. 1802). Married her cousin Samuel L. Gouverneur, President James Monroe's private secretary, in the White House in 1820. He was appointed postmaster of New York City by John Quincy Adams.

Graham, John (1774–1820). A Virginia-born Kentuckian, he served as secretary of legation in Madrid 1801–3, secretary of the Orleans Territory 1804–7, chief clerk at the State Department 1807–17, and minister to Portugal, 1819. He married Susan Hill.

Granger, Gideon (1767–1822). U.S. postmaster general 1801–14.

Greenup, Mary Catherine Pope (1752?-1807). Daughter of Nathaniel Pope of Virginia; wife of Kentucky congressman Christopher Greenup.

Grouchy, Emmanuel (1766–1847). A *maréchal* in Napoleon's Grand Armée, he fled to the United States after Waterloo, returning to France following the general amnesty of 1821.

Groves, William. Philadelphia schoolmaster.

Gurley, John Ward (1787?-1808). Orleans Territory attorney general 1803. Died in a duel with Philip L. Jones in 1808.

Hackley, Harriet Randolph. Sister of Thomas Mann Randolph and Anne Cary Randolph; wife of Richard S. Hackley, a Virginia-born New York City merchant who became U.S. consul to San Lúcar, Spain, in 1806 and vice consul at Cádiz in 1808.

Hagner, Peter. Third auditor of the treasury.

Halsey, Mrs. Wife of Thomas Lloyd Halsey (ca. 1776–1855) of Providence, R.I. JM appointed him U.S. consul at Buenos Aires in 1812.

Hamilton, Paul (1762–1816). A Revolutionary War veteran and South Carolina planter who had been governor of his state, Hamilton was secretary of the navy 1809–12. He married Mary Wilkinson in 1782, and they had six children, including Margaret Wilkinson Hamilton Seabrook.

Hand, John. A Philadelphia ship captain who delivered goods for JM and Latrobe.

Hanson, Louisa Serena. *See* Weightman, Louisa Serena Hanson

Hanson, Samuel (d. 1830). Publisher of the *Columbia Chronicle* and cashier of the Bank of Columbia.

Harper and Brothers. A New York publishing business founded in 1817 by brothers John and James Harper.

Harrison, William Henry (1773–1841). A Virginia-born soldier and politician, he married Anna Symmes, daughter of Judge John Cleves Symmes. He served as governor of the Indiana Territory 1800–1813. In 1813 Harrison recaptured Detroit and defeated the British and their Indian allies at the Battle of the Thames. He served in the U.S. House 1816–19 and in the Senate 1825–28 and became U.S. president in 1840.

Harvey, Peter. A Philadelphia coachmaker.

Hawkins, Benjamin (1754–1816). U.S. senator from North Carolina 1789–95 and U.S. agent to the southern Indians 1797–1816.

Hay, Miss. A Baltimore belle.

Hay, Eliza Monroe (1786–1840), daughter of James and Elizabeth Kortright Monroe, married George Hay (1765–1830), U.S. district attorney for Virginia 1803–16.

Hayne, Rebecca Alston. Wife of Robert Y. Hayne (1791–1839), U.S. senator from South Carolina 1823–32.

Holmes, David (1770–1832). Served as a representative from Virginia in Congress 1797–1809, as governor of the Mississippi Territory 1809–17, as governor of Mississippi 1817–20 and 1826, and as U.S. senator from Mississippi 1820–25.

Hopkins, Cornelia Lee (b. 1780). Daughter of William and Hannah Philippa Ludwell Lee, she was related to Eliza Collins Lee by marriage and lived for several years at Sully, the Lee estate. In 1806 she married John Hopkins, a Virginia lawyer. The couple lived in Alexandria.

Howard, Benjamin (1760–1814). Kentucky congressman 1807–10 and governor of the district of Louisiana 1810–13; afterward brigadier general in the U.S. Army.

Howard, Charles P. and Jane Taylor. Orange County neighbors and friends of the Madisons.

Hughes, Christopher (1786–1849). Secretary to the American Peace Commission at Ghent 1814, member of the Maryland House of Delegates 1815–16, special envoy to Spain 1816, he held diplomatic posts until 1845. His wife, Laura Sophia Smith Hughes (d. 1832), was the daughter of Samuel Smith of Baltimore.

Hull, Ann McCurdy Hart (b. 1791). Daughter of Capt. Elisha Hart of Saybrook, Conn.; wife of Isaac Hull (1773–1843). He joined the navy in 1798 and served in the Quasi-War and the Tripoli conflict. When the War of 1812 began, he commanded the *Constitution*, which destroyed the *Guerrière* in the first naval battle of the war. He headed the Boston Navy Yard 1815–23, commanded the Pacific Station 1824–27, served as commandant of the Washington Navy Yard 1829–35, and was commander of the Mediterranean Station 1838–41. She accompanied her husband on his tours of duty in the Pacific Ocean and Mediterranean Sea.

Hull, William (1753–1825). Revolutionary War veteran; governor of the Michigan Territory 1805–12. As brigadier general of the Army of the Northwest, he surrendered Detroit and was subsequently court-martialed for cowardice and neglect of duty and sentenced to death. JM remanded the sentence.

Hyde de Neuville, Anne-Marguérite-Henriette Rouillé de Marigny (1729–1849). Wife of Jean Guillaume Hyde de Neuville, French minister to the United States 1816–22. They lived in exile in the United States 1807–14.

Ingersoll, Charles Jared (1782–1862). Philadelphia-born son of Jared Ingersoll, he was a strong supporter of JM and a member of Congress 1813–15, after which he served as U.S. district attorney for Pennsylvania until 1829.

Jackson, Andrew (1767–1845). Son of Andrew and Elizabeth Hutchinson Jackson; widower of Rachel Donelson Robards; seventh president of the United States 1829–37.

Jackson, Francis James (1770–1814). Served as secretary to the British legations at Berlin and Madrid, ambassador to Constantinople, and minister to France and Berlin before his appointment as British minister to the United States in 1809. Jackson arrived in Washington in August 1809 but left that November.

Jackson, John George (1777–1825). He married, first, DPM's youngest sister, Mary Payne, and, second, Mary Sophia Meigs. Member of Congress from western Virginia (now West Virginia) 1803–10 and 1813–17, he was U.S. judge for the western district of Virginia 1819–25.

Jackson, Mary Elizabeth Payne. *See* Allen, Mary Elizabeth Payne

Jackson, Mary (Polly) Payne (1781–1808). Youngest daughter of John and Mary Coles Payne; sister of DPM and wife of John George Jackson.

Jackson, Mary Sophia Meigs (1793–1863). Daughter of Return Jonathan Meigs Jr. and second wife of John G. Jackson, whom she married in 1810.

Jáudenes y Nebot, José de. Spanish diplomat who served under Gardoqui in the 1790s.

Jennings, Paul. A slave born on the Madison plantation; son of an Englishman and a Madison slave. Daniel Webster bought him in 1846 and then manumitted him, after which he continued to help DPM in her old age and poverty. Author of *A Colored Man's Reminiscences of James Madison* (1865).

Johnson, Chapman (1779–1849). Born in Louisa County, Va., and educated at the College of William and Mary, he practiced law in Staunton, Va., and served multiple terms in the state senate. He was a member of the University of Virginia's Board of Visitors 1819–45 and served as its rector 1836–44.

Johnson, Thomas Baker (1779?-1843). Son of Joshua and Catherine Nuth Johnson; brother of Louisa Catherine Johnson Adams; brother-in-law of John Quincy Adams. Johnson was appointed postmaster of New Orleans in 1808.

Johnson, William, Jr. (1771–1834). South Carolina-born, Princeton-educated lawyer. Served several terms in the South Carolina legislature as a Republican. Married Sarah Bennett Johnson. U.S. Supreme Court justice 1804–34.

Jones, Eleanor. Wife of William Jones (1760–1831), congressman from Philadelphia 1801–3, secretary of the navy 1813–14, acting secretary of the treasury, president of the Bank of the United States 1816–19.

Jones, Joseph (1727–1805). Member of the House of Burgesses and the Continental Congress. Friend of JM; James Monroe's uncle. Judge of the Virginia General Court 1789–1805.

Jones, Lloyd (1768–1820). Brother of William Jones. Commander of the *Neptune* when it carried the U.S. peace negotiators to St. Petersburg and Ghent.

Jones, Walter (1777–1861). U.S. attorney for the District of Columbia 1802–21. A founder of the American Colonization Society.

Kantzow, Lucia Alice de Crossett, Baroness von. Wife of Baron Johan Albert von Kantzow, Swedish minister to the United States 1813–17.

Key, Thomas Hewitt (1799–1875). A graduate of Trinity College, Cambridge, Key was professor of mathematics at the University of Virginia 1825–27.

Kingston, John. Editor of *The New American Biographical Dictionary* (Baltimore, 1810), which included an essay on JM.

Knapp, Mary Phille. Old Philadelphia friend of DPM. She and her husband John moved to Washington in 1800, where he held a position as clerk in the comptroller's office in JM's administration.

Kozlov, Nikolai Iakovlevich (b. 1779). Russian consul general at Philadelphia 1811–18.

Krüdener, Baron Paul von. Russian minister to the United States 1827–36.

Labille, Louis. French upholsterer and paperhanger in Alexandria.

Lafayette, Marie Joseph Paul Yves Roch Gilbert du Motier, marquis de (1757–1834). Revolutionary War veteran. His son, George Washington Lafayette, accompanied his father on his 1824 tour of the United States.

Latrobe, Benjamin Henry (1764–1820). Architect and engineer who helped DPM furnish the White House in 1809.

Latrobe, Mary Elizabeth Hazlehurst (1771–1841). Daughter of Philadelphia merchant Isaac Hazlehurst, second wife of Benjamin Henry Latrobe, and an old Philadelphia friend of DPM. Their daughter was Juliana (Julia) Latrobe (1804–1890).

Law, Eliza Parke Custis (1776–1832). Eldest grandchild of George and Martha Washington. Wife of Thomas Law (1759–1834). They separated legally in 1804, after which she reverted to the name Custis, becoming Mrs. Eliza Parke Custis.

Lear, Frances (Fanny) Dandridge (1779–1856). Niece of George Washington, third wife of Tobias Lear (1762–1816), and a friend of DPM.

Lee, Elizabeth (Eliza) Collins (1769–1858). Daughter of wealthy Quaker Philadelphia merchant Stephen Collins and Mary Collins; married Virginia Federalist congressman Richard Bland Lee (1761–1826) in 1794. She was DPM's oldest and closest friend.

Lee, Mary Willis. Daughter of Dr. John Willis and JM's niece and ward, Nelly Conway Madison Willis. Married John Hancock Lee.

Lee, Sarah Juliana Maria. *See* Gales, Sarah Juliana Maria Lee

Lee, Susan Palfrey (1767?-1822), was a correspondent of DPM. She was the spouse of William Lee (1772–1840), U.S. commercial agent at Bordeaux 1801–16.

Legaré, Mary (b. 1795). Sister of Hugh Swinton Legaré, U.S. attorney general 1841–43. She moved in 1842 from Charleston, S.C., to Washington, where she lived with DPM for a time.

Leib, Michael (1760–1822). Member of the House 1799–1806 and of the Senate 1809–14. One of the "Malcontents"—an anti-Madison Republican.

Leiper, Thomas (1745–1825). A leading tobacco merchant in Philadelphia. In 1778 he married Elizabeth Coultas Gray.

Lenox, Peter (1771–1832). An entrepreneur in lumber and real estate and a Washington civic leader.

Levasseur, Auguste. The marquis de Lafayette's secretary.

Lindsay, Reuben (1747–1831). Justice of the peace, militia colonel, and planter in Albemarle County, Va.

Littell, John Stockton (1806–1875). Philadelphia author and editor.

Livermore, Harriet (1788–1868). Daughter of Edward St. Loe Livermore, a Federalist congressman, she made a great impression on Washington society during the social season of 1808. After a broken marriage engagement in 1811, however, she turned to religion and by 1824 was writing books and evangelizing in New England. In January 1827 she preached before Congress and in the next several decades made numerous pilgrimages to Jerusalem. She died in the Blockley Almshouse in Philadelphia.

Livingston, Edward (1764–1836). Member of Congress 1795–1801 and 1822–28, U.S. attorney for the district of New York 1801–4, U.S. senator 1829–31, secretary of state

1831–33, and minister to France 1833–35. His second wife was Louise Moreau de Lassy Livingston.

Livingston, Robert Le Roy (1778–1836). Federalist congressman from New York 1809–12; resigned to serve in the army.

Livingston, Robert R. (1746–1813). From a wealthy and powerful New York family, Livingston was a Republican supporter of Jefferson and JM. Appointed minister to France in 1801, he retired from politics in 1804.

Lomax, John Tayloe (1781–1862). Educated at St. John's College, Annapolis, he practiced law in Fredericksburg, Va. First professor of law at the University of Virginia, 1826–30. Associate judge of the Virginia circuit superior court of law and chancery 1830–57.

Lomax, Judith (1774–1828). Sister of John Tayloe Lomax. A poet and writer on religious themes, she published a volume of poetry in 1813, *The Notes of an American Lyre.*

Madison, Alfred (1790?-1811). JM's nephew, the son of William and Frances Throckmorton Madison, he became ill while a college student. At JM's suggestion he was sent to Philadelphia for treatment by Doctors Rush and Physick, but he died there.

Madison, Dolley Payne Todd (1768–1849).

Madison, James (1751–1836). Second husband of Dolley Payne Todd Madison. Political thinker, politician, and planter. Secretary of state 1801–9, president of the United States 1809–17.

Madison, James, Sr. (1723–1801). Father of JM.

Madison, Nelly Conway (1732–1829). Mother of JM.

Madison, Robert Lewis (1794–1828). Son of William and Frances Throckmorton Madison and nephew of JM, he stayed with the Madisons in the White House during the winter of 1812–13. Attended Dickinson College in Carlisle, Pa. Married Eliza Strachan in 1816. Member of the Virginia General Assembly 1821–23.

Madison, William (1762–1843). Younger brother of JM, he married Frances Throckmorton (1765–1832) in 1783; they had ten children. He married, second, Nancy Jarrell in 1834. Member of the Virginia legislature 1791–94 and 1804–11. Militia general in the War of 1812.

Martineau, Harriet (1802–1876). British writer. Toured the United States in 1834–36, when she visited the Madisons at Montpelier. Outspoken in her attacks on slavery before the tour, she was left by her experiences in the United States a confirmed abolitionist.

Mason, Anna Marie Murray. Wife of John Mason (1766–1849), son of George Mason of Gunston Hall. A Georgetown merchant, banker, businessman, Mason served as brigadier general of the Washington militia after 1802 and as commissioner general of prisoners during the War of 1812. Later he was president of the Bank of Columbia. The Masons lived with their ten children in a mansion on Analostan Island (now Roosevelt Island) in the Potomac River and entertained lavishly.

Mason, John Young (1799–1859). Member of Congress from Virginia 1831–37, U.S. district judge 1837–44, secretary of the navy 1844–45 and 1846–49, and U.S. attorney general 1845–46.

Mason, Murray (1808–1875). A son of Anna Marie Murray and John Mason, Mason entered the U.S. Navy as a midshipman in 1823 and held the rank of commander when he resigned in April 1861. Married Clara Forsyth, daughter of John and Clara Meigs Forsyth, in 1837.

Maury, Ann (1803–1876). Daughter of James Maury; friend of DPM.

Maury, James (1746–1840). Merchant and U.S. consul at Liverpool 1790–1830. He marketed JM's tobacco in England.

May, Frederick (1773–1849). Physician. Director and later president of the Washington Canal Company. Served in the first chamber of the Washington city council and was its president in 1807.

Mayo, Abigail DeHart (d. 1843). Wife of Col. John Mayo (1760–1818), who built the first bridge over the James River in Richmond; parents of Maria Mayo Scott.

Mayo, Maria. *See* Scott, Maria Mayo

McAlpin. There were two Philadelphia tailors surnamed McAlpin: James—who had done work for George Washington—and Andrew.

McKean, Sarah (Sally). *See* Yrujo, Sarah (Sally) McKean

McKean, Thomas (1734–1817). A Pennsylvania-born statesman and jurist, he was married twice: to Mary Borden in 1763 and to Sarah Armitage in 1774. Signer of the Declaration of Independence, member of the First and Second Continental Congresses, chief justice of Pennsylvania 1777–99, and governor 1799–1808. Father of Sally McKean Yrujo and Thomas McKean Jr. (b. 1779).

McLane, Catherine Milligan (1790–1849). Daughter of Philadelphian Robert Milligan; wife of Louis McLane, U.S. senator, minister to Great Britain, secretary of the treasury, and secretary of state.

McLean, Rebecca (b. 1811). Daughter of John McLean, postmaster general and later Supreme Court justice. Married Augustus H. Richards, a Philadelphia attorney, in 1829.

Meade, Richard Worsam (1778–1828). U.S. naval agent at Cádiz 1806–16.

Meikleham, Septimia Anne Randolph (1814–1887). Daughter of Martha Jefferson and Thomas Mann Randolph. Married a Scottish physician, David Scott Meikleham (1804–1849).

Melli Melli, Sidi Suleiman. Served as first Tunisian ambassador to the United States in 1805.

Merry, Elizabeth Death Leathes (d. 1824). Wife of Anthony Merry (1756–1835), British minister to the United States 1803–6, she was an amateur botanist who disliked her stay in the United States.

Mifflin, Samuel (1776–1829). Philadelphia merchant and industrialist. In 1800 he married Elizabeth Davis.

Milligan, George P. One of the secretaries of the U.S. mission at Ghent.

Milnor, James (1773–1844). Federalist congressman from Philadelphia 1811–13.

Mitchell (Michel). The White House butler, he returned to France in May 1813.

Moncure, Henry Wood (1800–1866). Son of William and Sarah Elizabeth Henry Moncure, he graduated from the College of William and Mary in 1822 and became a merchant with the firm of Dunlop, Moncure and Company in Richmond. He bought Montpelier from DPM in the 1840s.

Monroe, Elizabeth Kortright (1763–1823). Daughter of a New York merchant, in 1786 she married James Monroe (1758–1831), secretary of state 1811–17, president of the United States 1817–25, and a close friend of JM. The couple had two daughters,

Eliza, who married George Hay, and Maria Hester, who married Samuel L. Gouverneur.

Morfit, Henry Mason (1793–1868). Washington claims lawyer.

Morier, John Philip (1778–1853). Secretary to the ambassador to Constantinople 1799. Chargé d'affaires to the United States 1810 but left soon thereafter.

Morris, Anne Cary (Nancy) Randolph (1774–1837). Daughter of Thomas Mann Randolph Sr.; sister of Thomas Mann Randolph, Harriet Randolph Hackley, and other siblings. In 1809 she married Gouverneur Morris (1752–1816), member of the Continental Congress 1778–79 and the Constitutional Convention of 1787, U.S. minister to France 1792–94, U.S. senator 1800–1802.

Morris, Anthony (1766–1860). Philadelphia Quaker merchant; son of Samuel and Rebecca Wistar Morris. Married Mary Smith Pemberton; they had four children, Phoebe P. Morris, James Pemberton Morris (1795–1834), Rebecca Morris Nourse, and Louisa Pemberton Morris. Anthony Morris served as Speaker of the Pennsylvania Senate 1793–94 and director of the Bank of North America 1800–1806 and was a very old friend of DPM.

Morris, Phoebe P. Daughter of Anthony Morris and a friend and protégée of DPM, who frequently stayed at the White House.

Morton, Mary Eleanor Jane Smith. Daughter of Reuben Smith of Madison County, Va. In 1823 she married Jeremiah Morton (1799–1878), member of Congress 1849–51, who owned several plantations in Orange County, Va.

Moylan, Stephen (1737–1811). Aide-de-camp to George Washington and quartermaster general during the American Revolution. Rented DPM's Philadelphia house 1796–1807.

Nelson, Hugh (1768–1836). Son of Thomas Nelson, Revolutionary governor of Virginia. Moved to Belvoir in Albemarle County and married Eliza Kinloch in 1799. Judge of the General Court of Virginia 1809–11, U.S. congressman 1811–23, and minister to Spain 1823–25. Their son Francis K. Nelson married Ann (Nancy) Page, the daughter of Mann and Elizabeth Nelson Page, in 1823.

Newman, James (1806–1886). A noted agriculturalist who lived at Hilton, a plantation in Orange County, Va.

Nicholas, John (1757/8–1836). The eldest son of John Nicholas Sr. (1721–1795) and Martha Fry Nicholas. Revolutionary War veteran and Federalist from Albemarle County, Va. In 1788 he married Louisa Carter (d. 1816).

Nourse, Joseph (1754–1841). Register of the U.S. Treasury 1789–1829; dismissed by Andrew Jackson. Lived at Dumbarton House in Georgetown until 1813. His son Charles Joseph Nourse became chief clerk of the War Department in 1827 and lived at the Highlands outside Washington, D.C., with his wife, Rebecca Morris Nourse, daughter of Anthony and Mary Pemberton Morris.

Ogle, Anna Marie Cooke (1777–1856). Married Benjamin Ogle, son of Gov. Benjamin Ogle of Maryland.

Onís y González, Luis de (1762–1827). Minister of the Supreme Junta of Spain to the United States, he arrived in the United States in 1809. JM refused to recognize him until 1815. He remained in the United States until 1819.

Page, Jane Frances Walker (1799–1873). Sister of Judith Page Walker Rives and wife of Dr. Mann Page of Albemarle County, Va.

Page, Margaret Lowther (1744–1833). Second wife of John Page (1744–1808), Virginia politician and governor, who served in Congress with JM 1789–97. The Pages lived at Rosewell in Gloucester County, Va. Their children included John Page (d. 1838) and Barbara Page (ca. 1795–1864).

Pageot, Mary Lewis. Wife of Alphonse Pageot, French chargé d'affaires in Washington, and daughter of Jackson associate William B. Lewis.

Pahlen, Feodor Petrovich, Count (1780–1863). Russian minister to the United States 1810–11.

Parke, Thomas (1749–1835). Philadelphia Quaker and physician, director of the Library Company, member of the American Philosophical Society, and president of the College of Physicians in Philadelphia. Married Rachel Pemberton.

Patterson, Daniel Todd (1786–1839). A New Yorker who joined the navy in 1799, he served in New Orleans during the War of 1812. He commanded a squadron in the Mediterranean 1832–36 and was commandant of the Washington Navy Yard.

Patterson, William (1752–1835). Wealthy Baltimore merchant, first president of the Bank of Maryland, and among the first incorporators and directors of the Baltimore and Ohio Railroad. He married Dorcas Spear, sister of the wife of Gen. Samuel Smith. Their daughter was Elizabeth Patterson Bonaparte.

Patton, John Mercer (1797–1858). Member of Congress from Virginia 1830–38.

Paulding, James Kirke (1778–1860). A prominent literary figure from New York, secretary to the Board of Navy Commissioners 1815, and secretary of the navy 1838–41. Married Gertrude Kemble Paulding (1792–1841).

Payne, Anna. See Cutts, Anna Payne.

Payne, Anna C. (1819–1852). Niece of DPM, daughter of John C. Payne and Clara Wilcox, she was companion to DPM after JM died. Married Dr. James H. Causten in 1850.

Payne, John C. (b. 1782). Brother of DPM; son of John and Mary Coles Payne; in 1814 married Clara (Clary) Wilcox, daughter of Charles and Catharine Ryan Wilcox. They had eight children, including Anna C. Payne and William Temple Payne (1820–1843). They moved to Illinois in 1837.

Payne, Lucy. See Todd, Lucy Payne Washington

Payne, Mary. See Jackson, Mary (Polly) Payne

Payne, Mary Coles (1745?-1808). Daughter of William and Lucy Winston Coles, in 1761 she married John Payne (d. 1790), son of Josias and Anne Flemming Payne. Parents of DPM, Lucy, Mary, Anna, and John C. Payne.

Pedersen, Ann Caroline Smith (b. 1791). Daughter of William Loughton Smith (1758–1812), a Federalist congressman from South Carolina; in 1820 she married Peder Pedersen, Danish chargé d'affaires and consul general 1803–15 and Danish minister to the United States 1815–30.

Pemberton, Elizabeth (Betsy). See Waddell, Elizabeth (Betsy) Pemberton

Pemberton, John (1783–1842). Probably the youngest brother of Elizabeth Pemberton Waddell, he married Rebecca Clifford.

Peyton, Bernard. JM's commercial agent at Richmond.

Peyton, John Howe (1778–1847). A Virginia lawyer who married Susan Madison, niece of Bishop James Madison and a relative of JM, in 1804. Served multiple terms in the Virginia legislature.

Physick, Philip Syng (1768–1837). A prominent Philadelphia physician and surgeon as well as professor of surgery at the University of Pennsylvania.

Pichon, A. Emilie. Wife of Louis-André Pichon (1771–1850), second secretary of the French legation 1791–95 and chargé d'affaires 1801–5.

Pinkney, William (1764–1822). Served as U.S. minister to Great Britain 1807–11, attorney general 1811–14, U.S. minister to Russia 1817–18, and U.S. senator 1819–22.

Pleasonton, Stephen. State Department clerk under JM and later fifth auditor of the treasury.

Polk, Sarah Childress (1803–1891). Wife of James K. Polk (1795–1849), member of Congress from Tennessee 1825–39 and president of the United States 1845–49.

Porter, David (1780–1843). A Bostonian who joined the navy in 1798, he saw action in the Quasi-War, the Barbary War, and the War of 1812. In the last conflict he participated in operations in and around the Potomac River in 1814. In 1815 he built a home that he called Meridian Hill in the Washington area.

Porter, John. Philadelphia physician.

Preston, William. Brother of Francis Smith Preston.

Preston, William Campbell (1794–1860). Son of Francis Smith and Sarah Buchanan Campbell Preston. His mother was a close friend of Anna Payne Cutts. Born in Philadelphia, he graduated from South Carolina College in 1812. He lived in Virginia until his marriage to Maria Coulter in 1822, after which he moved to South Carolina and served as U.S. senator and college president. His second wife was Louise Penelope Davis Preston.

Pyne, Smith (1803–1875). Pastor of St. John's Protestant Episcopal Church, Washington, D.C.

Randall, Josiah (1789–1866). Jacksonian Democrat and Philadelphia politician.

Randolph, Anne Cary (Nancy). See Morris, Anne Cary (Nancy) Randolph

Randolph, David Meade (1760–1830). A Revolutionary War veteran, he was U.S. marshal for Virginia from 1790 to 1801, when Jefferson removed him from office. His wife was Mary Randolph Randolph.

Randolph, Ellen Wayles. See Coolidge, Ellen Wayles Randolph

Randolph, John, of Roanoke (1773–1833). Member of the House from Virginia 1799–1813, 1815–17, 1819–25, 1827–29 and of the U.S. Senate 1825–27. Jackson sent him as minister to Russia 1830. Brother of Richard Randolph, cousin of Anne Cary (Nancy) Randolph and Judith Randolph, and uncle of Tudor and John St. George Randolph.

Randolph, Judith (d. 1816). Daughter of Ann Cary and Thomas Mann Randolph Sr.; sister of Anne Cary (Nancy) Randolph, Harriet Randolph Hackley, Mary (Molly) Randolph Randolph, and Thomas Mann Randolph. She married her cousin Richard Randolph, by whom she had two sons. The older son, John St. George Randolph (1792–1857), was deaf and dumb and in 1816 was sent to an insane asylum, where he remained until his death. The younger son, Tudor Randolph (1796–1815), died while a student at Harvard College.

Randolph, Martha (Patsy) Jefferson (1772–1836). Daughter of Thomas and Martha Wayles Jefferson. In 1790 she married her second cousin Thomas Mann Randolph (1768–1828), who served in the U.S. House of Representatives 1803–7 and as governor of Virginia 1819–22. The couple had eleven children, among them Thomas

Jefferson Randolph (1792–1875), executor of his grandfather's estate and first editor of his papers; Cornelia Jefferson Randolph (1799–1871); Benjamin Franklin Randolph (1808–1871), who married Sarah (Sally) Champe Carter; and Meriwether Lewis Randolph (1810–1837).

Randolph, Mary (Molly) Randolph (1762–1828). Daughter of Thomas Mann Randolph Sr.; sister of Thomas Mann Randolph. Mary Randolph married her cousin David Meade Randolph. After her husband's finances collapsed in 1808, she ran a successful Richmond boardinghouse until she moved to Washington in 1820. In 1824 she published the first widely circulated American cookbook.

Randolph, Septimia Anne. *See* Meikleham, Septimia Anne Randolph

Rea, John. Philadelphia upholsterer who supplied much of the furniture for the President's House.

Ridgely, Henry Moore (1779–1847). Delaware Federalist congressman 1811–15.

Ritchie, Thomas (1778–1854). Editor and publisher of the *Richmond Enquirer* 1804–45 and the Washington *Union* 1845–51. A strong supporter of JM's administration, he later clashed with JM over constitutional issues.

Rives, Judith Page Walker (1802–1882). Daughter of Francis Walker and wife of William Cabell Rives (1793–1868), a Virginia planter and politician who wrote a three-volume biography of JM. They lived at Castle Hill, their plantation near Monticello. She wrote poetry, fiction, and travel pieces.

Roane, William Harrison (1788–1845). Member of Congress from Virginia 1815–17 and U.S. senator 1837–41.

Robinson, Frederick John, first earl of Ripon (1782–1859). One of the negotiators of the commercial treaty with Great Britain subsequent to the Treaty of Ghent.

Rose Hill family. Rose Hill was an estate that belonged to the Orange County family of Lawrence Taliaferro.

Rush, Catherine Elizabeth Murray (1783?-1854). Wife of Richard Rush (1780–1859), son of Dr. Benjamin Rush of Philadelphia. He was comptroller of the U.S. Treasury 1811–14, attorney general 1814–17, minister to Great Britain 1817–25, secretary of the treasury 1825–29, and minister to France 1847–49. The couple had eleven children.

Russell, Jonathan (1771–1832). Republican politician from Rhode Island. Chargé d'affaires in Paris 1810–11 and in London 1811. In 1814 JM nominated him to the court of Sweden and then to be one of the negotiators of the Treaty of Ghent.

Rutherfoord, Emily Ann Coles (1795–1871). Sister of Edward Coles and second cousin to DPM. In 1816 married John Rutherfoord (1792–1866), son of Thomas Rutherfoord, a Richmond merchant. He was acting governor of Virginia in 1841.

Scott, Maria Mayo (1789–1862). Eldest daughter of John Mayo, and a Richmond belle. In 1817 married Winfield Scott (1786–1866), brigadier general who led troops at Battles of Chippewa and Lundy's Lane and general in chief of the U.S. Army during the Mexican War. The couple had seven children. Their eldest daughter, Maria, died in 1833.

Scott, William, Baron Stowell (1745–1836). Judge of the High Court of Admiralty 1798–1828.

Seabrook, Margaret Wilkinson Hamilton (1796–1839). Daughter of Paul and Mary Wilkinson Hamilton; wife of Whitemarsh Benjamin Seabrook of South Carolina.

Sérurier, Louis-Barbé-Charles (b. ca. 1775). French minister to the United States 1811–16.

Shaw, Samuel (1768–1837). Physician and congressman from Vermont.

Short, William (1759–1849). Diplomat and financier from Virginia. Failed to win Senate approval of his nomination as minister to Russia in 1808.

Sigourney, Lydia Howard Huntley (1791–1865). Writer, educator, philanthropist; married Charles Sigourney. At one point the best-known woman writer and poet in the United States, she wrote or compiled fifty-six books.

Sim, Thomas. Washington physician.

Simmons, William. Accountant in the War Department.

Singleton, Rebecca Travis Coles (1784–1849). Second daughter of John and Rebecca Elizabeth Tucker Coles, she married Richard Singleton in 1812 and moved to South Carolina. Angelica Singleton Van Buren was their daughter.

Sioussat, Jean Pierre (1781–1864). Majordomo at the White House during JM's administration until the building's destruction in 1814, after which he clerked at the Bank of the United States and then at the Bank of the Metropolis. He was DPM's agent and friend in Washington after 1837.

Skipwith, Fulwar (1765–1839). Commercial and diplomatic agent of the United States in Paris 1796–1800 and U.S. commercial agent in Paris 1801–8. In 1802 he married Evelina Louisa Barlié van den Clooster. In 1810 he helped lead the West Florida revolt and briefly served as governor.

Smith, John Speed (1792–1854). U.S. representative from Kentucky 1821–23 and veteran of the War of 1812.

Smith, Margaret Bayard (1778–1844). Novelist and essayist. Wife of Samuel Harrison Smith, editor of the *National Intelligencer*.

Smith, Margaret Smith (d. 1842). Daughter of Congressman William Smith of Baltimore, Margaret Smith was a distant relative of her husband, Robert Smith, a member of Madison's cabinet. The couple had eight children, seven of whom died in childhood.

Smith, Margaret Spear. Wife of Gen. Samuel Smith of Baltimore.

Smith, Mary Eleanor Jane. *See* Morton, Mary Eleanor Jane Smith

Smith, Richard. Cashier of the Bank of the Metropolis and brother of Clement Smith, he was president of the Farmers and Mechanics Bank in Georgetown. He was a friend of DPM and her trustee in old age.

Smith, Robert (1757–1842). Secretary of the navy 1801–9, and secretary of state 1809–11. His wife was Margaret Smith Smith.

Smith, Samuel (1752–1839). A wealthy Baltimore merchant and leader of the Republican Party in Maryland, he was a militia general, a member of Congress 1793–1803 and 1816–22, and a senator 1803–15 and 1822–23. He was married to Margaret Spear Smith.

Smith, Samuel Stanhope (1751–1819). President of the College of New Jersey (now Princeton University) and a friend of JM.

Snyder, Simon (1759–1819). State legislator and governor of Pennsylvania 1808–17.

Sparks, Jared (1789–1866). As editor of the *North American Review* 1823–29, he became one of the leading social and literary figures in Boston. He corresponded frequently with JM and visited Montpelier when he was collecting letters for his edition of *The Writings of George Washington* and his *Life of Gouverneur Morris*.

Spear, Nancy. Member of a well-connected Baltimore family; her sister Margaret married Samuel Smith.

Stevenson, Sarah (Sally) Coles (1789–1848). Sister of Edward Coles and other siblings and second cousin of DPM. Married Andrew Stevenson, Speaker of the U.S. House of Representatives 1827–34 and U.S. minister to Great Britain 1836–41.

Steward, Sarah. One of the Madisons' slaves at Montpelier.

Stoddert, Harriet. *See* Campbell, Harriet Stoddert

Story, Joseph (1779–1845). A Harvard-educated lawyer, he was a member of Congress from Massachusetts 1808–9. JM appointed him an associate justice of the U.S. Supreme Court in 1811.

Stuart, Gilbert (1755–1828). Artist and portrait painter.

Sverchkov, Aleksei (1788–1822). Counselor of the Russian legation in Washington 1811–18, under Dashkov.

Sweeney, Mary. Washington seamstress and upholsterer. She worked on furnishings for the President's House and the Capitol.

Syme, Martha H. (d. 1824). A cousin of DPM through the Winston family.

Tallmadge, Matthias B. (1774–1819). A New York lawyer, he married Elizabeth Clinton, the daughter of George Clinton. Judge of the New York district court 1805.

Tayloe, Ann Ogle (1772–1855). Daughter of Benjamin Ogle, later governor of Maryland. In 1792 married John Tayloe III (1771–1828), who was born in Virginia and educated in Great Britain. He was one of the wealthiest men in the United States during its founding years. They lived at Mount Airy, the Tayloe plantation in Richmond County, Va., and at the Octagon House, their Washington, D.C., mansion. The Tayloes had fifteen children. Among them were John Tayloe IV and Benjamin Ogle Tayloe (1796–1868), husband of Julia Dickinson Tayloe (d. 1840), daughter of New York congressman John Dean Dickinson (1767–1841), who served in Congress 1819–23 and 1827–31. Benjamin Tayloe was attaché to the U.S. legation in Great Britain and private secretary to U.S. minister Richard Rush during the Monroe administration.

Taylor, James (1769–1848). A distant cousin of JM from Virginia who founded Newport, Ky., Taylor was a contractor for the U.S. Army during the War of 1812. He served as court clerk for Campbell County, Ky., and as a militia brigadier general.

Taylor, Robert (1763–1845). Orange County neighbor of the Madisons who handled their local legal affairs. He served in the U.S. House of Representatives 1825–27.

Taylor, Robert Barraud (1774–1834). A graduate of the College of William and Mary and a general in the War of 1812, Taylor practiced law in Norfolk, Va., and served in the House of Delegates. He was a member of the first Board of Visitors of the University of Virginia 1819–22.

Thornton, Anna Maria Brodeau (1774–1856), kept a diary of Washington 1800–1863. Wife of William Thornton (1759–1828), architect, doctor, civil servant. One of the founders of Washington, D.C., he was born in the Virgin Islands and educated in Great Britain. In 1786 he moved to Philadelphia, where he became a friend of JM and married. In the 1790s the Thorntons moved to the Federal City, where he designed the U.S. Capitol. They were prominent in Washington society and were close personal friends of the Madisons. The two families were neighbors while they lived on F Street.

Timoleon. Pseudonym for George Stevenson, who in 1810 and 1811 wrote occasional pieces in the Baltimore *Whig* attacking JM.

Tingey, Thomas (1750–1829). British-born captain in the U.S. Navy during the

Quasi-War. Commandant of the Washington Naval Yard 1800–1829. He married, first, in 1777, Margaret Murdock; they had three children. In 1812 he married Ann Bladen Dulaney, and in 1817 he married Ann Evelina Craven.

Todd, Dolley Payne. *See* Madison, Dolley Payne Todd

Todd, James. Brother of DPM's first husband, John Todd. Cashier of the Philadelphia National Bank until 1805, when he absconded with embezzled funds and went to Georgia. His sons, Samuel Poultney Todd and John N. Todd, served as pursers in the U.S. Navy.

Todd, James Madison (1818–1897). Son of Lucy Payne Washington and Thomas Todd.

Todd, John, Jr. (1763–1793). Lawyer. First husband of Dolley Payne.

Todd, John Payne (1792–1852). Sole surviving son of DPM by her marriage to John Todd.

Todd, Lucy Payne Washington (1777?-1846). Sister of DPM, in 1793 she married George Steptoe Washington (ca. 1773–1808), nephew of George Washington. They lived at their plantation, Harewood, and had four children: George Washington (b. 1797); Samuel Walter Washington (ca. 1799–1831), a physician who married Louisa Clemsen of Philadelphia in 1820; William Temple Washington (1800–1877), who married Margaret Fletcher of Kentucky; and George Steptoe Washington Jr. (1806–1831), who married Gabriella Augusta Hawkins of Frankfort, Ky. In 1812 she married Judge Thomas Todd (1765–1826) of Kentucky, a U.S. Supreme Court associate justice after 1807. She then had three more children: Madisonia Todd (1813–1887), William Johnston Todd (1815–1839), and James Madison Todd (1818–1897).

Todd, Thomas. *See under* Todd, Lucy Payne Washington

Tompkins, Daniel D. (1774–1825). Governor of New York 1807–17 and vice president under James Monroe.

Trist, Virginia Jefferson Randolph (1801–1882). Granddaughter of Thomas Jefferson. In 1824 she married Nicholas Philip Trist (1800–1874), who served in the Jackson and Polk administrations.

Tucker, George (1775–1861). Member of Congress 1819–25. Professor of moral philosophy at the University of Virginia 1825–45. A prolific author, he wrote a two-volume life of Thomas Jefferson.

Tucker, Lelia Skipwith Carter. Daughter of Sir Peyton Skipwith, on 8 Oct. 1791 she married St. George Tucker (1752–1827), judge for the federal district court of Virginia 1813–27. He had married his first wife, Frances Bland Randolph, the widow of John Randolph of Matoax and mother of John Randolph of Roanoke and other siblings, in 1778; she died in 1788.

Turreau de Garambouville, Louis-Marie (1756–1816). Turreau was a French revolutionary soldier whose campaign in the Vendée in 1793 led to his trial on charges of unnecessary cruelty. Minister to the United States 1804–11.

Tyler, John (1790–1862). Member of Congress from Virginia 1816–21 and U.S. senator 1827–36. Elected as Harrison's vice president in 1840, he succeeded to the presidency after Harrison's death but did not seek another term in 1844.

Vail, Aaron (1796–1878). Son of Aaron Vail, U.S. commercial agent at Lorient (d. 1815), and Elizabeth Dubois Vail. He was a U.S. diplomat.

Van Buren, Angelica Singleton (1816–1877). Daughter of Richard and Rebecca Travis

Coles Singleton, she married Abraham Van Buren, son of the president, in the fall of 1838.

Van Buren, Martin (1782–1862). Secretary of state 1829–31, vice president 1832–36, and president of the United States 1836–40.

Van Cortlandt, Philip (1749–1831). A Revolutionary War veteran and member of Congress from New York 1793–1809.

Van Ness, Marcia Burnes. Daughter of David Burnes of Georgetown and wife of John Peter Van Ness (1770–1846). Member of Congress 1801–3, he resigned to become a major in the militia of the District of Columbia, rising to the rank of major general during the War of 1812. President of the Washington city council in 1803, he served as mayor 1830–34. He was also president of the National Metropolitan Bank 1814–46.

Van Rensselaer, Stephen (1764–1839). Major general of militia in the War of 1812 and member of Congress 1822–29.

Vaughn, Sir Charles Richard (1774–1849). British minister to the United States 1825–35.

Viar, José Ignacio de. Special envoy to the United States from Spain 1788. In the 1790s he served under Gardoqui without holding diplomatic rank and later was consul general under Yrujo.

Waddell, Elizabeth (Betsy) Pemberton (1780–1859). Wife of Henry Lawrence Waddell (ca. 1775–1833), son of Henry Waddell, a New Jersey minister. In 1812 the Waddells moved to Summerseat, a farm outside Philadelphia in Bucks County.

Waggaman, George Augustus (1782–1843). U.S. senator from Louisiana 1831–35.

Waln, Mary Wilcox (d. 1841). A friend of Mary Elizabeth Hazlehurst Latrobe, she married a wealthy Philadelphia merchant, William Waln (1775–1826), in 1805.

Walsh, Robert (1784–1859). Founder and editor of the *American Review of History and Politics* and professor of English at the University of Pennsylvania 1818–28.

Warden, David Bailie (1772–1845). U.S. consul at Paris 1811–14.

Warren, John Borlase (1753–1822). British admiral and commander in chief of the American station 1813–14.

Washington, George Steptoe. *See under* Todd, Lucy Payne Washington

Washington, Lucy Payne. *See* Todd, Lucy Payne Washington

Watkins, Thomas G. Thomas Jefferson's personal physician 1819–26.

Watterston, George (1783–1854). Librarian of Congress 1815–29. Founded the Washington National Monument Society in 1833.

Weightman, Louisa Serena Hanson (d. 1839?), daughter of Samuel and Mary Kay Hanson. Married in 1814 to Roger Chew Weightman (1787–1876), a Washington printer and book dealer and mayor of Washington 1824.

Wethered, Mrs. John. Wife of John Wethered (1809–1888), congressman from Maryland 1843–45.

Wharton, Mrs. Wife of the Marine Corps commandant Franklin Wharton (1767–1818).

Whitecroft, Mrs. Wife of William Henry Whitecroft, treasurer of Washington, D.C.

Whittingham, William Rollinson (1805–1879). Fourth Protestant Episcopal bishop of Maryland.

Wickham, Elizabeth Selden McClurg. Wife of John Wickham (1763–1839), a celebrated Richmond lawyer, who was one of Aaron Burr's defense attorneys at his 1807 treason trial.

Wilcocks, Benjamin Chew (d. 1845). U.S. consul at Canton 1812.

Wilkins, William W. Philadelphia lawyer; DPM's counsel and friend.

Wilks, Mark (1760–1831). Governor of St. Helena 1813–15.

Williams, David Rogerson (1776–1830). Member of Congress from South Carolina 1805–9 and 1811–13. Governor of South Carolina 1814–16.

Willis, Miss. See Lee, Mary Willis

Willis, Nelly Conway Madison (1781–1865). Daughter of JM's brother Ambrose (d. 1793); JM's ward; married Dr. John Willis (1775–1812). She lived with their two children, John and Mary, at Woodley Plantation, near Montpelier.

Winder, William H. (1775–1824). General who commanded the defenses of Washington in 1814.

Wingate, Joshua. Collector of customs in Portland, Mass. (now Maine), and clerk in the War Department.

Wingate, Julia. Daughter of Dorcas Marble and Henry Dearborn.

Winston, Lucy Coles (1741–1826). DPM's aunt, she was the daughter of William and Lucy Winston Dabney Coles and the second wife of Isaac Winston (1745–1821) of Culpeper County, Va. Among their children were Martha Henry Winston, who married Peter Fontaine Armistead in 1806, and Dolley Coles Winston.

Wirt, William (1772–1834). Attorney general of the United States under James Monroe and John Quincy Adams. Author of *The Letters of the British Spy* (1803).

Wood, Joseph (ca. 1778–1830). Painter of miniatures and portraits.

Worthington, Charles (1739–1836). Physician. Member of St. John's Episcopal Church and the first president of the Medical Society of the District of Columbia. He married Elizabeth Booth of Jamestown, Va.

Wright, Frances (1795–1852). Writer, lecturer, philanthropist. With her sister Camilla she traveled in the United States from 1818 to 1820 and again in 1824. Wrote *Views of Society and Manners in America* (1821). Experimented with freeing and settling slaves in Nashoba, Tenn.

Yrujo, Sarah (Sally) McKean (1777–1841). Daughter of Pennsylvania governor Thomas McKean. In 1798 she married Carlos Fernando Martínez de Yrujo, marquis de Casa Yrujo (1763–1824), Spanish minister to the United States 1795–1807.

Yznardy (Yznardi; Iznardi), Josef. U.S. consul at Cádiz.

Index